The New

Institutionalism in

Organizational

Analysis

The New

Institutionalism in

Organizational

Analysis Edited by
Walter W. Powell and
Paul J. DiMaggio

The University of Chicago Press
Chicago and London

The University of Chicago Press, Chicago 60637
The University of Chicago Press, Ltd., London
© 1991 by The University of Chicago
All rights reserved. Published 1991
Printed in the United States of America

ISBN-13: 978-0-226-67709-5
ISBN-10: 0-226-67709-5

19 18 17 16 15 14 13 12 11 10   9 10 11 12 13

Library of Congress Cataloging-in-Publication Data

The New institutionalism in organizational analysis / edited by
   Walter W. Powell and Paul J. DiMaggio.
        p.   cm.
     Includes bibliographical references (p.   ) and index.
     1. Organization.   2. Social institutions.   3. Social change.
   I. Powell, Walter W.   II. DiMaggio, Paul.
   HM131.N47   1991
   302.3′5—dc20
                                          91-9999
                                            CIP

⊗ The paper used in this publication meets the minimum
requirements of the American National Standard for Information
Sciences—Permanence of Paper for Printed Library Materials,
ANSI Z39.48-1992

Contents

	Acknowledgments	vii
1	Introduction	
	Paul J. DiMaggio and Walter W. Powell	1

Part One: The Initial Formulations

2	Institutionalized Organizations: Formal Structure as Myth and Ceremony	
	John W. Meyer and Brian Rowan	41
3	The Iron Cage Revisited: Institutional Isomorphism and Collective Rationality in Organization Fields	
	Paul J. DiMaggio and Walter W. Powell	63
4	The Role of Institutionalization in Cultural Persistence	
	Lynne G. Zucker	83
5	The Organization of Societal Sectors: Propositions and Early Evidence	
	W. Richard Scott and John W. Meyer	108

Part Two: Refining Institutional Theory

6	Institutions, Institutional Effects, and Institutionalism	
	Ronald L. Jepperson	143
7	Unpacking Institutional Arguments	
	W. Richard Scott	164
8	Expanding the Scope of Institutional Analysis	
	Walter W. Powell	183
9	The Public Order and the Construction of Formal Organizations	
	Ronald L. Jepperson and John W. Meyer	204
10	Bringing Society Back In: Symbols, Practices, and Institutional Contradictions	
	Roger Friedland and Robert R. Alford	232

Part Three: Empirical Investigations

A. Constructing Organizational Fields

| 11 | Constructing an Organizational Field as a Professional Project: U.S. Art Museums, 1920–1940 | |
| | Paul J. DiMaggio | 267 |

12   Making Corporate Actors Accountable: Institution-
           Building in Minneapolis–St. Paul
           Joseph Galaskiewicz   293

B. Institutional Change

13   The Structural Transformation of American Industry: An
           Institutional Account of the Causes of Diversification
           in the Largest Firms, 1919–1979
           Neil Fligstein   311

14   Institutional Origins and Transformations: The Case
           of American Community Colleges
           Steven Brint and Jerome Karabel   337

C. Institutional and Competitive Forces

15   Organizational Isomorphism in East Asia
           Marco Orrù, Nicole Woolsey Biggart,
           and Gary G. Hamilton   361

16   Institutional Change and Ecological Dynamics
           Jitendra V. Singh, David J. Tucker,
           and Agnes G. Meinhard   390

           References   423
           Contributors   465
           Index   469

Acknowledgments

We owe a special debt to the American Sociological Association's Problems of the Discipline (POD) Program for a small grant that made it possible to hold the conference out of which this volume emerged, and to the Center for Advanced Study in the Behavioral Sciences for hosting that conference and in many other ways facilitating Powell's work on the project. (Actually, our debts to both the ASA and the Center for Advanced Study go back further, for the idea for the conference was inspired by and hatched at an earlier conference, also supported by a POD grant, that Lynne Zucker organized at UCLA in 1985, while DiMaggio was at the Center.) In recognition of our debt to the ASA, and of the POD program's unique contribution to cooperative efforts in social science scholarship, we have pledged royalties from the hardcover edition to the ASA for use in the Problems of the Discipline program. Special thanks are also due to the Program on Nonprofit Organizations at Yale, an institution that has generously supported our collaborative and individual work over the years.

We have accumulated numerous other debts in the production of this volume that are less easily repaid. To Doug Mitchell of the University of Chicago Press, we owe thanks for his confidence, good advice, unparalleled diplomacy, and patience. To Sharon Ray, we owe appreciation for her patience and diligence in compiling and keeping track of the references. Chick Perrow and Mayer Zald were part of this project from the beginning, serving as a kind of loyal opposition at the conference and offering valuable criticism and advice as the book manuscript took form. We acknowledge the helpful critical comments of many generous reviewers in notes to the introduction and our own chapters, but conversations and correspondence with Ron Jepperson, John Meyer, Dick Scott, and Lynne Zucker have been so helpful over such a long time that their contributions to our thinking cannot be isolated within particular chapters. We are lucky to work in an area peopled by such fine colleagues.

We owe a special debt to our authors, who, despite having many other obligations, went beyond the call of duty, often making numerous revisions, to produce substantial papers of the highest quality. We confess that we briefly harbored an impulse to put out a "quick and dirty" conference report; it was the exemplary work of the contributors, more than anything else, that raised our aspiration level. (We also thank them for their patience.)

Finally, we are grateful to our two favorite natural scientists, Marianne Broome Powell and Carol Mason, for putting up with this volume and its editors despite the fact that they are even busier than we are.

1 Introduction

PAUL J. DiMAGGIO AND
WALTER W. POWELL

Institutional theory presents a paradox. Institutional analysis is as old as Emile Durkheim's exhortation to study "social facts as things," yet sufficiently novel to be preceded by *new* in much of the contemporary literature. Institutionalism purportedly represents a distinctive approach to the study of social, economic, and political phenomena; yet it is often easier to gain agreement about what it is *not* than about what it *is*. There are several reasons for this ambiguity: scholars who have written about institutions have often been rather casual about defining them; *institutionalism* has disparate meanings in different disciplines; and, even within organization theory, "institutionalists" vary in their relative emphasis on micro and macro features, in their weightings of cognitive and normative aspects of institutions, and in the importance they attribute to interests and relational networks in the creation and diffusion of institutions.

Although there are as many "new institutionalisms" as there are social science disciplines, this book is about just one of them, the one that has made its mark on organization theory, especially that branch most closely associated with sociology. In presenting the papers assembled here, we hope to accomplish three things. First, by publishing together for the first time (in part 1) four often-cited foundation works, we provide a convenient opening for readers seeking an introduction to this literature.[1] Second, the papers that follow (especially those in part 2) advance institutionalism's theoretical cutting edge by clarifying ambiguities in the paradigm and defining the processes through which institutions shape organizational structure and action. These papers consolidate the work of the last decade and suggest several agendas for further investigation.

Third, the empirical contributions in part 3 illustrate the explanatory potential of institutional theory in an area in which it has been relatively silent: the analysis of organizational change. Two of these chapters (DiMaggio; Galaskiewicz) analyze the emergence of organizational fields; two (Fligstein; Brint and Karabel) explain significant transformations within existing fields; and the last two chapters (Orrù, Biggart, and Hamilton; Singh, Tucker, and Meinhard) explore the relationship between institutional processes and interorganizational competition.

Together, then, the contributions to this volume represent the new institutionalism's origins, its present, and its future. They set out fundamental ideas, define and clarify distinctive analytic frameworks, and explores themes of change, conflict, and competition that bring institutional analysis into closer contact with the concerns of organization studies and contemporary social theory.

This introduction provides a context for the papers that follow. We present neither an overview nor a critique of the new institutionalism in organization theory, nor do we offer a research agenda. The contributions to this book do those jobs very ably. What we shall do, in the following sections, is locate the "neoinstitutional" organization theory presented here, first, among the several contemporary institutionalisms, especially those of economics and political science, and, second, within the disciplines of sociology and organization studies, both with reference to the "old" institutionalism and to independent but convergent developments in sociological theory. We close this introduction with a discussion of several key open questions in institutional analysis and show how chapters in this volume speak to these issues.

The "New Institutionalism" in Disciplinary Context

The study of institutions is experiencing a renaissance throughout the social sciences.[2] In some quarters, this development is a reaction against the behavioral revolution of recent decades, which interpreted collective political and economic behavior as the aggregate consequence of individual choice. Behavioralists viewed institutions as epiphenomenal, merely the sum of individual-level properties. But their neglect of social context and the durability of social institutions came at a high cost, especially in a world in which "social, political, and economic institutions have become larger, considerably more complex and resourceful, and prima facie more important to collective life" (March and Olsen 1984:734).

The resurgence of interest in institutions also harkens back to an older tradition of political economy, associated with Veblen and Commons, that focused on the mechanisms through which social and economic action occurred; and to the efforts of functionalists like Parsons and Selznick to grasp the enduring interconnections between the polity, the economy, and the society. These older lineages fell into disfavor not because they asked the wrong questions, but because they provided answers that were either largely descriptive and historically specific or so abstract as to lack explanatory punch. The current effort to conjoin the research foci of these traditions with contemporary developments in theory and method is not merely a return to scholarly roots, but an attempt to provide fresh answers to old questions about how social choices are shaped, mediated, and channeled by institutional arrangements.

A different strand of institutional thinking comes from such fields as macrosociology, social history, and cultural studies, in which behavioralism never took hold. In these areas, institutions have always been regarded as the basic building blocks of social and political life. New insights from anthropology, history, and continental social theory challenge deterministic varieties of both functionalism and individualism, shedding light on how meaning is socially constructed and how symbolic action transforms notions of agency. This line of thinking suggests that individual preferences and such basic categories of thought as the self, social action, the state, and citizenship are shaped by institutional forces.

Within organizational studies, institutional theory has responded to empirical anomalies, to the fact that, as March and Olsen (1984:747) put it, "what we observe in the world is inconsistent with the ways in which contemporary theories ask us to talk." Studies of organizational and political change routinely point to findings that are hard to square with either rational-actor or functionalist accounts (see DiMaggio and Powell, ch. 3). Administrators and politicians champion programs that are established but not implemented; managers gather information assiduously, but fail to analyze it; experts are hired not for advice but to signal legitimacy. Such pervasive findings of case-based research provoke efforts to replace rational theories of technical contingency or strategic choice with alternative models that are more consistent with the organizational reality that researchers have observed.

Approaches to institutions rooted in such different soils cannot be expected to converge on a single set of assumptions and goals. There are, in fact, many new institutionalisms—in economics, organization theory, political science and public choice, history, and sociology—united by little but a common skepticism toward atomistic accounts of social processes and a common conviction that institutional arrangements and social processes matter. In this brief review, we focus only on a few of the major tendencies and contrast them with the "new institutionalism" in organizational analysis.[3]

The New Institutional Economics

The analytic tradition initiated by Coase (1937, 1960) and reinvigorated by Williamson (1975, 1985) has been taken up by economic historians (North 1981), students of law and economics (Posner 1981), game theorists (Schotter 1981), and organizational economists (Alchian and Demsetz 1972; Nelson and Winter 1982; Grossman and Hart 1987).[4]

The new institutional economics adds a healthy dose of realism to the standard assumptions of microeconomic theory. Individuals attempt to maximize their behavior over stable and consistent preference orderings, but they do so, institutional economists argue, in the face of cognitive limits, incomplete information, and difficulties in monitoring and enforcing agreements. Institutions arise and persist when they confer benefits greater than the transaction cots (that is, the costs of negotiation, execution, and enforcement) incurred in creating and sustaining them.

The new institutional economics takes the transaction as the primary unit of analysis. The parties to an exchange wish to economize on transaction costs in a world in which information is costly, some people behave opportunistically, and rationality is bounded. The challenge, then, is to understand how such attributes of transactions as asset specificity, uncertainty, and frequency give rise to specific kinds of economic institutions. According to organizational economists, institutions reduce uncertainty by providing dependable and efficient frameworks for economic exchange (North 1988).

Despite these shared assumptions there are points of divergence even within the new institutional economics. In particular, there are differences in treatments of transaction costs, contention over the optimality of institutions, and differential explanatory weight given to the state and ideology. Williamson (1985) sees opportunism (self-interest-seeking with guile) as a key source of transaction costs. By contrast, Matthews (1986) emphasizes the purely cognitive costs of organizing and monitoring transactions, even when participants are honest. North (1984) also defines transaction costs more broadly, viewing them as the general overhead costs of maintaining a system of property rights, under conditions of growing specialization and a complex division of labor.

Another unresolved issue concerns the extent to which institutions represent optimal responses to social needs. Throughout much of this literature there is, to use Kuran's (1988:144) term, an air of "optimistic functionalism, a mode of explanation whereby outcomes are attributed to their beneficial consequences." Williamson (1985), for example, implies that considerable foresight is exercised in the development of institutional arrangements and that competition eliminates institutions that have become inefficient. By contrast, Akerlof (1976) demonstrates that institutions may persist even when they serve no one's interests. For example, although everyone may be worse off under a caste system, rational individuals may comply with its norms because they do not want to risk ostracism. In other words, once institutions are established, they may persist even though they are collectively suboptimal (Zucker 1986).

Nelson and Winter (1982), who take an evolutionary approach, view institutions as end products of random variation, selection, and retention, rather than individual foresight. North (1988) argues that institutions are shaped by historical factors that limit the range of options open to decision makers; thus they produce different results than those implied by a theory of unlimited choices and strategic responses. Matthews (1986) argues that inertia plays an important role in institutional persistence. Even when institutions do not conform to the demands of a given environment, they may nevertheless endure because, as North suggests, the prospective gains from altering them are outweighed by the costs of making the changes. Thus, for North and others, the transaction costs of institutional change provide institutions with something of a cushion.

North is one of the few economists to attend to the importance of ideology and the state in maintaining institutions. As exchanges among individuals grow more specialized and complex, contracts require third-party enforcement, a demand that is met by political institutions, which play a positive role in specifying and enforcing property rights. But states vary greatly in the ways they define property rights, and citizens may view political institutions as more or less legitimate, depending on their ideologies. When ideological consensus is high, opportunistic behavior is curbed. When it is low, contracting costs are higher and more energy is expended on efforts at institutional change. Thus ideological consensus represents an efficient substitute for formal rules.

THE POSITIVE THEORY OF INSTITUTIONS

A new institutionalism has emerged in the field of politics in reaction to earlier conceptions of political behavior that were atomistic not only in their view of action as the product of goal-oriented, rational individuals (a position many "positive theorists" still share) but in an abstract, asocial conception of the contexts in which these goals are pursued. One strand of political science institutionalism (positive theory) focuses on domestic political institutions; another (regime theory) deals with international relations.

The positive theory of institutions is concerned with political decision making, especially the ways in which political structures (or institutions) shape political outcomes (Shepsle 1986). Atomistic versions of social-choice theory, to which this work responds, predicted unstable and paradoxical decisions under majority voting rules. Yet political life is not in constant flux; indeed, the key feature of U.S. politics is its pervasive stability (Moe 1987). What, then, accounts for this stability? The answer given by institutionalists in political science is that much of the instability inherent in pure majority voting systems is eliminated by legislative rules.

This approach complements the new institutional economics in its effort to link actor interests to political outcomes. The institutional arrangements that structure U.S. politics are viewed as responses to collective action problems, which arise precisely because the transaction costs of political exchange are high. Shepsle describes political institutions as "ex ante agreements about a structure of cooperation" that "economize on transaction costs, reduce opportunism and other forms of agency 'slippage,' and thereby enhance the prospects of gains through cooperation" (1986:74). Political institutions thus create stability in political life.

Most of the positive theorists' research deals with the relatively fixed structural features of the U.S. Congress—the agenda powers of congressional committees, and the rules that define legislative procedures and committee jurisdictions (Riker 1980; Shepsle and Weingast 1981, 1987; Weingast and Marshall 1988). The public-choice models that inform this work give special prominence to the mechanics of legislating, for example, the distribution of agenda-setting powers, the sequence in which proposals must be made, and the allocation of veto rights (Shepsle and Weingast 1987; Ostrom 1986; Shepsle 1986, 1988). Modeling in this tradition often employs principal-agent imagery to examine the efforts of one political actor (e.g., a congressional subcommittee) to control another (e.g., a federal agency).

The general picture provided by this insightful line of work is one in which congressional policy is highly dependent on the agenda-setting powers inherent in legislative rules. The explanation of the powerful gatekeeping role played by legislative committees "resides in the rules governing the sequence of proposing, amending, and especially of vetoing the legislative process" (Shepsle and Weingast 1987:86). The structure of political rules is fairly resilient to the ebbs and flows of the agendas of politicians, and the rules can easily live on when the original support for them wanes. As a result, legislative rules are seen as robust, resistant in the short run to political pressures, and in the long run, systematically constraining the options decision makers are free to pursue.

Political scientist Terry Moe has chided rational-choice institutionalism for emphasizing the formal mechanisms of legislative control to the exclusion of indirect, unintentional, and systemic methods (Moe 1987:291). Missing from the positive theory's models of rules and procedures are the dynamic, informal features of institutions. In an insightful analytic history of the National Labor Relations Board, Moe demonstrates how the agency transformed its own political environment, and highlights the vital mutual dependence that developed between the NLRB and its constituents. He also emphasizes the role of informal norms and standards of professionalism in shaping the board's relationship with Congress. Nevertheless, Moe concludes that, despite its flaws, the new institutionalism in politics and economics promises to provide a general rational-choice theory of social institutions. We are somewhat less optimistic, in part because Moe's excellent work demonstrates that this approach focuses on only the more formal and fixed aspects of the political process. While some concern is evinced for how institutions emerge, most of the analyses treat rules and procedures as exogenous determinants of political behavior.

INTERNATIONAL REGIMES

The second strand of political science's new institutionalism has emerged in the field of international relations. Here scholars have rejected a once popular anarchic view of international relations and have explored the conditions under which international cooperation occurs, and examined the institutions (regimes) that promote cooperation (Krasner 1983; Keohane 1984, 1988; Young 1986). International regimes are multilateral agreements, at once resulting from and facilitating cooperative behavior, by means of which states regulate their relations with one another within a particular issue area. Some of these international institutions (e.g., the United Nations or the World Bank) are formal organizations; others, such as the international regime for money and trade (the GATT or General Agreement on Trade and Tariffs) are complex sets of rules, standards, and agencies. Regimes are institutions in that they build upon, homogenize, and reproduce standard expectations and, in so doing, stabilize the international order.

The initial work on regimes borrowed freely from the language and conceptual artillery of game theory and institutional economics and took scarcity and competition to be basic features of the international system. Nation-states were regarded as self-interested utility maximizers that nevertheless experienced powerful incentives to enter into constraining agreements in order to maximize their long-term welfare (Young 1986). If no benefits were realized from international agreements or if cooperation could be sustained without cost, international regimes would not arise. The logic is similar to that of work on domestic politics: regimes appeared whenever the costs of communication, monitoring, and enforcement were low compared to the benefits derived. Thus, nations, in an effort to realize joint gains, agree to bind themselves to regimes that subsequently limit their freedom of action.

More recently, international relations scholars have come to question the value of the rational-actor approach to international institutions. As Keohane (1988:388) points out, it "leaves open the issue of what kinds of institutions will develop, to whose benefit, and how effective they will be." Clearly many international institutions are not optimally efficient and, were they to be reconstructed de novo, would undoubtedly look quite different. Imperfect regimes survive nonetheless because sunk costs, vested interests, and the difficulty of conceiving of alternatives make it sensible to maintain them.

Dissatisfaction with the rational-actor approach has led some scholars to develop a more sociological line of inquiry, which recognizes that "institutions do not merely reflect the preferences and power of the units constituting them; the institutions themselves shape those preferences and that power" (Keohane 1988:382; see also Kratochwil and Ruggie 1986; Krasner 1988). In this more process-oriented view, institutions constitute actors as well as constrain them, and interests emerge within particular normative and historical contexts. Understanding the way policymakers think about international rules and standards, and the political discourses they employ, is critical to any analysis of international politics.

Both the rational-actor and more sociological approaches to international institutions are better developed theoretically than empirically: there is little research on why regimes develop in some issue areas rather than others; nor do we know what factors explain regime persistence.[5] What is apparent is that international regimes are durable institutions that shape and constrain the relations among states, and that understanding how such institutions develop, persist, and expire is an important task.

POINTS OF DIVERGENCE

The disparities among the various approaches are nicely illustrated by their varying definitions of an institution. Political scientists in the rational-choice/game-theoretic tradition view institutions as temporarily "congealed tastes" (Riker 1980), frameworks "of rules, procedures, and arrangements" (Shepsle 1986), or "prescriptions about which actions are required, prohibited, or permitted" (Ostrom 1986). The new institutional economics, particularly the branch located in economic history, contends that "institutions are regularities in repetitive interactions, . . . customs and rules that provide a set of incentives and disincentives for individuals" (North 1986:231). The economics of organization conceives of institutions as governance structures, social arrangements geared to minimize transaction costs (Williamson 1985).

In the international relations literature, regimes are defined as "sets of implicit or explicit principles, norms, rules, and decision-making procedures around which actors' expectations converge in a given area of international relations" (Krasner 1983:2). What distinguishes this line of research from rational-choice approaches is its specifically normative element—standards of behavior are defined in terms of customs and obligations, a focus that draws this work much closer to the sociological tradition. Indeed, Young's (1986:107) definition of an institution—"recognized practices consisting of easily identifiable roles, coupled with collections of rules or conventions governing relations among the occupants of these roles"—is consonant with much recent work in sociology.

As we move from the new institutionalism in economics and public choice to the new institutionalism in regime theory and organization theory, the term *institution* takes on a different meaning. In the former approaches, institutions are the products of human design, the outcomes of purposive actions by instrumentally oriented individuals. But in the latter, while institutions are certainly the result of human activity, they are not necessarily the products of conscious design.

Consider the institution of sovereign statehood, a more than three-hundred-year-old notion that developed slowly over the course of centuries. The principle of sovereignty is well understood—it implies reciprocity among nation-states, it creates well-defined roles and statuses, and it implies membership in the international system. But the institution of the modern sovereign state is not traceable to the conscious efforts of specific social groups. Nor is the complexity of the modern state easily decomposable into smaller units of analysis; nor can it be adequately described by simple aggregation techniques. Indeed, such institutions are relatively constant in the face of considerable turnover among individual members and officeholders, and are often resilient to the idiosyncratic demands of those who wish to influence them.

The new institutionalism in organization theory and sociology comprises a rejection of rational-actor models, an interest in institutions as independent variables, a turn toward cognitive and cultural explanations, and an interest in properties of supraindividual units of analysis that cannot be reduced to aggregations or direct consequences of individuals' attributes or motives. In the sociological tradition, institutionalization is both a "phenomenological process by which certain social relationships and actions come to be taken for granted" and a state of affairs in which shared cognitions define "what has meaning and what actions are possible" (Zucker 1983:2). Whereas economists and public-choice theorists often treat *institution* and *convention* as synonyms, sociologists and organization theorists restrict the former term to those conventions that, far from being perceived as mere conveniences, "take on a rulelike status in social thought and action" (Meyer and Rowan, ch. 2; Jepperson, ch. 6; Douglas 1986:46–48).

In this sense, then, the sociological approach to institutions is more restrictive than that of economics and public choice: only certain kinds of conventions qualify. On the other hand, with respect to the sorts of things that may be institutionalized, sociology is much more encompassing. Whereas most economists and political scientists focus exclusively on economic or political rules of the game, sociologists find institutions everywhere, from handshakes to marriages to strategic-planning departments. Moreover, sociologists view behaviors as potentially institutionalizable over a wide territorial range, from understandings within a single family to myths of rationality and progress in the world system (Meyer and Rowan, ch. 2).

The new institutionalism in organization theory tends to focus on a broad but finite slice of sociology's institutional cornucopia: organizational structures and processes that are industrywide, national or international scope. Indeed, the new institutionalism in organizational analysis takes as a starting point the striking homogeneity of practices and arrangements found in the labor market, in schools, states, and corporations (DiMaggio and Powell, ch. 3; Meyer and Rowan, ch. 2). The constant and repetitive quality of much organized life is explicable not simply by reference to individual, maximizing actors but rather by a view that locates the persistence of practices in both their taken-for-granted quality and their reproduction in structures that are to some extent self-sustaining (see Zucker, ch. 4).

A second dividing line among the various "institutionalisms" follows from these definitional differences. Do institutions reflect preferences of individuals or corporate actors, or do they represent collective outcomes that are not the simple sum of individual interests? Most institutional economists and public-choice theorists assume that actors construct institutions that achieve the outcomes they desire, rarely asking where preferences come from or considering feedback mechanisms between interests and institutions. To be sure, actors' options are limited by sunk costs in existing arrangements, and their strategies may even yield unintended effects. But the thrust of these approaches is to view institutional arrangements as adaptive solutions to problems of opportunism, imperfect or asymmetric information, and costly monitoring.

The more sociologically oriented branch of institutionalism rejects this orientation for several reasons. First, individuals do not choose freely among

—9—

institutions, customs, social norms, or legal procedures. One cannot decide to get a divorce in a new manner, or play chess by different rules, or opt out of paying taxes. Organization theorists prefer models not of choice but of taken-for-granted expectations, assuming that "actors associate certain actions with certain situations by rules of appropriateness" (March and Olsen 1984:741) absorbed through socialization, education, on-the-job learning, or acquiescence to convention. Individuals face choices all the time, but in doing so they seek guidance from the experiences of others in comparable situations and by reference to standards of obligation.

Moreover, sociological institutionalists question whether individual choices and preferences can be properly understood outside of the cultural and historical frameworks in which they are embedded. People in different societies or institutional domains, at different times, hold varying assumptions about the interests that motivate legitimate action, the auspices under which persons or collectives may act, and the forms of action that are appropriate. The very notion of rational choice reflects modern secular rituals and myths that constitute and constrain legitimate action (see Jepperson and Meyer, ch. 9; Friedland and Alford, ch. 10).

A third point of contention between the economic/public-choice and sociological variants of institutional theory concerns the autonomy, plasticity, and efficiency of institutions. Do institutions adapt to individual interests and respond to exogenous change quickly, or do they evolve glacially and in ways that are not typically anticipated?

Some institutionalists in political science and economics recognize that institutions are not highly malleable. Institutional arrangements constrain individual behavior by rendering some choices unviable, precluding particular courses of action, and restraining certain patterns of resource allocation. For example, Shepsle (1986, 1989) has argued that such political institutions as Congress's committee structure and its seniority system must be obdurate if politicians are to make credible commitments. And economists Richard Nelson and Sidney Winter (1982) emphasize the role of rules, norms, and culture in organizational change and explicitly disavow the view that market competition ensures the selection of efficient organizational structures and processes. But such work, although important, is something of an exception; most public-choice theorists and economists who study institutions view them as provisional, temporary resting places on the way to an efficient equilibrium solution.

Organizational sociologists find adaptive storytelling less persuasive. In their view, behaviors and structures that are institutionalized are ordinarily slower to change than those that are not.[6] (Indeed, given the distinction between convention and institution noted above, this is almost a matter of definition.) Sociologists concur with rational-choice scholars that technical interdependence and physical sunk costs are partly responsible for institutional inertia. But these are not the only, or the most important, factors. Institutionalized arrangements are reproduced because individuals often cannot even conceive of appropriate alternatives (or because they regard as unrealistic the alternatives they can imagine).[7] Institutions do not just constrain options: they establish the very criteria by which people discover their preferences. In other words, some of the most important sunk costs are cognitive.

When organizational change does occur it is likely to be episodic and dramatic, responding to institutional change at the macrolevel, rather than incremental and smooth. Fundamental change occurs under conditions in which the social arrangements that have buttressed institutional regimes suddenly appear problematic (see Powell, ch. 8). Whereas economists and political scientists offer functional explanations of the ways in which institutions represent efficient solutions to problems of governance, sociologists reject functional explanations and focus instead on the ways in which institutions complicate and constitute the paths by which solutions are sought.

The New Institutionalism and the Sociological Tradition

The new institutionalism in organizational analysis has a distinctly sociological flavor. This perspective emphasizes the ways in which action is structured and order made possible by shared systems of rules that both constrain the inclination and capacity of actors to optimize as well as privilege some groups whose interests are secured by prevailing rewards and sanctions. Yet neoinstitutionalism in organizational analysis is not simply the old sociology in a relabeled bottle; it diverges in systematic ways from earlier sociological approaches to organizations and institutions. To explicate these differences, we begin this section with an account of the relationship between neoinstitutionalism and the old institutionalism in organization theory. This discussion leads to a consideration of affinities between the new institutionalism and broader currents in Anglo-American and continental social theory, particularly to developments in the theory of action.

THE NEW INSTITUTIONALISM AND THE OLD

If, in retrospect, one could assign a birth date to the new institutionalism in organizational studies, it would have to be 1977, the year in which John Meyer published two seminal papers, "The Effects of Education as an Institution" and "Institutionalized Organizations: Formal Structure as Myth and Ceremony" (with Brian Rowan, ch. 2), which set out many of the central components of neoinstitutional thought. To be sure, some of these ideas were visible in Meyer's ongoing research on the world system (Meyer and Hannan 1979); some appear in his brilliant paper on school "charter effects" in a 1970 edited collection; and Meyer's preoccupation with macro influences on local phenomena is evident in his early work on contextual effects in organizational research (1968). The 1977 papers, and the fruitful collaboration between Meyer and W. Richard Scott that followed (1983b), clarified and developed institutional principles in the context of formal organizations. By 1985, when Lynne Zucker convened a small conference on the subject at UCLA (Zucker 1987), the number of scholars intrigued by the effects of culture, ritual, ceremony, and higher-level structures on organizations had reached a sufficient mass for neo-institutional theory to be named and reified.

Neoinstitutionalism traces its roots to the "old institutionalism" of Philip Selznick and his associates, yet diverges from that tradition substantially (see Selznick 1949, 1957; and, for an appreciative but critical overview, ch. 5 of Perrow 1986). Both the old and new approaches share a skepticism toward rational-actor models of organization, and each views institutionalization as a state-dependent process that makes organizations less instrumentally rational by limiting the options they can pursue.[8] Both emphasize the relationship between organizations and their environments, and both promise to reveal aspects of reality that are inconsistent with organizations' formal accounts. Each approach stresses the role of culture in shaping organizational reality.

Given the decidedly rational and materialist cast of most alternative approaches to organizations, these similarities evince much continuity between the old institutionalism and the new. Yet the latter departs from the former in significant ways (summarized in table 1.1). In describing these differences, we emphasize core features; of course, individual exceptions can be found.[9]

The old institutionalism was straightforwardly political in its analysis of group conflict and organizational strategy. The leadership of the Tennessee Valley Authority, for example, co-opted external constituencies intentionally, trading off its creators' more populist agricultural designs to protect the rural electrification program (Selznick 1949). By contrast, the new institutionalism has usually downplayed conflicts of interest within and between organizations, or else noted how organizations respond to such conflicts by developing highly elaborate administrative structures (see Scott and Meyer, ch. 5). Although, as we note below, institutional and political approaches to organizational change are beginning to come into fruitful dialogue, the focus in the initial work was on aspects of institutions that tend to prevent actors from recognizing or acting upon their interests (DiMaggio 1988a).

It follows that although the old and new approaches agree that institutionalization constrains organizational rationality, they identify different sources of constraint, with the older emphasizing the vesting of interests within organizations as a result of political tradeoffs and alliances, and the new stressing the relationship between stability and legitimacy and the power of "common understandings that are seldom explicitly articulated" (Zucker 1983:5).

These differences are reflected in the treatment of organizational structure in

Table 1.1 The Old and the New Institutionalisms

	Old	New
Conflicts of interest	Central	Peripheral
Source of inertia	Vested interests	Legitimacy imperative
Structural emphasis	Informal structure	Symbolic role of formal structure
Organization embedded in	Local community	Field, sector, or society
Nature of embeddedness	Co-optation	Constitutive
Locus of institutionalization	Organization	Field or society
Organizational dynamics	Change	Persistence
Basis of critique of utilitarianism	Theory of interest aggregation	Theory of action
Evidence for critique of utilitarianism	Unanticipated consequences	Unreflective activity
Key forms of cognition	Values, norms, attitudes	Classifications, routines, scripts, schema
Social psychology	Socialization theory	Attribution theory
Cognitive basis of order	Commitment	Habit, practical action
Goals	Displaced	Ambiguous
Agenda	Policy relevance	Disciplinary

the two traditions. The old institutionalism highlighted the "shadowland of informal interaction" (Selznick 1949:260)—influence patterns, coalitions and cliques, particularistic elements in recruitment or promotion—both to illustrate how the informal structures deviated from and constrained aspects of formal structure and to demonstrate the subversion of the organization's intended, rational mission by parochial interests. The new institutionalism, by contrast, locates irrationality in the formal structure itself, attributing the diffusion of certain departments and operating procedures to interorganizational influences, conformity, and the persuasiveness of cultural accounts, rather than to the functions they are intended to perform (Meyer and Rowan, DiMaggio and Powell, this vol.).

Another fundamental difference between the two institutionalisms is in their conceptualization of the environment. Authors of older works (Selznick 1949; Gouldner 1954; Dalton 1959; Clark 1960a) describe organizations that are embedded in local communities, to which they are tied by the multiple loyalties of personnel and by interorganizational treaties ("co-optation") hammered out in face-to-face interaction. The new institutionalism focuses instead on nonlocal environments, either organizational sectors or fields roughly coterminous with the boundaries of industries, professions, or national societies (Scott and Meyer, ch. 5). Environments, in this view, are more subtle in their influence; rather than being co-opted by organizations, they penetrate the organization, creating the lenses through which actors view the world and the very categories of structure, action, and thought (see part 2).

Because institutionalization was a process in which constraining relations with local constituencies evolved over time, older institutionalists regarded organizations as both the units that were institutionalized and the key loci of the process. By contrast, neoinstitutionalists view institutionalization as occurring at the sectoral or societal levels, and consequently interorganizational in locus. Organizational forms, structural components, and rules, not specific organizations, are institutionalized. Thus whereas the old institutionalism viewed organizations as organic wholes, the new institutionalism treats them as loosely coupled arrays of standardized elements.

Other important differences follow from this: institutionalization, in the older view, established a unique organizational "character . . . crystallized through the preservation of custom and precedent" (Selznick 1949:182, 1957:38–55). Rooted in ego psychology, the notion of character implied a high degree of symbolic and functional consistency within each institution. Moreover, because the character-formation process operated at the organizational level, it could only increase interorganizational diversity. In the new view, institutionalization tends to reduce variety, operating across organizations to override diversity in local environments (DiMaggio and Powell, ch. 3; but see Zucker's postscript to ch. 4 and Scott, ch. 7). The organization's standardized components, however, are loosely coupled, often displaying minimal functional integration (Meyer and Rowan, ch. 2). Not only does neoinstitutionalism emphasize the homogeneity of organizations; it also tends to stress the stability of institutionalized components (Zucker, ch. 4). By contrast, for the old institutionalism, change was an endemic part of the organization's evolving adaptive relationship to its local environment (Selznick 1957:39).

Although both old and new institutionalisms reject a view of organizational behavior as merely the sum of individual actions, they do so on quite different grounds. For the old institutionalists, the problem is less with the assumption that individuals pursue material and, especially, ideal interests (defined, of course, more broadly than in utilitarian thought)—Selznick's bureaucrats and local influentials were canny, if not always successful, strategists—than with the notion that such individual striving leads to organizational rationality. Rather, organizations are "recalcitrant tools," and efforts to direct them yield "unanticipated consequences" beyond anyone's control. By comparison, the neoinstitutionalist rejection of intentionality is founded on an alternative theory of individual action, which stresses the unreflective, routine, taken-for-granted nature of most human behavior and views interests and actors as themselves constituted by institutions (see chapters by Jepperson and Zucker).

Underlying these differences is a considerable gulf between old and new in their conceptions of the cultural, or cognitive, bases of institutionalized behavior. For the old institutionalists, the salient cognitive forms were values, norms, and attitudes. Organizations became institutionalized when they were "infused with value," as ends in themselves (Selznick 1957:17). Participants' preferences were shaped by norms, reflected in evaluative judgments. Newcomers to an institution underwent "socialization," which led to "internationalization" of organizational values, experienced as "commitment."

The new institutionalism departs markedly from this essentially moral frame of reference. "Institutionalization is fundamentally a cognitive process" (Zucker 1983:25). "Normative obligations . . . enter into social life primarily as facts" that actors must take into account (Meyer and Rowan, ch. 2, this vol.). Not norms and values but taken-for-granted scripts, rules, and classifications are the stuff of which institutions are made. Rather than concrete organizations eliciting affective commitment, institutions are macrolevel abstractions, "rationalized and impersonal prescriptions" (Meyer and Rowan, ch. 2), shared "typifications," independent of any particular entity to which moral allegiance might be owed. Neoinstitutionalists tend to reject socialization theory, with its affectively "hot" imagery of identification and internalization. They prefer cooler implicit psychologies: cognitive models in which schemas and scripts lead decision makers to resist new evidence (Abelson 1976; Cantor and Mischel 1977; Bower, Black, and Turner 1979; Taylor and Crocker 1980; Kiesler and Sproul 1982); learning theories that emphasize how individuals organize information with the assistance of social categories (Rosch et al. 1976; Rosch 1978; Fiske 1982; Fiske and Pavelchak 1986; Kulik 1989); and attribution theory, where actors infer motives post hoc from menus of legitimate accounts (Bem 1970; Kelly 1971).

INSTITUTIONALISM AND THE THEORY OF ACTION

The differences between the old and new institutionalisms—in analytic focus, approach to the environment, views of conflict and change, and images of individual action—are considerable. They are all the more striking because they are so seldom noted: far from offering a sustained critique of the old institutionalism, neoinstitutionalists, when they refer to their predecessors, tend to acknowledge continuity and elide points of divergence (but see Zucker 1983:6; Scott 1987a:493–95).

What, then, is the basis of this profound change? To some extent, this shift in theoretical focus reflects historical changes that have transferred formal authority and organizing capacity from local elites to more "macro" levels (see Scott and Meyer, ch. 5). But this is only part of the story. Equally important is a dramatic transformation in the way in which social scientists have come to think about human motivation and behavior. The last two decades have witnessed a cognitive turn in social theory, a sea change comparable to the rejection of utilitarianism by turn-of-the-century theorists (Parsons 1937). The current developments represent a shift from Parsonsian action theory, rooted in Freudian ego psychology, to a theory of practical action based in ethnomethodology and in psychology's "cognitive revolution."[10] Although organizational analysts have often been in the vanguard in applying this new theory of action to substantive problems, they have rarely acknowledged the change.[11]

There has been little effort to make neoinstitutionalism's microfoundations explicit (but see Zucker 1987, ch. 2). Most institutionalists prefer to focus on the structure of environments, macro- to microlevel effects, and the analytic autonomy of macrostructures. Yet it is important, we believe, to develop a social psychological underpinning in order to highlight both gross differences between institutional and rational-actor models, and more subtle departures from established traditions in sociology and from such approaches to organizational analysis as resource dependence and strategic contingency theories.

We agree that the macro side of neoinstitutionalism, which is set out in detail by the contributions in parts 1 and 2, is central. Yet any macrosociology rests on a microsociology, however tacit; much of the distinctiveness of neoinstitutional work follows from its implicit images (which constitute the rudiments, at least, of a "theory of action" in Parsons' sense) of actors' motives, orientations toward action, and the contexts in which they act. It follows from this that to understand neoinstitutionalism, it is necessary to bring these assumptions to light.[12]

The work of Selznick and his colleagues bears a strong affinity to Parsonsian theory—not Parsons' work on organizations (1956) but the middle Parsons of the "general theory of action" (1951; Parsons and Shils 1951).[13] That theory was influenced profoundly by Parsons' reading of Freud, whom he viewed as converging with Durkheim "in the understanding of the internalization of cultural norms and social objects as part of the personality" (1937:11).

It is from Freudian object-relations theory that Parsons derived his emphasis on internalization, commitment, and the infusion of objects with value, all themes that are also prominent in Selznick's work. In Parsons' model, the relationship between parent and child serves as a prototype for social interaction. The inclination to conform to others' expectations arises from the child's "overwhelming sensitivity to the reaction of significant adult objects" (Parsons and Shils 1951:17). The mother's breast is the first object of cathectic attachment, but the child gradually learns to generalize needs from creature gratifications to socio-emotional rewards, and objects of cathexis from parents to other persons and, eventually, moral abstractions. With socio-emotional rewards as a lure, the child internalizes parental value-orientations and "introjects" standards of evaluation for the performance of roles, such that proper performance, by the self as well as by others, is seen as rewarding in its own right (Parsons 1951:201–48). Equipped with such values and needs-dispositions, as well as command of a symbolic system that renders communication possible, children grow into adulthood ready and able to conform to the expectations of alters and to play the social roles into which they have been cast. The integration of value-orientations within a collectivity is postulated as a functional imperative: roles are only "institutionalized when they are fully congruous with the prevailing culture patterns and are organized around expectations of conformity with morally sanctioned patterns of value-orientations shared by members of the collectivity" (Parsons and Shils 1951:23). "Institutional integration," that is, "the integration of a set of common value patterns with the internalized need-disposition structure of the constituent personality," is the "core phenomenon" at the base of social order (Parsons 1951:42).

This telegrammatic condensation hardly does justice to the richness and ingenuity of Parsons' account. Some of what we have left out—the numerous points at which Parsons introduces opportunities for conflict or fluidity into his system, or his discussions of additional mechanisms that complement normative consensus in ensuring social order—need not detain us here. What *is* worth noting is that the grounding of human behavior in morality and commitment, this selective inheritance from Freud, does not, as Parsons (1951:12) claims, emerge naturally from the action frame of reference; rather, it reflects a reductive strategy that minimizes crucial elements in Parsons' own definition of culture.[14] The roads not taken would have led to an enhanced appreciation of the purely cognitive aspect of routine social behavior.

In keeping with his tripartite scheme of orientations toward action, Parsons initially describes culture as including a cognitive realm (comprising ideas and beliefs), a cathectic (affective/expressive) dimension, and an evaluative element (consisting of value-orientations). Each of these aspects of culture could serve as objects of orientation or, by contrast, could be internalized as constitutive of orientations toward action. This schema is rich and sufficiently multidimensional to provide a basis for an exhaustive analysis of the ways in which cognition, affect, and values influence and are implicated in behavior (J. Alexander 1983). In developing the framework, however, Parsons makes a series of reductive moves that truncate radically the scope of his discussion. Of these, three are critical. First, culture as an object of orientation existing outside the actor is dismissed in favor of culture as an internalized element of the personality system, thus blocking analysis of the strategic use of culture in pursuing desired ends. Second, within culture's constitutive mode, Parsons shifts attention from cognitive to evaluative aspects by stressing "the internalization of value-orientations" and placing the inculcation of institutionalized role expectations at the center of analysis (Parsons and Shils 1951; Parsons 1951:37). Finally, cognition and cathexis are for most purposes conflated to a hybrid "cathectic-cognitive orientation" toward the situation of action that "always entails expectations concerning gratifications or deprivations" (Parsons and Shils 1951:11, 68–69). Thus Parsons rules out analysis of affectively and evaluatively neutral, taken-for-granted aspects of routine behavior ex cathedra, apparently for no better reason than to simplify the construction of his six pattern variables, to which "culture" is eventually further reduced. The result is that Parsons' break with utilitarianism is incomplete.[15] Action remains rational in the sense that it comprises the quasi-intentional pursuit of gratification by reasoning humans who balance complex and multifaceted evaluative criteria.

Parsons established a multidimensional paradigm that embraced the affective and evaluative dimensions of actors' orientations, and an unprecedentedly sophisticated form of role theory that linked individual and societal levels of analysis. He moved beyond narrow instrumental rationality, transcended the facile dichotomy between passions and interests, and endogenized and socialized motivation. These are no mean feats; but at the phenomenological level, in omitting the processes of cognition and adopting the stylized ego-alter paradigm, he reproduced utilitarianism's "as-if" style of reasoning and its rhetoric of gratifications and choice. It would be left to phenomenology and ethnomethodology to explore the cognitive-constitutive aspect of culture (Cicourel 1974; Heritage 1984, ch. 2).[16]

To summarize, Parsons' solution was incomplete for three reasons. First, he focused on the evaluative almost to the exclusion of the cognitive or cathectic aspects of culture and action-orientation.[17] Second, he implicitly treated action as occurring as if it were the product of a discursively reasoning agent.[18] Third, he assumed much more stringent requirements for both intra- and intersubjective consistency than recent work in psychology has shown to be the case.

These problems follow less from the analysis of the unit act at the heart of his theory than from the model's grounding in personality psychology. He can hardly be blamed for this, for he wrote before psychology's cognitive revolution revised earlier images of consciousness. His view of self, culture, and society as morally integrated entities and his definition of institutions as a "system of regulatory norms, of rules governing actions in pursuit of immediate ends in terms of their conformity with the ultimate common value-system of the community" (Parsons 1990:324) reflect the era in which he was writing. These assumptions and the theory of action that followed from them made sense to institutionalists like Selznick and helped them illuminate previously neglected areas of organizational life. Before long, however, two forces—ethnomethodology and the cognitive revolution—would make Parsons' language of norms and values less resonant and lead to a search for an alternative theory of social action.

One of these, cognitive psychology, has an indigenous branch, the Carnegie school, within organization theory. A key contribution of the Carnegie school has been to focus on the routine, taken-for-granted aspects of organizational life. We can find traces of cognitivism in Weber's theory of bureaucracy—his emphasis on the role of "calculable rules" in reducing uncertainty and rationalizing power relations, and his notion that bureaucracy thus differs from administration by notables, which, "being less bound to schemata," is "more formless" and "functions more slowly" ([1922] 1978:956–1005). But cognitive science per se was introduced to organization theory by Herbert Simon and James March (Simon 1945; March and Simon 1958; Cyert and March 1963).[19]

March, Simon, Richard Cyert, and their colleagues developed an array of insights that students of organization now regard as foundational elements: the importance of uncertainty and its reduction through organizational routines; the notion that the organization of attention is a central process out of which decisions arise; the concern with the implications for decision making when choices are made under conditions of ambiguity about preferences, technology, and interpretation; and the many insights that follow from the view of decision making as a political process involving multiple actors with inconsistent preferences. The new institutionalists in organization theory owe a considerable debt to the Carnegie school. We learned from Simon's (1945:88–90) early work that habit must not be seen as a purely passive element in behavior, but rather as a means by which attention is directed to selected aspects of a situation, to the exclusion of competing aspects that might turn choice in another direction. Simon's (1945:79–109) rich discussion of the role of premises in structuring the activities and perceptions of organizational participants also remains an enduring insight. March and Simon (1958) taught us that organizational behavior, particularly decision making, involves rule following more than the calculation of consequences. March and his colleagues' recent work on the "garbage-can model" has deepened our knowledge of the complexity of decision-making processes: organization members discover their motives by acting; problems and solutions are typically decoupled; and decisions often occur through oversight or quasi-random mating of problems and solutions (Cohen and March 1974; March and Olsen 1976; March and Weissinger-Baylon 1986).

The work of the Carnegie school represents a robust alternative to the canons of choice found in statistical decision theory and microeconomic theory. In their efforts to develop a theory of choice driven by attention allocation, March and Simon's primary focus was on decision making and other internal organizational processes. This preoccupation led them away from an explicit concern with organizational environments. Nonetheless, in the evolution of organizational analysis from Barnard to the Carnegie school we see a shift, parallel to the transition from the old to the new institutionalism, from a normative to a cognitive approach to action: from commitment to routine, from values to premises, from motivation to the logic of rule following.

Ethnomethodology and Phenomenology

Because they were not sociologists, March and Simon had no need to confront the Parsonsian paradigm; moreover, their work had limited impact, at first, on general (as distinct from organizational) sociology. Within the discipline itself, the challenge of analyzing cognitive aspects of behavior and the taken-for-granted element in cognition went unmet until the 1960s, when Harold Garfinkel, a Parsons student influenced as well by the phenomenology of Alfred Schutz, took on the task. Garfinkel developed an approach to social investigation, ethnomethodology, that he came to regard as an alternative to sociology; in return, sociology marginalized ethnomethodology as an exotic species of inquiry ill adapted to life east of the Sierras.[20] Yet despite the failure of Garfinkel's ambitious project on its own terms, his response to Parsons' normative theory of action has had a momentous impact.[21]

Garfinkel's work reopened the neglected problem of "order in symbolic systems" and sought to discover the nature of practical knowledge and the role of cognition in face-to-face interaction. Social order, he argued, does not derive automatically from shared patterns of evaluation and social roles, but is constituted, as practical activity, in the course of everyday interaction. Interaction is a complex and problematic process in which persons must work hard to construct a mutual impression of intersubjectivity. In their efforts to make sense together, conversational participants employ tacit background knowledge, cognitive typifications that Garfinkel refers to as "socially-sanctioned-facts-of-life-in-society-that-any-bona-fide-member-of-the-society-knows" (1967:76). Conversations are sustained by the inherent indexicality of language, the ability of participants to relate any utterance to some external knowledge that makes it interpretable.

Garfinkel departs from phenomenology in noting that contextual knowledge cannot sustain interactional order by itself, because the symbolic order is never perfectly shared. As Randall Collins (1981:995) puts it, utterances "are frequently ambiguous or erroneous, not always mutually understood or fully explicated." Thus conversation is not automatically sustained but is a "practical organizational accomplishment." People enter into conversation with an attitude of trust and a willingness to overlook a great deal, doing "accommodative work" to "normalize" interactions that appear to be going awry. Rules and norms possess large penumbral areas; an "et cetera clause" implicit in every rule leaves room for negotiation and innovation. Actors "ad hoc" when they encounter unexpected circumstances, and employ legitimating "accounts" to define behavior as sensible. Garfinkel developed this vocabulary in the context of a brilliant series of "breaching experiments" in which he and his students violated subtle constitutive expectations and noted the often dramatic consequences (Garfinkel 1967).

In what sense does ethnomethodology constitute a theoretical challenge to Parsons' model? To start with, Garfinkel shifted the image of cognition from a rational, discursive, quasi-scientific process to one that operates largely beneath the level of consciousness, a routine and conventional "practical reason" governed by "rules" that are recognized only when they are breached. To this he added a perspective on interaction that casts doubt on the importance of normative or cognitive consensus. The underlying attitude of trust and the willingness of participants to use normalizing techniques enable participants to sustain encounters even in the absence of real intersubjectivity, much less agreement (Cicourel 1974:53). Finally, intentionality is redefined as post hoc; whereas, for Parsons, action always has an evaluative aspect and a desired end, for Garfinkel action is largely scripted and justified, after the fact, by reference to a stock of culturally available legitimating "accounts."[22]

Garfinkel retains norms, but they are not the substantive ones that Parsons had in mind. Rather they are cognitive guidance systems, rules of procedure that actors employ flexibly and reflexively to assure themselves and those around them that their behavior is reasonable. Deviation from these general rules may elicit strong emotional reactions, but such norms are neither articulated to values of the sort summarized in the pattern variables, nor plausibly connected to commitment in Parsons' sense of object attachment. Far from being internalized in the personality system, the content of norms is externalized in accounts. As such, Garfinkel's rules more closely resemble the "scripts" or "production systems" of cognitive psychology (Schank and Abelson 1977; Klahr et al. 1987) than Parsons' norms and values.[23]

The 1960s also saw the emergence of another line of phenomenological thinking, Peter Berger and Thomas Luckmann's *The Social Construction of Reality*. This work had a more direct influence on institutionally minded organizational scholars, no doubt because it granted institutions a larger role in ensuring social order. Berger and Luckmann (1967:19) argue that the central question for sociological theory is "How is it possible that subjective meanings become objective facticities?" Like Garfinkel, Berger and Luckmann emphasize the centrality of "common sense knowledge" to interaction and the bracketing of doubt. "The validity of my knowledge of every day life," they contend, "is taken for granted by myself and by others until further notice" (p. 44).

Berger and Luckmann, like Parsons, slight the microconstruction of social order that so concerned Garfinkel. Practical reason is not their concern. Indeed, their account of institutions as constituted by "a reciprocal typification of habitualized actions by types of actors" (1967:54) is similar to Parsons' discussion of institutionalized roles, but with a crucial difference. Their analysis operates largely at the level of cognition, whereas Parsons emphasizes the evaluative and cathectic aspect and the integration of role requirements with the personality system. By contrast, Berger and Luckmann grant extraordinary power to institutions as cognitive constructions, suggesting that they "control human conduct . . . prior to or apart from any mechanisms or sanctions specifically set up to support" them (p. 55). Even the internalization of typifications, although guided by cathectic attachments and linked to normative legitimation, is essentially cognitive in nature.

Ethnomethodology and phenomenology together provide the new institutionalism with a microsociology of considerable power. Although this foundation has not been discussed extensively (but see the chapters by Jepperson, Scott, and Zucker, who rectify this neglect), it is implicit in Meyer and Rowan's treatment of "accounts," in their emphasis on the role of the "logic of confidence" in sustaining an illusion of intersubjectivity within schools, and in their definition of "institutionalized rules" as "classifications built into society as reciprocated typifications or interpretations."

This fusion of ethnomethodology and phenomenology is not a satisfactory theory of action, for it fails to offer convincing answers to several questions. First, why are actors willing to work so hard to sustain their images of reality and the interactions that confirm them? It is not enough to argue, as Berger and Luckmann do, that the exterior, objectified quality of shared typifications provides no alternative, for Garfinkel demonstrates that common sense alone is not adequate to produce successful interaction. Second, how do the microprocesses with which these theories are concerned produce social order? It cannot do to reduce social structure to an inventory of typifications or a set of constitutive rules. Socially provided and constituted scripts rarely prescribe action in a way that unambiguously establishes correct behavior. Third, what place do intentionality and interest have in the institutional order?

A full discussion of these issues would require a volume of its own. These problems have not been solved; nor, perhaps, are they likely to prove soluble within the framework of neoinstitutional theory. On the other hand, we can discern important developments in general social theory that bear decided affinities with the new institutionalism and are beginning to make their mark on it. It is to these approaches that we now turn.

ELEMENTS OF A THEORY
OF PRACTICAL ACTION

The new institutionalism is based at the microlevel on what we have called a theory of practical action. By this we mean a set of orienting principles that reflect the cognitive turn in contemporary social theory in two ways. First, new work in social theory emphasizes the cognitive dimension of action to a far greater extent than did Parsons and, in doing so, has been influenced by the "cognitive revolution" in psychology. Second, this work departs from Parsons' preoccupation with the rational, calculative aspect of cognition to focus on preconscious processes and schema as they enter into routine, taken-for-granted behavior (practical activity); and to portray the affective and evaluative dimensions of action as intimately bound up with, and to some extent subordinate to, the cognitive. In other words, the cognitive turn informs an emergent "theory of practical action" that both defines cognition differently than did Parsons and, at the same time, accords it much greater importance.[24]

The insights of ethnomethodology are integrated into a more multidimensional framework in the work of Anthony Giddens (1979, 1984, 1986). The mark of Garfinkel is evident in Giddens's notion of "structuration," the continual and necessary reproduction of social structure by "knowledgeable agents" in everyday life and the reciprocal indexing of their actions to shared typifications; in his emphasis on the "reflexive monitoring of conduct in the day-to-day continuity of social life" (1984:44); and in his distinction between practical and discursive consciousness, or between tacit and conscious reflexivity. Giddens emphasizes the role of routine in sustaining social structure and sketches the rudiments of a psychology of motivation in his notion of the "basic security system" as a fundamental component of the self. Drawing selectively on developmental ego psychology, Giddens contends that the control of diffuse anxiety is "the most generalized motivational origin of human conduct" (p. 54). The means of such control is adherence to routine, and the compulsion to avoid anxiety motivates actors to sustain the social encounters that constitute the stuff of both daily life and social structure. Thus Giddens provides a cognitive theory of commitment to scripted behaviors that does not rest on the norms and sanctions of the Parsonsian tradition.

Giddens's account, however, does little to explain why some interactions go better than others or why routines create particular stable patterns. Although Giddens repeatedly stresses the point that actors are knowledgeable, in marked contrast to the view of humans as "cultural dopes," his work thus far provides little insight into the sources of this knowledge. A solution to the problem of macro stability requires an integration of the cathectic, affective element of action that, although just under the surface in Garfinkel's treatment of morality, is never fully developed.

Two theorists, Erving Goffman and Randall Collins, have drawn on Durkheim to explore this dimension of practical consciousness (Collins 1988a). Goffman (1967) made a decisive contribution in adapting Durkheim's theory of society to the dyad, interpreting interaction as miniritual, ceremonial activity oriented to affirming the sacredness of selves. Parsons, too, believed that people valued proper role performance in and of itself. But Goffman innovated by relaxing the assumptions of intersubjectivity and value consensus, comparing the "ritual order" he analyzed to the "schoolboy order" of Parsonsian theory, wherein people must work hard for the credits they gain and cheating elicits sanctions. The ritual game, he argues, is "easier" on societies and people alike because "the person insulates himself by . . . blindnesses, halftruths, illusions, and rationalizations" (Goffman 1967:43). What is crucial in the ritual game is the sense of affirmation that exchange partners derive from successful encounters, the feelings of selfhood that are reinforced. Commitment is to the "interaction ritual" and the self, and not to specific values, the explicit object of interaction, or the incidentals of appropriate role performance.

Collins has incorporated Goffman's process-driven insights into a more encompassing theory. What most people call social structure, he argues, is constituted out of "interaction ritual chains" in which people, operating at the level of practical consciousness, invest cultural resources and emotional energies in ritual encounters that enact either hierarchy (when cultural and emotional resources are unequal) or solidarity (when these are evenly matched). Rather than viewing society as bound together by a functionally necessary moral consensus, Collins sees it as united and riven, to varying degrees, by emotional solidarity, emerging not out of the evaluative orientation of actors but from feelings of comembership or antagonism generated by repetitive interaction. Groups defined by class, gender, educational attainment, or occupation vary in their moral density, in their control of cultural resources, and in the number and dispersion of their interactions. These features in turn shape group members' styles of discourse, orientations toward deviance and punishment, and cosmopolitanism. Stability (in the sense of robust patterns of alliance and cleavage, rather than political or ideological stasis) emerges from the patterning of these interactions in time and space and from the enduring effects of solidarity, reinforced by recurrent rituals of varying intensity, where moral density is strongest (Collins 1981, 1988a).[25]

We have considered several contemporary theorists whose work, which bears an affinity to the new institutionalism, makes several key advances: it re-establishes the centrality of cognition; it emphasizes the practical, semiautomatic, noncalculative nature of practical reason; and it spurns the assumptions of intra- and intersubjective consistency that were prominent in Parsons' thought. But these gains have come at a cost. First, in overreacting to Parsons' exaggerated emphasis on norms, some sociological cognitivists have been slow to theorize the normative element of practical action, instead presenting images of action lacking in substantive content. Second, they have overlooked an important insight of Parsons, developed primarily in his argument about the decisive role of the cognitive orientation in economic decision making, that different institutional domains evoke cognitive, cathectic, and evaluative orientations to varied degrees. Third, they have failed to come up with an analytic construct as powerful as the role system to explain the relative fit between persons and the positions they occupy in the social division of labor. Even in these areas, however, advances can be detected from within the emerging practical action perspective.

Efforts to theorize the substantive bases of practical evaluation—why certain ideas, images, or symbols evoke strong affective responses, whereas others seem to operate at the cognitive level alone—have taken two forms.[26] First, some scholars have traced historically the rise and diffusion of what John Meyer calls the "Western cultural account," a Durkheimian complex of individualism, rationalism, and evolutionism, and linked the legitimacy and evocativeness of these referents, as employed in discourse, to changes in both social structure and culture (see the chapters by Jepperson and Meyer, and Friedland and Alford; also see Meyer 1988a and 1988b; Thomas 1989). At a more general level of abstraction, Mary Douglas (1986) has developed a sophisticated and intriguing argument attributing the legitimacy of institutions to their capacity to sustain "naturalizing analogies." Institutions, she argues, begin as conventions, which, because they are based in coincidence of interest, are vulnerable to defection, renegotiation, and free riding. To become institutionalized, a behavioral convention requires a "parallel cognitive convention to sustain it," an analogy that obscures its purely human origins. Equipped with such an analogic base, institutions appear as "part of the order of the universe and so are ready to stand as the ground of argument." But not all conventions can sustain naturalizing analogies, only those that "match a structure of authority or precedence" so that "the social pattern reinforces the logical patterns and gives it prominence" (Douglas 1986:52). Thus Douglas provides a basis for anticipating what kinds of institutions may arise and links the institutional order to patterns of social hierarchy.

The notion that the relative weights of cognition, affect, and evaluation change across various settings of action has been less developed, although here, too, we see recent progress. Scott and Meyer (ch. 5) distinguish between analytically independent institutional and technical dimensions of organizational environments: the more technically developed an environment, the greater the role for discursive and analytic cognition; the more institutionalized, the greater the roles of practical reason and, perhaps, evaluation. Bell (1973) suggests that economy, culture, and polity are organized around contradictory "axial principles" in postindustrial societies. Friedland and Alford (ch. 10) identify several institutional domains, each with its own "logic" of action emphasizing different bases of evaluation and, to some extent, the predominance of different action-orientations: cognitive in the market and bureaucracy, affective in the family, evaluative in religion.

The link between micro- and macrolevels of analysis has not received much explicit attention from practitioners of the new institutionalism, most of whom move back and forth among ethnomethodology, phenomenology, and conventional resource dependence arguments. Zucker (ch. 4) is the most ethnomethodological, suggesting that many typifications are "built up" from ground level by participants in interactions, although some (e.g., "organization") have general significance. Jepperson (ch. 6) too draws on ethnomethodology, echoing Giddens and Collins in viewing institutions as "stable designs for chronically repeated activity sequences." Jepperson and Meyer (ch. 9) are the most phenomenological, emphasizing shared typifications that vary across societies but are largely shared within nation-states. Scott and Meyer (ch. 5) and DiMaggio and Powell (ch. 3) employ more structural imagery and draw on the Carnegie school's notion of satisficing: the former emphasize incentives created by vertical authority structures that vary across organizational sectors; the latter stress horizontal networks that both focus attention and aid in the diffusion of shared typifications of organizational form.

Within the broader field of social theory, we come closest to a genuine alternative to Parsons' version of role theory in Pierre Bourdieu's (1977) theory of the *habitus*. Bourdieu's work has been an important part of the cognitive turn in social theory, emphasizing the doxic (taken-for-granted) elements of action, social classification, practical consciousness ("knowledge without concepts"

[1984:470]), and the situated, embodied reproduction of social structure (Bourdieu and Passeron 1977). The habitus is an analytic construct, a system of "regulated improvisation" or generative rules that represents the (cognitive, affective, and evaluative) internalization by actors of past experience on the basis of shared typifications of social categories, experienced phenomenally as "people like us." Because of common histories, members of each "class fraction" share a similar habitus, creating regularities in thought, aspirations, dispositions, patterns of appreciation, and strategies of action that are linked to the positions persons occupy in the social structure they continually reproduce. Institutions, in this view, are inseparable from the distribution of dispositions: an institution can "only become enacted and active" if it, "like a garment or a house, finds someone who finds an interest in it, feels sufficiently at home in it to take it on" (Bourdieu 1981:309).

The habitus construct is the cornerstone of Bourdieu's theory of practice. Its role is to explain how and why strategically oriented agents chronically reproduce and acquiesce to social structures that are not in their interest. With respect to the issues identified above, Bourdieu's argument makes four critical contributions. First, it provides an alternative account to role theory of the differentiation of cognitive understandings and behavioral norms along social-structural lines. Second, it moves beyond the Freudian imagery of "internalization" to posit a generative grammar of strategic behavior, rooted in but not fully determined by the past. Third, it is multidimensional in two senses: pointing to a substantive theory of practical evaluation rooted in differences in the habitus of class fractions; and providing an account of "rational" strategies of action as themselves institutionalized.[27] Fourth, it offers an alternative solution to the Parsonsian problem of the allocation of persons to social positions. To be sure, the habitus construct requires further development, and empirical questions about the precise forms of social boundaries with which variations in the habitus coincide and the ways in which the habitus is transformed over time remain open. Nonetheless, Bourdieu's framework offers a particularly balanced and multifaceted approach to action. Although his work is just beginning to influence organization theory (DiMaggio, ch. 11; Bourdieu and Boltanski 1975; Thévenot 1984; Boltanski 1987; Marceau 1989), much of it dovetails with and may contribute to a broadening and deepening of the institutional tradition.[28]

IMPLICATIONS OF THE NEW THEORY
OF PRACTICAL ACTION

Placed in the context of the transformation in the sociological theory of action we have described, the differences between the old and new institutionalisms in organizational analysis become understandable. The shifts in theoretical focus from object-relations to cognitive theory, from cathexis to ontological anxiety, from discursive to practical reason, from internalization to imitation, from commitment to ethnomethodological trust, from sanctioning to ad hocing, from norms to scripts and schemas, from values to accounts, from consistency and integration to loose coupling, and from roles to routines have quite naturally altered the questions that students of organizations have asked and the kinds of answers they have offered.

When institutions were seen as based on values and commitment, and formal organization identified with the relatively rational pursuit of goals, it made sense to ask how the "shadowland" of informal social relations provided a counterpoint to the formal structure. By contrast, if legitimacy is derived from post hoc accounts or symbolic signals, it is more sensible to focus on the institutionalized quality of formal structures themselves. Indeed, it is an emphasis on such standardized cultural forms as accounts, typifications, and cognitive models that leads neoinstitutionalists to find the environment at the level of industries, professions, and nation-states rather than in the local communities that the old institutionalists studied, and to view institutionalization as the diffusion of standard rules and structures rather than the adaptive custom-fitting of particular organizations to specific settings.

In other words, the differences between the old and new institutional approaches to organizations could not be less arbitrary. They reflect, are shaped by, and are themselves coming to influence widespread and convergent changes throughout social theory in fundamental images of human action and society.

New Directions in Institutional Theory

Although we are sympathetic to the trends we have described, our intention has been cartographic rather than celebratory. As should be clear from the foregoing, we suspect that something has been lost in the shift from the old to the new institutionalism. Although the prime importance of assimilating the cognitive revolution to sociological theory is undeniable, we agree with Alexander (1987) that the goal must be a sounder multidimensional theory, rather than a one-sidedly cognitive one. Indeed, one of the key purposes of the conference to which this volume can be traced was to expand the universe of discourse in institutional theory to include researchers whose work placed more emphasis on the strategic and political elements of action and institutional change. The result, both at the conference and in this book, has been to integrate more firmly organizational institutionalism with general sociology, to place interests and power on the institutional agenda, and to clarify and deepen the conversation about the form that a theory of institutional change might take.

One of the principal goals of this volume is to address head on the issues of change, power, and efficiency. Up until now, it is fair to say the new institutionalism has been most attentive to processes of legitimation and social reproduction. We have emphasized that organizational environments are composed of cultural elements, that is, taken-for-granted beliefs and widely promulgated rules that serve as templates for organizing. Institutional reproduction has been associated with the demands of powerful central actors, such as the state, the professions, or the dominant agents within organizational fields. This emphasis has highlighted the constraints imposed by institutions and stressed the ubiquity of rules that guide behavior. But institutions are not only constraints on human agency; they are first and foremost products of human actions. Indeed, rules are typically constructed by a process of conflict and contestation. Burns and Flam (1987) make this point forcefully when they argue that the major political struggles in modern societies revolve around the formation and reformation of rule systems that guide political and economic action.

Thus, although we stress that rules and routines bring order and minimize uncertainty, we must add that the creation and implementation of institutional arrangements are rife with conflict, contradiction, and ambiguity. The chapters in parts 2 and 3 tackle a series of fundamental questions: How do institutional arrangements shape the nature of collective action? How persistent are institutions—how mutable are institutionalized practices? When do different institutional logics challenge one another? What is the role of elites in maintaining existing institutions? Under what conditions are challengers and entrepreneurs able to refashion existing rules or create new institutional orders? And, finally, what are the tensions between arguments that emphasize the "stickiness" of institutions and approaches that assume an optimization logic, depicting institutions as the results of intentional actions or adaptive solutions to conflicting interests.

INSTITUTIONS AS SHAPERS OF INTEREST AND POLITICS

A theme that runs through many of the contributions to this volume is the notion that actors and their interests are institutionally constructed. Ann Swidler (1986) has argued that "culture" represents a tool kit from which people select both institutionalized ends and the strategies for their pursuit (see also Bourdieu 1981). Similarly, Scott (ch. 7) contends that "institutional frameworks define the ends and shape the means by which interests are determined and pursued." Cultural frames thus establish approved means and define desired outcomes, leading business people to pursue profits, bureaucrats to seek budgetary growth, and scholars to strive for publication. Friedland and Alford (ch. 10) agree that "utility maximization, satisficing, income maximization, profit maximization, risk power, even interest itself are all institutionally contingent." And Jepperson and Meyer (ch. 9) suggest that "functional needs" and social problems are only discovered and addressed when they fit within existing institutions.

Such arguments are ably documented with examples of historical change and cross-national variation in cultural definitions of actors, interests, and politics.

Yet they beg an important question: If institutions exert such a powerful influence over the ways in which people can formulate their desires and work to attain them, then how does institutional change occur? The answers to this question include those that work from within an institutional framework, and those that see the origins of change in processes that are not institutional.

Several authors take the first path in developing notions of "institutional contradiction." One form of contradiction is related to the way in which institutions fit together at the microlevel. Jepperson (ch. 6) emphasizes the nesting of institutions with one another. Greenwood and Hinings (1988), reintroducing Selznick's organizational character but with a cognitive spin, argue that organizational components and strategies fall into socially constructed, interdependent clusters, which they call archetypes. Zucker (1988b) contends that, within organizations, institutionalization of components spreads by a "contagion of legitimacy," as new elements linked to old institutions themselves become institutionalized. In other words, institutional elements constitute an interrelated network of mutually supportive or antagonistic parts.

This imagery has several implications for discussions of change. For one thing, it suggests that institutional models are unlikely to be imported whole cloth into systems that are very different from the ones in which they originate. This point is well illustrated by Westney's (1987) account of the innovations that late nineteenth-century Meiji emulators developed in the course of fitting Western models of the police, postal system, and newspaper into a preexisting Japanese institutional framework. For another, it suggests that tightly coupled institutions may be unstable in the face of external shocks. Moreover, as Zucker (1988b) contends, given the variation in local environments, strong institutionalization at the local level may interfere with the persistence of vital macroinstitutions.

The degree of coupling among institutions is ultimately an empirical issue. For example, while Zucker (1987) sees the dependence of professionals on organizations as preventing them from acting as a source of change, Scott (ch. 7) and Powell (ch. 8) argue that the competing claims of professionals create conflicts and heighten ambiguity. Disputes over professional jurisdiction generate uncertainty about which rules and routines are evoked in special situations. Similarly, DiMaggio (ch. 11) describes the relative autonomy of organizational levels, demonstrating that the same museum professionals who behaved docilely in their home organizations sponsored radical reform from field-level platforms.

Friedland and Alford (ch. 10) develop a quite different argument about "institutional contradiction." Society, they contend, comprises several different institutional orders, each with a central logic—a set of material practices and symbolic constructions—which constitutes its organizing principles and which is available to organizations and individuals to elaborate. Conflict occurs when institutional orders come into contradiction (as when people struggle over whether to treat women's work or the sale of body organs as falling under the rules of the marketplace, the family, or religion). Rather than pitting "rational" deinstitutionalizers against "conservative" institutions, politics concerns "the appropriate relationship between institutions" and the question of "by which institutional logic different activities should be regulated and to which categories of persons they should apply."

Friedland and Alford's perspective has much face validity. Interinstitutional conflict may be discerned in DiMaggio's (ch. 11) account of the democratic versus elite models of the American art museum in the 1920s and in Galaskiewicz's (ch. 12) discussion of business leaders' efforts to maintain a communitarian rather than a pure market model of the corporate role in Minneapolis.

EXTRAINSTITUTIONAL SOURCES
OF INSTITUTIONAL CHANGE

None of the authors regards institutions as entirely immutable or institutional change as a strictly endogenous process. Jepperson (ch. 6) and Fligstein (ch. 13) both mention the effects of exogenous shocks that block the reproduction of institutional patterns and thus induce change, and Jepperson considers collective action as a separate causal mechanism that can erode or eliminate institutions (although the form and object of such action may themselves be institutionalized). Meyer and Rowan distinguish between institutional effects and "the effects generated by the networks of social behavior and relationships which compose and surround a given organization." Scott and Powell acknowledge that institutional constraints always leave space for the autonomous play of interests and improvisation.

Power and interests have been slighted topics in institutional analysis. To be sure, Meyer and Rowan pointed to the power of the state and the collective mobilizing efforts of the professions. DiMaggio and Powell stressed how coercive processes, that is, the direct imposition of standard operating procedures by powerful organizations in a field, as well as more subtle pressures for conformity, limit variability. But little attention has been focused on how incumbents maintain their dominant positions or respond to threats during periods of crisis or instability. And we know even less about how skillful entrepreneurs put multiple institutional logics to strategic use. The chapters in this volume begin to redress this neglect.

Efforts to incorporate power into institutional arguments begin with two simple observations: (1) actors in key institutions realize considerable gains from the maintenance of those institutions; and (2) when organizational fields are unstable and established practices ill formed, successful collective action often depends upon defining and elaborating widely accepted rules of the game. Consequently, the acquisition and maintenance of power within organizational fields requires that dominant organizations continually enact strategies of control, most notably through either the socialization of newcomers into a shared world view or via the support of the state and its judicial arm.[29]

Fligstein makes this point nicely in arguing that certain corporate strategies were favored by CEOs with marketing and finance backgrounds because the strategies fit their interests and competencies. Successful executives developed conceptions of control that came to dominate their industries and defined appropriate standards of behavior. Brint and Karabel (ch. 14) note the fit between the vocationalizing agenda of community college administrators and their backgrounds and status concerns. DiMaggio describes museum professionals who sought radical changes in museum missions and policies that would tend to enhance their own positions relative to those of their trustees.

In all of these cases, advocates of change drew on institutionalized models and employed highly legitimate and stylized accounts, which we have no reason to doubt they believed, to advance their positions. But the options favored and terms of debate bore a decided affinity to the interests of the participants.

The three case studies of institutionalization—Galaskiewicz on corporate philanthropy, Brint and Karabel on community colleges, and DiMaggio on art museums—are remarkably convergent in suggesting how power and interests shape the evolution of organizational fields. Each identifies goal-oriented elite intervention at critical points in a field's development; each illustrates the construction of fieldwide organizations, with professionals playing leading roles, that exerted an autonomous impact on ideology and behavior; and each documents contests between institutional models that were shaped around strategic considerations. The point is not that the interests pursued were not in some sense institutionalized, but that for the explanatory purposes of each paper, the active political side of the story (which, in each case, has decisively institutional elements) is more germane.

Brint and Karabel suggest that neoinstitutionalists still have much to learn from Selznick's work, which focused directly on the exercise of power. "Our difficulties with the new institutionalism," they write, "have less to do with its tenets than with its silences." In some respects, the vocationalization of the community college is a textbook institutionalization story: a change in organizational mission sponsored by key elites as a contribution to the goals of justice and economic progress, it began slowly then diffused widely. But it is an institutional story with an odd twist: diffusion occurred only after sixty years of fruitless advocacy by community-college administrators and their allies. What explains, first, the continued but ineffectual efforts at vocationalization in the face of student opposition and, second, the project's eventual success? To answer this question, Brint and Karabel emphasize not only institutional models and rational myths, but also "the pursuit of organizational interests" and "the role of group struggle in shaping organizational structures and policies."

AN INSTITUTIONAL PERSPECTIVE ON
COMPETITION AND EFFICIENCY

The contributions to this volume reflect not just an effort to deal with politics and conflict, but a parallel attempt to come to terms with the problems of competition and efficiency. Typical of this effort is the rapprochement between institutionalism and the population ecology approach. Institutionalists are now much more willing to acknowledge the importance of competition and organizational selection than they once were (see Powell, ch. 8). Ecologists, for their part, now emphasize the importance of institutional factors in competition and explicitly disavow Panglossian models of organizational evolution (Hannan and Freeman 1989). Chapter 16 by Singh, Tucker, and Meinhard is a fine example of this convergence: using population models, the authors demonstrate the effects of institutional change on population dynamics and the salutory effect of institutional legitimacy on the survival rates of Toronto's voluntary social-service agencies. They suggest that competition for social fitness has a decided payoff.

Rather than deny the importance of competition, institutional theorists now emphasize the historical and intersocietal variability of competitive regimes and the role of institutions in constituting these regimes. Chapter 15 by Orrù, Biggart, and Hamilton illustrates this point vividly with its comparison of intercorporate coordination in Japan, Taiwan, and Korea. Firm structures and interfirm networks are "strikingly uniform or isomorphic within each economy, but different from each of the others—they express the organizing principles of that economy's environment." The authors challenge the notion that institutional and technical imperatives are inconsistent; by contrast, they find that institutional and technical considerations "converge harmoniously in shaping organizational forms." Rather than "hamper organizational efficiency," the "distinct conceptions of what constitutes appropriate economic activity" in their three East Asian cases "provide a basis for market order and for competitive relations."

Indeed, as Powell (ch. 8) and Scott (ch. 7) suggest, the early tendency of many neoinstitutionalists to identify technical features with for-profit firms and institutional forces with nonprofit or government agencies is no longer viable. The successful application of institutional models to the adoption of structural elements and practices by proprietary companies, illustrated by Galaskiewicz's chapter on corporate philanthropy and Fligstein's on corporate strategy in this volume, has become a growth industry. Recent efforts in this vein include treatments of the multidivisional firm (Fligstein 1985), patterns of corporate philanthropy (Galaskiewicz 1985a; Galaskiewicz and Burt 1991; Galaskiewicz and Wasserman 1989; Useem 1987), training and promotion procedures in law firms (Tolbert 1988; Tolbert and Stern 1989), the introduction and spread of matrix management (Burns and Wholey 1990), financial reporting methods

(Mezias 1990), legal departments of multinationals (Miyazawa 1986); due process procedures in corporations (Dobbin et al. 1988; Edelman 1990), human resource policies (Baron, Dobbin, and Jennings 1986), and management buyouts (Amburgey and Lippert 1989). All of these studies provide ample illustration of how institutional forces shape corporate structures and practices.

Do such findings mean that businesses are inefficient? The implications are far from obvious. On the one hand, early expressions of the new institutionalism explicitly contrasted institutional processes to those driven by efficiency considerations, contending that money spent on ceremonial or legitimating activities constituted "pure costs from the point of view of efficiency" (Meyer and Rowan, ch. 2; see also DiMaggio and Powell, ch. 3). But this argument is questionable for several reasons. First, we must distinguish between the processes by which an organization makes a change from the effects of the change it has made: a firm that adopts a product-related diversification strategy because it is accepted in its industry might well benefit materially from this decision. Second, we must ask whether institutionally driven choices (e.g., the adoption of a human resource management department) have any net impact on efficiency at all. Third, we must account for the income-producing effects of legitimacy rather than simply looking at the cost side: it may be highly efficient for a school district to spend a million dollars on ceremonial activities if the resulting legitimacy induces voters to endorse a $15 million bond issue.

The key thrust of institutional analysis is neither to expose the inefficiency of organizational practices nor to celebrate the nonoptimality of institutional arrangements. We are skeptical of arguments that assume that surviving institutions represent efficient solutions because we recognize that rates of environmental change frequently outpace rates of organizational adaptation. Because suboptimal organizational practices can persist for an extended period of time, we rarely expect institutions simply to reflect current political and economic forces. The point is not to discern whether institutions are efficient, but to develop robust explanations of the ways in which institutions incorporate historical experiences into their rules and organizing logics.

Acknowledgments

This introduction is a collaborative effort; the authors' names are listed in alphabetical order for the sake of convenience. We are grateful for perceptive written comments on earlier drafts of the introduction by Jeff Alexander, Steve Brint, Randall Collins, Ken Dauber, Ron Jepperson, John Meyer, Steve Mezias, Dick Nelson, Charles Perrow, Ken Shepsle, Don Shin, Harrison White, and Mayer Zald. The discussion of the positive theory of institutions owes much to presentations by Shepsle and Barry Weingast at a conference that Powell attended. The authors also benefited from careful readings of earlier drafts by participants in faculty/graduate-student workshops at Arizona and

Yale. The authors bear responsibility for such unclarity or unsatisfying treatments of controversial matters as remain.

Notes

1. Scott and Meyer have substantially revised their paper for this volume and Zucker has added a new postscript to hers. The chapters by Meyer and Rowan and DiMaggio and Powell appear in their original form.

2. For definitional discussions of *institution, institutionalized,* and *institutionalization,* see the chapters in parts 1 and 2, especially those by Jepperson (ch. 6) and Scott (ch. 7).

3. In doing so, we are more concerned with central tendencies than with exceptions. Although neoinstitutionalism in economics and political science emerged in opposition to atomism rather than models of rational action, many economists and political scientists have come to question (and in their models, to modify) key elements in the rational-choice approaches to institutions that have dominated their fields. On the other hand, approaches such as transaction-cost economics and agency theory have made inroads into organizational analysis and sociology. To make matters even more complicated, earlier uses of *institution* persist in sociology (where *institution* sometimes refers to such complexes of interrelated agents and activities as law, religion, medicine, the family, or the state), political science (where *institutional* work includes historical or richly descriptive accounts of such political units as state agencies or legislatures), and history (where *institutional* sometimes refers to studies of constitutions and kings). Our point is not that any discipline presents a unified front, but that variation in the treatment of institutions between disciplines tends to be greater than the variation within them.

4. Putterman 1986 provides an excellent overview of this literature and offers samplings of key papers in this tradition. As Richard Nelson has pointed out in a personal communication, the new institutionalism in economics contrasts sharply with what used to be known as "institutional economics." The latter, associated with such early twentieth-century scholars as John Commons and Thorstein Veblen, was quite sociological in its emphasis on custom, political economy, and the historical specificity of economic institutions.

5. See Young 1986 for a thoughtful review of early work on regimes. He is critical of the vagueness and the disconcerting elasticity of the key concepts, but he suggests this work represents an important new line of thought on international relations.

6. Under circumstances of rapid societal-level cultural change, however, organizations may incorporate new elements in the institutional environment at a rapid rate. We are grateful to John Meyer for this point, which is illustrated in Thomas 1989.

7. We thank Ron Jepperson for the latter point.

8. A process of system change is state-dependent when the probability and direction of change from one period to the next are a function of the state of the system at the initial period.

9. This is particularly the case with respect to the old institutionalism, the boundaries of which were constructed retrospectively to enclose a variety of works and authors who

did not regard themselves as members of a self-conscious school (Perrow 1986). In our discussion, we refer especially to the *loci classici* of the old institutionalism, Selznick's *TVA and the Grass Roots* (1949) and *Leadership in Administration* (1957).

10. Although *cognition* sometimes refers to the full range of mental activity, we follow current usage in distinguishing between cognition, on the one hand, and affective or evaluative processes on the other. By *cognition* we refer to both reasoning and the preconscious grounds of reason: classifications, representations, scripts, schemas, production systems, and the like.

11. Our argument here is only that the institutional theory of organizations has participated in a broader theoretical turn; we are not interested in questions of priority. A casual perusal of citation patterns and publication dates suggests that, except for the impact of Garfinkel and Berger and Luckmann on the early formulations of Meyer and Rowan and Zucker, the affinity between organizational institutionalism and these broader currents is largely one of convergence rather than influence. If anything, the cognitive revolution seems to have reached institutional theory before making its mark on social theory as a whole, probably due to the presence within organization theory of the seminal work of Herbert Simon and James March. The papers in this volume evince a diminishing parochialism within institutional theory as awareness of convergent work from outside the field of organization studies has grown (see Friedland and Alford, Jepperson, Jepperson and Meyer, Powell, and Scott).

12. We would distinguish our view, which is consistent with Collins's (1981) call for "microtranslation," from individual reductionism (i.e., positing motivated individual action as the ultimate cause of all social phenomena in an analytic sense). In keeping with this, we use the term *action* throughout to refer to social behavior, without any of the muscular, rational, or individual reductionist connotations that some have associated with that term. We are grateful to John Meyer, Ron Jepperson, and other readers of an earlier version for pressing us to make explicit our reasons for concentrating on microfoundations in this draft, and for clarifying the lack of consensus within institutional theory on the relative importance of the "micro" side.

13. In referring to the "middle" period, we follow Alexander 1987:53–72. Our discussion of Parsons draws on two major works (Parsons and Shils 1951; Parsons 1951) that were published after Selznick's *TVA and the Grass Roots* (1949). Parsons integrated object-relations theory into his model of action during the 1940s, however, and Selznick had access to his essays (e.g., Parsons 1945) during this period. Selznick 1957 also drew directly on work in ego psychology.

14. For an insightful discussion of how Parsons' treatment of social action neglects the ways that individuals construct their behavior out of an amalgam of cultural roles and normative values, see Camic 1989:63–69.

15. Indeed, Mayhew 1984 has illustrated how, despite Parsons' early criticisms of utilitarianism, the later work of Parsons progressively incorporated a utilitarian image of a modern social order. Both Mayhew 1984 and Bourricaud 1981 suggest that Parsons sought to extend the tools of utilitarian theory beyond the realm of the market to all modern forms of social organization. This "institutionalized individualism" (Bourricaud 1981) argues that processes of exchange are stabilized by constraining normative structures external to the exchange partners. Some readers may note the obvious parallels between this version of institutionalism and recent work in the new institutional economics. See Camic's (1986:1076) discussion for more on this point.

16. In an extraordinarily thoughtful and extensive set of comments on an earlier draft of this essay, Jeffrey Alexander suggests that Parsons' view of values and norms is far more consistent with cognitivists' images of scripts, rules, and classifications than we acknowledge and that Parsons anticipated much of the "practical theory of action" that we describe below. To be sure, Parsons' critique of utilitarianism, his portrayal of the analytic autonomy of levels of analysis, and his concern with the mutual orientation of actors are all fundamental precursors to the contemporary approaches we discuss; his contribution is easy to take for granted today precisely because it was so effective. On the other hand, we find it difficult to locate in Parsons' major writings evidence that he anticipated the trends we describe; we are struck, instead, by his emphasis on the moral aspects of value-commitments, the general fit between values and norms, and the quasi-rational manner in which actors pursue means-end chains. The issue is a difficult one, because Parsons did not have at his disposal the vocabulary that has developed over many years of work by the Carnegie school, ethnomethodologists, and cognitive psychologists, and therefore could not easily have expressed certain images of action even if he anticipated them. Moreover, as Alexander has noted, Parsons' work is complex and not always internally consistent. It may be safest to conclude that Parsons' discussions of values and norms, employing the language available to him, lend themselves to a reification of values, a treatment of persons as "oversocialized," and an essentially moral view of the evaluative dimension of actors' orientations to the means and ends of action. In other words, we believe we give an accurate account of "Parsonsianism" as it was received into American sociology, even if Parsons himself had a more complex view of the manner in which values and norms enter into action than we imply.

17. Cognition for Parsons is assimilated, as Warner 1978 tells us, to either a scientific mode of thought or a normative one. Warner 1978:1328 points out that the former analytic move rejects the notion that cognition has variable properties, while the latter effort recognizes the variable status of cognition but reduces it to little more than the status of a belief. As a result, the social actors in Parsons' scheme appear to lack either interpretive competence or practical consciousness. This passive individual has been aptly labeled a "cultural dope" by Garfinkel 1967:66–68.

18. A key premise of Parsons' *Structure of Social Action* (1937) is that action consists of a reasoned selection of means and ends by the application of guiding norms. Yet the unremitting thrust of his argument was to homogenize social action (Camic 1986). By omitting any consideration of the habitual nature of action, he severely handicapped his efforts to account for patterns of order in social relationships.

19. March and Simon drew some of the inspiration for their pathbreaking work from *The Function of the Executive,* written by Chester Barnard (1938), an AT&T executive seconded to the Harvard Business School. Barnard was a talented amateur scholar; *Functions* is theoretically undisciplined, full of sharp but not always consistent insights. The influence of Harvard, of Parsons, and of the Henderson circle and their appreciation of Pareto is evident in Barnard's systems approach. His voluntaristic model of attachment to the firm and his emphasis on passionate commitment as a source of organizational solidarity are consistent with Parsons' normative theory of action. But there is also a cognitive side to *Functions,* found in Barnard's analysis of decision making, in his prescient account of what would later become known as the "enacted environment," in his view of goals and subgoals as objects that leaders can manipulate, and in his notion of the "zone of indifference" within which workers comply unreflec-

tively with management directives. What Simon, March, and their Carnegie colleagues achieved was to purge Barnard of Parsons and to systematize and develop further the cognitive theory that was struggling to escape.

20. Garfinkel has published relatively little, and his writing often resists easy comprehension; his major work is *Studies in Ethnomethodology* (1967). Fortunately, the secondary literature is systematic and informative; see, especially, Heritage 1984, 1987 and Alexander 1987:238–70.

21. Alexander 1987 has distinguished between Garfinkel's early work, which represents an elaboration of Parsons' framework, and his later work, which repudiates it. Our comments refer to the second phase, which has had a more marked influence on contemporary theory.

22. A related line of argument in organizational behavior has been pursued by Weick in his work (1976) on loosely coupled systems, and by Staw and his colleagues (Staw 1981; Staw and Ross 1987) in their work on the escalation of commitment.

23. Within neoinstitutionalism, the position of norms and associated "sanctions" is a matter of some disagreement or, perhaps, ambiguity. Scott and Meyer contend that institutions rest on normative as well as cognitive foundations; DiMaggio and Powell (ch. 3) describe normative isomorphism, but, as Scott (ch. 7) argues, do not distinguish it clearly from cognitive effects. Zucker (postscript to ch. 4) is more strictly cognitive, arguing that the use of sanctions to defend a behavior pattern is evidence of weak institutionalization, insofar as high levels of institutionalization make sanctions unnecessary. Jepperson and Powell (chs. 6 and 8), by contrast, view the support of rewards and sanctions as an intrinsic aspect of institutions, but Jepperson specifies that such support occurs through "relatively self-activating social processes," while Powell relies more on the binding power of rules.

24. It may be useful to contrast this approach to rational-actor models and the Parsonian model of action with a concrete example, the increasingly well-worn case of the motorist stopping at a highway restaurant to which she expects never to return. A rational motorist would fail to leave a tip, calculating that the waiter who has been stiffed would have no opportunity to sanction her misbehavior. A Parsonian motorist would leave a tip because she had internalized the notion that this was good; she and the waiter would smile at one another as she did so in mutual appreciation of her appropriate role performance. A practical actor would also leave a tip, because that is what one does, but without experiencing a warm glow. If the practical actor stopped to think about it, she might fail to leave a tip (if her image of human action is derived from graduate economics courses) or she might leave one and feel good about it (if she is an ex-waitress or a Parsonian), but under most circumstances she won't give the matter much thought.

25. Few neoinstitutionalists have embraced Collins's work for two reasons (but see Jepperson, ch. 6). First, his best-known paper on the topic rather misleadingly rejects "cognitive" approaches to action because it identifies "cognition" with rational, discursive thought. In fact, Collins follows ethnomethodology in laying considerable emphasis on the "irreducibly tacit element in cognition and communication" (1981:991); what he rejects is a preoccupation with that part of cognition Giddens refers to as discursive consciousness, along with the "as-if" rationalist vocabulary of values and norms. Second, because of his emphasis on the interactional foundations of social organization and on the affective or ritual aspects of the micro-order, the work is sometimes misinterpreted as sharing the radical realism of some (but by no means all)

ethnomethodologists, that is, as regarding macroconcepts as "mere" epiphenomena of, or glosses on, an "essential" microlevel. In fact, although he regards the ritual aspect of interaction as primary, Collins (1981) acknowledges the role of accounts, macroreferences, and cultural resources in normalizing and structuring interactions. Because he assumes the polemical burden of challenging reified, quasi-rational accounts of social action, Collins opts to neglect the origins and use of shared typifications (but see his more recent work, especially Collins 1988a and 1988b). Nonetheless, his approach points to a solution to the problem of order that is more consonant with new research on cognition and more plausible than approaches that undervalue affect and ritual. In this volume, both Meyer and Rowan, and Friedland and Alford develop institutional arguments that incorporate attention to ritual and ceremony at a more macrolevel. Also see Meyer 1988a on the sacred modern self.

26. The need for such work is evident on empirical grounds. Given that anything that enters into human interaction can become the basis of a shared typification, why are some typifications (the nation, the family, private property) so much more compelling than others (counties, second cousins, the commons)? A purely cognitive theory of action, even one that integrates Giddens's ideas about the basic security system, cannot account for the dramatically different affective and normative responses of the subjects in Zucker's experiment under the "office condition" (ch. 4) and the participants in Milgram's obedience-to-authority research program (Milgram 1974).

27. On the former, see, especially, *Distinction* (Bourdieu 1984); on the latter, see, especially, *The Logic of Practice* (1990).

28. The natural affinity between Bourdieu's ideas and neoinstitutional theory is especially evident in Thévenot 1984; note also Jepperson's characterization of "institutionalization as a particular set of social reproductive processes" (ch. 6).

29. There are intriguing parallels between institutionalist thought and the Marxian tradition in this regard, and much room for a dialogue that has not yet taken place. Antonio Gramsci's notion of hegemonia (1971), the domination by elites of the consciousness of members of other classes, for example, directs attention to why some ideas and practices are institutionalized and others are not. Similarly, Michael Mann's (1973) depiction of the four-part process by which a social class achieves "consciousness"—recognition of itself as a class, awareness of the capitalist as an opponent, heightened salience of the class identity, and the identification of alternatives—has much in common with institutional accounts of change. These affinities have rarely been acknowledged for two reasons. First, authors in the Marxian tradition generally hew to an a priori model of class structure that is of limited applicability to many phenomena in which neoinstitutionalists are interested (especially at the organizational level). Second, Marxian analysts ordinarily view social change as the result of conflict between self-conscious, rational (corporate) actors (a tendency at its most explicit in contemporary "analytic Marxism" [Wright 1985; Elster 1982]), treating processes that institutionalists view as nearly universal as pathological departures from rationality ("false consciousness"). Nonetheless, the Marxian tradition has the virtue of focusing on the exercise of power (conscious or unconscious), on the means by which power is exercised, and on patterns of inequality of power common to most large-scale societies. We are grateful to Don Shin for reminding us of this, and to Chick Perrow for repeated exhortations to attend seriously to power and inequality, a point that we concur with and have tried to attend to elsewhere (see DiMaggio 1988a and Powell 1985b).

Part One

The Initial Formulations

2 Institutionalized Organizations: Formal Structure as Myth and Ceremony

JOHN W. MEYER AND BRIAN ROWAN

Formal organizations are generally understood to be systems of coordinated and controlled activities that arise when work is embedded in complex networks of technical relations and boundary-spanning exchanges. But in modern societies, formal organizational structures arise in highly institutionalized contexts. Professions, policies, and programs are created along with the products and services that they are understood to produce rationally. This process permits many new organizations to spring up and forces existing ones to incorporate new practices and procedures. That is, organizations are driven to incorporate the practices and procedures defined by prevailing rationalized concepts of organizational work and institutionalized in society. Organizations that do so increase their legitimacy and their survival prospects, independent of the immediate efficacy of the acquired practices and procedures.

Institutionalized products, services, techniques, policies, and programs function as powerful myths, and many organizations adopt them ceremonially. But conformity to institutionalized rules often conflicts sharply with efficiency criteria; conversely, to coordinate and control activity in order to promote efficiency undermines an organization's ceremonial conformity and sacrifices its support and legitimacy. To maintain ceremonial conformity, organizations that reflect institutional rules tend to buffer their formal structures from the uncertainties of technical activities by becoming loosely coupled, building gaps between their formal structures and actual work activities.

This chapter argues that the formal structures of many organizations in postindustrial society (Bell 1973) dramatically reflect the myths of their institutional environments instead of the demands of their work activities. The first part describes prevailing theories of the origins of formal structures and the main problem the theories confront. The second part discusses an alternative source of formal structures: myths embedded in the institutional environment. The third part develops the argument that organizations reflecting institutionalized environments maintain gaps between their formal structures and their ongoing work activities. The final part summarizes by discussing some research implications.

Throughout the chapter, institutionalized rules are distinguished sharply from prevailing social behaviors. Institutionalized rules are classifications built into society as reciprocated typifications or interpretations (Berger and Luckmann 1967:54). Such rules may be simply taken for granted or may be supported by public opinion or the force of law (Starbuck 1976). Institutions inevitably involve normative obligations but often enter into social life primarily as facts which must be taken into account by actors. Institutionalization involves the processes by which social processes, obligations, or actualities come to take on a rulelike status in social thought and action. So, for example, the social status of doctor is a highly institutionalized rule (both normative and cognitive) for managing illness as well as a social role made up of particular behaviors, relations, and expectations. Research and development is an institutionalized category of organizational activity which has meaning and value in many sectors of society; it is also a collection of actual research and development activities. In a smaller way, a No Smoking sign is an institution with legal status and implications as well as an attempt to regulate smoking behavior. Fundamental to the argument of this chapter is that institutional rules may have effects on organizational structures and their implementation in actual technical work which are very different from the effects generated by the networks of social behavior and relationships which compose and surround a given organization.

Prevailing Theories of
Formal Structure

A sharp distinction should be made between the formal structure of an organization and its actual day-to-day work activities. Formal structure is a blueprint for activities which includes, first of all, the table of organization: a listing of offices, departments, positions, and programs. These elements are linked by explicit goals and policies that make up a rational theory of how, and to what end, activities are to be fitted together. The essence of a modern bureaucratic organization lies in the rationalized and impersonal character of these structural elements and of the goals that link them.

One of the central problems in organization theory is to describe the conditions that give rise to rationalized formal structure. In conventional theories, rational formal structure is assumed to be the most effective way to coordinate and control the complex relational networks involved in modern technical or work activities (see Scott 1975 for a review). This assumption derives from Weber's (1946, 1947, 1952) discussions of the historical emergence of bureaucracies as consequences of economic markets and centralized states. Economic markets place a premium on rationality and coordination. As markets expand, the relational networks in a given domain become more complex and differentiated, and organizations in that domain must manage more internal and boundary-spanning interdependencies. Such factors as size (Blau 1970) and technology (Woodward 1965) increase the complexity of internal relations, and the division of labor among organizations increases boundary-spanning problems (Aiken and Hage 1968; Freeman 1973; Thompson 1967). Because the need for coordination increases under these conditions, and because formally coordinated work has competitive advantages, organizations with rationalized formal structures tend to develop.

The formation of centralized states and the penetration of societies by political centers also contribute to the rise and spread of formal organization. When the relational networks involved in economic exchange and political management become extremely complex, bureaucratic structures are thought to be the most effective and rational means to standardize and control subunits. Bureaucratic control is especially useful for expanding political centers, and standardization is often demanded by both centers and peripheral units (Bendix 1964, 1968). Political centers organize layers of offices that manage to extend conformity and to displace traditional activities throughout societies.

The problem: *Prevailing theories assume that the coordination and control of activity are the critical dimensions on which formal organizations have succeeded in the modern world.* This assumption is based on the view that organizations function according to their formal blueprints: coordination is routine, rules and procedures are followed, and actual activities conform to the prescriptions of formal structure. But much of the empirical research on organizations casts doubt on this assumption. An earlier generation of researchers concluded that there was a great gap between the formal and the informal organization (e.g., Dalton 1959; Downs 1967; Homans 1950). A related observation is that formal organizations are often loosely coupled (March and Olsen 1976; Weick 1976): structural elements are only loosely linked to each other and to activities, rules are often violated, decisions are often unimplemented, or if implemented have uncertain consequences, technologies are of problematic efficiency, and evaluation and inspection systems are subverted or rendered so vague as to provide little coordination.

Formal organizations are endemic in modern societies. There is need for an explanation of their rise that is partially free from the assumption that, in practice, formal structures actually coordinate and control work. Such an explanation should account for the elaboration of purposes, positions, policies, and procedural rules that characterizes formal organizations, but must do so without supposing that these structural features are implemented in routine work activity.

Institutional Sources
of Formal Structure

By focusing on the management of complex relational networks and the exercise of coordination and control, prevailing theories have neglected an alternative Weberian source of formal structure: the legitimacy of rationalized formal structures. In prevailing theories, legitimacy is a given; assertions about bureaucratization rest on the assumption of norms of rationality (Thompson 1967). When norms do play causal roles in theories of bureaucratization, it is because they are thought to be built into modern societies and personalites as very general values, which are thought to facilitate formal organization. But norms of rationality are not simply general values. They exist in much more specific and powerful ways in the rules, understandings, and meanings attached to institutionalized social structures. The causal importance of such institutions in the process of bureaucratization has been neglected.

Formal structures are not only creatures of their relational networks in the social organization. In modern societies, the elements of rationalized formal structure are deeply ingrained in, and reflect, widespread understandings of social reality. Many of the positions, policies, programs, and procedures of modern organizations are enforced by public opinion, by the views of important constituents, by knowledge legitimated through the educational system, by social prestige, by the laws, and by the definitions of negligence and prudence used by the courts. Such elements of formal structure are manifestations of powerful institutional rules which function as highly rationalized myths that are binding on particular organizations.

In modern societies, the myths generating formal organizational structure have two key properties. First, they are rationalized and impersonal prescriptions that identify various social purposes as technical ones and specify in a rulelike way the appropriate means to pursue these technical purposes rationally (Ellul 1964). Second, they are highly institutionalized and thus in some measure beyond the discretion of any individual participant or organization. They must, therefore, be taken for granted as legitimate, apart from evaluations of their impact on work outcomes.

Many elements of formal structure are highly institutionalized and function as myths. Examples include professions, programs, and technologies:

Large numbers of rationalized professions emerge (Wilensky 1965; Bell 1973). These are occupations controlled not only by direct inspection of work outcomes but also by social rules of licensing, certifying, and schooling. The occupations are rationalized, being understood to control impersonal techniques rather than moral mysteries. Further, they are highly institutionalized: the delegation of activities to the appropriate occupations is socially expected and often legally obligatory over and above any calculations of its efficiency.

Many formalized organizational programs are also institutionalized in society. Ideologies define the functions appropriate to a business—such as sales, production, advertising, or accounting; to a university—such as instruction and research in history, engineering, and literature; and to a hospital—such as surgery, internal medicine, and obstetrics. Such classifications of organizational functions, and the specifications for conducting each function, are prefabricated formulas available for use by any given organization.

Similarly, technologies are institutionalized and become myths binding on organizations. Technical procedures of production, accounting, personnel selection, or data processing become taken-for-granted means to accomplish organizational ends. Quite apart from their possible efficiency, such institutionalized techniques establish an organization as appropriate, rational, and modern. Their use displays responsibility and avoids claims of negligence.

The impact of such rationalized institutional elements on organizations and organizing situations is enormous. These rules define new organizing situations, redefine existing ones, and specify the means for coping rationally with each. They enable, and often require, participants to organize along prescribed lines. And they spread very rapidly in modern society as part of the rise of post-industrial society (Bell 1973). New and extant domains of activity are codified in institutionalized programs, professions, or techniques, and organizations incorporate the packaged codes. Some examples are the following.

The discipline of psychology creates a rationalized theory of personnel selection and certifies personnel professionals; personnel departments and functionaries appear in all sorts of extant organizations, and new, specialized personal agencies also appear.

As programs of research and development are created and professionals with expertise in these fields are trained and defined, organizations come under increasing pressure to incorporate R & D units.

As the prerational profession of prostitution is rationalized along medical lines, bureaucratized organizations—sex-therapy clinics, massage parlors, and the like—spring up more easily.

As the issues of safety and environmental pollution arise, and as relevant professions and programs become institutionalized in laws, union ideologies, and public opinion, organizations incorporate these programs and professions.

The growth of rationalized institutional structures in society makes formal organizations more common and more elaborate. Such institutions are myths which make formal organizations both easier to create and more necessary. After all, the building blocks for organizations come to be littered around the societal landscape; it takes only a little entrepreneurial energy to assemble them into a structure. And because these building blocks are considered proper, adequate, rational, and necessary, organizations must incorporate them to avoid illegitimacy. Thus, the myths built into rationalized institutional elements create the necessity, the opportunity, and the impulse to organize rationally, over and above pressures in this direction created by the need to manage proximate relational networks:

Proposition 1. *As rationalized institutional rules arise in given domains of work activity, formal organizations form and expand by incorporating these rules as structural elements.*

Two distinct ideas are implied here: (1*A*) As institutionalized myths define new domains of rationalized activity, formal organizations emerge in these domains. (1*B*) As rationalizing institutional myths arise in existing domains of activity, extant organizations expand their formal structures so as to become isomorphic with these new myths.

To understand the larger historical process it is useful to note that:

Proposition 2. *The more modernized the society, the more extended the rationalized institutional structure in given domains and the greater the number of domains containing rationalized institutions.*

Modern institutions, then, are thoroughly rationalized, and these rationalized elements act as myths giving rise to more formal organization. When propositions 1 and 2 are combined, two more specific ideas follow: (2*A*) Formal organizations are more likely to emerge in more modernized societies, even with the complexity of immediate relational networks held constant. (2*B*) Formal organizations in a given domain of activity are likely to have more elaborated structures in more modernized societies, even with the complexity of immediate relational networks held constant.

Combining the ideas above with prevailing organization theory, it becomes clear that modern societies are filled with rationalized bureaucracies for two reasons. First, as the prevailing theories have asserted, relational networks become increasingly complex as societies modernize. Second, modern societies are filled with institutional rules which function as myths depicting various formal structures as rational means to the attainment of desirable ends. Figure 2.1 summarizes these two lines of theory. Both lines suggest that the postindustrial society—the society dominated by rational organization even more than by the forces of production—arises both out of the complexity of the modern social organizational network and, more directly, as an ideological matter. Once institutionalized, rationality becomes a myth with explosive organizing potential,

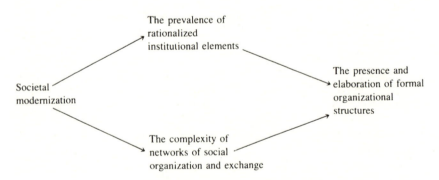

Fig. 2.1. The origins and elaboration of formal organizational structures.

as both Ellul (1964) and Bell (1973)—though with rather different reactions—observe.

THE RELATION OF ORGANIZATIONS TO THEIR INSTITUTIONAL ENVIRONMENTS

The observation is not new that organizations are structured by phenomena in their environments and tend to become isomorphic with them. One explanation of such isomorphism is that formal organizations become matched with their environments by technical and exchange interdependencies. This line of reasoning can be seen in the works of Aiken and Hage (1968), Hawley (1968), and Thompson (1967). This explanation asserts that structural elements diffuse because environments create boundary-spanning exigencies for organizations, and that organizations which incorporate structural elements isomorphic with the environment are able to manage such interdependencies.

A second explanation for the parallelism between organizations and their environments—and the one emphasized here—is that organizations structurally reflect socially constructed reality (Berger and Luckmann 1967). This view is suggested in the work of Parsons (1956) and Udy (1970), who see organizations as greatly conditioned by their general institutional environments and therefore as institutions themselves in part. Emery and Trist (1965) also see organizations as responding directly to environmental structures and distinguish such effects sharply from those that occur through boundary-spanning exchanges. According to the institutional conception as developed here, organizations tend to disappear as distinct and bounded units. Quite beyond the environmental interrelations suggested in open-systems theories, institutional theories in their extreme forms define organizations as dramatic enactments of the rationalized myths pervading modern societies rather than as units involved in exchange—no matter how complex—with their environments.

The two explanations of environmental isomorphism are not entirely inconsistent. Organizations both deal with their environments at their boundaries and imitate environmental elements in their structures. However, the two lines of explanation have very different implications for internal organizational processes, as is argued below.

THE ORIGINS OF RATIONAL INSTITUTIONAL MYTHS

Bureaucratization is caused in part by the proliferation of rationalized myths in society, and this in turn involves the evolution of the whole modern institutional system. Although the latter topic is beyond the scope of this chapter, three specific processes that generate rationalized myths of organizational structure can be noted.

The Elaboration of Complex
Relational Networks

As the relational networks in societies become dense and interconnected, increasing numbers of rationalized myths arise. Some of them are highly generalized; for example, the principles of universalism (Parsons 1971), contracts (Spencer 1897), restitution (Durkheim 1933), and expertise (Weber 1947) are generalized to diverse occupations, organizational programs, and organizational practices. Other myths describe specific structural elements. These myths may originate from narrow contexts and be applied in different ones. For example, in modern societies the relational contexts of business organizations in a single industry are roughly similar from place to place. Under these conditions a particularly effective practice, occupational specialty, or principle of coordination can be codified into mythlike form. The laws, the educational and credentialing systems, and public opinion then make it necessary or advantageous for organizations to incorporate the new structures.

The Degree of Collective Organization
of the Environment

The myths generated by particular organizational practices and diffused through relational networks have legitimacy based on the supposition that they are rationally effective. But many myths also have official legitimacy based on legal mandates. Societies that, through nation building and state formation, have developed rational-legal orders are especially prone to give collective (legal) authority to institutions which legitimate particular organizational structures. The rise of centralized states and integrated nations means that organized agents of society assume jurisdiction over large numbers of activity domains (Swanson 1971). Legislative and judicial authorities create and interpret legal mandates; administrative agencies—such as state and federal governments, port authorities, and school districts—establish rules of practice; and licenses and credentials become necessary in order to practice occupations. The stronger the rational-legal order, the greater the extent to which rationalized rules and procedures and personnel become institutional requirements. New formal organizations emerge, and extant organizations acquire new structural elements.

Leadership Efforts of Local
Organizations

The rise of the state and the expansion of collective jurisdiction are often thought to result in domesticated organizations (Carlson 1962) subject to high levels of goal displacement (Clark 1956; Selznick 1949; Zald and Denton 1963). This view is misleading: organizations do often adapt to their institutional contexts, but they often play active roles in shaping those contexts (Dowling and Pfeffer 1975; Parsons 1956; Perrow 1970; Thompson 1967).

Many organizations actively seek charters from collective authorities and manage to institutionalize their goals and structures in the rules of such authorities.

Efforts to mold institutional environments proceed along two dimensions. First, powerful organizations force their immediate relational networks to adapt to their structures and relations. For instance, automobile producers help create demands for particular kinds of roads, transportation systems, and fuels that make automobiles virtual necessities; competitive forms of transportation have to adapt to the existing relational context. But second, powerful organizations attempt to build their goals and procedures directly into society as institutional rules. Automobile producers, for instance, attempt to create the standards in public opinion defining desirable cars, to influence legal standards defining satisfactory cars, to affect judicial rules defining cars adequate enough to avoid manufacturer liability, and to force agents of the collectivity to purchase only their cars. Rivals must then compete both in social networks or markets and in contexts of institutional rules which are defined by extant organizations. In this fashion, given organizational forms perpetuate themselves by becoming institutionalized rules. For example, school administrators who create new curricula or training programs attempt to validate them as legitimate innovations in educational theory and governmental requirements. If they are successful, the new procedures can be perpetuated as authoritatively required or at least satisfactory. New departments within business enterprises, such as personnel, advertising, or research and development departments, attempt to professionalize by creating rules of practice and personnel certification that are enforced by the schools, prestige systems, and the laws. Organizations under attack in competitive environments—small farms, passenger railways, or Rolls Royce—attempt to establish themselves as central to the cultural traditions of their societies in order to receive official protection.

The Impact of Institutional Environments on Organizations

Isomorphism with environmental institutions has some crucial consequences for organizations: (a) they incorporate elements which are legitimated externally, rather than in terms of efficiency; (b) they employ external or ceremonial assessment criteria to define the value of structural elements; and (c) dependence on externally fixed institutions reduces turbulence and maintains stability. As a result, it is argued here, institutional isomorphism promotes the success and survival of organizations. Incorporating externally legitimated formal structures increases the commitment of internal participants and external constituents. And the use of external assessment criteria—that is, moving toward the status in society of a subunit rather than an independent system—can enable an organization to remain successful by social definition, buffering it from failure.

Changing Formal Structures

By designing a formal structure that adheres to the prescriptions of myths in the institutional environment, an organization demonstrates that it is acting on collectively valued purposes in a proper and adequate manner (Dowling and Pfeffer 1975; Meyer and Rowan 1978). The incorporation of institutionalized elements provides an account (Scott and Lyman 1968) of activities that protects the organization from having its conduct questioned. The organization becomes, in a word, legitimate, and it uses its legitimacy to strengthen its support and secure its survival.

From an institutional perspective, then, a most important aspect of isomorphism with environmental institutions is the evolution of organizational language. The labels of the organization chart as well as the vocabulary used to delineate organizational goals, procedures, and policies are analogous to the vocabularies of motive used to account for the activities of individuals (Blum and McHugh 1971; Mills 1940). Just as jealousy, anger, altruism, and love are myths that interpret and explain the actions of individuals, the myths of doctors, of accountants, or of the assembly line explain organizational activities. Thus, some can say that the engineers will solve a specific problem or that the secretaries will perform certain tasks, without knowing who these engineers or secretaries will be or exactly what they will do. Both the speaker and the listeners understand such statements to describe how certain responsibilities will be carried out.

Vocabularies of structure which are isomorphic with institutional rules provide prudent, rational, and legitimate accounts. Organizations described in legitimated vocabularies are assumed to be oriented to collectively defined, and often collectively mandated, ends. The myths of personnel services, for example, not only account for the rationality of employment practices but also indicate that personnel services are valuable to an organization. Employees, applicants, managers, trustees, and governmental agencies are predisposed to trust the hiring practices of organizations that follow legitimated procedures— such as equal opportunity programs, or personality testing—and they are more willing to participate in or to fund such organizations. On the other hand, organizations that omit environmentally legitimated elements of structure or create unique structures lack acceptable legitimated accounts of their activities. Such organizations are more vulnerable to claims that they are negligent, irrational, or unnecessary. Claims of this kind, whether made by internal participants, external constituents, or the government, can cause organizations to incur real costs. For example, with the rise of modern medical institutions, large organizations that do not arrange medical-care facilities for their workers come to be seen as negligent—by the workers, by management factions, by insurers, by courts which legally define negligence, and often by laws. The costs of illegitimacy in insurance premiums and legal liabilities are very real. Similarly, environmental safety institutions make it important for organizations to create formal safety rules, safety departments, and safety programs. No Smoking rules and signs, regardless of their enforcement, are necessary to avoid charges of negligence and to avoid the extreme of illegitimation: the closing of buildings by the state. The rise of professionalized economics makes it useful for organizations to incorporate groups of economists and econometric analyses. Though no one may read, understand, or believe them, econometric analyses help legitimate the organization's plans in the eyes of investors, customers (as with Defense Department contractors), and internal participants. Such analyses can also provide rational accountings after failures occur: managers whose plans have failed can demonstrate to investors, stockholders, and superiors that procedures were prudent and that decisions were by rational means.

Thus, rationalized institutions create myths of formal structure which shape organizations. Failure to incorporate the proper elements of structure is negligent and irrational; the continued flow of support is threatened and internal dissidents are strengthened. At the same time, these myths present organizations with great opportunities for expansion. Affixing the right labels to activities can change them into valuable services and mobilize the commitments of internal participants and external constituents.

Adopting External Assessment Criteria

In institutionally elaborated environments, organizations also become sensitive to and employ external criteria of worth. Criteria include, for instance, such ceremonial awards as the Nobel Prize, endorsements by important people, the standard prices of professionals and consultants, or the prestige of programs or personnel in external social circles. For example, the conventions of modern accounting attempt to assign value to particular components of organizations on the basis of their contribution—through the organization's production function—to the goods and services the organization produces. But for many units—service departments, administrative sectors, and others—it is utterly unclear what is being produced that has clear or definable value in terms of its contribution to the organizational product. In these situations, accountants employ shadow prices: they assume that given organizational units are necessary and calculate their value from their prices in the world outside the organization. Thus modern accounting creates ceremonial production functions and maps them onto economic production functions: organizations assign externally defined worth to advertising departments, safety departments, managers, econometricians, and occasionally even sociologists, whether or not these units contribute measurably to the production of outputs. Monetary prices, in postindustrial society, reflect hosts of ceremonial influences, as do economic measures of efficiency, profitability, or net worth (Hirsch 1975).

Ceremonial criteria of worth and ceremonially derived production functions are useful to organizations: they legitimate organizations with internal participants, stockholders, the public, and the state, as with the IRS or the SEC. They demonstrate socially the fitness of an organization. The incorporation of structures with high ceremonial value, such as those reflecting the latest expert thinking or those with the most prestige, makes the credit position of an organization more favorable. Loans, donations, or investments are more easily obtained. Finally, units within the organization use ceremonial assessments as accounts of their productive service to the organization. Their internal power rises with their performance on ceremonial measures (Salancik and Pfeffer 1974).

Stabilization

The rise of an elaborate institutional environment stabilizes both external and internal organizational relationships. Centralized states, trade associations, unions, professional associations, and coalitions among organizations standardize and stabilize (see the review by Starbuck 1976).

Market conditions, the characteristics of inputs and outputs, and technological procedures are brought under the jurisdiction of institutional meanings and controls. Stabilization also results as a given organization becomes part of the wider collective system. Support is guaranteed by agreements instead of depending entirely on performance. For example, apart from whether schools educate students or hospitals cure patients, people and governmental agencies remain committed to these organizations, funding and using them almost automatically year after year.

Institutionally controlled environments buffer organizations from turbulence (Emery and Trist 1965; Terreberry 1968). Adaptations occur less rapidly as increased numbers of agreements are enacted. Collectively granted monopolies guarantee clienteles for organizations like schools, hospitals, or professional associations. The taken-for-granted (and legally regulated) quality of institutional rules makes dramatic instabilities in products, techniques, or policies unlikely. And legitimacy as accepted subunits of society protects organizations from immediate sanctions for variations in technical performance. Thus, American school districts (like other governmental units) have near monopolies and are very stable. They must conform to wider rules about proper classifications and credentials of teachers and students, and of topics of study. But they are protected by rules which make education as defined by these classifications compulsory. Alternative or private schools are possible, but must conform so closely to the required structures and classifications as to be able to generate little advantage. Some business organizations obtain very high levels of institutional stabilization. A large defense contractor may be paid for following agreed-on procedures, even if the product is ineffective. In the extreme, such organizations may be so successful as to survive bankruptcy intact—as Lockheed and Penn Central have done—by becoming partially components of the state. More commonly, such firms are guaranteed survival by state-regulated rates which secure profits regardless of costs, as with American public utility firms. Large automobile firms are a little less stabilized. They exist in an environment that contains enough structures to make automobiles, as conventionally defined, virtual necessities. But still, customers and governments can inspect each automobile and can evaluate and even legally discredit it. Legal action cannot as easily discredit a high school graduate.

Organizational Success and Survival

Thus, organizational success depends on factors other than efficient coordination and control of productive activities. Independent of their productive efficiency, organizations which exist in highly elaborated institutional environments and succeed in becoming isomorphic with these environments gain the legitimacy and resources needed to survive. In part this depends on environmental processes and on the capacity of given organizational leadership to mold these processes (Hirsch 1975). In part it depends on the ability of given organizations to conform to, and become legitimated by, environmental institutions. In institutionally elaborated environments, sagacious conformity is required: leadership (in a university, a hospital, or a business) requires an understanding of changing fashions and governmental programs. But this kind of conformity—and the almost guaranteed survival which may accompany it—is possible only in an environment with a highly institutionalized structure. In such a context an organization can be locked into isomorphism, ceremonially reflecting the institutional environment in its structure, functionaries, and procedures. Thus, in addition to the conventionally defined sources of organizational success and survival, the following general assertion can be proposed:

Proposition 3. *Organizations that incorporate societally legitimated rationalized elements in their formal structures maximize their legitimacy and increase their resources and survival capabilities.*

This proposition asserts that the long-run survival prospects of organizations increase as state structures elaborate and as organizations respond to institutionalized rules. In the United States, for instance, schools, hospitals, and welfare organizations show considerable ability to survive, precisely because they are matched with—and almost absorbed by—their institutional environments. In the same way, organizations fail when they deviate from the prescriptions of institutionalizing myths: quite apart from technical efficiency, organizations which innovate in important structural ways bear considerable costs in legitimacy.

Figure 2.2. summarizes the general argument of this section, alongside the established view that organizations succeed through efficiency.

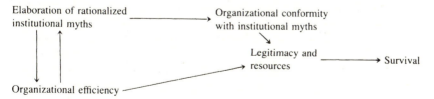

Fig. 2.2. Organizational survival.

Institutionalized Structures and Organizational Activities

Rationalized formal structures arise in two contexts. First, the demands of local relational networks encourage the development of structures that coordinate and control activities. Such structures contribute to the efficiency of organizations and give them competitive advantages over less efficient competitors. Second, the interconnectedness of societal relations, the collective organization of society, and the leadership of organizational elites create a highly institutionalized context. In this context rationalized structures present an acceptable account of organizational activities, and organizations gain legitimacy, stability, and resources.

All organizations, to one degree or another, are embedded in both relational and institutionalized contexts and are therefore concerned both with coordinating and controlling their activities and with prudently accounting for them. Organizations in highly institutionalized environments face internal and boundary-spanning contingencies. Schools, for example, must transport students to and from school under some circumstances and must assign teachers, students, and topics to classrooms. On the other hand, organizations producing in markets that place great emphasis on efficiency build in units whose relation to production is obscure and whose efficiency is determined not by a true production function, but by ceremonial definition.

Nevertheless, the survival of some organizations depends more on managing the demands of internal and boundary-spanning relations, while the survival of others depends more on the ceremonial demands of highly institutionalized environments. The discussion to follow shows that whether an organization's survival depends primarily on relational or on institutional demands determines the tightness of alignments between structures and activities.

Types of Organizations

Institutionalized myths differ in the completeness with which they describe cause and effect relationships, and in the clarity with which they describe standards that should be used to evaluate outputs (Thompson 1967). Some organizations use routine, clearly defined technologies to produce outputs. When output can be easily evaluated, a market often develops, and consumers gain considerable rights of inspection and control. In this context, efficiency often determines success. Organizations must face exigencies of close coordination with their relational networks, and they cope with these exigencies by organizing around immediate technical problems.

But the rise of collectively organized society and the increasing interconnectedness of social relations have eroded many market contexts. Increasingly, such organizations as schools, R & D units, and governmental bureaucracies use variable, ambiguous technologies to produce outputs that are difficult to appraise, and other organizations with clearly defined technologies find themselves unable to adapt to environmental turbulence. The uncertainties of unpredictable technical contingencies or of adapting to environmental change cannot be resolved on the basis of efficiency. Internal participants and external constituents alike call for institutionalized rules that promote trust and confidence in outputs and buffer organizations from failure (Emery and Trist 1965).

Thus, one can conceive of a continuum along which organizations can be ordered. At one end are production organizations under strong output controls (Ouchi and Mcguire 1975) whose success depends on the management of relational networks. At the other end are institutionalized organizations whose success depends on the confidence and stability achieved by isomorphism with institutional rules. For two reasons it is important not to assume that an organization's location on this continuum is based on the inherent technical properties of its output and therefore permanent. First, the technical properties of outputs are socially defined and do not exist in some concrete sense that allows them to be empirically discovered. Second, environments and organizations often redefine the nature of products, services, and technologies. Redefinition sometimes clarifies techniques or evaluative standards. But often organizations and environments redefine the nature of techniques and output so that ambiguity is introduced and rights of inspection and control are lowered. For example, American schools have evolved from producing rather specific training that was evaluated according to strict criteria of efficiency to producing ambiguously defined services that are evaluated according to criteria of certification (Callahan 1962; Tyack 1974; Meyer and Rowan 1978).

STRUCTURAL INCONSISTENCIES IN INSTITUTIONALIZED ORGANIZATIONS

Two very general problems confront an organization if its success depends primarily on isomorphism with institutionalized rules. First, technical activities and demands for efficiency create conflicts and inconsistencies in an institutionalized organization's efforts to conform to the ceremonial rules of production. Second, because these ceremonial rules are transmitted by myths that may arise from different parts of the environment, the rules may conflict with one another. These inconsistencies make a concern for efficiency and tight coordination and control problematic.

Formal structures that celebrate institutionalized myths differ from structures that act efficiently. Ceremonial activity is significant in relation to categorical rules, not in its concrete effects (Merton 1940; March and Simon 1958). A sick worker must be treated by a doctor using accepted medical procedures; whether the worker is treated effectively is less important. A bus company must service required routes whether or not there are many passengers. A university must maintain appropriate departments independent of the departments' enrollments. Activity, that is, has ritual significance: it maintains appearances and validates an organization.

Categorical rules conflict with the logic of efficiency. Organizations often face the dilemma that activities celebrating institutionalized rules, although they count as virtuous ceremonial expenditures, are pure costs from the point of view of efficiency. For example, hiring a Nobel Prize winner brings great ceremonial benefits to a university. The celebrated name can lead to research grants, brighter students, or reputational gains. But from the point of view of immediate outcomes, the expenditure lowers the instructional return per dollar expended and lowers the university's ability to solve immediate logistical problems. Also, expensive technologies, which bring prestige to hospitals and business firms, may be simply excessive costs from the point of view of immediate production. Similarly, highly professionalized consultants who bring external blessing on an organization are often difficult to justify in terms of improved productivity, yet may be very important in maintaining internal and external legitimacy.

Other conflicts between categorical rules and efficiency arise because institutional rules are couched at high levels of generalization (Durkheim 1933), whereas technical activities vary with specific, unstandardized, and possibly unique conditions. Because standardized ceremonial categories must confront technical variations and anomalies, the generalized rules of the institutional environment are often inappropriate to specific situations. A governmentally mandated curriculum may be inappropriate for the students at hand, a conventional medical treatment may make little sense given the characteristics of a patient, and federal safety inspectors may intolerably delay boundary-spanning exchanges.

Yet another source of conflict between categorical rules and efficiency is the inconsistency among institutionalized elements. Institutional environments are often pluralistic (Udy 1970), and societies promulgate sharply inconsistent myths. As a result, organizations in search of external support and stability incorporate all sorts of incompatible structural elements. Professions are incorporated although they make overlapping jurisdictional claims. Programs are adopted which contend with each other for authority over a given domain. For instance, if one inquires who decides what curricula will be taught in schools, any number of parties from the various governments down to individual teachers may say that they decide.

In institutionalized organizations, then, concern with the efficiency of day-to-day activities creates enormous uncertainties. Specific contexts highlight the inadequacies of the prescriptions of generalized myths, and inconsistent structural elements conflict over jurisdictional rights. Thus the organization must struggle to link the requirements of ceremonial elements to technical activities and to link inconsistent ceremonial elements to each other.

RESOLVING INCONSISTENCIES

There are four partial solutions to these inconsistencies. First, an organization can resist ceremonial requirements. But an organization that neglects ceremonial requirements and portrays itself as efficient may be unsuccessful in documenting its efficiency. Also, rejecting ceremonial requirements neglects an important source of resources and stability. Second, an organization can maintain rigid conformity to institutionalized prescriptions by cutting off external relations. Although such isolation upholds ceremonial requirements, internal participants and external constituents may soon become disillusioned with their inability to manage boundary-spanning exchanges. Institutionalized organizations must not only conform to myths but must also maintain the appearance that the myths actually work. Third, an organization can cynically acknowledge that its structure is inconsistent with work requirements. But this strategy denies the validity of institutionalized myths and sabotages the legitimacy of the organization. Fourth, an organization can promise reform. People may picture the present as unworkable but the future as filled with promising reforms of both structure and activity. But by defining the organization's valid structure as lying in the future, this strategy makes the organization's current structure illegitimate.

Instead of relying on a partial solution, however, an organization can resolve conflicts between ceremonial rules and efficiency by employing two interrelated devices: decoupling and the logic of confidence.

Decoupling

Ideally, organizations built around efficiency attempt to maintain close alignments between structures and activities. Conformity is enforced through inspection, output quality is continually monitored, the efficiency of various units is evaluated, and the various goals are unified and coordinated. But a policy of close alignment in institutionalized organizations merely makes public a record of inefficiency and inconsistency.

Institutionalized organizations protect their formal structures from evaluation on the basis of technical performance: inspection, evaluation, and control of activities are minimized, and coordination, interdependence, and mutual adjustments among structural units are handled informally.

Proposition 4. *Because attempts to control and coordinate activities in institutionalized organizations lead to conflicts and loss of legitimacy, elements of structure are decoupled from activities and from each other.*

Some well-known properties of organizations illustrate the decoupling process: (1) Activities are performed beyond the purview of managers. In particular, organizations actively encourage professionalism, and activities are delegated to professionals. (2) Goals are made ambiguous or vacuous, and categorical ends are substituted for technical ends. Hospitals treat, not cure, patients. Schools produce students, not learning. In fact, data on technical performance are eliminated or rendered invisible. Hospitals try to ignore information on cure rates, public services avoid data about effectiveness, and schools deemphasize measures of achievement. (3) Integration is avoided, program implementation is neglected, and inspection and evaluation are ceremonialized. (4) Human relations are made very important. The organization cannot formally coordinate activities because its formal rules, if applied, would generate inconsistencies. Therefore individuals are left to work out technical interdependencies informally. The ability to coordinate things in violation of the rules—that is, to get along with other people—is highly valued.

The advantages of decoupling are clear. The assumption that formal structures are really working is buffered from the inconsistencies and anomalies involved in technical activities. Also, because integration is avoided, disputes and conflicts are minimized and an organization can mobilize support from a broader range of external constituents. Thus, decoupling enables organizations to maintain standardized, legitimating, formal structures while their activities vary in response to practical considerations. The organizations in an industry tend to be similar in formal structure—reflecting their common institutional origins—but may show much diversity in actual practice.

The Logic of Confidence
and Good Faith

Despite the lack of coordination and control, decoupled organizations are not anarchies. Day-to-day activities proceed in an orderly fashion. What legitimates institutionalized organizations, enabling them to appear useful in spite of the lack of technical validation, is the confidence and good faith of their internal participants and their external constituents.

Considerations of face characterize ceremonial management (Goffman 1967). Confidence in structural elements is maintained through three practices—avoidance, discretion, and overlooking (Goffman 1967:12–18). Avoidance and discretion are encouraged by decoupling autonomous subunits; overlooking anomalies is also quite common. Both internal participants and external constituents cooperate in these practices. Assuring that individual participants maintain face sustains confidence in the organization and ultimately reinforces confidence in the myths that rationalize the organization's existence.

Delegation, professionalization, goal ambiguity, elimination of output data, and maintenance of face are all mechanisms for absorbing uncertainty while preserving the formal structure of the organization (March and Simon 1958). They contribute to a general aura of confidence within and outside the organization. Although the literature on informal organization often treats these practices as mechanisms for the achievement of deviant and subgroup purposes (Downs 1967), such treatment ignores a critical feature of organization life: effectively absorbing uncertainty and maintaining confidence requires people to assume that everyone is acting in good faith. The assumption that things are as they seem, that employees and managers are performing their roles properly, allows an organization to perform its daily routines with a decoupled structure.

Decoupling and maintenance of face, in other words, are mechanisms that maintain the assumption that people are acting in good faith. Professionalization is not merely a way of avoiding inspection—it binds both supervisors and subordinates to act in good faith. So in a smaller way does strategic leniency (Blau 1956). And so do the public displays of morale and satisfaction which are characteristic of many organizations. Organizations employ a host of mechanisms to dramatize the ritual commitments which their participants make to basic structural elements. These mechanisms are especially common in organizations which strongly reflect their institutionalized environments.

Proposition 5. *The more an organization's structure is derived from institutionalized myths, the more it maintains elaborate displays of confidence, satisfaction, and good faith, internally and externally.*

The commitments built up by displays of morale and satisfaction are not simply vacuous affirmations of institutionalized myths. Participants not only commit themselves to supporting an organization's ceremonial facade but also commit themselves to making things work out backstage. The committed participants engage in informal coordination that, although often formally inappropriate, keeps technical activities running smoothly and avoids public embarrassments. In this sense the confidence and good faith generated by ceremonial action is in no way fraudulent. It may even be the most reasonable way to get participants to make their best efforts in situations made problematic by institutionalized myths at odds with immediate technical demands.

Ceremonial Inspection and Evaluation

All organizations, even those maintaining high levels of confidence and good faith, are in environments that have institutionalized the rationalized rituals of inspection and evaluation. And inspection and evaluation can uncover events and deviations that undermine legitimacy. So institutionalized organizations minimize and ceremonialize inspection and evaluation.

In institutionalized organizations, in fact, evaluation accompanies and produces illegitimacy. The interest in evaluation research by the U.S. federal government, for instance, is partly intended to undercut the state, local, and private authorities which have managed social services in the United States. The federal authorities, of course, have usually not evaluated those programs which are completely under federal jurisdiction; they have only evaluated those over which federal controls are incomplete. Similarly, state governments have often insisted on evaluating the special fundings they create in welfare and education but ordinarily do not evaluate the programs which they fund in a routine way.

Evaluation and inspection are public assertions of societal control which violate the assumption that everyone is acting with competence and in good faith. Violating this assumption lowers morale and confidence. Thus, evaluation and inspection undermine the ceremonial aspects of organizations.

Proposition 6. *Institutionalized organizations seek to minimize inspection and evaluation by both internal managers and external constituents.*

Decoupling and the avoidance of inspection and evaluation are not merely

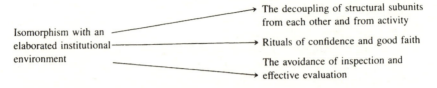

Fig. 2.3. The effects of institutional isomorphism on organizations.

devices used by the organization. External constituents, too, avoid inspecting and controlling institutionalized organizations (Meyer and Rowan 1978). Accrediting agencies, boards of trustees, government agencies, and individuals accept ceremonially at face value the credentials, ambiguous goals, and categorical evaluations that are characteristic of ceremonial organizations. In elaborate institutional environments these external constituents are themselves likely to be corporately organized agents of society. Maintaining categorical relationships with their organizational subunits is more stable and more certain than is relying on inspection and control. Figure 2.3 summarizes the main arguments of this section of our discussion.

Summary and Research Implications

Organizational structures are created and made more elaborate with the rise of institutionalized myths, and, in highly institutionalized contexts, organizational action must support these myths. But an organization must also attend to practical activity. The two requirements are at odds. A stable solution is to maintain the organization in a loosely coupled state.

No position is taken here on the overall social effectiveness of isomorphic and loosely coupled organizations. To some extent such structures buffer activity from efficiency criteria and produce ineffectiveness. On the other hand, by binding participants to act in good faith and to adhere to the larger rationalities of the wider structure, they may maximize long-run effectiveness. It should not be assumed that the creation of microscopic rationalities in the daily activity of workers effects social ends more efficiently than commitment to larger institutional claims and purposes.

The argument presented here generates several major theses that have clear research implications. The first thesis is that environments and environmental domains which have institutionalized a greater number of rational myths generate more formal organization. This thesis leads to the research hypothesis that formal organizations rise and become more complex as a result of the rise of the elaborated state and other institutions for collective action. This hypothesis should hold true even when economic and technical development are held constant. Studies could trace the diffusion to formal organizations of specific institutions—professions, clearly labeled programs, and the like. For instance, the effects of the rise of theories and professions of personnel selection on the creation of personnel departments in organizations could be studied. Other studies could follow the diffusion of sales departments or research and development departments. Organizations should be found to adapt to such environmental changes, even if no evidence of their effectiveness exists.

Experimentally, one could study the impact on the decisions of organizational managers in planning or altering organizational structures, of hypothetical variations in environmental institutionalization. Do managers plan differently if they are informed about the existence of established occupations or programmatic institutions in their environments? Do they plan differently if they are designing organizations for more or less institutionally elaborated environments?

Our second thesis is that organizations which incorporate institutionalized myths are more legitimate, successful, and likely to survive. Here, research should compare similar organizations in different contexts. For instance, the presence of personnel departments or research and development units should predict success in environments in which they are widely institutionalized. Organizations which have structural elements not institutionalized in their environments should be more likely to fail, as such unauthorized complexity must be justified by claims of efficiency and effectiveness.

More generally, organizations whose claims to support are based on evaluations should be less likely to survive than those which are more highly institutionalized. An implication of this argument is that organizations existing in a highly institutionalized environment are generally more likely to survive.

Experimentally, one could study the size of the loans banks would be willing to provide organizations which vary only in (1) the degree of environmental institutionalization, and (2) the degree to which the organization structurally incorporates environmental institutions. Are banks willing to lend more money to firms whose plans are accompanied by econometric projections? And is this tendency greater in societies in which such projections are more widely institutionalized?

Our third thesis is that organizational control efforts, especially in highly institutionalized contexts, are devoted to ritual conformity, both internally and externally. Such organizations, that is, decouple structure from activity and structures from each other. The idea here is that the more highly institutionalized the environment, the more time and energy organizational elites devote to managing their organization's public image and status and the less they devote to coordination and to managing particular boundary-spanning relationships. Further, the argument is that in such contexts managers devote more time to articulating internal structures and relationships at an abstract or ritual level, in contrast to managing particular relationships among activities and interdependencies.

Experimentally, the time and energy allocations proposed by managers presented with differently described environments could be studied. Do managers, presented with the description of an elaborately institutionalized environment, propose to spend more energy maintaining ritual isomorphism and less on monitoring internal conformity? Do they tend to become inattentive to evaluation? Do they elaborate doctrines of professionalism and good faith? The arguments here, in other words, suggest both comparative and experimental studies examining the effects on organizational structure and coordination of variations in the institutional structure of the wider environment. Variations in organizational structure among societies, and within any society across time, are central to this conception of the problem.

Acknowledgments

This chapter was originally published in the *American Journal of Sociology* 83(2): 340–63.

3   The Iron Cage Revisited: Institutional Isomorphism and Collective Rationality in Organizational Fields

PAUL J. DiMAGGIO AND
WALTER W. POWELL

In *The Protestant Ethic and the Spirit of Capitalism,* Max Weber warned that the rationalist spirit ushered in by asceticism had achieved a momentum of its own and that, under capitalism, the rationalist order had become an iron cage in which humanity was, save for the possibility of prophetic revival, imprisoned "perhaps until the last ton of fossilized coal is burnt" (Weber 1952:181–82). In his essay on bureaucracy, Weber returned to this theme, contending that bureaucracy, the rational spirit's organizational manifestation, was so efficient and powerful a means of controlling men and women that, once established, the momentum of bureaucratization was irreversible (Weber [1922] 1978).

The imagery of the iron cage has haunted students of society as the tempo of bureaucratization has quickened. But while bureaucracy has spread continuously in the eighty years since Weber wrote, we suggest that the engine of organizational rationalization has shifted. For Weber, bureaucratization resulted from three related causes: competition among capitalist firms in the marketplace; competition among states, increasing rulers' need to control their staff and citizenry; and bourgeois demands for equal protection under the law. Of these three, the most important was the competitive marketplace. "Today," Weber [1922] 1978:974) wrote, "it is primarily the capitalist market economy which demands that the official business of administration be discharged precisely, unambiguously, continuously, and with as much speed as possible. Normally, the very large, modern capitalist enterprises are themselves unequalled models of strict bureaucratic organization."

We argue that the causes of bureaucratization and rationalization have changed. The bureaucratization of the corporation and the state have been achieved. Organizations are still becoming more homogeneous, and bureaucracy remains the common organizational form. Today, however, structural change in organizations seems less and less driven by competition or by the need for efficiency. Instead, we contend, bureaucratization and other forms of organizational change occur as the result of processes that make organizations more similar without necessarily making them more efficient. Bureaucratization and other forms of homogenization emerge, we argue, out of the structuration (Giddens 1979) of organizational fields. This process, in turn, is effected largely by the state and the professions, which have become the great rationalizers of the second half of the twentieth century. For reasons that we will explain, highly structured organizational fields provide a context in which individual efforts to deal rationally with uncertainty and constraint often lead, in the aggregate, to homogeneity in structure, culture, and output.

Organizational Theory and Organizational Diversity

Much of modern organizational theory posits a diverse and differentiated world of organizations and seeks to explain variation among organizations in structure and behavior (e.g., Woodward 1965; Child and Kieser 1981). Hannan and Freeman begin a major theoretical paper (1977) with the question, "Why are there so many kinds of organizations?" Even our investigatory technologies (for example, those based on least-squares techniques) are geared toward explaining variation rather than its absence.

We ask, instead, why there is such startling homogeneity of organizational forms and practices, and we seek to explain homogeneity, not variation. In the initial stages of their life cycle, organizational fields display considerable diversity in approach and form. Once a field becomes well established, however, there is an inexorable push toward homogenization.

Coser, Kadushin, and Powell (1982) describe the evolution of American college textbook publishing from a period of initial diversity to the current hegemony of only two models, the large bureaucratic generalist and the small specialist. Rothman (1980) describes the winnowing of several competing models of legal education into two dominant approaches. Starr (1980) provides evidence of mimicry in the development of the hospital field; Tyack (1974) and Katz (1975) show a similar process in public schools; Barnouw (1966–68) describes the development of dominant forms in the radio industry; and DiMaggio (1982a, 1982b) depicts the emergence of dominant organizational models for the provision of high culture in the late nineteenth century. What we see in each of these cases is the emergence and structuration of an organizational field as a result of the activities of a diverse set of organizations and, second, the homogenization of these organizations, and of new entrants as well, once the field is established.

By *organizational field* we mean those organizations that, in the aggregate, constitute a recognized area of institutional life: key suppliers, resource and product consumers, regulatory agencies, and other organizations that produce similar services or products. The virtue of this unit of analysis is that it directs our attention not simply to competing firms, as does the population approach of Hannan and Freeman (1977), or to networks of organizations that actually interact, as does the interorganizational network approach of Laumann, Galaskiewicz, and Marsden (1978), but to the totality of relevant actors. In doing this, the field idea comprehends the importance of both *connectedness* (see Laumann, Galaskiewicz, and Marsden 1978) and *structural equivalence* (White, Boorman, and Breiger 1976).[1]

The structure of an organizational field cannot be determined a priori but must be defined on the basis of empirical investigation. Fields only exist to the extent that they are institutionally defined. The process of institutional definition, or "structuration," consists of four parts: an increase in the extent of interaction among organizations in the field; the emergence of sharply defined interorganizational structures of domination and patterns of coalition; an increase in the information load with which organizations in a field must contend; and the development of a mutual awareness among participants in a set of organizations that they are involved in a common enterprise (DiMaggio 1983).

Once disparate organizations in the same line of business are structured into an actual field (as we argue, by competition, the state, or the professions), powerful forces emerge that lead them to become more similar to one another. Organizations may change their goals or develop new practices, and new organizations enter the field. But in the long run, organizational actors making rational decisions construct around themselves an environment that constrains their ability to change further in later years. Early adopters of organizational innovations are commonly driven by a desire to improve performance. But new practices can become, in Selznick's words (1957:17), "infused with value beyond the technical requirements of the task at hand." As an innovation spreads, a threshold is reached beyond which adoption provides legitimacy rather than improves performance (Meyer and Rowan 1977). Strategies that are rational for individual organizations may not be rational if adopted by large numbers. Yet the very fact that they are normatively sanctioned increases the likelihood of their adoption. Thus organizations may try to change constantly; but after a certain point in the structuration of an organizational field, the aggregate effect of individual change is to lessen the extent of diversity within the field.[2] Organizations in a structured field, to paraphrase Schelling (1978:14), respond to an environment that consists of other organizations responding to their environment, which consists of organizations responding to an environment of organizations' responses.

Tolbert and Zucker's (1983) work on the adoption of civil service reform in the United States nicely illustrates this process. Early adoption of civil service reforms was related to internal governmental needs and strongly predicted by such city characteristics as the size of immigrant population, political reform movements, socioeconomic composition, and city size. Later, however, adoption is not predicted by city characteristics, but is related to institutional definitions of the legitimate structural form for municipal administration.[3] Marshall Meyer's (Meyer, Stevenson, and Webster 1985) study of the bureaucratization of urban fiscal agencies has yielded similar findings: strong relationships between city characteristics and organizational attributes at the turn of the century, null relationships in recent years. Carroll and Delacroix's (1982) findings on the birth and death rates of newspapers support the view that selection acts with great force only in the early years of an industry's existence.[4] Freeman (1982:14) suggests that older, larger organizations reach a point where they can dominate their environments rather than adjust to them.

The concept that best captures the process of homogenization is *isomorphism*. In Hawley's (1968) description, isomorphism is a constraining process that forces one unit in a population to resemble other units that face the same set of environmental conditions. At the population level, such an approach suggests that organizational characteristics are modified in the direction of increasing compatibility with environmental characteristics; the number of organizations in a population is a function of environmental carrying capacity; and the diversity of organizational forms is isomorphic to environmental diversity. Hannan and Freeman (1977) have significantly extended Hawley's ideas. They argue that isomorphism can result because nonoptimal forms are selected out of a population of organizations *or* because organizational decision makers learn appropriate responses and adjust their behavior accordingly. Hannan and Freeman's focus is almost solely on the first process—selection.[5]

Following Meyer (1983b) and Fennell (1980), we maintain that there are two types of isomorphism: competitive and institutional. Hannan and Freeman's classic paper (1977), and much of their recent work, deals with competitive isomorphism, assuming a system rationality that emphasizes market competition, niche change, and fitness measures. Such a view, we suggest, is most relevant for those fields in which free and open competition exists. It explains parts of the process of bureaucratization that Weber observed, and may apply to early adoption of innovation, but it does not present a fully adequate picture of the modern world of organizations. For this purpose it must be supplemented by an institutional view of isomorphism of the sort introduced by Kanter (1972:152–54) in her discussion of the forces pressing communities toward accommodation with the outside world. As Aldrich (1979:265) has argued, "the major factors that organizations must take into account are other organizations." Organizations compete not just for resources and customers, but for political power and institutional legitimacy, for social as well as economic fitness.[6] The concept of institutional isomorphism is a useful tool for understanding the politics and ceremony that pervade much modern organizational life.

THREE MECHANISMS OF INSTITUTIONAL ISOMORPHIC CHANGE

We identify three mechanisms through which institutional isomorphic change occurs, each with its own antecedents: (1) *coercive* isomorphism that stems from political influence and the problem of legitimacy; (2) *mimetic* isomorphism resulting from standard responses to uncertainty; and (3) *normative* isomorphism, associated with professionalization. This typology is an analytic one: the types are not always empirically distinct. For example, external actors may induce an organization to conform to its peers by requiring it to perform a particular task and specifying the profession responsible for its performance. Or mimetic change may reflect environmentally constructed uncertainties.[7] Yet, while the three types intermingle in empirical settings, they tend to derive from different conditions and may lead to different outcomes.

Coercive Isomorphism

Coercive isomorphism results from both formal and informal pressures exerted on organizations by other organizations upon which they are dependent and by cultural expectations in the society within which organizations function. Such pressures may be felt as force, as persuasion, or as invitations to join in collusion. In some circumstances, organizational change is a direct response to government mandate: manufacturers adopt new pollution control technologies to conform to environmental regulations; nonprofits maintain accounts and hire accountants in order to meet tax law requirements; and organizations employ affirmative action officers to fend off allegations of discrimination. Schools mainstream special students and hire special education teachers, cultivate PTAs and administrators who get along with them, and promulgate curricula that conform with state standards (Meyer, Scott, and Deal 1981). The fact that these changes may be largely ceremonial does not mean they are inconsequential. As Ritti and Goldner (1979) have argued, staff become involved in advocacy for their functions that can alter power relations within organizations over the long run.

The existence of a common legal environment affects many aspects of an organization's behavior and structure. Weber pointed out the profound impact of a complex, rationalized system of contract law that requires the necessary organizational controls to honor legal commitments. Other legal and technical requirements of the state—the vicissitudes of the budget cycle, the ubiquity of certain fiscal years, annual reports, and financial reporting requirements that ensure eligibility for the receipt of federal contracts or funds—also shape organizations in similar ways. Pfeffer and Salancik (1978:188–224) have discussed how organizations faced with unmanageable interdependence seek to use the greater power of the larger social system and its government to eliminate difficulties or provide for needs. They observe that politically constructed environments have two characteristic features: political decision makers often do not experience directly the consequences of their actions; and political decisions are applied across the board to entire classes of organizations, thus making such decisions less adaptive and less flexible.

Meyer and Rowan (1977) have argued persuasively that as rationalized states and other large rational organizations expand their dominance over more arenas of social life, organizational structures increasingly come to reflect rules institutionalized and legitimated by and within the state (also see Meyer and Hannan 1979). As a result, organizations are increasingly homogeneous within given domains and increasingly organized around rituals of conformity to wider institutions. At the same time, organizations are decreasingly structurally determined by the constraints posed by technical activities and decreasingly held together by output controls. Under such circumstances, organizations employ ritualized controls of credentials and group solidarity.

Direct imposition of standard operating procedures and legitimated rules and structures also occurs outside the governmental arena. Michael Sedlak (1981) has documented the ways that United Charities in the 1930s altered and homogenized the structures, methods, and philosophies of the social service agencies that depended upon it for support. As conglomerate corporations increase in size and scope, standard performance criteria are not necessarily imposed on subsidiaries, but it is common for subsidiaries to be subject to standardized reporting mechanisms (Coser, Kadushin, and Powell 1982). Subsidiaries are compelled to adopt accounting practices, performance evaluations, and budgetary plans that are compatible with the policies of the parent corporation. A variety of service infrastructures, often provided by monopolistic firms—for example, telecommunications and transportation—exerts common pressures over the organizations that use them. Thus, the expansion of the central state, the centralization of capital, and the coordination of philanthropy all support the homogenization of organizational models through direct authority relationships.

We have so far referred only to the direct and explicit imposition of organizational models on dependent organizations. Coercive isomorphism, however, may be more subtle and less explicit than these examples suggest. Milofsky (1981) has described the ways in which neighborhood organizations in urban communities, many of which are committed to participatory democracy, are driven to developing organizational hierarchies in order to gain support from more hierarchically organized donor organizations. Similarly, Swidler (1979) describes the tensions created in the free schools she studied by the need to have a "principal" to negotiate with the district superintendent and to represent the school to outside agencies. In general, the need to lodge responsibility and managerial authority at least ceremonially in a formally defined role in order to interact with hierarchical organizations is a constant obstacle to the maintenance of egalitarian or collectivist organizational forms (Kanter 1972; Rothschild-Whitt 1979).

Mimetic Processes

Not all institutional isomorphism, however, derives from coercive authority. Uncertainty is also a powerful force that encourages imitation. When organizational technologies are poorly understood (March and Olsen 1976), when goals are ambiguous, or when the environment creates symbolic uncertainty, organizations may model themselves on other organizations. The advantages of mimetic behavior in the economy of human action are considerable; when an organization faces a problem with ambiguous causes or unclear solutions, problemistic search may yield a viable solution with little expense (Cyert and March 1963).

Modeling, as we use the term, is a response to uncertainty. The modeled organization may be unaware of the modeling or may have no desire to be copied; it merely serves as a convenient source of practices that the borrowing organization may use. Models may be diffused unintentionally, indirectly through employee transfer or turnover, or explicitly by organizations such as consulting firms or industry trade associations. Even innovation can be accounted for by organizational modeling. As Alchian (1950) has observed:

> While there certainly are those who consciously innovate, there are those who, in their imperfect attempts to imitate others, unconsciously innovate by unwittingly acquiring some unexpected or unsought unique attributes which under the prevailing circumstances prove partly responsible for the success. Others, in turn, will attempt to copy the uniqueness, and the innovation-imitation process continues. (Pp. 218–19)

One of the most dramatic instances of modeling was the effort of Japan's modernizers in the late nineteenth century to model new governmental initiatives on apparently successful Western prototypes. Thus, the imperial government sent its officers to study the courts, army, and police in France, the navy and postal system in Great Britain, and banking and art education in the United States (see Westney 1987). American corporations are now returning the compliment by implementing (their perceptions of) Japanese models to cope with thorny productivity and personnel problems in their own firms. The rapid proliferation of quality circles and quality-of-work-life issues in American firms is, at least in part, an attempt to model Japanese and European successes. These developments also have a ritual aspect; companies adopt these "innovations" to enhance their legitimacy, to demonstrate they are at least trying to improve working conditions. More generally, the wider the population of personnel employed by, or customers served by, an organization, the stronger the pressure felt by the organization to provide the programs and services offered by other organizations. Thus, either a skilled labor force or a broad customer base may encourage mimetic isomorphism.

Much homogeneity in organizational structures stems from the fact that despite considerable search for diversity there is relatively little variation to be selected from. New organizations are modeled upon old ones throughout the economy, and managers actively seek models upon which to build (Kimberly 1980). Thus in the arts one can find textbooks on how to organize a community arts council or how to start a symphony women's guild. Large organizations choose from a relatively small set of major consulting firms, which, like Johnny Appleseeds, spread a few organizational models throughout the land. Such models are powerful because structural changes are observable, whereas changes in policy and strategy are less easily noticed. With the advice of a major consulting firm, a large metropolitan public television station switched from a functional design to a multidivisional structure. The stations' executives were skeptical that the new structure was more efficient; in fact, some services were now duplicated across divisions. But they were convinced that the new design would carry a powerful message to the for-profit firms with whom the station regularly dealt. These firms, whether in the role of corporate underwriters or as potential partners in joint ventures, would view the reorganization as a sign that "the sleepy nonprofit station was becoming more business-minded" (Powell 1988). The history of management reform in U.S. government agencies, which are noted for their goal ambiguity, is almost a textbook case of isomorphic modeling, from the PPPB of the McNamara era to the zero-based budgeting of the Carter administration.

Organizations tend to model themselves after similar organizations in their field that they perceive to be more legitimate or successful. The ubiquity of certain kinds of structural arrangements can more likely be credited to the universality of mimetic processes than to any concrete evidence that the adopted models enhance efficiency. John Meyer (1981) contends that it is easy to predict the organization of a newly emerging nation's administration without knowing anything about the nation itself, since "peripheral nations are far more isomorphic—in administrative form and economic pattern—than any theory of the world system of economic division of labor would lead one to expect."

Normative Pressures

A third source of isomorphic organizational change is normative and stems primarily from professionalization. Following Larson (1977) and Collins (1979), we interpret professionalization as the collective struggle of members of an occupation to define the conditions and methods of their work, to control "the production of producers" (Larson 1977:49–52), and to establish a cognitive base and legitimation for their occupational autonomy. As Larson points out, the professional project is rarely achieved with complete success. Professionals must compromise with nonprofessional clients, bosses, or regulators. The major recent growth in the professions has been among organizational professionals, particularly managers and specialized staff of large organizations. The increased professionalization of workers whose futures are inextricably bound up with the fortunes of the organizations that employ them has rendered obsolescent (if not obsolete) the dichotomy between organizational commitment and professional allegiance that characterized traditional professionals in earlier organizations (Hall 1968). Professions are subject to the same coercive and mimetic pressures as are organizations. Moreover, while various kinds of professionals within an organization may differ from one another, they exhibit much similarity to their professional counterparts in other organizations. In addition, in many cases, professional power is as much assigned by the state as it is created by the activities of the professions.

Two aspects of professionalization are important sources of isomorphism. One is the resting of formal education and of legitimation in a cognitive base produced by university specialists; the second is the growth and elaboration of professional networks that span organizations and across which new models diffuse rapidly. Universities and professional training institutions are important centers for the development of organizational norms among professional managers and their staff. Professional and trade associations are another vehicle for the definition and promulgation of normative rules about organizational and professional behavior. Such mechanisms create a pool of almost interchangeable individuals who occupy similar positions across a range of organizations and possess a similarity of orientation and disposition that may override variations in tradition and control that might otherwise shape organizational behavior (Perrow 1974).

One important mechanism for encouraging normative isomorphism is the filtering of personnel. Within many organizational fields, filtering occurs through the hiring of individuals from firms within the same industry; through the recruitment of fast-track staff from a narrow range of training institutions; through common promotion practices, such as always hiring top executives from financial or legal departments; and from skill-level requirements for particular jobs. Many professional career tracks are so closely guarded, both at the entry level and throughout the career progression, that individuals who make it to the top are virtually indistinguishable. March and March (1977) found that individuals who attained the position of school superintendent in Wisconsin were so alike in background and orientation as to make further career advancement random and unpredictable. Hirsch and Whisler (1982) find a similar absence of variation among Fortune 500 board members. In addition, individuals in an organizational field undergo anticipatory socialization to common expectations about their personal behavior, appropriate style of dress, organizational vocabularies (Cicourel 1970; Williamson 1975), and standard methods of speaking, joking, or addressing others (Ouchi 1980). Particularly in industries with a service or financial orientation (Collins 1979 argues that the importance of credentials is strongest in these areas), the filtering of personnel approaches what Kanter (1977) refers to as the "homosexual reproduction of management." To the extent managers and key staff are drawn from the same universities and filtered on a common set of attributes, they will tend to view problems in a similar fashion, see the same policies, procedures, and structures as normatively sanctioned and legitimated, and approach decisions in much the same way.

Entrants to professional career tracks who somehow escape the filtering process—for example, Jewish naval officers, women stockbrokers, or black insurance executives—are likely to be subjected to pervasive on-the-job socialization. To the extent that organizations in a field differ and primary socialization occurs on the job, socialization could reinforce, not erode, differences among organizations. But when organizations in a field are similar and occupational socialization is carried out in trade association workshops, in-service educational programs, consultant arrangements, employer–professional school networks, and in the pages of trade magazines, socialization acts as an isomorphic force.

The professionalization of management tends to proceed in tandem with the structuration of organizational fields. The exchange of information among professionals helps contribute to a commonly recognized hierarchy of status, of center and periphery, that becomes a matrix for information flows and personnel movement across organizations. This status ordering occurs through both formal and informal means. The designation of a few large firms in an industry as key bargaining agents in union-management negotiations may make these central firms pivotal in other respects as well. Government recognition of key firms or organizations through the grant or contract process may give these organizations legitimacy and visibility and lead competing firms to copy aspects of their structure or operating procedures in hope of obtaining similar rewards. Professional and trade associations provide other arenas in which center organizations are recognized and their personnel given positions of substantive or ceremonial influence. Managers in highly visible organizations may in turn have their stature reinforced by representation on the boards of other organizations, participation in industrywide or interindustry councils, and consultation by agencies of government (Useem 1979). In the nonprofit sector, where legal barriers to collusion do not exist, structuration may proceed even more rapidly. Thus executive producers or artistic directors of leading theaters head trade or professional association committees, sit on government and foundation grant-award panels, consult as government- or foundation-financed management advisers to smaller theaters, or sit on smaller organizations' boards, even as their stature is reinforced and enlarged by the grants their theaters receive from government, corporate, and foundation funding sources (DiMaggio 1983).

Such central organizations serve as both active and passive models; their policies and structures will be copied throughout their fields. Their centrality is reinforced as upwardly mobile managers and staff seek to secure positions in these central organizations in order to further their own careers. Aspiring managers may undergo anticipatory socialization into the norms and mores of the organizations they hope to join. Career paths may also involve movement from entry positions in the center organizations to middle-management positions in peripheral organizations. Personnel flows within an organizational field are further encouraged by structural homogenization, for example, the existence of common career titles and paths (such as assistant, associate, and full professor) with meanings that are commonly understood.

Each of the institutional isomorphic processes can be expected to proceed in the absence of evidence that it increases internal organizational efficiency. To the extent that organizational effectiveness is enhanced, the reason is often that organizations are rewarded for their similarity to other organizations in their fields. This similarity can make it easier for organizations to transact with other organizations, to attract career-minded staff, to be acknowledged as legitimate and reputable, and to fit into administrative categories that define eligibility for public and private grants and contracts. None of this, however, ensures that conformist organizations do what they do more efficiently than do their more deviant peers.

Pressures for competitive efficiency are also mitigated in many fields because the number of organizations is limited and there are strong fiscal and legal barriers to entry and exit. Lee (1971:51) maintains this is why hospital administrators are less concerned with the efficient use of resources and more concerned with status competition and parity in prestige. Fennell (1980) notes that hospitals are a poor market system because patients lack the needed knowledge of potential exchange partners and prices. She argues that physicians and hospital administrators are the actual consumers. Competition among hospitals is based on "attracting physicians, who, in turn, bring their patients to the hospital." Fennell concludes that

> Hospitals operate according to a norm of social legitimation that frequently conflicts with market considerations of efficiency and system rationality. Apparently, hospitals can increase their range of services not because there is an actual need for a particular service or facility within the patient population, but because they will be defined as fit only if they can offer everything other hospitals in the area offer. (P. 505)

These results suggest a more general pattern. Organizational fields that include a large professionally trained labor force will be driven primarily by status competition. Organizational prestige and resources are key elements in attracting professionals. This process encourages homogenization as organizations seek to ensure that they can provide the same benefits and services as their competitors.

Predictors of Isomorphic Change

It follows from our discussion of the mechanisms by which isomorphic change occurs that we should be able to predict empirically which organizational fields will be most homogeneous in structure, process, and behavior. While an empirical test of such predictions is beyond the scope of this chapter, the ultimate value of our perspective lies in its predictive utility. The hypotheses discussed below are not meant to exhaust the universe of predictors, but merely to suggest several hypotheses that may be pursued using data on the characteristics of organizations in a field, either cross-sectionally or, preferably, over time. The hypotheses are implicitly governed by ceteris paribus assumptions, particularly with regard to size, technology, and centralization of external resources.

A. ORGANIZATIONAL-LEVEL PREDICTORS

There is variability in the extent to and rate at which organizations in a field change to become more like their peers. Some organizations respond to external pressures quickly; others change only after a long period of resistance. The first two hypotheses derive from our discussion of coercive isomorphism and constraint.

Hypothesis A-1. *The greater the dependence of an organization on another organization, the more similar it will become to that organization in structure, climate, and behavioral focus.* Following Thompson (1967) and Pfeffer and Salancik (1978), this proposition recognizes the greater ability of organizations to resist the demands of organizations on which they are not dependent. A position of dependence leads to isomorphic change. Coercive pressures are built into exchange relationships. As Williamson (1979) has shown, exchanges are characterized by transaction-specific investments in both knowledge and equipment. Once an organization chooses a specific supplier or distributor for particular parts or services, the supplier or distributor develops expertise in the performance of the task as well as idiosyncratic knowledge about the exchange relationship. The organization comes to rely on the supplier or distributor, and such transaction-specific investments give the supplier or distributor considerable advantages in any subsequent competition with other suppliers or distributors.

Hypothesis A-2. *The greater the centralization of organization A's resource supply, the greater the extent to which organization A will change isomorphically to resemble the organizations on which it depends for resources.* As Thompson (1967) notes, organizations that depend on the same sources for

funding, personnel, and legitimacy will be more subject to the whims of resource suppliers than will organizations that can play one source of support off
against another. In cases where alternative sources are either not readily available or require effort to locate, the stronger party to the transaction can coerce
the weaker party to adopt its practices in order to accommodate the stronger
party's needs (see Powell 1983).

The third and fourth hypotheses derive from our discussion of mimetic isomorphism, modeling, and uncertainty.

Hypothesis A-3. *The more uncertain the relationship between means and
ends, the greater the extent to which an organization will model itself after organizations it perceives as successful.* The mimetic thought process involved in
the search for models is characteristic of change in organizations in which key
technologies are only poorly understood (March and Cohen 1974). Here our
prediction diverges somewhat from Meyer and Rowan (1977), who argue, as
we do, that organizations which lack well-defined technologies will import institutionalized rules and practices. Meyer and Rowan posit a loose coupling
between legitimated external practices and internal organizational behavior.
From an ecologist's point of view, loosely coupled organizations are more likely to vary internally. In contrast, we expect substantive internal changes in
tandem with more ceremonial practices, thus greater homogeneity and less
variation. Internal consistency of this sort is an important means of interorganizational coordination. It also increases organizational stability.

Hypothesis A-4. *The more ambiguous the goals of an organization, the
greater the extent to which the organization will model itself after organizations that it perceives as successful.* There are two reasons for this modeling.
First, organizations with ambiguous or disputed goals are likely to be highly
dependent upon appearances for legitimacy. Such organizations may find it to
their advantage to meet the expectations of important constituencies about how
they should be designed and run. In contrast to our view, ecologists would argue
that organizations that copy other organizations usually have no competitive
advantage. We contend that, in most situations, reliance on established, legitimated procedures enhances organizational legitimacy and survival characteristics. A second reason for modeling behavior is found in situations where
conflict over organizational goals is repressed in the interest of harmony; thus
participants find it easier to mimic other organizations than to make decisions
on the basis of systematic analyses of goals since such analyses would prove
painful or disruptive.

The fifth and sixth hypotheses are based on our discussion of normative processes found in professional organizations.

Hypothesis A-5. *The greater the reliance on academic credentials in choosing managerial and staff personnel, the greater the extent to which an
organization will become like other organizations in its field.* Applicants with
academic credentials have already undergone a socialization process in univer-

sity programs and are thus more likely than others to have internalized reigning norms and dominant organizational models.

Hypothesis A-6. *The greater the participation of organizational managers in trade and professional associations, the more likely the organization will be, or will become, like other organizations in its field.* This hypothesis is parallel to the institutional view that the more elaborate the relational networks among organizations and their members, the greater the collective organization of the environment (Meyer and Rowan 1977).

B. FIELD-LEVEL PREDICTORS

The following six hypotheses describe the expected effects of several characteristics of organizational fields on the extent of isomorphism in a particular field. Since the effect of institutional isomorphism is homogenization, the best indicator of isomorphic change is a decrease in variation and diversity, which could be measured by lower standard deviations of the values of selected indicators in a set of organizations. The key indicators would vary with the nature of the field and the interest of the investigator. In all cases, however, field-level measures are expected to affect organizations in a field regardless of each organization's scores on related organizational-level measures.

Hypothesis B-1. *The greater the extent to which an organizational field is dependent upon a single (or several similar) source(s) of support for vital resources, the higher the level of isomorphism.* The centralization of resources within a field both directly causes homogenization by placing organizations under similar pressures from resource suppliers, and interacts with uncertainty and goal ambiguity to increase their impact. This hypothesis is congruent with the ecologist's argument that the number of organizational forms is determined by the distribution of resources in the environment and the terms on which resources are available.

Hypothesis B-2. *The greater the extent to which the organizations in a field transact with agencies of the state, the greater the extent of isomorphism in the field as a whole.* This hypothesis follows not just from the previous one, but from two elements of state/private-sector transactions: their rule-boundedness and formal rationality, and the emphasis of government actors on institutional rules. Moreover, the federal government routinely designates industry standards for an entire field which require adoption by all competing firms. John Meyer (1980) argues convincingly that the aspects of an organization which are affected by state transactions differ to the extent that state participation is unitary or fragmented among several public agencies.

The third and fourth hypotheses follow from our discussion of isomorphic change resulting from uncertainty and modeling.

Hypothesis B-3. *The fewer the number of visible alternative organizational models in a field, the faster the rate of isomorphism in that field.* The predictions of this hypothesis are less specific than those of others and require further refinement; but our argument is that for any relevant dimension of organizational strategies or structures in an organizational field there will be a threshold level, or a tipping point, beyond which adoption of the dominant form will proceed with increasing speed (Granovetter 1978; Boorman and Leavitt 1979).

Hypothesis B-4. *The greater the extent to which technologies are uncertain or goals are ambiguous within a field, the greater the rate of isomorphic change.* Somewhat counterintuitively, abrupt increases in uncertainty and ambiguity should, after brief periods of ideologically motivated experimentation, lead to rapid isomorphic change. As in the case of A-4, ambiguity and uncertainty may be a function of environmental definition and, in any case, interact both with the centralization of resources (A-1, A-2, B-1, B-2) and with professionalization and structuration (A-5, A-6, B-5, B-6). Moreover, in fields characterized by a high degree of uncertainty, new entrants, which could serve as sources of innovation and variation, will seek to overcome the liability of newness by imitating established practices within the field.

The two final hypotheses in this section follow from our discussion of professional filtering, socialization, and structuration.

Hypothesis B-5. *The greater the extent of professionalization in a field, the greater the amount of institutional isomorphic change.* Professionalization may be measured by the universality of credential requirements, the robustness of graduate training programs, or the vitality of professional and trade associations.

Hypothesis B-6. *The greater the extent of structuration of a field, the greater the degree of isomorphism.* Fields that have stable and broadly acknowledged centers, peripheries, and status orders will be more homogeneous both because the diffusion structure for new models and norms is more routine and because the level of interaction among organizations in the field is higher. While structuration may not lend itself to easy measurement, it might be tapped crudely with the use of such familiar measures as concentration ratios, reputational interview studies, or data on network characteristics.

This rather schematic exposition of a dozen hypotheses relating the extent of isomorphism to selected attributes of organizations and of organizational fields does not constitute a complete agenda for empirical assessment of our perspective. We have not discussed the expected nonlinearities and ceiling effects in the relationships we have posited. Nor have we addressed the issue of the indicators that one must use to measure homogeneity. Organizations in a field may be highly diverse on some dimensions, yet extremely homogeneous on others. While we suspect, in general, that the rate at which the standard deviations of structural or behavioral indicators approach zero will vary with the nature of an organizational field's technology and environment, we do not develop these ideas here. This section suggests that the theoretical discussion is susceptible to empirical test and lays out a few testable propositions that may guide future analyses.

Implications for Social Theory

A comparison of macrosocial theories of functionalist or Marxist orientation with theoretical and empirical work in the study of organizations yields a paradoxical conclusion. Societies (or elites), so it seems, are smart, while organizations are dumb. Societies comprise institutions that mesh together comfortably in the interest of efficiency (Clark 1962), the dominant value system (Parsons 1951), or, in the Marxist version, capitalists (Domhoff 1967; Althusser 1969). Organizations, by contrast, are either anarchies (Cohen, March, and Olsen 1972), federations of loosely coupled parts (Weick 1976), or autonomy-seeking agents (Gouldner 1954) laboring under such formidable constraints as bounded rationality (March and Simon 1958), uncertain or contested goals (Sills 1957), and unclear technologies (March and Cohen 1974).

Despite the findings of organizational research, the image of society as consisting of tightly and rationally coupled institutions persists throughout much of modern social theory. Rational administration pushes out nonbureaucratic forms, schools assume the structure of the workplace, hospital and university administrations come to resemble the management of for-profit firms, and the modernization of the world economy proceeds unabated. Weberians point to the continuing homogenization of organizational structures as the formal rationality of bureaucracy extends to the limits of contemporary organizational life. Functionalists describe the rational adaptation of the structure of firms, schools, and states to the values and needs of modern society (Chandler 1977; Parsons 1977). Marxists attribute changes in such organizations as welfare agencies (Pivan and Cloward 1971) and schools (Bowles and Gintis 1976) to the logic of the accumulation process.

We find it difficult to square the extant literature on organizations with these macrosocial views. How can it be that the confused and contentious bumblers who populate the pages of organizational case studies and theories combine to construct the elaborate and well-proportioned social edifice that macrotheorists describe?

The conventional answer to this paradox has been that some version of natural selection occurs in which selection mechanisms operate to weed out those organizational forms that are less fit. Such arguments, as we have contended, are difficult to mesh with organizational realities. Less efficient organizational forms do persist. In some contexts efficiency or productivity cannot even be measured. In government agencies or in faltering corporations selection may occur on political rather than economic grounds. In other contexts, for example, the Metropolitan Opera or the Bohemian Grove, supporters are far more concerned with noneconomic values like aesthetic quality or social status than with efficiency per se. Even in the for-profit sector, where competitive arguments would promise to bear the greatest fruit, Nelson and Winter's work (Winter 1964, 1975; Nelson and Winter 1982) demonstrates that the invisible hand operates with, at best, a light touch.

A second approach to the paradox we have identified comes form Marxists and theorists who assert that key elites guide and control the social system through their command of crucial positions in major organizations (e.g., the financial institutions that dominate monopoly capitalism). In this view, while organizational actors ordinarily proceed undisturbed through mazes of standard operating procedures, at key turning points capitalist elites get their way by intervening in decisions that set the course of an institution for years to come (Katz 1975).

While evidence suggests that this is, in fact, sometimes the case—Barnouw's account (1966–70) of the early days of broadcasting or Weinstein's (1968) work on the Progressives are good examples—other historians have been less successful in their search for class-conscious elites. In such cases as the development of the New Deal programs (Hawley 1966) or the expansion of the Vietnamese conflict (Halperin 1974), the capitalist class appears to have been muddled and disunited.

Moreover, without constant monitoring, individuals pursuing parochial organizational or subunit interests can quickly undo the work that even the most prescient elites have accomplished. Perrow (1976:21) has noted that despite superior resources and sanctioning power, organizational elites are often unable to maximize their preferences because "the complexity of modern organizations makes control difficult." Moreover, organizations have increasingly become the vehicle for numerous "gratifications, necessities, and preferences so that many groups within and without the organization seek to use it for ends that restrict the return to masters."

We reject neither the natural-selection nor the elite-control arguments out of hand. Elites do exercise considerable influence over modern life, and aberrant or inefficient organizations sometimes do expire. But we contend that neither of these processes is sufficient to explain the extent to which organizations have become structurally more similar. We argue that a theory of institutional isomorphism may help explain the observations that organizations are becoming more homogeneous and that elites often get their way, while at the same time enabling us to understand the irrationality, the frustration of power, and the lack of innovation that are so commonplace in organizational life. What is more, our approach is more consonant with the ethnographic and theoretical literature on how organizations work than are either functionalist or elite theories of organizational change.

A focus on institutional isomorphism can also add a much needed perspective on the political struggle for organizational power and survival that is missing from much of population ecology. The institutionalization approach associated with John Meyer and his students posits the importance of myths and ceremony but does not ask how these models arise and whose interest they initially serve. Explicit attention to the genesis of legitimated models and to the definition and elaboration of organizational fields should answer this question. Examination of the diffusion of similar organizational strategies and structures should be productive means for assessing the influence of elite interest. A consideration of isomorphic processes also leads us to a bifocal view of power and its application in modern politics. To the extent that organizational change is unplanned and goes on largely behind the backs of groups that wish to influence it, our attention should be directed to two forms of power. The first, as March and Simon (1958) and Simon (1957) pointed out years ago, is the power to set premises, to define the norms and standards which shape and channel behavior. The second is the point of critical intervention (Domhoff 1979) at which elites can define appropriate models of organizational structure and policy which then go unquestioned for years to come (see Katz 1975). Such a view is consonant with some of the best recent work on power (see Lukes 1974); research on the structuration of organizational fields and on isomorphic processes may help give it more empirical flesh.

Finally, a more developed theory of organizational isomorphism may have important implications for social policy in those fields in which the state works through private organizations. To the extent that pluralism is a guiding value in public policy deliberations, we need to discover new forms of intersectoral coordination that will encourage diversification rather than hastening homogenization. An understanding of the manner in which fields become more homogeneous would prevent policymakers and analysts from confusing the disappearance of an organizational form with its substantive failure. Current efforts to encourage diversity tend to be conducted in an organizational vacuum. Policymakers concerned with pluralism should consider the impact of their programs on the structure of organizational fields as a whole and not simply on the programs of individual organizations.

We believe there is much to be gained by attending to similarity as well as to variation among organizations and, in particular, to change in the degree of homogeneity or variation over time. Our approach seeks to study incremental change as well as selection. We take seriously the observations of organizational theorists about the role of change, ambiguity, and constraint and point to the implications of these organizational characteristics for the social structure as a whole. The foci and motive forces of bureaucratization (and, more broadly, homogenization in general) have, as we argued, changed since Weber's time. But the importance of understanding the trends to which he called attention has never been more immediate.

Acknowledgments

This chapter was originally published in 1983 in the *American Sociological Review* 48(April): 147–60. The chapter incorporates several changes that are not in the 1983 version. The first iteration of the chapter was presented by Powell at the American Sociological Association meetings in Toronto, August 1981. The authors have benefited considerably from careful readings of earlier drafts by Dan Chambliss, Randall Collins, Lewis Coser, Rebecca Friedkin, Connie Gersick, Albert Hunter, Rosabeth Moss Kanter, Charles E. Lindblom, John Meyer, David Morgan, Susan Olzak, Charles Perrow, Richard A. Peterson, Arthur Stinchcombe, and Blair Wheaton. The authors' names are listed in alphabetical order for convenience. This was a fully collaborative effort.

Notes

1. By *connectedness* we mean the existence of transactions tying organizations to one another: such transactions might include formal contractual relationships, participation of personnel in common enterprises such as professional associations, labor unions, or boards of directors, or informal organizational-level ties like personnel flows. A set of organizations strongly connected to one another and only weakly connected to other organizations constitutes a *clique*. By *structural equivalence* we refer to similarity of position in a network structure. For example, two organizations are structurally equivalent if they have ties of the same kind to the same set of other organizations, even if they themselves are not connected; here the key structure is the *role* or *block*.

2. By *organizational change* we refer to change in formal structure, organizational culture, and goals, program, or mission. Organizational change varies in its responsiveness to technical conditions. In this chapter we are most interested in processes that affect organizations in a given field: in most cases these organizations employ similar technical bases; thus we do not attempt to partial out the relative importance of technically functional versus other forms of organizational change. While we cite many examples of organizational change as we go along, our purpose here is to identify a widespread class of organizational processes relevant to a broad range of substantive problems, rather than to identify deterministically the causes of specific organizational arrangements.

3. Knoke 1982, in a careful event-history analysis of the spread of municipal reform, refutes the conventional explanations of culture clash or hierarchal diffusion and finds but modest support for modernization theory. His major finding is that regional differences in municipal reform adoption arise not from social compositional differences, "but from some type of imitation or contagion effects as represented by the level of neighboring regional cities previously adopting reform government" (p. 1337).

4. A wide range of factors—interorganizational commitments, elite sponsorship, and government support in the form of open-ended contracts, subsidy, tariff barriers and import quotas, or favorable tax laws—reduces selection pressures even in competitive organizational fields. An expanding or a stable, protected market can also mitigate the forces of selection.

5. In contrast to Hannan and Freeman, we emphasize adaptation, but we are not suggesting that managers' actions are necessarily strategic in a long-range sense. Indeed, two of the three forms of isomorphism described below—mimetic and normative—involve managerial behaviors at the level of taken-for-granted assumptions rather than consciously strategic choices. In general, we question the utility of arguments about the motivations of actors that suggest a polarity between the rational and the nonrational.

Goal-oriented behavior may be reflexive or prerational in the sense that it reflects deeply embedded predispositions, scripts, schema, or classifications; behavior oriented to a goal may be reinforced without contributing to the accomplishment of that goal. While isomorphic change may often be mediated by the desires of managers to increase the effectiveness of their organizations, we are more concerned with the menu of possible options that managers consider than with their motives for choosing particular alternatives. In other words, we freely concede that actors' understandings of their own behaviors are interpretable in rational terms. The theory of isomorphism addresses not the psychological states of actors but the structural determinants of the range of choices that actors perceive as rational or prudent.

6. Carroll and Delacroix 1982 clearly recognizes this and includes political and institutional legitimacy as a major resource. Aldrich 1979 has argued that the population perspective must attend to historical trends and changes in legal and political institutions.

7. This point was suggested by John Meyer. We are grateful for his extensive comments.

4 The Role of Institutionalization in Cultural Persistence

LYNNE G. ZUCKER

"The only idea common to all usages of the term 'institution' is that of some sort of establishment of relative permanence of a distinctly social sort" (Hughes 1936:180). Specific explanations of cultural persistence have been varied, and frequently institutionalization and persistence have not been clearly separated conceptually. This chapter shows that a more fully developed conception of institutionalization derived in part from the ethnomethodological approach can be used to make clearer predictions about cultural persistence. Much of the confusion of earlier discussions of institutionalization centers on the use of intervening mechanisms to explain persistence. It is argued here that internalization, self-reward, or other intervening processes need not be present to ensure cultural persistence because social knowledge once institutionalized exists as a fact, as part of objective reality, and can be transmitted directly on that basis. For highly institutionalized acts, it is sufficient for one person simply to tell another that this is how things are done. Each individual is motivated to comply because otherwise his actions and those of others in the system cannot be understood (Schutz 1962; Berger and Luckmann 1967); the fundamental process is one in which the moral becomes factual.[1] Yet institutionalization is not simply present or absent; unlike many of the earlier approaches, institutionalization is defined here as a variable, with different degrees of institutionalization altering the cultural persistence which can be expected.

The research reported here investigates the effect of different degrees of institutionalization in constructed realities on cultural persistence in three distinct experiments, each one focusing on a different aspect of persistence. First, for cultural persistence, transmission from one generation to the next must occur, with the degree of generational uniformity directly related to the degree of institutionalization (transmission experiment). Second, once transmission has taken place, maintenance of the culture must occur, with the degree of maintenance directly related to the degree of institutionalization (maintenance experiment). Third, once maintenance has occurred, cultural persistence depends on the resistance to attempts to change, with the degree of resistance directly related to the degree of institutionalization (resistance-to-change experiment).

Cultural Persistence in
Institutional Theory

TRADITIONAL EXPLANATIONS OF
CULTURAL PERSISTENCE

Two traditional explanations of cultural persistence have received the most attention in the literature: the subsystem approach and the normative framework approach. The subsystem approach focuses on specific clusters or sectors, such as family, economy, or polity. Institutional subsystems, then, are separate spheres of activity, each with distinctive clusters of norms and each forming a distinct part of a typology of institutions. While the specific typology used varies widely (see Storer 1973; Bierstedt, Meehan, and Samuelson 1964; Merton, Brown, and Cottrell 1959), explanations for persistence rest on functional necessity (Angell 1936) or on self-interested desire for rewards (Blake and Davis 1964; Parsons 1939, 1940; Sumner 1906). However, both explanations have received strong criticism. First, it is difficult to determine functional necessity independently of persistence; in fact, persistence often is used as an indicator of functional necessity. Second, it has been found that some actions in institutions appear to require sanctions while others do not, so that direct social control cannot fully explain persistence.

The other major traditional approach focuses on the normative framework of institutions which persists because the norms are shared. No external motivation for conformity is necessary because norms which are central to institutions become internalized. The actor is internally motivated to do what he has to do (Parsons 1951; Berger and Luckmann 1967). However, the normative framework approach provides no criteria for separating processes which are institutionalized from those which are not. There is no independent measure of which norms are most important in a social system—it is only after a norm is internalized that it can be identified as institutionalized. Further, there are no explicit criteria for determining whether or not an act is internalized. Certainly, actions performed without direct social control will not necessarily be considered internalized. Yet it is not clear how to distinguish internalization of acts on any other basis.

When explaining persistence, both traditional approaches to institutions focus on the actor's compliance with the action prescribed by the institution. Recognition of functional necessity, self-interest, or internalization is thought to motivate the actor to comply. The actor plays no independent role in maintaining these institutions; rather they serve to constrain his behavior. The social structure (macrolevel) determines the behavior of individuals and small groups (microlevel) and exists independently of them. While the limitations of traditional approaches to institutionalization have been stressed, they are appropriate to deal with some aspects of institutionalization and the transmission of some kinds of meaning. In fact, they may provide good explanations when institutionalization is low.

THE ETHNOMETHODOLOGICAL
APPROACH TO INSTITUTIONALIZATION

A relatively recent approach, the ethnomethodological approach, provides a strikingly different view of the role played by institutions in cultural persistence, dealing explicitly with highly institutionalized action. Reality, while socially constructed, is "experienced as an intersubjective world known-or-knowable-in-common-with others," which exists historically prior to the actors and furnishes "the resistant 'objective structures'" which constrain action (Zimmerman and Pollner 1970:37). To arrive at shared definitions of reality, individual actors transmit an exterior and objective reality, while at the same time this reality, through its qualities of exteriority and objectivity, defines what is real for these same actors. Macrolevel and microlevel are inextricably intertwined. Each actor fundamentally perceives and describes social reality by enacting it and, in this way, transmits it to the other actors in the social system (Berger 1968). Generational transmission provides the clearest example of this process. The young are enculturated by the previous generation, while they in turn enculturate the next generation. The grandparents do not have to be present to ensure adequate transmission of this general cultural meaning. Each generation simply believes it is describing objective reality.

Hence, institutionalization is both a process and a property variable. It is the process by which individual actors transmit what is socially defined as real, and at the same time, at any point in the process the meaning of an act can be defined as more or less a taken-for-granted part of this social reality. Institutionalized acts, then, must be perceived as both objective and exterior. Acts are objective when they are potentially repeatable by other actors without changing the common understanding of the act, while acts are exterior when subjective understanding of acts is reconstructed as intersubjective understanding so that the acts are seen as part of the external world (see Berger and Luckmann 1967 on reification and objectivation).

Objectification and exteriority often covary, with an increase in one causally producing an increase in the other. Depending on the specific relationship between these two variables, the degree of institutionalization can vary from high to low. Hence, acts may vary in the degree to which they are institutionalized. When acts have ready-made accounts (Garfinkel 1967), they are institutionalized, that is, they are both objective and exterior. Ready-made accounts will not exist for acts unique to a single actor or for acts where intersubjective knowledge is low. While these accounts are socially created, they function as objective rules because their social origin is ignored (Schutz 1962). At the same time, ready-made accounts define the possible—institutionalization makes clear what is rational in an objective sense. Other acts are meaningless, even unthinkable (Meyer 1971). Thus, direct social control—whether through incentives or negative sanctions—is not necessary. In fact, applying sanctions to institutionalized acts may have the effect of deinstitutionalizing them. They may seem less objective and impersonal, less factual—and the very act of sanctioning may indicate that there are other possible, attractive alternatives.

But acts are not simply either institutionalized or not institutionalized. The meaning of an act may be perceived as more or less exterior and objective, depending on the situation in which the act is performed and/or depending on the position and role occupied by the actor. For example, acts which are dependent on a particular unique actor are low on institutionalization as in personal influence.[2] In contrast, acts which are performed by an actor occupying a specified position or role are high on institutionalization.

Settings can vary in the degree to which acts in them are institutionalized. By being embedded in broader contexts where acts are viewed as institutionalized, acts in specific situations come to be viewed as institutionalized. Indicating that a situation is structured like situations in an organization makes the actors assume that the actions required of them by other actors in that situation will be those typical of a more formal and less personal interaction. This assumption leads the actors to believe that acts will be more regularized and that the interaction will be more definitely patterned than if the situation were not embedded in an organizational context.

Any act performed by the occupant of an office is seen as highly objectified and exterior. When an actor occupies an office, acts are seen as nonpersonal and as continuing over time, across different actors (Hughes 1937). In addition, an office increases intersubjective knowledge of appropriate action (Weber 1947; Berger and Luckmann 1967). Both the position and role of the occupant establish conditions which maximize treating any act as an accurate reflection of a "fact of life." Thus, acts performed by occupants of an office are by definition institutionalized, though the degree of institutionalization may vary.

In contrast to office, personal influence is dependent on the particular unique actor. There is no rationale under which such an actor can be replaced without changing many of the expectations for behavior. When an actor exercising personal influence leaves the situation, the next actor cannot be classified as having the same quality or qualities. The effect of unique personal influence depends solely on the characteristics of the particular persons interacting. In no way is legitimacy derived from other actors or contexts. Each actor is taken as unique, and each one influences others independently on that basis. Acts performed by actors exercising personal influence are low in objectification and exteriority, hence low in institutionalization.

Implications of the Ethnomethodological Approach to Institutionalization for Cultural Persistence

As described above, three aspects of cultural persistence are directly affected by institutionalization: transmission, maintenance, and resistance to change. Institutionalization is thought to increase all three.

Transmission is defined as the process by which cultural understandings are communicated to a succession of actors. Cultural understandings may be transmitted either in a branching manner, in which each successive actor communicates the meaning to multiple actors, or in a purely sequential one, producing a chain of actors each of whom communicates the meaning only to the next actor on the chain. In any case, whether transmission occurs within a single "generation" or between "generations," it proceeds from actor to actor independent of any of the earlier transmitting actors.

It is argued here that transmission of acts high on institutionalization is not problematic. The actor doing the transmitting simply communicates them as objective fact, and the actor receiving them treats them as an accurate rendition of objective fact. However, depending on the degree of institutionalization of acts, transmission will vary. Some transmission will occur with personal influence (as shown in Jacobs and Campbell 1961); but since acts performed by actors exercising personal influence are low on exteriority and objectification (unique to the particular actor and not transferable to succeeding actors), personal influence will not have as great an effect on transmission as institutionalized context or office. That is, while some transmission occurs with personal influence, increasing objectification and exteriority will increase transmission.

Continuity of the transmission process will also increase institutionalization. The more the history of the transmission process is known, the greater the degree of continuity the actors assume. The history of transmission provides a basis for assuming that the meaning of the act is part of the intersubjective common-sense world. As continuity increases, the acts are increasingly objectified and made exterior to the particular interaction. The act is clearly repeatable, not tied to a unique actor or situation. The basic assumption, then, is that continuity casually produces objectification and exteriority.

Turning now to maintenance, one major assumption is that transmission of acts high on institutionalization is sufficient for maintenance of these same acts. While a large number of experimental findings illustrates the central role that direct social control plays in maintaining or modifying behavior, in these experiments the acts to be maintained are generally low on institutionalization; further, other methods of modifying or maintaining behavior are not examined.

In this theoretical approach, it is argued that the degree of institutionalization radically affects the role and impact of direct social control. For acts low on institutionalization, direct social control (or other intervening mechanisms, such as internalization) is necessary, while for acts high on institutionalization, all that is required is transmission. The institutionalization process simply defines a social reality that will be transmitted and maintained as fact.

The third aspect of cultural persistence which should vary with degree of institutionalization is resistance to change. Acts high on institutionalization will be resistant to attempts to change them through personal influence because they are seen as external facts, imposed on the setting and, at the same time, defining it. Acts performed by actors exercising personal influence, on the other hand, are seen as highly dependent, both on the particular actor and on the particular situation in which the influence attempt is made. Thus, once an act high on institutionalization is transmitted, attempts to change it through personal influence will not be successful and, in fact, may result in a redefinition of the actor rather than the act. Each one of these aspects of cultural persistence was examined in a separate laboratory experiment in which institutionalization could be varied.

General Experimental Design

The research problem requires a situation in which institutionalization of acts can vary from high to low. While the degree of institutionalization can vary in both ambiguous and unambiguous settings, it can be varied more readily in ambiguous settings (Cicourel 1964: ch. 7). Hence, this initial experimental investigation is limited to the less problematic ambiguous setting. In addition, it is necessary that all actors in the situation be committed to obtaining an appropriate understanding of the situation (Garfinkel 1967: ch. 1), though not necessarily committed to the task itself. Further, the task must be one which does not have preexisting relevance to organizational settings, to minimize the possibility of normative, obligatory responses. The more tenuous and unbelievable the connection between the experimental setting and organizational settings, the more likely that differences can be attributed to a cognitive understanding of the "facts of life" rather than obligatory conformity. Finally, the setting must be sufficiently flexible to permit examination of transmission of a preestablished set of norms to actors new to the situation.

A setting which is ambiguous, generates commitment to obtaining a common understanding of the situation, does not have preexisting relevance to organizations, and can be flexibly designed is the autokinetic situation (Sherif 1935).[3] The autokinetic effect is a visual illusion—a stationary pinpoint of light presented in a totally dark room appears to move, smoothly or erratically. In his early studies, Sherif (1935) found that subjects alone developed a judgment standard for the apparent movement and that the particular standard was peculiar to the individual. Over time (three sessions in one week), this standard remained highly stable. He also found that in group situations individuals did not form their own judgment standards but, rather, that the group as a whole established a standard peculiar to that group.[4]

By varying Sherif's basic design, Jacobs and Campbell (1961) developed a transmission situation consisting of a series of stages, referred to as generations, each of which contains two people, one who has judged the previous set of light exposures and one who is new to the situation. In the first generation, the person identified as having just participated in a preceding generation is a confederate who judges the light as moving considerably farther than subjects do who respond alone to the light (the "control" group). The confederate represents an existing enculturated definer of the situation, transmitting a distance judgment standard to the first subject. In the next generation, the confederate leaves the experiment, a new subject is brought in, and the enculturated subject transmits to the new subject. The same procedure is followed in succeeding generations.

Jacobs and Campbell (1961:342–43) were concerned with "manipulating cultural strength" by varying the number of "culture-bearing" confederates and by varying the number of naïve subjects. For each experimental condition, generations were continued until the judgments were approximately equal to those in the control condition (judging light movement alone). While Jacobs and Campbell had anticipated producing strong cultures, their findings did not support this prediction. After the last generation with the confederate, the arbitrary norm was transmitted in some degree only to the fourth or fifth generation. Little difference was found between conditions with different numbers of confederates.

In the research reported here, it was expected that varying institutionalization would produce more striking differences. Instructions were used to create three levels of institutionalization. The higher the level of institutionalization the higher the transmission, maintenance and resistance to change of cultural understanding expected. Each of the aspects was examined in a separate experiment. Table 4.1 presents a summary of the overall design for the three experiments.

Transmission Experiment

The transmission experiment tests the proposition that the greater the degree of institutionalization, the greater the generational uniformity of cultural understandings. It was predicted that the generational uniformity of cultural understandings would be least with personal influence, highest with organizational context and office and intermediate with organizational context alone.

Table 4.1 Transmission

	Order of Response	
	First	Second
1st generation	Confederate	Subject 1
2d generation	Subject 1	Subject 2
3rd generation	Subject 2	Subject 3
Maintenance	Subject 3 (alone)	
Resistance to change	Confederate	Subject 3

Note: Maintenance and resistance-to-change experiments are conducted when subject 3 returns one week after the transmission experiment.

SUBJECTS

A total of 180 female subjects were used, with 45 subjects participating in each of the three experimental conditions and 45 subjects in the control condition. Three generations were used, with fifteen replications in each condition.

APPARATUS AND PROCEDURE

The experiment took place in a completely darkened room to facilitate perception of the autokinetic phenomenon. To provide a constant exposure time, the light was operated by a timer, coupled with a motor, as in the Jacobs and Campbell study. Each naïve subject was read the instructions for the appropriate condition prior to entering the experimental room. In the control condition, the instructions focused on the task, with no information about social characteristics or understandings:

> This is a study of visual perception. It requires judgments made with limited information. In a few minutes, you will be brought into the next room. In this room is an apparatus that will project a small light. After the light appears, it begins to move. Let me explain what you will be doing. You must judge the distance that the light moves from the time that it appears until it is turned off. You will repeat this procedure a number of times. Each time the light is shown, you will be asked to judge the distance the light moved in inches along a straight line connecting the starting point and the ending point. After each time the light is turned off, you will be asked to say how far the light moved.
>
> Try to make your judgments as accurate as possible.
>
> Please fill out the card on the desk. As you will notice, it has been numbered. To assure anonymity in this study, each participant is assigned a number and all names are removed from any records.

The personal influence condition closely followed the Jacobs and Campbell (1961) instructions and included the full description of the task as in the control condition instructions:

> This study involves problem solving in groups. You will be participating with another person. There are already two people at work in the next room. . . .
>
> To simplify the recording procedure, the person who is already in the room will be asked for her judgment first. At this point, you will be asked for your judgment second. After a while, the other person will leave, you will take her place, and a new person will be brought in. Then you will be asked for your judgment first.

The organizational context condition instructions incorporated organizational context and continuity (modified from Weick and Gilfillan 1971), otherwise retaining the same wording as the personal influence condition:

> This study involves problem solving in model organizations. You will be participating with another organizational member. Your two-member organization is meant to be a small-scale model of much larger organizations, and it has many of the same characteristics they do.
>
> Most large organizations continue even though individual members, or even whole divisions, may be replaced, due to changing jobs, retirement, reorganization, etc. The model organization in which you will participate also will have this feature: members who have been in it for a while will drop out, and new members will join, but the job will go on. Thus, performance of any single member may not be important to the organization as long as the job continues to be done.
>
> There is already a two-member organization operating in the next room. In a few minutes, one of the members will leave, and you will be brought in. After you have worked together with the other member for some time, you will take her place. Then a new member will be brought in as a replacement, becoming part of the organization.

The office condition instructions were built directly on the organizational context instructions, adding an office:

> Large organizations also place members in different positions, often according to the amount of time spent in the organization. The model organization in which you will participate also has this feature—the member who has spent the most time in the organization will be the Light Operator. When she leaves, you will become the Light Operator.
>
> As you may already have guessed, the group member labeled Light Operator will be responsible for turning the light on after each member gives her judgment on the previous movement. The Light Operator in each case must depress a button to activate the light. From then on, the timing and motion of the light is controlled automatically until the next trial.
>
> To simplify the recording procedure, the Light Operator will be asked for her judgment first. She will be called Member 1. At this point, you will be asked for your judgment second. You will be

called Member 2. After a while, the Light Operator will leave, you will take her place as Light Operator, and a new member will be brought in. Then you will be asked for your judgment first, being called Member 1.

In each case, the subject was asked to fill out a numbered card designed to enhance the continuity manipulation in the instructions. In the personal influence condition, low on continuity, the number assigned to each subject was 3; in the organizational context and office conditions, each subject was assigned number 103; while in the control condition, number 21 was assigned to each subject, representing neither low nor high continuity.

After the subjects were led into the experimental room, they were seated side by side eight feet from the light box. All subjects were blindfolded before entering the room and between generations so that no visual contact with other subjects was made. The experimenter communicated with the subjects using a microphone system and prompted responses with a name or number (depending on condition). In the personal influence and organizational context conditions, the experimenter controlled the timer and prompted responses by using the subject's first name. In the office condition, however, the subject who had been in the room longest controlled the timer placed next to her in the second set of thirty trials. The subject simply depressed a button which activated the light for a fixed period of time. Responses were prompted by "Member 1" and "Member 2" in the first trial, then simply "1" and "2."

The light was presented and the subjects' responses (judgments of the light movement in inches) recorded for a block of thirty trials. After each block of trials, the senior member of the group was taken out, the other member moved to the right seat, and a new member was brought in. In the first generation, the experienced member was a confederate who had been instructed how to respond. The confederate was instructed to make judgments with a mean of 12 and a range of 9 to 15 (from Sherif 1967).

After each generation, the subject taken from the room was conducted to an interview room. If she was the last subject in the transmission experiment (each group consisted of three generations), she was not interviewed but scheduled to return again one week later.

RESULTS

Control Condition

The control condition was designed to provide a baseline for all experimental data collected, with a single subject responding alone to the light for 90 trials. This makes it clear what degree of change occurred when a higher initial standard of judgment was provided by a confederate in the experimental conditions. It was found that the mean response of the 45 subjects in the control condition was highly consistent across the three blocks of 30 trials (4.37, 3.95, 3.95

inches). Thus, unlike results reported by Sherif (1935) and Jacobs and Campbell (1961) which showed a steady and significant decline in judgments, the mean judgments of the 45 control subjects in this experiment did not show a significant decline. Hence, the baseline response can be defined as the average of all judgments (90 trials): 4.16 inches.

Experimental Conditions

The predictions that transmission (and, hence, generational uniformity) would be greater in the organizational context condition than in the personal influence condition, and greater in the office condition than in the organizational context condition, are examined in two main ways. First, the response levels of later generations are compared. Second, mean response levels of naïve subjects over the three generations are compared to test the predicted ordering of the experimental conditions.

Turning first to the discussion of the transmission coefficient, the use of mean response levels of successive naïve (new) subjects to predict response levels of later generations was suggested by Jacobs and Campbell's (1961) data. Although not noticed by them, in their data for all four conditions the relative rate of decline in response level toward the baseline remains essentially constant between generations in the same conditions. This is most clearly illustrated in their figure 2 (Jacobs and Campbell 1961:345): with a baseline of 3.8 inches, the naïve subject made mean judgments (in 30 trials) of 12.4, 9.3, 7.1, and 5.8 inches. Examining the ratio of elevations above the baseline in successive generations, it can be seen that it remains essentially constant:

$$\frac{9.3 - 3.8}{12.4 - 3.8} = .64;$$

$$\frac{7.1 - 3.8}{9.3 - 3.8} = .60;$$

$$\frac{5.8 - 3.8}{7.1 - 3.8} = .61.$$

In designing the experiment reported here, it was assumed that this decline, so characteristic of the Jacobs and Campbell data and also clear in Sherif (1967:264–68), is a general characteristic of generational transmission in the autokinetic situation. The essentially constant geometric decline toward the baseline permits prediction of the response levels of later generations, so that it is not necessary to collect data on all generations.

Before turning to the specific results in this experiment, the measure of relative rate of decline in response levels should be more generally expressed as a transmission coefficient. This measure of transmission is based on a comparison of the response levels of the naïve (new) subjects in each generation, where response level is defined as the mean of a subject's judgments over thirty trials. The transmission coefficient then can be defined as the ratio of elevations above the baseline of successive naïve subjects:

$$T_i \frac{S_i + B}{Si - B} \ (i = 1,2),$$

where S_j is the average response of the jth subjects in the naïve position and B is the baseline response. One desirable property of the transmission coefficient defined in this manner is that it permits prediction of the generation at which the response level will approximate the baseline allowing a more direct reflection of experimental findings. Since actual experimental data cannot be expected to be completely constant, an average transmission coefficient, defined as follows, will be used:

$$T = \frac{T_1 + T_2}{2}.$$

Table 4.2 presents the average transmission coefficients (T) for the three generations in this experiment.[5] The transmission coefficients for each pair of generations (T_1 and T_2) in each condition were essentially constant. There was a greater difference between the coefficients in the personal influence condition than between those in the other two conditions, possibly because the response level in the third generation closely approximates the baseline response.

Figure 4.1 presents the extrapolated response levels based on the average transmission coefficient, T, for each experimental condition as well as the actual experimental data on which the coefficients were based. The predicted differences between the three conditions are clearly found. In the personal influence condition, the extrapolated response level approximates the baseline response in the 7th generation, while in the organizational context condition, the extrapolated response level does not approximate the baseline response until the 29th generation. Even in the 38th generation, in the office condition, the extrapolated response level does not yet approximate the baseline response.

Table 4.2 Transmission Coefficients Defining Rate of Decline of Response Level for Each Experimental Condition

Transmission Coefficients	Institutionalization		
	Personal Influence	Organizational Context	Office
T_1 (first to second generations)	.49	.87	.92
T_2 (second to third generations)	.37	.89	.97
T (average coefficient)	.43	.88	.94

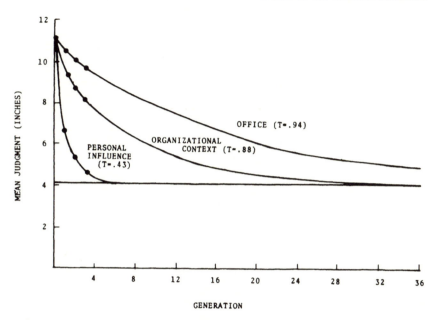

Fig. 4.1. Extrapolated response levels based on transmission coefficients determined by the first three generations in each condition.

Now direct comparisons between the mean response levels of naïve subjects are made to permit significance tests of the predicted ordering of the experimental conditions. Table 4.3 presents these mean response levels by condition. The predicted ordering for the magnitude of response level was obtained:

Personal influence < organizational context < office.

In the personal influence condition, the mean response level of naïve subjects declined rapidly so that it was only slightly above the baseline by the third generation (4.58 compared to 4.16 for the baseline response).

In order to evaluate the magnitude of the differences in response level by condition, analysis of variance was used. Because comparisons between different levels of institutionalization involve differences between generations as

Table 4.3   Mean Response Level of Naïve Subjects
over Three Generations in the Transmission Experiment

	Institutionalization		
	Personal Influence	Organizational Context	Office
Generation			
First	6.53	9.44	10.51
Second	5.31	8.77	10.00
Third	4.58	8.25	9.79

Table 4.4 Analysis of Variance Test on the Mean Response Level of Naïve Subjects

Source of Variance	Sum of Squares	df	Mean Square	F	Significance Level[a]
Between groups					
A (condition)	514.75	2	257.37	74.83	$p < .001$
Subjects within groups	144.45	42	3.44		
Within groups					
B (generation)	37.96	2	18.98	9.42	$p < .001$
B × subjects within groups	169.30	84	2.02		

a. Under the more conservative, negatively biased test.

well as differences associated with institutionalization itself, customary two-way analysis of variance is not appropriate. Instead, analysis of variance for the special case of the two-factor experiment with repeated measures on one factor is used in table 4.4 (Winer 1962:298–318). The data provide clear support for the statistical significance of the main effects due to institutionalization.[6]

To recapitulate briefly, the transmission experiment tests the proposition that if institutionalization is increased, then generational uniformity of cultural understandings will be greater. From the preceding analysis of the data, it is clear that the effects of institutionalization occurred as predicted. Further interpretation of results will be deferred until all three experiments have been described. Before turning to the maintenance experiment, results bearing on the effectiveness of the experimental manipulations are reported.

EFFECTIVENESS OF THE EXPERIMENTAL MANIPULATIONS

As described earlier, the instructions read at the beginning of the experiment were designed to manipulate the degree of institutionalization. Since this is the only manipulation of the independent variables for all three experiments reported here, it is crucial to assess its effectiveness. Therefore, rather than attempt to assess this directly, a number of other variables which were expected to vary directly with the degree of institutionalization were chosen to validate the manipulation. Specifically, it was predicted that increasing institutionalization should increase the subjects' subjective certainty of the accuracy of their judgments, subjects' reported ease in estimating light movement, and subjects' reported expectations that their answers should be the same as those of the experienced subject (the transmitter of cultural understandings). In addition, it was predicted that the occupant of the office position would be seen as less personal; the highly institutionalized position should increase the role distance and significantly affect perception of attributes of the occupant of that position.

Parts of the postexperimental questionnaire and the adjective list (given before the questionnaire) were designed to determine whether these additional dependent variables designed to measure validity did indeed vary with the degree of institutionalization. Turning first to the questionnaire results, subjects were asked three questions reflecting perception of institutionalization. First, subjects were asked, "How certain were you of the accuracy of your judgments?" They were shown a separate card on which was drawn a seven-point scale, where 1 represented "Certain" and 7 indicated "Uncertain." Certainty was predicted to increase with increasing institutionalization, because it reflected certainty in the accuracy of the group standard, not individual judgment. Subjects in the more institutionalized conditions were predicted both to be more certain of their judgment and to change more toward the confederate's judgments from the baseline response in the transmission experiment, a prediction contrary to the assumption made in many psychological studies where certainty is thought to increase resistance to change (Boomer 1959).

Second, subjects were asked about ease of judgment: "Was it difficult to estimate the distance the light moved?" It was predicted that the more institutionalized and, therefore, certain about accuracy, the easier estimating light movement should be. In the absence of objective criteria for determining difficulty of judgment, assessment of difficulty would rest on a trial-by-trial examination of difficulty in reaching a decision. Where certainty in the accuracy of group standards is high (in the more institutionalized conditions), decisions should be less difficult. Hence, in this case, certainty determines difficulty rather than difficulty determining certainty as most studies assume (Coleman, Blake, and Mouton 1958; Kretch and Crutchfield 1962; Freedman, Carlsmith, and Sears 1974).

The third question asked in the postsession interview which reflected perception of institutionalization was, "Did you feel that your answers should be the same as the other person in the first set of judgments?" It was predicted that the greater the degree of institutionalization, the more frequently the subject would report that her responses should be the same as the other person in the "experienced" or transmitter position. The more institutionalized, the more subjects should feel normatively constrained to transmit the confederate's standard.

The responses on these three questions on the postexperiment questionnaire are summarized in table 4.5. Each of the three sets of findings is in the predicted direction. Subjects were much less certain of their accuracy in the personal influence condition than in either of the more institutionalized conditions. While subjects in the organizational context condition were less certain of their accuracy than subjects in the office condition, the difference was not striking. Turning now to the responses to the question "Was it difficult to estimate the distance the light moved?" as predicted, fewer subjects in the office condition reported difficulty than in the organizational context condition. Nearly all subjects in the personal influence condition reported difficulty. Finally, over half of the subjects in the personal influence condition did not feel normatively constrained to give the same response as the confederate, compared to less than a

Table 4.5 Questionnaire Responses by Experimental Condition

| | Institutionalization | | |
Question	Personal Influence	Organizational Context	Office
Mean certainty score[a]	5.35	3.62	3.22
Number reporting judgment difficulty	41	26	16
Number not feeling answer should be same as experienced subjects[b]	28	11	3

Note: N in each condition is 45.
a. The smaller the number, the more certain of own judgment accuracy. Scale is 1 to 7.
b. Question reversed so that all predicted magnitudes in the table would be in the same direction.

quarter of the subjects in the organizational context condition. Only 7 percent in the office condition did not feel normatively constrained.

The adjective checklist was designed primarily as a check on the office manipulation. Six adjective pairs were chosen to indicate role distance and the nonpersonal nature of office. Comparing the person occupying the experienced-position in the office condition with the person occupying that position in the personal influence condition for each of these adjective pairs, the subjects in the office were characterized more frequently as decisive, cold, unsociable, dominant, methodical, and unemotional. Each of these differences, except the unsociable-sociable comparison, is significant by the t-test.[7]

Maintenance Experiment

The maintenance experiment was designed to test the proposition that the greater the degree of institutionalization, the greater the extent of maintenance of cultural understandings without direct control. The subjects in the personal influence condition were expected to maintain the transmission experiment response level least well, with subjects in the office condition maintaining it to the highest degree and subjects in the organizational context condition intermediate.

SUBJECTS

The third subject from each group in the transmission experiment returned one week later, hence the total subjects available for the maintenance experiment were fifteen subjects per condition, for a total of forty-five subjects.

APPARATUS AND PROCEDURE

The same apparatus was used as in the transmission experiment as well as the same procedures, with the following exceptions: (1) it is not a transmission situation, hence the generational design was not used; (2) the subject responded alone for the thirty trials.

The subject was read instructions (the same for all subjects in the maintenance experiment, regardless of experimental condition) identical to those used in the control condition, except that they were prefaced with the phrase "As you will remember." The subject was told that the other person scheduled for the same time had not arrived yet and in order to refresh her memory about the task, she would judge the light movement alone until the other person arrived.

RESULTS

Analysis of the results is based on comparison between the same subject's responses in the last thirty trials in the transmission experiment and the thirty trials in the maintenance experiment. The mean differences in response levels between these two phases are presented in table 4.6. The ordering of magnitude of the differences is as predicted:

Personal influence < organizational context < office.

However, it was not predicted that the means would actually increase very slightly in the organizational context and office conditions.[8]

Analysis of variance was used to examine the difference between response levels of the same subject in the transmission phase and the maintenance phase. These results are presented in table 4.7. The data provide clear support for the statistical significance of the main effects on maintenance of cultural understandings due to institutionalization.

Resistance-to-Change Experiment

The resistance-to-change experiment was designed to test the proposition that the greater the degree of institutionalization, the greater the resistance to change in cultural understandings through personal influence. A change in the definition of the situation is attempted.

After the trials alone (maintenance experiment), a confederate was brought in, identified as the late other subject. The confederate, responding first, attempted to establish a lower-than-baseline response level, permitting measurement of resistance to change. The confederate's judgment had a mean of approximately 1.5 and a range of .5 to 2.5 inches. It was predicted that judgments in the personal influence condition would be less resistant to change than judg-

Table 4.6 Differences in Response Level in the 30 Trials in the Maintenance Experiment

Difference between Transmission and Maintenance Experiments	Institutionalization		
	Personal Influence	Organizational Context	Office
Third Subject	.78	− .08	− .47

Table 4.7   Analysis of Variance Test on the Difference in Response Level of the Same Subject in the Transmission and Maintenance Experiments

Source of Variance	Sum of Squares	df	Mean Square	F	Significance Level
Between groups	12.35	2	6.17	5.27	$p < .01$
Within groups	49.18	42	1.17		

ments in the organizational context condition and that judgments in the organizational context condition would be less resistant to change than judgments in the office condition.

SUBJECTS

The resistance-to-change experiment was a continuation of the maintenance experiment and therefore had the same subjects.

APPARATUS AND PROCEDURE

Again, the same apparatus was used. The same procedure was used as in the maintenance experiment except that a confederate was brought in. Thirty trials each were given, the confederate responding first, since "she didn't have the refresher session." No other instructions were given.

RESULTS

A comparison between the thirty trials in the maintenance experiment and the thirty trials for the same subject in the resistance-to-change experiment provided the basis for analysis of the results. The mean difference in response levels between the two experiments is presented in table 4.8. The ordering is as predicted, with the personal influence condition having the greatest change, the organizational context condition less change, and the office condition the least change.

Analysis of variance was used to examine the differences between response levels of the same subject in the maintenance experiment and the resistance-to-change experiment. Table 4.9 presents the results. The data provide clear support for the predicted effects of institutionalization on resistance to change.

Table 4.8   Difference in Response Level between the Maintenance and Resistance-to-Change Experiments

	Institutionalization		
	Personal Influence	Organizational Context	Office
Third Subject	1.59	1.03	.05

Table 4.9 Analysis of Variance Test on the Difference in Response Level of the Same Subject in the Maintenance and Resistance-to-Change Experiments

Source of Variance	Sum of Squares	df	Mean Square	F	Significance Level
Between groups	18.23	2	9.11	16.27	$p < .001$
Within groups	23.53	42	.56		

Thus, the analysis of results in the resistance-to-change experiment uniformly supports the predictions made.

Conclusions and Implications

The predictions derived from an ethnomethodological approach to institutionalization receive strong support in the results of the three experiments reported here. Each specific finding has a number of implications for research on institutionalization and poses significant issues which have not been sufficiently addressed in other, more traditional, theoretical approaches to the problem of cultural persistence.

TRANSMISSION OF CULTURAL UNDERSTANDINGS

Given that cultural understandings are socially constructed, the problem is to explain why some are so permanent and universal while others are unique to person, place, or time. The transmission experiment was designed to test specific ideas about the mechanisms underlying generational uniformity, identifying the degree of institutionalization (both objective and exterior) as a determinant of this uniformity.

A number of alternative explanations of the results could be made, but none is as convincing as the ethnomethodological explanation on which the experiment was based. Specifically, creating an organizational context may implicitly lead the naïve subjects to believe that they are expected by the experimenter to conform to the "more experienced" subject. On the basis of the experimental procedures alone, this seems unlikely, since in every condition naïve subjects know at the outset that they will occupy the other position. Further, the task itself is unrelated to organizational settings. The strongest refutation, however, can be made on the basis of the assessment of the effectiveness of the experimental manipulations. Other aspects of institutionalization unrelated to organizational context were found to covary with degree of institutionalization: certainty of accuracy, reports of difficulty in judging light movement, and expectations that answers should be the same as the "experienced" subject.

Status value theories (Berger, Cohen, and Zelditch 1966, 1972) would predict the results obtained for the office condition alone, though not fully since the naïve subjects know they will occupy the office after one set of trials. However, since positions are differentiated, it could be argued that the occupant of the low position is more likely to be influenced by the occupant of the high position. However, the scope of the theoretical approach presented here is quite different, predicting not only the direction of influence in the office condition, but also the relative magnitude of influence which depends not on status value but on institutionalization.

MAINTENANCE OF CULTURAL UNDERSTANDINGS

Maintenance frequently has been described as occurring only when direct social control is present. Direct sanctions produce compliance; as long as the expected behavior is in the actor's self-interest, it will be maintained. Even the internalization and self-reward conceptions depend on direct sanctions to establish the behavior initially and/or to maintain the behavior in those actors not fully "socialized."

In the theoretical approach presented here, it is asserted that the more institutionalized, the greater the maintenance without direct social control. The effects of institutionalization can be seen most clearly when no sanctioning process is present. In the experiments reported here, social influence was present, but should operate uniformly in all conditions. The differences found, then, can be attributed to the relatively high dependence of acts low on institutionalization on social control mechanisms compared to the strikingly low dependence of acts high on institutionalization. The greater the degree of institutionalization, the less likely sanctions will exist. For example, laws regulating black-white interaction in the South were enacted only after the institution of slavery was challenged (Woodward 1957).

RESISTANCE TO CHANGE

Resistance to change is fundamentally affected by institutionalization, regardless of sanctions. The confederate's below-the-baseline responses serve to positively sanction lower responses by the subjects, yet it was found that only when the degree of institutionalization was low (the personal influence condition) did this sanctioning cause the subjects to reduce their response to below the baseline.

These results are, on one level, nonintuitive, since the subjects closer in response level to the confederate change the most. Subjects in the personal influence condition essentially adopted the new judgment standard: the situation was redefined. However, those subjects further from the confederate's response level changed much less. As predicted, they resisted the confederate's attempt to redefine the situation.

The results of this experiment contradict other approaches most directly. In other approaches, resistance to change, regardless of source or content, comes directly or indirectly from the strength of the previous sanction. The subsystem approach assumes that resistance to change is a function of the distribution of rewards; if more rewards are associated with one action than with another, the more highly rewarded action will be exhibited. Therefore, those actions that are more highly rewarded will be more resistant to change. The normative framework approach argues that resistance to change is a function of internally generated motivation, either internalization or self-reward. Generally, this internal motivation is seen as deriving from previous sanctions applied to some actions and not to others. Neither of these traditional approaches to institutionalization could predict or explain the results obtained in the resistance-to-change experiment.

GENERAL IMPLICATION

The findings reported in this chapter are thus consistent with previous arguments, serving to modify parts of the traditional approaches to institutionalization. The findings reported here do not suggest rejection of the traditional approaches but rather serve to conditionalize them by restricting the set of situations to which they apply. That is, it is not that these other approaches should be rejected but rather that the class of situations to which they apply should be more precisely specified. These other approaches do not deal adequately with highly institutionalized action: the mechanisms they use are more important when the degree of institutionalization is low.

The theoretical approach developed in this chapter, based on the ethnomethodological approach, provides a more complete explanation of highly institutionalized action. In three experiments, persistence of cultural understandings has been shown to vary directly with the degree of institutionalization. The degree of institutionalization—depending on personal influence, organizational context, or office—directly affected three major aspects of persistence: generational uniformity, maintenance, and resistance to change. Thus, a theory which explains highly institutionalized action also permits more accurate and complete predictions of cultural persistence.

In conclusion, the findings reported in three experiments provide strong and consistent support for the predicted relationship between degree of institutionalization and cultural persistence. As predicted, it was found that the greater the degree of institutionalization, the greater the generational uniformity of cultural understandings, the greater the maintenance without direct social control, and the greater the resistance to change through personal influence.

Postscript: Microfoundations of Institutional Thought

Neoinstitutionalists ordinarily operate at the macrolevel, focusing on the role of an institutionalized environment ("the state" or "law" or "constitutional orders") in legitimizing organizations and their structures (Zucker 1987; Meyer

1987). Such work, well represented in this volume, often emphasizes increasing isomorphism among organizations subject to similar institutional pressures (DiMaggio and Powell, ch. 3; Scott and Meyer, ch. 5) and often focuses on the content, rather than the process, of institutionalization. Most macrolevel institutional research examines indicators of the effects of the institutional environment on some aspect of organizational structure or activity (see Meyer and Scott 1983b; Zucker 1988b). The process by which this occurs remains a "black box."

By contrast, the microlevel approach represented in my 1977 paper and in subsequent papers (Zucker 1983; Tolbert and Zucker 1983; Zucker 1987) focuses upon institutionalization as a *process* rather than as a state; upon the cognitive processes involved in the creation and transmission of institutions; upon their maintenance and resistance to change; and upon the role of language and symbols in those processes. Although microinstitutionalism is largely complementary to, rather than competitive with, macroinstitutionalism, several important differences deserve attention.

Degrees of Institutionalization

The original insight in the cognitive approach to institutions was that actions vary in the extent to which they are perceived as exterior and objective, that is, that institutionalization is a continuous rather than a binary variable. My 1977 study demonstrated how small variations in exteriority and objectivity could create varying amounts of institutionalization. By contrast, most work at the macrolevel has taken institutionalization for granted and simply examined its often nonintuitive effects. Such an approach replaces *process* with *effects* as the object of institutional research and tends to focus on dysfunctional or irrational aspects of institutional systems (e.g., myth and ceremony in Meyer and Rowan, ch. 2), and away from the potential efficiency gains inherent in repeatable routines easily transmitted to organizational newcomers and maintained easily over time (Zucker 1977; Nelson and Winter 1982).

Institutionalization versus Resource Dependence

Cognitive measures of the degree of institutionalization have another advantage: they are analytically independent of the sanctioning capacity of the external environment. Measures of the degree of institutionalization constructed solely at the macrolevel often confound institutionalization with resource dependence: for example, firms adopt affirmative-action personnel structures to the extent they are dependent on federal contracts for revenues (Dobbin et al. 1988); and universities adopt administrative structures in response to changes in resource flows from private and public sources (Tolbert 1985). Without micromeasurement strategies, one cannot tell whether such adoptions reflect institutionalization per se (i.e., exteriority and objectiveness) rather than clever strategic responses to external constraint.

STRATEGIC VARIATION IN RESPONSE
TO INSTITUTIONAL ENVIRONMENTS

In contrast to the conventional emphasis of macroinstitutionalism on organizational homogeneity, direct investigation of transmission and maintenance processes yields insights into the variability of organizations' strategic responses to similar institutional environments. For example, law firms all face highly institutionalized systems of legal training and credentialing which, from the macroperspective, should engender isomorphism among law firms in recruitment and supervision of attorneys. But Tolbert (1988) finds different strategies among law firms: some recruit heavily from a single law school, while others recruit from several different schools. Socialization and supervision strategies vary accordingly, with firms recruiting from a single school relying on less formal, more tacit kinds of control. In other words, variation in strategic response to the same environment can engender differentiation rather than isomorphism. To specify the conditions under which either of these occur requires a focus on internal institutional process. Microinstitutionalism offers a potent, but as yet undeveloped, alternative to the influential transaction-costs and agency-theoretic approaches favored by economists.

DEINSTITUTIONALIZATION

There has been little work on the processes by which institutions disappear. The results of my 1977 experiment were surprising in the ease with which institutional effects were created: an instructional manipulation of a seemingly trivial action embued the system with meaning. As the results of my third experiment indicated, such effects were much more difficult to destroy. Institutionalization often occurs accidentally, as a by-product of the creation of other structures; deinstitutionalization is seldom accidental. Once institutionalized, structure or activity may be maintained without further action: institutionalized elements become embedded in networks, with change in any one element resisted because of the changes it would entail for all the interrelated network elements. (Thus it is hard to abolish grades in college classes because graduate schools depend upon apparently comparable measures of student achievement in making admission decisions [Zucker 1986; Nadel 1953].) Every institutionalized system tends to carry "baggage" of related structures and activities that become institutionalized over time—a process I have elsewhere (1987) referred to as the "contagion of legitimacy."

CONCLUSION

Without a solid cognitive, microlevel foundation, we risk treating institutionalization as a black box at the organizational level, focusing on content at the exclusion of developing a systematic explanatory theory of process, conflating institutionalization with resource dependency, and neglecting institutional variation and persistence. Although important insights can be gained by examining the content of institutions, there is an ever-present danger of making the neoinstitutionalist enterprise a taxonomic rather than an explanatory, theory-building science. Institutional theory is always in danger of forgetting that labeling a process or structure does not explain it.

Acknowledgments

This chapter, with the exception of the postscript, was first published in 1977 in the *American Sociological Review* 42(5): 726–43. The author wishes to thank Morris Zelditch, Jr., John W. Meyer, and Anne M. McMahon for their assistance throughout the research reported in this chapter. In addition, she thanks the following people for extensive comments on an earlier version of this chapter which the author presented at the West Coast Conference on Small Group Research in Victoria, Canada, April 1975: Phillip Bonacich, Mel Pollner, and Ralph H. Turner. Finally, a special thanks to Paul DiMaggio for editing and commenting on the postscript.

Notes

1. Ethnomethodologists deal both with emergent culture, facing the problem of creating new culture, and with existing culture, facing the problem of cultural persistence. It is this second thread of ethnomethodology which is selected for further examination in this chapter. When emergent culture is the focus, then the problem of establishing facticity becomes the central problem. It is here that the moral character of social facts becomes the central concern (Garfinkel 1967). When the social facts are not well established, their transmission is problematic and may well depend on an obligatory, moral response to a specific situation. However, when social facts are well established, the moral character becomes less significant than the cognitive. It is this situation that is examined further here.

2. Personal influence is used throughout this chapter to mean direct influence between actors who perceive each other as equals. Influence between actors who are seen as occupying differentiated roles or who are seen as interacting in a specialized setting governed by consensual rules is not considered to be personal influence.

3. There is much support in articles published since Sherif's original study for the claim that the underlying effect is highly variable, including studies of the physiological basis of the effect (Marshall 1966; Gregory and Zangweil 1963; Farrow et al. 1965). The effect is so unstructured that it frequently has been proposed as a projective technique (Cornwell 1966; Rechtschaffen and Mednick 1955).

4. As demonstrated in an earlier study (Alexander, Zucker, and Brody 1970), expectations that the light movement will be patterned and stable account for judgmental convergence. When subjects' expectations are altered, either through instructions explaining the autokinetic illusion or through overhearing a confederate give divergent judgments of a light they could not see, it was found that subjects' judgments did not

converge. However, Sherif's basic instructions, used in the experiments reported in this chapter, lead subjects to exhibit judgmental convergence.

5. While it is technically possible to use two generations—one ratio of elevation above the baseline—three generations were used to test the assumption that the decline was also constant in the experiment described here.

6. The mechanism underlying differential transmissions was also explored, comparing response levels of the same subjects when in the naïve and experienced positions. Results are available from the author by request.

7. Tables are available from the author by request.

8. Absolute differences are used because any changes, even an increase in response level, are due to the subject's perception of the common understanding in the situation. The slight increase in means in the two more institutionalized conditions is probably due to a "ceiling effect." Responses overall were maintained to a high degree. When developing the design used here, it was assumed that judgment standards artificially established through a confederate plus a one-week time span would be less well maintained than earlier studies found. Such was not the case. In future experiments, the problem of near-perfect maintenance may be avoided by using a more structured, less ambiguous setting in which an artificial definition of the situation would be less well maintained.

5 The Organization of Societal Sectors: Propositions and Early Evidence

W. Richard Scott and
John W. Meyer

This chapter takes seriously the assumption that organizations are affected by their environments, and it works to expand our conception of what environmental features are salient for explaining organizational structure and performance. Organization-environment models dominant during the 1970s—which we review—underestimated the extent to which organizations are connected to and affected by larger systems of relations. These systems, we argue, are increasingly organized at broader and wider levels so that local organizations are connected into nonlocal and vertical hierarchies as well as into the horizontal, community-level systems that have received attention. We also suggest that previous environmental models gave attention to technical features of environments but neglected the importance of institutional elements within environments.

Building on the insights derived from three bodies of work—on community structure, policy implementation, and agency coordination—we argue the utility of isolating wider interorganizational systems for study. In particular, we propose the concept of *societal sector* as a useful way of bounding such systems. A societal sector is defined to include all organizations within a society supplying a given type of product or service together with their associated organizational sets: suppliers, financiers, regulators, and so forth.

The primary work of this chapter is to identify salient dimensions or characteristics of sector structure, suggest factors accounting for these features, and most importantly, propose hypotheses that link sector characteristics with the number, variety, structure, and functioning of the organizational units operating within the sector. The structure of the sector within which an organization is located is taken to be an important aspect of the environment of the organization. When possible, we summarize empirical work relevant to the hypotheses proposed. The hypotheses are discussed, illustrated, and tested primarily with reference to public sectors in the United States, but we believe that the proposed schema and arguments have potential applications to private sectors and, particularly, to the analysis of similar sectors—whether public or private—in different societies.

Review of Earlier Approaches to Organizations-Environments

INADEQUACIES OF PREVIOUS MODELS

Organizational paradigms dominant throughout the 1970s dealt inadequately with the patterns of connectedness and disconnectedness among organizations. While there was great progress during the 1960s and 1970s in focusing attention outside the formally defined boundaries of organizations to take account of environmental stimulants and constraints and interorganizational exchanges and ties, the prevailing models were limited in important respects. The dominant models during this period included the following:

Organizational Set Models

This family of models conceptualizes the environment from the standpoint of a specific "focal" organization (see Blau and Scott 1962:195–99; Evan 1966). An organization is viewed as connected to varying "counter" organizations that provide critical resources and/or information requisite for its functioning. Depending on the relative value and scarcity of these resources, the resulting interorganizational system is conceived as a set of power and dependence relations. Economic interdependencies are seen as giving rise to political processes and attempted solutions. Analytic attention is focused on the types of strategies pursued by the focal organization in adapting to varying circumstances (see Dill 1958; Thompson 1967; Aldrich and Pfeffer 1976; Pfeffer and Salancik 1978). The primary limitations of models of this type have been that they tend to focus attention on direct rather than indirect connections and flows among organizations; also, by viewing the environment from the vantage point of a single organization, they tend to obscure the characteristics of the larger system of relations of which the focal organization is only a component unit.

Organizational Population Models

This group of models isolates for analysis aggregates or collections of organizations viewed as similar in form or function, for example, all universities or all newspapers in a given area (see Hannan and Freeman 1977; Aldrich 1979). The concept of population is analogous to that of species in biology. Varying criteria have been proposed to identify the members of an organizational population, including common structural features, similar patterns of core work processes, and similar responsiveness to environmental variation. Hence, attention is focused on competing forms of organization. Ecological models assume that because of the inertial properties of organizational structure, most change in organizational forms comes about through the replacement of one form of organization by another: less successful are replaced by more successful forms. The adjustment of organizational forms to environmental conditions is presumed to occur primarily through selection rather than adaptation processes (see Aldrich and Pfeffer 1976; Hannan and Freeman 1984).

Population ecology models tend to assume that competitive processes dominate relations among the units comprising the population and give little or no attention to cooperative relations developing among dissimilar organizations. Thus, these earlier models ignored important aspects of organization-environment relations. More recently, however, organizational ecologists have begun to stress "community" models that incorporate both competitive and symbiotic or cooperative connections among organizations in similar and diverse populations (see Carroll 1984; Astley 1985). While continuing to emphasize longer-term change processes via selective mechanisms, these models resemble interorganization field models.

Interorganizational Field Models

This group of models focuses on the nature of relations linking a collection of diverse organizations into a common system or network. Most models of this type have examined the relations occurring among similar and dissimilar organizations located within the same geographical area, such as a community or metropolitan area. Unlike the other types of models reviewed, this approach attends to the nature of the patterns exhibited by the relations among organizations. Indeed, in these models the focus is more often on the nature of the relations among organizations than on the organizations themselves. (For examples, see Litwak and Hylton 1962; Warren 1967; Turk 1977.) However, with but few exceptions, these field models have concentrated on horizontal linkages among organizations—linkages among organizations lacking formal authority over one another—and on connections among organizations within a relatively narrowly delimited geographical area, such as an urban community. Propositions from exchange theory and network theory are commonly employed to guide data collection and analysis. And recent work has emphasized the adaptive capacities of such systems (see Galaskiewicz 1984).

Each of these three types of models, while supporting important modes of analysis associated with valuable insights into the structure and functioning of organizations, has limitations. Assuming the perspective of a selected, focal organization, as is characteristic of organization set models, directs attention away from the structure and features of the larger system of relations within which many organizations function. The population ecology model aids in the examination of competitive relations among similar organizations but tends to conceal or ignore the supportive relations that develop among both similar and dissimilar organizations and affect their chances for survival. And the early interorganizational field models—in application if not in principle—stressed the importance of horizontal ties among organizations in a local region, thus ignoring vertical (hierarchical) and extralocal linkages among organizations.

Finally, all of the early organization-environment models emphasized the importance of the technical flows among organizations. Organizations were viewed primarily as production systems, and their structures were seen as shaped primarily by their technologies and technical aspects of their environments (see Perrow 1967; Thompson 1967; Galbraith 1973). Environments were conceived as task environments: as sources of information and stocks of resources necessary for task implementation. While such views are not wrong, they are clearly incomplete and limited. New conceptions emerging in the 1970s focused attention on the social and cultural aspects of organizations and their environments. They reflect an increasing awareness that no organization is just a technical system and that many organizations are not primarily technical systems. They call attention to the importance of the institutional environments of organizations.

The type of model developed in the present chapter differs from its predecessors in a number of respects: (1) attention is directed not only to the linkages among specific organizations but also to the larger structure of relations within which these organizations may function; (2) linkages among both similar and dissimilar organizations are of equal interest; (3) both horizontal and vertical linkages are included; (4) both local and nonlocal connections are examined; and (5) both technical and institutional aspects of organizations and environments are viewed as salient.

FORERUNNERS OF THE
PROPOSED MODEL

It is possible to identify three streams of work that anticipate some features of our own approach. Interestingly enough, all of this work had its origin outside the mainstream of organization theory. These lines of work have only recently begun to converge and to influence the models developed to explain the structure and functioning of organizations. The first, proposed by Warren, was developed to examine the structure of communities. The second, reflecting the work of numerous analysts, primarily political scientists, emerged in connection with the study of public policy issues and outcomes. The third approach was developed primarily by social workers and urban reformers concerned with improving the operation of human services agencies. We briefly review each of these approaches.

Warren's Community Patterns

As early as 1963, Roland Warren developed a theoretical model to support examination of the structure of American communities. At the heart of his model is the distinction between the "horizontal" and the "vertical" pattern of relations linking social units within and among communities. Warren (1972:161–62) describes the distinction as follows:

> We shall define a community's *horizontal pattern* as the structural and functional relation of its various social units and subsystems to each other. The term 'horizontal' is used to indicate that, roughly speaking, the community units, insofar as they have relevance to the community system, tend to be on approximately the same hierarchical level (a community unit level, as opposed to a state, regional, national, or international level of authority, administration, decision-making, and so on). . . .
>
> We shall define a community's *vertical pattern* as the structural and functional relations of its various social units and subsystems to extra-community systems. The term 'vertical' is used to reflect the fact that such relationships often involve different hierarchical levels within the extracommunity system's structure of authority and power. The relationships are typically those of a system unit to the system's headquarters, although several intervening levels may occur.

Warren notes that his typology differentiates among patterns of relations, not types of units: most social units, including organizations, are involved in both horizontal and vertical connections. The horizontal-vertical distinction is viewed as related to the well-known task-maintenance (or instrumental-affective) distinction (see Bales 1953; Parsons and Bales 1960). Thus, Warren (1972:163) argues that, in general, task performances by the community's constituent organizations—for example, schools, churches, factories, banks—tend to link them vertically with nonlocal systems, while integration and maintenance functions tend to be carried out utilizing relations that horizontally link units within the same community. Of more relevance for our purposes, Warren argues that the vertical, extralocal patterns are more likely to be rationally constructed and hierarchically arranged while the horizontal, locality oriented patterns are apt to be informally structured, with marketlike competitive and exchange processes, rather than authority, determining the influence of the various units (Warren 1972:242–43, 273).

It is Warren's overarching thesis that American communities are currently undergoing a "great change" that involves "the increasing orientation of local community units toward extracommunity systems of which they are a part, with a corresponding decline in community cohesion and autonomy" (1972:53). That is, in Warren's view, the structure of American communities is more and more dominated by the vertical pattern of relations linking its social units to external systems rather than by the horizontal patterns of relations among units in the same locality. This thesis guided Warren's later empirical research focusing on the Model Cities program. This research investigated the extent to which local "community decision" organizations in a number of separate cities were tied into a broader societal context and structured by external forces in reacting to and implementing the program (see Warren, Rose, and Bergunder 1974).

Warren's principal research arena is the community, and as noted he asserted that the dominant force shaping community structure, at least in the United States, was the nature of the linkages that relate local organizations to external regional, state, or national systems. It is surprising then that in the area of organization theory Warren has been associated with that set of interorganization field models that has devoted primary attention to the patterns of horizontal relations among organizations sharing the same locality. We attribute this (mis)conception to the impact of his paper published in *Administrative Science Quarterly,* a leading journal devoted to organization theory and research. In this influential article, entitled "The Interorganizational Field as a Focus for Investigation," Warren (1967) restricted attention to the horizontal patterns of relations among community organizations, defining several modes of interrelations and illustrating them with data from a study of community-level planning organizations in three cities. Warren (1967:399, n. 10) was careful to call attention to the limited scope of his analysis in a footnote: "although the present analysis confined itself to interaction among organizations at this community level, the vertical relations to organizational systems outside of the community, as, for example, the federal government, should not be overlooked."

Apparently, however, this self-imposed limitation—as well as Warren's other theoretical and empirical work on community structure—was overlooked by a generation of organizational analysts, and the truncated model employed in the *Administrative Science Quarterly* was taken for the whole. Thus, in spite of his own considerable efforts, Warren's influence on interorganizational theory and analysis has been to focus attention on informal, horizontal ties among organizations in the same locality to the neglect of formalized, vertical, extralocal connections. We propose to correct this oversight and to reinforce Warren's larger vision of interorganizational systems.

Public Policy Studies

The 1960s and 1970s witnessed the development and rapid growth of public policy analysis. Early work within this field focused on the determinants of public policy decisions—the characteristics of political actors, the nature of the political and bureaucratic context, the activities of interest groups—as well as on the decision process itself (see, e.g., Wildavsky 1964; Lindblom 1968; Allison 1971). More recently attention shifted to include not only policy decisions but their implementation since, in one policy arena after another, examination revealed that, far from being automatic, the implementation of public policy decisions is highly problematic. (See, e.g., Moynihan 1969 on poverty programs; Neustadt and Fineberg 1978 on public health measures; Estes 1979 on services for the aged.) Some analysts made implementation issues their primary focus (see, e.g., Pressman and Wildavsky 1973; Bardach 1977; Weatherly 1979), and it is this work that foreshadows our own efforts.

An emphasis on implementation directs attention to the administrative structures linking decision makers with recipients of rules or services. The decisions involved are public policies set at national or state levels that are intended to be, in the most usual case, carried out at local levels. The implementation apparatus is necessarily constituted as an interorganizational system: a set of vertically ordered and horizontally coordinated linkages coupling administrative units at higher levels with service or enforcement units at lower levels as well as units at one location with those at others. The units involved may be public or private organizations.

Several common themes may be discerned in the work of those analysts who have attempted to characterize these implementation networks as they function at the present time in the United States. We note three: (1) the distinctive and changing structure of the federal system; (2) the difficulty in getting semi-autonomous units within a policy area to cooperate in pursuit of a common policy; and (3) the problem in coordinating the efforts of independent units operating across several policy arenas.

Observers of the U.S. political scene have long noted that the administrative structures of governmental agencies operating within a given policy area tend not to be simple, lean, "rational" bureaucracies, but relatively complex, competing, and overlapping systems. A major contributing factor to this situation is our federalist system that has historically limited the power and jurisdiction of the national bodies in favor of promoting a strong, independent role for states and local bodies (see Grodzins 1966; Elazar 1972). While originally intended to operate in separate arenas, the various layers of the federal system increasingly compete and overlap in the functions they perform. To capture this evolution, Grodzins (1961:3–4) suggests that the "layer cake" structure of the federal system with its separate zones of jurisdiction has been transformed of late into a "marble cake":

> Wherever you slice through it you reveal an inseparable mixture of differently colored ingredients. There is no neat horizontal stratification. Vertical and diagonal lines almost obliterate the horizontal ones, and in some places there are unexpected whirls and an imperceptible merging of colors, so that it is difficult to tell where one ends and the other begins. So it is with federal, state, and local responsibilities in the chaotic marble cake of American Government.

This federalist structure contributes to a second, more general problem: the difficulty of getting multiple and quasi-independent organizations to cooperate in implementing a common policy. Downs (1967) speaks of the "leakage of authority" as programs designed by politicians move down into agencies staffed by career civil servants and, more generally, as programs must attempt to obtain the support of diverse collections of officials with varying goals and interests. Bardach (1977:46) broadens this picture to include not only administrative agencies but multiple constituencies and their interests:

> The array of relevant actors in the implementation process is large and diverse, including, in addition to governmental bureaus, their clients, private contractors, professional associations, publicists, and so forth. All of these actors are quite capable of articulating their own special fears and anxieties. It is perhaps this broad focus that distinguishes the study of "implementation," a subject of fairly recent interest, from the more traditional subject matter of public administration.

The "complexity of joint action" among independent or semiautonomous organizations is compellingly illustrated by Pressman and Wildavsky's (1973) analysis of the implementation of one project, under the auspices of the Economic Development Administration, intended to support public improvement projects and provide employment to minority workers. The goals were noncontroversial, and there was strong consensus on moving forward with a construction project in Oakland. Nevertheless, they describe a complex approval/decision process encompassing some seventy major agreements and extending over a period of more than three years that resulted in much less money being spent on construction and many fewer minority jobs created than was intended.

A third problem identified by policy analysts is the lack of coordination among different agencies operating in related policy arenas and within the same geographical area. Policies tend to be formulated and solutions sought in isolation from one another. There is a trend toward the "sectoralization" of policies (Wildavsky 1979:72). That is, policies, programs, and agencies are increasingly defined in limited, functionally differentiated terms. But while these various arenas can be analytically separated and theoretically distinguished, they often overlap in their operations or in their effects. Thus, rapid transit programs can have an impact on urban renewal, and taxation policies on both. This problem both harkens back to Warren's description of the dominance of vertical (single policy systems) over horizontal (integration across policy systems) patterns in communities as well as carries us forward to consider the concerns of human services system analysts.

Human Services Systems

The 1960s witnessed an explosion of national social programs designed to improve the welfare of disadvantaged groups as well as improve the functioning of locally based services in this society. Among the programs enacted within the space of a few years were the following: aide to disadvantaged students, local law enforcement, manpower training, antipoverty programs, urban renewal, community mental health, and hospital care for the poor and aged.

Although these programs were launched with much fanfare and great optimism in the Kennedy-Johnson era, unexpected deficiencies and problems soon became apparent. Apart from the difficulties of implementation encountered within specific programs, analysts and critics increasingly decried the lack of coordination among the various agencies and programs. Among the criticisms: client needs did not coincide with the packages of services provided, and the persons in need could not readily move among programs. Duplication of effort in some arenas was matched by the complete absence of services in others. In many arenas, the sheer number and variety of agencies and the rapidity with they they came, went, and were reorganized generated great complexity and accompanying confusion and ignorance on the part of both providers and clients (see, e.g., Aldrich 1972; Baker and O'Brien 1971; Gardner and Snipe 1970; Reid 1969; Rosengren and Lefton 1970).

A particular problem was the inability of local communities to accommodate and integrate these new public actors. As Sundquist (1969:24) comments: "The proliferation and vast expansion of federal assistance programs in the 1960s soon overwhelmed the local coordinating institutions that were in existence— local governments, primarily, and area planning bodies, and such private organizations as councils of social agencies." And just as the original problems of poverty, disadvantage, and substandard community services had become defined as a national problem, so accordingly, "it soon became apparent to the planners of those programs that the weakness of the community institutions was itself a *national problem* that demanded a national solution" (Sundquist 1969:24–25).

Thus, beginning in the late 1960s and continuing to the present time, there have been extensive efforts to develop centralized coordinating strategies and mechanisms, both within and across service domains. Sundquist (1969:25) notes that "by 1967 more than a dozen types of federally initiated, local coordinating structures could be counted." These ranged from community action agencies to area health planning agencies. The number and variety of these coordinating mechanisms have continued to grow, with efforts occurring at all levels: federal, state, regional, and local (see Gans and Horton 1975; Heintz 1976; Lehman 1975; Morris and Lescohier 1978; Rogers and Whetten 1981). Indeed, the current emphasis appears to stress coordination among programs as much if not more than the programs themselves. Such a posture likely reflects shifts in the political and fiscal climate commencing in the late 1970s and continuing into the 1980s as much as any concerns about deficiencies in program operation. As Brown (1983) suggests, the "breakthrough" policies and politics of the 1960s that sought to get government involved in new domains has given way to the "rationalizing" policies and politics in the 1980s, as attention turns to reforming and improving current programs. Morrissey, Hall, and Lindsey (1982:2) amplify:

A decade of recession and inflation in the 1970s, in combination with the current climate of social and fiscal conservatism, has eroded the support base for large-scale intervention programs, but issues of services coordination are still salient today. Public policies are now predicated on austerity and consolidation, and current forecasts indicate that few large social programs or new human services initiatives will be funded. Instead, relatively modest programs that make limited demands on scarce resources have been advanced to coordinate existing health and welfare services.

These three bodies of work—on community structure, policy implementation, and agency coordination—differ in vocabulary and point of view but agree on one broad conclusion: vertical connections currently dominate lateral connections among organizations, at least among organizations operating in the public sector. We prefer not to embrace this conclusion although it is certainly an interesting hypothesis to keep in mind. We instead find much support in this work for the more modest assumption that vertical and nonlocal linkages among organizations must not be overlooked if we are to understand the structure and functioning of organizations in contemporary society. We are gratified to note that this conclusion has also been reached by other students of organizations (see, e.g., Benson 1975, 1981; Aldrich and Whetten 1981; Knoke and Laumann 1982).

The work we have reviewed provides important evidence of the growing interconnectedness of organizational systems—both private and public—in American society. And it provides valuable descriptive information about the variety of forms such connections may take, including information about changes over time. With this material as background, we are ready to commence a more systematic discussion of a theoretical model that identifies societal sectors as an important focus of organizational research and describes a number of concepts and propositions to guide investigations of these systems. Where available, we also note relevant empirical evidence.

Defining Societal Sectors

THE CONCEPT OF SECTOR

A *societal sector* is defined as (1) a collection of organizations operating in the same domain, as identified by the similarity of their services, products or functions, (2) together with those organizations that critically influence the performance of the focal organizations: for example, major suppliers and customers, owners and regulators, funding sources and competitors. The adjective *societal* emphasizes that organizational sectors in modern societies are likely to stretch from local to national or even international actors. The boundaries of societal sectors are defined in functional, not geographical terms: sectors are comprised of units that are functionally interrelated even though they may be geographically remote. The concept of sector incorporates and builds on the economist's concept of industry: all sellers of one type of product or service—or, more abstractly, all those firms characterized by a close substitutability of product usage who, as a consequence, exhibit demand interdependence. However, the concept of sector is broader than that of industry since it encompasses the different types of organizations to which these similar providers relate.

Attempts to classify organizations using the criterion of similarity of product or function are plagued by numerous problems, of which three merit comment. One problem is posed by the level of specificity at which the criteria of similarity is applied. Are we to focus on air travel or transportation? On acute care units or all medical services? This problem is perhaps most easily addressed by being quite explicit about the nature—including level of specificity—of the criteria used, and by recognizing that analyses and conclusions will be strongly influenced by the choices made (see Aldrich and Pfeffer 1976:99–101). This problem is somewhat eased by an important property of organizational systems, namely, that their complexity tends to assume a hierarchical form in the sense that units defined at higher levels are composed of clusters of units at lower levels (see Simon 1962). For example, transportation as a category of services subsumes air travel and other alternative means of locomotion. This tendency toward hierarchically organized clusters is exploited by the well-known Standard Industrial Classification (SIC) system developed by the U.S. Bureau of the Census (Office of Management and Budget 1972). This four-level system classifies all units providing goods and services into ten broad functional divisions (e.g., mining, manufacturing, services), next into groups (e.g., within the services division, health services, legal services, educational services), then into individual industries (e.g., within health services there are offices of physicians, nursing and personal care facilities, and hospitals), and finally into providers of more specific products or services (e.g., within hospitals there are general medical and surgical hospitals, psychiatric hospitals, and so on). The concept of societal sector could be applied to a collection of organizations identified by criteria at any one of these levels.

A second problem confronting all attempts to identify "similar" products or services is that of substitutability. It is often the case that products and services greatly dissimilar in form or composition may be addressed to the same need or function. Along the continuum of form versus function, we stress the criterion of function: we wish to include within the same sector units supplying products or services that are apparently dissimilar but functionally equivalent. For example, faith healers and wholistic and other "alternative" health providers would be included within the health care sector. There may be disagreements among participants and observers as to what functions are being performed by a given collection of organizations. Such disagreements create definitional problems, but they also signal ambiguities or disputes over domain definition. That is, a significant characteristic of any sector is the amount of consensus among its members as to the nature of the domain and its constituent members (see Thompson 1967; Braito, Paulson, and Klonglon 1972).

A third problem is one that confronts any attempt to apply classification criteria: the concrete units are often broader or more diffuse than the classes identified. In our case, having decided to emphasize function, we must recognize that all organizations are not functionally specific. Indeed, there is a well-known tendency for contemporary firms and agencies to diversify, producing products or services for widely differing purposes and markets. One approach to addressing this problem is that devised by the developers of the SIC. They propose that the units classified should not be companies but "establishments"—an economic unit generally at a single physical location and more likely to be engaged in a single type of activity. It may be possible, data sources permitting, to go further in this direction and include only selected components or subunits of organizations. For example, in defining the mental health sector, we would surely want to include specialized psychiatric units within community hospitals (although it would probably not be possible to include all those mental health patients treated in "scatter beds" within general hospitals). But dropping to the level of the establishment or subunit is not always feasible and, even when possible, may not eliminate the problem of multiple functions. We will no doubt often be forced to embrace the second SIC principle and settle for including or excluding units from the sector depending on their "primary" functional activity.

The SIC classification principles help deal with problems of boundary definition for societal sectors: determining what organizational units are to be regarded as within the focal sector. However, our interest in sector characteristics per se again allows us to turn this problem into a useful variable at the sector level. We can assess the extent to which the organizational units within a given sector are functionally specialized as opposed to performing a more diffuse and undifferentiated set of functions. Clearly, sectors vary considerably along this dimension.

As noted, the concept of societal sector is broader than that of industry for we wish to include also those organizations comprising the "set" of the focal industry group—those organizations that support and/or constrain their activities. For example, the housing sector would consist of all of the public and private organizational units, relations, and flows relevant to maintaining and adding to the supply of housing. Such a definition would encompass units from many different industries, for example, components of the construction, finance, public administration, and insurance industries. Thus, the definition of *societal sector* is similar in many respects to that of *public policy sector* (see, e.g., Dye 1981; Wildavsky 1979), although we prefer not to link our definition closely to the content of and controversies over current public policies.

Within the organizational literature, the concept of sector is similar to Hirsh's (1972, 1985) concept of "industry system," Benson's (1975) "interorganizational network," and DiMaggio and Powell's (1983) "organizational field." (For a discussion of the similarities and differences among these related definitions, see Scott 1983:160–64.)

While we have chosen to depart from the specific definition of industry as developed by economists, we follow their lead in our general theoretical orientation. In spite of the definitional and operational difficulties economists have encountered, they have found the concept of industry to be highly serviceable as a way of apprehending one of the relevant environments within which firms operate, recognizing that "the behavior of the firm can depend crucially on the organization of its industry" (Sherman 1974:215). We encounter similar definitional problems in defining *societal sector*, but hope to show that this conception also identifies a salient environment—that the structure and behavior of an organization depend importantly on the characteristics of the sector in which it operates.

THE TREND TOWARD SOCIETAL SECTORALIZATION

The concept of societal sector suggests the presence of organizational systems that are, at least to some degree, functionally differentiated. In the extreme and oversimplified case, we would observe all of the activities associated with a given function—for example, the provision of medical care—being performed by a specialized and hierarchically organized set of interrelated organizations. All medical care would be performed by these specialized structures; none would be provided by such diffuse social arrangements as families, and none would be provided by organizational forms devoted to the service of other functions—for instance, there would be no industrial physicians or school nurses. Of course, in reality we observe a much lower overall level of specialization: functions are performed by multiple structural arrangements, and particular structures perform multiple functions. And we observe much variation in degree of specialization across sectors within a society. For example, at the current time in the United States, the mental health services sector exhibits a low degree of specialization: less than 20 percent of mental health services delivered are provided by specialist mental health providers and facilities (see Regier, Goldberg, and Taube 1978; Scott 1986).

An important assumption underlying this model is that contemporary societies increasingly exhibit functionally differentiated sectors whose structures are vertically connected, with lines stretching up to the central nation-state. This view stems from the work of social analysts such as Bell (1973) and Wildavsky (1979), who conceive of society as a system of organizations tending toward rationalization guided by an increasingly powerful, active, and inclusive organization—the nation-state. Alford and Friedland (1985) have labeled this perspective the "managerial" worldview. A variety of social changes in the world—economic integration and competition, expanded ideologies of justice and equality, improved systems of technical control—supports a process of centralization, and of centralization under rather explicit organizational controls. Of course the extent to which such differentiation and centralization have occurred is a matter to be empirically determined. There exists much variation across sectors within a society as well as across societies.

The best current accounts of existing differences in sector organization reside in the political science literature where an expanding body of work is developing on (1) the nature and extent of the organization of private interests in a society, (2) their relation to the central state, and (3) the manner and degree of interest concertation achieved. The most highly developed and explicit form of interest articulation is found in the "corporatist" state. As stated by Schmitter (1974:93–94),

> Corporatism can be defined as a system of interest representation in which the constituent units are organized into a limited number of singular, compulsory, noncompetitive, hierarchically ordered and functionally differentiated categories, recognized or licensed (if not created) by the state and granted a deliberate representational monopoly within their respective categories in exchange for observing certain controls on their selection of leaders and articulation of demands and supports.

That is, in a more corporatist arrangement, competing, overlapping and pluralistic interests within a given sector become more hierarchically organized into "peak" associations, which in turn have access to and are accorded special status and powers by the nation-state. Particular attention is given in this work to the role of business and trade associations as they act to tame competitive tendencies among firms within a sector in order to advance the interests of the sector as a whole against that of other interests. And there is an awareness in this literature of the unique qualities of the nation-state as one type of corporate actor and, at the same time, as one type of organizational environment. As Streeck and Schmitter (1985:20) point out:

> [In the conventional organizational literature] the peculiar facilitative role of the state . . . does not seem to be adequately captured in terms of a relationship between the association and one environment among others. "Public status" refers to the, direct or indirect, acquisition of a unique resource that no other environment but the state has to offer: the ability to rely on legitimate coercion. Organization theory tends to be "state-free" in the sense that it does not systematically recognize this

crucial distinction—crucial, in any case, for understanding the emergence of a corporative-associative order.

In comparison with other more highly organized corporatist societies, such as the Scandanavian countries, Switzerland, the Netherlands, and, to a lesser extent, West Germany and France, the United States has moved a relatively short distance toward this form of centralization. As Wildavsky (1979:71–72) points out:

> How can interest groups grow into sectors when prevailing American ideology as well as existing institutions militate against it? Federal structure, reinforced by the separation of powers, makes centralization and coordination of interest groups difficult to achieve, and the suspicion of "special interests" leads to restrictions on their efforts. . . . "Peak" associations—one interest, one group—have been slow to start in the United States.

Still, evidence suggests that centralizing trends are under way in U.S. society, and, as we will note, they take on a somewhat special cast in this country.

Determinants and Consequences of Sector Organization

The general approach we employ is to identify several characteristics of societal sectors in order to (1) consider the determinants of these characteristics at the sector level; and (2) examine the relations between these characteristics and the properties of organizations functioning within the sectors. Primary attention is given to the latter task: we emphasize sectors as an important type of environment influencing the structure and performance of component organizational units. A number of hypotheses are generated and are described and illustrated. We also report any evidence that has developed since they were first proposed. We believe that all of the propositions are testable employing either a cross-sectional (e.g., comparing the medical care with the educational sector in the United States), a cross-societal (e.g., comparing the medical care sectors in the United States and United Kingdom), or a longitudinal design (e.g., comparing the state of the medical care sector in the United States in 1940 and 1980). To date, our own empirical efforts have been restricted to cross-sectional and longitudinal comparisons within a single society—the United States.

TECHNICAL VERSUS INSTITUTIONAL SECTORS

Defining Technical and Institutional Environments

In our previous work, we have argued the utility of distinguishing between technical and institutional environments of organizations (see Meyer and

Rowan 1977; Meyer, Scott, and Deal 1981; Meyer and Scott 1983b; Scott 1987b). These distinctions are applicable to sectors as one level of environment. By definition, *technical* environments are those in which a product or service is produced and exchanged in a market such that organizations are rewarded for effective and efficient control of their production systems. In the purest case, such environments are identical to the competitive markets so dear to the hearts of neoclassical economists. Organizations operating in such environments are expected to concentrate their energies on controlling and coordinating their technical processes and are likely to attempt to buffer or protect these core processes from environmental disturbances (see Thompson 1967).

Institutional environments are, by definition, those characterized by the elaboration of rules and requirements to which individual organizations must conform if they are to receive support and legitimacy. The requirements may stem from regulatory agencies authorized by the nation-state, from professional or trade associations, from generalized belief systems that define how specific types of organizations are to conduct themselves, and similar sources (see Meyer and Rowan 1977; DiMaggio and Powell 1983). Whatever the source, organizations are rewarded for conforming to these rules or beliefs.

Combining Technical and Institutional Environments

It is important to stress that technical and institutional environments should not be viewed as mutually exclusive states: they can and do coexist. (See the related arguments in Powell, ch. 8.) Although they are somewhat negatively correlated, they are not strongly so, and it is useful to cross-classify them so that various combinations can be identified, as depicted in figure 5.1.

Figure 5.1 portrays such a cross-classification, with each variable limited to two states: strong and weak. Illustrative types of organizations found in each combination of environmental states are listed. Organizations such as utilities, airline companies, and banks are viewed as subject to highly developed technical *and* institutional pressures. They face both efficiency/effectiveness demands as well as pressures to conform to procedural requirements. As a result, we would expect their administrative structures to be larger and more complex than those of organizations facing less complex environments. In general, organizations of this type carry out tasks that combine complex technical requirements with a strong "public good" component.

By contrast, most manufacturing concerns are primarily subjected to strong technical requirements with weaker but varying degrees of institutionalized pressures, relating to such matters as health, safety, pollution controls, and so forth. Most professional service organizations, such as schools, mental health clinics, churches, and law firms, operate in strong institutional and weak technical environments, although again varying levels of technical controls are present.

Institutional Environments
Stronger   Weaker

		Stronger	Weaker
Technical Enivronments	Stronger	utilities banks pharmaceuticals general hospitals	general manufacturing
	Weaker	mental health clinics schools, legal agencies churches	restaurants health clubs

Fig. 5.1. Combining technical and institutional environments. *Source:* Scott 1987b:126, table 6.1.

Where neither technical nor institutional environments are highly developed, it is difficult for organizations to develop or flourish. Forms such as personal service units (e.g., health clubs) that emerge under these conditions tend to be small and unstable. It appears that strong and stable organizational forms can arise in either technical or institutional environments, but that one of these two sets of constraints/supports must be present.

Admittedly, it is often difficult to distinguish empirically technical from institutional rules and procedures. This is because those who formulate institutional rules strive to make them appear technical in nature. We live in an age in which technical capability is held in high esteem (see Ellul 1964; Berger, Berger, and Kellner 1973). Thus, social workers are expected to follow detailed procedures in determining eligibility for services or in providing specific therapies to clients; lawyers must conform to highly elaborated procedural requirements in drawing up a will or incorporating a new enterprise. Such requirements are formulated so as to appear technical in character, although no criteria for evaluating outcomes exist independent of those that assess conformity to the specified procedures.

Institutional procedures often ape technical ones; conversely, many technical procedures, over time, become institutionalized, as Selznick (1949) noted. Procedural rules that, when established, had a firm technical justification may persist long after their useful technical contributions are past.

Both technical and institutional environments give rise to "rational" organizational forms, but each type is associated with a different conception of rationality. Technical environments emphasize a rationality that incorporates a set of prescriptions for matching means and ends in ways that are efficacious in producing outcomes of a predictable character. Institutional environments embrace a rationality that is suggested by the cognate term *rationale:* providing an account that makes past actions understandable and acceptable to others, that renders the organization accountable for its past actions.

This brief overview of the distinction between technical and institutional environments and its implications for organizational structure can be summarized in six propositions. The first four are adapted from Meyer, Scott, and Deal (1981:153–54).

H1 Organizations in technical sectors will attempt to control and coordinate their production activities, buffering them from environmental influence.

H2 Organizations in technical sectors will succeed to the extent that they develop efficient production activities and effective coordinative structures.

H3 Organizations in institutional sectors will not attempt to closely control or coordinate their production activities, but will seek to buffer or de-couple these activities from organizational structures.

H4 Organizations in institutional sectors will succeed to the extent that they are able to acquire types of personnel and to develop structural arrangements and production processes that conform to the specifications of established norms and/or authorities within that sector.

Hypotheses 1 and 2 stem from Thompson's (1967) seminal discussion. They are widely embraced and have been elaborated by organizational analysts (see Scott 1987b:182–85), but they have been treated more as orienting assumptions than as testable hypotheses. Hypothesis 3 was first proposed by Meyer and Rowan (1977), who also provided illustrative data from schools to support their arguments (see Meyer and Rowan 1978). More systematic evidence regarding the structural properties of schools has been reported by Meyer et al. (1978) and by Firestone and Herriott (Firestone 1985; Herriott and Firestone 1984). The study by Meyer and colleagues, based on data from 188 elementary schools in thirty-four districts in the San Francisco Bay area, reports low levels of consensus on school policy matters within schools and districts but relatively high levels of consensus among role groups (e.g., principals, teachers, superintendents) across schools. These results are consistent with the argument that schools are not highly structured by means of organizational mechanisms (e.g., rules, tight supervision) but are ordered by broader institutional belief systems. The study by Firestone and Herriott, based on multiple respondent survey data from over a hundred schools, examines the patterning of various types of coordination (coupling) and concludes that secondary schools give more evidence of loose coupling than do elementary schools, which exhibit more centralized authority systems and higher levels of goal consensus. These results are thus only partially supportive of hypothesis 3. These analysts also explore a variety of types of coupling mechanisms and thus raise useful methodological questions about how extent of coupling can best be operationalized.

Indirect evidence pertaining to hypothesis 4 comes from a study conducted by Rowan (1982), although his unit of analysis was not organizations but programs within organizations. His analysis of data from a sample of school districts in California shows that programs supported by a "balanced" institutional environment—a situation in which there was consensus concerning the legitimacy of a program among legislative bodies, professional associations, and teacher training institutions—were not only more likely to be adopted by school districts but were also more likely to be retained, to survive over time, compared to programs lacking such consensual support. More direct evidence is provided by a study of voluntary social service organizations in Toronto conducted by Singh, Tucker, and House (1986). Using indicators such as listing in the *Community Directory of Metropolitan Toronto* and receipt of a charitable registration number issued by Revenue Canada as evidence of endorsement by institutional authorities, this study shows that organizations acquiring these approvals were more likely to survive over the period of study than those lacking such indicators of legitimacy.

Two additional hypotheses are suggested by the preceding discussion.

H5 Organizations functioning in sectors that are highly developed both institutionally and technically will develop more complex and elaborate administrative systems and will experience high levels of internal conflict.

To illustrate, organizations such as tertiary care hospitals and defense contractors that confront high levels of both institutional and technical demands are likely to exhibit dual authority systems or matrix structures; levels of conflict are reported to be high in these situations (see Neuhauser 1972; Davis and Lawrence 1977; Scott 1982b).

H6 Organizations functioning in sectors that are not highly developed either technically or institutionally are expected to be relatively small in size and weak in terms of their capacity for survival.

Examples of such organizations include restaurants, health clubs, and similar personal service establishments. Freeman and Hannan (1983) have suggested that restaurants might be regarded as the "fruit flies" of the organizational world since their expected life span is so brief. However, organizations in this category are always potential targets for increased societal support and organizational upgrading, with the creation of new technologies or new "rational myths" (Meyer and Rowan 1977) providing institutional support. An instance of such an organizing and rationalizing process based on the elaboration of institutionalized rules and beliefs is currently under way in the United States in the sector of services for the aged, as informal familial arrangements increasingly give way to more organized and publicly financed and regulated care arrangements (see Scott 1981b; Alexander 1988).

SECTOR LEVELS

An important characteristic of sector structure is the number and locus of levels at which organizational units have developed. The five most commonly observed levels within a society at which units may form are the following: (1) national or societywide offices, associations, headquarters; (2) regional or multistate authorities, associations; (3) state offices, associations; (4) substate areas, districts, councils; and (5) local units, branch offices, establishments.

In arenas dominated by public organizations, these levels are readily illustrated. The U.S. public school system is formally organized at all levels although only modestly so at the regional or multistate level. Thus, individual schools in local areas are organized into school districts, which in turn operate primarily under state authority. Regional programs are less highly developed, operating in selected, specialized areas such as athletic associations or educational research centers. At the national level, there exists a cabinet-level office and a specialized federal agency devoted to education, albeit national authority over educational institutions is limited to specific domains such as programs for the educationally disadvantaged. A variety of professional associations and unions are also organized at district, state, and national levels. (For a discussion of levels of authority in the sector of higher education, see Clark 1983.)

Private firms and industries are also increasingly organized into vertically structured systems operating at multiple levels. Thus, many manufacturing units or retail outlets are frequently only establishments of companies that operate under the authority of companies organized at regional, national, and even international levels. The major divisions of multidivisional corporate organizations are often structured on a regional basis. In addition to these ownership patterns, many companies combine efforts in local, regional, and national associations that operate to stiffle competition and promote common interests (e.g., chambers of commerce, trade associations—see Aldrich and Staber 1988). And both resource-dependence perspectives and class cohesion theory point to a variety of evidence ranging from interlocking directorates, joint ventures, and mergers to patterns of banking loans and stock ownership in order to challenge the dominant "portrait of the American economy as a loosely connected system of autonomous large firms unconstrained by outside owners or by each other" (Glasberg and Schwartz 1983:311).

A widely accepted proposition from open systems theory is that

H7 Organizations located in more complex and uncertain environments develop more complex internal structures—holding constant the complexity of work processes.

Sectors vary in the extent of their complexity and organizational coherence, and we would expect these differences to affect the structural features of organizations operating within a sector. Thus, within a sector, as superordinate units develop to manage or regulate local units, we would expect to observe changes in the structural features of these units. In particular, changes in the structure of organizational environments are expected to produce changes in the administrative components of organizations since these are structures that perform boundary-maintaining and boundary-spanning functions.

Consistent with these expectations, Powell (1988) has contrasted the situation confronted by publishers of scholarly books with that of public television stations. While organizations in both sectors are engaged in dispensing cultural products, the TV stations face a more diverse and less coherent set of constituencies and pressures than do those publishers for whom "the supply and demand sides are joined. The industry serves only one community—the academy" (p. 124). Powell compared the administrative structures of one book publisher and one public television studio of comparable size and operating budget. The publisher had only three departments and one policy-making committee while the TV company had four divisions, each with six to eight departments and several major policy-making committees. Powell (1988:126) concludes: "Organizations, such as WNET, that are located in environments in which conflicting demands are made upon them will be especially likely to generate complex organizational structures with disporportionately large administrative components and multiple boundary-spanning units."

When a multiple-level system exists, however, an important question to be addressed is *where*—at what sector level—are the predicted organizational effects likely to be manifested? If complex and conflicted environments are expected to be associated with administrative complexity of the component organizational units, which units are most likely to be affected? It is possible to argue that units at all levels will be affected—complexity at higher levels producing complexity at lower levels throughout the system, following the principle of isomorphism (see DiMaggio and Powell 1983). On the other hand, only some levels may be affected, organizational forms at one level serving to manage or absorb complexity in the environment and acting to buffer lower, subordinate units from its effects. Research on public schools conducted by investigators at Stanford has provided some evidence pertinent to this question.

In a study utilizing survey data from twenty elementary school districts in the San Francisco Bay area, Rowan (1981) found a strong positive association between the amount of special federal and state funds received per student and the size of the administrative staff of the school district, controlling for district size. A later study conducted by Scott and Meyer (1987) compared public, Catholic parochial, and private schools. Private schools were found to exhibit either no or only minimal structure above the local school level. Partly as a consequence, they revealed considerably higher administrative ratios at the school level than parochial or public schools. Although the Catholic schools studied were organized at the areawide level—into diocesan structures—the educational aspects of these structures were quite small and underdeveloped relative to public school districts. We attribute this difference in part to the fact that Catholic schools faced simpler administrative environments: they received no state funds, and any federal funds received were administered by the public districts and routed directly to individual schools serving qualified students (see Encarnation 1983). Like Rowan, we found that the complexity of public school districts varied directly with the number of special state and/or federal programs in which the district was involved. In addition, we found that administrative complexity at the individual school level was also positively associated with the number of public programs in which they participated for middle and secondary, but not for elementary, public schools. Apparently, complexity at the district level acts to buffer elementary schools more so than middle or secondary schools from the effects of environmental complexity. The evidence from middle and secondary schools provides support to the notion of loose coupling among levels of educational units: each level adjusts somewhat independently to the demands posed by the environment.

Sector Decision Making

Two sets of distinctions are proposed to characterize, first, the types of decisions and, second, their distribution across the units comprising the sector. Three types of decisions are identified: (1) *programmatic* decisions refer to the right to determine the purposes or goals toward which sector activities are to be directed; (2) *instrumental* decisions refer to the right to determine the means or procedures to be employed in pursuing sector objectives; and (3) *funding* decisions refer to the right to determine what level of funds are to be expended and/or how funds are to be allocated among program activities and across units within the sector. And three dimensions are identified to capture variation in the distribution of decision-making rights within a sector. First, *centralization-decentralization* of decision making refers to the extent to which decisions are made at higher rather than lower levels within a sector (see also Aldrich 1978). While the degree of centralization of decision making varies greatly across sectors and societies, it appears that, for the United States, there has been an increase in the centralization of decision making during this century in virtually all sectors—although in most arenas decision making remains more decentralized in the United States than in other industrialized societies. This trend appears in sectors dominated by private organizations as well as those characterized by heavy public involvement. In the former case, increased centralization is associated with increased levels of economic concentration within industry groups as well as with the widespread rise of tactics such as interlocking directorates and the creation of formal and informal associations to reduce uncertainty and support interorganizational action (see Pfeffer and Salancik 1978; Aldrich and Staber 1988). In the public sectors, the increased tendency of state and, particularly, national governments to support and regulate a wider array of products and services is widely recognized.

It appears that centralization of decision making within sectors exhibiting extensive public involvement has not proceeded evenly with respect to the three types of decisions:

H8 Within public sectors in the United States, funding decisions are more highly centralized than are programmatic decisions, and programmatic decisions more highly centralized than are instrumental decisions.

This generalization reflects in part the superior taxing abilities of higher as compared to lower levels of government. It also reflects the reality that it is easier to move money than to change behavior (see Wildavsky 1979:48). But most critical is the wide-spread development of and support for professional occupations in this society. As a corporate group, professionals in their associations demand and command discretion and control over programmatic and instrumental decisions falling within their claimed sphere of competence. These associations have enormous influence in the setting of product, service, and personnel standards in a wide variety of sectors (see Freidson 1986:185–208). And, as individual practitioners, professionals jealously guard their discretion over instrumental decisions. Thus, we would argue:

H9 The more highly professionalized a sector, the more likely that instrumental and programmatic decisions will be decentralized.

Strong professional groups oppose and have successfully resisted attempts to centralize even funding decisions. Thus, for example, the American Medical Association successfully opposed the introduction of national health insurance and long delayed the development of the Medicare and Medicaid programs (see Starr 1982).

Centralization of programmatic authority is also weakened by the divisions of authority in a federalist system. Because the central government in the United States lacks authority to command in a number of arenas, it must utilize mechanisms such as the grant-in-aide to induce subordinate governance levels to comply. As Derthick (1972:84) notes in her discussion of the New Towns program, because of the "division of authority among governments in the federal system, the federal government cannot order these governments to do anything. It gets them to carry out its purposes by offering incentives in the form of aid, which they may accept or not, and by attaching conditions to the aid."

Thus, the type of centralization exhibited within a sector has important consequences for the structure of controls operating within that sector. We argue:

H10 The centralization of decision making concerning funding, in the absence of centralized programmatic or instrumental decision making, is associated with the development of vertical interlevel controls exercised through accounting mechanisms (see Meyer 1983a).

When funding is centralized, but programmatic authority is not, control is exercised by financial officers and accountants. As Meyer (1983a:187–88) describes the current situation of control in U.S. public education, "We have the rise of what may broadly be called the "accountants"—the personnel who manage the funding and reporting relations with central power. The central functionaries do not have the direct authority to set policies, and so justify their expenditures through narrower technical rules." Thus, in school systems for example, funding is tied to attendance data, with close attention paid to its proper accounting; in hospitals, federal reimbursement is based on diagnostic categories that determine how many days of inpatient care are to be compensated. Funding decisions do not directly prescribe programmatic and instrumental decisions but create pressures and place constraints on them and, in the limiting case, can virtually determine them.

The rise of the accountants is documented in a study conducted by Rowan (1982). Utilizing longitudinal data from a random sample of thirty city school districts in California, he examined changes in staff composition at five-year intervals from 1930 to 1970. Consistent with hypothesis 10, Rowan (1982:49) concludes:

> The most pronounced tendency of districts in the sample was to differentiate positions with business and personnel functions. The proportion of districts with these specializations rose from 0% in 1930 to 83% with business positions and 67% with personnel positions in 1970. Such a marked pattern of growth reflects not merely the growth in scale of operations within school districts, but also an increased concern with financial accountability and with credentialing and labor management contingencies.

The second dimension, *fragmentation-unification* of decision making, refers to the extent to which decisions are integrated or coordinated at any given level of a sector. While centralization refers to vertical integration, unification refers to horizontal or lateral integration. There is no necessary association between these dimensions. Sectors that have become increasingly centralized may still exhibit a high degree of fragmentation. This combination of centralization and fragmentation is especially likely to occur in societal sectors under certain political conditions:

H11 Liberal political regimes that encourage a pluralist approach to decision making and that emphasize the separation of powers within nation-state structures are likely to exhibit higher levels of fragmentation of decision making within sectors as well as between sectors.

The medical care and the educational sectors provide good examples of societal sectors in the United States that are characterized by high levels of fragmentation (see Meyer 1983a; Scott 1982b). Although in recent years both sectors have exhibited increased centralization as considerable decision-making authority has been shifted from local to state to national levels, the degree of integration at these levels remains low. A large number of programs and requirements have been generated but they are highly specific in focus, are associated with differentiated agencies and constituencies, and sometimes work at cross-purposes. Sergiovanni and colleagues (1980:162–64) describe fragmentation existing at the federal level in the early 1980s in U.S. educational programs:

> One could, in fact, question whether it is even accurate to speak of "federal policy" in education. Certainly there is no single center of planning and coordination within our nation's capital. Programs which bear upon education emerge, rather, from literally dozens of agencies and congressional committees. . . . The Office of Civil Rights has been instrumental in enforcing desegregation guidelines. Head Start, Follow Through, and Upward Bound programs make their home in the Office of Economic Opportunity. Dependents' schools on overseas military bases are administered by the Department of Defense, and many Indian children attend schools administered by the Bureau of Indian Affairs within the Department of Interior.

(For descriptions of fragmentation in the health care sector, see Somers 1969 and Kinzer 1977.)

Fragmentation is especially likely to be focused around programmatic and funding decisions: specific programs become attached to or generated by particular agencies, and each program is linked to a specific set of funding mechanisms. But fragmentation can also form around instrumental decisions, as when agencies specialize in performing or supporting different types of therapies or instructional methods. Fragmentation is signified either by a large number of uncoordinated loci of decision making at a given level or by a large and varied number of routes or channels used to transmit decisions, reports, or funds from one sector level to another.

Since the effects of fragmentation on sector organization are expected to be similar to those of federalization, we define this third dimension before developing hypotheses and reporting evidence: *federalization-concentration* of decision making refers to the extent to which decisions are made independently at multiple levels within a sector. Just because programmatic decisions regarding educational policy are made at the national level does not necessarily preclude programmatic decisions in the same domain being made at state and/or local levels. In the U.S. educational sector, increasing federal activity has not displaced but appears to have stimulated and strengthened state agencies (see Murphy 1981; McDonnell and McLaughlin 1982), and the influence of local interests has not been supplanted but only supplemented by the increased involvement of state and federal agencies. One set of authorities has been layered over another, with each claiming authority on differing legitimacy bases—"national interest," constitutional vesting, the "religion of localism" (see Scott and Meyer 1988). The contemporary variant of federalism, as already noted, is one in which varying levels of government within a sector may exercise independent and overlapping jurisdiction over the same types of decisions. Thus, Coleman and Hoffer (1987) characterize the earlier environment of the public school as more often consisting of a "functional community" in which social norms evolved out of the local community social structure in contrast to today's environment, described as an "open network," such that schools operate in a context of incompatible values and conflicting claims of authority.

When the various types of decisions within a sector are centralized, unified and concentrated, we would expect to observe a relatively straightforward set of vertical line controls among organizations at differing levels within the sector and relatively lean administrative components at each level. Our prediction is that

H12 Organizations operating in sectors characterized by centralized, unified, and concentrated programmatic decision making are expected to be tightly coupled across levels and to exhibit relatively small administrative components at each level.

Examples in the United States of such arrangements include public sector agencies like the Social Security Administration (SSA) that administers Social Security benefits through a set of departments and agencies operating at federal, state, and local levels, and the Internal Revenue Service, responsible for administering the income tax program.

As already noted, instances of sectors involving both public and private organizations that exhibit higher levels of centralization, unification, and concentration are found in other societies organized in a corporatist arrangement, in which private interests become structured into peak associations, exercise public (state-authorized) authority, and are thus able to achieve a "concertation" (unification) of decision making. Streeck and Schmitter (1985) provide an enlightening discussion of the control advantages enjoyed by this form of "private interest government" as compared to more conventional modes of public authority.

Most sectors in the United States, by contrast, are currently characterized by relatively high levels of fragmentation and federalization, and by variable amounts of centralization. Such conflicting and inconsistent environments are expected to generate more complex interlevel and intraorganizational structures at many if not all levels. Specifically, we expect that

H13 Organizations operating in sectors characterized by fragmented or federalized programmatic decision making are expected to exhibit complex linkages across levels and elaborated and enlarged administrative components at each level.

Examples of these sectors include welfare services, education, and medical care. The chief attribute of these sectors is their organizational multiplicity and variety, with agencies and programs piling up in ways that are sometimes supplementary, but more often duplicative or overlapping, and occasionally conflicting. Local organizations responding to these elaborated environments themselves develop more complex and convoluted structures.

Several studies provide evidence relevant to this prediction. A study by Stackhouse (1982) based on a national survey of secondary schools in the United States found that schools operating in states exhibiting higher levels of centralized and unified policy decisions exhibited smaller administrative components than schools participating in centralized but fragmented state environments. And a study by Meyer, Scott, and Strang (1987) combined data from several national sources describing school district structure and funding during the 1970s. The investigators made the assumption that, in general, state-level funding represented a less centralized and more unified environment while federal-level funding signified a more centralized and more fragmented environment. The amount of federal funding received was found to be positively associated with size of district administration, while the amount of state funding was negatively correlated with the size of administration.

By contrast, the association between environmental fragmentation and administrative complexity was reported to be negative rather than positive in a study of agricultural cooperatives in Hungary conducted by Carroll, Goodstein, and Gyenes (1988). Fragmentation of decision making was assessed by calculating the distributional inequality of influence within four decision making domains across fourteen agents, as well as by a measure assessing the number of autonomous village councils to which the cooperative was subject. Results showed significant and negative correlations between both measures of fragmentation and the administrative ratio of the cooperatives. Carroll, Goodstein, and Gyenes discuss several alternative explanations for the discrepancy in findings between this and previous studies.

In discussing the problem of defining societal sectors, we noted that they vary in the extent of their functional differentiation: organizations in some sectors are more limited and restricted in the types of activities they perform than are organizations in other sectors. We can now suggest a possible source of this variation:

H14 The more centralized, unified, and concentrated programmatic and funding decision making within a sector, the greater the extent to which organizations within that sector will be limited and specific in the types of functional activities they perform.

The argument is that unified and centralized authority supports the creation of a limited, functionally specific system of organizations. New initiatives are resisted unless they are consistent with the existing mission. If they are adopted, it is done in a centralized manner and they are imposed consistently on all appropriate subordinate units. By contrast, fragmented and federalized sectors present relatively easy targets for various waves of new programs and reforms, so public schools, for example, are likely to individually and variously incorporate purposes as varied as nutrition, public health, birth control, and civil defense (see Meyer 1983b).

Some systematic evidence pertaining to this prediction is provided in the study contrasting the program and curricular goals of public and private schools (Scott and Meyer 1988). We found that public schools at the secondary level were more likely to claim an emphasis on both college preparation and vocational training, while private and parochial schools at the secondary level reported concentrating their training on college preparation. Thus,

> Catholic and other private secondary schools focus their programs on building the college-bound middle class person. Public schools tend to add to this goal a very different emphasis on serving students who will probably end up in working class positions in society. The finding reflects a truism about American public education—for the most part, public schools can do little to choose their constituencies or the purposes appropriate to them. (Scott and Meyer 1988:154–55)

The division of labor among organizations within a sector is also expected to be affected by these same sector characteristics. A hypothesis formulated by our colleagues Elaine Backman and Michal Tamuz predicts that

H16 The more centralized, unified, and concentrated decision making within a sector, the fewer the number of different organizational forms within the sector and the greater the variance among them.

Again, unified and centralized authority permits decision makers to design and create a system of organizations governed by "rational"—that is, orderly and systematic—criteria. A division of labor that "makes sense" can be charted. Backman and Tamuz employ this proposition to help account for the differences they observed between sectors providing prison services—a relatively unified sector exhibiting a limited number of rather clearly differentiated facilities— and the mental health services sector—a fragmented sector exhibiting a large number of overlapping and diffusely defined facilities (see Tamuz 1982; Scott and Lammers 1985).

SECTOR CONTROLS

Closely related to sector decision-making characteristics are the modes of control exercised within sectors by higher over lower units. Three major types of control may be distinguished, based on what indicators are employed to assess performance (see Donabedian 1966; Suchman 1967; Scott 1977): (1) *Structural* controls focus on "organizational features or participant characteristics presumed to have an impact on organizational effectiveness, including administrative [features] that support and direct production activities" (Scott 1977:84), for example, measures of the adequacy of facilities and equipment or the qualifications of personnel. (2) *Process* controls "focus attention on the activities performed by organizational participants, and assessment consists of determining the degree of conformity to these performance standards" (Scott 1977:82), for example, quantity measures of numbers of clients served or units produced or quality assessments against some specified standard of performance. And (3) "*Outcome* indicators focus attention on specific characteristics of materials or objects on which the organization has performed some operation" (Scott 1977:75), for example, measures of patients' mortality or morbidity in health care organizations or measures of students' information or skills in educational settings.

H16 Organizations functioning in sectors that are highly developed technically but not institutionally will be subjected primarily to interlevel controls emphasizing outcomes.

For example, the Environmental Protection Agency (EPA) attempts to specify emission standards for the regulation of pollution from automobiles. The objective is to specify the quality of air to be obtained, not the method of achieving it or the qualifications of workers who are to produce the desired effect. Of course, as has been often observed, initial attempts to utilize outcome controls in many sectors often shift over time to emphasize process controls, for example, air quality standards are replaced by equipment specifications or by prescribed numbers of inspections (see Wildavsky 1979).

H17 Organizations functioning in sectors that are highly developed institutionally but not technically will be subjected primarily to interlevel controls emphasizing structural measures.

In sectors like education and mental health, primary emphasis is placed on such structural controls as accreditation, certification, and licensure.

H18 Organizations functioning in sectors in which decision making is centralized but fragmented or federalized are likely to be subjected primarily to interlevel controls emphasizing processes.

Authorities that must share control with other units, as in the case of fragmented or federalized sectors, are rarely in a position to require changes in outcomes.

What they can do is require evidence that effort is being expended in the pursuit of their goals. Process controls—emphasizing numbers of clients processed and numbers of services administered—provide such evidence.

H19 The exercise of structural controls is more compatible with the loose coupling of administrative to production tasks than is the exercise of process controls, and the exercise of process controls is more so than the exercise of outcome controls.

Indeed, a major contribution of the loose coupling literature on organizations (e.g., March and Olsen 1976; Meyer and Rowan 1977; Weick 1976) is to remind us that structural features of organizations can vary somewhat independently of processes conducted, and processes, of outcomes achieved.

Conclusion

The central argument of this chapter is that organizations are embedded in larger systems of relations. These systems increasingly exhibit a vertical structure, with decisions about purposes and funding more highly centralized and more formally structured today than in the past. Vertical linkages among organizations are an increasingly prevalent and salient fact of societal structures.

Just as significant as the existence of these vertical connections is their variety. Societal sectors vary in many important respects: whether they are dominated by institutional or technical processes; the number of levels at which organizations have developed; the structure of decision making; and the nature of interlevel controls. These dimensions, plus others still to be identified, are expected to strongly influence the number and types as well as the structure and performance of organizations within each sector. Thus, for example, regulatory processes may be expected to assume quite different guises and to have different effects in the medical care sector than in the civil aeronautics sector, reflecting not only differences in political processes (see Wilson 1980) and economic mechanisms (see Noll 1971) but organizational arrangements.

To develop and illustrate these ideas, we have concentrated attention on the current organization of public sectors in the United States, although we believe the schema will prove helpful in analyzing the structure of other sectors, other societies, and other times. The United States presents the unusual and interesting case of a society historically organized in a decentralized manner—with great emphasis on individual freedoms, local autonomy, market processes, and curbs on public power—that has undergone considerable centralization in this century. Attempts to centralize, however, have exhibited great variety, as illustrated by Sundquist (1969:13) in his description of the wave of centralization occurring during the Great Society reforms:

> When the federal structure was transformed in the 1960s, it was not recast according to anybody's master plan. Nobody had one. . . . Each statute had its own administrative strategy. Some programs followed the older model of federalism; most were patterned on the new. Formula grants coexisted with project grants. Established agencies vied with new ones as the recipients of the federal funds, in a welter of relationships and patterns that varied from agency to agency and program to program.

In addition to describing variation by sector and over time—variation our model is designed to capture—Sundquist's portrait reveals an absence of centralized and unified programmatic authority at the national level: programmatic authority is often fragmented and federalized, and when centralization occurs it has tended to take the form of funding controls (see Meyer and Scott 1983b).

The absence of centralized and unified programmatic authority gives rise to control systems that are cumbersome and complex for many reasons. First, attempts to exercise control primarily through fiscal systems tend to create an elaborate system of indirect controls: reimbursement formulas, report and accounting requirements, data collected for documentation and justification rather than production purposes. Second, when controls are fragmented and federalized, there are many controlling agencies each with only a piece of the action and each with an independent connection to all the organizations under their jurisdiction. The analytic and decision-making procedures within each of these agencies may be highly rational, but the combined effect on the subordinate units of the cumulated requirements can produce confusion bordering on administrative chaos (see Sproull 1981). Third, fiscal and fragmented decision making tends to rely on structural and process controls that, we argue, are associated with loose coupling between administrative and production tasks. Reacting to their perceived lack of control over production tasks (and outcomes), there is often an escalation of control attempts in these sectors. Fourth, when authority is fragmented and federalized, coordination efforts are often frustrated. Again, Sundquist (1969:19) provides a good description of this condition:

> As the need for coordination began to be felt by planners and administrators within the federal government—and as external criticism mounted—the government responded by moving to create an elaborate structure of coordination, both in Washington and at the community level (with some innovation, too, at the regional and state levels). In doing so, the government chose to rely almost wholly upon systems of mutual adjustment rather than of central direction, upon what could be attained through negotiation among equals rather than through the exercise of hierarchical authority.

Presumably, the government "chose" mutual adjustment because programmatic authority was not and could not be centralized or unified in these sectors. (Or, as Benson's 1981 version would have it, the "interorganizational feudalism" observed in many sectors of U.S. society results from the inability of the central governmental structures to overcome the vested private interests exercising control in each.) Our somewhat ironic conclusion is that less authority produces more controls. The absence of programmatic authority within a sector undergoing centralization produces more elaborated and extensive control systems and, in consequence, more complex administrative components in the constituent organizational units.

One final comment. Although we have emphasized the costs associated with fragmented and federalized systems, we do not wish to be regarded as advocates of bureaucratic centralism. In a liberal society, there are many good reasons for dividing and decentralizing power, even at the cost of administrative inefficiency. And even from the narrower perspective of effective administration, it is well to remember that administrative systems must serve many values, only one of which is efficiency. Experienced observers of the political scene, such as Grodzins and Landau, have pointed to important administrative functions served by federalism and duplication: "Morton Grodzins concluded from his seminal study of federalism that 'a little chaos' is a good thing—the whole system is more responsive when jurisdictional lines are not clear and exclusive, because a citizenry thwarted at one level of government can have recourse to another" (Sundquist 1969:27). Similarly, Powell (1988:125) notes the advantages associated with the multiple and complex funding and regulatory controls to which public TV is subject: "With respect to public access, public TV has social benefits that may outweigh the administrative costs. The current fragmented system probably provides more open airwaves than would be the case if the system was financed solely by either government, private foundations, corporate philanthropy, or member contributions."

Grodzins and Powell cite the values of access and responsiveness. Landau (1969:351) points to the importance of error correction and reliability:

> it may be quite *irrational* to greet the appearance of duplication and overlap by automatically moving to excise and redefine. To unify the defense departments, or the several independent information-gathering services of the government, or the large number of agencies engaged in technical assistance, or the various anti-poverty programs, or the miscellany of agencies concerned with transportation, or the great variety of federal, state and local administrations that function in the same areas may rob the system of its necessary supports. It can be hypothesized that it is precisely such redundancies that allow for the delicate process of mutual adjustment, of self-regulation, by means of

which the whole system can sustain severe local injuries and still function creditably.

To the extent that centralization of power and resources results in increasing homogenization of structural forms within an organizational sector (see DiMaggio and Powell 1983), then one must be concerned with the loss of this diversity. As Hannan and Freeman (1989:7) point out, such a reduction may diminish

> the capacity of a society to respond to uncertain future changes. Organizational diversity within any realm of activity such as medical care, microelectronics production, or scientific research, constitutes a repository of alternative solutions to the problem of producing sets of collective outcomes. These solutions are embedded in organizational structures and strategies.

The loss of such organizational capacity and future adaptability may be too great a price to pay for current economies in administration.

Acknowledgments

This paper was first published about seven years ago (see Scott and Meyer 1983). In this revised version, the authors have attempted to modify and update the arguments in light of subsequent work, but at the same time to retain some of the flavor of the original piece as it reviewed the organization-environment literature of the 1970s and attempted to chart a new direction for development into the 1980s.

Preparation of the original version was supported in part by funds from the Educational Policy and Organizational Division of the National Institute of Education (Grant No. OB-NIE-G-80-0111) administered through the Institute for Research on Educational Finance and Governance, Center for Educational Research, Stanford University. The analyses and conclusions do not necessarily reflect the views or policies of either institute.

The original work benefited from the comments and suggestions of Elaine Backman, Mary Bankston, Eleanor Ferguson, Mitchell LaPlante, Allyn Romanow, John Sutton, Sharon Takeda, Michal Tamuz, and David Weckler, most of whom met with us in an informal seminar to develop these ideas and design studies to probe them.

In revising the chapter, the authors have been assisted by discussions with and comments from Bruce L. Black, Andrew Creighton, Paul J. DiMaggio, Frank R. Dobbin, Ronald L. Jepperson, David Strang, Lynne G. Zucker, and especially Walter W. Powell.

Part Two

Refining Institutional Theory

6 Institutions, Institutional Effects, and Institutionalism

Institution and institutionalization are core concepts of general sociology. Across the social sciences, scholars reach for these terms to connote, in one fashion or another, the presence of authoritative rules or binding organization. As I write, for example, the university where I work is holding a series of symposia on institutional racism. This series presumably differs from one that might be held on racism—or so at least its announcements suggest. The symposia seem to concentrate more on historical, organizational, and structural features of racism—institutional racism—features distinct from the race-related orientations and preferences of individuals.

This usage conforms with what may be the core denotation of *institution* in general sociology, that is, an institution as an organized, established, procedure.[1] These special procedures are often represented as the constituent rules of society (the "rules of the game"). They are then experienced and analyzable as external to the consciousness of individuals (Berger, Berger, and Kellner 1973:11). This most general denotation may help us understand why some scholars have even identified sociology with the study of institutions. Durkheim did so, for example, calling sociology "the science of institutions" (e.g., [1901] 1950:1x). And one commentator on Weber suggests that "the theory of institutions is the sociological counterpart of the theory of competition in economics" (Lachmann 1971:68).

But the import and centrality of the concept of institution (and of its related terms) have not guaranteed clear and thoughtful usage. Some scholars invoke *institution* simply to refer to particularly large, or important, associations. Others seem to identify institutions with environmental effects. And some simply equate the term with "cultural" effects, or with historical ones.[2]

This conceptual variety and vagueness is striking. It is also troubling, given the recent emergence of various "new institutionalisms" across the social sciences: in political science (e.g., March and Olsen 1984), in economics (Langlois 1986), in psychology (Farr and Moscovici 1984), and now in organizational analysis (e.g., this volume). Before such institutionalisms themselves become institutionalized—reified as distinct "theoretical strategies," codified in textbooks, and taken as given by practitioners—we had better take stock. In this spirit, this chapter is largely concerned with the conceptualization of institutions, institutional effects, and institutionalism. My intentions are twofold. First, I intend to describe a core structure within the semantic field of institutional terms. I recommend that we employ exclusively these core meanings and avoid a number of current conceptualizations, many of which serve only to confound institutional terms with other concepts or build untested empirical claims into our definitions. Second, by employing this clarification, I attempt to specify the distinguishing features of institutionalism as a line of theory.

In brief, I argue that institutionalization best denotes a distinct social property or state (and I attempt to specify this property), and that institutions should not be specifically identified, as they often are, with either cultural elements or a type of environmental effect (sections 1 and 2 below). It then becomes possible to represent institutionalization as a particular set of social reproductive processes, while simultaneously avoiding the opposition of institutionalization and "change" (section 3). And it becomes possible to represent institutionalism in an entirely straightforward way, as arguments featuring higher-order constraints imposed by socially constructed realities, and to distinguish it from other lines of argument (sections 4 and 5).

While this chapter concentrates on basic conceptualization, it is decidedly substantive in its aspirations. I hope to provide materials of immediate utility for communicating about, organizing, and advancing substantive arguments. (Concepts without propositions do not constitute theory, as Homans properly reminded Parsons, but propositions linking ill-formed concepts also can represent much wasted effort.) My examples and applications are drawn from organizational analysis, but the basic conceptual issues are entirely general ones.[3]

1. Institutions and Institutionalization

I begin with examples of objects commonly thought to represent institutions. Consider the following list:

marriage	academic tenure
sexism	presidency
the contract	the vacation
wage labor	attending college
the handshake	the corporation
insurance	the motel
formal organization	the academic discipline
the army	voting

First note some differences between these objects. Some can be referred to as organizations, others not. Some may seem more "cultural," others more "structural." But the objects share important commonalities that encourage us to group them together. All are variously "production systems" (Fararo and Skvoretz 1986), or "enabling structures," or social "programs," or performance scripts. Each of these metaphors connotes stable designs for chronically repeated activity sequences. This basic imagery is at the core of sociological uses.[4]

We can tighten our conceptualization of institutional terms considerably by pursuing these metaphors. *Institution* represents a social order or pattern that has attained a certain state or property; *institutionalization* denotes the process of such attainment.[5] By *order* or *pattern,* I refer, as is conventional, to standardized interaction sequences. An institution is then a social pattern that reveals a particular reproduction process. When departures from the pattern are counteracted in a regulated fashion, by repetitively activated, socially constructed, controls—that is, by some set of rewards and sanctions—we refer to a pattern as institutionalized.[6] Put another way: institutions are those social patterns that, when chronically reproduced, owe their survival to relatively self-activating social processes. Their persistence is not dependent, notably, upon recurrent collective mobilization, mobilization repetitively reengineered and reactivated in order to secure the reproduction of a pattern. That is, institutions are not reproduced by "action," in this strict sense of collective intervention in a social convention. Rather, routine reproductive procedures support and sustain the pattern, furthering its reproduction—unless collective action blocks, or environmental shock disrupts, the reproductive process.

This qualification ("unless . . . ") is important. The discussion so far might suggest that institutionalization is either equivalent to, or a form of, stability or survival. But this identification is inaccurate. If one holds a pattern to be institutionalized, one points to the presence of ongoing reproductive processes whereby "departures from normal forms of action defined by the [institutional] design tend to be counteracted" through routines (Fararo and Skvoretz 1986:224). But whether these processes actually succeed, and ensure the pattern's survival, is an entirely separate matter. For example, in certain conditions, high institutionalization can make a structure more vulnerable to environmental shock (from internal or external environments). Tocqueville's analysis of the "Old Regime and the French Revolution" provides a classic example: the French state was highly institutionalized, but in a way that made it highly vulnerable to environmental change (it was a "house of cards," in Tocqueville's phrasing) (Tocqueville [1856] 1955).

Consider again the above entries in the list of putative institutions. We consider voting to be an institutionalized social pattern in (say) the United States, while not in (say) Haiti. We do so in large part because voting in the United States is embedded in a host of supporting and reproducing practices and is not highly dependent (as it is in Haiti) on repeated political intervention for its employment. Similarly, the academic discipline is an institution within the modern university system because it is linked to other similarly institutional practices that, taken together, constitute the university system. These institutional practices require, again, relatively little "action"—repetitive mobilization and intervention—for their sustenance. (More on the differences between institutionalization and "action" in a moment.)

These examples remind us additionally that institutionalization is a relative property: we decide whether to consider an object to be an institution depending upon analytical context. The examples just above suggest one dimension of this general relativity: whether a practice is an institution is, (1), relative to particular contexts. But we can extend and formalize this relativity a bit more.

Within any system having multiple levels or orders of organization, (2), primary levels of organization can operate as institutions relative to secondary levels of organization. A microcomputer's basic operating system appears as an institution relative to its word-processing program (especially to a software engineer). In collectivities, constitutional procedures may appear institutional relative to practices of formal organization, and the latter practices institutional relative to unorganized social practices.

Further, whether an object is an institution is (3) relative to a particular dimension of a relationship. In certain respects, Yale University is more institution to New Haven than to most other communities (it is a prominent fixture of the local environment); yet in other respects, Yale is less an institution in New Haven than elsewhere (Paul DiMaggio notes, only half kidding, that the prestige of an Ivy League university seems to equal the square root of the distance from it). Parents are more institutions to their own children, than to other kids, as taken-for-granted realities; yet children may contest their own parents' authority more than that of others' parents.

Finally, whether an object is an institution is, (4), relative to centrality. In systems, cores are institutions relative to peripheries. The regime of international politico-economic coordination is more an external, objective, constraint for Ghana than for the IMF. An association can be more an institution—more a fixed feature of an external environment—for a nonmember than for a member.

The details and dimensions are here less important than the general point—that the same term, "in a different reference" (MacIver 1931:16), may, or may not, denote an institution. Whether we consider an object an institution depends upon what we are considering to be our analytical problem.

How Do Institutions Operate?

Institutions are not just constraint structures; all institutions simultaneously empower and control. Institutions present a constraint/freedom duality (Fararo and Skvoretz 1986): they are vehicles for activity within constraints (thus the imagery of "production systems" suggested by Fararo and Skvoretz). All institutions are frameworks of programs or rules establishing identities and activity scripts for such identities.[7] For example, the formal organization, considered as an institution (March and Simon 1958:2–4; Stinchcombe 1973), is a packaged social technology, with accompanying rules and instructions for its incorporation and employment in a social setting. Institutions thus embody "programmed actions" (Berger and Luckmann 1967:75) or "common responses to situations" (Mead [1934] 1972:263). Institutionalized programs then produce expectational bonds or "reciprocal expectations of predictability" (Field 1979:59). Put informally: institutions operate primarily by affecting persons' prospective bets about the collective environment and collective activity.[8]

Through their effects on expectations, institutions become taken for granted, in some fashion. The qualifier ("in some fashion") is a crucial one: while most discussions directly associate institutionalization with "taken-for-grantedness" (e.g., Zucker, ch. 4, this vol., and 1983), this phenomenological concept is an ambiguous and underanalyzed one. Taken-for-granted objects are those that are treated as exterior and objective constraints (see, e.g., Berger and Luckmann 1967; Zucker 1983). But such facticity can take on a number of quite different forms. First, taken-for-grantedness is distinct from comprehension, as is well recognized (e.g., Berger and Luckmann 1967:60): a pattern may be treated as exterior, objective, constraining, whether or not persons feel they understand the pattern well. But also, and less recognized, taken-for-grantedness is distinct from conscious awareness: one may take for granted some pattern because one does not perceive it, or think about it; alternatively, one may subject the pattern to substantial scrutiny, but still take it for granted—if in a quite different fashion—as an external objective constraint. Further, taken-for-grantedness is distinct from evaluation: one may subject a pattern to positive, negative, or no evaluation, and in each case (differently) take it for granted.[9]

When analysts refer to institutions as taken for granted, they may have a more specific idea in mind. They are suggesting that institutions are those standardized activity sequences that have taken for granted rationales, that is, in sociological parlance, some common social "account" of their existence and purpose. Persons may not well comprehend an institution, but they typically have ready access to some functional or historical account of why the practice exists. They also have an expectation that further explication is available, should they require it. Institutions are taken for granted, then, in the sense that they are both treated as relative fixtures in a social environment and explicated (accounted for) as functional elements of that environment.[10]

To What Should
Institutionalization Be Opposed?

It may further clarify our understanding of what institutionalization is if we consider what it is not. If a social object is not institutionalized, to what analytical class might it be said to belong?

Since institutionalization is a property of an order, it can be opposed, in the first instance, to the absence of order—in effect, to social entropy. But beyond this rather trivial contrast (and secondly), institutionalization can also be distinguished from the absence of reproductive processes. For example, we may find some social patterns that are the recurrent products of elementary social behavior (as pictured by Homans, or in contemporary biosociology). We may wish to consider some generic prestige or esteem processes, or common social patterns that emerge in cases of institutional breakdown, as examples (Homans 1961: ch. 16). In addition, some social patterns are repeated or persistent unintended consequences of social interaction, rather than chronically reproduced patterns. For example, consider the repetitive operation of some general sociological regularity, like the "social distancing" processes driving some patterns of housing segregation. In these cases, we may find a persisting social pattern, but it is not secured through the self-activating reproduction processes characteristic of institutions.

Third, institutionalization can be distinguished from other forms of reproduction. For example, we may wish to consider deep socialization (e.g., internalization) as a process distinct from institutionalization and as an alternative medium for the reproduction of social patterns. (It would be useful to have a typology of main social reproduction forms.) Here I wish to concentrate on just one contrast: between institutionalization and "action," as I have defined it above, as two different reproduction forms. A social pattern is reproduced through action if persons repeatedly (re)mobilize and (re)intervene in historical process to secure its persistence. In some Latin American countries, democracy is sustained (when it is sustained) by action in this sense, rather than by the institutional processes that largely promote it in (say) the United Kingdom. "Action" is a much weaker form of reproduction than institutionalization, because it faces all the "logic of collective action" problems well established in the literature (e.g., Olson 1965).

Similarly, when Dahrendorf speaks of the "institutionalization of class conflict" (1964:267ff.), he is arguing that class action is supplanted: that the political interaction between classes proceeds largely without recurrent attempted interventions by organized classes into social processes and, additionally, that "class conflict" may be sustained in the absence of persisting class subcultures or class consciousness. (Whether he is right or wrong in so arguing is, here, irrelevant.) Class relations become less immediately political, since they become naturalized as a stable feature of constraining environment—they become institutionalized.

This institutionalization/action contrast is a central one. If one participates conventionally in a highly institutionalized social pattern, one does not take action, that is, intervene in a sequence, make a statement. If shaking hands is an institutionalized form of greeting, one takes action only by refusing to offer one's hand. If attending college has become an institutionalized stage of the life course, a young person takes action more by forgoing college than by enrolling in it. The point is a general one: one enacts institutions; one takes action by departing from them, not by participating in them.

To summarize so far, without attempting a tight definition: institutions are socially constructed, routine-reproduced (ceteris paribus), program or rule systems. They operate as relative fixtures of constraining environments and are accompanied by taken-for-granted accounts. This description accords with the metaphors repeatedly invoked in discussions—metaphors of frameworks or rules. These imageries capture simultaneous contextual empowerment and constraint, and taken-for-grantedness.

EXAMPLES OF ARGUABLY LESS PRODUCTIVE CONCEPTUALIZATIONS OF INSTITUTIONAL TERMS

I have argued that institutionalization is best represented as a particular state, or property, of a social pattern. I now need to distinguish this conceptualization, briefly, from other current depictions.

Some analysts render institutionalization as a "property" idea, as I do here, but associate it with the properties of legitimacy, or formal organization, or contextuality. Each of these associations seems misguided. Legitimacy may be an outcome of institutionalization, or it may contribute to it, but illegitimate elements can clearly become institutionalized (organized crime, political corruption, fraud, etc.).[11] Similarly, while we may wish to consider formal organization as an institution, or argue that formal organization can carry or generate institutions (e.g., Zucker 1987), or that some organizations have become institutions (the Red Cross), it is arbitrary to identify institutionalization with formal organization. We have good reason to consider voting and marriage to be institutions, for example, and they are not formal organizations.

Further, while some analysts equate contextual or environmental effects with institutional ones, they are analytically quite distinct. All institutional effects have contextual qualities, as we have seen (the quality of external, objective, constraint), but not all contextual effects are institutional ones.[12] Many contextual effects are aggregative in character, for example, rather than institutional. We may consider a number of international market effects on national economies as being contextual effects; while such markets have institutional foundations, we typically do not consider their effects as immediately or proximately institutional.

Context invokes a spatial contrast: external, widespread, or global, versus local. Some analysts use institutionalization not to invoke context but to delimit a particular level of analysis, most often a macrolevel. *Macro,* like contextual, can specify a wide span of both time and space, or alternatively—in what I think is a tighter usage—it can invoke an hierarchic comparison: more highly organized versus less highly organized.[13] In any case, identification of institution with any one level of analysis is also misleading. Some institutional effects are not macro-organized—for example, some of the "interaction rituals" captured by Goffman. These patterns may be widespread and therefore have contextual qualities, but they are institutionalized at submacro orders of organization. (More on these issues in a later section.)[14]

A third category of definitions differentiates institutions by associating them with particular social domains or controls. In organizational analysis, especially, many commentators associate institutions in one way or another with "culture," that is, with normative effects, ideas, conceptions, "preconscious understandings," myths, ritual, ideology, theories, or accounts. This conceptualization greatly confuses discussion and development of institutional arguments because any of the various social control structures can be more, or less, institutionalized; no one in itself encapsulates institutionalization. "Culture"—typically represented as those forms of "consciousness" with socially coordinating effects—may be more or less institutionalized. (For example, one might consider single parenting as a significant cultural pattern, but still not wish to represent it, at least yet, as a highly institutionalized one.) All institutions embody social rationales or accounts, but this is no reason to identify institutions with the class of rationales or accounts. It may be that analysts tend to equate institutionalization with culture for a historical reason: in the modern nation-states, much institutionalization is carried by cultural rules (as argued, e.g., in Meyer, Boli, and Thomas 1987).[15] But institutionalization is better reserved as an abstract property that can characterize many forms of social coordination.[16]

2. Forms and Degrees of Institutionalization

FORMS OF INSTITUTIONALIZATION

One can delimit three primary carriers of institutionalization: formal organization, regimes, and culture. Perhaps most discussion has concentrated on institutional effects emanating from formal organization, for example, studies of the effects of work organization on individual conformity (Kohn 1969).

There are then two primary types of informally organized institutionalization. The first I denote by the term *regimes*, referring to institutionalization in some central authority system—that is, in explicitly codified rules and sanctions—without primary embodiment in a formal organizational apparatus. A legal or constitutional system can operate as a regime in this sense, but so can, for example, a profession (or for that matter, a criminal syndicate). With regimes, expectations focus upon monitoring and sanctioning by some form of a differentiated, collective, "center."[17]

Institutionalization can also be carried by "culture": here simply those rules, procedures, and goals without primary representation in formal organization, and without monitoring and sanctioning by some "central" authority. These rules are, rather, customary or conventional in character. Institutionalizing in culture produces expectations about the properties, orientations, and behavior of individuals, as constraining "others" (Mead) in the social environment.

In saying that institutions can be carried in different ways, I have distinguished between different types of rule or control structures (organization, regime, culture).[18] Institutions can certainly have a complex embodiment: in both regime and culture, for example (citizenship). But we need some such distinctions for a number of reasons. First, they force us to keep separate institutionalization, as a property, from particular types of rule or control structures. Also, institutions having different primary carriers (e.g., the handshake in "culture") may operate in different fashions. Further, we may wish to distinguish collectivities, or historical periods, by their relative reliance on the differing modes of institutionalization. For example, consider the claim that the history of the modern Western world is driven particularly by institutions "devolving from a dominant universalist historical culture" (Meyer, Boli, and Thomas 1987:27).

DEGREES OF INSTITUTIONALIZATION

Can we generate a rough metric of institutionalization? For example, how might we compare the relative institutionalization of the following institutions in contemporary American society: the liberal state, racial discrimination, the corporation, sexism?[19] This topic represents a persistent weak point in institutional discussion, and I do little to remedy the problem here, beyond delimiting the issue.[20]

We can pull together some clues about how to proceed from the literature. Goffman's "total" institutions are entirely encompassing structures, highly sequestered from environments and tightly integrating various aspects of life around a singular plan (Goffman 1961). Berger and Luckmann provide more general imagery when they suggest that total institutionalization is, archetypically, liturgy—the total absence of "action." All "problems" are common; all "solutions" socially constructed and reified; all expectations common and publicly hegemonic (Berger and Luckmann 1967:80).[21] With total institutionalization, "the only distinctive contribution an individual can make is in the skill and style of performance" (Shibutani 1986:16).

This imagery suggests that one can perhaps best conceive of degrees of institutionalization in terms of relative vulnerability to social intervention. An institution is highly institutionalized if it presents a near insuperable collective action threshold, a formidable collective action problem to be confronted before affording intervention in and thwarting of reproductive processes.

A given institution is less likely to be vulnerable to intervention if it is more embedded in a framework of institutions. It is more embedded if it has been long in place (so that other practices have adapted to it) or more centrally located within a framework (so that it is deeply situated). It is more embedded if it is integrated within a framework by unifying accounts based in common principles and rules. Further, the greater the linkage of this institution to constraints conceived to be socially exogenous—namely, to either socially exogenous (transcendental) moral authority or presumed laws of nature—the less vulnerability to intervention.[22]

The degree of institutionalization is also dependent on the form of taken-for-grantedness. If members of a collectivity take for granted an institution because they are unaware of it and thus do not question it, or because any propensity to question has halted due to elimination of alternative institutions or principles (e.g., by delegitimating them through reference to natural or spiritual law), the institution will be decidedly less vulnerable to challenge and intervention, and will be more likely to remain institutionalized.[23]

3. Institutional Change

There are a number of distinct types and processes of institutional change. Remembering the principle that every entry is an exit from someplace else, we can distinguish four major types of institutional change: institutional formation, institutional development, deinstitutionalization, and reinstitutionalization.[24]

Institutional formation is an exit from social entropy, or from nonreproductive behavioral patterns, or from reproductive patterns based upon "action." Examples of these three exits, respectively, might be the institutionalization of the self, as it is differentiated from nature and the gods (e.g., in the Greek period [Snell 1960]), of sexuality (as discussed by Foucault 1978 or Elias 1978), and of class conflict (Dahrendorf 1964).

Institutional development (or elaboration) represents institutional continuation rather than an exit—a change within an institutional form. An example might be the expansion of citizenship, as charted by Marshall (1964).

Deinstitutionalization represents an exit from institutionalization, toward reproduction through recurrent action, or nonreproductive patterns, or social entropy. The crescive deinstitutionalizations of gender, or of community corporate structures, as central socio-organizational vehicles, are examples.

Reinstitutionalization represents exit from one institutionalization, and entry into another institutional form, organized around different principles or rules. The long-term transformation of religion in Western societies, captured in discussions of secularization, is an example of the reinstitutionalization of a persisting social force.

There are a number of distinct ways in which institutions, once established, can change (i.e., develop, become deinstitutionalized, be reinstitutionalized) (see generally the discussion in Eisenstadt 1968:418–20). Institutions can develop contradictions with their environments (as pictured in ecological thinking), with other institutions (as pictured by Marx), or with elementary social behavior (as pictured by Homans 1961: ch. 16; see also Friedland and Alford, ch. 10, this vol.). These contradictions, or, separately, exogenous environmental shocks, can force institutional change by blocking the activation of reproductive procedures or by thwarting the successful completion of reproductive procedures, thus modifying or destroying the institution. Institutions can embody endogenous change as well: for example, procedural rationality, as a social institution itself, drives social change by routinizing it.

4. Institutional Effects and Institutionalism

Institutional effects are those that feature institutions as causes. The imagined institutional effects may be upon institutions, as dependent variables (e.g., the effects of the state on science), or upon dependent variables that are not in themselves represented as institutions (e.g., the effects of changes in the educational system upon consumer choices). One can thus identify two major classes of institutional effects.

Institutional *explanations* are those featuring institutional effects, or that weight institutional effects highly relative to other effects, or that isolate institutionally caused features of an analytical object. Institutional *theories* then are those that feature institutional explanations. *Institutionalism* is a theoretical strategy that features institutional theories and seeks to develop and apply them.

It may be best to try to capture institutionalism by contrasting it with other lines of theory. One way to differentiate sociological arguments is by noting the degree to which they represent units as socially constructed, and by the levels of analysis most commonly employed in their causal propositions. The "levels" dimension distinguishes roughly between methodologically structuralist and individualist imageries; the "constructedness" dimension distinguishes between phenomenological and realist conceptions of causal units and processes. These two dimensions define a simple table of lines of theory (see fig. 6.1).[25] Institutionalism invokes institutions as causes, so it necessarily emphasizes both high social construction and higher-order effects. In the catchphrases employed here, institutionalism thus tends to be both "phenomenological" and "structuralist." I first discuss the two dimensions abstractly and then explicate each cell of the figure with examples; I provide fullest development of the institutionalism cell.

Highly socially constructed units are opposed to putatively natural or noncontextual ones. That is, high constructedness denotes that the social objects under investigation are thought to be complex social products, reflecting context-specific rules and interactions. In low-construction (here, "realist") imagery, units may enter into social relations that influence their behavior, but the units themselves are socially pregiven, autochthonous.[26] In high-construction (here, "phenomenological") imagery, the units' existence is itself a framework-

Degree to Which Units Socially Constructed	Featured Levels of Analysis	
	Low Order (Individualist)	High Order (Structuralist)
High Construction (Phenomenological)	**1** "Organizational culture"; symbolic interaction	**2** Institutionalism
Low Construction (Realist)	**3** Actor &/or functional reduction attempts: neoclassical economics; behavioral psychology; most neoinstitutional economics; some network theory	**4** Social ecology; resource dependence; some network theory

Fig. 6.1. Lines of theory in organization analysis.

specific social creation—in phenomenological parlance, units are "constituted." These units may then be separately influenced by social ties as well.[27] In high-construction imagery, one cannot isolate subunit "foundations" of social organization; one rather seeks deep or core rules. The causal imageries are quite distinct: a natural base, a social superstructure, in realist lines; a nested system of social programs, in phenomenological ones. This fundamental difference is not captured by conventional (and questionable) idealist/materialist or structure/agency distinctions.[28]

By levels of analysis, the second dimension, I refer to the levels of social organization most commonly featured in causal propositions, namely, higher versus lower orders of organization. This dimension taps differences over how social influence or construction processes take place. Methodologically individualist lines try to invoke only low orders of social organization in their explanations and thus seek single-level explanations; they give relatively micro-orders causal primacy over more macro-orders of organization in this fashion. Structuralist lines allow for independent and unmediated effects of multiple orders of organization, and often, though not necessarily, see higher orders as having greater causal potency than lower orders.[29]

Figure 6.1 can be put to quite general use, but here its cells present examples from organizational analysis. Consider the cell entries as ideal-typical tendencies. The lines of theory represented in cell 3, for example—low-low: individualist/realist—attempt to reduce organizational properties directly to primitively social units (low construction), linked primarily by interactions within a single, usually low, order of organization. With low values on both dimensions, the cell entries, not surprisingly, tend to come from outside of sociology—these lines of argument, at the limit (e.g., in the neoclassical theory of the firm) admit neither social content nor structure. So firms in this line of argument are represented as units showing little social construction (at the limit, as "black boxes"), affected primarily by each other (homogeneous units), and linked by causal processes operating through low orders of organization (at the limit, through markets conceived as aggregative containers, without much structure).[30]

The lines of argument in cell 4 (higher levels, low construction: structuralist/realist) differ from cell 3 primarily by injecting additional, and higher, orders of organization into their causal imageries. In these lines, firms may be the organizational counterpart to "fruit flies"—that is, largely natural entities—but they face environments having substantial structure and heterogeneity (e.g., multiple types of resource and selection constraint, represented at different orders of organization—as in resource dependence and ecological ideas). Interactional ties can be networks linking heterogeneous units (e.g., firms to individuals or states as well as to other firms).

The lines of thought in cell 1 differ from those in cell 3 in a separate way. In these individualist/phenomenological lines of argument, rather than adding levels and considering higher-order causal effects, cell 1 ideas depart from the "black box" imageries. Firms here can be histories, or cultures. In phenomenologically inspired social psychologies, for example—as in the ideas of Weick (1969), or in "organizational culture" research—the entities linked to one another are highly constructed: for example, identities or roles with complex local histories and specificity. In the "levels" dimension, however, the cell 1 ideas run parallel to those in cell 3. Causal imagery typically invokes single rather than multilevel analysis, and the primary causal forces invoked seem to operate at a relatively local level, linking a fairly homogeneous set of units (e.g., local negotiation of identities, or effects of past organizational culture upon the present one).

Cell 2 represents institutionalism (high-high: structuralist/phenomenological), departing from the reduction attempts of cell 3 along both dimensions. In institutionalist imagery, firms can be, among other things, embodied cultural theories of organizing (March and Simon 1958:2–4; Stinchcombe 1973; Meyer and Rowan, ch. 2, this vol.). Some examples of institutionalism may help clarify its characteristics. I start with some examples from outside of organizational analysis and then suggest some from within.

In historical sociology, institutionalism is apparent in the recently reinvigorated exploration of the formation and development of capitalism, individualism, and democracy. For example, arguments that individualism emerges as part of collective political and religious frameworks (and in part from the substantive contents of Christian doctrine), rather than from aggregations of persons' reactions to microlevel and immediate social experiences, are characteristically institutionalist ones. So are arguments that hold Christendom to be a driving force in the development of Western capitalism, not just by "pacifying" social relations by providing some normative framework (Mann 1986), but by constructing and stimulating economic relations through specific institutional-ized cultural tenets (Meyer 1988a). Institutionalist arguments are apparent in those depictions of "modernization" as the incorporation of an ideological package of institutions and accounts rather than a threshold effect of accumulated experiences and reactions (Inkeles and Smith 1974). In social psychology, Swanson, Goffman, and Berger and Luckmann all develop institutionalist lines in emphasizing the ways in which variation in collectivity types can constitute different forms of self (e.g., Swanson 1986; Goffman 1974; Berger, Berger, and Kellner 1973). Distinct institutionalist arguments are also apparent in the study of institutions themselves, such as education or the family. Note the argument that education affects society not only indirectly through socialization or credentialing of individuals, but also directly through the (higher-order and social construction) effects of education on other institutions, for example, through the creation of an educated society, theories of personnel, and a "scientized polity" (Habermas 1970; also see Meyer 1977).

This volume provides a number of examples of institutionalist argumentation in organizational analysis (and Scott, ch. 7, this vol., catalogs a range of institutionalist causal mechanisms). The institutionalist emphasis on constructedness and high-order effects is apparent in its recurrent stress upon the dependence of formal organizing on special institutional conditions (e.g., Stinchcombe 1965; Meyer and Rowan, ch. 2, this vol.); in arguments about the incorporation of organizational practices from environments rather than the intraorganizational generation of such practices (Tolbert and Zucker 1983); in institutionalist emphasis upon the import of social as well as ecological ties between organizations (e.g., DiMaggio and Powell, ch. 3, this vol.; perhaps also White 1981); in the argument that differences in firms across nation-states may represent instances of broader forms of organizing specific to types of polities (Jepperson and Meyer, ch. 9, this vol.); in the suggestion that while contemporary societies may be full of organizations, and that while formal organization may be an institution within them, these societies are not best considered to be "societies of organizations" (Jepperson and Meyer, ch. 9, this vol.).

These institutionalist arguments generally not only stress the structuring quality of rules or frameworks, but also attribute causal import to the particular substantive contents of the rules invoked—frames are not just formal structures. Fararo and Skvoretz usefully distinguish institutional from network theory by indicating that institutional arguments are structural ones that also "[preserve] the content of social action and interaction"; "social relations are content-filled control structures" (Fararo and Skvoretz 1986:242, 230). For example, we can observe the emphasis placed upon the social history of elements; in practice, this can amount to invoking lagged dependent variables as causes. In addition, emphasis on construction entails attention to social reflexivity as itself an independent source of social structuration, that is, the operation of publicly prominent social analysis of and discourse about social processes, as, in itself, a potential structuring force.[31] In this dimension (degree of constructedness), institutionalist arguments then differ markedly from those that posit units with largely autonomous and naturally emanating experiences, reflections, choices, preferences, actions—both by calling the autonomy and inevitable emanation into question and, independently, by questioning and restricting the causal potency of these non- (or less-) constructed elements. Neither actor nor activity is thought to be primordial; there is then little tendency to consider either as foundational of social structure. Rules or frames are the basic elements of social structure, in institutionalist imagery, rather than some class of asocial subunits.

In its emphasis on multilevel causal connections and on high or macroorder effects, institutionalism differs from arguments that rely primarily on aggregative processes (e.g., the collective as largely an additive outcome of microlevel states), on "demographic" depictions of structure (structural features as reflecting relative proportions of sets of subunits [Stinchcombe 1968: ch. 3]), and on causal models that largely feature single-level explanations (e.g., microlevel outcomes associated with microlevel causes). The higher-order effects can operate in a contextual or environmental manner, or as a strict collective effect, that is, as in the effects of a "center" or core of a system, represented as a higher order of organization, on a periphery of the system.

5. Institutionalism and Actors

This discussion has attempted to explicate the distinctive character of institutionalism in organizational analysis and to link these properties to a general institutionalism in social science. Note I have not attempted to assess the relative merits or explanatory success of institutionalism versus the other lines of argument represented in figure 6.1 (though I have suggested some distinctions that should have immediate utility for evaluating the logical status of various arguments). Nor have I attempted to assess the scope relations of the various lines, that is, to determine whether the lines of theory directly compete, or have different explananda, or reveal any complementarities. At the very least, however, the above discussion should raise strong suspicions about common oppositions of institutional and "actor," or "interest," arguments. Such a contrast may confound a number of quite distinct issues.

Consider institutional and "rational-choice" arguments; they are often said to exist in sharp opposition. But note that self-proclaimed rational-choice arguments often feature institutional constraints (in connection with opportunity costs) as central causes (Friedman and Hechter 1988; Elster 1986), and institutional arguments often invoke adaptive responses to change in institutional conditions (see Scott, ch. 7, this vol.). Do these two lines of argument truly amount to competing paradigms? Alternatively, they might represent competing ways to invoke institutional effects, or reflect disagreements about proper microfoundations of macroeffects, to mention just two alternatives. The literature is unclear.

Some issues seem straightforward. Institutionalism, like any set of causal arguments, must be capable of providing "microtranslation" (Collins 1981) of its propositions, that is, samples of the lower-level processes embodied in higher-order effects (in effect, statements about activities or behaviors of persons). Some institutionalist lines of argument—particularly the early institutionalism of, for example, Durkheim, or those institutionalist arguments advanced by Parsons, or the primitive institutionalism of "culture and personality" studies—largely neglected microtranslation, or failed the microtranslation test (e.g., the childhood socialization arguments of the early culture/personality studies). But the new institutionalisms seem no less capable of providing microtranslations than noninstitutionalist arguments, though they may provide different ones. Institutionalism may not advance conventional arguments about "actors" or "action" (more on this in a moment), but such conventions by no means define the totality of legitimate causal arguments.[32] Similarly, successful influence attempts by a delimited "actor," carrying a specific "interest," represent only one category of possible social change explanations, and successful change arguments need not be limited to it. Institutionalism also contributes a distinctive set of ideas to the class of change arguments (e.g., the idea of institutional contradiction, in Marx, or in Friedland and Alford, ch. 10, this vol.). (See the conspectus of institutionalist causal mechanisms provided by Scott, ch. 7, this vol.)

The conceptualization suggested in section 1, above, opposed institutionalization, in part, to "action"—in the specific sense there defined—but not to actors. Institutional arguments need not be directly contrasted with actor and interest accounts; rather, they represent, in part, a distinctive line of argument about actors and interests. Institutional accounts argue, as discussed above, that actors cannot be represented as foundational elements of social structure.[33] They suggest, typically, that actors and interests are highly institutional in their origins and operation and, moreover, that in modern polity forms they are often constructed institutions themselves (as, e.g., in Jepperson and Meyer, ch. 9, this vol.). Institutionalism suggests that social systems vary in the extent to which "action" is carried by actors, in the canonical sense of autonomous rational egoists, operating in private capacities. In modern systems much action is conducted by authorized collective agents of one sort or another. Systems also can vary in how much "action" they sustain, and in the degree to which social reproduction is dependent upon action, relative, for example, to institutional processes.

Action references often become the social-theoretic analogue to the economist's automatic (and nonexplanatory) invocation of preferences and utility. In response, institutionalism has tended to "defocalize" actors (DiMaggio 1988a) purposefully, because undue focus on actors has seemed to impair the production of sociology. But this discussion is not yet well developed by either those in or outside of institutionalism, so debate on these matters has been shallow.

6. Reprise

Institutions and institutional effects are core to general sociology rather than peripheral to or competitive with it. Institutional effects should not be narrowly associated with explanations of stability or thought to be irrelevant to change; institutions can be powerful sources of both stability and change. And while institutionalization can be opposed, in part, to "action," it is not well distinguished from actor or interest effects.

There are ironies here. Perhaps the discussion of both institutions and action has remained insufficiently developed due to institutional processes. American sociology's long-standing reification of action (Münch 1986), rooted in the larger institutional matrix of American society, has promoted the taken-for-grantedness of action and has simultaneously hindered scholarly perception of institutional effects.

Acknowledgments

This chapter reflects the author's discussion or correspondence with Elaine Backman, Randall Collins, Carol Conell, Walter W. Powell, John W. Meyer, David Strang, and Morris Zelditch, Jr. It also draws on written comments provided by Carol Conell, Paul J. DiMaggio, and Francisco Ramirez on an earlier version. More specific acknowledgments are provided in the text.

Notes

1. MacIver 1931:15–17 distinguished sharply between an association, as an organized group, and an institution, as an organized procedure.

2. See Eisenstadt 1968 for a catalog of uses of the term, Znaniecki 1945 for a rich historical discussion of institutional thinking, and Scott 1987b for an overview of the use of the concept in organizational analysis.

3. This chapter draws on a large number of works, but especially upon Fararo and Skvoretz 1986; Zucker, this vol. and 1983; and Meyer, Boli, and Thomas 1987. Also, Sartori 1984 and Cohen 1980: ch. 7 provide powerful and complementary insights on the requisites of good conceptualization—insights this chapter attempts to employ.

4. This imagery is reflected in the work of a great variety of social theorists, including Mead 1934:261ff., Parsons 1951, Gerth and Mills 1953, Berger and Luckmann 1967, Durkheim [1901] 1950, Davis 1949, Hayek 1973, Goffman 1974, Buckley 1967, Eisenstadt 1968, March and Olsen 1984, Douglas 1986, MacIver 1931, Giddens 1984:375 and 1982:10, Bierstedt 1970:320, Shibutani 1986:16, and Stinchcombe 1986a:904–5.

5. Here I follow Zucker 1983 in representing the terms as process and property variables, though I do not follow her in the details of conceptualization.

6. I have freely adapted a characterization provided by Fararo and Skvoretz 1986. I have also drawn upon Przeworski and Sprague 1971. I should add that institutions are not equivalent to norms. Many theorists have distinguished norms from institutions by making the latter, but not the former, self-policing. See, e.g., Schotter 1981:10–12; also Parsons, e.g., 1951:20; a norm is institutionalized, according to Parsons, *if* it is rewarded and sanctioned.

7. "Institutionalized situations with their moral and practical arrangements create individuals' obligations and powers, create activities" (Stinchcombe 1986a:905).

8. For examples of many additional, parallel, formulations, see Berger and Luckmann 1967:60 (institutions embody "what everybody knows," "recipe knowledge"); Lachmann 1971:13 (they are "orientation maps" of the future actions of others); and Parsons (institutions produce agreement on specific courses of action that a situation demands).

9. It seems especially arbitrary to associate institutions (as current discussions often do) with absence of thought or with positive evaluation. This practice smuggles untested empirical claims into our conceptualization and then impairs theoretic debate. For example, both Mary Douglas and Lévi-Strauss seem to associate institutions with absence of thought (with "unthink") (Douglas 1986; Lévi-Strauss 1966). So modern societies, revealing greater discourse about social practices, are presumably less institutionalized than nonmodern (e.g., tribal) ones. (Tribal systems for Lévi-Strauss are "cold" cultures, with their social institutions enmeshed with nature and without the endogenous contradictions generating change.) Contrast Stinchcombe, who argues that modern societies have both greater reflexivity and greater institutional self-replicating capacity (1968:115). We need to treat such differences as substantive theoretical ones, to be adjudicated empirically, rather than eliding them by treating them definitionally.

10. Comments by Francisco Ramirez, on a previous version of this chapter, stimulated this paragraph. He provides an excellent example, discussing the pre–Vatican II mass: "No one would dispute its institutional character. The mass was always enacted, never the product of collective action. The mass was celebrated in Latin; the sequence of events was rigidly prescribed. Each event had a name. What the priest had to do in enacting a given event was set forth in a written script; what the undifferentiated others had to do in reaction (stand, kneel, bless yourself) was also carefully prescribed. The only variable was the content of the sermon (now called a homily) and whether the script was sung. . . . From an alien perspective a zombie-like production. But without attributing a high degree of comprehension to the participants (not everyone took a course in liturgy or even knew that the color of the vestments used in a given day had precise symbolic meaning), just about every participant could tell you that the mass was about worshiping God and that you were supposed to go to mass on Sundays and other days of obligation. The participants were not merely going through standardized interaction sequences without having some shared story-line as to what the practice was all about."

11. Walter Buckley is compelling in his insistence upon distinguishing institutionalization from legitimation: some "social problems," he says, "are so pervasive, stable, and difficult to root out precisely because they are 'institutionalized.' That is, they involve complex interpersonal, and often highly organized, networks of expectations, communications, normative interpretations, interests, and beliefs, embedded

in the same sociocultural matrix as are 'legitimized' structures" (1967:161, also 145, 129–30).

12. That is, contextual effects often refer to effects of the proportional distribution of individuals across groups within a collectivity, or to the rates of interaction between individuals in different social locations. See, e.g., Przeworski 1974. For examples of such arguments, see Blau 1977.

13. *Macro* can refer to spatial extensiveness or large numbers, but also to a high order of organization within a structure having multiple orders of organization (a high order being a complex of lower orders: chapters are in part complexes of paragraphs, which are themselves organizations of sentences). Thus *macro* can refer to effects of a collective or system "center," relative to a periphery, as well as to global (extensive) effects upon a locality. The two usages are often conflated.

14. Note the ambiguous usage of *environment* in the organizational literature. Sometimes the term invokes context imagery (e.g., fields of organizations), other times macro (hierarchic ordering) imagery (e.g., references to law), sometimes both (e.g., "the institutional environment"). This is confusing.

15. A number of authors, including those just cited, may in fact confound these historical arguments with conceptual ones. This conflation was certainly a core impairment of Parsons' theorizing.

16. It is difficult to categorize and evaluate Stinchcombe's discussion of institutionalization—roughly, the process of binding power to a value (1968, esp. pp. 181–88). For him, an institution is best considered a structure in which powerful people are committed to some value (p. 107), or those values and norms that have high correlations with power. This imagery is evocative, but I do not find it sufficient for conceptual purposes, for two reasons: the imagery ties institution too closely to two relatively unstable concepts (power and value); it also directs one to focus unduly on formally organized institutions (as in Stinchcombe's own examples). In a recent book review, Stichcombe employs a conceptualization much closer to the one recommended here (1986a).

17. *Center* in the sense of Shils 1975 or Eisenstadt 1968, not in a geographic sense.

18. These distinctions are not meant to represent different levels of analysis or organization.

19. One cannot properly engage in holistic comparison of institutionalization; the question What is the relative institutionalization of the contemporary United Kingdom and France? as historical particulars, does not lend itself to pursuit. It seems more legitimate (and in principle productive) to compare the relative institutionalization of institutions within collectivities, or types of institutions across societies, or of analytical types of social orders. One can compare, for example, the degree to which types of political regimes are institutionalized across comparable societies (as many often do; Huntington 1968 is largely on this topic). Or one can try to compare the relative institutionalization of various "nonmodern" (e.g., tribal, feudal) versus "modern" (i.e., the rationalized, rich, individualist) types of societies.

20. Most treatment of this topic in the literature has been implicit or, if explicit, informal and cursory. Parsons 1982 discusses the issue en passant and informally; Eisenstadt 1968 does so as well. Meyer, Boli, and Thomas 1987 provides a provocative but one-paragraph discussion. Huntington 1968 provides an extended treatment of degrees of political institutionalization. He associates greater institutionalization with greater adap-

tiveness, complexity, differentiation, insulation, and unification. He also provides some operationalization of these ideas, for comparing the institutionalization of governmental regimes. Welfling 1973 uses Huntington's work in an empirical study of the institutionalization of African party systems. Huntington's ideas may have broader utility, but they would seem to require greater tightening and generality. Wuthnow 1987: ch. 8 discusses the institutionalization of science in the seventeenth century and associates this institutionalization with organizational autonomy, procurement of a resource base, development of an internal system of communication and organization, and external legitimation. Shefter and Ginsberg 1985 provides an insightful, but entirely informal, discussion of the "institutionalization of the Reagan regime," associating institutionalization with a secure resource coalition, successful performance, agenda control, a legitimating ideology, and policies benefiting supporters. (However, they tend to confound institutionalization with survival, as do many treatments.)

21. Compare: "When everything is institutionalized, no history or other storage devices are necessary: 'The institution tells all' " (Schotter 1981:139).

22. Compare Mary Douglas (1986:46ff., I paraphrase): a convention is institutionalized if any question about it receives an answer discussing the nature of the universe.

23. Meyer, Boli, and Thomas 1987:37 discusses the elimination of alternatives.

24. DiMaggio 1988a provides a similar listing.

25. In working out this figure, I have drawn upon conversations with John W. Meyer.

26. I am unhappy with the label "realist," but have no better alternative at hand. "Realism" has taken on the connotations I wish to suggest. There are actually two distinct forms of realism. The first, a naturalistic realism, exemplified in rational-choice-type arguments, sees units as having high social autonomy and represents them as primordial building blocks of social structure. The second, social structural realism, sees units as highly constrained by the positions they occupy within networks of statuses and roles (e.g., White, Boorman, and Breiger 1976). But these latter arguments remain a variant of realism because they do not see the units themselves (or the networks) as outcomes of social construction or constitution processes. They see the networks as representing "concrete" patterns of interactions (a common word, indicative of realist imagery); the units linked by these infrastructural networks are exogenous to the theory.

27. Phenomenological arguments allow for two distinct types of institutional effects: institutions can act as rules or instructions generating and defining social objects; they can independently operate as regulators of social processes. Compare Fararo and Skvoretz 1986:243.

28. Thus this "constructedness" dimension should not be conceived as representing differences on "where to draw the exogeneity/endogeneity line" or on where to stop trying to explain. The dimension captures far more substantial differences: differences over what the exogeneity is. In "realist" lines, the exogenous domain (of explanatory variables) is nonsocial—composed of asocial psychological states, or givens of nature (see Langlois 1986: ch. 10 on the aspirations for exogeneity in general equilibrium theory). "Phenomenological" arguments differ by calling into empirical question the supposed nonsocial character of the realist's exogenous variables, and thus by greatly restricting the range of nonsocial exogenous variables. In phenomenological arguments, the exogenous variables driving social endogenous variables can also be social ones—

but represented at a different level of social organization, or reflecting some different dimension of sociality, than the endogenous social variables.

29. Structuralism denies that a microtranslation (Collins 1981) of a structural effect is equivalent to a set of macro-organized variables linked by an intervening microrelationship (and thus would deny Coleman's 1986 treatment of structural effects). The difference between this methodological structuralism and individualism thus centers on the number and proper treatment of composition effects in social orders. (For a rare polemic in favor of methodological structuralism, see Mayhew 1980).

30. Neoinstitutional economics, as represented, e.g., by Williamson, begins to depart from cell 3 along the "constructedness" dimension, but remains largely within this cell.

31. Thus institutional propositions include (but are not limited to) "theories of theorization effects" (Bourdieu 1977:178). For example, Pfeffer, in his organizational analysis text, following Zucker, gives a number of examples of institutional effects that occur because a process is viewed by organization members as institutionalized in formal structure (Pfeffer 1982:241, 242, 244).

32. I need to reiterate that microtranslation must be distinguished sharply from microreduction. The capacity for such translation is a requirement for a causal theory, and a guard again obfuscation; reduction, in contrast, represents perhaps an ultimate theoretic aspiration, but is not a requirement of theoretic adequacy. Further, providing microtranslations does not require provision of microfoundations, if this term is taken literally. *Foundations* may be a misleading metaphor for social science. The foundations of a building can stand without a superstructure; in the social world, however, the typical "foundations" imagined do not have this free-standing capacity. This point is behind Marx's excoriation of the "Robinson Crusoe" reasoning in classical economics, and behind Durkheim's reminder that there would be no modern "individual" without the (collective) "cult" of individualism.

33. It goes without saying that persons are the only ontological elements of social structure—unless one follows Hegel, of course. But this is a matter entirely separate from the epistemological and methodological issues we are discussing.

7 Unpacking Institutional Arguments

W. Richard Scott

The development of a new theoretical framework requires diverse talents and efforts. There are the creative insights of the founders, the imaginative applications of the new converts, the meticulous designs and tests of the empirical researchers, and the challenging queries and expressed doubts of the critics. All contribute to the enterprise.

Yet another type of constructive effort involves the attempt to clarify arguments and distinguish among varieties of work within the theoretical framework. As theories grow, they also become more differentiated. Generically similar but diverse forms of arguments develop. More attention must be devoted to consolidating existing arguments and to clarifying new and different arguments. While these activities may be less exciting and dramatic than those involving the generation of new arguments or applications, they are no less essential to the progress of the theoretical enterprise.

Institutional theory as developed and applied by sociologists interested in the analysis of organizations has grown rapidly in the past decade.[1] There has been sufficient development, and sufficient theoretical differentiation, so that efforts to take stock and consolidate previous contributions—to provide a firmer base for present and future developments—become more necessary and valuable. This is the work to which I propose to contribute in the present chapter.

This chapter is in two parts. In the first, I attempt to describe changes that have occurred over time in the ways in which organizational theorists have conceived of the environments within which organizations operate. I emphasize, in particular, the introduction of cultural and structural elements and changes in the level of analysis. Differences exist in conceptions of how diverse are the symbolic or cultural elements involved and how organizational environments are to be bounded. In the second section, I survey recent empirical studies of institutional effects in order to examine what causal arguments are being made by researchers as they attempt to explain how institutional environments affect organizational forms and functions. A number of different causal mechanisms are identified and discussed.

The Conception of Organizational Environments

THE RECONCEPTUALIZATION OF ENVIRONMENTAL ELEMENTS

Picking up a distinction proposed by Zucker (1987) in her recent overview of institutional theory, I focus primarily on that strand of work concerned with examining the effects of institutional environments on organizational structures rather than with examining the internal generation of institutionalized forms within organizations.

Perhaps the single most important contribution of institutional theorists to the study of organizations is their reconceptualization of the environments of organizations. With the advent and widespread adoption of open systems models of organizations during the 1960s, the importance of environmental factors in shaping and supporting organizational forms became apparent. Earlier models, however, emphasized technical facets—resources required by the organization's production system to transform inputs into outputs. Although some versions stressed environments as sources of information, this concept was interpreted narrowly to identify knowledge required in the production process—for example, predictability of inputs; knowledge of cause-effect relations; analyzability of search processes. Technology was in the saddle and seen as shaping organizational structure.

Introducing Cultural Elements

This conceptual hegemony was shattered in 1977 by the work of Meyer and Rowan, although their work drew on important antecedents. Their influential article called attention to a neglected facet of environments: institutionalized beliefs, rules, and roles—symbolic elements capable of affecting organizational forms independent of resource flows and technical requirements.

In their concept of institutionalization Meyer and Rowan appropriated the definition and usage of Berger and Luckmann (1967), who emphasize that shared cognitive systems, although created in interaction by humans, come to be viewed as objective and external structures defining social reality. The more institutionalized the cognitive categories and belief systems, the more human actions are "defined by a widening sphere of taken-for-granted routines" (Berger and Luckmann 1967:57).

Although, in their foundation work, Berger and Luckmann were concerned with identifying and describing the general processes by which social reality is constructed and maintained, in later work Berger and colleagues focused on the subset of belief systems that are distinctive to modernization. In a book that has been surprisingly neglected by later institutional theorists (perhaps because its title, *The Homeless Mind,* sounds like an existentialist tract left over from the 1950s), Berger, Berger, and Kellner (1973) identify three broad types of institutions underlying and supporting modern modes of consciousness: knowledge systems and cognitive styles associated with (1) technological production, (2) bureaucratic administration, and (3) pluralization or differentiation of life-worlds. Knowledge systems supporting bureaucratic forms, for example, include beliefs in delimited spheres of competence, the importance of proper procedure, and impersonality. Associated cognitive styles include an emphasis on orderliness, autonomous organizability, predictability, affective neutrality, and moralized anonymity. Berger and colleagues are here concerned with identifying those generalized belief systems and mind sets that support the existence and spread of bureaucratic forms into virtually every sphere of modern life. The prevailing assumption is that "in principle, everything is organizable in bureaucratic terms" (1973:50).

It is this general view of bureaucracy as an institutional form—or, more compellingly, as "the preeminent institutional form in modern society"—that is embraced and amplified by Zucker (1983:1):

> Organizations not only are pervasive but also have largely redefined modern society. The initial adoption, closely linked to improved efficiency in manufacturing and utilities, succeeded in legitimating formal, rational structure. Seen in objective, nonpersonal terms, and as an exterior, taken-for-granted element of the social system, organizational form became institutionalized. It diffused outward to other kinds of collective activity, including political systems and, most recently, social movements. (P. 24)

Zucker adds the proposition that rational organization structure acquired legitimacy through its early association with improving industrial efficiency, but otherwise embraces Berger's conception of a generalized "ideal-type" symbolic model stressing formal rationality as underlying the spread of organizations.

General vs. Specific Cultures

Meyer and Rowan (1977:343) also start off with this generalized conception: "In modern societies, the elements of rationalized formal structure are deeply ingrained in, and reflect, widespread understandings of social reality." And most of their formal propositions are formulated at this quite general level. For example, "Proposition 1. As rationalized institutional rules arise in given domains of work activity, formal organizations form and expand by incorporating these rules as structural elements" (1977:345). However, they also introduce the concept of rational myths, a notion that moves in the direction of suggesting that rationality may not be all of a piece but differentiated, coming in various forms and guises. They note, "norms of rationality are not simply general values. They exist in much more specific and powerful ways in the rules, understandings and meanings attached to institutionalized social structures" (1977:343).

Even more to the point, their discussion is punctuated with multiple and diverse examples of potential sources of rationalized myths: public opinion, educational systems, laws, courts, professions, ideologies, technologies, regulatory structures, awards and prizes, certification and accreditation bodies, governmental endorsements and requirements. Although not systematically pursued, it is strongly implied that there is not one but many institutional environments and that some would-be sources of rationalized myths may be in competition if not conflict. Thus, an important step is taken to move from a generalized to a differentiated model of institutional contexts: from a conception of *the* institutional environment to one of multiple, alternative institutional environments.

Institutional and Technical Environments

Additional progress was made when, in subsequent conceptualizations, institutional environments were distinguished more and more explicitly from technical environments. Early definitions were vague: technical environments involved "complex technologies" and "exchanges" while institutional environments involved "rules" and "socially defined categories" (Meyer, Scott, and Deal 1981:152). Later formulations have provided increasingly explicit criteria for distinguishing between the two types of environments. Thus, Meyer and I propose that "*technical* sectors are those within which a product or service is exchanged in a market such that organizations are rewarded for effective and efficient control of the work process" (Scott and Meyer 1983:140). And that, by contrast, "*institutional* sectors are characterized by the elaboration of rules and requirements to which individual organizations must conform if they are to receive support and legitimacy from the environment" (p. 140). Even more explicitly, "Technical environments exercise output control over organizations. . . . In institutional environments organizations are rewarded for establishing correct structures and processes, not for the quantity and quality of their outputs" (Scott 1987b:126; see also Scott and Meyer 1983:149).

This last criterion is very similar to one proposed by Berger, Berger, and Kellner in their effort to distinguish technological from bureaucratic cognitive styles. They argue that technological consciousness admits the "separability of means and ends" (1973:27), whereas,

> Bureaucracy posits the non-separability of means and ends. . . . In bureaucracy the means are typically as important, or nearly so, as the ends. It is not just a question of getting somebody a passport but of getting it to him by the proper means. . . . The proper means and pro-

cedures are given a positive moral value, and in many cases it is assumed that even if the legitimate end is obtained by illegitimate means, the damage done by this to the bureaucratic agency far outweighs any positive benefit from the action. (1973:53)

Developing a more precise set of criteria for differentiating between the two types of environments permitted another modification—I think, improvement—in our treatment of these distinctions. It became increasingly clear to Meyer and me that the presence of one set of elements did not preclude the presence of the other type. The distinctions are more usefully treated as dimensions along which environments vary rather than as dichotomous states. Indeed, cross-classifying the two dimensions yields an interesting typology of environments in which some organizations such as utilities and banks are viewed as subject to both strong technical and institutional pressures; other organizations such as health clubs are seen as subject to weak technical and institutional environments; organizations such as competitive manufacturing companies confront relatively technical but weak institutional pressures; and organizations such as schools and churches operate in relatively strong institutional but weak technical environments. The typology appears to have heuristic utility in that we have been able to generate a number of hypotheses concerning the likely structural impact of these varying combinations of environmental pressures (see Meyer and Scott, ch. 5; Scott 1987b).

The line of work stemming from Berger and colleagues and continuing through Meyer and Rowan up to the present that emphasizes the symbolic—both cognitive and normative—aspects of the environment has significantly altered previous conceptions of organizational environments. Models giving exclusive attention to technical features have been challenged to incorporate cultural elements. There is increasing recognition that no organization is just a technical system and that many organizations are not primarily technical systems.

The increased attention to institutional factors has both contributed to and borrowed from the renewed interest in the sociology of culture. The "new cultural" emphasis, which is exemplified by the work of Berger, Bourdieu, Douglas, Foucault, and Habermas, views culture as "the symbolic-expressive aspect of human behavior" (Wuthnow et al. 1984:3; see also Wuthnow and Witten 1988). Culture is not confined to the subjective, inner thoughts or values of individuals or to some amorphous notion of a collective consciousness, but is recognized as constituting its own objective reality—albeit a socially constructed reality. And the importance of culture is no longer seen as consisting exclusively in its impact on the social structure. Rather, cultural systems can not only be studied as interesting social phenomena in their own right; they can influence the social world independently of their effect on social structures by affecting the meanings attributed to these structures (Wuthnow et al. 1984).

Thus, Meyer and Rowan (1977) argue that the formal structure of an organization has significance apart from its effect on the behavior of organizational participants since it signifies rationality and purposive order, increasing the legitimacy of its operations in the eyes of participants and constituents. Finally, Swidler's (1986:273) image of "culture as a 'tool kit' of symbols, stories, rituals and world-views, which people may use in varying configurations to solve different kinds of problems" is consistent with our insistence that there can exist multiple and competing versions of institutionalized belief systems from which, to some extent, organizations can select (see Scott 1990). This argument is amplified in the next section.

Legitimacy

An associated change in the models of how organizations relate to environments is the renewed emphasis on, and partial reconceptualization of, the concept of legitimacy. Beginning with Parsons (1960) who early emphasized that the correspondence of the values pursued by the organizations must be congruent with wider societal values if the organization is to receive legitimation and hence have an acknowledged claim on societal resources, legitimacy has been largely interpreted as pertaining to societal evaluations of organizational goals. This is the conception embraced by Pfeffer and colleagues (see Dowling and Pfeffer 1975; Pfeffer and Salancik 1978). In contrast to this focus on evaluations based on the importance or appropriateness of organizational goals, Berger and colleagues (Berger, Berger, and Kellner 1973) stress the cognitive aspects of legitimation, in particular, the theories or explanations that connect means with ends. Legitimation concerns the problem of "explaining or justifying the social order in such a way as to make institutional arrangements subjectively plausible"—the problem of motivating actors to enact actions by locating them "within a comprehensible, meaningful world" (Wuthnow et al. 1984:50).

Berger and colleagues argue that acquiring legitimation is especially crucial as well as problematic for organizations operating in institutional environments—in their terms, for bureaucratic in comparison to technological structures—because of their abstract formality.

> Here, organization can be set up autonomously, that is, as following no logic but its own. . . . As a result, the processes of bureaucratic organization have a high degree of arbitraryness. . . . there is nothing that intrinsically prohibits the passport agency from deciding that ten rather than three bureaucrats must approve every passport application. (1973:50–51)

As a consequence, such organizations have a special need for procedural legitimation and are especially vulnerable to attacks on the plausibility of their work arrangements and procedures.

Consistent with the open systems model of organizations, explanations, justifications, and meaningful accounts are more likely to be imported from the environment than to be manufactured from within. As colorfully amplified by Brown (1978:375): "All of us to some degree design or tailor our worlds, but we never do this from raw cloth; indeed, for the most part we get our worlds ready to wear. This is perhaps most often the case when the world in question is that of formal organizations." If we now add the notion introduced above of an increasingly complex and differentiated symbolic environment, we come to what I regard as an improved conception of legitimacy stemming from the institutionalist perspective:

> We take the view that organizational legitimacy refers to the degree of cultural support for an organization—the extent to which the array of established cultural accounts provide explanations for its existence. (Meyer and Scott 1983a:201)

Or, stated as the converse:

> The legitimacy of a given organization is negatively affected by the number of different authorities sovereign over it and by the diversity or inconsistency of their accounts as how it is to function. (1983a:202)

The conception of a differentiated and competitive institutional environment also supports the view that organizations are not passive actors being imprinted by cultural templates. Rather, just as is the case within their technical environments, organizations may be expected to exercise "strategic choice" (see Child 1972) in relating to their institutional environments. And various environmental agents may be expected to compete with one another for the loyalties of any particular organization. The choices available to organizations may range, at the modest pole, from deciding what types of insurance coverage to supply employees to, at the extreme, selecting the type of institutional environment with which to connect. As an example of the latter, consider the choices available to the manager of a training program created to train workers to do simple carpentry. Such managers confront the potential option of defining their programs as occupational training, occupational therapy, or recreation. Depending on the decision, their organization will be located in quite different institutional environments, varying in regulatory pressures, funding arrangements, and many other important respects. They will justify their claims for external support employing quite different arguments (legitimation of ends); they will employ trainers with differing qualifications and credentials and utilize different rationales and logics to justify their training procedures (legitimation of means). And, as noted, the force of such arguments in promoting legitimacy will be determined by the amount of consensus within the relevant sector or field regarding the appropriateness of the means selected to achieve the desired ends.

Introducing Structural Elements

In addition to adding cultural or symbolic factors as critical elements characterizing the environment of organizations, Meyer and I (Meyer and Scott 1983b) have proposed that increased attention be given to what we have termed the "relational frameworks" within which organizations are located. In a similar vein, DiMaggio and Powell (1983), adapting Giddens's (1979) concept, have called attention to the increased "structuration" of interorganizational relations. Both conceptions point out that organizations are not only involved in a set of exchange relations with other social actors; they are also located in a network or framework of relations which their own activities create but which also acts to shape and constrain their possibilities for action. Both conceptualizations emphasize the potential importance of distant as well as proximate connections and of vertical (power-authority) as well as horizontal (competitive-cooperative) relations. And both sets of theorists argue that the relational contexts or the structural connections among organizations are becoming increasingly organized. As Meyer and I (1983b:15) conclude: "The environments of formal organizations are, to a surprising degree, themselves formally organized." However, we also insist that there is much variation in how much and what kinds of structure are present in different organizational environments. The amount and type of environmental structure are to be empirically determined.

A growing number of analysts, including Burt (1983) and DiMaggio (1986a), have demonstrated the utility of network analysis, including structural equivalence techniques, in capturing this facet of organizational environments. Most importantly, institutional arguments enrich the theoretical foundation for employing network methodologies in assessing interorganizational systems.

To end the stream of consensus, differences exist between the predictions of Meyer and Scott and those of DiMaggio and Powell concerning the effects of organizational environments on structure. DiMaggio and Powell (1983) propose the master hypothesis that as the environments of organizations become more structured, organizational structures within them become more homogeneous. Indeed, although they usefully identify three different mechanisms of influence operating among organizations in the same environment—coercive, memetic, and normative—all are predicted to have the same effect—increased structural isomorphism.

By contrast, Meyer and I argue that under some conditions, more highly structured organizational environments may create increased diversity of form. For example, we suggest that in environments lacking much centralized authority, organizational forms may exhibit increased similarity (because of competitive and memetic processes). But as authority becomes more centralized, decision makers may decide to create a variety of more specialized organizational forms, increasing organizational diversity by design (coercion) (Scott and Meyer, ch. 5).

Within a given environment, the connection between shared cultural systems and the presence of a structural framework is likely to be problematic. Often environmental elements will have the power to impose a structural arrangement in a given environment but lack the power to create a consistent symbolic system. DiMaggio and Powell (1983:147) are right in identifying the state and the professions as "the great rationalizers of the second half of the twentieth century." They also correctly suggest that the former is more likely to be associated with the use of coercion and the latter with normative—although, I would propose, even more with cognitive—modes of influence. This in turn suggests that nation-states may be primarily in the business of creating rationalized structural frameworks while the professions are more likely to be engaged in creating rationalized cultural systems. Whether or not these two systems are convergent will depend, then, on the nature of the relation between the state and the profession or professions active in that environment at any given time. While this formulation is admittedly simplistic, it does attend to DiMaggio's (1988a) plea that institutional theorists more clearly identify what actors or agents are involved when institutional effects are asserted. In addition, it suggests that varying types of actors not only use different types of influence mechanisms but also affect different types of targets. Finally, it reinforces an important point noted above regarding the variety of cultural systems in institutional environments. There is not one but many forms of rationality, and there may be competing conceptions as to how a particular environment is to be appropriately structured. For example, state administrators are more likely to create bureaucratic arrangements that centralize discretion at the top of the structure and allow relatively little autonomy to officials. By contrast, professional actors, both individual and corporate, will prefer weaker and more decentralized administrative structures that locate maximum discretion in the hands of practitioners. Both forms embody rational assumptions and modes of consciousness, but give rise to quite different structural arrangements (see Alford 1975; Scott 1985).

BOUNDING ENVIRONMENTAL ELEMENTS

For years organizational analysts could treat environments as residual—as everything that is "not system." But when, under open system models, environments became important causal forces, it was necessary to be more explicit about their definition. In particular, there is need to "bound" them—to define their limits and identify their constituent elements so that their characteristics may be assessed.

We have reviewed in detail elsewhere the important early models developed to specify the boundaries of organizational environments (see Scott and Meyer, this vol., ch. 5; Scott 1987b:119–25). Organizational *sets* seem best suited to supporting analyses focused on the power-dependency relations that arise out of the exchange of resources and information (see, e.g., Evan 1966; Thompson 1967; Pfeffer and Salancik 1978). Organizational *populations* are useful in examining the differentiation of organizational forms that arise out of competitive interactions (see, e.g., Hannan and Freeman 1977; Aldrich 1979). And the identification of *interorganizational fields* has helped us to examine the kinds of differentiation and system linkages that arise among a diverse set of organizations sharing a common locality (see, e.g., Warren 1967, 1972; Turk 1977).

Such models represent an important advance on formulations that attempted to identify generalized environmental forces or dimensions, as DiMaggio (1986a:337) has noted:

> This shift from an environment described in general terms as turbulent, stable, or munificent, to a field constructed from measurement of attributes or relations of a specific set of organizations, provides important analytic advantages. . . . It is less useful to learn that an organization's environment is "munificent" or "turbulent" than to identify the organizational sources of such munificence or turbulence. Second, the effects of environmental variables may depend on the position that an organization occupies in its field.

Nevertheless, each of these earlier models is seriously flawed when considered as a basis for institutional analysis. The organizational set identifies environmental boundaries on the basis of exchange of resources critical to a given, "focal" organization. The organizational population restricts attention to competitive interdependence among similar types of organizations. And the interorganizational field employs geographical boundaries—usually based on political definitions, for example, metropolitan jurisdiction—thus excluding nonlocal influences.

In recent years, several investigations have proposed a new generation of similar models, with varying labels, that are more consistent with and supportive of institutional conceptions. I have suggested the generic term "functional organizational fields" to identify these models (see Scott 1987b:124). Other labels include "industry system" as employed by Hirsch (1972, 1985), "societal sector" utilized by Meyer and me (Scott and Meyer, ch. 5), and "organizational field" as defined by DiMaggio and Powell (ch. 3). In all of these models, boundaries are defined in functional rather than geographic terms. All begin by identifying a group of organizations producing similar products or services (much like the concept of population as employed by the ecologists or industry group as employed by economists) but include as well their critical exchange partners, sources of funding, regulatory groups, professional or trade associations, and other sources of normative or cognitive influence. Nonlocal as well as local connections, vertical as well as horizontal ties, and cultural and political influences as well as technical exchanges are included within the organizational field of forces viewed as relevant.

Many problems remain for the investigator who attempts to operationalize this conception of environmental boundaries: What degree of connection or influence is required to include an organizational actor within the functional field? How specific are the criteria we use in assessing "similarity" of products or services (a broader or more abstract criterion will greatly increase the size and complexity of the field identified)? How do we handle the problem that large, differentiated, and/or diversified organizations participate in multiple functional fields? How do we assess and bound cultural patterns, which are often less visible and more subtle and invasive than structural connections? These and similar difficulties will challenge researchers for some time to come.

In spite of these operational difficulties, I am in full agreement with DiMaggio's (1986a:337) imperialistic assertion that "the organizational field has emerged as a critical unit bridging the organizational and societal levels in the study of social and community change." The functional field serves as a useful basis for both bounding the environment of an organization whose structure or performance is to be examined from an institutionalist perspective as well as defining a significant intermediate unit—a critical system in its own right—to be employed in macrosociological analyses.

Connecting Institutional Environments and Organizational Structures

I turn now from considering how institutional theorists have attempted to conceptualize the environments of organizations to examine some of the arguments advanced by institutional analysts to explain the effects of environments on organizations.[2] While all institutional theorists assert that such effects occur, a review of the current research literature suggests that there exists little agreement among them as to how and why and where—in what parts of the structure—such changes occur.

While I have not attempted to conduct a comprehensive survey, my reading of various institutional analyses has identified several different accounts of structural influence. The accounts vary in one or more respects: (1) what types of environmental elements are singled out for attention; (2) what influence or causal mechanisms are identified; and (3) what aspects of organizational structure are affected. The categorization scheme places major emphasis on the causal arguments advanced. In the following discussion, seven different arguments are identified.

THE *IMPOSITION* OF ORGANIZATIONAL STRUCTURE

Some sectors or fields contain environmental agents that are sufficiently powerful to impose structural forms on subordinate organizational units. Nation-states do this when mandating by law changes in existing organizational forms or when creating a new class of administrative agencies. Corporations also do this when acquiring new companies or reorganizing existing divisions. DiMaggio and Powell (1983) refer to this type of influence as "coercive," but it may be useful to employ more fine-grained distinctions. Under the category of imposition, I would distinguish between two types: imposition by means of authority versus imposition by means of coercive power. We would expect changes in structural forms imposed by authority to meet with less resistance, to occur more rapidly (see Tolbert and Zucker 1983, on the diffusion of municipal reforms in those three states that adopted civil service requirements for all cities), and to be associated with higher levels of compliance and stability than those imposed by force. The structural changes should also be less superficial and loosely coupled to participants' activities than those imposed by coercive power. While institutionalists share with others—for example, resource dependency theorists—an interest in power processes, an institutional perspective gives special emphasis to authority relations: the ability of organizations, especially public organizations, to apply legitimate coercion (see Streeck and Schmitter 1985).

THE *AUTHORIZATION* OF ORGANIZATIONAL STRUCTURE

A related but distinct type of institutional mechanism involves the authorization or legitimation of the structural features or qualities of a local organizational form by a superordinate unit. The feature that distinguishes this mode from the case of imposition is that the subordinate unit is not compelled to conform but voluntarily seeks out the attention and approval of the authorizing agent. As DiMaggio and Powell (1983) note, this type of "normative" pressure is especially likely to be found in professional sectors. Thus, voluntary hospitals in the United States are not required as a condition of their operation to receive accreditation from the Joint Commission on Accreditation of Hospitals, but most find it in their own interests to seek out such legitimation. (Accreditation has also become a condition for eligibility for reimbursement from public funds, but it is important to analytically distinguish authorization from inducement effects, described below.) In their study of the population of voluntary social service agencies operating in Toronto, Canada, during the period 1970–80, Singh, Tucker and House (1986) used as measures such authorization mechanisms as a listing in the *Community Directory of Metropolitan Toronto* and receipt of a charitable registration number issued by Revenue Canada. Such voluntarily sought indicators were treated as signifying "external legitimacy"—as announcing that the organizations listed had been "endorsed by powerful external collective actors" (Singh, Tucker, and House 1986:176). The Toronto study provides strong evidence that receipt of such endorsements was associated with improved life chances: listed organizations showed significantly higher survival rates than those that were unlisted over the period surveyed.

I employ the term *authorization* in this context in order to directly connect this mechanism with an earlier treatment of authority norms. In our discussion of the sources of authority, Dornbusch and I (Dornbusch and Scott 1975:56–63) define *authorization* as the process by which norms supporting the exercise of authority by a given agent are defined and enforced by a superordinate unit. Authority is legitimated power; legitimated power is normatively regulated power. When an organization's use of power is authorized it is, presumptively, both supported and constrained by the actions of officials superior to it and in a position to oversee its appropriate use.

In many arenas there are multiple possible sources of authorization. For example, private schools may seek accreditation from public education agencies but also have the option of being certified by numerous private professional and trade associations. Organizations must determine with which, if any, external sponsors to connect. There are often costs as well as gains associated with these choices. Organizations may have to modify their structures and/or activities in various ways in order to acquire and maintain the support of external agents; at a minimum they must provide information and access to the representatives of these bodies. The prevalence of authorization processes across a wide variety of sectors, however, suggests that, for many types of organizations, the gains associated with these external connections far outweigh the costs.

The *Inducement* of Organizational Structure

Many organizational fields do not contain agents having power and/or authority to impose their own structural definitions on local organizational forms. But they may be in a position to provide strong inducements for organizations that conform to their wishes. Relatively weak nation-states, like that in the United States, often resort to such marketlike control tactics because they lack the authority to impose their programs on subordinate units. (This weakness is especially likely to occur when these units are located in a different layer of the federalist "layer cake" from the control agent. For example, federal educational agencies lack authority over their counterparts in individual states.) To employ a distinction Meyer and I have found useful, the U.S. government frequently is able to obtain authority over *funding* decisions within a given societal sector such as educational services or health care but not over *programmatic* decisions, which remain under the control of state or local organizational officials or professional agents (see Meyer and Scott 1983b).

Inducement strategies create structural changes in organizations and organizational fields by providing incentives to organizations that are willing to conform to the agent's conditions. Typically, the funding agency specifies eligibility conditions: conditions for receiving funds in the form of grants, contracts, tax benefits, and so forth, or reimbursement for work performed. The recipient organization usually must provide detailed evidence concerning continuing structural or procedural conformity to requirements—accounts of who performed the work, how the work was performed, on whom the work was performed—in the form of periodic reports. Complex accounting control systems are employed because more straightforward command-and-compliance authority is lacking. The agent can control what the organization is doing only if and when the organization is using the agent's funds to do it.

DiMaggio's study (1983) of the effects of controls exercised by the National Endowment for the Arts provides a carefully researched example of this type of influence strategy. This study, along with that conducted by Meyer, Strang, and me on federal funding of educational programs, points to an important feature of this approach affecting where the structural changes are most likely to occur. Inducement strategies create increased organizational isomorphism (structural similarity), but more so at the intermediate than the operative organizational field level. The major effects reported by DiMaggio are on the state's art councils—their existence, form, and functions being specified by NEA as a condition for eligibility of funding—rather than on the arts organizations themselves. Similarly, the major effects of federally funded programs we observed in our research on educational systems were found at the level of the states' educational agencies and the district offices rather than at the level of the individual school—although most of the programs examined were designed to influence the behavior of school teachers, not state and district administrators (Meyer, Scott, and Strang 1987).

For many reasons, organizational structures created by inducements are unlikely to have strong or lasting effects on the organizational performances they are intended to affect. In the usual case, they constitute only one of many funding streams on which the organization relies to sustain its performance, and organizational participants have been observed to have a strong aptitude for "comingling" funds from varying sources while carrying on their normal operations in pursuit of organizationally defined purposes (see Sproull 1981). The funding agent's distinctive purposes are more likely to be reflected in the preparation of organizational "accounts"—both fiscal and retrospective reporting—than in the performance of workers. An additional explanation of the weakness of inducement strategies is suggested by the social psychological literature that reports that participants' internal motivation and commitment is weakened, not reinforced, by receipt of external incentives (see Deci 1971; Staw et al. 1980).

The *Acquisition* of Organizational Structure

Probably the influence process most widely studied by institutional analysts has involved the acquisition—the deliberate choosing—of structural models by organizational actors. Whether because of the effect of memetic or normative mechanisms, organizational decision makers have been shown to adopt institutional designs and model their own structures on patterns thought to be, variously, more modern, appropriate, or rational.

In analyses by Tolbert and Zucker (1983) of the adoption by municiple agencies of civil service reforms and by Fligstein (1985) of the spread of multidivisional forms among large United States corporations, the diffusion of a novel organizational pattern was observed across a field of similar, autonomous organizations. When a new structural pattern is voluntarily adopted by organizational managers—in contrast to the situations described above in which the major impetus for the change comes from outside the organization—then analysts must attempt to rule out an obvious competing explanation: that the changes are embraced for efficiency reasons—because they are expected to improve technical performance. This is easier said than done. The approaches employed to date are indirect, and the results are subject to varying interpretations. For example, Tolbert and Zucker argue that "internal"—for example, demographic—characteristics of cities predicted adoption of civil service reforms in earlier but not later periods, asserting that the former officials were driven by "rational" motives—an interest in excluding immigrants from political power and improving control—while later adopters were motivated by conformity pressures—a concern to appear up-to-date. However, it could be that later city officials confronted different types of internal governance issues to which civil service reforms were viewed as a rational solution.

In comparison with imposed or induced structural changes, one would expect acquired changes to be less superficial. Organizational managers should be more committed to them and in a better position than external agents to encourage their adoption and implementation or, if necessary, to inspect and enforce conformity to them. Williamson (1975), among others, has argued that organizational managers have superior audit capacities compared to external regulators or exchange partners.

The *Imprinting* of Organizational Structure

While there have been relatively few empirical studies of imprinting—the process by which new organizational forms acquire characteristics at the time of their founding which they tend to retain into the future—this phenomenon has been much discussed since it was first introduced by Stinchcombe (1965) in his seminal essay. He offers illustrative evidence concerning the imprinting process by noting how the basic features associated with various industries—the characteristics of the labor force, establishment size, capital intensity, relative size of the administrative bureaucracy, ratio of line to staff workers, proportion of professionals within the administration—varied systematically by time of founding. In a later study, Kimberly (1975) showed that the type of program, staffing, and structures employed within a population of rehabilitation organizations varied according to when the units were established.

The mechanism posited to account for these results embodies Berger and Luckmann's (1967) central argument that organizations acquire certain structural features not by rational decision or design but because they are taken for granted as "the way these things are done." This taken-for-granted character of the form is then argued to be an important basis for its persistence over time.

The *Incorporation* of Environmental Structure

We have been taught by March and others (e.g., March 1981; March and Olsen 1984) that everything that happens is not necessarily intended, that every outcome is not the result of a conscious decision process. This insight helps account for some of the effects of institutional environments that I and my colleagues have described in a number of recent studies (see Meyer and Scott 1983b; Scott and Meyer 1988; Meyer et al. 1988).

It is a well-known proposition in open systems theory that organizations will tend to map the complexity of environmental elements into their own structures (Buckley 1967). We have pursued empirically a specific instance of this argument: that "organizations operating in more complex and conflicted environments will exhibit greater administrative complexity and reduced program coherence" (Scott and Meyer 1988:129). To test this prediction, we examined the organization of societal sectors that are both centralized and fragmented—a situation, we argue, that creates disproportional administrative complexity in the structure of local organizations attempting to relate to them (see also Meyer and Scott 1983b).

The argument here is not that environmental agents require by power and/or authority such administrative development (although they sometimes do), nor is it that environmental agents necessarily provide incentives for administrative elaboration (although they sometimes do so), nor is it that organizational managers consciously decide to add components to their administrative structures in order to deal more effectively with a differentiated environment (although, again, they sometimes take such actions). Rather, it is that via a broad array of adaptive processes occurring over a period of time and ranging from co-optation of the representatives of relevant environmental elements to the evolution of specialized boundary roles to deal with strategic contingencies, organizations come to mirror or replicate salient aspects of environmental differentiation in their own structures. They incorporate environmental structures.

This type of institutionalization process, in which organizational structure evolves over time through an adaptive, unplanned, historical process, is perhaps most consistent with Selznick's (1957) version of institutionalization. And in its emphasis on unintended resultants, history-dependent causal determinants, and inertial structural residues, it also shares much in common with the "new institutionalism" in political science as described by March and Olsen (1984).

THE *BYPASSING* OF ORGANIZATIONAL STRUCTURE

Yet another view of the relation between institutional environments and organizational structure developed out of our research on schools. We have proposed that, in important respects, much of the orderliness and coherence present in American schools is based on institutionally shared beliefs rather than on organizational structures (see Meyer, Scott, and Deal 1981).

Of course, it is the case for schools, pursuant to virtually all of the arguments summarized up to this point, that institutional beliefs, rules, and roles come to be coded into the structure of educational organizations. As Meyer and Rowan (1978:96) argue: "In modern society . . . educational organizations have good reasons to tightly control properties defined by the wider social order. By incorporating externally defined types of instruction, teachers, and students into their formal structure, schools avoid illegitimacy and discreditation."

In research on the belief systems and the existence of rules reported by various classes of school participants—superintendents, principals, teachers—we discovered that there existed a good deal of consensus across these role groups as to the extent of educational policy regarding curricular materials, grades, student conduct, and similar matters. This is not surprising in a highly institutionalized context. However, such agreements were little affected by organizational boundaries: teachers and principals within the same school as well as teachers, principals, and superintendents in the same district did not show higher levels of consensus on educational policies than that present across the role groups generally—groups whose members were selected from a diverse sample of schools in an urban metropolitan area.

It appeared that the high level of "overall agreement about the extent of formal policies and the areas to which they apply" was the result not of organizational but of institutional processes:

> According to this view, agreements on the nature of the school system and the norms governing it are worked out at quite general collective levels (through political processes, the development of common symbols, occupational agreements). Each school and district—and each teacher, principal, and district officer—acquires an understanding of the educational process and division of labor, not from relating to others within the same organizational unit, but from participating in the

same institutional environment, from sharing the same educational "culture." (Meyer, Scott, and Deal 1981:159–60)

Today I would amend the argument to include students and parents among the primary carriers of the cultural belief system.

Such shared conceptions and symbols provide order not only by being mapped into organizational forms and procedures but also by their direct influence on the beliefs and behaviors of individual participants, making their organizational representation less essential. They are embedded in the cultural infrastructure. Organizational structures may only be required to support and supplement cultural systems that exercise a direct influence on participants.

According to such an argument, the existence of strong institutional environments may, under some conditions, *reduce* rather than increase the amount or elaborateness of organizational structure. Cultural controls can substitute for structural controls. When beliefs are widely shared and categories and procedures taken for granted, it is less essential that they be formally encoded into the organizational structure.

Conclusion

I have argued in this chapter that institutional theorists have transformed our conceptions of the salient environments of organizations; in particular, they have emphasized the importance of symbolic—both cognitive and normative—systems and structural features of organizational environments. They have also introduced new criteria for the bounding of organizational environments. In my summary of these developments in the first section of the chapter, I emphasized the importance of recognizing that most types of organizations confront multiple sources and types of symbolic or cultural systems and that they exercise some choice in selecting the systems with which to connect. Future studies could usefully focus attention on characterizing the variety of institutional sources (e.g., professions, nation-states), noting their preferred modes of influence (e.g., creating structural linkages versus cultural systems), and examining the styles of rationality they endorse (e.g., centralized rule-following versus decentralized discretion).

In the second section, I reviewed empirical studies that revealed a variety of mechanisms and a number of diverse arguments as to how institutional elements affect organizational structures. Since the arguments made are quite varied—and at least some of them make competing predictions—I suggest that institutional analysts need to become more articulate about the alternative paths utilized by institutional processes in exerting their effects and the factors determining such choices. The seven specific mechanisms I have detected in the empirical literature may nor may not hold up under further scrutiny as distinct types of institutional forces. Nevertheless, I would argue that sorting out and clarifying these arguments is an essential accompanyment to the continued development of institutional theory.

Acknowledgments

This chapter is a revised version of a paper prepared for a Conference on Institutional Change held at the Center for Advanced Study in the Behavioral Sciences, Stanford, California, May 15–16, 1987. In making revisions, the author has benefited from the comments and suggestions of Ronald L. Jepperson, John W. Meyer, and Walter W. Powell.

Notes

1. Excluded from review are related developments in political science (e.g., March and Olsen 1984) and in economics (e.g., Williamson 1981). These variants both draw on and depart from sociological work in ways too complex to review in this chapter.

2. An earlier version of this section first appeared in Scott 1987a.

8 Expanding the Scope of Institutional Analysis

WALTER W. POWELL

I argue that the full power of the institutional perspective has yet to be realized, due in part to ambiguities in some of the initial contributions to this line of work and to the fact that a somewhat stylized version of institutional theory—a restricted institutionalism—has thus far been explicated. My goal in this chapter is to tackle these shortcomings and to suggest ways to expand institutional analysis. I take issue with some of my previous work, done collaboratively with Paul DiMaggio, as well as with that of others who have employed institutional ideas with considerable flair and intellectual profit. My aim is not simply to be contentious, but to enable us to make progress in refining and sharpening our arguments.

Specifically, I contend that there are three areas in which the research program is in need of improvement: (1) Current work in the field makes too much of the differences between so-called market-driven sectors and institutionalized sectors. Institutional and competitive processes are not necessarily oppositional. As Braudel (1982:227) has noted, "it is too easy to call one form of exchange economic and another social. In real life, all types are both economic and social." (2) Although the observation that organizational practices and structures are loosely coupled with outcomes and policies is a key insight, it has led to what I believe is an inappropriate view that institutionalized organizations are relatively passive, inefficient manipulators of symbols rather than substance. A more productive line of research would focus on why less than optimal arrangements persist over time. And (3) we need an enhanced understanding of both the sources of heterogeneity in institutional environments and the processes that generate institutional change. The literature suggests a static, constrained, and oversocialized view of organizations.

A Restrictive Institutionalism?

Much of the empirical research thus far has focused on nonprofit organizations and public agencies (schools, the mental health sector, health care, cultural institutions, etc.). Perhaps inadvertently, this attention to the public and nonprofit sectors has led to what I believe is an unfortunate partitioning of the organizational universe. Meyer, Scott, and Deal (1981) suggest that there are technical and institutional sectors, while DiMaggio and Powell (1983), as well as Tolbert and Zucker (1983), posit two forces: competitive and institutional isomorphism. These were intended as analytical distinctions; obviously the two forms cluster in different ways across different fields. But many readers saw these categories as descriptions of different kinds of organizations. Such a view, however, cedes too much terrain to market processes. In addition, it implies that competitive settings are the turf where rational-actor models are most appropriate, and that institutional settings are dominated by satisficers who strive only to reduce uncertainty and ensure their continued existence.

A brief review of the various dimensions that have been employed in the literature will help us see how readers could have confused an analytical distinction with an empirical question. Meyer, Scott, and Deal (1981) argued that organizations differ in the extent to which their success is dependent upon solving technical problems or coping with institutional demands. The survival of some organizations depends more on achieving high standards of efficient internal production, while the survival of other organizations requires conformity to the normative codes of the relational networks in which they are embedded. Technical environments are those in which organizations are evaluated by their outputs. These firms closely monitor production and buffer their technical cores from environmental influences. Institutional environments are composed of organizations that are judged more by the appropriateness of their form than by their outputs. In institutional environments, organizations compete for social fitness rather than economic efficiency.

But if we view technical and institutional sectors as dichtomous alternatives, we run into trouble. To illustrate, let us make a stylized comparison of mental health clinics and the commodities market according to the dimensions of technical and institutional environments. Which faces a stronger institutional environment? The mental health clinic would seem to be the obvious choice. The mental health field is highly professionalized, subject to the regulatory jurisdiction of numerous local, state, and federal authorities as well as various semipublic accreditation bodies. Funding and support are often dependent upon legislative approval. The outputs of a mental health clinic are not closely monitored, nor are clinics likely to be richly rewarded for highly efficient use of their resources. There is little, if any, evaluation of the efficacy of treatment because the technology of mental health treatment is ambiguous and its outputs difficult to define, much less to measure. The very nature of the work process buffers clinics from efficiency tests; at the same time, however, the lack of understanding about mental health treatment renders the clinics vulnerable to conflicting external demands.

Commodities markets are a purportedly classic example of anonymous spot market exchanges. In spot markets prices adjust to changes in supply or demand

and market forces rule, unmediated by personal relationships or institutional factors. Traders are rewarded for effective and efficient performance. They are confronted with a continuous conflict of interest with all other traders for transactions at the most advantageous price. But this mode of economic exchange is buttressed by a number of both macrolevel and microlevel regulatory structures, without which trading would be too volatile to even pursue (Abolafia 1984; Leblebici and Salancik 1982). Trading abuses are to some extent policed by both federal rules (e.g., the U.S. Securities and Exchange Commission and the Commodity Futures Trading Commission) and the proscribed behaviors of the Exchange. Admission to the trading floor is restricted as well. But it is at the microlevel where reputational and relational considerations combine to monitor self-interested behavior and curb abuses. The standard transaction looks as follows:

Buyer → Broker → Brokerage house → Floor trader
↓
Clearing house
↓
Seller ← Broker ← Brokerage house ← Floor trader

Amid the noise and the shouting, an intricate series of transactions takes place, without even the benefit of a handshake. Large sums of money are spent on the wave of a hand, and floor traders keep track of numerous deals in their heads. What keeps this system from continuously breaking down, from falling prey to opportunism, fraud, and manipulation? How are traders not overwhelmed by the volume and volatility of their work? This market exchange is, in many respects, a highly institutionalized activity. The system is not some large impersonal trading floor, but rather a series of repeated transactions among small networks of trading partners who depend on one another to execute today's task faithfully because the expectation is that they will return to the trading floor tomorrow.[1] As Baker (1984) has shown in his study of the national securities market, one trades with people in proximity in order to reduce risk. In contrast to the predictions of microeconomics, Baker (1984) found that tightly knit micronetworks promote reliable communication that dampens price volatility.

This brief comparison of commodities markets and mental health clinics illustrates how difficult it is to neatly separate economic and institutional processes. Even the most competitive of activities is possible only because of micro- and macrolevel institutional arrangements that insure the reproduction of economic exchange. And organizations using poorly understood technologies, such as psychiatric treatment, are subject to output controls, such as case load quotas.

Similar confusion stems from the DiMaggio and Powell (ch. 3) two-stage model of organizational change. We argued that organizational fields have characteristic life cycles, with youthful periods in which efficiency properties dominate and mature periods in which institutional isomorphism governs survival. This suggests that early adoption of an innovation can be predicted in terms of the technical needs of potential adopters. But once some threshold of institutionalization is attained, adoption provides legitimacy rather than improved performance. Several empirical studies, dealing with such topics as the adoption of civil service reforms by city governments (Tolbert and Zucker 1983), the growth of city finance agencies (M. Meyer, Stevenson, and Webster 1985), and the adoption of personnel units and job evaluation programs (Baron, Dobbin, and Jennings 1986), lend support to his model of change.

There are, however, several shortcomings to this argument. First, it implies that conformity to institutional pressures is relatively easy and inexpensive. This smoke and mirrors form of adaptation (see Hannan and Freeman 1989:34) suggests that legitimation is merely a signaling process. Second, such an explanation erroneously portrays the initial practice as a kind of natural solution to technical imperatives. It ignores the many roads not taken, the alternative choices not pursued. As many organization scholars have suggested, there was nothing inevitable or natural about the way modern industrial organization evolved in the late nineteenth and early twentieth centuries (Piore and Sabel 1984; Fligstein 1990b). Third, the criteria for what is a good technical solution are often open to dispute. Engineers, economists, entrepreneurs, and environmentalists may all speak with authority, but they will be a most discordant chorus. Finally, the two-stage model obscures the entire process of institutional sponsorship through which some innovations come to be defined as useful and find broad acceptance.[2]

Alternatives: An Expanded Institutionalism

If these initial arguments are not entirely satisfactory, what other options might prove more fruitful? One alternative, suggested by Scott (see ch. 7 as well as ch. 5), is that institutional and technical factors are not dichotomous, but rather dimensions along which environments vary. Both types of environments place pressures on organizations to which they must be responsive in order to survive. Some sectors, such as banking or transportation, face both strong competitive demands as well as pressures from various regulatory bodies and consumer groups to conform to procedural requirements. If we are to pursue Scott's lead, we need to develop arguments about how technical and institutional pressures will influence the degree of heterogeneity and homogeneity in different organizational fields, and how such compositional effects influence the rates of diffusion of various practices from one firm to another.[3]

Another approach would be to uncover the varied ways in which institutional factors buttress or attenuate the competitive struggle among organizations. Support from political and social elites is a powerful stabilizing force. Government regulation protects many organizations from competitive pressures. Some organizations are buffered by the fact that they fund current activities with healthy sales from well-established product lines. In such cases, organizations may not need to outperform others in order to survive. But even among market-driven organizations, productive efficiency may have relatively little to do with survival. Hannan and Freeman (1989) suggest that selection in organizational populations does not necessarily favor the most efficient producers.[4] They argue that a number of strategic factors—market share, product reputation, successful advertising, physical location, patent protection, and the presence of legal threats—may be more consequential. Even the most efficiency-minded organizations rely on socially constructed beliefs such as more is better. Moreover, as Friedland and Alford suggest in chapter 10 of this volume, profit and risk are culturally constructed categories whose definitions vary widely across nation-states and within particular time periods.

A third approach is to show how political and institutional forces set the very framework for the establishment of economic action; these processes define the limits of what is possible. This view goes beyond the argument that the invisible hand operates with a light touch, or that economic action is embedded in social relations, and suggests that institutional processes help shape the very structure of economic arrangements. The rules of the wider environment determine not only what organizations can do, but which organizations can exist. There is not a grand natural selection process that determines efficient outcomes, but instead an unfolding process where the basic choices are limited and shaped by institutional and political processes.

Roy (1986) makes a strong case for the view that the government historically created—not just legalized—the modern corporation. His argument suggests that organizational forms—private and public corporations, partnerships, and nonprofit organizations—are socially constituted in both a legal and political sense. The U.S. government played a crucial role in the creation of the corporate form. The state provided the legal underpinnings of the corporate form of property, offered financial assistance to fledgling corporations, removed various barriers to a national market, and helped dampen the opposition of anticorporate forces. The state also played a similar role in the development of the nonprofit sector. Hall (1987) describes how a combination of religious and social elites and state and federal governments created the notion of stewardship, of private responsibility for the public good. He demonstrates how from 1865 on the advocates of private power concentrated their energies in two closely related areas: building private business corporations capable of operating on a national scale and transforming nonprofit institutions, especially colleges, into organizations that would facilitate their goal of expansion.

Once organizational forms are established, the role of the state, professional groups, and various organizational elites does not recede. As we have argued, the state and the professions have become the great rationalizers of this century (DiMaggio and Powell, ch. 3). They construct and legitimate organizational goals, standardize and distribute resources (tax laws, monetary policy, support for the banking system), and develop and maintain systems of bureaucratic control (personnel policy and labor law). More specifically, such varied activities as the adoption of the multidivisional form (Fligstein 1990b), accounting practices (Hopwood 1983; Covaleski and Dirsmith 1988; Meyer 1986), personnel policies (Baron, Dobbin, and Jennings 1986), and corporate philanthropy (Galaskiewicz 1985a; Useem 1987) are strongly shaped by institutional expectations and pressures. As firms grow in size and become involved in industry activities as well as dense networks of exchange, the institutionalized expectations of other firms, consumers, and the government exert greater influence on their behavior (Jacobs, Useem, and Zald 1991). Indeed, ecologists Carroll, Delacroix, and Goodstein (1988) argue that the expectations and the power of the modern state impose constraints on the diversity of organizational forms that can be adopted. In addition, the state often provides blueprints for acceptable means of organizing.[5]

The critical agenda for institutional analysis should be to show how choices made at one point in time create institutions that generate recognizable patterns of constraints and opportunities at a later point. Examples of these processes are abundant. The role of the International Monetary Fund in promulgating central banking procedures that now limit the choices available in confronting the debt crisis or the salutary effects of the World Health Organization's efforts at creating national health ministries, which are now crucial in the fight against AIDS, are two important contemporary illustrations.

Our contribution to the study of organizations will be greatly enriched if we are able to discern the sources of institutional patterns, their subsequent elaboration and potency, the degree to which these forces are sustained, and the kinds of settings where they operate with the greatest resonance. This agenda is consonant with the core insights of the institutional approach: modern organizations are more likely to arise, expand, and survive in those settings where the social environment creates and sustains the basic building blocks of formal, rational organization.

The argument that institutional patterns limit future options is, however, not only an assertion that applies to social structures. It is equally relevant to individuals. A key institutional insight is that individual preferences and choices cannot be understood apart from the larger cultural setting and historical period in which they are embedded.[6] To the extent that we accept the idea that individual self-definition is partly constituted by a wider institutional structure,[7] we challenge the notion that such recurring social forms as the labor market or the democratic polity are created and sustained by the aggregate choices of utility-maximizing individuals. As Meyer, Boli, and Thomas (1987:15) observe, these forms of organization are both widespread and extraordinarily durable. It is hard to imagine that the values and knowledge of large numbers of disparate individuals would be so uniform were there not widely accepted norms about appropriate behavior and models of action.

My call for an expanded institutionalism requires that the focus of empirical research should not be confined to the public and nonprofit sectors, and that more attention be directed to such core sectors of the economy as manufacturing and finance. A broadened theoretical agenda is required as well. We need to develop arguments as to why outcomes at some given point in time cannot be understood in terms of the preferences of actors existing at that same point in time, but must be explained as the product of previous choices, that were shaped by institutional conventions and capabilities. This requires much more sophisticated analysis of how institutions, by precluding some options and facilitating others, shape individual identities and public discourse.

Institutional Reproduction

The initial attention to nonprofits and the public sector meant that many of the organizations were characterized by poorly understood technologies, operated in environments with modest technical demands, and experienced weak selection pressures. An important insight that emerged from this work is that pressures for efficiency are variable—they are felt with differential force in different organizational fields. These studies underscored the discrepancy between what organizations say they do and what they actually do. Loose coupling between procedures and purposes was found at many levels—between formal and informal organization, across different hierarchical levels, between espoused policy and observed outcomes (March and Olson 1976).

These were important findings, and they remain so. But the manner in which they have been interpreted and disseminated in the organizational literature strikes me as somewhat peculiar. Institutional arguments have become associated (inappropriately, in my opinion) with notions that organizations are not concerned with task performance; instead organizations are viewed as manipulators of appearances, seeking only legitimacy. Others have used institutionalism as a residual explanation, useful for explaining outcomes when more instrumental explanations proved inadequate. The individuals who inhabited institutionalized fields were regarded as unsure of their interests or unable to realize them, thus making them susceptible to mimetic influences. Institutional arguments and perspectives such as rational choice or population ecology were portrayed as oppositional.

My own view is that this "institutionalization of the institutional perspective" is misguided. It highlights specific findings at the expense of the basic argument that institutional pressures stem from more general societalwide processes of rationalization. It ignores the insight that if organizations can manipulate the symbols they present to the external environment, then they must also be adept at producing and controlling symbolic elements as well.

Clearly some of this "misreading" is the result of a lack of clarity in some of the original statements. For example, DiMaggio and Powell suggested that "structural change in organizations seems less and less driven by competition or by the need for efficiency" and that "isomorphic processes proceed in the absence of evidence that they increase internal organizational efficiency" (see this vol., ch. 3). Zucker (1987:445) contended that institutionalized organizations "serve many important legitimating functions, but the core tasks are not performed as well as they would be in a market-oriented organization, and basic organizational objectives are also often deflected."

Sometimes institutional theorists suggested that institutional processes both were inefficient *and* enhanced survival prospects. Scott and Meyer (this vol., ch. 5) maintain that "organizational conformity to the institutional environment simultaneously increases positive evaluation, resource flows, and therefore survival chances, and reduces efficiency." Meyer and Rowan (this vol., ch. 2) and DiMaggio and Powell (ch. 3) both argue that organizations adopt practices or structures mandated by their environment, even when these elements are poorly suited for the task at hand. The reason for this conformity to external demands, however, is to ensure organizational survival, because these external agents are typically suppliers of key resources. The obvious question is how can practices that increase survival prospects also be regarded as inefficient? And if organizations are rewarded for compliance with external demands, how can we argue that conformity is not based on the calculating behavior of those who are seeking legitimacy?

Often in the very same papers where these equivocal statements appear, sensible amendments follow. For example, Scott and Meyer note that adherence to procedural specifications is one way in which stable organizational forms can be created and legitimated in conflict-ridden arenas. DiMaggio and Powell contend that organizations are rewarded for being similar to other organizations in their fields because it makes it easier to conduct exchanges, to attract personnel, to maintain a good reputation, and to be eligible for contracts and grants. The solution to this conundrum, as Jerry Davis (pers. com.) has pointed out to me, is to "rephrase the problem as one of joint optimization." Organizations adopt structures and practices that are in some respects suboptimal in order to gain needed resources. Organizations always have to consider numerous factors of production, any one of which might be used "inefficiently" in absolute terms but which combine with other factors to produce satisfactory outcomes.

I want to suggest that these ambiguities are due in part to our failure to attend to the issues of institutional persistence or reproduction. How are practices and structures perpetuated over time, particularly in circumstances where utilitarian calculations would suggest they are disfunctional? Why are practices reproduced when superior options are available? Why are less-than-optimal arrangements sustained, even in the face of opposition? As a starting point, let me suggest four avenues of institutional reproduction: (1) the exercise of power, (2) complex interdependencies, (3) taken-for-granted assumptions, and (4) path-dependent development processes.

Practices and structures often endure through the active efforts of those who benefit from them. Indeed, Stinchcombe (1968:107) defines an institution as "a structure in which powerful people are committed to some value or interest." He alerts us to the fact (often downplayed in institutional arguments) that "power has a great deal to do with the historical preservation of patterns of values." For good theoretical reasons, institutionalists have been reluctant to label something maintained solely through the exercise of power an institution. But it is clear that elite intervention may play a critical role in institutional formation. And once established and in place, practices and programs are supported and promulgated by those organizations that benefit from prevailing conventions. In this way, elites may be both the architects and products of the rules and expectations they have helped devise. But practices can also take on a life of their own and persist without active elite support. Chapter 11 by DiMaggio is an excellent case study of the successful institutionalization of a professional project—a particular model of what the art museum should represent and who should be its custodians.

A good deal of the influence of the modern professions stems from their control over the selection of new recruits, the socialization of successors, and control over the conditions of incumbency. Once such a system of control and reproduction is in place, it almost inevitably attempts to expand its jurisdiction (Abbott 1988). Skilled institution builders who gain from such a system of power will typically expend considerable effort to maintain their dominance. The professional project can be employed by others, however, as a resource to justify alternative courses of action. What is missing in both research on the professions and institutional analysis is a good understanding of the ecology of competition: Why are the claims of some occupational groups readily accepted, while those of others rejected or questioned? Why is the exercise of professional or elite power buttressed by institutional sponsorship and effectively reinforced by carrots and sticks in some cases, but not others?

Reproduction is not necessarily contingent upon recurrent collective mobilization, a point underscored by Jepperson in chapter 6. Persistence may not depend upon active agency because a particular practice or structure is so embedded in a network of practices and procedures that change in any one aspect requires changes in many other elements (see Thompson 1967 on long-linked technologies and serial interdependence). This is the standard inertia argument for why U.S. automakers were reluctant to retool their assembly lines, even in the face of considerable evidence that large, gas-guzzling autos would soon be in less demand (Abernathy 1978). When interdependencies extend across organizational boundaries to other organizations, particularly in the case of hierarchical relations (e.g., to the central office, to higher authorities such as the state, or to central coordinating agencies), then practices become quite resistant to efforts at change. The literature in economics on standard setting and network externalities (Katz and Shapiro 1985, 1986; Arthur 1989) aptly illustrates the technological interdependencies that accrue once the choice of a technology or industrywide set of rules is made. The more other users there are, the less likely will firms be willing to undergo change to a new regime, even when the new technology is superior. This argument can easily be extended beyond the realm of technology. Common procedures that facilitate interorganizational communication may be maintained, even in the face of considerable evidence that they are suboptimal, because the benefits associated with familiarity may easily outweigh the gains associated with flexibility. Altering institutional rules always involves high switching costs, thus a host of political, financial, and cognitive considerations mitigate against making such changes.[8]

Social patterns may also reproduce themselves without active intervention when practices and structures come to be taken for granted, hence they are not questioned or compared against alternatives (see the discussion of practical action in our introduction). Institutional patterns shape behavior such that some courses of action are perceived as natural and legitimate. I take this point to be a key one of Giddens's (1984) structuration theory: institutions provide shape to the moral definitions of the purposes and regulations of recurrent social life. Thus, in enacting their roles in the workplace, the worker and the manager may never think about the institutional arrangements (of power, control, status, etc.) that these work roles and settings imply.

Organizational procedures and forms may persevere because of path-dependent patterns of development in which initial choices preclude future options, including those that would have been more effective in the long run. These processes occur both at the level of the individual organization and at the collective level of the industry or the field. Path-dependent arguments help account for one of the most interesting observations in organization theory: Stinchcombe's (1965:153–64) classic paper on founding processes, which suggested an imprinting of basic structural features—labor force composition, firm size, capital intensity, etc.—that vary systematically by time of founding and remain fairly constant over time.

Organizational memory and learning processes not only record history, they shape its future course; the direction of that path depends greatly on the processes by which memory is maintained (Levitt and March 1988). Learning in organizations is often superstitious, that is, organizations become committed to routines that are shaped by early and often arbitrary successes (Nystrom and Starbuck 1984; Powell 1986). Success is frequently the enemy of experimentation and leads to competency traps—circumstances in which favorable performance with an inferior procedure or technology leads an organization to accumulate additional experience with it, thus keeping knowledge of a more advantageous procedure or technology too limited to make it rewarding to use (Levitt and March 1988).

The economic historians Brian Arthur and Paul David, in a provocative set of papers, have modeled the surprising manner in which historical small events can become magnified by positive feedback. As a result, the economy, under conditions of increasing returns, can dynamically lock itself in as a result of chance decisions to a technological path that is neither guaranteed to be efficient, nor easily altered, nor predictable in advance. Research on path-dependent processes has focused primarily on competition between generic technologies (such as the turn-of-the-century contest between steam- and gas-powered engines), on competing standards (e.g., the QWERTY keyboard typewriter, or computer programming languages or software), on rival sponsored technologies (VHS versus BETA video recorders), and on competing distribution systems. This branch of economic history may strike some as rather arcane, but it shares with institutional theory a critical insight: practices and procedures have positive external effects; consequently choices made by one organization are very much influenced by the choices of others. These external economy effects have the potential for multiple equilibria and "lock-in."

Paul David (1986) observes that path-dependent processes are often governed by historical accident or the particular sequences of choices made close to the beginnings of a process. A path-dependent sequence of economic changes is one in which important influences upon the eventual outcome can be exerted by small, fortuitous events. Several key features are common to path-dependent processes: (1) strong technological interrelatedness, (2) increasing returns, or positive feedback, and (3) irreversibility of investment due to learning and habituation.

Brian Arthur (1989, 1990) demonstrates that many technologies show increasing returns: the more a technology is adopted, the more it is improved, and the greater its payoff. When this occurs and adoption cumulates, the choice of the technology becomes structurally rigid and locked in. Even though individual choices are sensible, there is no guarantee that the particular outcome selected from among many alternatives will be the "best" choice. And because of the lock-in feature, later competing improvements cannot be easily capitalized on. The increasing returns to adoption arise from a number of sources: learning by using, interorganizational interdependencies, scale economies, informational increasing returns, and technological interrelatedness. But the technology that "takes the market" need not be the one with the longer-term higher payoff to adopters.

Path-dependent models suggest that institutional arrangements are not likely to be flexible; they cannot change rapidly in response to perturbations in the environment. The self-reinforcing feedback mechanisms that support path-dependent processes make it difficult for organizations to explore alternative options. While these models have principally been applied to technology adoption, their significance is potentially broader. Arthur (1987) has demonstrated their utility for explaining agglomeration economies such as the success of Silicon Valley, as well as their relevance for international trade and industrial organization (1988a, 1988b). Similarly, the applicability of path-dependency notions to bandwagon effects in science, mass communication, and popular culture seems clear. As a general explanation of the extent to which practices and procedures become more attractive, more developed, and more widespread, the more they are adopted, path-dependent arguments hold considerable promise for the explanation of institutional persistence.[9]

This discussion illustrates several of the various ways in which institutional arrangements that are not necessarily optimal may nevertheless persist over time. Once particular sets of social arrangements are in place, they embody sunk costs—economic and psychological—that cannot be recovered. Shared expectations arise that provide psychological security, reduce the cost of disseminating information, and facilitate the coordination of diverse activities. Efforts at change are often resisted because they threaten individuals' sense of security, increase the cost of information processing, and disrupt routines. Moreover, established conceptions of the "way things are done" can be very beneficial; members of an organizational field can use these stable expectations as a guide to action and a way to predict the behavior of others. These are not necessarily stories about inefficiency or maladaptation, but rather plausible accounts of how practices and structures reproduce themselves in a world of imperfect information and increasing returns.

Explaining Heterogeneity and Change

In chapter 3 of this volume, we argue that institutionalization is a constraining process that forces units in a population to resemble other units that face the same constraints. Our image of how this process unfolds is best summarized by the statement that "organizational actors making rational decisions construct around themselves an environment that constrains their ability to change further in later years." In this formulation, institutional isomorphism appears as somehow external to human action, as a source of binding constraint. We neglected, however, to emphasize that each form of constraint is, in varying ways, also a form of enablement. Constraints open up possibilities at the same time as they restrict or deny others.[10] Our efforts at developing a theory of practical action (see introduction) are a step at remedying this omission.

I also want to suggest that much of the imagery of institutional theory portrays organizations too passively and depicts environments as overly constraining. There is a wide range of institutional influences, and internal responses to these pressures are more varied than is suggested by our initial arguments. Indeed, actors may use institutionalized rules and accounts to further their own ends, seeking legitimation for changes that enhance their prestige and power. Moreover, as we know from work in resource dependency theory (Pfeffer and Salancik 1978), organizations frequently attempt to resist or alter external demands that are placed upon them.

SOURCES OF VARIATION

What are the sources of variation in organizational responses to institutional pressures? Why do some institutionalized practices vary in the rate and extent of their diffusion, and why are some externally legitimated processes quickly adopted, while others fail to be endorsed or to receive only token support? Institutionalization is always a matter of degree, in part because it is a history-dependent process. Organizational fields are created at different times and under distinctive circumstances; thus they evolve according to divergent trajectories and at varying speeds. In addition, organizations may accommodate conflicting institutional demands in different ways. They may compromise with or resist external pressures, play one source of legitimacy and support off against another, or comply with some expectations while challenging others (see Powell and Friedkin 1986; Covaleski and Dirsmith 1988). If we recognize that institutional environments are complex and trace the sources of conflicting demands, then we can account for the circumstances when institutionalization is contested or incomplete. In order to make progress on these questions, we need a better understanding of the factors that promote heterogeneity in institutional environments as well as the forces that generate institutional change. In this last section, I outline several key sources of heterogeneity in organizational environments.

Resource Environments Vary Greatly

Most organizations obtain inputs—resources, legitimacy, personnel—from other organizations. Employees are hired after finishing their studies in educational organizations or completing their training with vocational programs or labor unions; finance capital is sought from banks and venture capitalists; supplies and materials are obtained from firms in other industries, sometimes located in other countries. Even within relatively tightly bounded organizational fields, no two firms will have the exact same pattern of resource flows. Complex resource environments create heterogeneity and allow for the possibility for organizations to respond strategically to external demands. When the boundaries of organizational fields are murky or penetrated by members of other fields (for example, medical care technology involves hospitals as well as high-tech firms), heterogeneity in organizational forms and practices will be even greater.

There Are Key Differences in the Structure of Industries and in How Organizations Relate to the State

Not only do industries vary enormously in terms of their size, dependence on exports, product and market life-cycle differences, labor and capital intensity, and so forth, but there is considerable divergence in the amount of direct and indirect state intervention in industry. Some government policies apply to all or most organizations, but many policies are either industry-specific or have unequal impact. Variation in business-state relations will lead to divergent patterns of organizational response to state mandates.

*American Society Generates Many
Levels and Types of Organizations,
with Overlapping Responsibilities,
Organizational Interpenetration,
and Systems of Partial
or Fragmented Governance*

Multiple levels of government—federal, state, and local—and different kinds of government agencies compete for control and provide dissimilar kinds of regulation as well as inducements. Contradictory pressures and overlapping jurisdictions create organizational heterogeneity and complexity (see Scott and Meyer, ch. 5; also Meyer 1986; Powell 1988). Competing demands from divergent segments of the environment lead organizations to develop specialized units to deal with the particular demands of different external constituencies. Organizations located in environments in which conflicting or incongruent demands are made upon them will be especially likely to generate complex organizational structures with disportionately large administrative components and multiple boundary units. While these substructures may look very much alike in organizations exposed to comparable demands, few organizations will face exactly the same set of pressures; thus, at the organizational level, there may well be wide diversity in form and practice.

*Government Requirements Are Not
Always Felt by Organizations
as Direct Coercion*

Paradis and Cummings (1986) suggest that the DiMaggio and Powell notion of coercive isomorphism emphasizes mandate at the expense of compromise and bargaining. Their study of the evolution of hospices led them to suggest that government did not simply impose its standards on newly designed social service entities. A process of negotiation and compromise occurred; bureaucrats and advocates try to hammer out solutions that are somewhat responsive to the demands of both parties. The more these compromises are fine-tuned to individual cases, the greater the heterogeneity within a field.

*Occupational and Professional
Projects Vary*

There is wide variation in the basis of the claims for legitimacy made by diverse occupations as well as disparate success in mobilization. Some occupations seek support externally, mobilizing through professional associations or craftlike guilds. When professions are successful, admission and access are commonly restricted and control over training and the credentialing process is garnered. In contrast, other occupations are less grand in their claims and seek instead to control the work process within their own functional departments. Such groups seek internal autonomy rather than external control. Thus different occupations and professions have competing conceptions as to how an organization ought to be structured. Professional and occupational diversity leads to heterogeneity and conflict within organizational fields.

> *Sources of Constraint Vary in Direct Relation to the Capability of Organizations to Shape or Influence the Nature of Institutional Expectations*

In chapter 3, DiMaggio and Powell identify three mechanisms of influence—coercive, mimetic, and normative—that shape organizations operating in the same field. Although we linked these mechanisms to different sources of influence, we argued that each mechanism had a comparable effect: increased homogenization in organizational practices and forms. But this formulation is too broad. As Scott (ch. 7) suggests, patterns of influence are felt with different force. Several factors are critical determinants of the potency of institutional pressures: whether constraints are based on recognized sources of authority, coercive power, or normative expectations (see Scott's discussion of multiple sources of authority); whether constraints are tied to fiscal or programmatic controls (see discussion in ch. 5, and the illustration of this in Powell 1988); and whether sources of influence are accepted with enthusiasm or actively resisted. Multiple, conflicting constraints provide opportunities for various kinds of organizational forms to be established. These cross-cutting institutional pressures provide a space for entrepreneurs to construct an organization out of a diverse set of legitimated practices.[11]

PATTERNS OF INSTITUTIONAL CHANGE

Early work in institutional theory was more attentive to organizational change than to sources of heterogeneity. For example, in chapter 3 we argue that things that are institutionalized tend to be relatively inert, that is, they resist efforts at change. Our view suggests that change is neither frequent nor routine because it is costly and difficult. When change does occur, we contend, it is likely to be episodic, highlighted by a brief period of crisis or critical intervention, and followed by longer periods of stability or path-dependent development. Periods of deregulation, for example, are likely to be followed by an era of consolidation. Major changes often occur when legal or other rule-maintaining boundaries are relaxed. But once an institutional order is back in place, it tends to reconstitute itself, walling itself off from outside influences.

This, in turn, can lead to highly rigid institutional arrangements, which may develop internal contradictions and again become vulnerable to challenge.

We suggested that most organizational innovations arise from outside of institutional channels. Within organizational fields, the locus of change will originate in those units that are least subject to isomorphic pressures. In the absence of incentives embedded in existing institutional arrangements, innovation and diversity will be more likely to come from the periphery of organizational fields or from outside sources. The case of workplace reform in the United States is an apt example.

In the United States, new forms of participative management ór workplace reform initially met with limited success. Most attempts at job redesign during the 1970s took place in new, typically nonunion, plants, while very little reform was accomplished in established firms (Kochan, Katz, and McKersie 1986). Other kinds of workplace changes took hold in family-owned firms (e.g., Cummins Engine) or in failing companies (where worker ownership was tried as a last resort). Innovative human resource management policies sprung from new industries (e.g., high tech), still early in their product life cycle (Kochan, McKersie, and Katz 1986). These developments were not surprising; new social practices routinely face both active resistance and recalcitrance on the part of those comfortable with the status quo. As Cole (1985:563) observes, "the major institutional actors—management, unions, government—displayed little interest in introducing new work structures." It was not until the late 1970s and early 1980s that core U.S. manufacturing firms, facing serious economic losses and daunting foreign competition, began to seriously consider and implement alternative forms of work organization.

The argument that sources of change and innovation come from the periphery has an obvious parallel with ecological arguments that contend that organizational change comes about through the replacement of existing populations by new organizational forms (Hannan and Freeman 1989). Hannan (1986b:89–90) endorses the proposition that general norms of rationality and specific organizational agents (such as the state, business schools, and professional associations) create strong pressures for structural homogeneity; however, he also suggests a countertendency. To paraphrase his argument, if the population of individuals who demand the services of organizations is heterogeneous, and if organizations are becoming more homogeneous, thus limiting the range of their outputs, then there will be a growing demand for products and services that is unfilled. This creates opportunities for "outlaw" entrepreneurs to experiment with new organizational forms. To the extent that the new forms are successful, change is introduced into organizational populations.

Hannan and Freeman (1989) suggest another explanation for organizational change when they point to the role of "multiplier" organizations. Some kinds of organizational innovations generate dramatic changes in the rates of founding of other organizations. The creation of the stock market was a notable example. Similarly, venture capital firms played a key role in the extraordinary expansion of high-technology companies in the 1960s and 1970s. What other kinds of explanations—more or less compatible with the basic tenets of the institutional approach—would help account for why some institutional practices fall into disfavor, why some innovations seem to spring from highly institutionalized organizations, and why processes of diffusion and imitation can lead to novel kinds of arrangements?

Unsuccessful Imitation

Attempts at replicating the practices of other organizations often result in unintended changes. This is most common when organizational routines or forms are transplanted across sociopolitical contexts: from blue-collar work to white-collar; from one profession to another; and from one nation-state to another (Westney 1987). In such cases, cultural differences as well as subtle (or perhaps overt) forms of resistance may create either local modifications or unplanned changes. As a result, *partial diffusion* may occur or new hybrid arrangements may take hold.

Recombination

Organizations located in complex environments, particularly those subject to both strong institutional and technical pressures, may model themselves after a highly diverse set of organizations. Novel recombinations may occur when organizations borrow from dissimilar sources.

Incomplete Institutionalization

The influence of external pressures may be partial, inconsistent, or short-lived. For example, government agencies, corporate sponsors, or community groups may have the influence to encourage the adoption of particular practices but lack the power to mandate them. In such cases, support for new policies may be strategic, that is, organizations will embrace them as long as it is in their own interests. Various collective actors, such as professional associations, trade associations, and other sources of reference group influence, may be able to promulgate ideas for change, but not require them. Similarly, government may legislate certain policies (such as equal opportunity employment), but leave the actual implementation of the policy unspecified. As a result, practices may become only weakly institutionalized. In each of these cases, practices that appear to have institutional support will have unequal staying power. As a result, policies may be introduced but not reproduced, or practices may take a firm hold for a short period, only to quickly wane when their source of normative support erodes.

The Recomposition of
Organizational Fields

A less common but quite dramatic form of institutional change occurs when the boundaries of established fields are rearranged. This process can unfold in a geographical fashion or as a result of political upheavals. Quite often, the two processes go in tandem. Such upheavals are most likely when established practices no longer confer benefits or serve to reduce uncertainty to the members of a field. For example, the de-evolution of some federal authority down to the level of states and municipalities during the Reagan era had a marked effect on the nature of government power. The various states and municipalities promulgated a much wider array of policies, sometimes serving as laboratories for governmental experimentation and other times rolling back the influence of state policies and turning initiatives over to the private or nonprofit sectors. Another example of both a geographic and political redefinition of a field is unfolding in Europe, as the European community moves toward integration in 1992 and the creation of an internal market. When the structure of fields changes in such a profound fashion, established organizations scurry to protect their interests and to reestablish rules and practices that favor the status quo. But boundary changes also bring upstarts to the fore and create the possibility for a redefinition of rules and assumptions that favor newcomers or challengers at the expense of incumbents.

Obviously, not all forms of social change can be explained from an institutional point of view. Many kinds of change—be they physical, ecological, or political—come as exogenous shocks. Stinchcombe (1965) has emphasized how both the expansion of a society's resource base (via population growth and/or economic development) and political crises either call into question or renounce existing ways of doing things and create the opportunity for all manner of new organizational arrangements. The key question is how much can institutions alter their practices and reshape their environment in response to exogenous shocks or internal stresses? Explicit attention to sources of heterogeneity and change should enable us to learn jut how pliable and adaptive institutions are.

Summary and Implications

The goal of this chapter has been to chart a new path for institutional analysis. My intention has not been to dismiss previous arguments, but to suggest profitable new questions that need to be tackled. We need to expand the domain of our efforts so that we can better understand the different institutional logics that are salient in a wide variety of organizational fields. Institutional arguments are applicable to a much broader terrain than the public or nonprofit sectors that have been the standard focus of extant research. We have tended to neglect the myriad ways in which professional groups and organizations can shape the institutional environment in which they operate.

We need much more research and theory on processes of reproduction. What kinds of social processes have irreversible tendencies? Are some practices or beliefs "sticky downward," that is, are certain things like the concept of citizenship rights, self-sustaining? Why is it that once established, some beliefs and procedures are relatively immune to challenge, while others are easily delegitimated? In what respects is competition the enemy of established institutions? Why is knowledge that can be monopolized more likely to become institutionalized? A key task, then, is to explain variation in the strength of institutional rules. Why do some institutional arrangements sanction or endorse specific goals and then specify the vehicles for attaining them, while other institutional pressures are more diffuse and thus subject to much greater experimentation and incremental adjustment?

To the extent that we develop a richer account of the structural sources of heterogeneity in institutional environments, we will be better suited to explain episodes of change. At what point are institutional orders stressed beyond their capacity to resist challenges and absorb new elements? When do the bundles of procedures and practices that make up an institutional regime lose their coherence and develop internal contradictions? Actions taken to respond to challenges and crises often lead to the establishment of new institutional powers and precedents. Yet at this point we know relatively little about how organizational fields change their structure and content.

We need to remain mindful, however, that a broadened institutional approach has definable limits. Not every cultural element or environmental influence is an institutional effect, a point Jepperson hammers home in chapter 6. The organization's literature commonly conflates institutional pressures with any kind of contextual effect. Institutional arguments, however, are inherently complicated because any analysis of forms or procedures that have attained a rulelike, self-sustaining character must recognize that these arrangements are both dependent variables at time t and independent variables at time $t + 1$. To explain how social actors and the patterns of action they engage in are institutionally anchored, we need both detailed ethographic studies that reveal how institutional practices come to be legitimated and large-scale, longitudial studies that explore the staying power of institutional arrangements. Much remains to be done, but the end product—a robust institutionalism—is worth the effort.

Acknowledgments

This chapter was written while the author was a fellow at the Center for Advanced Study in the Behavioral Sciences. During that period, financial support was provided by the National Science Foundation grant number BNS 84-11738 and the Exxon Education Fund. The author has benefited from com-

Walter W. Powell

ments by or discussions with Paul DiMaggio, Mark Granovetter, Ron Jepperson, Robert Keohane, Steve Krasner, Harrison White, and Mayer Zald.

Notes

1. Recent research in the sociology of markets (by scholars such as Abolofia, Baker, and Granovetter) focuses not on discrete transactions but instead highlights the vital role of reputation. This work illustrates how difficult and impractical it is to isolate an individual transaction from an actor's overall reputation.

2. As Meyer, Scott, and Deal 1981:175–76 points out in a discussion of unresolved theoretical problems, "technical organizations satisfy their environments with all sorts of commodities of abstract value that turn out to be concretely useless."

3. It would be useful to study how institutional influences have changed over time. For example, case studies of industries prior to state involvement or research on the origins of trade associations could provide insight into the process of institutionalization.

4. Hannan and Freeman 1989:37 contends that "selection processes are multidimensional and that efficiency in production and marketing, broadly defined, is only one of the relevant dimensions." The authors share the view of many political sociologists and institutional theorists that, in many circumstances, political and social ties are more important to survival than efficiency.

5. Ecologists have become quite responsive to the notion that institutional factors operate at the population level and can thereby shape competitive processes. The findings of Carroll and Huo 1986 show that institutional variables strongly affect the rates of founding and failure of newspaper organizations in the Bay Area. Hannan and Freeman 1987 contends that legitimation produces positive density dependence, that is, the strength of institutional rules endorsing rational organization affects the case of founding national labor unions. Tucker et al. 1988 (also see ch. 16 of this vol. by Singh, Tucker, and Meinhard) demonstrates how major institutional changes can dramatically alter the ecological dynamics within a population of social service organizations. The authors concentrate on the role of the state in establishing the conditions that stimulate organizational founding. In a companion paper, Singh, Tucker, and House 1986 shows that the endorsement of powerful collective actors helps reduce the mortality rate as organizations age, while the loss of external legitimacy significantly increases the likelihood of failure. The impact of legitimacy persisted when they controlled for organizational form, resource scarcity, munificence, and population density. This strand of research underscores the point that the analysis of institutional factors is fundamental to the study of formal organization. Although ecologists have operationalized the institutional environment in ways that are not wholly satisfactory to institutional theorists (see Zucker's 1989 critique), there is clearly an important area of consensus: institutional processes and ecological processes can be complementary.

6. In his rejoinder to Coleman's (1986) controversial outline of a theory of action, Sewell (1987) notes that arguments based on individual interests ignore "the burgeoning and multiple literatures on the social or cultural construction of the individual and of individual values" (p. 168). This literature, found in Marxism, in cultural anthropology

(e.g., Geertz 1973; Rosaldo 1980; Shweder and LeVine 1984), and in Foucault 1978 and Bourdieu 1977, maintains that individual interests are historically and culturally produced.

7. Obviously, societies differ considerably in the degree to which individual roles and characteristics are socially prescribed. The religious martyrs in Iran under the Ayatollah or the loyal employees of large Japanese firms are stark contrasts with the gold rush speculators on the Amazon frontier.

8. See Sundstrom 1988 for an interesting discussion of both economic and sociological reasons for institutional persistence.

9. Arthur 1990 suggests that there is a fundamental difference between those sectors of the economy that are heavily resource-based (e.g., agriculture, mining, bulk-goods production) and those that are knowledge-based. The former are subject to diminishing returns, while the latter entail increasing returns. In the latter case, increased production brings not only a drop in unit costs but more experience and greater understanding. But complex knowledge-based production is also much more subject, he argues, to lock-in processes, whereby chance events coupled with positive feedback determine technological trajectories.

10. Socialization is perhaps the best example of a process that fuses constraint and enablement. The literature on unobtrusive controls and premise setting speaks to this point (Simon 1957; Perrow 1977; Powell 1985a).

11. Good illustrations of this process can be found in such empirical studies as Rowan 1982, Powell and Friedkin 1986, and Covaleski and Dirsmith 1988.

9 The Public Order and the Construction of Formal Organizations

RONALD L. JEPPERSON AND
JOHN W. MEYER

Two decades ago, the determinants of the structure and expansion of formal organizations seemed straightforward. Functional and evolutionary ideas depicted formal organizing as a routine outcome of efficiency-generating competition of natural actors. Since this time, however, organizational theory has become more self-critical. Now even those rooted in neoclassical economics point out the institutional requisites of economic organization, some arguing that Western property rights and organizing forms are rare and unlikely constructions (esp. North 1983, 1987; also Hicks 1969; and, for commentary, Barzelay and Smith 1987). Outside of neoclassical theory, almost all current lines of thought reflect prominent attention to organizational environments (Scott 1987b).

But uncertainty about how to think about wider environments—in effect, about how to conceptualize society, its institutions, and institutional effects—leaves us without good answers to some classical questions about formal organizing:

> When, and why, does formal organizing arise and expand? What general implications follow from the manifest historical linkage of formal organization to the modern West? Current discussion largely avoids these issues, due to its implicit functionalism (whether politically left or right); we are thus without plausible explanations of organizational construction.
>
> Why do we find great commonalities in organizing forms and trajectories across the different Western systems? These commonalities—for example, in the great late nineteenth-century "organizational revolutions"—are an embarrassment to functional (or conflict) theories, which tie organizing to varying local interests or power structures.

What accounts for the prominent differences in amounts, domains, and traits of formal organization across modern nation-states? Much theory ignores systemic historical and political sources of such diversity (diversity that is known, in fact, to be great).

One reason for our relative silence about such questions is that we retain a limited view of the environment of organizing, seeing it mainly as a system of resources adjoining organizations, or their elemental actors and technologies, at some boundary. An excessive realism—freighted with assumptions about the prior and autochthonous existence of actors, technologies, and organizations—generates an impoverished view of the organizing environment and in turn makes it difficult to explain contextual commonality or diversity in organizing.

Current institutional thinking offers insights that may help. The core institutionalist contribution is to see environments and organizational settings as highly interpenetrated. In institutionalist imagery, first, actors and technical functions, taken as prior by other theories, are represented as being constituted by social environments, that is, given form and legitimacy by them, and then both enabling and constraining organizational form. The American "individual citizen," in both legal theory and social practice, is a most easily organizable entity. But this individual also has rights and powers that constrain organizing (blocking slavery, for instance). Similarly, the socially constructed interaction called therapy makes new additions to organizations possible, while also constraining them by defining professional personnel and procedures.

Second, environments are interpenetrated with formal organization directly: organizations exist as social ideologies with social (usually legal) licenses. Third, institutionalism suggests that the interpenetration of environments with organizing (and its actors and technical functions) is especially great with those features of social environments that are themselves highly rationalized, that is, with elements of what was traditionally called "civil society." Formal organization is not only interdependent with, but interpenetrated with, the various elements of rationalized society: modern actors and their "interests," legitimated functions and their functionaries, and agents of the modern collectivity such as state elites, and legal and professional theorists and practitioners.

Fourth, institutional theory makes explicit that both formal organizational systems and the rationalized society are dependent upon the modern polity, as it is embodied in the nation-state and the wider world system. Rationalized structures, from organizations to actors to technical functions and functionaries, derive their resources, meaning, and legitimacy from their linkages to modern rules of the public good.

Modern national polities vary in form. They vary especially in the ways they construct the rationalized society—the rationalized actors and functions (or technologies) that are available ingredients for and constraints upon formal organizing. Much variation in the amounts and forms of formal organizing in a modern polity can be accounted for by variations in social rationalization, such as (*a*) the construction of legitimate actors with autonomous interests; (*b*) the construction of legitimated technical or functional elements (e.g., corporate occupational groups, sciences, or professions); or (*c*) the degree to which such structures are absorbed directly in an expanded state organization.[1]

This chapter develops arguments about the ways in which formal organizing depends on the modern polity. Organizing is everywhere largely a precipitate of this polity and part of the substructure of the rationalized society it builds. Homogeneity around the world in organizing reflects homogeneity in the outlines of nation-state polities, and variation reflects polity variation. We proceed by developing our general argument about interpenetration (section 1), and about common organizational consequences of the Western nation-state model (section 2). We then turn to variation—the primary focus of this chapter—variation in the ways in which the modern polity form is institutionalized in different nation-states (section 3), and in consequent organizational variation (section 4). Finally (section 5) we discuss institutional processes of change in the polity, rationalized society, and (thus) in organizational systems.

The argument here contrasts sharply with powerful legacies of nineteenth-century theory. Unlike classical social and economic theory, we do not see organization as a natural product of "private" actors and interests. Rather, we see the actors, interests, and functions involved as publicly legitimated, as are the constructed organizations: modern organization is a creature of public authority. (The very term *private* indicates the delegation to, and public penetration of, society, which so characterizes the modern polity.) Modern society is, in a half-truth, a society of organizations. It is also the society of rationalized non-organizational elements—modern persons, professions, sciences, legitimate interests—which construct and constrain organizations.

Throughout, our usage of the term *formal organization* is conventional (see, e.g., Stinchcombe 1973:24 and 1965:142 for conceptualization). By *modern polity* we mean the system of rules conferring societal authority in pursuit of collective ends, establishing agents of collective regulation and intervention (Swanson 1971). We have in mind processes such as monetarization and democratization—the construction of markets and rights—and the institutionalization of goals such as collective progress and justice. By *rationalized society* we refer to the reconstruction and systematization of the elements of society around polity goals and integration: the construction of citizen-individuals, professions and other social technologies, sciences, and so on.[2] In our usage, the modern polity is a socially binding ideology, taking the form of a functional theory; the rationalized society is made up of the elements of such a model constructed in reality.

1. Formal Organizing and Rationalized Society in the Modern Polity

FORMAL ORGANIZING AND RATIONALIZED SOCIETY

Rationalized formal organization requires the great institutional structures of the rationalized society (Meyer and Rowan, ch. 2, this vol.). Any role system is likely to be embedded in some sort of institutional context, whether the role system is one of individual habit and taken-for-granted meanings, of group customs, or local (e.g., "organizational") culture. But rationalized formal organizing depends specifically upon a rationalized societal context, one in which the particular ingredients of formal organizing are formed and widespread, namely, calculating actors with codified interests, legitimate social functions, knowledge systems, and so on. More and more social domains and activities become subject to the normative standard of means-ends calculation (Moore 1979:1, 30).

THE MODERN POLITY, SOCIAL RATIONALIZATION, AND ORGANIZATIONAL RATIONALIZATION

The modern collective action model is a distinctive rule system organizing persons and their activity in terms of universalistically defined resources, and means to collective ends. There is recent and reinvigorated discussion of the rise to dominance of this polity form.[3] We do not enter this discussion here, but we do rely upon it as essential analytical context: the important outcome is that a distinctive polity form, a creation of the Europe-based world system, develops and expands worldwide.[4]

This polity reorganizes social life around two fundamental dimensions of rationalization: that of collective sovereignty and identity (defining the legitimated public agents, e.g., "actors," in society); and that of collective tasks or functions (defining and integrating human activity around universalized goals of justice and progress). Persons and activities are interpenetrated with collective authority and legitimacy; further, they are linked through elaborate social means-ends schemas and technologies. All the successful modern polities mobilized by rationalizing both their constituent political elements, and the collective functional responsibilities of (and relations between) these elements.

The institutions of the modern polity, in our conceptualization, include the state but are not limited to it. They also include, notably, a "public sphere" of collective discourse and social movements, and a rationalized, or "civil," society of publicly chartered but formally "private" bodies and agents (e.g., corporations, enterprise managers, science, professions, and modern individuals).

The modern polity then provides many opportunities, empowerments, resources, and legitimations enabling formal organization of all sorts of activities in terms of the claimed collective good. Polity centers construct and legitimate the necessary goals (e.g., the pursuit of material wealth), means/ends technologies (scientific forms of production or of education), standardized and universalized resources (monetarization), principles of collective sovereignty (property rules), and systems of rationalized control (models of hierarchy, principles of labor contracts). When these constructed elements are widespread and linked to universalized depictions of the moral and natural worlds, rationalized organizing is greatly facilitated.

ACTIVITY WITHOUT POLITY LINKAGE

Aspects of modern society that are not securely linked to polity rules embodying myths of the universal collective good—as in group, organizational, or subcultures—tend not to generate much rationalized organizational structure or much evolution of the rationalized society. Thus attempts to construct formal organization outside the modern polity (as with communes, the Hutterites, the Amish Mennonites, or various mafias) are notoriously unstable. Unrationalized "organizational cultures," similarly, do not persist or spread well. Legal, scientific, cultural, and administrative supports from a wider polity are crucial requirements of both social and organizational rationalization. Social entities or functions given collective standing as agents or aspects of the public interest, such as modern citizens or professions or associations (business, consumer, or environmental protection groups), are much more likely to become nodes of organizing than are social groups or activities without such standing.

THE WORLD SYSTEM AND
FORMAL ORGANIZING

Throughout its history, the nation-state polity has been integrated within a states system and a broader Eurocentric world polity. This broader polity is revealed in knowledge and religious systems; shared definitions of collective ends, means, and resources; and common models of control structures and sovereignty (see Bull and Watson 1984; Meyer 1987; and Mann 1986).

The evolving density of this competitive and isomorphic system—whether one sees it as driven by endogenous properties of the units or by the world institutional frame—generates a great deal of expansion and penetration. New social domains enter common imageries of progress and justice; new functions and groups in social life attain actor or member status. Unexpected properties of humans and their activity (sexual reproduction, education, mental health) are accounted and regulated by nation-state rules and ideologies, and reported on the world stage as universally significant events relevant to generalized images of progress (the GNP) or justice (equality).

Licenses and regulations occur mainly at the nation-state level, even with giant multinationals. World organization is very rapidly expanding, but is still only secondarily engaged in the direct constitution of organizations, actors, and functions. But by structuring so much modern value and activity in a system of explicit cultural, political, military, and economic competition and competitive isomorphism, the nation-state system (*a*) further intensifies the rationalization of society, but especially (*b*) increases the likelihood that this rationalization will lead to or be vested in formal organizing. It drives formal organizing both in the state, as state apparatus, and in society, as "private" formal organization.

SUMMARY

These ideas help explain why formal organization exists at all, either in state or in society—a clearly crucial phenomenon that postrationalist organization theory has almost given up as beyond explanation. Older theory, to be sure, assumed that formal organizing occurs because it is functional, more or less as claimed; current theory is more skeptical—on very good grounds—but can then no longer explain why formal organization is present. Our line of argument proposes that a wider polity (often worldwide) of universalistic collective definitions plays a governing role, combined with an expanding set of subunit national societies competing and copying each other within this frame. The slow evolution of natural law understandings does not sufficiently account for the expansion of formal organizing: there is a definite historical thrust to codify means and ends and controls in formalized structures, pressure for formal organization in both state and society. From this point of view, formal organizing is a sort of manic outburst of rationality created under considerable competitive urgency and, for the same reason, unlikely to work as chartered. (If social arrangements were naturally efficacious, why would messianic organization be perceived as necessary?) One can see the manic quality of formal organizing most clearly in the peripheries of the modern system, where external pressures make elaborate organization seem crucial in the struggle against failure and entropy.

2. Organizational Consequences of the Modern Polity Form: Some Commonalities

For many areas of social life, what is striking about the modern national polities under consideration is their commonality in the structuring of social activity and social identities. This commonality may be especially notable in those areas of social life built around rules of efficiency or effectiveness in means/ends relations. Comparative studies of education, for instance, suggest much more variation in the organization of its control (both by the world polity and nationally), than in the structuring of its goals and means/ends relations. We focus in this section on important institutional commonalities in another system of activity in which means/ends relations are prominent, both in social activity and in collective conceptions—the economy. We stress throughout how the economy is formed within, and interpenetrated with, the broader polity, and how common polity elements seem to account for many commonalities in formal organizing within this constructed economic realm.

THE ECONOMY

Images depicting the economy as a "private" domain are misleading ones; older images of a "public household" are probably more apposite theoretically. So-called private organizations, private actors, or private functional groups mainly represent public or collective authority and responsibility delegated to subunit agents or functionaries. Thus, modern polities have two sets of collective agents managing economic organization: state officials, and business enterprise managers. Corporate managers are social authorities, and their authority has, fundamentally, a delegated character (see esp. Lindblom 1977: pt. 5). In the modern polities, much social "action" is carried out not by the canonical actors depicted in economic theory, but largely by authorized agents of collective interests—perhaps especially in what is called the economy.

There is a great deal of isomorphism in the ways in which national polities build this public household. Relatively early, polity rules rationalize society around constructed "factors of production," and in rather standardized ways: Wuthnow (1980) suggests, for example, that science and technology are institutionalized as early as the seventeenth century; capital and labor have even earlier adumbrations.

This early rationalization, and the interpenetration of public and private, seems to be a direct institutional legacy of Christendom's "religious capitalism" (Collins 1986b): the operation of the Church as simultaneously polity and development agency, and of Christendom as dominant public culture (Collins 1986b; Mann 1986). This polity and culture both allowed and promoted an extraordinary degree of "private" economic property and activity, outside the ambit of political intervention or control (Mann 1986:399 and passim). Substantial economic rationalization, and an initial organizational intensification, was well in place before the formation of distinct national states. The intensification nodes were the city-state subpolities within the broader European polity—units most prominently organized as economic civil societies.

Formal organizing outside of the Church and the state did not expand until bounded national legal orders and pacified societal terrains, operating as competitive production projects, were well established. While modern economic organization has an extranational heritage, it takes on national forms: we typically point to *national* production systems, *national* class structures. These national systems, as new "power containers" (Giddens 1984:262), generated and sustained modern formal organizing, a development much energized by their simultaneous competition as war capitalisms and their embeddedness in a common elite culture bequeathed initially by Christendom (McNeill 1982). Formal organizations then represented the new and expanding public "intermediate entities" (Coleman 1974:27) between the primordial polity institutions, individual and state: formalized treaties in a competitive environment.

All the emergent polities in this European world system constructed "capital" as a legitimated public interest and formed the public household around it. Various classes, class fractions, class coalitions, status groups, and mixes thereof acquired agency for this legitimated factor across national systems and over historical time. Rarely was this agency carried by single, stable, bounded classes (although factors were more closely associated with singular classes in early capitalisms than in advanced ones). Mann notes, for example, that after the fourteenth century "the market ceased to be primarily an instrument of the class of lords and became an instrument of *property and capital in general*" (Mann 1986:411, emphasis added). The embedding of public authority in this general principle of capital well antedates industrial capitalism and is again rooted in the West's distinctive earlier form of religious capitalism. Our very ability (and propensity) to analyze these economies as concatenations of abstract production "factors" is a historical legacy—a reflection of the politically constructed and systemic character of these economies.

THE NINETEENTH-CENTURY ORGANIZATIONAL REVOLUTION

The nineteenth-century organizational revolutions that generated new intermediate organizing entities reflected broad political projects to redefine the intersection of public agency and private life. These projects were created and most rapidly pursued in the liberal polities of the European world system (i.e., the United States and England, where elite ideological agreement on economic growth was most easily formed), but were quickly adopted, in distinct fashions, in competitor regimes. Arguments that adduce only efficiency considerations or narrowly rendered actor/interest explanations have been unable to produce compelling accounts of the nineteenth-century expansion of formal organizing: Douglass North, for example, now argues that neoclassical economics "does not and cannot explain the dynamics of change" (North 1981:57 and 1983; also, for commentary, Barzelay and Smith 1987).

The evolution of company law represented an initial departure from narrow private property rules toward public charters, public liability laws, and the state redefinition of efficiencies, that is, toward a form of public organization (Horwitz 1977; Barzelay and Smith 1987; Hurst 1982). The corporation was originally a legal device extending public power to "private" individuals (i.e., those outside of government), in the name of the public good; early corporate law did not distinguish between public and private domains and functions. The new organizational form was then greatly expanded, and in a limited sense re-privatized, with the move from special to general incorporation.

The reconstruction of the "private" realm involved in the creation of autonomous organization of capital was in continuous interdependence with the rationalization and public penetration of nonorganizational society. The organizational revolution simultaneously involved extraordinary public expansion: the creation of official sociologies and psychologies, and the public entry into features of society previously unacknowledged (as stressed in recent social history, e.g., by Foucault).

It is remarkable, given the disparate internal political histories, that by the last quarter of the nineteenth century, quite similar forms of economic organization had been considered and chartered in the United States, England, and the Continent. The legal similarities were much greater than similarities of practice: use of the limited-liability corporate form expanded rapidly in nineteenth-century United States (and in England), but was still exceptional in the late nineteenth century on most of the Continent (Ashworth 1975:93–96). The expansion was quick, as our arguments would predict, where legal and political actors could represent changes in corporate form as serving both public purposes and property rights. The underlying homogeneity across countries was sustained by competitive monitoring and diffusion, and driven by the larger Eurocentric polity.

While these legal developments give the appearance of polities instrumentally controlled by economic classes, this appearance is in fundamental respects misleading. First, nineteenth-century states and courts, in the United States and England as well as elsewhere, were active in selecting and promoting some business practices and directions over others. This selection was pursued with substantial autonomy. The new corporate form was not an inevitable evolution of early company law (Friedman 1973). Second, to the extent that the law (or the state) operated as an "instrument" of a social force, it operated as an expression of a broad public agency and broad "capital" project, rather than a direct instrumentality of specific mobilized classes. Gentry classes in both England and the United States, for example, eventually lost such agency. Investors and entrepreneurs were able to speak with legitimated authority as special carriers of the societal project of economic production. Third, the instances of legal homogeneity across systems are not well accounted for by narrowly gauged class accounts, given the substantial heterogeneity of class structures across the nineteenth-century polities under consideration. Unequal power was certainly reflected in the legal evolution, but the processes were not narrowly interest-driven.

THE TWENTIETH-CENTURY
INSTITUTIONALIZATION OF
FORMAL ORGANIZATION

As formal organizing became institutionalized in economies and other social domains in the twentieth century, it displaced previous communal, kin-based, and traditional associational forms (see esp. Zucker 1983). This institutionalization represented a further rationalization of social actors and functions. The rationalized associational society and formal organizing converge, for example, becoming more interdependent and receiving more common legal treatment and standing. Associations become (as in one review definition) those formally organized named groups in which most members do not receive financial compensation for their participation (Knoke 1986:2). And formal organizations move toward becoming associations, especially in the liberal polities; corporations, for example, increasingly become financial entities controlled by associational boards. The managerial revolution, partially differentiating ownership from control, rationalizes by further detaching the agency for "capital" from family or specific-class embeddedness. Social elements are further converted into functional factors in these ways.

All the polity forms under consideration become "asymmetric societies" (Coleman 1982) with this institutionalization of formal organizing. Natural persons seem eclipsed by corporate persons of various sorts (the main theme of Coleman 1974, 1982). These polities become both mass societies and massively organized ones. All become more individualist, while organizing the expanded individualism through new collectivisms. Marx's prophecy of great structural simplification of the economy has been entirely confirmed (but not his expectations about the political consequences of this simplification).

It nevertheless seems a mistake to represent these societies as societies of organizations, that is, as systems in which organizations largely represent, construct, or control their own environments (see Zucker 1983:12 and passim; Perrow 1986:173–74 and passim). Formal organizing, in the very process of its expansion and institutionalization, has also become immersed in greater societal and ideological controls (Meyer 1983b). The organizational displacement of earlier forms simultaneously contributes to the building up of the individual as member of rationalized society and the expansion of the polity as an institutional structure. Natural persons certainly become both more connected to and more dependent upon various corporate persons, as rightly stressed in the organizational society accounts. But they also become empowered as members of a diffuse "public" to expect and participate in various forms of intervention in and penetration of the organizational sector. The polity and rationalized society expand as formal organizing expands—in law, in collectively mobilized participation, and in an expanded state. Polities are the primary loci of institutionalization, we suggest, rather than organizations in themselves (and rather than diffuse "environments").

Consider in these systems the character of *interest structures*. Modern polities construct and enforce institutionalized systems of interdependent, national, interests or functions. All have a fairly similar set of interests, and legitimated voices, available to people: capital, labor, citizen or public, consumer. Classes have even more attenuated connections to economic factors of production (if one defines classes, as we think is most useful, in a fairly strict Marxian sense, as in Wright 1979). Those individuals who remain incorporated into the economic system have similar portfolios of legitimated economic interests, made up of different proportions (to be sure) of interdependent elements: capital, labor, consumer, and citizen.

Basic interests become linked to the functional elements or factors of the rationalized society; "actors" are constructed, and action taken, in terms of these prior, limited, and highly institutionalized interests. The kinds of personas that embody the different interest portfolios—for example, whether "labor" exists as a personified interest, represented in a subculture or peak association—differ greatly by polity form. But the fundamental interest systems of modern polities are quite similar.

Institutionalized systems of interest and/or function greatly modify the operation of power in modern societies. All these polities are systems of massive power, in the sense of resource mobilization. And all base inequalities of power in differential proximate control over resources. But there has been a great decline, in the broad historical sweep, in the power of resources that are not tied to roles and legitimated authority. Much power is converted into institutionalized authority (such as that of business elites [Lindblom 1977; Block 1977]): it is truly "structural power." Thus power holders claim they are highly constrained in their maneuver and influence, and analysts continue to report and suffer difficulty in locating the founts of power in these systems—largely because they neither detect nor seek its institutionalization and transformation.[5]

3. Main Forms of the Modern Polity

We have so far discussed polity and organizational commonalities. But nation-state polities are not simple copies of a more extensive world polity, though they are prominently influenced by it. Their positions in the wider competitive system vary, and the particular forms of national polity—and, as a consequence, the inclinations to organize formally and the forms of organizing that are employed—are highly dependent upon such positions. The commonplace ideas that commercial zones become liberalized polities, while military/political ones become statist or corporatist ones, reflect such recognition. We try to develop such ideas, and their further organizational implications, here in sections 3 and 4.

Earlier we described the modern polity as mobilizing persons and activities (*a*) under collective control and sovereignty, and (*b*) around collective means and ends ("functions"). All the modern polities rationalize both collective sovereignty and collective functions, so that people and activity are seen as contributing to the collective good. Parallel developments may be characteristic of a good many mobilized political systems in human history; what is distinctive about Western Christendom, and the subsequent modern polity, is its intensification or interpenetration (as Mann 1986, following Weber, notes). People and activity in society are not simply to be brought under passive control: individual persons and their activities in nature are to carry important parts of the collective project, in their own right. This Western propensity, greatly developed by the Reformation and Counter-Reformation, made it possible to locate central parts of the Western polity *within* mobilized and rationalized *society*, rather than in central political organization only. Now analysts often unreflectively render this process as socioeconomic development or modernization.

The modern polities vary along the two core dimensions.[6] Along the first dimension, some modern systems incorporate persons as what American theorists call individual actors, by linking them tightly to the collectivity as a project and then validating them as carriers of sovereign capacity and commitment. Social and public activity are then not greatly differentiated. Other modern polity forms authorize individuals and subgroups, in their socially "private" capacities, in a much weaker way: as members with natural and functional rights, and less as empowered actors. In this latter case, society and its history—and its current collective carriers and functionaries—are the analogues of the American theorist's actor. (And thus public and private activity and actors are more differentiated.)

The second dimension of variation concerns the degree to which the polity directly specifies and controls collective tasks and functional relations. Some modern polities attempt to specify and institutionalize societal functions through central sociopolitical processes, tightly controlling their emergence, relative legitimation, and change: for example, the activities, and relations between, occupations, technologies, professions; or the specific contents of public goods. In others, public functions and interests are epiphenomenal outcomes, or outgrowths, of the ongoing operation of society as a natural community or association. The attempt to regulate collective history through central polity processes (e.g., using either state or communitarian mechanisms) is much more limited.

Four major historical trajectories then emerge, demarcating different modern polity forms, as in the following classification (fig. 9.1). The typology yields, along the diagonals, two statist polity forms and two society-based forms.

One polity type both authorizes social subunits as public actors and institutionalizes collective functions, and thus necessarily comprises a formal

Degree of Authorization of Social Subunits as Public Actors	Degree of Collective Institutionalization of Public Functions and Functional Relations	
	Low	High
High	1 Liberal/individualist	2 Statist society
Low	3 Segmental (state outside society)	4 Corporatist

Fig. 9.1. Four main types of modern rationalized polity.

organizing model (the "high-high" cell 2). Here we have the polity as unified rational organization of both legitimated social actors and functions—the statist society (Badie and Birnbaum 1983; Dyson 1980). The state exists as both the model of organizing rationality and the location for the articulation of the general will of society's actors (the Jacobin vision). The modern French polity is thus the most representative example. Belgium, Canada (esp. French Canada), and Italy (esp. northern) embody this model to lesser degrees and in differing ways. The state organizes both aspects of rationalization: persons and interests, activities and functions. Society is validated as ultimately sovereign and as the object of progress (as the Western project requires), but is seen as irrational and chaotic in itself. In practice, it sits in opposition to state organization and acts to limit it. Relatively less rationalized organizing is found in society independent of the state, and large organizations that arise are in one way or another made directly part of, or dependent upon, the state structure.

A weaker statist form institutionalizes some elements of rationality, but in a structure segmented from and relatively external to society (thus the "low-low" cell 3, because of the weak polity-penetration of society). Latin American states often have this character, as do some one-party states. Society itself is denigrated and sustains low rationalization. The state exists as largely an external project, linked to and legitimated by the Church, the external world system, or a distant societal future. Stepan (1978) calls the Latin American form "organic statism," with various military, intellectual, or class elites deriving authority externally and taking frequent action (e.g., coup attempts) on this basis. The state organization grows, but society itself incorporates weak organizing forms.

The two remaining forms arise historically from the sacralization of society rather than the state, a process rooted in the Protestant reformation settlements. The liberal form (especially American) organizes around legally constituted actors, attributed with both sovereignty and technical capacity (cell 1). The United Kingdom and Australia embody this form in varying ways; also, centuries of British and American hegemony have spread properties of this form widely and encouraged attempts to define it as the quintessence of modernity. Rational organization expands as product of institutionalized actors, whose choices or interests have collective standing and whose resultant constructions are given legal license and protection. Much legal, religious, and educational attention is given to the control and socialization of these empowered actors. The interests expressed by actors then come under less formal or explicit legal and social control. With a system organized around people and groups legitimated not only as members, but as constituent actors with substantial sovereignty and choice, a state role for forming and controlling interests and choices is (comparatively) limited.

The corporatist form (cell 4) reflects exactly the opposite society-based resolution; German history, with its estate legacy, is particularly representative (esp. Wilhelminian Germany, but also the Bonn Republic and Austria; elements of this model are also present in Switzerland and the Nordic countries). Here modernity arises through collective rationalization and institutionalization, not of subunit actors but of social functions and specialized activities, and the corporate groupings performing them—variously occupations, classes, strata, regions, communities, professions. Individuals gain standing not as actors with autonomous interests, but as functionaries—as members of groups with legitimated functional needs and responsibilities. Much organization is thereby generated, but of a distinct form, as we discuss below in section 4.

Our isolation of a few basic forms of sociopolitical organization depends entirely upon "sampling on the dependent variable," though in this case we do not err methodologically, since world history has done the sampling. The consolidation of polity forms, and the greater continuities that some achieve relative to others, actually represents legacies of competitive success in the world system. Other polity forms—purer corporatist ones, unadulterated by individualism (to take just one example)—have failed to spread or survive as well, defeated by military or economic competition.

Our polity examples suggest that certain countries represent relatively singular polity forms (France, United States, Germany), while other countries have more colloidal polities, mixed either regionally (e.g., northern versus southern Italy) or in their institutional matrix (e.g., Canada, with its liberal *and* statist heritages). Some countries seem harder to capture with this simplifying typology (e.g., the USSR), but the polity distinctions nevertheless seem to help greatly in sorting variation in organizational systems—the topic to which we turn.

4. Consequences of Modern Polity Variation for Formal Organizing

All the modern polity forms rationalize social actors and functions, but they differ in how they organize and locate this rationalization. This variation produces differences in (*a*) the *amount* of formal organizing that will take place, and the *domains* in which formal organizing will occur; (*b*) the types of *structures* that formal organizing will employ; and (*c*) the form of *interpenetration* of formal organizing with polity and society. These differences have patterning and magnitude sufficient to amount to distinct formal organizational systems or regimes.

RESEARCH FINDINGS ON VARIATION IN FORMAL ORGANIZING

Research efforts in comparative organization have generated a number of findings that guide us here.[7] Nationality has emerged as a powerful predictor of both organizational practices and individuals' attitudes toward organization. Managers' passports, for example, are the best single predictor of their dispositions about organization structure and problem solving: differences remain prominent even within multinational corporations (Laurent 1983). Within countries, widely disparate organizations and organizational domains seem to share distinct national traits (as captured, for example, in Crozier's studies of France). Researchers are often driven by these traits to infer the presence of "implicit models of organization" governing both practices and orientations.

A common sketch of country clusterings of models and practices emerges. Lammers and Hickson (1979), in their review of studies through the late 1970s, collect a set of largely paired-country comparisons (e.g., United States–Britain, Germany–United States, Britain-France, United States–Italy), comparisons that suggest underlying persistent patterns. They distinguish Latin, Anglo-Saxon, and "traditional" clusters of countries in terms of variation in organizing structures, rules (such as flexibility or explicitness), and boundaries (separation of organizational from nonorganizational roles). Laurent, in his studies of the managerial orientations (OECD, but primarily European and North American), detects a north-south axis distinguishing clusters with instrumental versus collectivist models of organizing. U.K. and U.S. managers reveal more instrumental views, French and Italian more collectivist images, with Germanic orientations in between (Laurent 1983). In his reviews of literature on structural variation, and in his own research on employee organizing attitudes in a multinational with branches in forty countries, Hofstede found four relevant country clusters: Latin, Germanic, Nordic, and Anglo. These clusters differ both in the kinds of organizing structures employed and in attitudes toward organizational power, rules, individual roles, and organizational goals (Hofstede 1980).

Hamilton and Biggart, in comparative investigations of industrial structure and state economic activity in East Asia (1988; also Orrù, Biggart, and Hamilton, ch. 15, this vol.), argue that Japan, South Korea, and Taiwan reflect three distinct models of economic organization. In Japan, the political center coordinates strong intermediate economic authorities (such as the *zaibatsu* industrial groups). South Korea's statist-bureaucratic capitalism embodies an ideology of central societal administration. In Taiwan, the state acts as an "exemplary center" amid a Chinese family-capitalism network.

These patterns, while remarked upon more and more, have not yet received much theoretical attention. (The work just cited is a notable exception,[8] as is Dobbin 1986.) Analysts have concluded that national cultural or societal structure shapes organizational models, but they generally recognize that clear partitions discriminating causes and effects, and processes connecting them, are not well elaborated (Rose 1985:77–82). Competing theoretical arguments about such variation are thus not readily apparent in the field.

Explaining National Organizational Variation

The four polity forms outlined above capture well the variation that comparative researchers are detecting. For our central causal imagery, we suggest that what the polity institutionalizes in rationalized society will be standardized and taken for granted for the purpose of formal organizing. The basic form of polity institutionalization (institutionalizing subunit social actors, or societal functions, or both) establishes a constraining framework for formal organizing: formal organizing builds around these materials. Organizers are driven to adapt to the polity and rationalized societal institutions in shaping organizational structure.

Organizational structure can be distinguished by the degrees to which it specifies (*a*) vertical and lateral differentiation of, and authoritative control over, *persons;* vis-à-vis (*b*) vertical and lateral differentiation of, and coordination of, *activities.* This distinction yields a range of organizational structure, from low structuration of both persons and activity, through various intermediary mixes, to high structuration of both—generating the various organizational types well known in the literature (Scott 1987b; see also the Aston work, especially Pugh 1976).

It should be apparent that this conceptualization of formal organizing is an analogue to our earlier treatment of polity structure. The two models map onto each other in the following way. If organizational structuration develops within, and is stimulated by, a constraining and empowering polity evolution, its primary forms should be dialectical counterparts of the polity's institutional form. For example, if organization develops within a polity that institutionalizes subunit *actors,* it will likely congeal around organizational specifications and elaborations of *activities:* it can (and must) incorporate the polity-established actors. Conversely, polity institutionalization of public functions will direct formal organizing toward controls over *persons:* for organizing to occur, it must structure action from the assembly of polity-provided functions.

Further, the character of polity institutionalization should affect the *degree* of formal organizing, in systematic fashion. We see this connection as dialectical as well: if a polity institutionalizes primarily along one or the other dimensions of rationalization (i.e., if it is either of the two "high-low" polity forms), formal organizing will be greatly stimulated, filling out the contents of rationalized societal structure. In contrast, both the high-high and the low-low polity forms will limit organizational structuration, either by supplanting or suppressing it (the high-high form), or by failing to stimulate it (the low-low form).

Three propositions integrate this reasoning and enable us to link our earlier conceptualization of polity structure to variation in fundamental organizational forms:

(1) Polity institutionalization of social subunit actors produces (*a*) extensive formal organizing, with organization (*b*) building upon pregiven actors by elaborating the coordination of *activity*.

(2) Polity institutionalization around collectively specified social functions (*a*) produces much formal organizing as well, but (*b*) with sharper authoritative control and differentiation of *persons*.

(3) Polity institutionalization around both dimensions of rationalized social structure produces both (*a*) less formal organizing and, (*b*) where organization does occur, explicit rationalized structuration of *both* persons and activity.

We now try to explicate our reasoning—and spell out causal processes—by presenting empirical examples of variation across the four polity types.

THE LIBERAL/INDIVIDUALIST POLITY

Amount and Domain of Formal Organizing

Licensing individual persons as legitimate and rational social actors, with interests having collective standing, facilitates the creation of a great deal of formal organization. The United States provides the archetypal example here. The domains in which formal organizing occurs spread across the social map in this polity form. First, in a system in which individuals are handed the loaded gun of legitimated actorhood and legitimated interests, each individual must recognize that others are similarly empowered. The first interest (and collective obligation) of all in the Tocquevillean society is to attain control over everyone else, that is, to capture the socialization and social control of actors themselves. Formal organizing thus clusters in the first instance around actors. An enormous amount of such organization is constructed: religious organizations, courts and criminal systems, local government, parties, massive educational efforts, moral improvement and self-control associations, temperance movements, mental health associations, and so on. Even in other domains—for instance, economic—huge sectors tied to personnel activity arise.

Second, the liberal system also generates much organization around legitimated interests, in the ordinary sense: the formation of economic organizations is greatly stimulated by law and culture. Third, much formal organizing develops around the control of the political system and the law, since these structures directly constitute and reconstitute actors and interests. Overall, then, such systems are densely filled with rationalized formal organization.

Structure

The organizational structures created by this system are sprawling ones. Formal organizing must incorporate societally empowered actors, embodied solutions looking for problems. This constraint limits the possible formality of and authority in formal organizing. The pregiven actors substitute for much definition of organizational status and authority. With actors supplied by society, and substantive goals set by formal organizing, loose organizational structures can sustain themselves: the modal organization in this polity type is expanded and differentiated both laterally and vertically, but loosely integrated, and weakly tied together by its vertical authority relations.

Much organizing is built up at lower levels by people "acting," with the action only loosely linked to centers by organizational authority. Organizations tend to become interpenetrated, managing and incorporating the wider variety of legitimated actors created in such a system; distinctions between different organizing forms (e.g., associations versus organizations) become particularly blurred.

Organizing and Polity

The liberal polity itself is not a rational organization. Rather its confederal structures often look chaotic—Skowronek's (1981) "state of courts and parties" in the United States, for example (Meyer and Scott 1983b). Some formal organizing is called public, some private, but from a wider point of view the whole interorganizational system is a public control structure. Public and private interpenetrate and are not clearly differentiated. Especially in such systems, power concentrates in society and is institutionalized as social authority (e.g., "the privileged position of business," and society's structural dependence upon it [Lindblom 1977]). Given the license people have as actors with public standing, more interests are claimed in these systems, each interest providing potential grounds for formal organizing. But these many interests tend also to be comparatively homogeneous in form and content. The polity form directs people toward rights claims and legal mobilization, and makes delegitimation of other actors and claims difficult; this marketlike ecology produces a strategic narrowing and convergence of foci, claims, and agendas.

Without societal institutionalization of and around collective functions, interests do not readily congeal around broad functional categories such as class. There is less of such functional (e.g., "class") consciousness in these systems, and "interest intermediation" (Schmitter 1979) occurs less readily through the construction of collective functional personas such as Labor or Capital.

THE CORPORATIST POLITY

Amount and Domain of Organizing

Representing the other Reformation linkage of polity and society, the corporatist polity constructs not actors and interests, but people and groups as agents performing legitimated social functions. (We concentrate here on central European corporatism.) Even now, what in the United States is defined as a legitimate private interest is in Germany presented as a substantively valuable social function. The organizational effects here, too, involve the construction of a great deal of formal rational organization, but structures and domains and sequences vary. Formal organization clusters around social functions, linked closely to vertical authority patterns legitimating the functions: occupational groups, for instance, look less like interest groups and more like status elements in a public ceremony (carrying a *Beruf*). The urgent pressure is less for social control of actors than for the social control of functional integration—thus exaggerated myths, not about people and personality (as in the United States), but about authority, and about the national community with its putative requirements.

Structure

Formal organizing must assemble social functions and associated statuses. In fundamental respects, for example, corporatist organizing occurs in a pregiven occupational space. Organization evolves as rational bureaucracy, with linkages to political, economic, and cultural centers, and with less emphasis on participation and differentiation at the bottom. In such a system, differentiation at the bottom always has threatening elements, and the appearance of top-down delegation is crucial. In practice, organization may be relatively decentralized. Functional differentiation is actually more lateral than vertical, linking responsibility for activity to statuses exogenously ascribed with distinct competences and knowledge. The stress on myths of control creates very different imagery than the American depiction of local actor autonomy. A "logic of professionality" obtains, rather than the "logic of administration" of more statist systems (Rose 1985:75, quoting Maurice, Sellier, and Silvestre 1982).

Organizing and Polity

The corporatist polity, like the liberal one, is a "societal" rather than statist form, and it too drives public and private together. But it does not create liberal public privatism; rather, people discover themselves in functional theories, as members of occupations, classes, families, gender identities, regions, communities, estates, and the like. Their claims are substantive ones, not procedural—the requirements of functional groups (e.g., state protection, as with cartels); the requirements of people in order to function properly in their groups (commonly, welfare claims). People in such a system gain entry as in all modern intensifying polity forms. But they do so not as actors who properly socialized interests, but as elements with needs and natural rights, and as elements with rightful claims upon duties of others. The corporatist form is more a welfare than a participation system: social welfare claims, rights, and services expand more rapidly than educational, religious, and political participation (Flora and Heidenheimer 1981).

Both state and social organization share the same pattern in the corporatist polity: less apparent differentiation, more hierarchical dramatization. Power is also suffused in societal authority, but in a society that finds more expression in, and that penetrates, a state apparatus. Social authority and interests cluster around social functions, generating a community of interdependent yet competing interest personas. Recognized functions are fewer than the liberal form's interests, but they tend to be much more highly and formally organized. Capital and labor more readily find personas in these systems, and there is more allied functional "consciousness." The dominant form of interest intermediation is then corporatism, strictly considered—societally authorized bargaining between peak associations (Schmitter 1979).

THE NATIONAL STATIST SOCIETY

Amount and Domain of Organizing

Polities institutionalizing both actors and functions at the national level in a society-penetrating state apparatus, but also legitimating rational and bounded actors in society itself, set up an oppositional system. State organizations expand, in elaborate and rationalized form. (France provides the ultimate model of the state for many theorists; see, e.g., Badie and Birnbaum 1983.) Formal organizing arises in society, linked to, subordinate to, and defined in terms of state-represented action and functions. But there is less formal organizing in society itself than in other systems, and fewer societal domains receive formal organizing; charismatic organizational rationality tends to be a monopoly of the state. The canonical formal organization that does appear clusters around state-categorized actors or functions. People in society act by mobilizing in opposition both to the state and to the expansion of rationalized formal organization.

Structure

Formal organizing must incorporate pregiven, state-defined, function-specific actors. So formal organizing emerges in isomorphic relation to state structure—the "bureaucratic phenomenon" (Crozier's theme). For autonomous formally organized action to occur, organizing must specify internally both authority (the linkage to state categories) and activity (to convert state-defined authority into organizational action). The rationalization of organization, combined with societal opposition to it, tends to mean that decoupling in such systems is extreme.

Organizing and Polity

Statist systems sharply distinguish public and private, by institutionalizing the former in the state and the latter in society. Myths, rhetorics, and ideologies reflect this differentiation; thus personal identity, while located in the (private) society, requires establishing a stance or posture vis-à-vis the (public) state. Individuals are both carriers of state-centered grades—the statist systems contain definite caste elements and tonalities—but also embodiments of rationalized but asocial and antinomian energies and drives. The statist-society system depicts organization as an overt power structure, and thus an inescapable source of alienation; managers are controllers who "alternate authoritarianism and seduction" (Faucheux, Amado, and Laurent 1982:354, 362).

Power in this polity form (and in the second statist one that follows) is more concentrated in an apparatus than in the societal systems, and vested in agents who have authority in the Castle on the Hill. The French state, for example, is classically strong as an organization, relatively buffered from societal penetration, but is relatively weak in its capture of society (Badie and Birnbaum 1983). The dialectic of state and society generates a distinct interest structure. Interests in society are many, but they do not have immediate public standing. Interests compete to achieve institutionalization in state apparatus and categories, and thereby to define a general will—if necessary, by capturing and manning the apparatus. This produces highly abstract and stylized interests, organized not around communal functions, as in the corporatist systems, but around lines of action and intervention upon the state-cum-society. (The various "lefts" and "rights" were a French invention, and such categorizations continue to be most salient in this polity form.) Consciousness is organized around a limited set of such action lines, and interest intermediation takes on a "party" form (rather than the associational mobilization of the liberal polities, and the "corporatist" intermediation of the corporatist ones).

THE STATE OUTSIDE SOCIETY

Typical Latin American polities institutionalize neither social actors nor social functions in society. Institutionalization largely occurs in a segmented state apparatus, largely outside of society. But the state organization—exogenously legitimated—tends itself to be relatively fragmented: an assembly of competing bureaucratized elites deriving their justification from externally defined missions.

Here the least rationalized formal organizing occurs. The organization that does occur is more "traditional" in character, incorporating socially primordial groups, or state bureaucratic elements, with little autonomy generated and sustained for the organization in itself. Formal organizing occurs less in a society differentiated from state, but occurs in a state-and-formal-organizing domain, differentiated from a society containing primordial organizing.

Interests are often exogenous in legitimacy claims and often take a zero-sum character. Power and interest intermediation are more cabalistic than in the other systems, with less conversion into legitimated authority. Capital, for instance, has less (and more exogenous) legitimacy in terms of the collective good.

5. Institutional Sources of Change in Formal Organizing

Throughout we have been discussing processes that both maintain and change systems. It is difficult to discuss "change" separately from other aspects of the operation of a system. In social science, change is most often conceived as a separate matter by those who posit causal variables that are (putatively) free from institutional embeddedness, and thus potentially exogenous forces, for example, genetics, primordial human motives, asocial human experience, ecological circumstances, and, in earlier lines of thought (notably Hegelian), transcendental initiatives. An institutional point of view in no way denies that some forces are properly conceived as exogenous to institutions.[9] But we focus specifically in this section on institutional sources of change in formal organizing, both because we see such change as highly institutional in its primary driving forces, and because we believe that noninstitutional accounts greatly exaggerate its less-institutional features.

INSTITUTIONAL SOURCES OF CHANGE

External

Nation-state polities in the West have always been situated in a dense and competitive network of economic exchange, political and military competition and imitation, and cultural isomorphism. The isomorphism itself facilitates local change through competition and diffusion. As new commodities arise in the system (e.g., computers), every member attempts to incorporate them—and more successful members do so more successfully. As new devices of political coordination or control are created (e.g., tax systems or military techniques), similar efforts are made everywhere. As expanded cultural institutions arise (e.g., mass and elite education in the last century, movements for ethnic and racial incorporation in the 1950s and 1960s, or the women's movements in the 1970s), there is much diffusion. Either the social construction of new acting groups in the citizenry (women, children, minorities) or of new social functions (control of air and water pollution, recreational facilities, new commodities, or new therapies) can generate such effects. Most of the institutional change now occurring in any given polity can be predicted more readily from knowledge of the wider world environment than from an understanding of internal structure—a point obvious everywhere else in the world (as newspaper coverage clearly reveals) aside from the hegemonic United States.

Internal

Nation-state polities incorporate logics of progress and justice that continually fuel new expansions, at least under favorable conditions of world expansion (an important condition). These logics create the often-noted "rational restlessness" (Weber) of these systems. They contain not just groups and functions, but groups and functions justified in terms of larger and evolving collective goals. The creation, for instance, of citizenship as a general collective good rather than a specific absolute status licenses all sorts of parties and agents to push for elaboration of institutions: in all modern systems, new groups (children, women, fetuses, the dying, the disturbed), or their agents, can make such claims. Similarly, once some function, such as education, gains standing, a variety of parties can push for elaboration on grounds of justice or progress (usually both)—thus driver training, sex education, or (even) sociology. The legal, moral, religious, political, and economic institutional supports are already at least partly in place.

Institutional Causal Processes

The modern licensing of individuals and groups as actors or members, and of interests or functions, as imbued with collective goods, creates agents of institutional change. The various sciences play empowered roles, particularly in importing changes from the external system and interpreting them as producing public goods for the local collective. Even behind the Iron Curtain, economists import versions of Reaganomics, sociologists and journalists doctrines of new forms of equality, psychologists new human needs. Physical scientists and engineers bring in both techniques and definitions of problems. In systems in which justifications rest so heavily on doctrines of effectiveness and justice in an evolving real world, the carriers of knowledge have high standing as agents of the collective interest. Their justifications are crucial to most institutional changes in modern systems.

But ordinary social "actors" or "functionaries" also have standing, either as carriers of valid "interests" or recognized "functions." Such agents transmit exogenous institutional change (e.g., women's rights, or the necessity of a national computer industry), but also elaborate extant institutions. In practice most new "interests" or "functions" arise from groups or functionaries that already have standing and responsibility, and are elaborations of "interests" and "functions" that already have such position. For example, a central theme in the modern literature on social movements is that such mobilization rarely arises from the genuinely peripheral, who generally remain unorganized.

Institutional interventions are as much or more governed by (and distorted in terms of) logics of claimed progress and justice than narrowly driven by interests per se. Success of claims is predicated not so much by relative power than by relative institutionalized authority broadly considered. (In sociological analyses, the term *power* is commonly used to refer to authority that the analyst wishes to delegitimate.) And many institutional changes in formal organizing flow from broad national and world polity shifts, which then penetrate organizational domains.

CHANGE IN THE DIFFERENT POLITY
FORMS

National polities, differing fundamentally in their social organization, differ also in the dominant sources and forms of institutional change in formal organizing. Each polity type generates characteristic uncertainties and attempted resolutions of them. Liberal systems, lacking a specified definition of social interests and functions, elaborate knowledge systems that support and stabilize interests. Corporatist systems generate societal theories too, but focus especially on distributional justice: functions are more directly controlled in these systems, but questions of rights are contested. Both types of statist systems construct negotiations of relations between state and society. That is, as new issues arise, these systems organize them in characteristic ways, and at least the more dominant polities successfully reproduce their structures over long periods of time (see Dobbin 1986 on industrial policy patterns). More peripheral countries, variously pressured by the world stratification system, sustain less continuity in organizing; further, their change sources are more purely external.

In the United States, with its licensed actors and interests, change is pursued by people who learn to posture in this way; even scientists speak as interested citizens with a bit of technical expertise rather than as direct embodiments of central authority. The agents—here, often lawyers—who act, act for actors and their interests, and only weakly as agents of official central authority (e.g., the courts). But they comport themselves as public agents nevertheless, producing the direct assertions of public good common in American public discourse. Even business firms address the public as citizens concerned about the U.S. economy (many fly flags, in this country, or offer citizen commentaries as advertisements) rather than more truculently claiming "private" rights and interests.

In France, change differs. Legitimate standing to engage in rationalized collective action is held more narrowly by the state; authority to define problems and solutions is more rationalized and bureaucratic. Institutional change emanates more powerfully from people posing as agents of the state, as it adapts to world competition, and as it reacts to the power contests formed when episodic waves of protest and disorder emerge from society. These patterns form cycles of institutional stability and disruption that have long histories ("stable instability" [Siegfried 1956]).

In Wilhelminian Germany, classically (and still, if less purely, in the Bonn Republic) prominent agents of change are the functional groups and their structures: classes, corporate industrial groups, the military, the intellectuals (as collective functionaries, not as citizens), and even specific occupational and regional and local groupings. Change takes the form of expanded claims of functional import (and often stigmatization of the import or moral responsibility of other groups) and of natural rights derived from these functions. At its base, the system recurs to a "natural," and vitally important, depicted human community, and claims based on natural communal needs have conspicuous standing.

In modernized segments of the third world, fragmented elites, each with externally validated claims to the embodiment of collective purpose, take action—often against each other, and often against the putative decadence or backwardness of society. Elites, making rationalized claims, are actors, more than in an integrated state apparatus or empowered society. Change then flows from continually evolving exogenous definitions of the state and also from the exigencies of attempted domination of society.

ORGANIZATIONAL OUTCOMES

Institutional changes, in the successful competitors to which most researchers attend, tend to bring polities toward isomorphism in many respects. But they also tend to reinforce the distinctive patterns of organizational structure that we have described (Dobbin 1986). Liberal individualism in successful competitors expands by the construction of ever more actors and interests. Its organizational system incorporates these in ever more extended divisions of "labor," or treaties about functions. Corporatisms re-create and change the relevant corporate groups—as when Continental corporatist countries, now blocked from much military posturing, incorporate economic, regional, and sometimes ethnic groups as functional constituents. In statist systems, new functions and groups appear as elements of the state. In weak organic statist systems in the third world, however, the prediction of organizational continuity is less valid, due to the lower rationalization and institutional penetration of society. Here the exogenous character of the "modern" makes for a good deal of instability in organizational form.

6. Postscript

In contrast to the latent functionalism of current theory, we see functional models as constituting the modern polity: at its core, it is just such a model embodied in normative and cognitive principles, and institutionalized variously in the practices of the modern systems. We consider modern actors and functional groups to be constructed through such institutionalization, carrying their collective dependence continually with them, maintaining the modern order and, under some conditions, reifying it in the symbolic structures we call formal organizations.

Our arguments also suggest why modern theories postulating actors actually have so little to say about them, or their interests—treating one or the other as explanatory catchalls—and further, why modern functional theories are so vague about collective functions. These lines of theory build around reifications. That is, they tend to incorporate reflections of society's institutionalized models as premises in analytical models. Ritual invocations of putative theories of action then both produce and require theoretic silences about actual action and interests. The recurrent attempts to derive formal organizing from putatively "natural" actors or functions, without attention to social sources or historical process, now seem naïve.

Similarly, the line of thought in this chapter suggests why "cultural" theories have not seemed attractive alternatives. Most macrolevel arguments about cultural effects have treated culture as some vague composite or collective effect. We have tried to supply more specific causal imagery: the culture involved, we argue, is the system of rules built up in the modern polity. Whether this causal imagery is "cultural" then remains largely a semantic, and unimportant, issue.

This chapter certainly does not supply a complete alternative theory. Thus we have not attempted to specify how definitions of collective good are produced, or how societal functions gain legitimated standing, or how contending models for institutionalization might have competed. Positions on such questions would certainly complement and extend our discussion, but our present argument in no way requires them.

For those who might contemplate a fuller argument, we add one thought on the politics of Western institutionalization. All the modern polities were certainly "contested terrains." But the contest occurred at the system level—between legitimated institutions. Much consequential conflict results because of polity features we have conspicuously stressed. First, these polities embody authorized subunits that are unequal: the associated conflict drives much rationalization. Second, many struggles are over how the forms and rules of wider polities are to be adapted to the exigencies of local settings: how world structures are incorporated into nations, and how world and national rules are incorporated into subnational contexts. Further, a basic contradiction in these polities flows from the empowerment of both collectivities and individual persons as rational moral projects. Individuals, in these systems, have rights, responsibilities, and capacities, not only as social members, but as independent units as well. The virtue of the collectivity is not autonomous, but linked to the development and equality of individual subunits. This tension generates much of the political change, and hence organizational change, that we observe.

Organizational theory, developing without a clear idea of society, has tended to leave these "old" institutionalist insights behind. Perhaps the "new" institutionalism should recover them.

Acknowledgments

The authors have drawn upon ideas in Meyer and Scott 1983b, March and Olsen 1984, and Thomas et al. 1987 and have benefited from comments provided by readers of previous versions of this chapter: M. Barzelay, J. Boli, C. Conell, F. Dobbin, S. Eisenstadt, N. Fligstein, G. Hamilton, J. March, W. Powell, and M. Zald.

Notes

1. Our general argument is perhaps closest to those stressing the import of societal "authority patterns" for understanding economic organization, e.g., Bendix 1956, Hamilton and Biggart 1988.

2. On rationalization, we draw upon Weber [1927] 1950: chs. 22, 29; Stinchcombe 1986b; Kalberg 1980; Moore 1979:1, 30; and Habermas 1984:ch. 2.

3. The legacy of Christendom and the Roman Empire is often mentioned (Anderson 1974; Mann 1986; Hall 1986; Eisenstadt 1985; Collins 1986b), as are the competitive conditions of Europe (Anderson 1974; Tilly 1975; Skocpol 1979) in the absence of political integration (Wallerstein 1974, and many others), and within the distinctive European physical ecology (Jones 1981; McNeill 1982).

4. The canonical modern systems (unremarkably) are then found in Western Europe and North America, but they are also present outside this zone. Post–World War II Japan is clearly a representative as well, albeit with a very distinctive articulation of the modern interpenetrated individualism and collectivism. Many of the Latin American countries represent the modern polity form in aspiration and constitutional design, with varying degrees of actual social institutionalization and penetration (further discussed in sec. 3). The USSR represents a peripheral variant of the modern model; it is certainly a rationalist collective project, but it is only ritually individualist, largely absorbing "the people's" sovereignty in a unified collective actor. Many of the African systems are nation-states in name and external standing only, without much internal rationalization of social-political elements (i.e., unrationalized tribal elements) or much interpenetration of "private" and public purposes. India's polity, in contrast, is more modern in form, with more rationalized sociopolitical relations between the powerful caste and ethnic elements. Nepal or Burma, in different ways, are largely nonmodern polity forms, investing sovereignty outside the people, and without a (profane) society linking a (sacred) individual and cosmos through a progress project.

5. Thus the kinds of investigations well pursued and reported by Domhoff (e.g., 1983), while useful in revealing networks of influence, often seem to tap more superficial conduits of power. After all, is the Bohemian Grove really constitutive of the power structure of these systems? We concur with Knoke on this point: with an individual focus, "lost is the sense of an overarching structure of relationships among

corporate organizations and more diffuse collectivities, which may properly be seen as the ultimate repositories of power resources in a national system. Individual incumbents of the top command positions in various institutional hierarchies are usually constrained in their roles as fiduciaries, or agents, of the organization to behave in ways unrelated to their personal biographies or personal interests (although the two sets of interests undoubtedly coincide extensively)" (Knoke 1981:308–9).

We note that investigations originating in Marxian lines of thought have also converged upon this position. See, e.g., the rather striking conclusion reported by Przeworski and Wallerstein, who have been conducting a sustained theoretical and empirical investigation of "theories of the state": in an advanced capitalist society, they say, "a government which is a perfect agent of workers would not behave much differently from a [government that is] a perfect agent of capitalists" (Przeworski and Wallerstein 1986:244).

6. This section draws variously upon Jepperson's dissertation (in progress) and upon Meyer 1983b.

7. Throughout this section we draw upon Laurent 1983; Hofstede 1980; Rose 1985; Faucheux, Amado, and Laurent 1982; Lammers and Hickson 1979; Pugh 1976; Scott 1987b.

8. Hamilton and Biggart link the variation they describe to legitimated societal authority practices. In the aftermath of institutional disruption (World War II, the Korean War, the consolidation of Chiang's regime in Taiwan), political elites reformulated and adopted earlier models of legitimate authority in order to further polity stability. This causal account seems broadly compatible with the general line of argument we are presenting in this chapter.

9. Features of physical and social ecology, conjunctural events, environmental "shocks" of various sorts (climate, OPEC, AIDS), biogenetic constants and their social correlates (e.g., free riding), ontogenetic constants and their correlates (such as generational replacement), features of human intervention in nature ("praxis")—all may be represented, in particular instances, as institutionally exogenous. But an institutional view greatly endogenizes human experience, action, and reaction; this position may very well distinguish it from other viewpoints, especially from characteristic American reifications of action (see Münch 1986; Jepperson, ch. 6, this vol.). Moreover, an institutional position argues that human experience and reaction are more likely to operate as change inducers when they have standing in institutionalized collective rules, as relevant to collective goods. Social systems seem to have great capacity to be unresponsive to uncodified functional requirements, or to human suffering that lies outside definitions of the collective and its good (historically, for instance, the needs of the peasantry).

10 Bringing Society Back In: Symbols, Practices, and Institutional Contradictions

ROGER FRIEDLAND AND
ROBERT R. ALFORD

The social sciences are in the midst of a theoretical retreat from society. The retreat has taken two paths, one toward the utilitarian individual and the other toward the power-oriented organization. In this chapter we argue to the contrary, that it is not possible to understand individual or organizational behavior without locating it in a societal context. But to posit the exteriority of society in a nonfunctionalist, nondeterminist manner requires an alternative conception of society as an interinstitutional system. We conceive of institutions as both supraorganizational patterns of activity through which humans conduct their material life in time and space, and symbolic systems through which they categorize that activity and infuse it with meaning.

The central institutions of the contemporary capitalist West—capitalist market, bureaucratic state, democracy, nuclear family, and Christian religion— shape individual preferences and organizational interests as well as the repertoire of behaviors by which they may attain them. These institutions are potentially contradictory and hence make multiple logics available to individuals and organizations. Individuals and organizations transform the institutional relations of society by exploiting these contradictions.

Retreat from Society: Society as Marketplace

The most radical retreat from society has been toward the instrumental, rational individual, whose choices in myriad exchanges are seen as the primary cause of societal arrangements. Public-choice theory, agency theory, rational-actor models, and the new institutional economics all reflect this premise. Rational-choice theorists derive organizational arrangements—whether party, state, family, or firm—from the rationality of individuals in exchange, each attempting to maximize his or her utility by exchanging scarce, usually material, resources. Organizational structures—like parliaments, municipalities, or firms—are analyzed as arenas in which these scarce resources are produced and allocated, or as structured by the functional limits of exchange such as bounded rationality and the problems of achieving trust among strangers.

The new institutional economists argue that large corporate hierarchies emerge due to the difficulties of efficient exchange where transaction costs are high—those exchanges with uncertain outcomes, few actors, and highly localized knowledge (Williamson 1975). The origin and diffusion of these corporate hierarchies lie in their contribution to efficiency through reduced uncertainty and individual opportunism. Agency theorists analyze organizations as a network of voluntaristic contracts. Organizational structures are derived as solutions to problems of opportunism where self-interest and the costs of surveillance might otherwise interact to produce shirking (Alchian and Demsetz 1972; Moe 1984; Perrow 1986).

Similar arguments are made about the organization of the state as well as the groups and classes that would use its authority (Hechter 1983; Elster 1985). In the United States, for instance, public-choice theorists analyze the emergence of multiple municipalities in a metropolitan area as an efficient response to the problem of delivery of public goods to differentiated residential communities. In this market for public goods, the electoral patterns of voice and migratory choices of exit produce an equilibrium in which each municipality provides a bundle of public goods at a tax price which conforms to the preferences of the median voter (Borcherding and Deacon 1972; Deacon 1978).

Those who study individual behavior in precapitalist, prestate societies or in nonmarket, nonstate institutional arenas attempt to save the premise of individual instrumental rationality by expanding the sources of utility which individuals try to optimize: prestige, honor, power, holiness, security, wives, or whatever. Anthropologists typically assume that individuals economize on honor, whether they obey the rules by which it is measured and acquired, as in the case of Goode, who argues that people attempt to maximize esteem through social exchange, or manipulate the rules when it is to their benefit to do so, as in the case of Malinowski's Trobrianders or Leach's highland Burmese (Hatch 1989).

This line of analysis has been forcefully influenced by neoclassical economics, which has marginalized institutional analysis, opting instead for the elegant, deductive, and transhistorical models that that theory made possible. By bracketing the market, they could convert economics into a science of allocation and understand the market as a mechanism to aggregate preferences that came from elsewhere. Neoclassical economic theory takes preferences to be exogenous, ordered, and stable. The formation of preferences is outside the analytic concern of the discipline because, economists argue, individuals make independent, rational choices to maximize their utility. But once one moves away from material goods, calibrated through relative prices, the neoclassical apparatus is in dangerous waters precisely because it does not have a theory of utility formation. Without priced commodities, the postulate of rational utility maximization quickly becomes tautological, a liberal trope, not subject to falsification. Economics cannot have a theory of utility formation because it understands individuals as the market constructs them or, more importantly, as the market enables them to constitute themselves (Friedland and Robertson 1990).

A market, we believe, is not simply an allocative mechanism but also an institutionally specific cultural system for generating and measuring value. Many of the most important dimensions of economic life—material security, prestige, meaningful work, sociability, craftsmanship—do not have explicit prices. The utilitarian and contractarian philosophical foundations of neoclassical economics operate with a means-ends, subject-object dualism which assumes that individuals are instrumentally rational, that they evaluate their participation in social relationships based upon the costs and benefits they impose upon them.

If voting appears to economists as a nonrational form of behavior when analyzed on a cost-benefit basis, the decision to work is no less problematic. Work provides identities as much as it provides bread for the table; participation in markets is as much an expression of who one is as what one wants. Economists typically assume that work is a disutility to be traded off against leisure or income. Work contains all kinds of positive utilities—whether as expression of an identity (I work or I am a metal worker), a relative performance (I am a good metal worker), social value (It is good to be a metal worker), gender (It is good for a man to be a metal worker), or social status (It is better to be a metal worker than a salesperson). These utilities are socially and historically structured. The extent to which there are problems monitoring, measuring, and controlling performance—the major determinants of the displacement of the market by bureaucratic hierarchies in transaction cost economic explanations—will be contingent upon the utilities that individuals obtain from work. Without a theory of utility formation, explanations of when activities will be coordinated through markets, hierarchies, or "clans" are inevitably limited. It is arguable that a market economy could not operate efficiently if individuals were really instrumentally egoistic, participating lawfully only when the probable benefits of guile are outweighed by their costs. Some contemporary market failures may in fact be the result of market success.

This failure to explain the formation of preferences is linked to the assumption of independent individuals who interact solely through exchange. If preferences are socially constructed, not only socialized but socially structured, then markets cannot operate in a Pareto optimal manner. The evidence of retrospective rationality, that people form preferences based upon the options open to them, explodes neoclassical welfare economics from the inside out. Then, markets are merely aggregating utilities which have been shaped by those markets themselves.

Moreover, utility formation is institutionally specific. Analysts who convert all activities into marketlike activities, into problems of economization, argue that values should be formed and distributed with full cognizance of costs and benefits. A market relativizes all costs and benefits, and derives those costs and benefits from prices which must depend on the preexisting, market-based distribution of income. The marginalist approach, like the market itself, marginalizes power, in part, because it marginalizes meaning (Reddy 1987). Other institutional realms—families, states, religions—are more likely to generate values, and hence utilities, as absolutes which cannot be traded off against alternatives. Relativization through price transforms the bases of their coherence. Individuals are indeed confronted with instrumental choices within each of these institutional realms, and within each the exercise of choice expresses a different kind of individuality. Instrumental and expressive behavior are always linked. For example, a model that assumes that a household is a firm attempting to optimize output cannot account for the relatively invariant household division of labor between husband and wife, particularly the lack of male responsiveness to the time demands of household work (Berk 1985). As Berk argues, households not only produce goods, they produce gender, the "doing" of which is inseparable from the household's production function. Economists tend to argue that they study rational making of choices, while other social scientists study the irrational bases that prevent people from choosing. We argue that the opposition is not between rational and irrational, but between different transrational orders.

The State-Centered Approach

The other line of retreat from society has been toward the organization, whose drive toward rationalization and control over its environment and its consequent conflicts with other organizations are seen as primary. The dominant organizational theories isolate organizations from their institutional or societal contexts. Resource dependency theory assumes that organizations have strategic autonomy to negotiate the uncertain resources available in their environments in the interests of organizational survival and power (Pfeffer and Salancik 1978). The major counter theory, population ecology, deprives organizations of their strategic autonomy by converting society into an unspecified, abstract set of resources which are either lean or poor, fine-grained or coarse, turbulent or placid. The evolution of this environment selects, through differential birth and death rates, those organizational forms which effectively exploit the various niches the environment provides. Due to structural inertia, organizations are largely incapable of strategic adaptation. This model has little theory about the development of these niches, let alone their definition, which is independent of the organizations which occupy them. In these approaches, society is reduced to either an abstract environment or an interorganizational field.

Extending the logic of resource dependency theory, recent analyses of the state view it as a dominant organizational structure attempting to control a problematic international and domestic environment, thereby restructuring the society over which it claims to rule. Such an approach is an improvement over those which reduce the state to a representative government or an imperfect market medium. In the work of Theda Skocpol, the preeminent representative of this genre, the state is understood as the dominant organization within society, an organization with a "basic need to maintain control and order" (1985:9).

Skocpol is as obsessed with demonstrating potential state autonomy from societal forces, particularly class actors, as an earlier generation of political scientists and sociologists was with the policy relevance of partisan politics. In her model, the variables that explain state policy are those that affect the organizational capacities of the state. State autonomy varies across time, societies, and policy arenas, depending upon the resources—particularly financial ones—which the state controls.[1]

She asserts that the "extranational orientations of states, the challenges they may face in maintaining domestic order, and the organizational resources that collectivities of state officials may be able to draw on and deploy [are] . . . features of the state [which] help to *explain* autonomous state action" (1985:9, emphasis added). But these are not factors which explain autonomous state action; they are aspects of autonomous state action. A set of assumptions is transformed into a theory. This mode of argumentation reshuffles the major concepts embodied in the assumption of state autonomy by trying to define both the independent and dependent variables as state attributes, without resorting to any "societal" factors to help explain state actions.

Skocpol rejects "society-centered" theories because they convert the state into a captive instrument of voters, interest groups or classes, or into a functional medium which expresses the requirements of society whether ordered by class or consensus. Such approaches cannot understand the autonomy and independence of the state (1985:4). Thus she criticizes the neo-Marxist perspective, arguing that historical developments after World War I brought the state back in inexorably as an "autonomous organizational actor" (1985:6). "National macroeconomic management became the norm" and "public expenditures burgeoned" in all of the "advanced industrial capitalist democracies" (1985:6). This assumes what it is designed to show. Has macroeconomic management worked? Quite clearly not, as states have become vulnerable to cross-national flows of capital and commodities which have eroded their capacity to manage their national economies, to finance public expenditures, or to maintain the current regime in power. State structures and strategies can perdure because they are even less subject to selection mechanisms than are corporate forms. The size, structure, and strategies of states cannot a priori be used to justify a theoretical assertion about state autonomy. Without demonstrating their actual causes and consequences, their origin and persistence cannot be used to defend the assertion of state autonomy.

Neither the origins nor the uses of state autonomy are just material problems in the technology of domination. State-centered theories tend to reduce the meaning of governance and political participation to interests in power or resources used by elites to elicit obedience and assent. Skocpol thus marginalized the meaning of participation in revolutions in order to avoid the assumption that societies are normatively integrated or that revolutions were somehow "made" by ideologically driven revolutionaries (1979). Thus it was possible for her to discuss the French revolution without ever considering the doctrine of natural rights or Catholicism.

In another example, Orloff and Skocpol explained why the United States was slower than Great Britain in developing a welfare state, stressing differences in party elite competition and state centralization (1984). Orloff and Skocpol appeal to the "logic of state-building, in the struggle of politicians for control and advantage, and in the expectations groups have about what states with specific organizational structures should or could do" (1984:746). Here, they introduce beliefs and values as "expectations," but the main emphasis is on elite strategies inside state organizations and political parties.

While the role of belief or ideology is recognized empirically, these disappear theoretically. Popular opinion is never referred to as a causal factor explaining the adoption of welfare programs. Yet references to what can only be regarded as widespread public beliefs are scattered throughout the essay: "climate of a broad elite and governmental acknowledgement of a problem"; "a firm negative presumption" in the New Deal Era about public spending; a "general reaction of Congress, along with local and economic interest groups"; a "public commitment in place" in Britain to welfare; Americans "doubted" or "feared" corruption and therefore opposed social spending; and "echoes of this revulsion (against governmental handouts) reverberated into the Progressive era." These formulations are all empirical recognition of symbols, belief systems, even values, as factors which shape state policy. However, they are not accorded theoretical status because they are assumed to be shaped by elites in state and party organizations, and at best are intervening variables between elite capacities and public policies. It may be true that public opinion is not a basis for party competition because, as they assume, parties select issues and shape policy alternatives for the mass electorate, not vice versa. However, state policies are not only technical solutions to material problems of control or resource extraction; they are rooted in changing conceptions of what the state is, what it can and should do. They thus argue that the "climate of opinion" among key elites in both the United States and Britain favored social insurance and pensions. These conceptions are not simply legitimations of what must be done; nor are they just blueprints shared by elites and those they rule about what should be done. State power is rooted not only in the technologies of coercion and control, but in its symbolic organization.

Skocpol's view is from the commanding heights, at state headquarters where goals are formulated and strategic decisions made, not in the calculus of individuals and groups in the streets, fields, factories, or bedrooms nor in the institutional contradictions between capitalism, democracy, family, and state. State autonomy is asserted, its instances cataloged, but its origins remain opaque. Society is reduced to an untheorized environment, composed of organizational actors who control resources of relevance to state power. No larger system of interinstitutional relations constrains the structure and action of the state. Society has been reduced to an interorganizational field, the state to an autonomous organizational structure endowed with an abstract drive for power and control. The state's accumulation of resources and their conversion into autonomy or power, the challenge to state control, depend not simply on the iterations of a rational game for power, but upon the institutional structure of society which shapes the rule by which resources are accumulated, transformed into capacities for action, and made available as motives by which that action is made meaningful. Even in war, when the technologies of destruction count most, the categorical construction of us and them matters almost as much. Whether the enemy are to be subjugated or incorporated, a people without souls to be made into property, victims to be sacrificed on the top of large pyramids, an evil race to be destroyed—these are part of the symbolic technology of power. The institutional specificity of state power should be clearest at those times when it is being transformed. Starting with a deinstitutionalized organization, even if it is the state, one can only partially understand those transformations.

The Historical Limits of Reductionism

Our conceptions of individuals and organizations have been decisively shaped by institutional transformations. Take the example of the instrumental individual who maximizes income, utility, or whatever, although the point could be made for the power-oriented, rationalizing organization as well. Methodological individualism contends that only individual behavior is observable, that supraindividual social structures are nonobservable reifications. But the emergence of the individual as a category and the content of selfhood and rationality itself have all been historically and institutionally transformed. In the history of nations, Marcel Mauss remarked in his last essay, "those who have made of the human person a complete entity, independent of all others save God, are rare" (Mauss 1985:14).[2]

The historical transformation of individuality in ancient Greece is instructive. The ancient, preclassical Greek did not ascribe agency to an inner, unified personality or self (Barbu 1960; Snell 1960). The psychological language of

Homer's *Iliad* (8th century B.C.E) suggests that human beings did not imagine themselves as unique selves, whose motivations governed their behavior, but as internally fragmented, their behavior determined by gods (Snell 1960). Individuals saw themselves as expressions of the social roles they occupied. Over the course of three centuries, from Homer to Euripides, the individual emerged, his subjectivity valued, his personality heralded as an agency of rationality (Momigliano 1985).[3] This transformation is rooted in institutional changes which are strikingly familiar: the rise of a monetized commercial economy where the accumulation of wealth was divorced from birthright; the emergence of romantic love among both men and women;[4] the construction of states enforcing written laws which ascribed culpability to the individual rather than kin group; the achievement of a democratic order where the authority of the law was rooted in the assent of the citizenry; and the rise of a more personalized, as opposed to civic, religious system.

To derive these institutional transformations from the individuality they made possible is to return to the presociological individual derided by Emile Durkheim.[5] These institutions created, sacralized, and indeed provided the categories (intent, rights, rationality, liberty, guilt, madness, citizen, soul, love) through which individuality was lived. The modern state's fundamental duty, Durkheim wrote, was to "progressively call the individual into moral existence."[6] Without an autonomous, self-conscious individual, there could be no polis. But without the polis, individuality would mean something else.

As anthropologists have made clear, our notions of individual choice and agency are contingent modern products. Over and over again, ethnographers of non-Western societies report discursive knowledge and verbal accounts of self and other individuals which are more concrete, less abstract, more context-dependent than those in the contemporary West (Schweder and Bourne 1984; Levy 1973). People in many of these societies are less likely to conceptualize individuals independently of the roles they occupy and the contexts in which they are situated. Compared to the Western descriptions of persons, those in India, for instance, are temporally and spatially contingent on social context, not abstract attributes like honest or courageous. In these societies, an abstract conception of the individual as a unique entity, shorn of social context and worthy of value in and of himself, is either unknown or ill developed (Geertz 1975). The differences do not appear to be related to absences of linguistic tools, informational closure, or cognitive backwardness.[7] In Japan, a highly industrialized nation, the concept of individualism was a foreign introduction, for which there is still no adequate translation. Its translation still has the pejorative connotation of self-centeredness. For whatever reason, some societies do not conceptualize, let alone value, an abstract individual. Clearly the achievement of individuality was as much a cultural transformation as it was the natural outcome of the division of labor.

The Western experience of individuality, of choice, of freedom, has been institutionally and historically shaped by the emergence of capitalism, state, democracy, the nuclear family, and the Christian religion. Capitalism produces and distributes through individual exchanges of labor and capital and establishes factory regimes which provide individual workers with property rights in jobs (Burawoy 1983). The rise of the state progressively constituted the individual as an abstract legal subject with rights—specified independently of social structure—before the law, responsible for his or her actions, and through forms of communication which privatized the exchanges between state and society (Piven and Cloward 1980; Rokkan et al. 1970). These state-based constructions of the individual have been internationalized through the interaction of nation-states (Giddens 1986). The ideology and institutions of democracy exalt the autonomous rights of the individual to participate as a citizen in public life, in particular through secret individual ballots. The emergence of the nuclear family regulates mate selection on affective grounds independent of property, production, or politics. And the rise of Christianity posited the existence of a unique individual soul with an eternal disposition, whether or not that disposition could be influenced or revealed by behaviors on earth (Eisenstadt 1983).[8] As Paul's letter to the Galatians indicates, faith had replaced law as "our custodian": "But now that faith has come, we are no longer under a custodian; for in Christ Jesus you are all sons of God, through faith. . . . There is neither Jew nor Greek, there is neither slave nor free, there is neither male nor female, for you are all one in Christ Jesus" (Galatians 3.25–29). In Christianity, the historical individual has a relationship—however mediated—to God, and more important, to a sacred man in the person of Jesus. The church is symbolized as the body of Christ, a community of individuals on earth (Dumont 1982).[9]

One cannot derive a theory of society from the historical individuality that those institutional transformations created. The transhistorical individual cannot have ontological priority in the theoretical representation of society. Beginning with individuals as rational-instrumental actors takes as a theoretical premise an analytic category which has been shaped by institutional transformation. As a result, dominant institutional logics are imported in such a way as to become invisible assumptions. And as we argue, specifying the institutional bases of individual and organizational identities, interests, and actions is not simply a problem that plagues those who study societal transformation over the long durée. It is also a problem for contemporary social analysis.

The Autonomy of Levels

The project we propose is the development of a nonfunctionalist conception of society as a potentially contradictory interinstitutional system. An adequate social theory must work at three levels of analysis—individuals competing and negotiating, organizations in conflict and coordination, and institutions in contradiction and interdependency. Institutions must be conceived of as simultaneously material and symbolic. However, no institutional order should be accorded causal primacy a priori. To restore meaning into social analysis in a way which is neither subjectivist, functionalist, nor teleological, the notion of institutional contradiction is vital.

As we argued in *Powers of Theory*, three levels—individuals, organizations, and society—constitute the home domain of the dominant theoretical perspectives in political sociology, that is, pluralist, managerial, and class (Alford and Friedland 1985).[10] Each theoretical perspective only theorizes the relationship between state and society from the level which constitutes its home domain.

Pluralists analyze individuals in competitive interaction constrained by consensual normative bonds, ultimately rooted in individual motivations, expectations, and systems of individual interaction. Managerialists analyze the formation, operation, and relationships between elite-controlled bureaucratic structures. These organizations have an autonomy both from the societal structures in which they are located and from the individuals who compose them, and attempt to rationalize the internal and external conditions of their existence. Class theorists analyze society in terms of the contradictions within and between institutions. Institutions cannot be analyzed in isolation from each other, but must be understood in their mutually dependent, yet contradictory relationships. The structure of capitalism, based upon private ownership and legally free wage workers, not only is internally contradictory, tending inevitably toward economic and political crisis, but is externally contradictory in its relationship to state, democracy, and family.

Each theory has a home domain of analysis where it *is* analytically powerful. Each theory empirically observes the other levels of analysis, but it does not theorize their emergent properties. For example, pluralists believe that the requisites of democracy in a labor union, a small town, and a capitalist nation-state are equivalent, or derive bureaucratic structure from the limits of individual exchange and competition. Managerial theorists derive the logic of capitalism from the requisites of rationalization of the bureaucratic firms that compose it. Class theorists have difficulty studying the bases of state autonomy, let alone the political organization of class. Each theoretical perspective has places it cannot see, territory it cannot map. While this typology was designed for mapping the terrain in political sociology, the problems it raises pertain to social theory in general.

Theories that make individuals primary tend, at the extreme, to become open-ended, solipsistic, and voluntaristic approaches in which the entire world is renegotiated in every social interaction. They are excessively subjectivist or posit abstract conceptions of human "nature" which are invariant across time and space—like utility maximization. Theories which make organizations central tend either to overstate an omnipresent, disembodied power which enables elites to discipline and punish without resistance, or to assume that they have extraordinary latitude to make strategic choices determined only by their access to material resources. They will, for example, by an analysis of the state as the dominant organization, help us understand its capacities to make strategic choices, develop particular solutions to problems, and adopt effective interventions but not understand the range of variation within which those strategic choices are likely to vary nor the sources of the problems it must solve.

Those theories which make society primary tend toward a structural functionalism in which society has a deterministic relationship to individuals and organization. In evolutionary versions, the structural properties of the system point teleologically toward modernity, rationalization, or revolution. Thus the growth of state power in the West is variously understood as a response to the societal requisites of integration, the requirements of coordination, or socialization of the costs of capitalist crisis. In these functionalist approaches, the state is not theorized as an organization or a network of individuals and groups. Or democracy is understood as a natural form for an organic division of labor, a perfect mechanism by which to rationalize leadership succession, or the efficient shell for the hegemony of capitalism. The possible tensions between levels of analysis and institutional orders tend to be absent. Thus ironically most econometric models of individual behavior do not model individual variation as a measurement problem, treating it rather as a residual from a deterministic structural relationship.[11] Such theories are unable to specify the microfoundations of macrostructure, or vice versa.

All three levels of analysis are necessary to adequately understand society. Each level of analysis is equally an abstraction and a reification; each is implicated in the other; none is more "real" than any other.[12] Individual action can only be explained in a societal context, but that context can only be understood through individual consciousness and behavior. We conceive of these levels of analysis as "nested," where organization and institution specify progressively higher levels of constraint and opportunity for individual action. The relevant temporal frame in which it makes sense to study variation is longest for institutions and shortest for individuals. The relevant spatial extent over which activities can be organized is greatest for institutions and least for individuals. The symbolic world can only be constructed theoretically at the institutional level.

A New Institutionalism?

To position individuals and organizations in society, we require mediating concepts. The institutional level provides a critical bridge. Institutions are conventionally understood as supraorganizational patterns of organizing social life rooted in shared norms (Shibutani 1986:16). With its emphasis on an exterior normative, as opposed to an interior cognitive, order, this definition is inadequate.[13] To sustain heavy intellectual traffic, the notion of institution requires reconstruction, and particularly a rethinking of the relationship between symbol and practice. We would argue that institutions must be reconceptualized as simultaneously material and ideal, systems of signs and symbols, rational and transrational. Institutions are supraorganizational patterns of human activity by which individuals and organizations produce and reproduce their material subsistence and organize time and space. They are also symbolic systems, ways of ordering reality, and thereby rendering experience of time and space meaningful. In this section, we critically review efforts in organizational theory to analyze the supraorganizational, normative sources of organizational structure. We then put forward an alternative conceptualization of institution, including the notion that society is constituted through multiple institutional logics.

The evidence suggests that patterns of individual and organizational behavior vary institutionally. Bureaucratic structures are not readily reproducible across sectors and nations. Studies of the adoption of new organizational forms—like the multidivisional form, personnel practices, and due process rights for employees in corporations or civil service in municipalities—find that while an organization's technical or social attributes may account for their early adoption, their effect declines over time. Thus, for example, analyzing the period 1880 to 1935, Tolbert and Zucker (1983) found that attributes of municipalities determined adoption of civil service procedures until 1915, after which their adoption was no longer contingent upon municipal attributes (see also Baron, Dobbin, and Jennings 1986). Once this form was institutionalized, its adoption became normative, a source of organizational legitimacy independent of its immediate organizational functionality, or any other criterion of internal rationality.

Thus organizational structures appear to be institutionally patterned in ways which cannot be explained by competitive interaction between organizations, technology, or organization-specific environmental conditions. The new institutionalists in organizational theory argue that the processes by which organizational forms tend toward homogenization cannot be explained by their contributions to efficiency, particularly as an organizational field evolves (DiMaggio and Powell 1983; Meyer 1981). Institutional analysts have specified the mechanisms—professionalization, state regulation, requirements for trust, mimicry under conditions of uncertain technology—by which institutionalization takes place. From an institutionalist perspective, organizations which adopt the appropriate forms perform well not because they are most efficient, but because these forms are most effective at eliciting resources from other organizations which take them to be legitimate. Conformism may secure access to resources, but not because of superior efficiency (DiMaggio and Powell 1983:154).

While institutionalists have studied the fact of organizational homogeneity and the mechanisms by which isomorphism is accomplished, they have not begun to study why the institutional arenas are patterned in the way that they are or the conditions under which new institutional forms develop (DiMaggio and Powell 1983; Zucker 1983; Meyer and Hannan 1979; Meyer and Rowan 1977; Meyer and Scott 1983b). In short, they do not have the theoretical tools by which to understand the institutional content whose diffusion they do analyze, or the conditions under which particular forms are institutionalized or deinstitutionalized.

In part, that incapacity is due to models which posit a supraorganizational field which is normatively integrated, where the adoption of particular forms is not explained by the adaptive political actions of individuals or organizations. In an important essay, DiMaggio (1988a) calls for a synthesis of political and institutional approaches. Without politics, he argues, it is not possible to explain either the sources of institutionalization or deinstitutionalization.

DiMaggio argues that institutional models need not consider the interests and actions of actors because the models are most appropriate to those conditions where actors are unable either to recognize or rationally act upon their interests. Under these conditions, norms and preconscious assumptions about the nature of reality are likely to shape action independently of individual or organizational interests. Institutional theorists attempt to explain the diffusion of new organization forms. Uncertainties inherent in the technology (as in education or planning) or in the environment (as with rapid immigration) shape the diffusion of new organizational forms. Or the power of certain actors may cause organizational change, as when the inclusive authority of the state establishes due process procedures in employment (Edelman 1985).

But DiMaggio's analytic strategy does not adequately explain the success and failure of institutionalization. The approach assumes an institution-free conception of interest and power, and maintains the materialist-idealist dualism in which actors have objective interests, which can be understood independently of the actors' understandings. If actors do not understand their interests or how to realize them, they become susceptible to institutional influence. Or the approach implies that actors have material powers which enable them to enforce new institutional patterns on organizational and individual behaviors. For the institutionalists, defining the boundaries of an organizational field, within which there are strong pressures for conformity, is difficult and potentially tautological. The approach seems to assume that formal attributes of organizational fields can be specified independently of the institutional arena in which they are located. But, we would argue, it is the content of an institutional order that shapes the mechanisms by which organizations are able to conform or deviate from established patterns. These institutional orders, and the specific relations between them, delimit types of organizational fields.

The fundamental assumption is that when interests are stable, there is no need to explain their institutional origins. But the opposite may be true as well. Not only change, whether cataclysmic or glacial, but the stability of interests must also be explained. Institutional sources must be found for the stability and routinization of interests just as much as their transformation.

A new theory of institutions is required, not because certain conditions require interest-free models, but because interests are institutionally shaped. Utility maximization, satisficing, income maximization, profit maximization, risk, power, even interest itself are all institutionally contingent. Thus Hirschman has argued that the concept of interest as rational self-centeredness on the part of prince and entrepreneur emerged in the seventeenth and eighteenth centuries with the institutional transformation of state and economy. Interest was construed as an alternative to the destructiveness of "passions" to which rulers and masses were subject. Hirschman argues that the interest concept itself played a "role . . . in shaping behavior codes for individual men and women in society" (Hirschman 1986:38).[14]

Today, the categories of material action, such as profit or debt, for example, are culturally and politically constructed categories whose definition changes historically with shifts in accounting procedures and tax laws.[15] For example, critics argue that contemporary accounting procedures which were developed for external financial reporting—which emphasize direct labor costs and short-term returns—have prevented large U.S. corporations from making the long-term investments in new capital equipment necessary to maintain competitiveness in the world market (Holusha 1987). The cultural constructions involved in U.S. capital markets in the definition of performance and risk are readily apparent to the players in that market, which makes them of no less material consequence. Thus recent regulatory pressures on U.S. financial intermediaries to report the market, as opposed to book, value of their assets and liabilities will affect both depositor and investor decision making. The initial social reconstruction of reality to avoid the material consequences of default through such conceptual devices as the rescheduling of debt and then the collective process by which Latin American loans were written off are illustrative. Or the stigmatization of junk bonds not used for takeovers and leveraged buyouts is a reflection of labeling of what constitutes investment-grade paper by powerful actors. This in turn raises the costs of capital for smaller firms. Material advantage is sought in terms of cultural categories which are institutionally located, frequently contested, and sometimes reordered. These categories become normative and thereby shape not only the calculus of utility maximization but probably the formation of preferences as well.[16] There is an instrumental politics to the ways in which the categories change, certainly, but once they have become institutionalized they shape the rules by which rationality is perceived and exercised.

The kinds of "politics" possible in different institutional arenas also depend upon societal structure. The limits, the instruments, and the structure of power vary institutionally. Those limits and how they change should be a key issue. It is the institutional origins and consequences of uncertainty and power that are theoretically problematic.[17] Neither uncertainty nor power is sufficient to explain institutional transformation. Millions of women are today uncertain whether they shall ever find mates, but that has not led to institutional changes in marriage or the criteria of attractiveness or sexuality. Citizens are uncertain whether the next war will destroy us all, but that has not produced serious infringements on national sovereignty and national monopolies of the instruments of mass violence. States are more powerful today than ever before in terms of the reach of their administrative apparatus, yet they are unable to regulate effectively the deployment of the human and material resources within their territorial boundaries.

Uncertainty, risk, power, and interest can be conceptualized and measured independently of the institutional environment in which they are observed. But the analytic powers of such constructs must be specified. What constitutes uncertainty and hence the tolerable levels of risk are institutionally defined in historically specific ways. So too, just as power is a theoretically contested concept within the social sciences, power as concept and praxis is culturally and institutionally contingent. Thus, the persistent tendency for Americans to construct decentralized state structures, to separate governmental powers, to prevent the emergence of national banks, and to foster market regulation aimed at preventing market concentration derives in part from a culturally contingent concept of power, embedded in a notion of liberty derived from the original settlers' experience of a highly intrusive, regulative English state. The American concept of freedom is a negative one (freedom *from*), whereas the Continental European concept is a more positive one (freedom *to* or capacity), and hence facilitated the fashioning of concentrated institutional powers in pursuit of various objectives (Sharpe 1973a, 1973b). This institutional approach is not inconsistent with the impact of actors who occupied particular social locations, who had "interests" in particular structures. But American culture partially constituted those interests and provided symbolic resources upon which they could draw to defend them.

Institutional transformations are simultaneously material and symbolic transformations of the world. They involve not only shifts in the structure of power and interests, but in the definition of power and interest. DiMaggio makes this point when he says, "In other words, the institutionalization of an organizational form required institutional work to justify that form's public theory: legitimating accounts that organizational entrepreneurs advance about labor markets, consumer markets, expertise, and distinctive products or services" (1988a:25). A given public theory works when the world has been appropriately constructed. Categorical structures only make "sense" when they organize our lives. The deployment of material resources not only involves real material relations; it also communicates meanings. The inability of non-Western societies to absorb the technologies and material goods of the West without profound cultural transformation indicates the problem. So does the West's inability to absorb non-Western values without material transformation.

DiMaggio is certainly right when he contends that institutional theory is not currently adequate to explain "the origins, reproduction, and disappearance of institutionalized social and organizational forms" (1988a:16). But we will not succeed by going back to utilitarian individuals anxious to maximize something or avoid uncertainty, or to survival-oriented organizations trying to maintain power over their environments, in both cases abstracted from their institutional contexts. These two dynamics that DiMaggio discerns in most of the new institutionalist work are important to an adequate explanation, but they are not sufficient. To explain institutionalization, we must rethink the meaning of institutions.

Deep Play and Hard Work: Reconceptualizing Institutions

The classical social theorists all believed that the world was built from the ground up, from the material conditions of human life which they believed existed prior to the consciousness its participants had of them. The ideal world reflected, legitimated, or functionally concealed that real material structure of society. Durkheim's religion of individuality, of the irreducible value of the human being, derived from the unique and differentiated roles in a rising organic division of labor. Weber's officials legitimated their dominance by convincing subordinates of the rationality of the structures they controlled. Marx's capitalists and workers understood their relationship in the market as free exchange concealing the exploitation transpiring daily behind their backs. This materialist-idealist, or base-superstructure, theoretical dichotomy has been the appropriate way for theorists to apprehend the "real" social world for much of the nineteenth and twentieth centuries. This model must be reconstructed by asserting the centrality of the symbolic in the organization of social life.

Perhaps the most profound challenge to structural approaches to society has come from interpretive or cultural analyses, which have emphasized the metaphorical mechanisms by which we not only understand the world, but by which we literally live. These approaches reject the materialist-idealist duality that has characterized Western social theory. In their view, cultural symbols are both media and sources of individual behavior.

In Clifford Geertz's interpretations of the Balinese cockfights, for example, individuals do not simply jockey for power, wealth, and status (Geertz 1973). The fight is a dramaturgic expression of the nature of status and power in Balinese society. The cocks, held between the legs of the owners, stroked and incessantly evaluated, are repeatedly pushed into the ring, where they rip at each other with specially sharpened spurs until one dies. Enormous sums of money can change hands at each match, sums that are irrational from an individualistic, utilitarian perspective. The higher the sums, the more evenly matched the cocks are arranged to be, and the more likely the odds on which the bet is made are even. The greater the sum of money at stake, the more the decision to bet is not individualistic and utilitarian, but collective—one bets with one's kin or village—and status-oriented. Those who bet together love, live, or irrigate together. Here money is not just a measure of utility, but "a symbol of moral import" (p. 433). Because such matches are arranged to be equal, in the long run there is no redistribution of wealth.

In Geertz's analysis, these cockfights are a means not only to express the status structure and rivalries of Balinese society, but to create them. The cockfight not only provides a vehicle for understanding daily life—the ascriptive status competition, the murderous male impulses contained below the formalized politesse of Bali, the atomized, nondirectional organization of time—it creates the subjectivities upon which that daily life depends. "Art forms generate and regenerate the very subjectivity they pretend only to display" (p. 451).[18]

But all life involves such art forms, such rituals—where the media by which values are expressed, the rules for the attainment of ends, and the valuation and conceptualization of those ends are symbolically constructed and yet allow men and women to survive in the material world. Lévi-Strauss pointed out the ways in which a stomach could be filled and a cosmology revealed simultaneously through food preparation and eating practices. Similar arguments could easily be made for games, clothing, travel, architecture, urban planning, sexuality, conquest, distribution, child rearing, not to mention worship. In modern society, instrumental behaviors oriented to power, wealth, or sexuality express social cosmology just as much as marginal rituals like cockfights, gossiping in markets, or the processions of monarchs and potentates (Geertz 1983).

The Logic of Institutions

Each of the most important institutional orders of contemporary Western societies has a central logic—a set of material practices and symbolic constructions—which constitutes its organizing principles and which is available to organizations and individuals to elaborate. The institutional logic of capitalism is accumulation and the commodification of human activity. That of the state is rationalization and the regulation of human activity by legal and bureaucratic hierarchies. That of democracy is participation and the extension of popular control over human activity. That of the family is community and the motivation of human activity by unconditional loyalty to its members and their reproductive needs.[19] That of religion, or science for that matter, is truth, whether mundane or transcendental, and the symbolic construction of reality within which all human activity takes place. These institutional logics are symbolically grounded, organizationally structured, politically defended, and technically and materially constrained, and hence have specific historical limits.

Commodity producers attempt to convert all actions into the buying and selling of commodities that have a monetary price. Capitalist firms cannot exchange unpriced human activities that may be rational for an organization or useful to individuals. Bureaucratic state organizations attempt to convert diverse individual situations into the basis for routine official decisions and cannot easily handle conflicting claims over the substantive ends toward which bureaucratic rationality is directed or demands for popular participation in them. Parliaments and electoral institutions convert the most diverse issues into decisions that can be made either by majority vote or consensus among participants, and cannot directly recognize claims of authority based on technical expertise or class privilege. Families attempt to convert all social relations into reciprocal and unconditional obligations oriented to the reproduction of family members. Families are not infrequently threatened when market-based inequalities, universal bureaucratic rules, or religious differences become the basis of affiliation, obligation, or loyalty. Contemporary Christian religions attempt to convert all issues into expressions of absolute moral principles accepted voluntarily on faith and grounded in a particular cosmogony. Christianity cannot handle easily the organization of social life made possible by the accumulation of power through bureaucratic mechanisms, including its own, nor can it easily manage the relativization of values through democratic or market mechanisms.

The central institutions of contemporary Western societies—capitalism, family, bureaucratic state, democracy, and Christianity—are simultaneously symbolic systems and material practices.[20] Thus institutions are symbolic systems which have nonobservable, absolute, transrational referents and observable social relations which concretize them. Through these concrete social relations, individuals and organizations strive to achieve their ends, but they also make life meaningful and reproduce those symbolic systems. Social relations always have both instrumental and ritual content.[21] The materialist-idealist dualism, which has suffused so much of social theory over the last century, hobbles our capacity to understand.

Private property, for example, is a nonobservable symbolic relation concretized through ownership, a social relationship by which human beings control certain activities and the disposition of material goods in time and space. The buying and selling of commodities is simultaneously a symbolic and an instrumental behavior. Similarly, love is concretized through forms of sexual interaction ranging from marriage to specific forms of courtship and sexual stimulation. Marriage or lovemaking are both symbolic and instrumental behaviors. Democracy is concretized through voting, which is both a way in which people ritually enact the symbolic system and a means by which they attempt to control those who rule them. Or God is concretized through prayer and other ritual behaviors in church. And these ritual behaviors too have both an instrumental aspect by which people attempt to assure their position in the universe as well as obtain particular benefits on earth, as well as the obvious symbolic consequences.

This does not mean that when one buys, makes love, votes, or prays that property, love, democracy, or God really exists or really obtains as a result of those behaviors. It means that the behaviors make sense to those who enact the behavior only in relation to those transrational symbolic systems and that those symbolic systems only make sense in terms of the behavior. To believe that "the people rule," "a nation decides," "love conquers all," "the market is efficient," is no more rational than to hold that "God watches over us all." This does not mean there is any one-to-one relationship between behavior and meaning simply because of an institutional location of that behavior. Any given behavior can carry with it alternative meanings. Sexual intercourse, for example, can be an expression of affection, of passion, of power, of a divine commandment to reproduce, or of property.

The routines of each institution are connected to rituals which define the order of the world and one's position within it, rituals through which belief in the institution is reproduced. Voting and inaugurations; the signing of contracts; marriages and divorces; the issuance of budgets and plans—each involves real social relationships through which instrumental behavior is accomplished. But each too entails symbolic and ideological constructions of more than instrumental consequence.

When social analysts have analyzed the "symbolic" or "ritual" role of different kinds of activities, like planning, they have often studied those instances where the activity does not organize material life, where it is a hollow legitimation, for example, a way to co-opt potential opponents in an ineffectual exercise (Alford 1975; Edelman 1967; March and Olsen 1984). But through the quotidien and most institutionalized ritual behaviors, individuals reproduce the symbolic order of the institution and the social relationships that connect this world to a transrational order. Individual participation in various social relations should be analyzed not only in terms of the material interests that operation of the institutions serves, but in terms of the symbolic meaningfulness of that participation. Just as differentiated religions have their cosmological systems which account for the origin of the world and the words by which they understand it, so too do the most important institutions—whether they be national histories of the state, public theories of the market, or romantic myths or analytic psychologies of sexual and family life.

Institutional transformations are therefore associated with the creation of both new social relationships and new symbolic orders. Social revolutions, for example, restructure both the organizational relationships between the state and society, and the symbolic order of the society. Lynn Hunt has persuasively argued in her study of the French revolution that the new symbolic behaviors of the revolution were not simply the means of power, but their ends (1984). The new categories of ideology and citizen were ritually created. A new political culture made possible the emergence of new organizational forms and political elites. Political mobilization arises not only out of the organizational capacities of groups, which are stressed by resource mobilization theorists of social movements, but out of the violation of meanings, or disruption of the organizational conditions necessary for meaningful life, which they neglect. The defense of "daily life" as a source of political mobilization as posited by Richard Flacks (1988) is relevant to this latter concern. And the worldviews of those social movements which aim at institutional transformation shape the kinds of strategies they are likely to use (Friedland and Hecht 1989, 1990).

Intimately related to the materialist-idealist dualism in social theory is the dualism between means and ends. The retreat from society has been associated with an analytic strategy that builds upon a supposed universalism of means, as opposed to the historical particularism of ends which increasingly fall outside the purview of the social sciences. But this science of means lacks meaning. The new institutionalist work has demonstrated the normative organization of means, such as the diffusion of multidivisional forms among corporations, or manager forms of government among municipalities. Through these means, the studies indicate, organizations obtain legitimacy, but no necessary efficiency.

Institutions constrain not only the ends to which their behavior should be directed, but the means by which those ends are achieved. They provide individuals with vocabularies of motives and with a sense of self. They generate not only that which is valued, but the rules by which it is calibrated and distributed. Institutions set the limits on the very nature of rationality and, by implication, of individuality. Nonetheless, individuals, groups, and organizations try to use institutional orders to their own advantage.

This conception of institution is consistent with recent work in cognitive psychology which argues that individuals do not approach the world in an instrumentally naïve way, but rather learn routines, that their individual strategies and behaviors contain within them certain institutional priors. Rationality as well as the appropriate contexts of its use are learned. This conception is also consistent with Mary Douglas's recent argument in *How Institutions Think* (1986).[22] This volume is a slashing critique of rational-choice theory for neglecting the institutional constraints on individuals' conceptions of their needs, preferences, and choices. Whereas rational-choice theorists assume a sovereign individual whose preferences are not of theoretical concern, Douglas argues that both rational and irrational decisions are influenced by the "hold that institutions have on our processes of classifying and recognizing" (1986:3). Society is thought as it is enacted, and social solidarity depends upon the extent to which "classifications, logical operation and guiding metaphors" are held in common. Douglas argues that institutions require a cognitive base that naturalizes and rationalizes the conventions which constitute the institution. Thus systems of classification are a form of social praxis.

Institutional routines do not derive solely from bounded rationality, the requisite of trust, or uncertain technologies. Public-choice theory uses simplistic decision rules derived from the market to generate the formation of institutional structures from which those decision rules were originally derived. From an egoistic rational point of view, it is impossible to explain individual decisions to vote given its high costs, minimal impact on the outcome, and probability that benefits will be obtained even in its absence. If the political behavior of citizens can be accurately analyzed using a model of benefit maximization at minimum cost such that free-rider dilemmas abound, or if equity theory accurately explains the labors of love, then the institutional logic of capitalism has penetrated deeply into society. It is arguable that this rationality has contributed to the decline in electoral participation and the growing instability of familial relationships. Why do the unconditional loyalties which are the ideal of familial relations not provide a model for collective forms of political action? When such loyalties are recognized, as in the Mafia or political machine, they are regarded as deviant, traditionalistic, or pathological. A similar logic makes it appropriate to analyze mate selection and fertility choices as marketlike decisions, where children can be conceptualized as inferior goods (Becker 1981).

In his important critique of the undersocialized theories of economists and their importation of oversocialized models of institutional structure, Mark Granovetter stresses that both market exchange and bureaucratic hierarchy are embedded in social relations which affect their operations (Granovetter 1985). But how these relationships affect exchange and hierarchy is still ambiguous. In the essay, he points out that these relations may hinder *or* facilitate the operation of each structure. Thus social networks enable firms to acquire information about potential employees without hiring them, while other social networks make centralized control difficult within the firm. Social networks may facilitate interfirm exchange under the conditions where the new institutional economists would predict internalization through hierarchy. However, social networks per se do not have any content and as such do not entail interests, values, motives, beliefs. And as he himself points out, the asymmetrical nature of these social relations must be clearly taken into account. However, without content—that is, the distinctive categories, beliefs, and motives created by a specific institutional logic—it will be impossible to explain what kinds of social relations have what kind of effect on the behavior of organizations and individuals. The meaning of participation in these social relations must be understood. That content can best be understood by situating those social relations within a particular institutional context. Otherwise, the "embeddedness" approach can easily be assimilated to a rational individualist perspective wherein individuals maximize utility through sociability, prestige, or power or to the functionalism of the new institutional economics wherein social relations are

limits to the ideals of family relations.

derived, just like hierarchy, through the limits of exchange. Without the content of these social relationships, we are unable to understand what trust—so central to these discussions—actually means.

To this point, we have argued that institutions are constituted by symbols and material practices, and that society is composed of multiple institutional logics which are available to individuals and organizations as bases for action. However, our conception of culture is neither consensual nor functionalist. In the following section, we explore the politics of culture.

The Politics of Culture

One of the central problems in social theory is the analytic status of culture, usually considered as both normative systems of values and cognitive systems of classification and theory. The dominant sociological tradition has been materialist in the sense that culture is understood as a "reflection" of underlying social relations. Symbols are reduced to their material foundations. This ranges from the most transparent case of culture as routinized behavior to more baroque formulations in which shared understandings of the economy, for example, are distorted and legitimating representations of exploitation.

More recent interpretive traditions, centered in anthropology, give ontological primacy to culture as an explanatory factor. One of the most serious drawbacks of almost all interpretive approaches in cultural anthropology and in the text-based hermeneutical analyses of society is that they lack politics. Michel Foucault shattered the subject-object dualism of the human sciences, delineating as he did the materiality of discourse. In his archeologies, he drew the historical connection between power and discourse, bridged through the concept of discipline which included technologies of control, mechanisms of normalization and reconstitution of the human subject, and new kinds of human sciences. The subject's movement in space, in time, his very identity and needs, are seen as shaped by the normalizing power of the state. These analyses focus on power, but without agency, without conflict. Although he analyzes the historical disjunctures in dominant discourses, Foucault is as trapped in historical time as Lévi-Strauss is frozen in ethnographic space. The inhabitants of the asylum are silent; we only hear the voices of their most sophisticated keepers, usually backed by the power of the state.[23] Dominant discourses are not contested; they move across time according to an alchemical logic of sign and symbol. The residents of the prison, the asylum, the mental hospital are not—by design—analyzed as human beings, as subjects.

The discourses not only constitute individuals, they seem to determine them. Statements, we are told by Deleuze, constitute both subjects and objects (1988). As a result, we do not understand the process of how people ended up in these normalizing organizations, or the choices through which people became participants in these historically variant discourses and thereby contributed to that history. Without actors, without subjectivity, there is no way to account for change.[24] And without multiple institutional logics available to provide alternative meanings, subjects are unlikely to find a basis for resistance. In Foucault's approach, governmentality is a modern form of discourse and institutional practice aimed at the regulation of populations with the objective of increased collective productivity. Its science is political economy; its dominant technical means are the security apparatuses of the state (Foucault 1983, 1979). Foucault's power-centered analysis of modern society unhinges "governmentality" and "bio-power" from any particular institutional configuration. Foucault's insistence on delocalizing discourse and power must depoliticize it. Such an analysis is perfectly compatible with his denial of the subject. We should not be forced to choose between an acultural analysis of power and an apolitical analysis of culture.

Our argument, in contrast, is that individuals can manipulate or reinterpret symbols and practices. Ethnomethodological studies of microinteractions in both interpersonal and organizational settings have shown that people are highly sensitive to context in rule use. Under some conditions, they are artful in the mobilization of *different* institutional logics to serve their purposes. Sometimes rules and symbols are internalized and result in almost universal conformity, but sometimes they are resources manipulated by individuals, groups, and organizations.

The success of an attempt at institutional change depends not simply on the resources controlled by its proponents, but on the nature of power and the institutionally specific rules by which resources are produced, allocated, and controlled. The institutional nature of power provides specific opportunities for not only reproduction, but transformation as well. For example, the recent emergence of the hostile takeover through U.S. capital markets is an institutional change which is changing the ways in which power is exercised within and between corporate organizations, interest is conceptualized, organizations are defined, and resources in the economy are allocated. Although opposed by the most powerful actors in the economy, this artful use of property law changed the allocation of resources in the economy.

The meaning and relevance of symbols may be contested, even as they are shared. Individuals, groups, and organizations struggle to change social relations both within and between institutions. As they do so, they produce new truths, new models by which to understand themselves and their societies, as well as new forms of behavior and material practices. As Mauss pointed out, debates about the true nature of Christ were intimately connected to cultural conflicts over the social construction of individuality. They parallel contemporary debates between, for example, psychoanalysts, behaviorists, and linguists about the nature of agency. These arguments diffuse into social practices—in law, in the welfare state, in urban planning, in education—and thereby help constitute the individuality about which they argue. Through the actions of individuals and organizations, the institutional structures of society are not simply reproduced, but transformed.

When institutions are in conflict, people may mobilize to defend the symbols and practices of one institution from the implications of changes in others. Or they may attempt to export the symbols and practices of one institution in order to transform another. Analysts such as E. P. Thompson and Michael Hechter have pointed to the ways in which groups use particular institutional orders—religion and territorial governance—to reach for power within both state and capitalism (Hechter 1975; Thompson 1963). Thus the sources of change and resistance within institutions are just as likely to be found in the contradictions between them.

We would argue that the bases of individual and organizational autonomy, and some of their most characteristic internal tensions, derive from the contradictory relationships between institutions. Thus the ancient Greek dramatists first represented individual choice through role conflict, as in the case of Sophocles' Antigone who is torn between familial duty to bury her brother and a political obligation not to bury a traitor (Hollis 1985).[25]

This analysis suggests a critique of two traditional approaches to the relationship between individual and society: role theory and rational-actor models. Role theory abstracts the role from the person and the institutional memberships that he or she must manage. Because humans live across institutions, it is necessary, unlike in role theory, to specify the institutional conditions under which individual behavior can be explained by a person's role as worker, voter, or lover. Conversely, rational-actor models which generalize microeconomic theory to all institutional arenas abstract person from role, assuming an egoistic, calculating actor that can be specified independent of the multiple roles that constitute the self. Because the meanings and relevance of individuality and rationality depend upon the specific institutional context, it is also necessary to specify the institutional conditions under which it makes sense to analyze individual behavior in these terms.

Because institutional symbols and claims can be manipulated and their meaning and behavioral implications contested, any activity—take voting, for example—can carry multiple meanings or motivations. Thus the decision to vote can convey, at the individual level of analysis, membership in a national community, an instrumental attempt to attain state benefits, a routine obligation of citizenship, a belief in a particular ideology or worldview. The ambiguous and contested nature of symbols circumscribes the applicability of abstract models of individual or organizational behavior. There is no one-to-one relationship between an institution and the meanings carried by the practices associated with it. Thus it is unlikely that capitalist economies, bureaucratic states, or nuclear families obey systemic laws which can be specified ahistorically.

As one moves from the societal to the individual or organizational level of analysis, instrumental images of rationalizing, maximizing, satisficing, or scheming behavior *are* more appropriate. The ways in which individuals or organizations do so are institutionally constrained, but they are not determined. The combination of multiple levels of analysis and contradictory institutional logics prevents a priori functionalist or consensual interpretations.

The Politics of Institutional Contradiction

The major institutions of contemporary society are interdependent and yet also contradictory. Thus, for example, bureaucratic states may depend upon democratic mechanisms to legitimate their decisions and to buffer and routinize the external political environment, but the extension of democratic procedures also threatens to undermine the coherence of the rational bureaucracy, whether in the adoption of consistent policies or the exercise of force in the relation between states. Or capitalist markets may depend upon families in order to minimize the costs of supplying a labor force, but at the same time, the labor market may undercut the capacity of families to support reproduction. These are just examples, but they suggest to us that institutional contradictions are the bases of the most important political conflicts in our society; it is through these politics that the institutional structure of society is transformed. A key task of social analysis is to understand those contradictions and to specify the conditions under which they shape organizational and individual action.[26]

Some of the most important struggles between groups, organizations, and classes are over the appropriate relationships between institutions, and by which institutional logic different activities should be regulated and to which categories of persons they apply. Is access to housing and health to be regulated by the market or by the state? Are families, churches, or states to control education? Should reproduction be regulated by state, family, or church? Or more recently in the case of Baby M, do rights of contract supersede those of biological parentage? Does equal protection apply to competition in the labor market? Should women be treated by the same exchange principles as men in the market? Do the rights of citizenship apply to the economy or do those of the market apply to the state? Can money be used to acquire grace or expiate wrongdoing? Should church offices be purchasable or heritable? Should foreign policy decisions be determined by independent state bureaucracies, multinational firms, or popular institutions? Although these struggles are acted out by groups and organizations, their consequences alter the interinstitutional relations constituting a society.

Through individual, organizational, and class politics, institutional contradictions may be politicized and institutions transformed. For example, in the United States, feminists have extended the logic of the capitalist market into the family, perhaps partly in response to the erosion of the unconditional loyalties which previously characterized it. The household division of labor is re-specified "contractually" between husband and wife; indeed the use of contract has been formalized in a significant number of marriages. Feminists thus stress the unpaid, potential monetary value of a woman's labor in the household and what it would cost a family to purchase those services in the marketplace.

Capitalists and workers have attempted in different ways to extend the logic of democracy to capitalism. Thus in the early twentieth century, capitalists successfully achieved the legal status of a juridical person for the corporations they owned, thereby limiting their personal liability and allowing mobilization of capital through stock markets. More recently, workers in many capitalist societies have pushed for the democratization of the workplace and the extension of "citizenship" rights of due process and even participation to the employment relation in private firms.[27] Workers attempt to redefine the social relations of production as defined by democratic rights of citizenship rather than contractual property rights. In the United States, which is weakly unionized, there is evidence that class politics have institutional, as opposed to merely organizational, effects. In her study of the diffusion of due process in the workplace, Lauren Edelman studied the diffusion of grievance procedures which eroded the "employment at will" common-law doctrine which had regulated the relationship between owners and workers (Edelman 1985). In her contrast of the diffusion of union and nonunion grievance procedures, two things stand out. First, unionized organizations were no more likely than nonunion organizations to adopt grievance procedures, and second, there was little difference in the functional form of diffusion between union and nonunion sectors. Both followed roughly an exponential growth curve. These findings suggest that class conflict can operate not only within organizations, at the "point of production," but institutionally through their effects on corporate and legal practices which affect the definitions of workers "rights" throughout the economy.

One source of class struggle can be conceived as a contradiction between use value, presumably grounded in the logic of the family, and exchange value, rooted in the logic of capitalism. The implication is that working-class consciousness may develop out of the importation of an institutional logic external to capitalism. When workers struggle for wages, for rights of representation, for influence in the workplace, for public control over capital investment, they appropriate the logic of other institutions in order to transform the places where they work—the logic of the family and human needs, the logic of democratic citizenship and participation, the logic of rationality enforced by the state. Thus, for example, both Smelser, a structural functionalist, and Joan Scott, a feminist theorist, have pointed to how changes in the organization of production disrupted normative patterns of family life, leading to working-class political mobilization, although Smelser reconceptualizes it as a reactive symptom of insufficient institutional differentiation (Smelser 1959; J. Scott 1984). Others have pointed to the ways in which wage structures were established to defend particular organizations of gender or family cycle (Robertson, forthcoming).

The politicization of institutional contradiction appears in socialist societies as well. Before perestroika, in a number of societies at the periphery of the Soviet Union, reformers—whether Solidarity in Poland or planners in Czechoslovakia and Hungary—were already attempting to extend the logic of democracy to the administered economy. Valtre Komarek, a long-time planner and director of the Institute for Forecasting of the Academy of Sciences, who had been charged with planning Czechoslovakia's likely future, emphasized the importance of his country's democratic tradition as the basis of adaptation to technological change.

> If up to now our society has shown a strong trend to centralized manipulation of human beings as objects, this has to be changed into a situation where human beings become sovereign subjects. Without this, at this stage of technological change, no modern society is possible. . . . We need a greater radius of action for each individual. . . . It is our centuries of democratic tradition that has enabled them [the Czechs] to work in nonstandard conditions. (Quoted in Kamm 1987:4)

Thus reform was promoted and experienced not as a contradiction between capitalism and socialism, but between democracy and bureaucracy.

Recent anthropological work on China also suggests the importance of historically specific institutional contradictions. Dissecting what she calls "the cultural economy of power," Mayfair Yang delineates three modes of exchange in the contemporary Chinese economy: state distribution, commodity markets, and a gift economy—the last a system of *guanxi,* rooted in Confucian kinship ethics (Yang 1989). Yang notes: "Each mode follows its own rules of operation, its own corpus of etiquette and good form in social relations, produces its own system of valuation and rates of exchange, and represents a unique style of the tactics and strategies of domination" (1989:32). While these institutional orders each give rise to specific "microtechniques of power," Yang contends these techniques are not institutionally confined, but can be used by individuals outside of their institutional locus to gain advantages and even subvert the logic of other institutions.[28] The possibility of "tactical" subversion is established by the personal discretion inherent in the distributive state economy. Unlike a commodity, a gift is not an object, alienable from its owner, and thus independent of the social relationship in which it is exchanged. Yang argues that the practice of *guanxi* is rooted in a culturally specific relational conception of the person, where identities are constructed through the medium of "face," or internalization of others' judgments. *Guanxi* depends upon creating identities, whatever the basis, between people such that norms of mutual obligation can be activated. Gift giving is an aggressive material and symbolical construction of commonality, of "insideness," from which obligation logically flows. Through gifts, lower-status persons take possession of powerful persons whose substance they have penetrated with their own. The accumulation of symbolic capital can compensate for lack of material wealth or bureaucratic office. Individuals make use of the institutional logic of kinship to penetrate state definitions of needs and social categories.

The premise of institutional contradiction derives from class theory. Contemporary class theorists, particularly those influenced by critical and Gramscian theory, have understood class conflict as simultaneously culturally and materially generated through institutional contradiction. However, they have assumed that the limits of institutional arrangements are functionally determined by the requirements of capitalism. As a result, class theory has been incapable of understanding the multiple contradictions of democratic capitalist societies. Thus, for example, some class theorists have converted the contradiction between democracy and capitalism into a problem in the legitimation of capitalism. They assume that a capitalist economy has a systemic tendency toward crisis, a logic independent of the consciousness of the agents who enact it. Without normative regulation from outside, the system cannot reproduce itself. Thus Habermas has referred to the democratic aspect of the state as a "legitimation" system (Habermas 1975). More recently, he has maintained that there is a contradiction between rational communication achieved through language and the rationalized systems based upon purposive rationality—state and capitalist economy—which coordinate action through money and power (Habermas 1984). Habermas, like Parsons, depoliticizes the organization of production by assuming that the forms that emerge are determined by the requirements of technical efficiency. The conflictive normative dimensions of the economy or society are lost from view.[29]

Claus Offe also argues that capitalism generates the dynamics of the social system, yet it "neutralizes meaning" upon which its reproduction increasingly depends (Offe 1984:82). The apparently autonomous, unconscious laws of capitalism require normative, noncommodified forms of intervention which intrude upon it. Offe argues that the rationality of the state has no meaning except in terms of its consequences for capitalism. Offe thus subordinates the bureaucratic and democratic aspects of the state to the functions they perform for capitalism.

Not only do these analyses privilege the capitalist economy as the dominant institutional order, but they make culture a functional element in the maintenance of capitalist social order. Each institutional order is both potentially autonomous and contradictory with others. We do not believe that societal crises derive primarily from the tendency to export the internal contradictions of capitalism. Rather they may equally derive from external institutional contradictions between democracy, capitalism, state, family, and religion.

Conclusion

If the institutional constraints on behavior are not specified, the social sciences risk becoming ideologies of the institutions they study. Foucault has pointed to the double relation between truth and power, between forms of knowledge and power relations, between the development of the human sciences and the state (Foucault 1980). When social scientists import the dominant institutional logics into their analyses of individuals and organizations in unexamined ways, they unreflectively elaborate the symbolic order and social practices of the institutions they study. These elaborations subsequently become factors in the reproduction of these institutions and thus contribute to their hegemony, whether through socialization of institutional personnel or formulation of public policy (Giddens 1986, 1984).[30]

By becoming part of the grounding assumptions of social theory, the systematic ways in which individuals act out of these logics take on the aura of natural law, which is not unlike the way in which ordinary individuals themselves experience them. It is not accidental that public-choice theory has flourished and that one of its American champions has been crowned as a Nobel laureate at the same time that efforts are under way to disengage the state from major areas of distribution and production. The power of theory in part reflects the dominance of the institutions from which it derives its models. Categories of knowledge contribute to and yet depend upon the power of the institutions which make them possible. Without understanding the historical and institutional specificity of the primary categories of analysis, social scientists run the risk of only elaborating the rationality of the institutions they study, and as a result become actors in their reproduction.

Acknowledgments

Paul DiMaggio has been our inspiring nudge. The authors are deeply indebted to him and to numerous colleagues with whom they have discussed this essay: Mayfair Yang, Frances Fox Piven, Richard Hecht, Elvin Hatch, Ron Jepperson, Claus Offe, Alex Hicks, Harvey Molotch, Magnus Stenbeck, David Swartz, Michael Burawoy, Donald Palmer, Erik Wright, Satish Deshpande, Judith Stacey, Bill Friedland, Wendy Mink, Michael Brown, Mayer Zald, Andy Szasz, David Wellman, and Wally Goldfrank, as well as audiences at various universities who have offered useful comments and criticisms.

Notes

1. Skocpol argues that a "state's means of raising and deploying financial resources" is the most important single factor explaining a state's "capacities to create or strengthen

state organizations, to employ personnel, to coopt political support, to subsidize economic enterprises, and to fund social programs" (1985:17). Why this is the most important factor she does not argue.

2. Mauss traces the origin of the "social fact" of the person to the development of Roman citizenship, and the attachment of legal rights to persons, linked to the history of the persona, as a right to a set of names. Mauss sees a historical movement from personnage, to personne, to self.

3. When Homer wrote, biography did not exist. By the fourth century it was a distinct literary genre.

4. Sappho, the lyric poet whom Plato referred to as the "tenth Muse," made personal requests to Aphrodite and was thought to have committed suicide because of her unrequited love of a boatman.

5. Durkheim wrote that in the view of the French economists of his day, "there is nothing real in society except the individual; it is from him that everything emanates and it is to him that everything returns. . . . The individual . . . is the sole tangible reality that the observer can attain, and the only problem that science can pose is that of discovering how the individual must behave in the principal circumstances of economic life, given his nature" (Lukes 1972:80).

6. From his *Leçons de sociologie,* in Lukes 1972:271.

7. See Shweder and Bourne 1984 for the Indian case. While these analysts showed that Indians were intellectually able to abstract, they did not do so with respect to the concept of the person. Unfortunately, the researchers did not specify the context in which an abstract concept of the person might be more or less likely to develop.

8. Unlike Judaism, whose sacred texts narrate a collective history, Christianity's text is sacred biography. S. N. Eisenstadt argues for the importance of an axial age which split mundane and transcendent orders in several civilizations. Indicative of this transformation, God was no longer symbolized in human terms. This transformation established the possibility of a direct individual relationship with the transcendent order and thus established the symbolic conditions necessary for individuality. See Eisenstadt 1983.

9. Dumont argues that the progressive individuation reaches its height with Calvinism, which identifies human will with the will of God (Dumont 1982).

10. This study both failed to take the symbolic content of social structure seriously and neglected key institutional orders of the modern world, particularly religion and family. The book is also missing a last synthetic chapter. We offer this essay as partial compensation.

11. Stenbeck stresses the importance of alternate Raschian measurement techniques for assessing person variability in structures of meaning in order to determine scalability. These techniques are built on the assumption of a probabilistic relationship between societal structure and individual action rather than on a deterministic one (Stenbeck 1986).

12. Bureaucratic organization, for example, assumes abstract individuals, else it would not be possible to separate persons from offices.

13. We are indebted to Paul DiMaggio for this point.

14. Hirschman also argues that the analytic concept of interest has become a "vacuous tautology" (1986:50).

15. The construction of this indicator of performance is even more arbitrary within organizations (Eccles and White 1988).

16. Cross-national variations in rates of return might provide a particularly fruitful avenue for institutional analysis. The Japanese case of low rates of long-term return is a relevant puzzle. That the government absorbs long-term risks may not be an adequate explanation. Economists are increasingly recognizing the limits of neoclassical return on equity models to explain asset price variation. This area too suggests a fruitful area for institutional analysis.

17. Giddens makes the same kind of analytic approach when he stresses that the importance of "ontological security" derives from the routines of daily life, which, if disrupted, make people available for new institutionalization.

18. Schneider has written a trenchant critique of Geertz's account of the cockfight in which he argues that Geertz conflates significance and signification and provides no evidentiary base that the Balinese experience the meaning of the cockfight in the way that Geertz does or says they do (1987). But other than pointing out the incidence of cockfights elsewhere, Schneider has not shown that the Balinese *do not* experience them, whether discursively or nondiscursively, that way.

19. Where the boundaries are drawn, whether parochially as a "private" nuclear family, ethnicity, religion, nation, "master race," or all humanity, is problematic.

20. This list is only meant to be suggestive. While institutional boundaries are contested and hence fluid, they should in principle be observable in patterns of material and symbolic practice. This is not to say there is not a set of technical functions that any society must accomplish, only that the functions do not uniquely determine the institutional structure through which they are accomplished. In some sense, our title—"Bringing Society Back In"—is a misnomer, for while institutional orders may coincide in time, they do not necessarily cohere in space. Giddens is quite right to argue that it is the ability of the state to territorially bound other institutions in space that comprises the object of sociology—society.

21. This is not to say that under certain conditions. participation in these social relations may make life meaningless and individuals unable to achieve their ends. The existence of ideologies represents struggles over institutional boundaries and definitions of reality.

22. While Douglas recognizes the existence of the incompatible principles which organize different institutions (1986:126), she does not theorize them, given her concern to establish the basis of social solidarity in shared categories of knowledge.

23. Yet in *Madness and Civilization,* the one time they act—the objection of other prisoners to their common confinement with the mad—that action is deemed central to the transformation of the categorical system.

24. In his last work on the history of sexuality, Foucault takes up the subject of resistance to power, which he argues is not only universal, but "interior" to the power relation. See Foucault 1980.

25. As Hollis notes, "They choose as persons who are their masks, not as individuals who play their parts" (1985:222).

26. Our account here emphasizes interinstitutional, as opposed to intrainstitutional, contradictions. We began to analyze the internal contradictions within the state of its democratic, capitalist, and bureaucratic aspects (Alford and Friedland 1985). The theoretical challenge is to understand the relationship between internal and external institutional contradictions, as these are lived by persons and managed by organizations, such that the interinstitutional structure of society is either reproduced or transformed.

27. This, of course, was the expectation of T. H. Marshall, who predicted a gradual expansion of citizenship rights, or what we would call the logic of democracy, sequentially through juridical, political, social, and eventually economic realms (Marshall 1964). Conversely, Marxists argued that other social activities would increasingly fall under the logic of capitalism through commodification, as in the understanding of voting as a market exchange, the privatization of public services, and the tying of social benefits to labor market position.

28. Yang defines microtechniques in Foucault's sense as "forms of power relationships having the effect of disciplining and normalizing the population" (1988:30). Here Yang draws on Foucault's notion of governmentability. In fact, her text can be read as an empirical challenge to Foucault's state-centered institutional analysis of modern society, which unhinges "governmentality" and "bio-power" from any particular institutional configuration. For the microtechniques are strongly correlated with institutional orders, and their multiplicity, as in the case of gift giving, does not "discipline" the population, but is a means by which the population may evade the determination of "needs" by the state.

29. Parsons too stresses the formal rationality of production.

30. Giddens makes this point regarding the concept of balance of power and national sovereignty in the relationships among states (1986).

Part Three

Empirical Investigations

A. Constructing Organizational
   Fields
B. Institutional Change
C. Institutional and Competitive
   Forces

11 Constructing an Organizational Field as a Professional Project: U.S. Art Museums, 1920–1940

Paul J. DiMaggio

A key development in organizational sociology during the past two decades has been the increasing prominence of such concepts as industry, sector, population, domain, and field (Burt 1983; DiMaggio and Powell, ch. 3, this vol.; Hannan and Freeman 1989; ch. 5; Scott, ch. 7, this vol.). These constructs are central to efforts to explain patterns of interorganizational competition, influence, coordination, and flows of innovation because they define the boundaries within which these processes operate.

The question of where organizational fields come from has received little attention, however. This issue is particularly important for institutional theories of organizational change, for two reasons. First, institutional theory focuses on processes of mutual influence among organizations. Field boundaries, as they are perceived by participants, affect how organizations select models for emulation, where they focus information-gathering energy, which organizations they compare themselves with, and where they recruit personnel. Second, institutional theory pays particular attention to organizations like government agencies and trade associations that stand outside an industry per se, but within a sector or field, and influence or constrain the goods- or service-producing organizations within it. The related emergence of a collective definition of a set of organizations as an "industry," of formal and informal networks linking such organizations, and of organizations committed to supporting, policing, or setting policy toward the "industry"—what Powell and I refer to as the "structuration" of organizational fields—is a crucial step in the institutionalization of organizational forms (DiMaggio and Powell, ch. 3, this vol.; DiMaggio 1983).

Structuration processes are historically and logically prior to the processes of institutional isomorphism to which most institutional research has attended and, as I have argued elsewhere, are likely to entail quite different causal dynamics (DiMaggio 1988a). In other words, to understand the institutionalization of organizational *forms,* we must first understand the institutionalization and structuring of organizational *fields.* Where institutional processes have the greatest impact on organizational change, such fields are not simply investigators' aggregative constructs, but are meaningful to participants and include specialized organizations that constrain, regulate, organize, and represent at the level of the field itself. The neglect by researchers of structuration processes provides a one-sided vision of institutional change that emphasizes taken-for-granted, nondirected, nonconflictual evolution at the expense of intentional (if boundedly rational), directive, and conflict-laden processes that define fields and set them upon trajectories that eventually appear as "natural" developments to participants and observers alike (see Brint and Karabel, ch. 14, this vol.).

The purpose of this chapter is modest: to describe some moments in the structuration of one organizational field, U.S. art museums. Much of the story will not surprise students of institutions. The national diffusion of art museums was accompanied, as we would expect, by the emergence of fieldwide organization and developing consensus about many aspects of museum form and function. A central agency, the Carnegie Corporation, offered pivotal support to the structuration of the field. And members of a professionalizing occupation—museum workers—were instrumental at every step of the process. But the account also highlights three aspects of institutionalization which have thus far received scant attention.

The first has to do with models of diffusion. Studies of the diffusion of new organizational forms usually emphasize organizational imperatives and local decisions, implicitly suggesting that organizational forms are standardized through the effortless evolution of commonsense understandings about how to organize. By contrast, among the museums we see substantial discord about key aspects of museum form and function as well as the emergence of a national infrastructure—at which professional organizations supported by philanthropic foundations are at the core—committed to speeding and shaping the diffusion process.

The second lesson concerns tensions within the institutionalization process. Institutional theorists have focused upon the tendency for organizational forms to become more legitimate as they win wider acceptance. In the museum field, however, the price of acceptance was the mobilization of a constituency, including professionals and social reformers, with interests that diverged from those of the founding local elites. In other words, the diffusion process not only legitimated the museum as an organizational form, but at the same time legitimated conflict over the interpretation of the museum's mission.

Third, professionals were at the forefront of such debates, as scholarship about organizational professionals would lead us to expect. What is striking, however, is how little conflict occurred *inside* organizations and how much was played out *at the level of the field*. Professionals seem to have possessed a dual consciousness that enabled them to function as conservatives in organizational roles at the same time they used fieldwide organizations to launch attacks on the system that employed them.

The role of professionals is central to all three points, for they dominated both reform efforts and fieldwide organization. Although there are many studies of established organizational fields and many of professionalization, the former rarely take a historical perspective, whereas the latter rarely consider the influence of professionalizing occupations on interorganizational relations. To combine these perspectives requires a design that enables one to study both organizations that employ professionals and also professionally controlled organizations in the former's environment. This chapter is based on archival research, most of it in two organizations: the Carnegie Corporation of New York, a philanthropic foundation that supported aspiring professionals as a means of encouraging interorganizational coordination and change in the museum field; and the Pennsylvania Museum of Art, which employed several leading professional activists during this period, received generous funding from the Carnegie Corporation and other philanthropies, and served as a laboratory for the professional project of museum workers. Archival research of this kind permits a deeper focus than reconstruction of publicly available accounts, yet greater breadth, both geographically and over time, than does conventional ethnography.

Institutional Context

American art museums originated in the late nineteenth century as educational institutions dedicated to refining national taste and improving industrial design by exhibiting objects of beauty to which most Americans would not otherwise have had access (Harris 1962; Fox 1963; Zolberg 1974). This early emphasis on education shifted markedly toward acquisition and connoisseurship as soon as aesthetic standards were articulated and art works embodying these standards came within the grasp of American collectors. By 1920, the art museums' organization reflected the ideal and status interests of the urban social elites who governed them. The dominant model of the art museum, set forth by Benjamin Ives Gilman (1918), secretary of the Boston Museum of Fine Arts, was the product of a struggle that reoriented the museum from an educational institution to a curatorial one. This transformation entailed the classification of art work into a narrowly defined "high art" category and a more inclusive category of "nonart," and the exclusion of the latter (e.g., gewgaws, instructional plaster reproductions) from museum collections. It also involved the elaboration of an etiquette of appropriation, and a justifying ideology of connoisseurship, that defined authentic artistic perception in a manner that reinforced the status claims of elite patrons while devaluing the aspirations of the less educated and well to do (DiMaggio 1982a, 1982b).

Counterposed to the dominant model was an alternative vision of the art museum influenced by the experience of public libraries and department stores (Grana 1963:95–111; Zolberg 1986), best described in the work of John Cotton Dana (1917). Dana, a central figure in the professionalization of library work who pioneered the use of open stacks in public collections, was director of the Museum of the Newark Library Association and a leading reformer (Kingdon 1948; Cahill 1944; Alexander 1983:377–411).

These two models differed from one another in almost every respect (see table 11.1). Gilman's museum was devoted to the object: to its collection and conservation, and to the selection and sacralization of that which was worthy to bear the status of art. The museum ideal of the progressive reformers (reflected in museums at Newark and Rochester) stressed broad public education and, as means to that end, frequent special exhibitions and generous interpretation of the works exhibited.

The models differed as well in their definitions of art and education. Gilman espoused a restrictive view of what M. A. Abrams (1985) has called "art-as-such": the notion that true art is rare, timeless, disinterested, nonutilitarian, and qualitatively different from nonart. By contrast, progressives like Dana defined art broadly to include well-designed objects of use, regarded art as inseparable from its social context, and welcomed the exhibition of casts and well-rendered reproductions. (Dana believed most museums exhibited an "undue reverence for oil paint" and suggested that the major contribution of American art was the design of the American bathroom [Dana 1917:20; Cahill 1944]).

According to Gilman, the museum's aim was to permit the direct, unmediated perception of the work of art by the visitor, whom he called "the disciple." Only the slimmest interpretative materials were tolerated, lest they contaminate the relationship between the perceiver and the object. Such a view privileged the perceptions of the educated public and the upper classes, who could acquire through socialization or training what the museum was forbidden to impart. Artistic consumption was ritualized and perception ranked according to authenticity as adjudicated by the social circle of collectors and allied curators who controlled the museum (DiMaggio 1982b). By contrast, museum reformers sought to demystify art, believed in the validity of multiple readings of art works, focused on education rather than connoisseurship, and advocated the use of whatever interpretative materials contributed to this end.

These differences reflected and reinforced divergences in the two models' conceptions of the museum's public and the constituencies to which museum officials were most responsive. Conventional museums were governed by patrons, trustees, and donors, with the help of aesthetic specialists, and oriented their programs to the needs and interests of local elites, collectors, and the educated middle class. Museums influenced by the reform model defined their community to include the broad general public, but especially manufacturing

Table 11.1 Two Models of the Art Museum

	Gilman Model MFA, Boston	Data Model Newark, Branches
Mission	Collection Conservation Selection/sacralization	Education Exhibition Interpretation
Definition of art	Art-as-such Strongly bounded Rare objects	Art-for-use Weakly bounded Well-designed objects
Legitimate perception	Connoisseurship Direct, unmediated Ritual Hierarchical	Learning Aided by interpretation Pluralistic
Education	Low priority Primarily juvenile Special programs for members and scholars	Highest priority Primarily adult Special programs for trade or ethnic groups
Major publics	Local elites Collectors Educated middle class	General public Manufacturing groups Designers Craft workers
Control	Patrons Trustees Donors Aesthetic professionals	Museum professionals Educators, exhibitors State influence
Strategy	Rapid growth in collection, moderate growth in budget, no attendance growth, through service to collectors, patrons, scholars, and educated middle class	Rapid growth in attendance and budget, low growth in collec- tion, through service to indus- try, trades, and public schools
Building	Elegant, awe-inspriring Classical models	Simple, accessible Department store model
Living artists	Exclusion	Inclusion

Sources: Gilman 1918; Dana 1917.

groups, designers, and craftsmen. Such museums were more willing to accept the public accountability associated with support by government and permitted museum workers, including specialists in education and exhibition technique, to play a larger role.

Control, in turn, dictated the implicit strategies that museums pursued. The typical art museum of the 1920s sought to increase its collections as rapidly as possible and to boost its budget in order to acquire more art and preserve what it acquired. (Even during the Great Depression, 50 percent of art museum expenditures went toward acquisition [Coleman 1939:194].) By contrast, the reformers sought to follow the strategy successfully employed by public libraries: rapid expansion of budget and staff through extension of public service and attendance and increases in municipal support.

Finally, the traditional model's focus on insulating art and its patrons from nonart, the market, and the larger public was reflected both in the proliferation of classical museum buildings, often in remote locations, and in the virtual exclusion of living American artists and their work from the museum and its galleries. Reformers advocated functionally designed museums, built on the model of department stores and located in busy commercial neighborhoods, and exhibitions including the work of living American artists.

The components of the reform position can be traced to the nineteenth century—London's South Kensington Museum, the arts and crafts movement, the librarians' professionalization project—and were aimed at art museums with increasing frequency after 1895 (Goode 1897; Dana 1917). But it was only with their embrace by the professional vanguard of museum work that they became influential enough to win sponsorship from national foundations.

Factors Facilitating the Rise of Professionalism

As I have suggested, institutional theory has neglected the contradictory tendency of successful institutionalization projects to legitimize not just new organizational forms, but also new categories of authorized actors whose interests diverge from those of the groups controlling the organizations, and new resources such actors can use in their efforts to effect organizational change. Indeed, it was the very success of the art museum as an organizational form in the 1920s that provided cadres and resources for those who wished to change it.

By 1930 the United States had 167 art museums, of which 60 had been created during the previous nine years (Coleman 1932, cited in Adam 1939:49); the country was in the midst of a museum-building boom, which, despite the Great Depression, would bring the total to 387 by 1938 (Coleman 1939:663). So accepted was this new form that the Ogburn Commission, appointed by President Hoover, reported, "Today a museum is found in every city in the United States of more than 250,000 inhabitants" (Keppel 1933:994). Between 1920 and 1930, private gifts of $100,000 or more to arts institutions (almost all to "museums or art centers") soared from $2.6 to $18 million, and the capitalization of American art museums rose from $15 million in 1910 to $58 million by 1930 (Keppel and Duffus 1933:24, 65).

With increases in wealth and size, the museums hired more paid staff, including specialists in public education, and divided them into separate departments. In 1924 only one in four art museums offered any educational services; by 1930, directors of public art museums were obliged to employ at least one full-time educator, and such leaders as the Metropolitan, Cleveland, and

Detroit museums boasted sizable teaching staffs (Bach 1924). The proliferation of museum staff created a pool of potential participants in the museum workers' professional project.

The 1920s were marked, as well, by increasing municipal support for art museums. Many museums followed the precedent of the Metropolitan, which looked to the city for its building, maintenance, and educational budgets, while trustees financed the collections, salaries, and scholarship. For some new or reorganized museums, such as the Detroit Art Institute and the Pennsylvania Museum of Art, dependence on tax dollars was even greater. For trustees, municipal aid softened recurrent demands for contributions. For museum professionals, city patronage provided some promise of release from the exacting grip of trustee control. Municipal support strengthened the hand of staff who sought greater investments in education: a contemporary study reported that museums with substantial public support "make more educational contacts in their communities" (Cooke 1934:6).

These developments reflected a broad expansion of interest in art during the 1920s. The value of imported art works rose sharply during the second half of that decade, to more than 1 percent of all imports between 1927 and 1929 (Keppel and Duffus 1933:17). Census figures reveal a rise in the number of artists, sculptors, and art teachers from 20,800 in 1920 to 35,600 in 1930 (p. 19).

The professionalization of museum work was fueled directly by the expansion of higher education in the fine arts. Whereas in 1876 only seven colleges or universities offered courses in art history or appreciation and in 1916 fewer than one in four provided such instruction, by 1930 few accredited institutions failed to do so (Bach 1924:30; Hiss and Fansler 1934:18). This expansion had three major effects. The first was to produce consumers of the art museum's services. The second was to produce experts: 50 percent more graduate theses were submitted in the arts and archaeology between 1920 and 1930 as in all the years before 1920 (Hiss and Fansler 1934:39). The third was the consolidation of art history courses, previously scattered among several academic specialties, into departments of art history or fine arts. Consolidation heightened interaction among faculty at different universities and drew universities closer to museums, as several key departments (notably Harvard, Yale, Princeton, and New York University) developed programs to train potential museum workers in connoisseurship and art history.

If academic museum training programs created an independent cadre of experts concerned with but not employed by museums, professional reformers still needed an independent source of capital to fuel their efforts. Significantly, the 1920s hailed the beginnings of scientific philanthropy as several large foundations, especially those associated with the Rockefeller and Carnegie fortunes, expanded the size and influence of their professional staff in an attempt to enhance the efficiency of their giving. Whereas such foundations had previously served as extensions of their founders, by the 1920s new leadership endeavored to harness their activities to the search for scientific solutions to social problems (Lagemann 1983; Radford 1984). The ideological fit between the foundation administrators' progressive faith in planning and expert control in the interest of public service, and that of museum reformers, made the former potent allies of the museum workers' collective mobility project.

The Carnegie Corporation and Professional Control

These facilitating factors swelled the ideological, human, and financial resources available to aspiring professionals in and around museums. By the late 1920s a dense underbrush of organization dominated by museum staff and academic art historians had grown up around the art museum field. As universities embraced the arts, a consortium of regional associations of school art teachers came under the leadership of university faculty, renamed itself the College Art Association, and developed into the disciplinary voice of art historians. The American Federation of Arts, founded in 1909, became an active supplier of exhibitions to women's clubs and art museums around the country. Art museum directors formed a group of their own and held regular meetings. The American Association of Museums (AAM), a society of museum workers and trustees whose activities had been limited to holding annual meetings at which members lectured one another on museum philosophy and technique, increased and diversified its membership and activities, establishing and staffing a national office at the Smithsonian Institution. Professionally dominated associations of this kind increased the level of communication among professionals and enhanced their organizational skills, thus reducing the cost of further organization (Marrett 1980; Wiewel and Hunter 1986).

The most important of these organizations was the AAM. Because it was not simply a professional society, instead seeking organizational as well as individual members and including sympathetic trustees on its governing council, it could claim to speak for the museum field. At the same time, it was controlled by professionals, who had the time and energy to cultivate it, and it pursued the projects and reforms they favored. Indeed, the purpose of the association's expansion was to mount "an educational campaign to bring about a more general realization of the significance of the modern museum as a fundamental factor in an educational system capable of adequately meeting the present day need."[1] Between 1923 and 1932, the association enlarged its membership from 81 to 208 museums and from 365 to 909 individuals.[2] The AAM's focus on research, coordination, and pilot projects in the area of museum management and education won the favor of progressive foundations. By 1929, it had received substantial support from the Laura Spelman Rockefeller Memorial, the Rockefellers' General Education Board, and the Carnegie Corporation.[3]

Of these foundations, none was more active in support of the arts than the

Carnegie Corporation of New York, which, under the presidency of Frederick Keppel (1923–41), mounted the first concerted effort to treat the arts as a coherent field susceptible to central influence and direction, that is, as an object of policy (DiMaggio 1988b). Under Keppel, Carnegie made more than $13 million in grants to the arts and museums, representing more than 80 percent of all such foundation assistance during this period (Jubin 1968; DiMaggio 1986b). The corporation contributed generously to professional associations and coordinative agencies: by 1938 it had given nearly $700,000 to the American Federation of Arts, almost $200,000 to the AAM, and nearly $120,000 to the College Art Association (Lester 1940:39–41; Jubin 1968).

Carnegie president Keppel and many of his trustees believed that the arts, defined broadly after the fashion of the reformers, were essential elements in the good life and that with proper planning, infusions of expertise, and enlightened leadership, art museums could become as vital to public education as libraries (support for which was from Andrew Carnegie's time a cornerstone of the foundation's program). Their faith in central planning made it logical for Keppel and his colleagues to aid organizations that operated at the national level; their confidence in experts drew them to universities and professionals. Consequently, Carnegie's grants contributed to professionalizing museum work as a means of coordinating the museum field. The result was an organizational field largely defined by the informal or associational activities of museum professionals, rather than by formal ties among the museums that employed them.

To illustrate this argument, let us consider how the Carnegie Corporation's grants supported each of five key dimensions of professionalization (condensed from Wilensky 1964 and Larson 1977) and four dimensions of structuration (DiMaggio 1983). Note that the same grants simultaneously supported activities that advanced professionalism and structured the organizational field.

PROFESSIONALIZATION

Production of University-Trained Experts

Keppel's first advisory committee on the arts (1924) was dominated by academic art historians and critics, and his first major grants in the area were $100,000 to support Paul Sachs's training course at Harvard and a grant to create art-history teaching sets (books, photographs, lantern slides) for distribution to colleges and universities (Anderson 1941; Jubin 1968). By 1941, 140 U.S. institutions had received these sets, at a cost to Carnegie of $625,000. The foundation also made general-purpose grants (for endowment, chairs, teaching equipment, or library materials) totaling more than $1.75 million to assist or to establish fine arts departments in 46 American colleges and universities. The institutions that trained the largest number of museum staff—

Harvard, New York University, Princeton, and Yale—received grants of $100,000 or more.

Creation of a Body of Knowledge

The Carnegie Corporation made many grants to colleges and universities to support art historical scholarship and the application of scientific technique to the analysis and preservation of art works. Carnegie sponsored "surveys" of the arts and museum activities—some through the American Association of Museums—studies by psychologists of the efficacy of different exhibition methods, research on museum education, and efforts to develop intelligence tests of artistic aptitude (e.g., Bach 1924; Meier 1926; Robinson 1928; Rea 1932; Hiss and Fansler 1934; Melton 1935; Ramsey 1938; Adam 1939; Coleman 1939).

Organization of Professional Associations

We have already seen the extent of the Carnegie Corporation's assistance to fieldwide organizations. The American Association of Museums became, in effect, a client of the Corporation, relying on Carnegie for approximately one-third of its operating expenses throughout the depression. The Corporation also supported the AAM's publication and research activities.

Consolidation of a Professional Elite

The Carnegie Corporation's programs facilitated the emergence of an elite in several ways. First, its grants to universities sponsored the development of training programs, especially Harvard's under Paul J. Sachs, whose students constituted an informal network that dominated the art museum field for decades (Ciniglio 1976). Second, the Corporation's use of museum directors and staff as members of advisory groups enhanced the prestige and multiplied the professional contacts of those chosen. Third, Keppel was himself consulted by museum trustees in search of directors. When the Metropolitan filled its coveted directorship in 1940, both finalists were among those whom Keppel had recommended.[4]

Increasing the Organizational Salience of Professional Expertise

By emphasizing educational activities in its funding, the Carnegie Corporation empowered those staff who were capable of developing eligible programs. Before the 1920s, trustees controlled the resources museums needed: they gave money and art, knew other potential patrons and collectors, and had the political clout to garner municipal aid. By contrast, because Keppel's contacts (outside of New York) were with professionals rather than trustees, Carnegie's museum program placed directors in the unwonted position of gatekeepers with respect to important assistance.

STRUCTURATION

Increases in the Density of Interorganizational Contacts

The Carnegie Corporation's support for the American Association of Museums' regional and national conferences and advisory activities, and the Corporation's own convocations of museum professionals, increased the intensity of interaction among museums. Even isolated museums fell into contact with professional activists as a result of the Corporation's grant making. Figure 11.1 depicts the path traveled by Laurence V. Coleman, director of the AAM, as he carried out research for *The Museum in America: A Critical Study* (1939). Note that Carnegie's programs spurred informal interaction among museum professionals rather than formal relations among museums.

Increases in the Flow of Information

Carnegie's museum programs increased the flow of organizationally salient information by increasing the volume of research findings, sponsoring educational programs for museum professionals, and funding the publication of books, periodicals, and directories.

Emergence of a Center-Periphery Structure

By making grants to selected museums for pilot projects (and to the AAM to publish a periodical that reported such projects' results), the Carnegie Corporation and other foundations drew attention to successful applicants in a way that enhanced their position in the field as a whole. Similarly, Carnegie's support of the professional elite further reinforced the centrality of their institutions.

Collective Definition of a Field

By focusing in its grant making on the contribution of art museums as a group, supporting the American Association of Museums, funding production of directories of museums (Everard 1932) and museum workers (Bingham 1933), and supporting the collection and reporting of data on museums (e.g., Rea 1932), the Carnegie Corporation program reinforced the awareness of museum professionals and trustees that they were part of a collective enterprise, and thus the likelihood that they would look to one another as models and as sources of innovation.

In reviewing the implications of the Carnegie Corporation's activities for the professionalization and structuration of the environment surrounding art museums, I have not meant to imply that Keppel and his colleagues set out to achieve these ends in a coherent manner or that the Carnegie program was single-hand-

Fig. 11.1 Laurence Vail Coleman's trip to gather data for *The Museum in America: A Critical Study*. From his report to the Carnegie Corporation, August 6, 1935.

edly responsible for them. Such a view would be misleading for three reasons. First, although Carnegie played the major role as a center around which structuration could occur, it was joined by the Rockefeller philanthropies and, in the 1930s, by the federal government's arts projects, which further focused museum managers' attention on the national level. Second, Carnegie's museum grant-making was far-ranging, even scattered; the pattern, taken as a whole, was not the product of conscious design. Third, and most important, the Carnegie museum programs were as much a *resource* for professional reformers as they were an expression of the Corporation's own intentions. To understand this latter point, it is useful to look inside the Carnegie Corporation and its decision-making process.

The Case of the Branch Museum

None of the Carnegie Corporation's initiatives reflected the reform professionals' challenge to the standard model of the American art museum so clearly as did its support for the creation of neighborhood branch museums, a cause John Cotton Dana had long championed. The manner in which Carnegie came to sponsor Dana's scheme reveals both the influence that professional activists exercised in the Corporation's deliberations and the adventitious nature of the program development process during the Keppel years.

Frederick Keppel's preference, for reasons both of administrative efficiency and of diplomacy, was to delegate grant requests and program development to associations of experts. When possible he worked through formal organizations: the American Library Association for the Corporation's program of assistance to university libraries; and for the program in adult education, the American Association of Adult Education. Keppel had hoped to use the American Association of Museums in the same way, but was overruled by his trustees, who urged him to constitute a less formal body, which he designated the Museum Education Advisory Group.[5]

The advisory group's composition is revealing. All nine were AAM members, and five had been AAM officers, councilors, or committee chairs. The chairman, Clark Wissler, was a curator at the American Museum of Natural History. John Cotton Dana headed the list of members, followed by Charles R. Richards, director of the General Education Board's Industrial Arts Division and before that AAM's first full-time director. To gauge Keppel's reliance on AAM activists we can compare his advisers to a list of seventeen "leading museum men" compiled by Paul Sachs (the most influential museum man of his time) as part of the campaign to establish the Museum of Modern Art.[6] The two lists naturally differ: Keppel's was restricted to museum workers with special interest in education, included three from science and history museums, and drew heavily on the New York area. Despite their greater seniority and eminence, however, only four of Sachs's seventeen influentials (compared to five of

Keppel's nine advisers) had been AAM officers or councilors. Five men on Sachs's list were not even AAM members, although Sachs himself traveled within the AAM orbit and within one year would be the association's president.

The advisory group's proximity to the AAM was reflected in its recommendations to the Corporation. Of just over $300,000 in grants authorized by the group over its two-year existence, approximately $120,000 went to the AAM, another $30,000 to an AAM-sponsored study by a Yale psychologist, and $80,000 to the Pennsylvania Museum, the director of which was AAM president Fiske Kimball.[7]

Having drawn his advisers from the professional reform ranks, Keppel gave them free reign in designing a program and evaluating proposals to the Carnegie Corporation, intervening only to prevent administrative embarrassment. In a memorandum prepared for the second meeting of the Museum Education Advisory Group, John Cotton Dana recommended branches as a way to revive the appeal of museums, which he called "almost negligible." Only when "the aid they give to education . . . is seen to grow in extent and quality," wrote Dana, will "the income of museums from public funds be increased."[8] But Dana, who would die in July 1929, was too ill to attend the group's meetings. Reluctant to exercise the initiative Keppel had given them, the other advisers evaluated proposals and avoided the task of program design.

They were stirred to action only when one member pressed upon them an ill-conceived proposal for a National School Museum to lend art reproductions to public schools. Although a joint committee of the AAM and the National Education Association produced the plan, it was unpopular with the AAM members, who feared such an agency would jeopardize their own fragile but lucrative relations with local school systems. Urged privately by AAM president Kimball to reject the proposal, but, like his own advisers, reluctant to offend an advisory group member, Keppel suggested to Wissler that he appoint a consultant to study the matter.[9]

The man retained for this post was Paul Marshall Rea, who had written path-breaking studies of museums for the U.S. commissioner of education before the First World War and who, as president of the AAM between 1919 and 1921, mounted the successful effort to establish the association in Washington with a permanent staff (Coleman 1939:40). The year before, Rea had fallen out with his trustees at the Cleveland Museum of Natural History, resigned, and gone to work for Fiske Kimball at the Pennsylvania Museum of Art, where he designed an accounting system and headed a slender educational program.[10]

Rea set zealously to his task. Within one month he persuaded the advisory group to broaden his mandate by making him staff investigator on all proposals and, more important, to permit him to undertake research "charting the field and defining underlying principles of the educational work of museums."[11] Once the vexing matter of the National School Museum was settled by its proponent's death, Rea devoted nearly all of his time to this synoptic effort.

The advisory group's members were uncompensated and sporadic participants in the Carnegie program, and Keppel himself was preoccupied with other matters. Not surprisingly, therefore, Rea exercised increasing initiative in the group's deliberations.[12] In November 1930, two years after the group's first meeting, Rea presented orally the results of his study. Armed with a bewildering array of regression analyses, Rea noted diminishing returns in attendance to both population and expenditures. The solution, he argued, was the plan Dana advanced years before: decentralize museums into small neighborhood branches, where they can reach people easily and directly. "The real field of the Corporation," said Rea, "is to look for and help generously any institution in supporting branches."[13]

In a written presentation prepared for the group's next meeting, Rea tried to commit the foundation to constructing several systems of branches, an undertaking that lay outside the group's mandate to focus on educational programs and beyond the sums that Carnegie's trustees would commit to museum work. Some members of the advisory group preferred a more gingerly approach; Keppel made it clear that the Corporation would fund no bricks and mortar, only program activities on an experimental basis. These reservations, however, were strategic, administrative, and consistent with the Corporation's routine preference for pilot projects and limited discretionary budgets for new programs. No one challenged Rea's claim that branch museums would, at little cost, increase museum attendance fourfold (an estimate later revised to 1,600 percent [Rea 1932:176]). Nor did anyone seriously dispute Rea's two working assumptions, which together reflected the professional ideology of scientific efficiency in the service of social improvement. First, implicit in Rea's exclusive focus on attendance figures was the assumption that the art museum's overriding goal was educating the mass public. Second, Rea asserted that the "museum problem" was basically one of "the scientific management of facilities." His work's major contribution, he told his colleagues, was that it had "opened up a rather dazzling vista of . . . a real science of museum management."[14]

The advisory group authorized Rea to pursue negotiations with Fiske Kimball to start a branch at the Pennsylvania Museum of Art in Philadelphia. Kimball persuaded his trustees to sponsor a proposal, the advisory group endorsed it, and Keppel steered it through Carnegie's board. On May 8, 1931, America's first branch art museum opened its doors.[15]

The Carnegie Corporation's support for the branch museum represented neither foundation control of professionals nor professional manipulation of the Corporation. Instead the grant to the Pennsylvania Museum reflected a complementarity of interests melded together in a "garbage-can decision process" (Cohen, March, and Olsen 1972). The foundation's orientation toward adult education and demonstration projects and the interest of Keppel and several key trustees in the arts attracted them to the use of museums as agencies of popular instruction. The Corporation's lean staff structure and many competing programs led Keppel to seek ideas and guidance from organized experts. Once he did so, it was important to keep a constituency together if the Corporation's pilot programs were to have extensive effect, so Keppel would not risk antagonizing his chosen advisers by rejecting their proposals. Nor would he risk his standing before his trustees by presenting them with plans he knew to be unacceptable. Consequently, he monitored his advisory group to ensure that they stayed within the wide bounds he had placed around them but did not press them to sponsor any particular plan. When a hardworking, ambitious consultant, Rea, recommended that the Corporation focus on branch museums, an institutional innovation that perfectly embodied the professional critique of the typical museum model, the museum professionals in the advisory group quickly agreed.

So did Keppel. Although there is no evidence that he expected the group to reach this conclusion, he must have known when he appointed Dana that the branch idea would surface. And within the parameters set by the Corporation's budget, he cooperated with Rea in launching the Pennsylvania experiment. Wissler accurately predicted to Keppel the nature and amount of the grant several weeks before the advisory group authorized Rea to pursue the matter with Kimball and nearly three months before Pennsylvania submitted a proposal; far from intervening to prevent it, Keppel assisted in the negotiations. Moreover, he subsequently, and unsuccessfully, lobbied the Metropolitan Museum to experiment with branches, offering a grant of $100,000 for that purpose.[16] Had the depression not dramatically trimmed the resources over which Keppel had effective control, it seems likely that additional grants would have been made.

That the Museum Advisory Group recommended and the Carnegie Corporation adopted a program to support branch museums was the result of fortuitous events, staffing decisions, and changing patterns of participation. What was foreordained, once the Corporation chose its advisers from among the vanguard of professional museum reform, was that the group's recommendations would reflect the ideology and professional aspirations of museum workers.

Professionals in and out of Organizations

The branch museum case illustrates the capacity of professionals to mobilize in the environment around organizations that employ them. By refocusing the museum's mission on public education, legitimating new forms of expertise in educational and exhibition work, altering staff structures of museums, and directing them toward municipal and foundation funding, museum decentralization, had it succeeded, would have enhanced professional control over key skills and resources and deemphasized the skills and resources (art collections, family philanthropy, connoisseurship) dominated by trustees.

Yet the same professionals who organized at the field level to effect institutional change were neither alienated nor oppositional in their organizational roles. Following the branch example into the organization that implemented it allows us to observe the *intra*organizational behavior of some of the key figures who participated in the environment that Carnegie and the AAM helped structure.

The Pennsylvania Branch experiment was successful but abortive. The branch was located in the Sixty-ninth Street shopping district of Upper Darby, a rapidly growing Philadelphia suburb. In addition to Carnegie's $45,000, Sixty-ninth Street's developer, John H. McClatchy, gave the Pennsylvania Museum rent-free use of a building that had served as the Sixty-ninth Street Arts and Crafts Community Center and pledged $30,000 in escalating donations to the branch over five years. Among the conditions imposed by McClatchy, who hoped that the new museum would stimulate popular enthusiasm for the shopping district, were that the branch change exhibitions frequently and the museum hire a competent man "to take charge of the place, and . . . in various ways to conduct exhibitions in a manner to arouse neighborhood interest."[17]

Kimball found such a man in Philip Youtz, an architect and Columbia University instructor whom Carnegie had funded to organize adult classes at neighborhood branches of the New York Public Library. Youtz threw himself into planning the branch, which sat amid "a busy center where people naturally congregated . . . in the midst of the noise and hubbub of a populous business street." The little museum stayed open until ten o'clock every night, including Sunday, so as to be accessible to working men and women. The branch's layout was "like that of a successful store," with two large windows opening to the street. To further symbolize the openness of the place, Youtz tore down the walls of administrative offices and urged staff to stroll about, discussing exhibits informally with visitors.

Exhibitions were rotated even more briskly than required, with seventeen presented during the first twelve months. Youtz alternated exhibits of useful objects with conventional musem pieces and modern art, attempting to both elevate taste and fit programs to community interests. By May 1932 the branch had logged an attendance of 217,000, over one-quarter that of its spacious parent, without lowering attendance in the central building, bearing out Carnegie's hopes and Rea's claims (Youtz 1932).

Despite this promising beginning, the branch museum was short-lived. The Pennsylvania Museum was hit by city budget cuts that reduced its income from $271,000 in fiscal 1931 to $102,000 two years later.[18] Developer McClatchy, too, faced financial setbacks. In November 1931 he announced he could no longer afford to ensure the branch's plate glass window.[19] In January 1932, despite Youtz's plea that he seek funds for additional branches, Kimball instead asked Keppel for operating support for the main museum.[20] Youtz, suspecting the experiment might be terminated within the year, appealed to Keppel for a new assignment.[21] By June 1932 straits were so dire that a supplier repossessed the branch's water cooler.[22] In September, McClatchy told Kimball he could neither continue to forgo rent on the building nor make good on the gifts he had pledged.[23] Within a month, the branch closed its doors. Kimball put Youtz in charge of exhibitions at the central museum (from whence he quickly left to become associate director of the Brooklyn Museum) and applied what was left of the Carnegie grant to operating expenses.

Given the innovation's radical character, the lack of ardor or rancor in the Pennsylvania Museum's embrace of the branch is striking. Public statements and interorganizational communications of those involved emphasized professional reform at the same time their internal memoranda and behavior followed routine operating procedures of a museum organized according to the traditional model.

Consider, for example, Fiske Kimball's communications with professional associates in Carnegie's Museum Education Advisory Group and the AAM and his actions as director of the Pennsylvania Museum. His first proposal to the Carnegie Corporation (cosigned by two trustees) announced that

> the modern museum must interpret its collections actively and even bring its treasures, in varied ways, to the public outside its walls. . . . The Museum has a civic duty to establish a department of public educational work—so that the Museum shall offer to the community not merely a rarified aesthetic entertainment for the few, but a training in taste, an inspiration to creative work, and education both to the manufacturer and craftsman and to the consumer—that is, to everyone.[24]

Moreover, Kimball expressed strong support for the branch experiment throughout its brief life. His final report assured the Carnegie Corporation that "the extraordinary success of the experiment . . . was widely recognized in the museum world, and the potential advantage of museum decentralization through systems of branches conducted on these lines is regarded as fully established."[25] Reviewing Paul Rea's book for his professional peers, Kimball asserted that the "extraordinary success of this first true branch museum gives every promise that future development in museum service to the community lies along the lines indicated by Rea" (Kimball 1933:4).

Kimball supported the branch as best he could, but he did so without slacking from the courtship of wealthy collectors that occupied most of his time (Roberts and Roberts 1959). Clearly he was just as committed in practice to the acquisitive/curatorial museum as he was in rhetoric to decentralization and reform. When budget cuts threatened, Kimball was quick to protect the museum's core activities at the expense of public education.[26] When the depression worsened, it was the branch museum and, early in 1933, the educational program that were eliminated.

Disjunctions between inter- and intraorganizational rhetoric and action were not restricted to executives. Youtz rivaled Dana and Rea in his public excoriations of the traditional museum. Shortly after beginning his work in Philadelphia, he addressed the annual meeting of the American Association of Museums:

> Hitherto, museums have not really wanted the public. . . . They have been definitely oriented toward the wealthy collector to whom they looked for accessions, not to the common man in the street. . . . The man whose salary is less than, say, a hundred thousand a year, and who cannot be driven to the museum door by a liveried chauffeur, ascends the steps of the American museum and enters its great halls with an initial inferiority complex that leaves him cowed from the start. (Youtz 1931:2)

Addressing the AAM in 1932, Youtz inveighed against art museums for installing their collections "according to the tastes and interest of the staff and trustees" and warned that to continue to receive public support, museums would "have to become more democratic, which may mean modelling their buildings on the department store rather than on the renaissance palace" (Youtz 1932:8).

Yet Youtz operated pragmatically in Philadelphia, winning support and cooperation from several of the museum's conservative trustees. In contacts with board members, he subdued his populist rhetoric, opining that "it is probably still an open question as to whether people at large can be educated."[27] Despite his solicitude for "the common man," Youtz dismissed an opportunity to open a second branch in a working-class neighborhood because "the public which we would have to draw upon would be particularly apathetic to art."[28]

Apparent inconsistencies between professional rhetoric and administrative pragmatism were plentiful throughout the reform ranks. Keppel, who had his own problems with trustees, could advocate museum decentralization and write that John Cotton Dana was "among the major prophets of his generation" at the same time he supported Frank Jewitt Mather and Paul Sachs in their successful effort to establish a distinctive cognitive basis for museum professionalism *not* in education and in opposition to patron prerogatives, but in art historical scholarship and the cultivation of dependent collectors (Keppel 1926:42; Zolberg 1986). Metropolitan Museum secretary Henry Kent originated the branch idea, but when Keppel offered Carnegie support for a Lower East Side branch of the Metropolitan, Kent worried about insurance costs and the dignity of the setting, and the museum rejected the offer.[29] Even Rea, the unyielding ideologue of museum progressivism, quarreled with his trustees in Cleveland because they wished "to popularize the Museum rather more rapidly than Rea thought wise at the expense of its more scientific inquiries."[30]

Confronted with this inconsistency, it is tempting to dismiss such men as hypocrites. Instead, I would suggest that professional activism and organizational work were compartmentalized roles that evoked distinctive forms of rationality, forms of discourse, and orientations toward action. Reformers' behavior in the workplace was pragmatic, driven by organizational routine, and oriented to the solution of concrete problems defined by organizational superiors or posed by the resource environment. Thought and action in work contexts were characterized by practical rationality (Sahlins 1976; Giddens 1984), resting within parameters set by taken-for-granted assumptions about the acceptability of behavior to superiors or trustees, so that professionals failed to consider innovations that would threaten either their own employment or organizational survival. Grounded in routine, organizational tradition, networks of affect and loyalty, and common understandings of the possible, intraorganizational communication employed a restricted code (Bernstein 1971), with authority claims grounded in the speaker's formal position and assumptions of value or purpose remaining implicit.

By contrast, *inter*organizational contexts were characterized by formal equality and professional control. The absence of organizational superiors permitted a decontextualization of discourse and bracketing of organizational routines and survival imperatives. Within such settings, professional rationality was discursive (Giddens 1984); professional talk favored an elaborated code (Bernstein 1971), reflecting what Gouldner (1978) called the "culture of critical discourse," emphasizing the right to question the rationality of existing arrangements on the basis of technical criteria and basing authority claims on expertise rather than formal position. Whereas organizational speech could never be separated from the relationships between speaker and listener, the professionalized environment offered sites for the development of critical alternatives to existing organizational arrangements. Because professionally sponsored innovations could be developed as pilot programs, the professionalized environment served as a staging area from which activists asserted increased authority over the organizations that employed them, in the absence of significant intraorganizational conflict.

Conclusion

Students of institutions can draw several lessons from this case study. None of them call into question the major thrusts of institutional theory, but they do suggest refinements and processes in need of additional attention.

First, studies of the institutionalization of organizational forms have tended to focus on diffusion at the local level, using organizations or geographic areas as units of analysis (e.g., Tolbert and Zucker 1983; Fligstein 1985). As such work would lead us to expect, the art museum came to be taken for granted as something any major city must have. In contrast to the local imagery of such studies, however, we have seen that the diffusion of museums was guided and shaped by the emergence of fieldwide structures at the national level, outside the boundaries of particular museums, and that this professionally constructed environment was the site of much organizing by actors who wished to change the museum's structure and mission. The significance of such environments is highlighted as well in two other chapters in this section: Galaskiewicz's study of corporate philanthropy in Minneapolis (ch. 12) and Brint and Karabel's chapter on the vocationalization of the community college (ch. 14).

Second, studies of institutional diffusion have emphasized that organizational forms become more legitimate as they spread, focusing on the form per se rather than on variation among organizations of a given form with respect to structure, programs, and missions. In the museum case, we observe a contradictory dynamic whereby the legitimation of the form empowered and authorized the museum reform movement, which offered delegitimating criticism of existing museums. In other words, institutionalization bears, if not the seeds of its own destruction, at least openings for substantial change (see also Brint and Karabel, ch. 14, this vol.).

Third, institutional theorists have focused on the general and apolitical process whereby ideologies that are societal in reach shape the form of new organizations. In particular, Meyer, Boli, and Thomas (1987; see also Jepperson, ch. 6, this vol., and Jepperson and Meyer, ch. 9, this vol.) argue that organizational forms are shaped by a "Western cultural account" requiring organizers to justify their actions on the basis of widely accepted rational myths of justice and progress. The museum case illustrates this point: the museum reform movement borrowed progressive ideology quite explicitly to justify itself in terms of the values of efficiency and democracy. Nonetheless, the case also demonstrates a rather wide scope for conflict over the practical implications of the "Western cultural account," as museum reformers and traditionalists struggled over the programs that equity required and the goals in terms of which efficiency would be measured. Discourse about museums was full of often unreflective allusions to organizational models from other fields. But the choice of models—whether the museum was more appropriately likened to the library, the department store, or the symphony orchestra—was an object of fateful debate (see also Friedland and Alford, ch. 10, this vol., on contending logics of action).

To what extent are these points generalizable beyond the example at hand? The most striking feature of the museum case is the extent to which the creation of a national field was intertwined with the efforts of museum workers to define a profession and increase their own authority. Indeed, the case is consistent with the observation that professionals often come into conflict with the organizations that employ them (Goldner and Ritti 1967; Larson 1977; Scott 1982a:156; Freidson 1986; Perrow 1986). In the case of the art museum, relatively little conflict occurred *within* the employing organizations, however. Professionals stimulated change less at the intraorganizational level than *by mobilizing to construct an environment they could control at the level of the organizational field.* In view of this, it is no surprise that studies have often found that bureaucratically employed professionals fail to display alienation from their employers (Hall 1968; Perrucci and Gerstl 1969; Hastings and Hinings 1970; Tuma and Grimes 1981). Only a minority of professional employees are actively involved in fieldwide struggles, some leading activists work outside core employing organizations (e.g., in universities or professional associations), and most professional activists compartmentalize their organizational and environmental roles and activities. If the museum case is any guide, such studies yield negative findings because they look for conflict at the wrong level of analysis—inside the organization rather than within a professionally constructed organizational field.

Where else would we expect to find the dynamics that the museum case exhibited? It is noteworthy that many key actors in the movement to professionalize museum work were museum directors, techno-bureaucratic professionals (Larson 1977) with formal authority in their organizations. Administrative professionals are in a strategic position to dominate fieldwide structures because they can claim to act for organizational as well as for professional interests. Other kinds of professionals are less likely to attain dominant positions within, for example, trade associations and must instead mobilize through professional associations to influence training and credentialing institutions and regulatory agencies. Nonadministrative professionals, who in large and differentiated organizations frequently try to wrest autonomy not just from managers but from one another (Abbott 1988), also mobilize externally, but may be less likely to gain the sponsorship of powerful external constituencies.

Administrative professionalism is especially prominent in fields dominated by nonprofit organizations. Nonprofits are less likely than proprietary firms to be oligopolists, less likely to be highly competitive, and more likely to depend upon institutional as opposed to technical sources of legitimacy. Moreover, the affinity between the legitimizing accounts of professionals and of nonprofit organizations—both based on claims to expertise, a service ethos, and disinterest in pecuniary gain—provides an ideological resource to professionals in the nonprofit sector (Majone 1980). Furthermore, whereas interorganizational contacts among for-profit firms evoke suspicions of collusion, interaction among nonprofit firms and their employees is hailed as "coordination" (Weiss 1981).

National differences in modes of organizing also influence the capacity of professionals to mobilize (Jepperson and Meyer, ch. 9, this vol.). Scott and Meyer (ch. 5, this vol.) distinguish between fields with bureaucratic and those with professional "sovereigns," the latter of which characterize societies with weak central states and fragmented administrative systems. Cole (1985), for example, describes the effects of differences in environmental organization on the adoption of quality circles in Japan, Sweden, and the United States. Whereas efforts at institutional change were organized by business associations in

Japan and by government/union coalitions in Sweden, in the United States a weaker movement was mounted by technical experts seated in professional associations, universities, and advocacy and consulting organizations. The relatively weak central states of the United Kingdom and, especially, the United States enhance the capacity of professionals to structure environments in those countries (Abbott 1988).

If administrative professionals in nonprofit organizations are well situated to seek institutional change from positions in fieldwide structures that they construct and dominate, similar forms of environmental organizing have also characterized professions located in proprietary firms, however. Consider the case of personnel management. Like museum workers, industrial engineers and human-relations experts served their employers faithfully at the same time that professional and academic elites developed professional societies and publications that advanced positions critical of corporate owners and top executives (Stark 1980; Jacoby 1985; Meiksins 1984). Despite their subordinate positions in employing organizations, the efforts of successive movements of personnel specialists have changed the ways in which corporations recruit, control, and develop the careers of their employees (Merkle 1980; Baron, Dobbin, and Jennings 1986).

These observations are necessarily speculative. Students of institutions should direct systematic attention to the role of professionalization in the institutionalization of new organizational forms and, more generally, to the institutionalization of the fieldwide environments around those forms. Such attention will, I suspect, reveal substantially more interest-driven conflict and more problematic outcomes than much of the imagery of institutional theory has thus far suggested.

Acknowledgments

Thanks are due Maria Arias, Steven Brint, Eliot Freidson, Peter Hall, Ellen Condliffe Lagemann, Michelle Lamont, Kathleen McCarthy, Charles Perrow, Woody Powell, and participants in the NSF/Center for Advanced Study conference on institutional change for helpful comments on earlier drafts of this chapter. The author is grateful to the Carnegie Corporation for access to their archives and to Patricia Hanes and her staff for their patient assistance in using the Carnegie collections; to the director and staff of the Rockefeller Archive Center for use of the Laura Spellman Rockefeller Memorial Collection; to Louise F. Rossmassler for assistance in using the archives of the Philadelphia Museum of Art; to the Archives of American Art for use of the Philip Youtz collection; and to Mrs. Richard Stillwell for permission to consult the Paul Sachs Papers in the Columbia University Oral History Collection. Naturally, none of these persons or organizations are responsible for the author's interpretations or for errors of omission or commission.

Notes

1. Untitled petition circulated at May 23–26, 1921, meetings of AAM in Cleveland, requesting grant from the Carnegie Corporation to establish and staff a permanent AAM office; Carnegie Corporation Archives, filed under American Association of Museums, 1918–1928. (Because the Carnegie Corporation Archives have been moved to Columbia University, documents may no longer be in the locations indicated.)

2. Report of the Assistant Treasurer, American Association of Museums, December 31, 1926, Carnegie Corporation Archives, filed under American Association of Museums, 1918–1928; "American Association of Museums: Membership Growth," Carnegie Corporation Archives, filed under American Association of Museums, 1929–1935.

3. "Foundation Grants of AAM, 1923–1929," attachment to letter from Chauncey Hamlin to Frederick P. Keppel, May 8, 1929; Carnegie Corporation Archives, filed under American Association of Museums, 1918–1928.

4. Memorandum of Interview, Frederick P. Keppel and George Blumenthal, at Metropolitan Museum, December 11, 1939; Carnegie Corporation Archives, filed under Metropolitan Museum of Art. The finalists were Francis Henry Taylor and Horace Jayne (Tomkins 1970).

5. Agenda for Carnegie Corporation Trustees Meeting, April 9, 1924, Carnegie Corporation Archives; Confidential Minutes, Conference Group on Museum Education, December 5, 1928, Carnegie Corporation Archives, filed under Advisory Group on Museum Education.

6. Paul Sachs to Alfred Barr, February 10, 1931; in "Tales of an Epoch: The Reminiscences of Paul J. Sachs," vol. 1, Columbia University Oral History Research Office.

7. Clark Wissler, Report of Advisory Group on Museum Education, typescript dated June 1932; Carnegie Corporation Archives, filed under Advisory Group on Museum Education.

8. Appendix to Confidential Minutes of the Conference Group on Museum Education, December 5, 1928; Carnegie Corporation Archives, filed under Advisory Group on Museum Education.

9. Carl Rathmann to Frederick Keppel, April 2, 1929; Confidential Minutes of Meeting of Committee on Museum Education, May 25, 1929; Fiske Kimball to Frederick Keppel, August 28, 1929; Memorandum of Interview, Fiske Kimball and Frederick Keppel, September 9, 1929; Confidential Minutes of Meeting of Committee on Museum Education, November 23, 1929; Carnegie Corporation Archives, filed under Advisory Group on Museum Education.

10. Morse Cartwright to Frederick Keppel, March 19, 1928; Newton D. Baker to Frederick Keppel, October 17, 1928; Carnegie Corporation Archives, filed under Advisory Group on Museum Education; Kimball 1929:28.

11. Minutes of the Advisory Group on Museum Education, February 15, 1930: Carnegie Corporation Archives, filed under Advisory Group on Museum Education.

12. Memorandum of Interview, Robert M. Lester with Paul Marshall Rea and Clark Wissler, October 2, 1930: Carnegie Corporation Archives, filed under Advisory Group on Museum Education.

13. Confidential Minutes of the Meeting of the Advisory Group on Museum Educa-

tion, October 31 and November 1, 1930; Carnegie Corporation Archives, filed under Advisory Group on Museum Education.

14. Confidential Minutes of the Meeting of the Advisory Group on Museum Education, October 31 and November 1, 1930; John M. Russell's notes on the meeting of the Advisory Group on Museum Education, October 31 and November 1, 1930, dated November 11, 1930; Abstract of Minutes, February 20 and 21 meeting of the Advisory Group on Museum Education; Paul Marshall Rea, "A Proposed Report of Advisory Group on Museum Education to the Carnegie Corporation of New York," typescript, February 1931; Carnegie Corporation Archives, filed under Advisory Group on Museum Education.

15. Memorandum of Interview, Frederick Keppel and Fiske Kimball; Fiske Kimball to Frederick Keppel, March 16, 1931; Eli Kirk Price and Fiske Kimball to "Gentlemen," March 16, 1931; Robert M. Lester to Eli Kirk Price, April 17, 1931; Carnegie Corporation Archives, filed under Pennsylvania Museum of Art. "The Carnegie Corporation Chooses 69th Street's Community Center as the Site of the First Branch Art Museum," Philadelphia *Evening Bulletin*, April 24, 1931; Philadelphia Museum Archives, Record Group 6, PMA: 69th St. Branch—Pamphlets, publications. "The New Sixty-Ninth Street Branch of the Pennsylvania Museum of Art," undated press release; Philadelphia Museum Archives, Record Group 6, PMA: 69th St. Branch—Press releases re: opening and organization of Branch, May 1931–October 1932. The Newark Museum opened what it called branch museums in 1929, but these were spaces within public libraries comprising three or four exhibition cases each, rather than separate museum buildings. The Newark Museum first installed exhibition cases in branch libraries, although on an even more modest scale, in 1917. See *The Museum* (bulletin of the Newark Museum) 1, 1 (1917):30; and 2, 11 (1930):95–96. I am grateful to Sarah Ford for sharing these items with me.

16. Memorandum of Interview, J. M. Russell and Clark Wissler, January 28, 1931; Carnegie Corporation Archives, filed under Advisory Group on Museum Education. Memorandum of Interview, Frederick Keppel and Henry W. Kent, April 13, 1931; Henry W. Kent to Frederick Keppel, March 9, 1931; Memorandum of Interview, Henry Kent and Frederick Keppel, April 8, 1931; Memorandum of Interview, Frederick Keppel, William Sloane Coffin, and Roberta Fansler, March 30, 1933; Carnegie Corporation Archives, filed under Metropolitan Museum of Art.

17. John H. McClatchy to Fiske Kimball, March 3, 1931; Fiske Kimball to John H. McClatchy, March 5, 1931; Philadelphia Museum of Art Archives, Record Group 6, PMA: 69th Street Branch, General Correspondence, A–Z, 1932.

18. Report from Pennsylvania Museum of Art to Carnegie Corporation, received May 17, 1933; Carnegie Corporation Archives, filed under Pennsylvania Museum of Art.

19. Philip Youtz to file, November 24, 1931; Pennsylvania Museum of Art Archives, Record Group 6, PMA: 69th Street Branch: Floor plan, schedules, equipment.

20. Philip Youtz to Fiske Kimball, January 13, 1932; Philadelphia Museum of Art Archives, Record Group 6, PMA: 69th Street Branch, Youtz and Kimball, 1931–1932. Memorandum of Interview, Fiske Kimball and Frederick Keppel, January 14, 1932; Carnegie Corporation Archives, filed under Pennsylvania Museum of Art.

21. Philip Youtz to Huger Elliott, January 1932; Philadelphia Museum of Art Archives, Record Group 6, PMA: 69th Street Branch, general correspondence, A–Z,

1932. Philip Youtz to Frederick Keppel, March 29, 1932; Carnegie Corporation Archives, filed under Pennsylvania Museum of Art.

22. Philip Youtz to the Charles E. Hires Company, June 2, 1932; Pennsylvania Museum of Art Archives, Record Group 6, PMA: 69th Street Branch: Floor plan, schedules, equipment.

23. Philip Youtz to Fiske Kimball, September 17, 1932; Philadelphia Museum of Art Archives, Record Group 6, PMA: 69th Street Branch, Youtz and Kimball, 1931–1932. Memorandum of Interview, Fiske Kimball and Philip Youtz with Frederick Keppel, September 29, 1932; Carnegie Corporation Archives, filed under Pennsylvania Museum of Art.

24. Fiske Kimball, Eli Kirk Price, and John S. Jenks to Frederick Keppel, November 1, 1927; Carnegie Corporation Archives, filed under Pennsylvania Museum of Art.

25. Report to Carnegie Corporation by Fiske Kimball, March 24, 1934; Carnegie Corporation Archives, filed under Pennsylvania Museum of Art.

26. Kimball warned Youtz in October 1931 that the trustees would not accept another conditional grant from the Carnegie Corporation until economic conditions improved. Fiske Kimball to Philip Youtz, November 6, 1931; Philadelphia Museum of Art Archives, Record Group 6, PMA: 69th Street Branch, Youtz and Kimball, 1931–1932.

27. John S. Jencks to Philip N. Youtz, January 14, 1932; Philadelpia Museum of Art Archives, Record Group 6, PMA: 69th Street Branch, general correspondence, A–Z, 1932. Philip Youtz to J. Stogdell Stokes, February 27, 1932; J. Stogdell Stokes to Philip Youtz, March 11, 1932; Philadelpia Museum of Art Archives, Record Group 6, PMA: 69th Street Branch, general correspondence, staff memorandum, 1932. Record of Interview, Frederick Keppel and John Story Jenks, November 22, 1940; Carnegie Corporation Archives, filed under University of Pennsylvania: University Museum.

28. Philip Youtz to Fiske Kimball, October 21, 1931; Philadelphia Museum of Art Archives, Record Group 6, PMA: 69th Street Branch, Youtz and Kimball, 1931–1932.

29. Henry Kent to Frederick Keppel, March 9, 1931; Carnegie Corporation Archives, filed under Metropolitan Museum of Art.

30. Newton D. Baker to Frederick Keppel, October 17, 1928; Carnegie Archives, filed under Advisory Group on Museum Education, 1928–1930.

12 Making Corporate Actors Accountable: Institution-Building in Minneapolis–St. Paul

Much of the literature within the institutional tradition portrays the organization as a passive, reacting entity entrapped or responding to coercive or cultural forces in its environment (Scott, ch. 7, this vol.; Zucker 1987). The influence of the institutional environment can be subtle, working its way into the organization through rationalized myths, or direct, coming as an indictment on a felony charge. In either case, researchers in this tradition have eschewed the notion that organizations are purposive, rational actors which are goal directed and in control of their own fate (Jepperson, ch. 6, this vol.). This brand of environmental determinism makes the institutional perspective attractive to organizational sociologists who have tired of overly chauvinistic and rational theories of organizational behavior.

This chapter takes institutional analysis in a different direction. It focuses on collective action and institution-building at the interorganizational field level. It presents a case study that shows how field leaders can act purposively (albeit under conditions of bounded rationality) to construct and create institutions which in turn control and govern organizations' actions. Organizations, and particularly business corporations, are driven by short-term self-interest; given the proper set of incentives, however, they will pursue strategies which serve collective interests rather than self-interests. Our focus then is on how, within organizational fields, programs or rule systems come about which are neither imposed by external authorities nor absorbed from the larger culture, but rather are built or created by system participants and lead actors to pursue collective goals.

This chapter focuses in particular on corporations as participants in urban social systems. It is well known that business corporations, and especially multinationals, often are at odds with communities in which they do business or employ workers. In that respect our case study is an anomaly. It focuses on the efforts of business leaders in one metropolitan area to create or institutionalize a pattern of social control which would result in enhanced corporate public service activity at the local level. Since the established institutionalized means of encouraging corporate charitable contributions based on peer pressure and informal networks was breaking down, new methods of social control had to be institutionalized to sustain corporate public service activity. Our case study not only describes the sequence of events which led to the institutionalization of these new control systems, but also tries to identify the factors which led to their development, focusing on the resources and interests of business leaders and changes in the control of local corporations.

Institution-Building as a Sociological Phenomenon

What do we mean by institution-building and how do we go about studying it? According to Janowitz (1978:400), institution-building refers to "those conscious efforts to direct societal change and to search for more effective social controls which are grounded in rationality." Actors participate in the creation of these new systems voluntarily, and efforts are aware of and even guided by scientific thought. Students of institution-building focus on roles which different actors assume, the mechanisms which motivate actors to perform their roles accordingly, the myths or rationalizations that are put into place to ensure the legitimacy of the new arrangements, and the methods whereby the system reproduces itself.

In studying institution-building, researchers must be aware of several issues. First, institution-building is not restricted to the public sector. New institutional arrangements are constantly being created within the private sector. Indeed professional associations and their governance structures epitomize efforts at institution-building. Church hierarchies are institutional forms as old as the polity itself. The market is also a kind of private-sector institution whose rules are set by market participants (see Leblebici and Salancik 1982). Second, researchers studying institutions must place events into a historical context. Institutions—as a network of roles, sanctions, and ideologies—may be studied in and of themselves, but they cannot be understood completely without an understanding of the environment in which they operate and evolve. Institutions are embedded and thus built within the context of larger institutions (Jepperson, ch. 6, this vol.). Efforts to regulate the behavior of professionals, a congregation, traders, or corporations must be legitimated in terms of societal institutions, the most important of which is the law. In contrast to the mechanistic functionalist view (e.g., Parsons 1956), we envision these efforts at legitimation as being conscious and sensitive to the sanctions that larger systems can impose upon them (see DiMaggio and Powell 1983). Thus although we may strive to generalize our description of how institutions are constructed, there will always be a set of very particular historical or contextual circumstances of which researchers must be aware.

Third, researchers must be careful to keep the analytical distinction between the micro– and macro–social orders clear. With respect to institutions the macro-order is made up roles, incentive systems, and ideologies or belief systems (Hernes 1976). The micro-order is made up of preferences, capacities, and expectations of individuals. While it may be tempting to identify patterns at the macrolevel and to infer that they are the product of purposeful actors pursuing some well-reasoned strategy at the microlevel, such inferences can lead to premature and erroneous conclusions. Although the models of neoclassical economic theory would have one think otherwise, micro– and macro–social orders are often loosely coupled. It often takes a considerable amount of time for individual actions to bring about changes in the larger social system. It is equally tempting to focus on action at the microlevel—explicit efforts at negotiating new programs or rule systems—and to infer that these actions are prompted by pressures emanating from the macro–social order. Action at the microlevel is constrained by the opportunities and limitations defined at the macro-order. Yet we believe that it is dangerous to overestimate the impact of social structure or culture on action and to underestimate the interpretative and creative capacities of actors. Looking for causal explanations in the context only again ignores the fact that the micro-order is only loosely coupled to the macro-order.

Finally, students of institution-building have several analytic options open to them. First, researchers can describe the various stages of development. Here step or stage models are proffered where the sequence of events leading to some change in the institutional order is described in detail. As research examines more and more cases, the sequence is refined and a general pattern is identified. Second, researchers can try to identify (1) the underlying social processes which result in institutional change and (2) the roles that social structures play in facilitating or stymieing change. In other words, they can engage in causal analysis. For example, neo-Marxist theory has been the most successful at doing this at the local community level (e.g., Molotch and Logan 1987). Underlying contradictions in the production process create conditions for the emergence of new institutional forms. In contrast, our preferred strategy is to explain how new institutions develop out of the preferences and as strategic actions of individual actors. Third, researchers can take a normative approach to studying institutional change. They can prescribe to change agents how to build new community organizations (e.g., Alinsky 1969), revamp neighborhood schools (Janowitz 1969), stimulate local economic development (Taub 1988), or fight juvenile crime (Shaw 1940). As Janowitz (1978) points out, there is a long tradition in sociological practice which has offered activists advice on how to reorganize local institutions and engage in self-help.

Corporations and the
Urban Community

Since Warner and Low (1947) and Lynd and Lynd (1929, 1937), urban sociologists have been aware of the gradual withdrawal of corporations from local community affairs (see also Stein 1960 and Warren 1963). For the most part these early studies described how extralocally based business conglomerates purchased local firms, centralized decision making in some distant locale, gradually withdrew from civic involvement, and played only minimal and highly instrumental roles in community decision making (e.g., Merton 1949; Schulze 1961; and Mott 1970). The local community became simply an employment site or a marketing area in a national distribution network. Corporations became involved in community affairs only if their interests were directly threatened.

Current research on corporate-community relations shows that not much has changed. In particular, it has focused on the layoffs and plant closings that have left communities at the verge of bankruptcy or on inner city neighborhoods without needed employment opportunities (Perrucci et al. 1988). Furthermore, large corporations have been blamed for polluting our cities' rivers, streams, and air. The rationale for tolerating such behavior is that big business means more jobs. Yet some critics have argued that the public dollars needed to provide the infrastructure to attract big business are not offset by the number of new jobs created (Molotch 1976). This is especially true of high-tech or continuous-processing firms. Thus wooing business to an area often results in a net loss for the locale (for a different point of view, see Peterson 1981).

One reason corporations can get away with such things is the advantageous market position of large, multinational corporations. Molotch's (1976) classic work on the "city as a growth machine" drew attention to the competition for large corporate investments that takes place among cities across the country (see also Suttles 1984; Molotch and Logan 1987). Because they are independent of any geographically defined market, multinationals have several locational options. If companies are dissatisfied with local conditions, they can move their facilities elsewhere. Unlike earlier manufacturers who needed to cluster their facilities close together, high-tech and service industries have no need to locate their research or corporate facilities in any one place. With the advent of truck and inexpensive air transportation and high-speed telecommunication systems, there is no need for manufacturers to cluster either. One community becomes just as attractive as another, and areas are forced to compete with one another. To use the language of Hirschman (1972), corporations have a ready "exit" option. If local actors utilize either the local state government or local markets to impose sanctions upon corporations, companies can threaten to leave and take their jobs and tax revenues with them.

Furthermore, Molotch and Logan (1987:251–54) argue that the transnational scale of modern corporations means that the range of a firm's operations straddles the sovereignty of many units of government. Headquarters, assembly plants, distribution centers, legal status are all located in different places. If a government attempts to increase taxes on corporate profits, corporations can engage in numerous tactics to protect themselves, for example, transfer pricing. "Capital becomes difficult to trap because it dissolves, moves, redefines its internal relations, transforms itself into something else" (Molotch and Logan 1987:252). The consequence is that with all this liquidity the local government becomes less and less capable of protecting or safeguarding residents. Even if local or state governments wanted to tax or regulate corporate nuisances, they would be unable to.

To make matters more difficult, corporations (as opposed to natural persons) are immune to *social* controls. If individuals "blackmailed" their community to extract economic concessions or engaged in unfair labor practices, one could appeal to their sense of propriety and responsibility to the community or citizenship. The difference with respect to corporations is that they are amoral. An important thesis in Coleman's (1974) *Power and the Structure of Society* is that corporate actors enjoy many of the privileges of natural persons, but are immune from the social controls that constrain the behavior of natural persons. Under the law, corporate actors can own land, be taxed, sue or be sued, consummate transactions, make profits, and incur debts. In these respects corporate actors are no different than natural persons. The key difference between corporate actors and natural persons is that the former have no conscience. Communities of natural persons can bring shame on a natural person, exclude him from their cocktail parties, and even threaten him with exclusion from the moral community if he does not act in a way they think appropriate. Corporate actors do not have social selves. Social sanctions can be levied against the agents of the corporate actor, for example, the plant manager or even the CEO and directors, but the corporation is still bound—in fact, legally bound—to pursue the interests of its shareholders within the limits of the law. While the natural persons in the larger community can make life unpleasant for its agents, the corporate actor itself remains immune from these social controls. Because they are immune from the social control of natural persons in the community, corporate actors can leave a community if they are unhappy; they can also abuse the physical environment, withdraw from community affairs, or "muscle" local officials without fear of social retribution.

From what has been said it appears that communities of natural persons are destined to be held hostage by corporations. However, there are cases where business corporations have joined together and developed new governance structures which imposed normative controls upon members (see Ouchi 1984). Although participation in these efforts at self-control is voluntary, having joined, each actor is subject to the jurisdiction of these associations. The payoff is some sort of collective good, with the larger community or at least the larger business community benefiting. There are certainly free-rider problems and questions of accountability (are corporations violating the shareholders' trust?), but the important point is that new institutions have been created by corporate actors themselves to regulate and control their own behavior.

This chapter examines the efforts of one corporate community—Minneapolis and St. Paul—to establish a control system to encourage and sustain corporate contributions to charity. We are not the first to note the rampant institution-building taking place in the Twin Cities (see Ouchi 1984). Efforts were made in that community to ensure that companies acted in other socially responsible ways as well. However, this chapter looks only at those efforts at institution-building aimed at maintaining and increasing corporate commitment to the support of nonprofit organizations.

The Context for Institution-Building in Minneapolis–St. Paul

In this section we discuss one business community's efforts to institutionalize practices to routinize and ensure continued corporate contributions to charity. The case we discuss is special because the initiative was taken by individuals in the business community; it was not forced or introduced by outside change agents. While the discussion focuses only on efforts to sustain levels of corporate contributions, the agenda of the organizers was broader, hoping to institutionalize socially responsible behavior throughout the business community. We draw on research by Galaskiewicz (1985a, 1985b, 1987) done on corporate-community relations in Minneapolis–St. Paul.

To fully understand the Twin Cities case it is useful to know that between 1970 and 1980 important changes occurred in the control of the largest publicly held companies headquartered in the Twin Cities. Between 1970 and 1975 there was a noticeable decrease in the percentage of Fortune firms in the Twin Cities whose CEO was born in Minnesota: the figure dropped from 47.6 percent in 1970 to 30.4 percent in 1975. In the same period three firms hired a nonfamily professional manager as CEO, replacing the founder or his progeny, and three firms were acquired by out-of-state interests. By 1980, 38.1 percent or eight of the twenty-one firms on the 1970 Fortune lists either were acquired by extra-local interests, had a family member replaced by a professional manager as CEO, or had a professional manager born in Minnesota replaced by a professional manager born elsewhere. Loss of control over local corporations to professional managers or outsiders was finally taking place in the Twin Cities. Needless to say, other cities had faced a similar problem decades earlier. If history repeated itself, local corporate actors would withdraw from community affairs and orient themselves toward national and international markets (see Schulze 1961; Mott 1970).

A gradual withdrawal of Twin Cities companies from community affairs would be catastrophic, because these companies had become such an integral part of the local community. Just at the time when local control over local firms was slipping, there appeared a host of articles in the national and business press on the social responsibility of Twin Cities companies. For example, articles appeared in *Fortune* ("Minneapolis Fends Off the Urban Crisis," January 1976), the *Wall Street Journal* ("A Midwestern City Where Fine Arts Flourish," September 15, 1977), the *Chicago Tribune* ("A Club That Means Business," June 26, 1979), the *Boston Globe* ("Where the Arts Flourish: Minneapolis," May 4, 1980), the *New York Times* ("Minnesota a Model of Corporate Aid to Cities," July 27, 1981), and the *Harvard Business Review* ("In Minnesota, Business Is Part of the Solution," July–August 1981).

The cities of Minneapolis and St. Paul and the state of Minnesota shared in the spotlight. In another *Wall Street Journal* article ("A Northern City That Works: How Minneapolis Manages It," August 5, 1980) it was reported that Chicago was no longer the city that works and that Minneapolis had taken its place. In 1980 the *Chicago Tribune* ("Our Cities: Some Bests and Worsts," April 4, 1980) did an extensive analysis of the quality of life in eleven American cities. Minneapolis was cited as having the best municipal government, the best city planning office, the best civic leadership, the best downtown mall, and the best innovation in urban living (the downtown skyway system). In 1984 *Time Magazine* printed a feature article ("Minnesota's Magic Touch," June 11, 1984) praising the partnership between government, business, labor, and educational leaders that had worked to develop new high-technology enterprises in the state of Minnesota. Clearly the cities and the state had a great deal to lose if their companies lost interest in local affairs, inasmuch as much of the success of the region depended on the involvement and active participation of its major companies.

Our research focused primarily on the charitable contributions of locally headquartered Twin Cities publicly held corporations in 1980 and 1981. At the time of our research, corporate contributions were at an all-time high. The Minnesota Council on Foundations (Berner 1983) surveyed 78 companies in Minnesota and reported that they gave $63.4 million in 1982. The Council for Financial Aid to Education and the Conference Board compile annual statistics on corporate contributions for twenty-one metropolitan areas. Based on company giving as a percentage of pretax net income, Twin Cities companies ranked first in 1977, 1979, and 1980. In 1978 and 1981 they ranked second. In 1978 the *New York Times* ("Philanthropy, the Business of the Not-So-Idle Rich," July 23, 1978) claimed that some thirty-three corporations in Minneapolis give 5 percent of their income to philanthropy, out of a nationwide total of thirty-seven that reportedly do so. Indeed among the more noteworthy 5 percent givers in 1982 were Dayton-Hudson, Munsingwear, and H. B. Fuller. Among 2 percent givers were Honeywell, General Mills, Pillsbury, International Multifoods, Peavey, and Bemis.

Strategies for Institutionalizing
Corporate Public Service Activity

Our thesis is that this high level of community involvement and the very real possibility that it would be short-lived prompted a shift from a corporate grants economy based on informal peer (or old boy) networks, peer pressure, and social sanctions to a corporate grants economy based on bureaucratically institutionalized roles and formally organized reward systems. Legitimated and prompted by a cadre of business executives who had "roots" in the area and affiliations with many of the area's Fortune firms, a number of innovative strategies were implemented between 1975 and 1981 to ensure the high levels of corporate contributions among Twin Cities firms for the decade to come.

INSTITUTIONALIZING PUBLIC RECOGNITION

In our study we found that company giving in 1980 and 1981 was still heavily influenced by the social proximity of the chief executive officer to a cadre of twenty-eight older community leaders, many of whom were former executives of local firms and very involved in local philanthropic activities (Galaskiewicz 1985b). Based on our analysis and interviews with this cadre of philanthropic leaders, we concluded that many corporate contributions in the Twin Cities were the product of peer pressure exercised by these leaders. In fact, this is probably why corporate giving in the late 1970s and early 1980s was greater in Minneapolis–St. Paul than elsewhere in the United States. Executives who were in the social and civic networks of the philanthropic elite were more likely to be solicited and given recognition by this elite if their firms contributed more to charity. One of our more interesting findings was that companies were informally recognized by this elite as especially successful business ventures if either they had greater profits or gave more money to charity.

The problem with peer pressure, however, is that it is premised on the assumption that there is a prestigious elite motivated to solicit business executives and to applaud or scoff as firms heed or ignore their solicitations. In the Twin Cities the elite was growing old. In 1981 the average age of the twenty-eight living members of the elite was 64.6 years, and the successors to the older philanthropic elite did not appear to have the same social credentials and interests as their predecessors. In the course of the philanthropic elite interviews, we asked respondents to give us the names of the five or six individuals they believed would be instrumental in increasing corporate contributions in the next decade. Those who received two or more votes were dubbed the new corporate philanthropic elite. We found that the new elite included a slightly smaller proportion born in Minnesota, a smaller proportion of entrepreneurs and company founders, and a larger proportion of professional managers. In both the old and new elites, 10 individuals were the sons, grandsons, or sons-in-law of the founders of their companies. However, in the old elite, 9 of these 10 offspring were executives of Fortune 500 or 50 firms. In the new elite only 3 of the 10 offspring were executives of Fortune 500 or 50 firms. Thus in contrast to the old elite, members of the new elite were either professional managers of Fortune 500 firms who had no local ties or individuals with "blue blood" backgrounds but no corporate clout.

Peer pressure is also based on the assumption that those being pressured care if they are applauded or hissed. With the shift in corporate leadership there was the danger that the executives coming into management positions might be indifferent to the prodding and applause of *local* philanthropic leaders, even if the latter were from the best families. As noted earlier, in 38.1 percent of the twenty-one Fortune 500 or 50 firms listed in 1970, the founder or his progeny had stepped down as CEO, managers with local roots were replaced by managers from outside the area, or local firms were acquired by out-of-state companies by 1980. If CEOs become indifferent to those who are soliciting their company's charitable dollar, peer pressure will be ineffective in maintaining high levels of corporate contributions.

In what may be seen as an alternative to the "old boy" network, the Minneapolis Chamber of Commerce held its first annual awards luncheon for companies that reported contributing 5 percent of their pretax profits to charity in 1976. Ever since then, Chamber of Commerce members who verify that they are giving at the 2 percent or 5 percent level are recognized by the Chamber as being in the Two or Five Percent Club, invited to a civic luncheon, and given an award in front of a public audience with press and political officials present. After a lunch and remarks by distinguished speakers, new members of this club are introduced and given a memento.

The circumstances surrounding the creation of the Five Percent Club are of special interest, because representatives of the corporate philanthropic elite were directly involved. The principals included David Koch, CEO and chairman of the board of Graco Incorporated and president of the Minneapolis Chamber of Commerce from 1975 to 1976; Charles Krusell, executive director of the Minneapolis Chamber of Commerce; Wayne Thompson, senior vice president of environmental development of Dayton-Hudson Corporation; and Bower Hawthorne, vice president of public affairs of the Minneapolis Star and Tribune Company. The latter two principals are key because their respective superiors at that time were Kenneth Dayton and John Cowles, Jr., both of whom were in the philanthropic elite and very active in community affairs. The idea for the Five Percent Club came from Krusell and Thompson, whose own company, along with the Minneapolis Star and Tribune Company and Graco, was already giving at 5 percent. David Koch has said that the "the goal of the effort was to give visibility to the success stories in the community (i.e., successful companies). It was good for business for the citizens and voters to take notice of what we do. We also wanted to justify a publicly held company doing this sort of thing" (pers. com.).

Just by giving 2 percent or 5 percent of pretax net income to charity, any firm in the community could now win the applause of significant others in the business community and share the spotlight with guest speakers who were brought in for the occasion (e.g., John D. Rockefeller, Juanita Kreps, John Filer, and Walter Haas). Now every firm had the opportunity to be applauded, and thus every firm had some motive to give. Furthermore, by printing the names of the Five Percent and Two Percent Club members and releasing the list to the metropolitan press, the Chamber of Commerce made peer giving a public event.

We would argue that the transformation of peer recognition into public recognition effectively took social control out of the locker rooms and club rooms and put it in the public domain. Elites still acknowledge the especially generous company, but now the larger community is applauding as well. There is no second-guessing what will win a firm some applause; everyone can qualify for the honor, and the recognition one wins is citywide and extends well beyond the business community.

Institutionalizing an Ethic of Enlightened Self-Interest

In the early to mid-1980s the business press and the management literature argued that an ethic of enlightened self-interest was alive and well in American business circles. In 1984 the *Wall Street Journal* declared that enlightened self-interest now guides corporate decisions in making donations. No longer are contributions "based on the whims of top officers, on country club connections and on tradition" (Wall 1984:1). Firms give so that their long-term interests will be served. In 1981 an article in *Fortune* stated that "few corporations engage in philanthropy because others need money, as though a corporation were a well-heeled uncle who should spread his good fortune around the family. For the most part, corporations give because it serves their own interests—or *appears* to" (Smith 1981:121, emphasis added). The argument is familiar: "Society expects business to accomplish a variety of social goals, and it must accomplish these goals if it expects to profit in the long run. The firm which is most sensitive to its community needs will, as a result, have a better community in which to conduct its business . . . a better society produces a better environment for business" (Davis 1973:313). The watchword is, "What's good for society is good for our company" (Hay and Gray 1974:140).

Although the rhetoric of enlightened self-interest has emphasized the benefits that individual firms might realize in the future, skeptics in the management literature have correctly pointed out that it is still almost impossible to measure these benefits and that espousing this ethic is still irrational from an economic point of view. For example, McGuire struggled with the problem of measuring and evaluating the profit effect of enlightened self-interest. He finally had to conclude that enlightened self-interest at best represented "a crude blend of long-run profit and altruism" (1963:143). Keim (1978) concentrated on the unresolved free-rider problems. He cites Wallich and McGowan (1970) who argue that firms may rationalize enlightened self-interest on the basis that stockholders now have diverse portfolios and thus a broad interest in the benefits that a large group of firms, even an industry, might realize if companies acted in a socially responsible way. "Thus investment decision criteria for any firm should be expanded to include consideration of a social or group rate of return in addition to a private return" (Keim 1978:34). However, as Keim points out, in actuality investors hold stock in more than one but not in every corporation. Thus for them to advise managers to use a social or group rate of return for criteria in decision making is irrational: "If investors have less than completely diversified portfolios, clearly owners would always prefer a company in which they had little or no interest to bear the cost of social investments with public or non-excludable benefits" (Keim 1978:35).

In 1978 Twin Cities business executives created a local forum—a nonprofit venture called the Minnesota Project on Corporate Responsibility (MPCR)—where corporate leaders could come together to discuss issues of corporate responsibility with each other and with people outside of business. In 1982 the goals of MPCR were (1) to provide educational programs for executives of Minnesota corporations on the changing nature of corporate responsibility; (2) to conduct forums for the exchange of ideas on issues affecting various corporate stakeholders (e.g., employees, consumers, stockholders, communities, and governments); (3) to serve as a catalyst to foster greater cooperation among business, government, and community organizations; and (4) to encourage private-sector initiatives and the formation of public-private partnerships wherever appropriate.

The early stimulus for the MPCR came in 1976 at a conference for business community leaders at Itasca State Park near Bemidji, Minnesota. At this conference, George Lodge of the Harvard Business School lectured on a "new ideology"—an ideology of communitarianism—that was allegedly sweeping across the country, and on business's failure to come to grips with and interpret this ideology on its own terms. Lodge subsequently returned twice to meet with an informal group of senior executives. A second catalyst was a conference in the fall of 1977 that featured Henry Schacht of Cummins Engine. Business and community leaders from the Twin Cities met to discuss the responsibilities of business in a changing society and to foster effective initiatives and possible programs that would reflect these responsibilities. This resulted in the creation of the MPCR steering committee headed by Thomas Wyman, then CEO of Green Giant. The first meeting of the project took place in fall of 1978.

From its inception a number of prominent business leaders have been associated with MPCR, including several Fortune 500 and Fortune 50 executives. For example, John S. Pillsbury of Northwestern National Life Insurance, Judson Bemis of Bemis, Inc., and James A. Summer of General Mills attended the 1976 Itasca Seminar, and Bruce Dayton of Dayton-Hudson Corporation, Thomas Wyman of Green Giant, and Edson Spencer of Honeywell all subsequently met with Lodge on his later visits to Minneapolis.

From 1978 until 1982, MPCR's core curriculum consisted of a base course and several electives. Until 1981, executive seminars were conducted mainly at the Spring Hill Conference Center approximately fifteen miles west of downtown Minneapolis. The base course was a two-day seminar that focused on the fundamentals of corporate responsibility using the corporate stakeholder concept as a framework for discussion. Electives were one-day seminars and were more topical. They addressed such subjects as corporate culture, public/private partnerships, and international business responsibilities. Special CEO programs were offered from time to time, and once each year chief executives gathered for a day-long session to discuss a major corporate responsibility issue.

Indeed, in our statistical analysis we found that Twin Cities companies whose executives publicly rationalized contributions as necessary for the long-term survival of their business gave more money to charity during the period from 1979 to 1981, controlling for their pretax net income and their executives' social proximity to the old philanthropic elite. Furthermore, we found that companies whose managers espoused an ethic of enlightened self-interest tended to be firms that participated in the MPCR. Upon further inquiry we also found that the more contacts a firm's executives had with the philanthropic elite, the more likely it was to participate in MPCR's programs. Thus peer pressure appears to have been important in recruiting firms to the project's programs, but it was participation in the project and not proximity to the elite which explained who espoused an ethic of enlightened self-interest and, in turn, who gave more money to charities.

INSTITUTIONALIZING CONTRIBUTIONS WITHIN THE FIRM

Since World War II, companies have increasingly retained the services of contributions officers or professionals to oversee the contributions function within firms. Prior to that, contribution-budget and allocative decisions were made mostly by the chief executive officer, one of his staff, or another high corporate executive (Bertsch 1982:7).

According to the Conference Board (Troy 1982), a staff person is considered to be a professional if she or he works full time (51 percent or more of his or her time) on contributions or has a contributions or foundation title. Troy notes that

> the most basic responsibilities of the contributions officer are screening requests, executing grant approval, and handling related correspondence, payment procedures, and record keeping. As budgets grow, budget preparation and administration, development of policy and procedures, and coordination of the work of the contributions committee and foundation board are added responsibilities.
>
> As time and staffing permit, those in fully professionalized functions develop a long-range contributions plan, and designate a part of their budget for the development of projects which they investigate and initiate. They develop a process for using the expertise of other corporate personnel in planning, proposal screening, and evaluation,

and institute a program for communicating the contributions story inside and outside the corporation. (Troy 1982:3)

In the course of our interviews with Twin Cities corporations, we obtained background information on full-time and part-time contributions people. In none of the companies with fewer than two hundred employees did we find people who devoted at least 50 percent of their time to contributions or had contributions or foundation titles. Therefore, the following discussion only refers to the sixty-nine participating companies that had more than two hundred employees in 1980. Of these, we obtained information from 59 firms on the percentage of time devoted to contributions by those individuals most involved with donations. Full-time ($\geq$ 50 percent time) were found in 32.2 percent (19) of those firms. We obtained information from 67 firms on the job titles of those primarily responsible for contributions. Staff with contributions or foundation titles were found in 29.9 percent (20) of these firms. In 34.8 percent (24) of the 69 participating firms with over two hundred employees, there were 32 people who either were working full time on contributions or had contributions or foundation titles.

Summarizing the differences between the professional and nonprofessional staff, the contributions professional was more likely to be a woman, to live in the city (as opposed to a suburb), and to have previously worked for a nonprofit organization, the government, or in the direct delivery of human services. Furthermore, the contributions professional was more likely than the nonprofessional to belong to professional associations related to contributions activities and to attend conferences on these topics.

At the time of our study (1979–82), three formal organizations served the needs of corporate contributions professionals. The first was the Minnesota Council on Foundations, a nonprofit organization which was organized in 1969 and incorporated in 1975. In 1982 its goals were to enhance and strengthen private philanthropy and to promote responsible and informed giving. More than a hundred members represented private, corporate, operating, and community foundations as well as corporations with contributions programs. The Business Action Resource Council (BARC) began in 1976 as the Council on Corporate Responsibility and became part of the Minneapolis Chamber of Commerce shortly thereafter. In 1982 its goals were to encourage social responsibility in business, to act as a forum where people who are responsible for corporate contributions can share information with one another, and to inform corporate donors of community needs and encourage their cooperation in meeting these needs. Most of its members in 1982 were contributions professionals from local Twin Cities firms. In 1982, Women and Foundations/Corporate Philanthropy—Minnesota Network was an unincorporated group of men and women who were contributions professionals or trustees of private foundations. In 1982 its goals were to increase the amount of money for programs on behalf of women and girls and to enhance the status of women as decision makers within private philanthropy.

The significance of contributions professionals and their professional associations in the Twin Cities lies in their commitment to scientific philanthropy. This means that giving should be directed where it can have the greatest impact on social welfare. We see that Twin Cities contributions professionals tended to have a social welfare or government background. In our analysis we also found a strong zero-order correlation between the professionalization of the contributions staff and the degree to which the applications and disbursement procedures are formalized and routinized.

In the course of our research we found that the relationship between the philanthropic elite and professionalism was complex, suggesting that the latter was only indirectly affected by the former. The more professional the contributions staff, the more money companies gave to charity, independent of executive proximity to the philanthropic elite and pretax earnings. However, proximity to the elite was unrelated to professionalism, once we controlled for the size of contributions. If we were to speculate, we would guess that peer pressure gave rise to greater contributions and that the greater size of the contributions budget pressured companies to professionalize their staff. Thus while support structures outside the firm (e.g., BARC at the Chamber) were supported by leaders in the grants community, the decision to professionalize contributions staff was probably made internally by managers in an effort to routinize and rationalize this corporate function.

More importantly, we found evidence that these professionals shaped one another's priorities and those of their respective firms. In a pattern similar to that described by DiMaggio and Powell (1983), Galaskiewicz and Burt (1991) found that corporate-giving officers who were more central in their discussion network tended to recognize and have similar evaluations of nonprofit organizations in the Twin Cities. Furthermore, they found that giving officers who belonged to the same professional associations tended to evaluate nonprofits similarly. Giving officers who were in structurally equivalent positions also tended to recognize and evaluate positively the same nonprofits. Thus a system was being created whereby different funders in the community, through their network contacts, could come to some consensus as to which nonprofits should be funded and which should not (see also Galaskiewicz 1985a).

Finally, we found that nonprofits tended to receive more corporate funding in toto, if a larger number of corporate-giving professionals recognized and thought well of them. This effect was independent of the nonprofits' expenditures, the value of government grants and contracts, and the elite's use and/or service to the nonprofits. Clearly then professional roles and professional networks made a difference in this grants economy, for the perceptions and opinions of those who actively managed corporate contribution programs made a difference in the allocation of dollars to nonprofits. Once certain nonprofits became faddish in contribution circles and network contacts helped crystallize opinions about those organizations, a consensus emerged and corporate dollars were forthcoming.

From Old Boy Networks to
Formalized Patterns of Social Control

How did this flurry of institution-building relate to the loss of control of local corporations and their potential withdrawal from community affairs? As stated earlier, we believe that these formally institutionalized structures were instituted to replace the more informal elite-based social institutions that had been at the heart of the corporate grants economy. With companies becoming more corporate and less dominated by natural persons with loyalties to the local area, new ways of ensuring continued corporate support of community institutions were needed if local nonprofits were to continue to enjoy the support they had received in the past.

To illustrate, the old system operated on the assumption that primary-group networks, extending out from a set of motivated and committed business leaders, would act as conduits through which expectations would be communicated and applause and recognition would be expressed. In the new system any firm, simply by giving 2 percent or 5 percent of its pretax earning and filling out a form for the Chamber of Commerce, could win the applause of significant others in the business community and even in the community as a whole. By recognizing 5 percent and 2 percent givers, the Chamber of Commerce formally proclaimed to all that corporate contributions were acceptable, proper, and expected corporate behavior and that businesses were worthy of public acclamation because they had met this standard. Essentially public relations were to replace the recognition that cronies gave to one another in the locker room and club room.

The old system also operated under the assumption that donors would come to understand the purpose of their contributions through participation in elite subcultures. In the new system all businessmen, by participating in seminars or educational programs on corporate responsibility, could broaden their perspective on the goals of their corporations and the role that contributions should play. By institutionalizing the learning process in structures like MPCR the opportunity had been made available for all to learn about enlightened self-interest. Earlier we discussed how the MPCR was a vehicle through which executives who had been narrowly preoccupied with their firms' bottom lines could have an opportunity to understand the larger role that business plays in the community, the society, and world. This opportunity was now available to every firm; the elite were no longer the only ones privy to such insights.

Looking at our data, however, we found that companies in the center of the peer network were not more likely to embrace enlightened self-interest as a way to rationalize contributions. This surprised us, because we expected to find some old-boy network influences on how companies rationalized contributions. However, these firms were more likely to participate in the MPCR, and companies participating in the seminars were more likely to rationalize contributions as enlightened self-interest. One interpretation of these findings is that peer-group socialization into values of enlightened self-interest had already begun to break down. The weak association between proximity to the elite and values of enlightened self-interest could be evidence of this. Instead, peer-group pressures may have been rechanneled to recruit companies into the more formally organized arenas in which they then learned the orthodoxy through group discussions, presentations, and so on. Peer pressure was still important, but its indirect contributions to the socialization process were different than we had expected.

Finally, the old system operated on the assumption that corporate executives would be solicited by their peers and actively involved in making decisions on allocations within their firms. In the new system, professional boundary-spanning personnel received written requests from nonprofit-grant writers and took an active part in directing the flow of charitable dollars. With the institutionalization of professional organizations like the Business Action Resource Council, the Minnesota Council on Foundations, and Women and Foundations/Corporate Philanthropy, formally organized arenas were created to enable these professionals to learn about improving their job performance, about community priorities, and about one another's companies.

Moving to professionalized giving may just mean the creation of a new peer network made up of the new professionals. In this network control would be exercised over members just as control was exercised by the elite over local CEOs. We presented evidence of this earlier in our discussion: nonprofits which were recognized and respected by more contributions professionals tended to receive more corporate contributions. Even more important, contributions professionals who were central or structurally equivalent in discussion networks tended to recognize and value the same nonprofits in the community. In other words, not only did these networks carry a great deal of weight and directly influence the amount of money that nonprofits received from business organizations, but they also shaped the way corporate almoners came to view nonprofits in the community.

In sum, we argue that the high level of corporate involvement in the community and changes in the control of the largest corporations in Minneapolis–St. Paul can explain why new institutional forms like the Five Percent Club, the Minnesota Project on Corporate Responsibility, and contributions professionals emerged when they did. It is also our belief that these changes were orchestrated by a cadre of business leaders who had both corporate clout and long-standing ties to the community. The former enabled them to recruit local business people into their Five Percent Club and Project on Corporate Responsibility. The latter gave them the motivation to assume the responsibility of organizing these efforts. Participants in this corporate community consciously built a new set of institutions, created a new incentive structure, formulated an ideology to legitimate these roles, and helped institutionalize corporate responsibility roles within local firms.

Nonetheless, the future of these new institutional constructs is unclear. The old constructs were successful because a business elite which had personal and professional roots in the area was motivated and involved. With the passing of the philanthropic elite, the influx of out-of-town managers, and the ever present pressures to rationalize all aspects of corporate behavior in terms of the dominant ideology—the bottom line—contributions could soon degenerate into a marketing or public relations strategy. At that juncture the contributions function would move from the community affairs department and corporate foundation into the marketing or PR department or even be contracted out to consultants. Gifts would be rationalized in terms of short-term sales instead of the long-term interest of the firm. If this happens, it would be interesting to see if institutions such as the Five Percent Club, the Minnesota Project on Corporate Responsibility, and donors' associations (such as the Minnesota Council on Foundations and BARC) fall by the wayside, redefine their goals, or continue to champion the ideals of their founders. Our research has clearly shown that an old boy network based on personal ties to corporate agents can act as an institutionalized control system that makes corporate actors behave responsibly. However, it is unclear if this new institutional order, based on motivating and controlling organizational actors, can succeed equally as well.

Conclusion

How can the Twin Cities case help advance institutional theory? First, we found that organizations pursue strategies that serve either their long-term self-interest or immediate collective interests if the proper set of incentives are in place. Organizational behavior is not only premised on strict cost-benefit calculi and individual firm rationality. In this respect, we have confirmed an important assumption of institutional theory which states that organizations will respond to social pressures emanating from the larger society and make strategic choices on those grounds.

Second, we found that systems of social control are created and enforced by interorganizational field leaders in a rational and purposive manner. If analysts find cultural elements in the corporation which reflect larger societal values, it is not necessarily the case that they entered the organization through the backdoor, undetected. Rather, cultural elements that may even run contrary to the dominant ideology of the firm can be consciously introduced into the organization by change agents. While some may still be more fascinated by the "taken-for-granteds" which worm their way into organizations, this study shows that conscious efforts to institutionalize meanings, values, and norms both within the organization and at the interorganizational field level are effective in changing organizational behavior.

Third, the study highlights the importance of embedding institutional analysis in a historical context and the importance of social learning. Obviously the efforts at instituting new methods of social control were in response to changing patterns of control within local firms and the role that companies had come to play in supporting nonprofits in this community. However, and perhaps more importantly, change agents were aware of developments in other cities and communities which had seen their firms taken over by outside interests and influences and their interest in the local community wane.

Fourth, our results exemplified the difficulties of doing causal analysis within the institutional framework, particularly when the interface between the micro- and macro-orders is complicated. At the microlevel we noted that companies were responsive to the peer pressure and selective incentives of the corporate philanthropic elite. We noted how individual executives searched for ways to motivate greater contributions, attended meetings, and sponsored new associations. We noted how contributions professionals "networked" among themselves and how this influenced their perceptions and evaluations of nonprofits in the community. At the same time, at the macrolevel we noted the publicity which local corporations and the Twin Cities were receiving in the national press, the dependency of local nonprofits on corporate contributions, and changes in the control of local corporations. It becomes confusing when trying to offer a cogent explanation of why these systems of social control were institutionalized when and where they were. One cannot focus solely on the microlevel or solely on the macrolevel variables. Both are important, and both have an interactive effect on outcomes. As institutional theory attempts to build holistic theories of organizational behavior, it will increasingly be forced to craft models that incorporate elements of both social orders.

Acknowledgments

Funding for this research was provided by the National Science Foundation (SES 800-8570) and the Program on Nonprofit Organizations, Yale University. Special thanks to Paul DiMaggio for his very useful comments on an earlier draft and ultimately to Morris Janowitz, who provided the theoretical framework utilized in this chapter.

13 The Structural Transformation of American Industry: An Institutional Account of the Causes of Diversification in the Largest Firms, 1919–1979

NEIL FLIGSTEIN

In 1919 the hundred largest U.S. corporations operated predominantly in one industry. By 1979, almost all of the firms on the list of the largest corporations were highly diversified. While the identities of the firms changed substantially, about half of those firms remained throughout the entire period. The population of the largest firms, thus, changed in two ways: those that remained large became diversified, and those that grew large did so through diversification. This chapter explores this process by first documenting these changes, then proposing an organizational view of them and demonstrating how that view can be used to explain the spread of diversification among the largest U.S. firms.

The ability to change the course of a large corporation depends on a complex set of actions, both internal and external to the organization. Some organizations altered their strategies, while others, in similar organizational fields, did not. It is clear from the historical record that both adaptation and selection occurred. The conditions under which certain actors alter the direction of their organizations and other actors do not are the focus of this analysis.

I discuss four mechanisms which promote or inhibit organizational change: the role of existing strategy, structure, and a given power distribution in inhibiting change and promoting organizational inertia; turbulence in organizational fields whereby actors with interests based on their position in the corporation can articulate new strategies and have the power to implement them; the role of new organizations entering into already existing fields in providing an example for other organizations; and forces of institutionalization. Then I consider the history of the large modern corporation to understand how these factors, at given historical moments, affect which organizations will be transformed. Next I present quantitative models that confirm the thrust of the historical discussion.

One strong trend in current organizational theory is to attempt to specify how organizational fields become normatively defined and how those definitions create the possibility for change and stability in the constituent organizations (see essays in part 1 of this volume). The work presented here clarifies recent work on institutionalization in three ways. First, I suggest that the processes by which organizational fields are created and transformed reflect the operation of the mechanisms just discussed. Second, I argue that institutional theories have overestimated the role of norms in the construction of organizational fields and underestimated the relative power of actors in organizations in this regard. Third, I argue that institutionalists have given ground too readily to market-based accounts of organizational change (a charge that concurs with the arguments made in the chapters by Powell and Orrù, Biggart, and Hamilton). This chapter uses an institutional perspective to study processes that are generally thought to be best explained by reference to market processes. I assert that organizational theory allied with the institutional perspective can contribute greatly to understanding how market processes are defined by the interaction of large-scale organizations. The process of diversification in large firms nicely illustrates this point.

Theoretical Reflections

Recent advances in organizational theory can be brought to bear in such a way as to aid our understanding of how and why social change can occur in large-scale institutions (Hannan and Freeman 1977; 1984; DiMaggio and Powell 1983; Meyer and Rowan 1977; Meyer and Scott 1983b; Fligstein 1985, 1987, 1990b; White 1981; Pfeffer 1981; DiMaggio 1988a). The following discussion proposes a way of viewing how organizations are constructed and embedded in their organizational fields. Once such a view has been presented, it can be used to inform an understanding of how diversification proceeded.

Organizations operate in three contexts of what could be called institutional spheres: the existing strategy and structure of the organization, the set of organizations comprising the organizational field, and the state. These are arenas where rules are created, meaningful action occurs, power relations are formed, and concrete forms of social organization are set in place. Rules imply commonly held definitions of the situation that act to constrain and shape actors' behavior. The ability to set rules is a result of power such that actors in single organizations or sets of organizations (including the state) can create rules. The first context is the organization itself. Every organization has in place a set of strategies (or goals), structures, technologies, and physical limits that shape and constrain action. These forms of organization reflect systems of power and operate to support those who control them. Every organization, however, must allocate its resources toward specific goals, and this usually entails conflict over how to achieve them. The actual form and strategy of any given organization, therefore, reflect how the historical resolution of these conflicts have been played out.

The internal structuring of the organization is both a source of great power and, at the same time, a constraint on action. There are two aspects of internal structure: formal and informal authority. Formal authority refers to a position in a hierarchical structure, while informal authority refers to claims by actors for power and expertise that potentially allow them to direct resources of the organization. Those who are in power act to preserve their positions through claims exercised through both formal and informal authority structures. Changes in organizational goals can only result when either a new set of actors gains power or it is in the interest of those in power to alter the organization's goals.

Organizations are embedded in larger groups of organizations that may be defined in terms of product lines, markets, or firm size. These other organizations can be suppliers, distributors, or competitors. The links between these organizations can be characterized in network terms, and the substance of the links can range from formal relations to personal friendships (DiMaggio 1986a). The other organizations in the environment can influence the actions of any given organization both through network links and various dependency relations (Pfeffer and Salancik 1978). Dependency does not just refer to material resources, but includes social relations that involve legitimation, competition, or cooperation. In an organizational field where competitor's actions can have consequences for one's market share, dependency also exists because the actions of others will affect one's own position. So, for example, if competitors shift strategies, then a given organization may be forced to respond in order to maintain or expand its position.

To the extent that a given organization defines its environment and to the degree that the environment is well defined, one can speak of an organizational field (see discussion of fields in DiMaggio and Powell, ch. 3, and Scott, ch. 7, this vol.). Fields contain all of the relevant organizations from the point of view of actors in any given organization. While it is theoretically possible to specify at one point in time which organizations exist in any given field, it may prove empirically problematic to do so. Organizational fields are constantly undergoing change, and therefore patterns of influence may be complex.

Generally, the stability of organizational fields is a major variable in determining the likelihood of change in any given organization. Where rules exist and a pecking order of organizations is well established, fundamental change is less likely. When new organizations enter established fields or fields are in the process of formation or disintegration, change is more likely. The actions of others in the organizational field can either legitimate current actions or else constitute reasons for change.

The idea of a field differs from the idea of a niche or the environment in one important sense. Both concepts imply an objective reality that is imposed on any given organization. The idea of a field suggests that the environment and the niche are themselves constructions of organizations and their key actors. When a number of actors in and across organizations come to agree on a particular definition of their field (often a definition enforced by the relative power of large organizations and/or rules provided by the state), then one can say that a field is more well defined and stable.

The third institutional context in which actions are framed concerns relations with the state. The state is a set of formal organizations that interact in much the same way as other organizations. One can distinguish between actions of the state and actions of other organizations in an organizational field because the state can actually set the rules of the game for any given organizational field, even though it is not a direct participant in the field. It can mediate among organizations in the field and attempt to act in the interests of all organizations in order to stabilize the fields. It can, therefore, alter the environment more profoundly and systematically than other organizations. The actors who control the state achieve power through different means than the actors who control private and nonprofit organizations. But once actors are in power, organizational dynamics become important determinants of action (see Skocpol 1985; Fligstein 1990b:17–19).[1]

The state is a great source of stability or change, both in the field and within any given organization. By defining the rules of the game in any given field, the state provides for continuity. If the rules are changed, then actors in the state can consciously manipulate the actions of organizations in the field. Sometimes the actions of the state provide shocks to the system that bring about unexpected consequences.

One important aspect of the concept of organizational field is the ability of a given organization or set of organizations to capture or direct the actions of the field. Organizations can control fields on the basis of two principles. First, the relative size of organizations gives their actors differential power to dictate the actions of others in any given field. Actors in larger organizations are more likely to get other organizations to go along with cooperative actions to the degree that they can threaten the smaller actors. Second, to the degree that all members benefit from the formation of stable rules governing legitimate actions in the field, cooperation is to be expected.

Private-sector firms use the state to organize their fields in a fashion that supports the interests of the already existing organizations. The ability of any given organization to dictate the rules of the field, or induce the state to set up rules for the field, will depend on the resources that organizations command and the types of network and dependency relations the organization has to other organizations. This points to one obvious conclusion of social life: one great cause of stability (or, as Hannan and Freeman 1984 called it, "inertia") is the interests of any given set of organizations and the actors in them in maintaining some distribution of power and resources.

This view differs somewhat from those posed by recent institutional theorists, which stress the normative aspects of organizational fields. The view proposed here focuses, instead, on the organizational field as a construction of powerful organizations that is based on the interests of those organizations. The stability of organizational fields from the perspective outlined here depends on the ability of a particular view of a field to be held in place by the actors with an interest in that view. Recently, DiMaggio (1988a) has attempted to combine a theory of agency with institutional theory. While this chapter presents a similar argument, it does not attempt to integrate a notion of agency and power with the idea of the organizational field.

There are two key questions to address: Why are actors constrained by the institutional contexts in which they operate, and why and when are they some-times able to alter those contexts? The internal organization, the organizational field, and the state provide conditions that constrain actors' behaviors and at the same time provide opportunities for innovative behavior. But in order for these conditions to operate, a model of actors in organizations is necessary because they must interpret their environment, both internal and external to the organi-zation, and have the power to act to sustain or alter their organization. Actors create a view of the world in order to simplify it. Most often, that view will be framed in terms of their interests; hence, their intepretation of any new situation will be framed in those terms. Those interests will generally reflect their posi-tion in a social structure as well as their ability to articulate a coherent view of the world based on that position.

This view of actors differs from accounts of action that are based on notions of rationality or bounded rationality. Approaches that use rationality assume actors have perfect information and are able to make decisions that maximize some ends. Bounded rationality stresses that actors do not have perfect infor-mation and instead search for satisfying solutions. Both approaches assume that information is a neutral commodity that actors acquire. Thus, in these views the world does not require interpretation. My argument suggests that environments are murky; thus actors have to provide interpretations of them. These accounts are a function of actors' interests and position in any given organization. Solu-tions to problems from this perspective, require a construction of that problem as well as a course of action consistent with it. This gives rise to the importance of two issues: cognition or perception, and the role of power in organizational change.

In order to make a decision to change an organization, individuals must per-ceive a need and source for that change. Quite often, the state or the organiza-tional field will create shocks that reflect either a reconstitution of the rules or models of new organizational strategies that undermine the rules. The source of ideas for change can also emerge from the position an actor occupies within an organization. That position might provide arguments or interpretations that would alter the organization's course by offering a particular construction of an organizational crisis and a solution to that crisis. Such a solution would often enhance the power of that position in the organization. The issue of perception or cognition provides another reason why there exists a great amount of stability or inertia in organizations. Actors have a way they view the world, and, unless some event of major proportions occurs that unambiguously changes their world, they will continue to act in a consistent fashion. Of course, actors can persist in their interpretations even when there is clear evidence that those views do not make sense of the field.

Once some set of organizations in a field has changed its strategies, and once others perceive that the change has resulted in some allegedly superior results, then other actors will follow suit. The changes may or may not be actually positive for other organizations, but what matters is that actors in other organizations perceive the need for change and construct views of their world based on perceived successes.

This view isolates several mechanisms by which actors are constrained by their organizations and by which they are able to transform their local and distal structures. I argue that organizations display great inertia because they are systems of power held together by the interests of key actors in business as usual. A given system of power benefits those who are in charge, and their view controls the organization and allows them access to the resources of the organization. To upset that balance is to court both individual and collective disaster, and therefore existing strategy and structure, in which actors' interests are embedded, are strong forces that promote inertia.

To the degree that organizational fields are stable and the state regulates the environment, one would expect that organizations would be unlikely to alter their courses of action. This stability is often based on a collective definition of the organizational field that requires nonpredatory competition (White 1981; Fligstein 1990b:98–115). If actors in organizations recognize the interests of other organizations and their actions take account of the behavior of others, then they will be less inclined to upset the status quo. If the environment is heavily regulated by the state, then stability is even more likely. Any new potential competitor must play by certain rules, thereby protecting the status quo. In this sense, inertia is the result of a stable system of power in an organizational field.

In order for organizational change to occur, those in charge must have both a perception of some new strategy and the power to act upon it. If organizational fields are turbulent or ill formed, the possibility for innovative behavior is high. But shocks or instability still require that actors develop a set of solutions based on their interpretation of the shock, which will generally reflect their position in the organization and the interests of that position. Innovative organizations will take two forms: an organization comes into existence with a new strategy or else actors in existing firms possess the power to shift strategy (Stinchcombe 1965; Hannan and Freeman 1977). When an existing system of power is transformed, it requires a perceived crisis, either in the organization or the field.

Organizations extensively monitor one another. They do so by reading the business press, which is usually quick to note major organizational changes, attending trade meetings, and using other sources of information (including, in extreme cases, espionage). Once a visible organization embarks on a new course of action, organizations in the field are more likely to adopt it if they perceive it to be effective. When a sufficient number follow suit, the strategy becomes institutionalized and spreads rapidly (on the mechanisms of this process, see DiMaggio and Powell, ch. 3, this vol.). If the significant actors in an organizational field adopt this course of action, others will follow suit and that new course of action will come to define successful behavior in the field.

To summarize, organizational change is likely to be the outcome of a small set of circumstances. The possibilities for change are commonly found in the period leading up to the establishment of an organizational field. In this situation, successful courses of action need to be constructed and imposed on other organizations. Once organizational fields are stable, change is most likely to occur when some shock is delivered. The shocks could result from actions taken by the state, other organizations, or macroeconomic conditions. Once the instability exists, organizational change will be the result of three types of factors: the power of actors with a new perception of the situation to act in already existing organizations, organizations that come into existence with the new strategy, and forces of institutionalization in an organizational field where actors in organizations follow the lead of other key organizations. Sorting out how and when these various forces are operating requires paying close attention to the point in the process where one is observing. What is an effect at one time point can be a cause at another (for a similar argument about institutional change, see Powell, ch. 8, this vol.).

The Case of Diversification

The spread of diversification strategies in the largest U.S. firms was an immense change for those firms. This section suggests how my proposed organizational view can be used to understand the causes of that change. Economists and business historians have provided an account of the change in product mix by the largest U.S. corporations, and these studies generally point to three factors that influenced diversification (Gort 1961; Chandler 1961; Rumelt 1974; Williamson 1975). First, markets present corporations with opportunities for diversification, and executives seize them. Second, firms leave industries that are growing more slowly and enter industries that are expanding rapidly (Gort 1961). Third, firms treat product mix as an investment portfolio and choose to invest in different industries in order to spread risk across investments (Williamson 1975).

The basic problem with all of these explanations is that they do not specify the structural and historical conditions under which diversification takes place. Chandler's managers perceive opportunities and take advantage of them. The question of why the 1920s presented such opportunities is not considered. The strategy of exiting declining industries and entering new ones is quite modern and begs an explanation of the conditions under which this is likely to occur. Indeed, until 1920 the dominant tactic of most firms was to attempt to control as much production as possible in a single product line. Finally, treating the firm as an investment portfolio reflects a certain way of looking at organizational activities. It already implies a perception of the world and an appropriate way to organize.[2]

I offer as an alternative an organizational view of the innovation of diversification. The overall strategy of a firm reflects, at any given point in time, important organizational facts. It shows who is in power and what view maintains that power, and provides an indicator of how the resources of an organization are being used. Any decision to fundamentally alter the deployment of internal resources represents a major structural change. These kinds of changes do not occur often; when they do, they provide us with an opportunity to examine the conditions under which actors can alter their social structures. The object of attention is the hundred largest U.S. firms at ten-year intervals from 1919 to 1979; these firms represent the core of the economy. Of course, their names and identities have changed substantially over the period. While 216 firms have made appearances on the list, 50 firms have appeared on every list (Fligstein 1987). Thus there have been both stability and change in the largest firms in the economy.

Historical Overview of Diversification

The dominant strategy in U.S. industry until 1920 revolved around attempts to control markets. The ups and downs of the economy in the late nineteenth century encouraged firms to enter into cartels. But cartels were illegal, and therefore their agreements were unenforceable contracts in U.S. law (Fligstein 1990b:38–58). As a result, firms entered into large-scale mergers in order to stabilize their fields. By and large, these tactics failed as firms were unable to construct barriers to entry in their industry, and government antitrust policies effectively policed the most anticompetitive behavior (Fligstein 1990b:75–98).

The only effective and legal market control tactic set in place by 1920 can be characterized as a manufacturing strategy with two components: price leadership by the largest producers in a field, and the vertical integration of production, which ensured leading firms of lower costs. Legal collusion was possible only under oligoply conditions. In that situation, a small number of firms would set prices and other firms would follow. Vertical integration was the attempt to control the production process by securing suppliers and customers through the use of a functional form of organization. The endpoint of this strategy was the large-scale production of a small set of products that could be strongly controlled by a hierarchical structure.

Stability was achieved in organizational fields through the use of both mechanisms. The largest firms enforced a price by their size and relative efficiency. If smaller firms undercut prices, larger firms could retaliate. The control of suppliers also made larger firms invulnerable and opened the possibility of cutting off supplies to other firms. From the point of view of smaller firms, following the price leader meant that prices were stable and everyone was guaranteed a profit. This strategy is a manufacturing strategy in the sense that its central goal is to guarantee a market for the product and to control all of the vital goods necessary for its production. I have previously shown that manufacturing personnel tended to control those firms where this strategy dominated. This tactic of price leadership provided price stability for many industries (including steel, oil, and meat-packing) and was one of the principle motivations for the 1920s merger movement (Fligstein 1990b:112–15; Eis 1978).

The decision to diversify required a different view of the firm and its fundamental business, a view that can be called a sales and marketing perspective. The central tactic was the attempt to promote firm growth through the increased sales of a wide range of products. This entails developing new markets both nationally and multinationally, differentiating products from competitors through advertising and differences in quality and quantity, and introducing new products to cushion the firm from stable or declining product markets. Diversification is only one component of the sales and marketing strategy. If the thrust of the manufacturing strategy was to produce a reliable, mass market product with a stable price, then the essence of the sales and marketing strategy was to produce a greater variety of products with identifiable images.

The roots of diversification were contained in the marketing revolution of the 1920s. At the time, one observer noted:

> A characteristic of many U.S. industries during the nineteenth century and the early twentieth century was mass production of more or less standardized articles, a system which reached its zenith in the Ford plant. That method of operation permitted the economic utilization of labor and resulted in great economies of production. Since 1920, however, a different set of conditions has been apparent, as indicated by the new tempo of demand, the rapidity of style changes, and the receptivity of consumers to new varieties of and types of products. These changes in demand can be attributed to the ingenuity of manufacturers in applying to ordinary uses new ideas, materials, and machinery which were developed during the war period, and to the devising of new products which rapidly attained popularity. The spread of the demand for many of these products was stimulated by the utilization of aggressive methods of marketing and promotion. (Copeland 1927: 329–30)

In 1921 the American Management Assocciation set up a Sales Executive Division that began to hold yearly meetings. The members of the executive board included the sales mangers of Burroughs, Swift, Proctor and Gamble,

American Radiator, Atlantic Refining, DuPont, Goodyear, National Cash Register, and Ralston Purina, among others (Fligstein 1990b, ch. 4). In the 1920s the group published a series of papers and polls that were quite revealing of their strategies. In one poll, members were asked, "What steps have you taken to stabilize sales either from year to year or season to season by adopting new marketing policies or sales methods?" The three answers most frequently given were diversification, attempts to find new markets for existing products, and continuous advertising (American Management Association 1926). Diversification was the product of a new outlook, an outlook that stressed the significance of growth through the increase in sales.

In an article written in 1928, the author observed:

> Mass production now exists, and will only exist as a result of constructive and accurate sales planning. It is not and will not be a primary cause of sales volume and industrial prosperity. In the skill of consumer market analysis and in the ability to make a product which will appeal to that market are the keys of business success. The problem of increased selling has developed a new type of consolidation. Under this form, groups of noncompeting products selling to the same general market or subject to the same kind of management have been brought together under one ownership. The Postum Company, the General Motors Company, and the Radio Corporation are examples. This type offers to the constituent member of the group either the economy of selling or increased power in the sales market. (Mazur 1928:631)

The natural winners of such a shift were sales and marketing personnel. A president of a large steel tube company wrote:

> I would in no way minimize the importance of the production role. Nor would I gainsay the necessity for sound purchasing. But these and every other movement of business seems to me and to this business so dependent on the several basic functions of sales that I believe a sales bringing-up is the best foundation for business leadership. (Hobbs 1924:32)

Given this concern with marketing, it is not suprising that 30.9 percent of the mergers in the 1920s (a period of substantial merger activity) contained an element of diversification (Eis 1978:81). By the Great Depression, diversification was becoming an accepted part of American business.

But it was the Great Depression that proved the value of the sales and marketing strategy, in general, and the diversification of products in particular. The general downturn in business provided a shock to stable organizational fields where the manufacturing strategy dominated. A large market share in times of a declining market did not produce growth. Indeed, the only tactic that lead to firm growth during the Depression was diversification (Fligstein 1990a). But for diversification to spread, actors had to perceive the new strategy and find the power to act. The period from the depression until the early postwar era saw the rise of sales and marketing personnel in large firms (Fligstein 1987). Firms led by sales, and marketing personnel increasingly diversified their product lines, attempted to differentiate their products from competitors, began to market extensively overseas, and implemented the multidivisional form as an organizational tool (Fligstein 1985; 1990b). Diversification became an accepted strategy as a result of the success of the firms that began diversifying in the 1920s and continued growing in the Depression.

The impetus toward product-unrelated strategies occurs in the postwar era. While one could view this strategy as an extension of diversification, I argue that product-unrelated diversification reflects a clean break with the past. This new approach can be called a finance strategy, reflecting the fact that the decision to enter new businesses is undertaken purely on financial criteria and no longer is concerned with the fit of product lines. Firms in the modern era no longer view themselves as operating in a particular business, but instead view any given business as an investment that must pay off. The rate of return on capital and the potential for that return are viewed as the most important facts by which any product line is evaluted. The basic mode of expansion in the era of financial strategies is no longer sales, but mergers. The decision to merge is made independent of whether or not a product fits with a firm's existing lines.

The major impetus to this new strategy was unintentionally provided by the federal government. In the 1940s and early 1950s, the Federal Trade Commission and the Justice Department initiated a burst of antitrust suits; in 1950, half of the hundred largest firms had some form of antitrust suit pending against them. At the time, the Celler-Kefauver Act was passed by Congress, making any mergers that increased concentration in any given line of business illegal. From 1950 onward, all vertical and horizontal mergers became problematic. The law was applied constantly and consistently to horizontal and vertical mergers throughout the 1950s and 1960s, and their volume decreased substantially (Mueller 1979; Fligstein 1990a:194–225). As a result, firms turned to product-related and -unrelated mergers.

The state thus changed the rules by which firms could expand. In stable organizational fields, even those dominated by product-related strategies, the option of absorbing additional market share in any given product line was foreclosed. The only option left for growth for the largest firms was diversification. By altering the rules, the federal government inadvertently set the stage for a large-scale merger movement that was almost entirely driven by the desire to diversify.

This strategy was best exemplified by the acquisitive conglomerates. A small group of men (Tex Thornton at Textron, Jim Ling at L-T-V, Harold Geneen at ITT, Charles Bludhorn at Gulf and Western) viewed their corporations in purely financial terms as stock portfolios of investments, each with differing rates of return. The basic growth strategy was to use existing assets to purchase other companies. Jim Ling pioneered the leveraged buyout, whereby the assets of the company being purchased were used as the basis of securing loans. This tactic enabled Ling and others to buy firms that were larger than they were. The financial strategies came to dominate the largest firms, and the product mix of those firms became substantially more unrelated.

Since the 1960s, a number of forces have counteracted this acquisitive strategy. First, the large unrelated firm often performed poorly, both in profitability and in sales and asset growth. Firms found themselves saddled with unprofitable divisions, and many companies rushed to disinvest. Second, financial entrepreneurs no longer feel the need to operate the companies they buy. The phenomenon of corporate raiders revolves around a set of actors who are content to buy and sell the stock of large companies with the goal of raising the value of their investment. There are two tactics: If a hostile takeover is resisted, entrenched management will often buy out raiders at a premium. If a merger is consummated, existing management is replaced and the firm may be liquidated for its assets or held as an investment. This means that the finance strategy is actually practiced not just in the large firms, but by groups of individuals who operate outside of corporate structures engaged in any form of production. Finally, worldwide competition has forced the large firm to pay more attention to production processes. Unfortunately, in most cases, this involves cutting costs and sacrificing investment in new plant, which only increases the likelihood of further deterioration of the capital stock. The mergers that have been occurring are not creating new jobs or plant capacity, but instead appear as financial ploys to increase short-run profitability at the expense of long-run viability.

Agents, Structures, and the Shifts in Strategy

Now I intend to link the theoretical arguments made earlier to the process of diversification of the large firms. First, there are great pressures to maintain the status quo. The present structure and purposes of an organization and the interests of actors in the organization who are served by those purposes are the greatest forces toward inertia. The emergence of new strategies requires some kind of shock to stable organizational fields. In the case of diversification, the Depression provided one such shock and later the federal government's antitrust policy generated another. But while these shocks provide conditions for change, actors in organizations must recognize these shocks and take actions to alter their strategies. This means either upsetting a stable organizational field or entering a new one.

I utilize the functional background of the president of the organization as a measure of both power and perception. A person with a certain functional background will perceive the problems of the organization in a certain way. A manufacturing person will tend to see the organization's problems in production terms, a sales and marketing person will tend to view the nature, size, and extent of the market as critical to organizational survival, and a financial person will see the basic profitability of firm activities as crucial. In a given crisis, different solutions will be proposed by these different actors. The ability of these actors to impose their solutions depends on the amount of influence their functional subunit has on the direction of the organization. The perception of what is going on and the solution are intimately connected to the ability to have power and act.

Sales and marketing and finance presidents favor diversification because the initial impetus toward diversification arose from a concern over selling products in various markets. Finance personnel pushed both related and unrelated diversification because they thought that investment in new product lines spreads risk and promises an overall higher rate of return on capital. One would predict that when instability existed in organizational fields, firms headed by sales and marketing and finance presidents would push to diversify.

Forces promoting institutionalization offer another way for new strategies to spread. One major source of information about what is profitable organizational behavior comes from organizations sharing similar structural positions. If those organizations are changing their strategies, then any given organization is more likely to change its strategy. The pressures that produce similarity of output can be either mimetic, coercive, or result from a cultural definition shared by actors in an organizational field (see DiMaggio and Powell, ch. 3, this vol.). In the case of diversification, firms pay the most attention to competitors because they provide examples of organizations in similar structural positions (White 1981). With the success of diversification of competitors during the Depression, firms began to follow suit. Similarly, when the federal government closed off opportunities to expand in a firm's main product market and other firms began to pursue merger tactics for growth, this strategy began to proliferate. One important issue is to identify whether new firms entered organizational fields with diversification strategies or older firms altered their strategies. Of course, both could be occurring simultaneously.

Since it is problematic to observe an organization's actual decision-making processes over long periods of time, gathering evidence to support this interpretation must require some simplification of the theory and the assumption of certain processes. For instance, one can measure variables that index organizational power and see if they correlate with outcomes. Similarly, one cannot easily observe the degree to which organizations coalesce into fields. But if the theoretical construct is meaningful, then the behavior of those who are supposed to be members of the field should affect other organizations. The theoretical model cannot be easily observed, but if it accounts for alterations in the goals or strategies of organizations, then measures of the mechanisms should predict outcomes.

It is important to specify more precise predictions about the link between independent and dependent variables, where the dependent variable is the overall strategy of the firms. Inertial effects exist consistently throughout the period 1919–79 as firms with a given strategy tend to maintain it. Environmental turbulence is indexed by considering the historical factors that produce more versus less turbulent environments. One expects more shifts toward diversification strategies during the Depression of the 1930s than previous to that period and in the decade following the Celler-Kefauver Act (1950–60). The shift to product-related strategies dominates in the earlier period and the shift toward product-unrelated strategies emerges in the latter.

The early movers to diversification strategies are organizations in which persons who choose a new strategy must create a new view about organizational goals. In the early period, (1919–39) the role of sales and marketing presidents in the shift to a product-related strategy should be most pronounced. Once firms begin to change strategies, the role of presidents in that shift should decline. Similarly, the presence of finance presidents should be most important in the 1948–59 period as a cause of diversification to product-unrelated strategies; as a sufficiently large number of firms choose that strategy, the presidential power base becomes less important.

Effects of institutionalization should pick up where the effects of the president's background falls off because as soon as a large enough number of organizations shift their strategies, other organizations will follow suit. Institutionalization should have the largest effects from 1939–48, when firms will be more likely to adopt a product-related strategy, and after 1959, when firms are more likely to follow firms that have adopted a product-unrelated strategy.

Data and Methods

The first issue is to define the sample and the time frame. I choose to study the hundred largest firms at the following time points: 1919, 1929, 1939, 1948, 1959, 1969, 1979. These time points were selected for two reasons. First, they reflect a sufficiently long time frame in which to study changes in strategy. Second, lists of the hundred largest nonfinancial corporations were available at those time points.[3] The data have the following structure. For every firm that appears, data were collected for the time point before the firm entered the list (if the firm enters after 1919) and for the time point after the firm exits the list (if the firm exited). The data were then organized into files reflecting changes over decades, that is, 1919–29, 1929–39, 1939–48, 1948–59, 1959–69, 1969–79.[4]

The dependent variable in the data analysis is the strategy of the firm at the second time point. Three categories were coded: product-dominant, product-related, and product-unrelated. Data sources for this information included Rumelt (1974) and *Moody's Manuals* (1920, 1930, 1940, 1950, 1960, 1970,

1980).[5] Strategy was assessed on the basis of actual product mix of the firm.[6] *Product-dominant* implied that more than 70 percent of the revenues were generated from a single industry group. *Product-related* implies that firms produce in product markets that are related or are market extensions (for example, a chemical company that produced paint and explosives). No single product line accounts for more than 70 percent of the output. *Product-unrelated* means that firms engage in unrelated businesses to produce a substantial proportion of their revenue (again, no one product could account for 70 percent of revenues). An example was Ling-Temco-Vought which built guided missiles, made steel, and owned a rental car company at one point.

All of the independent variables refer to measurement at the first time point, ten years earlier. The first factor operationalized is stability or inertia. The age of the organization was coded at the first time point. Hannan and Freeman (1984) have argued that the older an organization is, the less likely it is to alter its fundamental strategy. Similarly, at the first time point, asset size in millions of dollars (normed to 1967 dollars) is included. This test of population ecology theory is not definitive as sampling has occurred on the dependent variable (i.e., the largest firms by definition have large size and are probably older than the average firm in the economy), and therefore the test is limited to age and size effects in the largest firms. It should be noted that economists might make exactly the opposite argument (Gort 1961). As firms grow larger and older, they must find new opportunities in order to sustain growth.

The third and most important measure of inertia is strategy at the first time point. This measure is coded exactly as the dependent variable. Placing the strategy at the first time point in the equation means that we predict the likelihood of a change in strategy. The straightforward interpretation of the coefficient on strategy at the first time point is the effect of existing strategy.[7]

The measure of perception/power is the subunit background of the president of the firm at the first time point. The subunit that is in control of the large firm can best be inferred from the subunit background of the president of the firm (Fligstein 1987). From 1919 to 1949, manufacturing personnel and entrepreneurs dominated large firms. Beginning in 1939, sales and marketing personnel began to rise as a proportion of presidents, and their numbers peaked in 1959. Since 1949, finance presidents have come to dominate large firms, and by 1979 they form the single largest group. This analysis allows us to assess to what degree a president altered his organization's strategy in line with his interests in the organization.

This variable was operationalized by first collecting the president or chief executive officer's name for each firm at all relevant time points. These names came from *Moody's Manuals.* Then the president's entry was found in *Who's Who in America, Who's Who in Business and Industry,* and other sources.[8] The description of each president's career (i.e., previous job titles) allowed us to infer how he came up through the organization. The following categories were coded: manufacturing, sales and marketing, finance, general management, entrepreneur, lawyer, and unable to ascertain.[9] The measure refers to the first time point and has been collapsed into four categories: manufacturing, sales and marketing, finance, and other. Three dummy variables are used to reflect these categories, with the other group as the left-out category.

The measurement of institutionalization is more complex because it is necessary to make assumptions about which firms constitute the organizational field of any given firm. Industries are used as theoretical proxies for the organizational field of any given firm. Two variables were created to measure what was occurring in the field. The percentage of firms employing a product-related and product-unrelated strategy in a given industry (measured at the two-digit Standard Industrial Classification level) was coded at the first time point for every firm. The firm was not included in that calculation, although it was included in the calculation for the other firms, in the given industry in order to prevent effects that might be tautological.

For each decade from 1919 to 1948, a logit regression was run predicting the likelihood of a product-related strategy at the second time point. The reference category was a product-dominant strategy. Since there were too few product-unrelated firms on the list until 1948–59, it was impossible to obtain stable parameter estimates of the likelihood of firms having that strategy. The data analysis was performed with the binomial logit regression routine in GAUSS (1985).

The decades in 1948–79 were analyzed separately in the following way. The dependent variable contained three categories, and hence a multinomial logit technique was used. An ordered logit approach was not chosen because there was evidence that firms moved from product-dominant to product-unrelated and vice versa. This means that while there was a certain amount of order to the dependent variable, it was possible for a firm to not follow the pattern from less to more diversification. These data were analyzed with the mutinomial regression routine in GAUSS (1985). Cases with missing data were deleted for both sets of regressions.

Results

It is useful to consider the overall patterns of diversification before attempting to explain them. Three categories of diversification are defined here: product-dominant, product-related, and product-unrelated. Table 13.1 presents the means of the strategy measures over the sixty-year interval. In 1919, 90.2 percent of the firms had product-dominant strategies and the rest had product-related strategies. The number of product-dominant firms declined until 1948, when 66.1 percent of the firms still had that strategy. The boom years of the 1920s saw only a slight increase in diversification. The Depression era was the first major shift toward diversification in the largest firms, consistent with

Table 13.1 Means and Standard Deviations of Variables Used in the Analysis

Variables	1919–29	1929–39	1939–48	1948–59	1959–69	1969–79
% Dominant (t_2)	87.25	79.6	66.1	41.4	26.1	21.7
% Related (t_2)	12.75	20.4	33.9	52.6	56.5	50.4
% Unrelated (t_2)	—	—	—	6.0	17.4	27.8
Age (t_1)	20.13 (17.2)	21.3 (18.1)	29.3 (13.4)	38.35 (14.78)	43.1 (16.9)	51.6 (18.7)
Assets (t_1)	323.71 (480.41)	533.6 (627.5)	608.6 (760.9)	618.97 (723.6)	1197.2 (1560.0)	2251.5 (2389.0)
% Related (t_1)	9.8	13.9	19.6	33.3	53.5	56.0
% Unrelated (t_1)	—	—	—	2.6	9.6	20.7
% Manufacturing president (t_1)	26.5	33.3	35.7	26.4	26.3	24.1
% Sales president (t_1)	6.9	9.3	13.4	21.4	22.8	18.9
% Finance president (t_1)	8.8	7.4	6.3	12.0	16.7	22.4
% Industry (t_1)						
Related strategy (t_1)	9.63	14.81	20.05	32.1	52.8	47.6
Unrelated strategy (t_1)	—	—	—	2.9	8.1	18.2

Notes: Variables are defined in the text. Means are given; standard deviations are in parentheses.

the previous discussion. The first product-unrelated firms appear on the list in 1948.

By 1959, the product-related firms form a majority as diversification greatly accelerated over the 1948–59 period. Between 1959 and 1979, product-dominant firms continued to decline while product-related firms remained stable. The most remarkable change in the postwar era was the increase in product-unrelated firms from 6 percent of the firms in 1959 to 27.8 percent of the firms in 1979. By 1979, the product-dominant group contained the fewest firms. A number of other interesting findings emerge. First, over time the average age and asset size of firms on the list increase steadily. Second, the patterns of who controls the firms based on subunits conforms to our historical and theoretical discussion.

One of the most important questions is whether or not the new diversification strategies were the product of new firms entering the list or of old firms changing strategy. Table 13.2 provides an answer by presenting the percentage of firms that shift strategies and considering the pattern with respect to the firm's status on the list. While the firms that enter the list do not reflect firms that are being born, they do reflect firms that are growing rapidly. Table 13.2 assesses the degree to which firms with new strategies experience rapid growth, enter the list of the largest firms, and provide a role model for already existing large firms. One would expect that those firms that leave the list might disproportionately reflect older or stable strategies.

In the earliest periods (1919–39), one can see a high degree of stability in firm strategies. Most firms that began as product-dominant ended the decade without changing. Those firms that arrived on the list in 1929, 1939, and 1948 appear to have shifted categories to product-related more frequently than those firms that either left the list or stayed on it. Some of those remaining on the list, however, also changed their strategy, particularly during 1939–48. Those firms that left the list were disproportionately in the category of the dominant strategy, and they did not alter their strategies. Their lack of growth can be partially attributed to their inability to shift strategies. One consistent interpretation of these patterns is that rapidly growing firms entered organizational fields with product-related strategies. Once the advantage of these strategies became apparent, other firms diversified, particularly in the Depression and the following decade.

In the postwar era, there are similar patterns of change. Those firms that appeared on the list were more likely to have shifted strategies than those that left the list. Those that remained also shifted strategies. These conclusions are somewhat problematic as many of the cell sizes are quite small for both the leavers and comers.

To summarize, this evidence supports the view that organizations that grew to occupy the list of the hundred largest organizations did so by altering their existing strategies. Those firms that remained on the list also changed their ex-

Table 13.2 Changes in Corporate Strategy by Decades, by Status, 1919–1979

1919–1929

1929	Total Sample 1919			Stayers 1919			Leavers 1919			Comers 1919		
	Dominant	Related	Unrelated	Dominant	Related	Unrelated	Dominant	Related	Unrelated	Dominant	Related	Unrelated
Dominant	92.0	40.0	0.0	96.7	12.2	0.0	95.6	0.0	0.0	68.75	20.0	0.0
Related	8.0	60.0	0.0	3.3	87.2	0.0	4.4	100.0	0.0	31.25	80.0	0.0
Unrelated	0.0	0.0	0.0	0.0	0.0	0.0	0.0	0.0	0.0	0.0	0.0	0.0
N	100	15		61	9		23	1		16	5	

1929–1939

1939	Total Sample 1929			Stayers 1929			Leavers 1929			Comers 1929		
	Dominant	Related	Unrelated	Dominant	Related	Unrelated	Dominant	Related	Unrelated	Dominant	Related	Unrelated
Dominant	92.4	6.3	0.0	95.6	7.0	0.0	100.0	0.0	0.0	71.4	0.0	0.0
Related	7.6	93.7	0.0	4.4	93.0	0.0	0.0	100.0	0.0	28.6	100.0	0.0
Unrelated	0.0	0.0	0.0	0.0	0.0	0.0	0.0	0.0	0.0	0.0	0.0	0.0
N	93	16		69	14		10	1		14	1	

continued

Table 13.2 *Continued*

1939–1948

1948	Total Sample 1939			Stayers 1939			Leavers 1939			Comers 1939		
	Dominant	Related	Unrelated	Dominant	Related	Unrelated	Dominant	Related	Unrelated	Dominant	Related	Unrelated
Dominant	76.7	9.5	0.0	75.0	5.9	0.0	100.0	20.0	0.0	69.2	0.0	0.0
Related	22.1	85.6	0.0	23.5	88.2	0.0	0.0	80.0	0.0	30.8	0.0	0.0
Unrelated	1.1	4.8	100.0	1.5	5.9	100.0	0.0	0.0	0.0	0.0	0.0	0.0
N	90	22	3	68	17	1	9	5		13		

1948–1959

1959	Total Sample 1948			Stayers 1948			Leavers 1948			Comers 1948		
	Dominant	Related	Unrelated	Dominant	Related	Unrelated	Dominant	Related	Unrelated	Dominant	Related	Unrelated
Dominant	65.7	0.0	0.0	62.5	0.0	0.0	84.6	0.0	0.0	58.1	0.0	0.0
Related	32.7	92.5	0.0	37.5	100.0	0.0	7.7	85.7	0.0	41.1	60.0	0.0
Unrelated	1.4	7.5	100.0	0.0	0.0	100.0	7.7	14.3	100.0	0.0	40.2	100.0
N	73	40	3	48	28	1	13	7	1	12	5	1

1959–1969

1969	Total Sample 1959			Stayers 1959			Leavers 1959			Comers 1959		
	Dominant	Related	Unrelated	Dominant	Related	Unrelated	Dominant	Related	Unrelated	Dominant	Related	Unrelated
Dominant	63.4	6.4	0.0	70.4	6.7	0.0	66.6	0.0	0.0	37.5	12.5	0.0
Related	29.2	84.0	0.0	25.9	86.6	0.0	33.3	80.0	0.0	37.5	75.0	0.0
Unrelated	7.3	9.6	100.0	3.7	6.7	100.0	0.0	20.0	0.0	25.0	12.5	100.0
N	41	63	11	26	46	5	6	10	0	8	8	6

1969–1979

1979	Total Sample 1969			Stayers 1969			Leavers 1969			Comers 1969		
	Dominant	Related	Unrelated	Dominant	Related	Unrelated	Dominant	Related	Unrelated	Dominant	Related	Unrelated
Dominant	89.2	0.0	0.0	90.5	0.0	0.0	100.0	0.0	0.0	66.6	0.0	0.0
Related	7.2	87.3	4.2	9.5	87.2	0.0	0.0	100.0	0.0	0.0	81.8	25.0
Unrelated	3.6	12.7	95.8	0.0	12.8	100.0	0.0	0.0	100.0	33.3	18.2	75.0
N	28	63	24	21	47	11	4	5	9	3	11	4

Notes: Status refers to status over the decade. A stayer is a firm that appears on the list of the hundred largest firms at both time points; a leaver is a firm that leaves the list at the second time point; a comer enters the list at the second time point. Dominant, related, and unrelated strategies are defined in the text. Tables are percentaged downward in columns.

isting strategies, albeit at a slower rate. The firms least likely to change were those that did not grow. This implies that diversification was a strategy of highly growth-oriented organizations which spread to other large organizations when the actors in those organization perceived the advantage of doing so. Firms that were becoming diversified grew more rapdily than firms that were not. In order to remain a large and growing firm, managers in established large firms had to adopt the new strategy. Those that did not were likely to experience slower growth and eventual declines in relative size.

Table 13.3 presents the decade-by-decade results of the logistic regressions that predict strategy. To facilitate the discussion, the results are considered by variable over decade. The results for the first three decades reflect the likelihood of a firm having a product-related as opposed to a product-dominant strategy at the second time point. The last three decades use product-dominant strategies as the left-out category and the parameters refer to the odds of product-related and -unrelated strategies as opposed to a product-dominant strategy.

The impact of strategy at the first time point is strong, supporting the ecological view that organizations do not easily change their strategies (Hannan and Freeman 1977; Stinchcombe 1965). Preexisting strategy reflects a form of organization and power that tends to reproduce itself. Generally, the age and size of a firm at the first time point did not affect the likelihood of any given strategy at the second time point. Only in the 1939–48 decade are there statistically significant effects of these variables, and those effects suggest that older and larger firms were more likely to have product-related than product-dominant strategies. This result is consistent with Gort's data (1961) for a similar period and was the basis of his assertion that large firms sought out new product lines in order to keep growing. It is important to note that this effect appears to be historically restricted.

What then explains shifts in organizational strategies? The first variables to consider are those that index the subunit background of the president at the first time point. Consistent with my argument, manufacturing presidents are no more likely than the left-out group of presidents to participate in diversification. Sales and marketing presidents are likely to aid in diversifying their firms in the 1919–39 period, as predicted. After 1939 there are no statistically significant effects of sales and marketing presidents on shifts toward product-related strategies, consistent with the hypothesis that after a certain number of firms shifted strategies, others in their industry would follow suit, independent of a president with a certain background.

In the 1959–69 and 1969–79 panels, there is a statistically significant effect of the sales and marketing presidents causing shifts toward product-unrelated strategies. These last results are less obvious and require some consideration. One could speculate that sales and marketing personnel came to view product-unrelated diversification as in their interests. This may reflect the fact that they thought marketing techniques could be applied to all products and therefore

Table 13.3 Results of a Logit Regression Predicting Strategy by Decade for the Largest Corporation

Variables	1919–29		1929–39		1939–48		1948–59 (1)		1948–59 (2)		1959–69 (1)		1959–69 (2)		1969–79 (1)		1969–79 (2)	
	b	SE(b)	b	SE(b)	b	SE(b)	b	SE(b)	b	SE(b)	b	SE(b)	b	SE(b)	b	SE(b)	b	SE(b)
Age	−.001	.04	.01	.021	.03*	.014	−.01	.01	−.36	.31	.02	.03	.009	.04	.002	.002	−.005	.02
Assets	−.004	.005	.005	.005	.006*	.003	−.005	.006	−.018	.015	−.002	.003	−.002	.001	−.003	.002	−.000	.000
Related strategy	1.08*	.48	1.12**	.42	2.04**	.567	1.05**	.41	.99	.58	2.08**	.68	.67	.56	.85**	.25	.08	.06
Unrelated strategy							.02	.42	2.02**	.83	.009	.38	1.45**	.64	−.02	.08	.94**	.21
% Related strategy	.045*	.023	.02*	.01	.14*	.06	.16*	.07	−.06	.08	−.007	.02	.04	.04	.08*	.04	−.07	.10
% Unrelated strategy							−.22*	.09	.87**	.38	−.08	.06	.12*	.06	−.02	.02	.16*	.08
Manufacturing president	.156	.645	−.137	.497	−.35	.30	.51	.66	−.22	.57	−.11	.28	−.33	.28	−.06	.07	.03	.07
Sales president	.957*	.418	.694**	.144	.44	.23	.20	.72	−.77	.86	.41	.74	.68**	.33	−.10	.08	.13*	.06
Finance president	−.562	.912	.637	.423	.63	.98	−.89	.94	1.09**	.41	−.10	.32	.98**	.34	−.06	.07	.42*	.20
Constant	−.446		.18		.55		.04		−.28		.11		.006		.09		.06	
N	102		108		112		117		117		114		114					

Notes: Variables are defined in the text. Results from logistic regression: dominant strategy = 0; related strategy = 1 for 1919–29, 1929–39, 1939–48. Results from multinomial logit: dominant strategy = left-out category; related strategy = 1; unrelated strategy = 2 for 1948–59, 1959–69, 1969–79.

*p < .05.

**p < .01.

they were not wedded to any given product line. Finally, the last three panels show a positive effect of the presence of a finance president on the diversification strategy of large firms. Finance presidents perceived that the rules of their organizational fields had changed, and thus they promoted shifts in their firms toward product-unrelated strategies.

The last variable of interest concerns the effects of institutionalization. It was argued that as an increasing percentage of firms in a given industry increased their levels of diversification, other firms would follow suit. The percentage of firms in a given industry with a product-related strategy was positively related to a shift to a product-related strategy in five of the six panels. Similarly, the percentage of firms with a product-unrelated strategy was also positively related to a shift toward that strategy in all three of the postwar panels. The percentage of firms with a product-unrelated strategy actually negatively effects the odds of a firm shifting to a product-related strategy in the 1948–59 decade, implying that certain industries were more wedded to product-related strategies while others more readily adopted the new unrelated strategy.

The general pattern of the coefficients matches our theoretical expectations. Organizational inertia played a key role in sustaining a strategy in any given firm. But once actors with a different view of the organization's goals gained power during periods of turbulence in organizational fields, they were able to implement their new strategies. Finally, as the shift toward diversification occurred in the organizational field of any given firm, that firm was more likely to follow suit and shift strategies.

Discussion and Conclusions

The spread of diversification strategies reflects quite clearly the ability of actors to alter their social structures. Although many firms joined the list of the largest firms with a given strategy, and many firms on the list continued with their old strategies, there was substantial change in strategies for both groups of firms. Shifting to diversification strategies was a major cause of entrance onto the list of the hundred largest firms. It is apparent that those firms that did not shift strategy were more likely to leave the list.

Those firms that altered their strategies appeared to be responding to two forces. First, key actors in those organizations articulated a new view of the firm's strategy and had the power to implement that view. Second, other firms in the organizational field acted as role models so that key actors were able to bring about a change in strategy. Some form of shock in the organization's field was a necessary, although not sufficient, impetus to change.

The conceptual framework discussed in this chapter proves useful in understanding the spread of diversification. Stable organizational fields held in place by the relative power of various organizations provide great impetus to the reproduction of the status quo. Existing organizations in those organizational fields are systems of power that constrain actors and encourage them to reproduce the status quo. Yet these very same fields and internal organizational processes can provide the possibility for change. Shocks to the organizational field need to be interpreted by actors, and this brings about the possibility for change. But for actors to precipitate change, they must create an organizational "story" that solves these problems. Once those perceptions are spread across the field, there are pressures for other organizations to conform. This can aid the process of change by forcing any given organization and its leaders to comply with the new definition of what is appropriate.

This perspective raises many questions as well. The problem of cognition and its relation to power needs to be theorized and examined empirically. The key issue concerns whether views of the world evolve from interests or vice versa. The conditions under which actors who have power undermine a given structure of power need to be considered. Similarly, the conditions under which actors in a given organization who do not have power, come to gain power, and bring about shifts in strategy are not well understood.

The functioning of organizational fields is also not well understood, and much research remains to be done. One main issue concerns the way diffusion processes work and the role of networks as a source of diffusion. Similarly, the forms of dependency in organizational fields need to be explored more thoroughly. It is important to establish to what degree reciprocal relations exist in organizational fields and how that affects actors' abilities to frame and direct action. Obviously, new organizations (and their key actors) can enter existing fields and disrupt them. It is important to understand how those disruptions are perceived by actors in the field and what effect this perception has on action. One way to resolve some of these issues is to examine a well-defined organizational field and watch as that field is transformed over time, by either the entry of new organizations or the actions of existing ones.

I have shown that diversification was an economic process that depended upon the location of organizations in organizational fields. It was a historically specific process that was shaped by the existence of organizational fields and the shocks provided to those fields over time. The first movers to the new strategies were organizations led by persons with structural positions that favored diversification. Once their examples allowed them to redefine the rules of existing organizational fields, diversification spread. This conceptual view has shown its utility in this case. It is plausible to assert that such a view will be able to help us understand stability and change in organizations in the private, nonprofit, and public sectors.

Acknowledgments

The author thanks Gerhard Arminger for his suggestions on framing the data analysis strategy and Jim Baron, Paul DiMaggio, Doug McAdam, Jeff Pfeffer, and Woody Powell for their comments on the text. He also thanks David Chang for his assistance in performing the calculations.

Notes

1. It is not my intent here to develop an organizational theory of the state. In this chapter the state is taken as exogenous to already existing organizational fields. The actions taken by state agencies are seen as having an effect on maintaining the stability of a given field or creating uncertainty in that field. From the point of view presented here, a more thorough analysis of the state would require that attention be paid to the role of various state organizations, the political process, and the role of various organized groups in the formation of policy.

2. These alternative views are not systematically considered here. For a more thorough discussion, see Fligstein 1990b, ch. 4.

3. The sources come from Collins and Preston 1961 for the years 1919–48 and from *Fortune* magazine (1960, 1970, 1980) for the years 1959–79. This definition is broader than the *Fortune* definition, which requires that a firm be engaged in manufacturing for at least 50 percent of its revenues in order to be included on the list of the largest firms. The broader definition was chosen as Collins and Preston used it, and it proved easier to find data on the largest nonfinancial firms using the *Fortune* list than attempting to construct the *Fortune* definition back to 1919.

4. The year 1948 was chosen because Collins and Preston's list refers to that year. Their major source of data was the Federal Trade Commission 1957.

5. Rumelt 1974 uses a somewhat different distinction that can be collapsed into these categories. The coding was done by two independent coders, and Rumelt was used as a check. When the two coders disagreed, the author resolved the issue.

6. The 70 percent rule was chosen following Rumelt 1974. This study found that firms were either well above or well below the 70 percent line for a single dominant product—a somewhat arbitrary dividing point. One would like to have a more precise rule, but this proved impossible as data quality declines as one goes back in time. Further, it was often impossible to separate product lines by relative sales, since that data were unavailable. In this situation, the verbal descriptions of products produced were used to make an informed judgment. Distinctions between *product-related* and *product-dominant* imply products being produced across related two-digit Standard Industrial Classification (SIC) codes, while *product-unrelated* taps whether or not firms produced across two unrelated SIC codes.

7. Because the inertia effect will be directly estimated for each decade, the organizational demography effects will be zero or close to zero unless they turn out to be positively related to change. A structural inertia argument based on these variables would therefore predict null effects when they are included in the equation.

8. These include *New York Times* obituary columns, articles in the business press, and books or papers that considered the careers of some of the presidents.

9. The general management category implied that a person held positions across subunits, such as plant manager and vice president in charge of finance.

14 Institutional Origins and Transformations: The Case of American Community Colleges

Steven Brint and
Jerome Karabel

In this chapter, we examine the applicability of the new institutionalism in organizational studies to a case of institutional change: the transformation of American two-year community colleges from predominantly liberal arts to predominantly vocational training institutions. The community colleges are a good case for study using the framework of the new institutionalism, since there can be little doubt as to the predominance of "institutional" as opposed to "technically efficient" elements in their constitutions. They are, in fact, an excellent example of Meyer and Rowan's (1978) dictum that education in America "is understood to occur" when the ritual categories of teacher, student, curriculum, topic, and type of school "are properly assembled" (p. 65). Most community college students drop out before finishing even an associates degree, and there have been persistent doubts, even among the supporters of community colleges, about whether the level of instruction that goes on in community college classrooms is truly "higher" education.

Community colleges are one of the great success stories of American higher education. Enrolling fewer than ten thousand students in 1920, they now enroll over four million, including over half of all degree-credit students entering higher education as freshmen. The two-year colleges were radically transformed in the years between 1960 and 1980. In 1960, about three-quarters of community college students were enrolled in liberal arts transfer programs. By 1980, the ratio was very nearly reversed, with close to three out of four students enrolled in programs promising immediate employment in technical, administrative, and "semiprofessional" jobs. Community college administrators and educational experts began advocating such a transformation as early as the 1920s. Consequently, both the forty to fifty years of failure to transform the schools and the successful efforts of the late 1960s and early 1970s must be explained.

Thus far, the leading explanations for the transformation have focused on either *consumer-choice*—the idea that students wanted vocational training because of its increasing market value in relation to liberal arts—or *business domination*—the notion that business encouraged the transformation because of an increasing need for "semiprofessional" and technical labor. We think both of these explanations are inadequate to account for the change, so we offer as an alternative an organizational/institutional analysis of the transformation.

We begin by briefly summarizing the transformation of American two-year colleges.[1] We then discuss how institutional theory bears on the community college case *and* how, at the same time, the community college case bears on institutional theory. A key argument in this chapter is that the new institutionalism, as it has developed so far, is more applicable to the study of institutional form and functioning than to the equally important topics of institutional origins and transformations. Our chapter, therefore, can be read as an effort to extend institutional analysis to these latter areas.

The Transformation of the Two-Year Colleges

The first two-year colleges were founded at the turn of the twentieth century. For the first third of the century, the two-year colleges were an extremely heterogeneous lot. Some were religious colleges, some agricultural, some traditional liberal arts colleges. Though a majority were independent, some were attached to four-year colleges and others to public high schools. Most of the first colleges were private, and many of the first administrators—perhaps the majority—hoped eventually to build them into four-year baccalaureate-granting institutions. The most important of the early two-year colleges were those sponsored by university presidents and deans as bulwarks, against a rising tide of young adults seeking access to the nation's colleges. In the 1900s and 1910s, William Rainey Harper of the University of Chicago and Alexis P. Lange of the University of California were especially important figures in the effort to use two-year colleges as institutional "road blocks." These efforts in many respects set the tone for subsequent development.

Even where they developed independently of the designs of university administrators, however, two-year colleges faced an organizational environment dominated by four-year schools. The four-year colleges monopolized training for the most prestigious jobs, insofar as formal training was required for those jobs. Thus, students who could afford to attend a four-year college and could be admitted, usually enrolled in the higher-status schools. Two-year colleges had a "residual" role from the beginning. They were for less advantaged, less able, and less mobile students. Nevertheless, from the beginning the very great majority of these students—80 percent and above—envisioned continuing their educations at four-year colleges once they completed the two-year program. Liberal arts was the cornerstone of the two-year-college curriculum, and this accurately reflected the preferences of student consumers.[2]

Before embarking on any other projects, the two-year institution thus had to accomplish the formidable task of establishing itself as a "genuine" college. The import of this task was well appreciated by the earliest leaders of the junior college movement, who chose to pursue academic "respectability" through the only available path—emphasis on the liberal arts transfer function.

Locked into a subordinate position in the academic hierarchy from which they had no real prospect of escape, some leaders of the two-year-college movement began to develop in the mid-1920s the rudiments of an alternative strategy for the enhancement of their institutions' low status. These men recognized the reality that most of their students would never transfer to a four-year college and were genuinely concerned about the fate that awaited these students in a competitive labor market. Their solution, which in their view served both student and institutional interests, was to transform the junior college from a predominantly transfer-oriented institution into one principally dedicated to the provision of terminal vocational education. Emphasizing that there was only "limited room at the top," such early junior college leaders as Leonard Koos, Walter Crosby Eells, and Doak Campbell saw the two-year college's task as the firm but gentle redirection of most students toward "middle-level" jobs commensurate with their presumed abilities and past accomplishments.

The American Association of Junior Colleges (AAJC) played an important role in the vocationalization project. The association was founded in 1920, essentially as a support group for administrators with some common practical problems and a powerful sense of insecurity based on the junior colleges' lack of a secure institutional function. Soon after its founding, the association became the principal staging ground for the vocationalization plans of the junior college vanguard leaders. These leaders used the association's journal, conferences, and book-length monographs to extol the virtues of a standard form for the two-year colleges, which they called the "comprehensive" form. As they defined it, the "comprehensive" junior college was publicly supported, independent, low-cost and had a policy of open admissions. Above all, it had a greatly augmented vocational track leading to employment in "semiprofessional" occupations.

The junior college vanguard had its first successes in California, where comprehensive junior colleges were enthusiastically sponsored by the leading four-year schools. The demographic and ecological situation in California helped produce the success of the two-year college there. Faced with few private-sector competitors and a fast-growing population, California communities quickly embraced the two-year college as an aid to social and cultural opportunity with some potential also to further community economic development. The California system was the first to gain fiscal stability and steady growth, and its design was soon emulated across the country. The AAJC held its 1930 meeting in Berkeley to showcase the California system, and a 1932 Carnegie Foundation report, "State Higher Education in California," provided another authoritative stamp of approval for the California model.

In spite of a lingering identification with the culture of the liberal arts among many junior college faculty, most administrators quickly became enthusiastic supporters of vocationalization. In addition to the organizational advantages of a secure labor market niche, the vocationalization project had a clear psychological appeal for them as well. Resentful of being treated as inferiors by their "senior" college colleagues, junior college presidents were often eager to distance themselves from the leaders of four-year colleges. A drastic increase in vocational education solved the status deprivation problem by promising to move the two-year colleges from the bottom of the liberal arts academic hierarchy to the top of the entirely new occupational training hierarchy.

Whatever else might be said about community college vocational programs, it cannot be claimed that they were initiated in response to popular demand. On the contrary, administrators repeatedly noted the resistance of junior college students (and their parents) to increased vocational training. Yet despite this resistance, which persisted through the end of the 1960s, key junior-college administrators and researchers remained committed to the project. Indeed, much of the discussion about vocational education in the junior college literature of this period was devoted precisely to the issue of how to expand these programs despite the lack of student interest in them.

The "consumer-choice" model of educational change—whatever its utility for the period after 1970, when the supply of four-year college graduates outstripped employer demand—is utterly incapable of explaining either the origins of the vocationalization project or the unremitting commitment by junior college leaders to it in the face of persistent, albeit usually passive, student opposition.[3]

Nor can a "business-domination" model shed much light on the long-standing movement to vocationalize the junior college. Though active in trying to shape community colleges to their own purposes in many states since the mid-1970s, big business was for decades entirely indifferent to the junior college movement. Instead of having to fight off threats to their autonomy from domineering corporate giants, community colleges spent decades trying—usually without success—to convince large firms that they could be of use to them.[4]

After years of arduous effort, the vocationalization project of community college administrators finally began to yield dividends in the late 1960s. By this time, powerful outside sponsors—among them major private foundations and the federal government—had joined the push for expanded occupational training. The community colleges' successful growth as low-cost, convenient alternatives to four-year colleges awakened the interest of outside elites. Partly with the help of grants from these outside sponsors, administrators improved their capacity to promote change, using such mechanisms of enrollment redirection as guidance counseling, testing, student recruitment, and direct job linkages. By the late 1960s, the percentage of students in vocational programs nationally began to rise significantly for the first time.

What is striking about the increase in the relative size of vocational programs in the late 1960s is not the magnitude of change, which was modest, but that the change occurred before the much-publicized decline of the college labor market in the early 1970s. The rapid multiplication of vocational programs in this period was not a response to "consumer choice." These programs were initiated in the hope that creating a diverse and attractive array of vocational offerings would finally "cure" students of their fixation on bachelor's degrees. The efforts were aided more by large infusions of external support than by any documented upsurge in popular demand.[5]

The abrupt downturn in 1970–71 of the college labor market provided administrators with a powerful new justification for the expansion of occupational training. Largely under the impetus of the new market conditions, community college students began to view the liberal arts transfer programs in a new light during this period. For the first time in the history of the junior college, the popularity of vocational programs began to rival—and, in some cases, to surpass—that of the liberal arts transfer programs.

There is no question that the objective decline in the labor market for college graduates in the early 1970s was a principle reason why the vocationalization project of community college administrators finally took off. As long as holders of the B.A. were manifestly doing well, the much-bemoaned "degree fixation" of most junior college students was impossible to dislodge. In the context of a strong market for graduates of four-year colleges, vocational programs looked, if not dead-end, then decidedly second best.

Yet if the objective deterioration in the labor-market situation of college graduates was undeniably a powerful force, it is also true that students made decisions on the basis of *subjective perceptions* of their prospects. In the case of community college students, there is reason to believe that the disjuncture between objective economic trends and subjective perceptions of these trends may have been sizable. Reports in the national mass media virtually never mentioned the continuing advantages of those who completed four years of college—their higher salaries, greater chances of promotion, and lower rates of unemployment. Instead, the media presented an image of high economic returns to community-college occupational training that was utterly incompatible with available research evidence showing far more modest results for these programs. Students influenced by the media were likely to have a far rosier view of the market benefits of vocational programs than was warranted by the actual facts.

Market forces have their greatest impact when they are supported by vigorous administrative action. At the few institutions where the administration adopted a more neutral posture toward vocationalization—mostly in predominantly black colleges—occupational enrollments expanded at a slower rate. Indeed, had two-year-college administrators and their allies in the foundations and the government been as vigorous in cultivating liberal arts transfer programs as they were in channeling students away from them, it is entirely possible that the community college today would be more evenly balanced in its liberal arts and vocational enrollments.

Community Colleges and the New Institutionalism

The studies that comprise the new institutionalism in organizational studies are brought together chiefly by a shared antagonism to the idea that efficiency and market competition are the driving forces behind all organizational change, and by a shared agreement that much organizational structure and change derives from efforts to create or conform to categories and practices that give classificatory meaning to the social world. These propositions help explain the "loose coupling" between organizational structure and task performance in many settings and the reason organizational forms that are not maximally efficient may nevertheless grow, prosper, and shape an organizational environment.[6] In John Meyer's work, for example, educational organizations are the classic examples of order-affirming, as opposed to task-performing, organizations (Meyer and Rowan, ch. 2, this vol.). They create a grid of legitimate educational categories, which provides a kind of collective normative order while masking tremendous variation in competencies and task performance within categories. Although "institutional" (or order-affirming) elements are found in all organizations, the nonprofit and social services sphere—where goals are mixed and bottom-line considerations qualified—are the "institutional" spheres par excellence.

Among the new institutionalists, both Meyer and Lynne Zucker have, in different ways, emphasized that once a form becomes embedded, its ability to survive and prosper may be less dependent on its performance than on the reassuring sense of order it conveys. This observation quite clearly fits the community college case. Indeed, the community colleges became thriving operations at precisely the time when their task performance was, by most measures, rapidly deteriorating. Budgets and enrollments grew as dropout levels climbed and test scores plunged in the 1960s and 1970s. The colleges grew largely on the basis of their appeal as low-cost, geographically convenient, open-access, and multipurpose institutions. As they gained acceptance with the public and with state legislatures, their basic categorizing principles became institutionalized as a standard part of the American educational system. Moreover, once their place in the educational system was secure, administrators could worry less about survival and more about long-term organizational interest. In this sense, institutionalization also increased the capacity of managers to promote change.

Another cornerstone of the new institutionalism is a theoretical piece by DiMaggio and Powell (ch. 3, this vol.) on the process by which organizations come to resemble one another. This article is especially relevant to the community college case. DiMaggio and Powell show how organizational forms that have little to do with task performance efficiencies per se can nevertheless become standard in an organizational field. The article belongs in the "new institutional" corpus because it adopts the "institutionally accepted" versus "technically efficient" distinction and because it is skeptical of efficiency arguments as explanations for the triumph of organizational forms. DiMaggio and Powell argue that the standardization of forms and practices is as common in nonprofit as in profit-making spheres and that the major sources of standardization are not competitive, but the result of the power of dominant professional elites to disseminate a single normative standard, the natural tendency of administrators to emulate apparently successful forms, and the power of the state to enforce conformity.

The sources of standardization in the community college case are well described by DiMaggio and Powell. A self-conscious professional elite—the junior college vanguard—organized to persuade other administrators in favor of a single "best" system. This system caught on first in California. As a fast-growing and fiscally secure system, the California model soon elicited the admiration of less secure administrators in other parts of the country. This admiration quickly inspired emulation. At a somewhat later date, several state legislatures required the California form—publicly supported, open-admission, two-year "comprehensive" schools—in the legislation authorizing two-year-college development in their states.

As these remarks should make clear, some themes of the new institutionalism are highly relevant to the community college case and have helped us better understand it. This does not mean, however, that we see our work as fitting easily into the framework of the new institutionalism, as it has developed thus far.

Gaps in the New Institutional Theory

Our difficulties with the new institutionalism have less to do with the tenets of the theory than with its silences. From our perspective, the new institutionalism has been strongest in identifying distinctive organizational forms and their functioning. It has been less effective in generating ideas about why particular kinds of forms are chosen over possible alternatives, and why organizational forms change over time in particular directions.

We wish to make a distinction, then, between the sociology of institutional forms and the sociology of institutional change—the two sides of which, we believe, would together comprise a full sociology of institutions. The new institutionalism has contributed thus far mainly to the first side of the dichotomy, while our work is essentially concerned with the second. The distinction is a venerable one, of course. In 1901, Emile Durkheim wrote (in a view he subsequently modified) that sociology was preeminently "the science of institutions, their *genesis and functioning*" (Durkheim [1901]1950:56, our emphasis). In more recent years, both Philip Selznick (1949, 1957) and Arthur Stinchcombe (1968) have emphasized a similar duality in institutional studies.

The new institutionalists have not been entirely silent on the origins of institutional forms. Meyer and Thomas have, for example, traced much recent institutional development to the expansion of state jurisdiction and, in particular, to the establishment of new citizen and personnel categories developed in the course of connecting the individual to the state and the economy (Thomas and Meyer 1984; Thomas et al. 1987). Insofar as these treatments emphasize the normative order at the expense of group interests and organizational competition, they would, from our perspective, be considered somewhat deficient. In addition, these arguments may be insufficiently attentive to the powerful interests and regulating mechanisms influencing the kind of organizations and the kind of personnel categories that are and are not created.

Thus, to our minds, half of a full sociology of institutions remains, for the most part, still to be constructed. This is the half concerned, to use Durkheim's phrase, with the *genesis* rather than the *functioning* of institutions. Our work is an effort to begin to bring this side to light. To do so, we build primarily on the insights of the "conflict" tradition in sociology, rather than on the insights of the Durkheimian tradition which have proven so fruitful for the new institutionalism thus far.[7]

In many respects, our work may be thought of as part of a revival of a classical tradition in the sociology of organizations, whose roots may be found in the work of Robert Michels ([1915]1962) on political parties and Max Weber ([1922]1963) on religious organizations. In the postwar period, this tradition was carried on primarily in the work of Philip Selznick and his students at the University of California—the original "institutional school" of organizational studies in the United States. One of the key themes of this tradition, especially visible in Michels' work on the German Social Democratic party and in Selznick's study of the Tennessee Valley Authority, is that organizations have distinct interests of their own. These interests can take on an autonomous logic capable of diverting organizations from their initial goals.

There is another important point of contact between the original institutional school and our own work. Like the work of the Selznick school, our work emphasizes the details of an organization's interaction with its environment over time. From this perspective, it seems clear to us that neither the consumer-choice nor the business-domination model pays sufficient attention to the beliefs and activities of the administrators and professionals who typically have the power to define what is in the "interest" of the organizations over which they preside. By contrast, much of our analysis focuses on explaining why these administrators chose to vocationalize in spite of the opposition of student consumers and the indifference of potential sponsors in the business corporations. Very much in the tradition of the original institutional school, our analysis incorporates a careful consideration of the forces, both external and internal to the community college movement, that facilitated or hindered implementation of the policy at different historical moments.

Our work, while indebted to what might be called the "old institutionalism" in organizational studies, seeks to develop a more systematic framework for analyzing the forces bearing on institutional change. In this sense, it seeks a higher degree of rigor than was typical of the original institutional school.[8]

Toward a Theory of Institutional Origins and Transformations

In developing a framework for understanding institutional origins and transformations, it is necessary to distinguish between the genesis of a sense of institutional interest among organizational leaders and the actual realization of the organizational forms and programs suggested by that interest. In the community college case, the long shadow of student resistance fell between the conception of highly vocationalized two-year programs and the actual realization of this idea. In general, there is no obvious reason to assume a direct and easy connection between the generation of interests and their realization; accordingly we discuss the two processes separately. In the pages that follow we begin with an analytical treatment of the generation of institutional interest in the community college case and move on to an analytical treatment of the realization of institutional interests. We conclude by drawing out some of the implications of our approach.

What is distinctive about our analysis is that it simultaneously focuses on the power structures and opportunity fields in the larger society that shape organizational possibilities *and* on the efforts of organizational elites to take advantage of the environment to further their own interests as well as those of their organizations. In this way, the analysis situates organizational behavior within the larger economy and polity, while at the same time paying close attention to the organization-enhancing behaviors of administrators. A core element of the institutional approach is that it recognizes that organizations can take on a logic of their own and pursue their own distinctive interests. These interests are not reducible—as they are in most pluralist and Marxist accounts of politics— to those of competing groups in civil society. It follows that institutional policies and structures—whether in education or in other domains—do not reflect in mirrorlike fashion the distribution of power in the larger society. On the contrary, such policies and structures may, under some circumstances, embody less the interests of external groups than the logic of the organization itself.

THE ORIGIN OF INSTITUTIONAL INTERESTS

There are many instances when organizational interests are pregiven by legal decrees or market processes. In other cases—and the community college case is one—these interests develop only gradually. Institutional interests are generated in the context of structures and spaces. These are preeminently structures of power and spaces of opportunity in the environment. Our analysis, in this sense, suggests an image of organizational elites as constrained entrepreneurs. Our view might be summarized by paraphrasing from Marx's famous remarks in *The Eighteenth Brumaire:* organizations may make their own history, but they do not make it just as they please.

Not all administrative elites would have made the same assessment of interest as the early leaders of the junior college movement. Indeed, the temptation *not* to break the academic mold must have been strong for at least some of these former academic teachers. We argue, however, that the determination of organizational interests can be read with a high degree of probability out of the power structure and opportunity fields faced by new organizations seeking to become established. Our analysis also emphasizes the distinctive assets and liabilities that an organization brings to its environment and the socially conditioned mental sets of leaders during the decisive period when institutional interests are generated.

Structures of Power and Constraint

An institutional analysis of origins and transformations requires first an analysis of the power centers constraining organizational development and a theorization of why these constraints exist. As Paul Starr has noted in the case of medicine, the development of institutions "takes place within larger fields of power and social structure" (Starr 1982:8). A key task of the institutional analyst is to specify these fields and to show how they shape and constrain the pattern of development of organizations operating within a particular field. Since organizational forms develop over time, such an analysis will almost necessarily be historical in character.

In the case of the community colleges, three power centers decisively shaped the environment faced by leaders of the junior college movement.

The leading four-year colleges were the first important power center. By the time two-year colleges appeared, the four-year colleges and universities had virtually monopolized training for the higher-status and better-remunerated occupations in American society. Success in the competition for "training markets" is arguably the single most important determinant of a college's status. An institution closely linked to a powerful labor market—for example, as a medical school is linked to the medical profession—is effectively guaranteed to be a prestigious one. Conversely, an institution tied to a weaker labor market— for example, a state teacher's college—is likely to be, at most, of moderate status. From its inception, the fundamental problem faced by the junior college was that the most lucrative and the highest-status training markets were already monopolized by existing higher education institutions. Head-to-head competition with established colleges and universities for these markets, especially the more powerful and prestigious among them, was a hopeless enterprise—and yet higher education itself seemed identified with these markets. Much of the early history of the junior college—the ceaseless debate over "mission," the persistent ambiguity over "identity," and the constant pull of new training and student markets—can be understood as a process of gradual and uneven adjustment to this organizational reality.

In a way that was less keenly felt by two-year-college administrators themselves, the junior colleges were also structurally subordinate to business organizations. Educational institutions feed their students directly into a structure of jobs that is predominantly organized in our society by private business firms. Business firms must be willing to hire the graduates of higher education institutions in order for those institutions to maintain a long-term viability. By their very location in the social structure, large firms were in control of what was, from a community college point of view, an absolutely critical resource— the capacity to hire the "products" of the nation's colleges and universities— credentialed graduates. Thus, even in the absence of any active interest whatsoever, business—unlike labor—simply had to be taken into account. This capacity of business to influence the actions of other institutions in the absence of any direct intervention has been referred to as its *structural power*.[9] From this perspective, large corporations, by virtue of their very position in the American social structure, profoundly influence the behavior of other institutions—including institutions of higher education—without having actively to *do* anything at all.

In emphasizing the structural power of business, we do not wish to suggest that large corporations never attempt actively to impose their will on colleges and universities. Nor do we wish to suggest that they lack the capacity to organize themselves for collective action. Yet such instances of direct corporate control of higher education policy are, we believe, the exception rather than the rule. The power of business over institutions of higher education is at once more subtle and more profound than direct influence models would suggest. While active corporate intervention is in fact rare, those who preside over institutions of higher education can never long ignore what Charles Lindblom (1977) has referred to as "the privileged position of business."[10]

Governmental bodies represented a third powerful constraining force on the two-year colleges. Even for private colleges—and most of the two-year colleges were private before the 1930s—state governments were typically important for legitimating the colleges' activities through their accreditation procedures. For the public junior colleges, which constituted the majority of the larger institutions, state and local governments supplied virtually all of the resources which the colleges required to operate.

It would be a mistake, however, to see the state as simply imposing its will on institutions of higher education. In the case of community colleges, there were, to be sure, instances of pressure from the state to expand vocational training and of fiscal incentives for the implementation of preferred policies. Even more common, however, was a pattern in which the two-year colleges worked to curry favor with the state by pursuing policies that, they believed, would gain approval. Such behavior, when manifested by one institution toward another, more powerful institution, might be referred to as *anticipatory subordination*. In this sense, the responses of the community colleges to the state and business are similar. In both cases, the colleges have been keenly aware of the structural power of these commanding institutional spheres. In attempting to gain the approval of key state officials by anticipating their preferences, colleges and universities are well aware that presenting themselves as providing students with economically relevant training can usually be counted on to evoke a positive response.

Yet relations between the community colleges and governmental bodies have been at once more complex and more distant than most simple models of resource dependency would suggest. The interests of legislators in higher education go beyond, and sometimes conflict with, their interests in providing trained workers for industry. Legislators also want to provide access to educational opportunities, vehicles for community service activities, ways to attract commerce into particular areas, and agencies for raising the cultural level of their communities. Many of the nonvocational functions of the community colleges helped make them attractive to legislators. Their potential to contribute to industrial training was thus only one "selling point."

The inertial tendencies of the state budgetary process are also worth emphasizing (see Wildavsky 1964). Once community colleges became an accepted step in the academic procession, to use Riesman's (1958) phrase, close scrutiny of their activities was rare. The key for the community colleges was to create an accepted meaning and place for themselves in a chain of institutions with specified relations to one another that legislators could support without question. The degree of autonomy that colleges enjoyed tended to be most extensive during periods of economic and fiscal prosperity. During recessionary periods, state governments were often moved to push higher education in the direction of a more consistent and committed contribution to state economic prosperity.

Opportunity Fields

The process by which organizational managers construct institutional interests involves assessments not only of the power structures constraining activity, but also of the fields of opportunity that remain open. Opportunity fields may be thought of as including both the existence of potential market niches and the relative degree of organizational competition in these spaces of opportunity.

Our analysis here is consistent with the idea that organizations, much like biological species, "adapt" to their environments (with the important exception that we build in an analysis of the institutional power centers shaping the open "spaces"). One way of interpreting environmental adaptation theory is to say that organizations survive if they fit into niches in the ecology of existing organizations. Organizational development can be seen in this way as a search for the exploitation of free space in the environment. Environmental adaptation theories have the opposite strengths of power structure–oriented theories. They provide a useful perspective on the actions of organizational entrepreneurs, as viewed from the bottom up.[11]

The community colleges, as we have said, were born subordinate, and they were aware from the beginning of the power centers constraining their activities. Only gradually, however, did junior college leaders also become aware of their own potential opportunity fields. They began to see, in particular, that a potentially large market existed for their services among students new to higher education. These students, they understood, were generally "destined" for jobs in the middle of the occupational structure, not at its peaks.

Models connecting higher education and occupational training already existed for the two-year-college leaders, both at the high school level in the vocational programs and at the university level in the professional training programs. The colleges only needed to adopt these models to their own structural situation. Junior colleges saw in the large numbers of students wanting to attend college but unlikely ever to obtain a bachelor's degree a vast potential demand. And, like many another entrepreneurial enterprise, junior colleges sought to stimulate this demand.

In retreating from the academic hierarchy, the junior colleges strategically situated themselves for entry into a major emerging market. This was, to be sure, a less glamorous market than the one occupied by prestigious institutions of higher education linked to the professions and upper management. But it was also a relatively large one—and one in which the junior colleges would face relatively weak competition. Given the saturation of elite training markets by existing institutions, *vocationalization directed the junior college toward the most attractive market niche available.* This reality, embedded in the complex organizational ecology of American higher education, gave the junior college vanguard and their successors an enduring advantage over those who saw the proper role of the two-year college as primarily one of providing liberal arts transfer programs.

In general, the first two-year colleges—those that developed during the first third of the century—faced a favorably sparse organizational ecology. They operated at a time when the postsecondary education sector (outside of New England and the middle Atlantic states) was weakly developed, the population growing, and the occupational structure shifting away from farm and toward white-collar employment. To some degree, however, opportunity fields varied from state to state. Where private colleges were well developed and population relatively stable, opportunity fields tended to be limited. In states with growing populations and few colleges, opportunity fields were relatively open. In states with small populations, colleges of all sorts struggled to survive. Thus, the existing density of organizations had a significant influence on subsequent development of two-year colleges in both sparsely populated and well-populated environments. The junior college became a recognizable institution throughout the country because of the missionary work of AAJC leaders, but the institution faced quite different organizational ecologies in different parts of the country. Junior colleges increased most rapidly when the general population was booming and the existing population of higher education institutions was sparse. They increased more slowly when population growth was slow and/or strong private colleges dominated the higher education field.

Organizational Assets

Thus far we have concentrated on environmental influences on the determination of institutional interest. Important influences also originated within the organizations themselves. The most important of these were assessments of organizational assets (or competitive advantages) and the ideological influences and status pressures bearing on organizational leaders.

The community colleges never enjoyed the advantages of high levels of capitalization, nor were they generally able to appeal on the basis of the quality of instruction or facilities. But they did have some distinct assets, notably low cost and locational convenience. These gave the colleges important advantages in the competition for student consumers. The colleges also enjoyed the advantages of nonspecific charters, which encouraged flexible searches for market niches. As their institutions gradually grew in the interwar years, junior college leaders increasingly stressed their institutions' primary competitive advantages: low cost, ease of access, and appeal as a gateway *both* to privileged labor markets through the transfer track and to "semiprofessional" and "technical" employment through the occupational training tracks.

Organizational assets influence not only the success of an institution's efforts to survive and grow, but also the attractiveness of the vocationalization project to staff. Low cost and locational convenience, in particular, attracted many of the kinds of students most likely to convince faculty of the virtues of vocational preparation. This was important because the faculty were, at the beginning, predominantly oriented to the liberal arts and were, accordingly, more often aligned with student opposition to vocationalization than with administrative enthusiasm for it.

Mental Sets of Organizational Elites

In the case of the two-year colleges, the social experiences of leaders and the status strains they experienced also influenced assessments of institutional interests. It may be argued that these forces helped determine the specific lines along which institutional interests were pursued.

The earliest vocationalizing leaders were quite clearly part of the movement by late nineteenth- and early twentieth-century university presidents to elevate the status and change the function of their institutions by limiting enrollments, raising standards, and emphasizing research. They were themselves mostly university teachers, and they were in close contact with the thinking of top leaders of the elite universities. In effect, they were the ideological and practical allies of the university presidents. The arguments for exclusivity at the four-year-college level were second nature to the junior college vanguard.[12] For these leaders who, like the reforming university presidents, saw the junior colleges as terminal institutions for the majority of their students, giving "consumers" what they could use in the occupational market place was a natural, practical alternative to standard academic training.

There was, in addition, another and more general ideological affinity involved in the original plans to reform the junior colleges. This came from the leaders' identification with the "organizational revolution" in America society of the late nineteenth and early twentieth centuries. In a period of industrialization, urbanization, and fears of class conflict, private and public bureaucracies organized along strict hierarchical and functional lines and, devoted to social order, were seen by many middle- and upper-class Americans as a solution to the ills of the modern world. As the educational historian David Tyack has so persuasively argued, ideas of educators during this period were greatly influenced by this more general political and cultural movement. In Tyack's view, the reformers of the period sought to use bureaucratic organizations, whose authority was invested in virtuous officials, as a functional equivalent to the waning influence of Protestant religion, whose authority was invested in the virtuous individual. However this may be—and we are inclined to accept it at least as one important factor[13]—the junior college vanguard quite clearly took inspiration and gained moral energy from the many other organizational reformers of the period. The junior college with its emphasis on ordered hierarchy, educated "followership," and practical usefulness bears the indubitable stamp of the broader organizational revolution of late nineteenth- and early twentieth-century America.

Status pressures seem also to have played a role in the determination of institutional interests. There is ample evidence that two-year-college leaders resented their low status position in the academic hierarchy. It seems likely that these status strains encouraged a search for a new identity that would remove the two-year-college leaders from their "spoiled" academic identities. These reactions came from concrete experiences of status deprivation—persistently communicated by patronizing four-year-college officials—rather than from abstract calculation of material interest. The evidence is very strong that for many administrators, a logic of organizational interest was constructed to rationalize decisions originally made to escape the pinch of status deprivation.

Although these status concerns clearly influenced the actions of some early junior college administrators, it is essential to emphasize that experiences and alternatives were constrained by the net of power relations, opportunity fields, and organizational assets within which junior college leaders operated. Our analysis of the situation faced by early leaders brings out, we hope, the boundaries within which competing logics operated and, in the community college case, also why one logic, though nontraditional, enjoyed important advantages in competition with more traditional notions of educational purpose.

THE REALIZATION OF INSTITUTIONAL INTERESTS

Just as our analysis of the generation of organizational interest focused simultaneously on the environment and the organization itself, so too does our analysis of the process of implementing change. In the analysis of the rates and levels of change, our attention shifts, however, from the fundamental structural situation faced by the community colleges to the major forces encouraging or restraining change. On the environmental side, our emphasis is on labor markets as a primary regulative institution in the American system of higher education. On the organizational side, our emphasis is on the gradual development of what we call the "managerial capacity" to promote change.

Market Forces

Without doubt, the strong labor market for college graduates before 1970 presented the most significant obstacle to the vocationalization of the two-year colleges. Junior college leaders were clearly aware of this obstacle, though they tended to view the eminently reasonable desire of students to obtain a bachelor's degree as a form of "degree fixation." Our analysis clearly indicates that the decline of the college labor market was the most important influence on the success of the vocationalization project beginning in 1970. In the absence of widespread collective protest, student resistance to vocationalization melted away with the decline of the college labor market in the early 1970s.

Having discussed market pressures at length, we need not dwell on them further except to make one important clarification. Our appreciation of the importance of market forces does not render our analysis simply a more sophisticated version of the idea that consumer choice propelled change. In the first place, junior college administrators chose to pursue a policy inimical to consumers for at least forty years before it became appealing to them. Second, administrators were sometimes able to change enrollments even in the absence of favorable market conditions. Third, external elites helped support vocationalization for reasons that had little or nothing to do with student demand. Finally, consumer anxieties were channeled along distinctive lines that, for many, had little to do with their own interests in the labor market, but had a great deal to do with the preferences of organizational managers. Thus, while markets create pressures on the choices of individuals, administrators and their allies have some independent scope as well, and they may, in addition, be able to supply the most influential interpretations of the implications of market changes.

Managerial Capacity

If labor market conditions were crucial influences on the rate of institutional transformation, so too were the more emerging capacities of managers to promote change. Managerial capacity typically builds over time with the aid of new resources, improvements in techniques, the growth of staff cohesiveness, and cumulative experience.

In the community college case, managerial capacity developed most clearly with the refinement of testing, guidance, recruitment, and job placement activities beginning in the 1930s. In many instances, the energetic development of this "social technology" for changing student preferences could and did lead to changing enrollment patterns, even in the absence of encouraging labor market conditions. Already by the late 1920s, a few determined and energetic California junior college presidents had shifted a large proportion of their enrollments to occupational training programs. In many states, significant changes in the vocational-to-transfer ratios were evident *before* the shift in the college labor market of the early 1970s. We have attributed much of this shift to improvements in the mechanisms for changing preferences. The AAJC played a very active role in disseminating and improving these mechanisms. New resources from foundations and the federal government beginning in the late 1950s and early 1960s enhanced the capacity of managers to develop and promote occupational programs. Vocationalization might have occurred without these funds, but it certainly would not have occurred as quickly as it did.

Elite sponsorship is often considered a principal cause of institutional (or policy) success. Indeed, a whole school of thought in political sociology[14] has been dedicated to showing the links between successful policies and elite sponsorship. In organization studies, the resource dependency model of organizational development (Pfeffer and Salancik 1978) encourages similar assumptions. Our findings are consistent with an emphasis on the importance of elite sponsorship,[15] but partially reverse the causal argument. In the case of the community colleges (and, we suspect, in many other cases), elite sponsorship did not precede but followed organizational success. Not until the colleges had proved their popularity and viability did they become potential candidates for such sponsorship.

Elite sponsorship did not make growth possible; in the beginning at least, growth made elite sponsorship possible. At the same time, elite sponsorship, when it came in the early 1960s, did certainly encourage the success of the vocationalization project.

Additional Influences on the
Rate of Change

Market pressures and managerial capacities were the most important influences on the progress of organizational change, but they were not the only influences. At times, at least four other factors played a role: (1) status group conflict, (2) national rallying events, (3) demographic changes, and (4) the entrance of new competitors for training markets.

When conflict between groups developed, it formed out of divergent status cultures. The most important of the groups struggling against the vocationalizing administrators were minority students and staff as well as the early opponents of vocationalization among college faculty. Minority opposition had a mainly localistic impact, but it was rather more important than faculty opposition because of the ideological support it could draw upon in minority communities.[16] By contrast, the other major conflict group—liberal arts–oriented faculty—was relatively disorganized and isolated. Dismayed by the preparation of many students and sometimes insecure about their academic status, faculty members were prone to sacrifice their belief in liberal arts in the face of an at least equal commitment to traditional academic standards.

During national rallying periods, pressures toward a common (rather than an occupationally specialized) curriculum increased. The effects of national crisis can be seen in trends toward the substitution of general education for occupational training during the early Depression era, during World War II, and during the early years of the cold war. On the basis of this evidence, we suggest that during widely perceived national crisis periods, educational emphases tend to shift from training and allocation to socializing efforts, with a renewed emphasis on "common national values."

It is sometimes argued that changes in the *kinds* of students attending two-year colleges have had direct effects on the types of programs offered by the colleges. This demographic argument holds that influx of less able or lower SES students encourages vocationalization as a response to the special needs and interests of these students. Increase in part-time and older students are thought to have similar effects for similar reasons.[17]

Our evidence suggests that demographic influences have been variable; their effect has depended, to a great degree, on the state of labor market demand for college graduates. In the 1950s, the community colleges began to attract large numbers of lower SES students for the first time. These students also tended to score lower than four-year-college students on standardized tests of academic aptitude. Nevertheless, the community colleges were not transformed by this demographic change in the student population because the four-year-colleges were not producing enough graduates to meet the demand for college-educated labor. Demographic changes encouraged vocationalization only during the period of overproduction of college-educated labor. Thus, our findings suggest that when markets for college labor are expanding, demographic changes have little effect. When they are declining, they have considerable effect, perhaps not so much as a direct causal influence as in providing a basis for rallying support for change.

Organizational competitors were an additional influence on the rate of change. Like the effects of students' changing demographic characteristics, the effects of competition were also variable. Strong preexisting competitors often effectively eliminated possible lines of development.[18] On the other hand, weak competitors often encouraged accelerated efforts to monopolize open opportunity fields. In this way competitors were sometimes a spur rather than an obstacle to institutional change. This occurred in Massachusetts, for example, when the state colleges first became interested in competing with the community colleges for the market niche for middle-level technical manpower. Instead of shifting the two-year colleges away from occupational training, the new competition focused energy on the development of new and stronger links with potential training markets. Thus, our evidence suggests that well-capitalized (and especially well-capitalized preexisting) competitors tend to block change. Weak competitors, however, tend to accelerate change by providing an external threat against which administrators can rally support.[19]

Conclusion

The analysis of the transformation of American community colleges presented in this chapter, while converging in important ways with the new institutionalism, is very different in emphasis. Unlike the new institutionalists, we are concerned with the origins and transformations of institutions rather than with their form and functioning. We are consequently indebted at least as much to an older tradition in the sociology of organizations, whose roots may be found in the work of Robert Michels ([1915]1962) and Max Weber ([1922]1978). This tradition, which was carried on in postwar American sociology principally in the works of Philip Selznick (1949, 1957) and his students, often focused on the forces that shaped the development of organizations and institutions over time.

This theme of "goal displacement" is central to our analysis of the transformation of the junior college from an institution initially stressing liberal arts transfer education to one emphasizing terminal vocational programs.[20] Our starting point—which we share with many scholars working within the framework of the new institutionalism—is to situate the institution under study within its own organization field. In our version of institutional analysis, however, we view organizational fields as *arenas of power relations,* with some actors—generally those possessing superior material and/or symbolic resources—occupying more advantaged positions than others. In the case of the two-year college, we have emphasized how its structural subordination to four-year colleges persistently shaped its trajectory of development.

We have thus emphasized that while organizations may pursue their own distinctive interests, they do so under conditions of powerful constraint. A fundamental tenet of our approach—whether it is applied to education, the media, or medicine—is that the "command posts" of any society significantly shape the possibilities faced by subordinate institutions. In market societies, the most important of these command posts are typically the state and major private corporations. In the community college case we have analyzed, the four-year colleges were also of great importance.

Though the transformation of the community colleges reveals relatively little overt struggle between groups, we wish to emphasize that those who use an approach that situates organizational activity in a larger structure of power relations must be sensitive to the capacity of politically mobilized classes or status groups to limit and direct the pursuit of organizational interests. Generally speaking, the greater the degree of mobilization of politically relevant groups in "civil society," the less autonomy administrators have to pursue their own distinct organizational—or professional—interests. A comprehensive institutional model of change thus must take into account both the pursuit of organizational interests and the role of group struggle in shaping organizational structures and policies.[21]

Yet within the context of these constraints, the institutional perspective we have developed in this chapter accords considerable import to the interests, beliefs, and activities of managers in the organizations under scrutiny. It is these people who typically set organizational policy and devise strategies to promote organizational survival and prosperity. In contrast to models of structural change that see business and labor as the major social actors, the institutional approach thus accords an autonomous role to a third major social group—the full-time professionals, typically unpropertied but highly educated, who have primary administrative responsibility in organizations. Our emphasis on the construction of organizational interests is therefore logically connected to a focus on the situation of the "new middle class" of professionals and managers as it bears on the definition of organizational interests.[22]

In recent years, a number of historically grounded works have appeared—in particular, Tyack (1974; Tyack and Hansot 1982) on elementary and secondary education; DiMaggio (1982a, 1982b) on the arts; Starr (1982) on medicine; Larson (1977) and Abbott (1988) on professions; and Chandler (1977) on modern corporate organization—that might be seen, along with our own, as constituting a revival of the "old institutionalism" in organizational studies. Each of these studies is sensitive to implications of structured power relationships for the development of organizations as well as to the force of market and technical efficiencies. Each is also sensitive to the tendency of organizations to take on lives of their own, in some cases at odds with the expressed purposes for which they were founded. To this extent, the revival of the old institutionalism has already begun to point the way for the fuller new institutionalism that we expect to find in the coming years. It also powerfully complements the fundamental insight of the existing new institutionalism that far more is involved in organizational patterns than the design implied by the criterion of technical efficiency.

Acknowledgments

The research reported in this chapter was supported by the National Institute of Education (NIE-G-77-0037) and the National Science Foundation (SES-80-25542 and SES-83-19986). The authors take full responsibility for the views expressed herein.

Notes

1. The summary section of this chapter is a condensation of the argument from our book *The Diverted Dream: Community Colleges and the Promise of Educational Opportunity in America, 1900–1985* (New York: Oxford University Press, 1989).

2. Before World War I, two-year colleges briefly entertained the idea that they would eventually become the exclusive feeders to the upper-division level of the universities, much as high schools had become the exclusive feeders into the freshman year of college. This aspiration was encouraged for a short time by the efforts of some university presidents to "amputate" the freshmen and sophomore years so as to specialize in higher-level work along the lines of the German research universities. During World War I, the loss of tens of thousands of young men to the military cut the enrollment of the nation's colleges and universities, and led university presidents to reconsider their plans to abandon the freshman and sophomore years.

3. Apart from vocationalization, the "consumer choice" model also fails to explain another major structural change in American higher education involving the two-year colleges—the radical increase in the overall proportion of students attending them. The postwar era has seen strong popular demand for low-cost, geographically accessible, open-access colleges. But there is no convincing evidence that the public was demanding the expansion of two-year as opposed to four-year colleges. This shift was a consequence of a series of "master plans" made by state authorities, especially after the late 1950s, to divert the bulk of the tidal wave of "baby-boom" students away from the four-year colleges. What we have here, then, is neither a structural necessity nor a response to the wishes of educational "consumers," but rather a *policy choice*. Where such a choice was not made—as, for example, in Indiana or Utah—the proportion of students in two-year institutions remained low.

4. In contrast to major national corporations, local business showed somewhat more interest in junior colleges, especially in institutions located in their own communities. But even local business was courted by the junior colleges and had to be convinced to hire their graduates.

5. Several nonmarket mechanisms were used to increase the proportion of students in vocational programs before 1970. Some of these mechanisms—such as the disproportionate allocation of resources to vocational programs and the motivated selection of campus presidents committed to vocationalization—helped shape student choices indirectly without explicitly controlling them. Guidance counseling and testing also often had the effect of shifting student "demand" toward occupational training. At times,

more radical steps were also taken, such as the several instances we found of quota-setting on liberal arts enrollments. These practices, while not common, suggest that at least some community colleges, in their eagerness to increase enrollment in occupational programs, were willing to restrict the initial choices of their supposedly sovereign student "consumers." Again, junior college administrators were, in many cases, motivated by a sincere concern for the welfare of the large majority of students who left junior colleges with neither the credits necessary for transfer nor marketable skills.

6. Our understanding of the new institutionalism has been greatly enhanced by Zucker 1987 and Perrow 1986:265–72.

7. The best-known work of this first generation of institutional analysts includes Selznick's own study of the TVA (1949), Messinger's (1955) study of the Townsend movement, Gusfield's (1955) study of the Women's Christian Temperance Union, Clark's studies of adult education (1956) and the junior college (1960b), Perrow's (1963) study of the YMCA, and Sudnow's (1964) study of court procedures in California. For an excellent overview of the Selznick school, see Perrow 1986: ch. 5.

8. Our work also strives to avoid biases of 1950s sociology that sometimes flaw the work of the "old institutionalism." In particular, we find the organic and functional metaphors favored by the Selznick school to be of only limited value in social analysis. Nor do we share the tendency in Selznick's later work to accept "responsible, value-oriented" elites as necessarily "knowing best." We analyze elites not only as value-oriented leaders, but as interested parties and as agents of historically specific forms of social organization.

9. It is obviously *not* our view that big business controls American higher education. We are thus in disagreement with that long and colorful tradition of social scientific and journalistic commentary, inaugurated by Thorstein Veblen's *The Higher Learning in America* (1918), that portrays American universities as creatures of corporate capital.

Our own position on the relationship between the system of higher education and business accords colleges and universities considerably more autonomy than do works in the Veblen tradition. It closely parallels Lindblom's (1977:175) when he writes: "To understand the peculiar character of politics in market-oriented systems requires . . . no conspiracy theory of politics, no theory of common social origins uniting government and business officials, no crude allegation of a power elite established by clandestine forces. Business simply needs inducements . . . if it is to do its job."

10. If the structural power of business limits the autonomy of colleges and universities, it does not eliminate that autonomy. A tight correspondence between the educational system and the economy is by no means inevitable in a capitalist society; the examples of Italy (Barbagli 1982) and Sri Lanka (Dore 1976), where the number of graduates produced by the system of higher education has persistently exceeded the demand for them, make this quite clear. Though capitalism may therefore preclude certain educational outcomes, it by no means dictates which among many possible policies will be chosen. Moreover, the pressures toward correspondence may be somewhat greater in state socialist societies because nonutilitarian status cultures originally drawn from aristocratic ideals of refinement are a less strong force than in the capitalist societies of Western Europe and North America. See Weber [1922]1978; Collins 1979.

11. In Hannan and Freeman's (1977) summary of the adaptation perspective, adaptation is a process of adjustive learning in which organizations or subunits of organizations (usually managers or dominant coalitions) scan the relevant environment for oppor-

tunities and threats, formulate strategic responses, and adjust organizational structure accordingly. Once an adequate theory of the power structure has been developed, the adaptation perspective provides a useful heuristic for understanding how organizations seek out opportunities and therefore secure positions (or niches) for themselves within partially populated organizational environments.

However, a discussion of the forces creating the structure of the free space in an organizational field is effectively absent from most adaptation theories. Consequently, we believe this approach begs a number of important questions. Above all, it does not allow us to consider very well the question of why some organizations become powerful enough to help shape the environment faced by other organizations; see Perrow 1986:210–11.

12. The sympathies of early junior college leaders with the reforming university presidents are emphasized by Goodwin 1971, Zwerling 1976, and Brint and Karabel 1989: ch. 2.

13. Tyack and Hansot 1982 has shown that many of the organizational reformers in the educational arena were themselves sons and daughters of devoutly religious Protestant parents. Many of the same influences Tyack and Hansot see working at the elementary and secondary school level can be seen working also in the junior college movement. Our study shows, for example, that a high percentage of junior college leaders were themselves Protestant ministers, or were at least from religious backgrounds. Among the key works on the early twentieth-century "organizational revolution," see Hofstadter 1955, Hays 1964, and Wiebe 1967.

14. See, for example Domhoff 1967, 1970. Domhoff's emphasis on the political influence of elites and elite resources articulates with the well-known theoretical work of the Italian elite theorists Pareto, Mosca, and Michels. Putnam 1976 and Dye 1986 are among the more influential contemporary advocates of the position.

15. According to Pfeffer and Salancik 1978, three factors are critical in determining the dependence of one organization on another: the importance of the resource controlled by the external source, the extent of the latter's discretion on the use of the resource, and the extent of possible alternative avenues of access to the resource.

We do not agree that the power relations are entirely based on "resources." In particular we do not agree that material resources alone are critical. Taxpayers provided virtually all of the resources to community colleges but had almost no say over the direction taken by the colleges. Neither government nor business was as influential in determining the direction of the community colleges as were the colleges and universities, which supplied no resources, or the "community college vanguard," which was energetic and organized but poor in material resources until the late 1960s.

This paradox is explained by drawing a distinction between direct resource influences and what might be called contextual influences. Even if an organization is not dependent on another for vital material resources, it may be dependent on it if the latter organization defines an important context in which the former operates. The community colleges were subordinate to both the four-year colleges and employing organizations, though, strictly speaking, they depended on neither for resources. The four-year colleges held the power to define the criteria of academic quality and had tended to monopolize training for the elite segments of the labor market. Business organizations exercised great influence because they defined the employment context in which community college students would move after completing their training.

16. In a reaction against an earlier version of "revisionist" scholarship that frequently portrayed educational policy as an imposition by elites on an inert working class, more recent revisionist accounts (see, for example, Nasaw 1979; Wrigley 1982; Hogan 1985) have stressed the role that class and ethnic conflict have played in shaping American education. We believe this perspective has made a significant contribution to understanding educational history, but in the case of the junior college, our research disclosed relatively little conflict of this sort.

17. The demographic argument is made most forcefully by Cross 1971 and Lombardi 1978 and 1979. Some critics of the community colleges have also made demographic arguments of this type, though they tend to interpret demographic changes not as a direct cause of tracking, but as providing an excuse for it. See, for example, Bowles and Gintis 1976: ch. 9; Nasaw 1979.

18. This sealing off of possibilities occurred, for example, in California where the high schools resisted a well-supported plan to graft the junior and senior high school years onto the two-year colleges. It also occurred in the many states which flirted with transferring the lower division college years to the junior colleges—an idea which was definitively abandoned after the First World War.

19. Our findings on status group competition are consistent with this generalization. Weak internal opposition—as, for example, by academically oriented faculty in the early years of the two-year colleges—seems to have had an energizing effect on the junior college vanguard. Strong internal opposition, on the other hand, could easily have encouraged the kind of stalemate and factionalization that often places organizations at a competitive disadvantage. See Gamson 1975: ch. 5.

20. In pursuing this theme of goal displacement in the junior college, we are indebted to Burton Clark's classic 1960 study, *The Open-Door Colleges*. This study, whose most famous contribution was its analysis of the "cooling-out" function in higher education, situated the junior college in relation to its external "environment" and, like a number of other studies conducted by students of Selznick during this period, emphasized that actual organizational practices diverged from expressed organizational goals.

21. For examples of a mode of analysis of institutional change that attempts to synthesize the traditional Weberian emphasis on organizational interests with the emphasis in recent versions of conflict theory (both neo-Weberian and neo-Marxist) on status-group and class conflict, see Karabel's analyses of open admissions at the City University of New York (Karabel 1983) and of the rise of Jewish quotas at Harvard, Yale, and Princeton (Karabel 1984).

22. In emphasizing the strategic position of credentialed professionals in the life of modern bureaucratic societies, the institutional approach has points of convergence with the "new class" theories of such analysts as Gouldner (1979) and Konrad and Szelenyi (1979). Such a focus need not, of course, be accompanied by an uncritical endorsement of "new class" theory; Brint 1984, for example, presents evidence suggesting that a "new-class" framework does not adequately explain the political attitudes of American professionals.

15 Organizational Isomorphism in East Asia

Marco Orrù,
Nicole Woolsey Biggart,
and Gary G. Hamilton

The new institutionalism has attracted attention as an alternative to, or significant modifier of, resource dependency and population ecology approaches to the study of organizational environments. Resource dependency theorists (Pfeffer and Salancik 1978) stress the environmental constraints generated by organizational interdependence as organizations attempt to secure resources necessary for survival. Population ecologists (Hannan and Freeman 1977, 1981; Aldrich 1979) focus instead on the survival of organizational forms under given environmental conditions. While these two approaches to the study of organizational environments have different units of analysis (focal organizations versus populations) and different assumptions about the efficacy of human agency in determining outcomes (the utility versus the futility of strategic action), they share a common concern with *technical* environments. Technical environments include production and control technologies, patterns of interorganizational exchange, regulatory processes, and other factors that lead to relatively more or less efficient or effective forms of organization.

The new institutionalism departs from these technically oriented approaches by turning our attention to *institutional* environments, the socially constructed normative worlds in which organizations exist. It is a theoretical perspective that focuses on organizational conformity with social rules and rituals rather than with the technically efficient processing of inputs and outputs. It is a perspective concerned more with legitimacy than efficiency.

Each of these different theoretical approaches shares a common concern, however, with organizational structure or form. In different ways each argues that environmental pressures shape organizations and, moreover, that organizations in the same environment will become structurally similar as they respond to like pressures; that is, they will demonstrate *isomorphism* (DiMaggio and Powell 1983). Technical environments shape organizations through *competitive isomorphism* or competition over scarce resources. In the heat of competition, organizations adopt efficient structures and practices or risk failure to relatively better-adapted rivals. Institutional environments shape organizations through social pressure and result in *institutional isomorphism.* Organizations in a common institutional environment begin to look like each other as they respond to similar regulatory and normative pressures, or as they copy structures adopted by successful organizations under conditions of uncertainty. They adopt organizational forms because they have been dictated by patron organizations such as funding agencies or because a given form becomes generally accepted practice in their sector. Institutional pressures have no direct concern with efficiency, although maverick organizations that fail to conform may risk survival as surely as an inefficient firm.

Analytically, there is no reason any organization might not be as subject to competitive factors as to institutional factors. In fact, however, theorists have tended to see organizations as more subject to one sort of pressure rather than another (Perrow 1985b:152). Although Aldrich suggested the influence of institutional factors in his overview of the ecological perspective (1979), population ecologists have not taken these factors seriously (see Carroll and Huo 1986; Hannan and Freeman 1984 for exceptions). At the very least, most theorists have chosen to study one type of organizational environment rather than another, based on the presumption of dichotomous environmental pressures. In support of this view, DiMaggio and Powell claim that competitive isomorphism "is most relevant for those fields in which free and open competition exists," such as manufacturing firms in a market economy (1983:150), while institutional isomorphism is likely among organizations which seek "political power and institutional legitimacy," for example, schools and government agencies. Scott and Meyer agree that some organizational sectors, such as banking, may be subject to both technical and institutional factors but argue that where that is the case there will be "higher levels of internal conflict" as organizations try to cope with the competing demands of legitimacy and efficiency (1983:140–41). The possibility that technical and institutional environments might converge in an organizational setting has been contemplated theoretically, but it has not been seriously entertained in empirical analysis.

With this chapter we hope to broaden the horizons of the new institutionalism both empirically and theoretically by challenging the current presumption of the dichotomy or necessary antagonism of technical and institutional environments. Using data about East Asian businesses we make two general, theoretical claims. First, we claim that the institutional approach need not be limited in its application to organizational environments where institutionalization is most predictable; rather, institutional arrangements have a paramount role and can be observed at the very core of market-regulated, technically dominated environments. We argue that, in East Asia, private businesses operate according to substantively distinct institutional models that differentially shape organizational behavior and structure.

Our second, related claim is that the institutional and technical components of environments need not be at odds with each other, nor do they need to be mutually exclusive; to the contrary, they can converge harmoniously in shaping organizational forms. Institutional arrangements do not necessarily lead to loss of efficiency or effectiveness in organizational forms; our research shows, rather, that the institutional traits of different East Asian businesses are one of the ingredients (if not the key ingredient) to their economic success and organizational fitness. We challenge Scott and Meyer's hypothesis (1983:141) that internal conflict is the result of simultaneous technical and institutional demands. On the contrary, we claim that institutional pressures can contribute to the emergence and the maintenance of market order both within and between competitive organizations.

Our data suggest that large business groups in South Korea, Taiwan, and Japan operate according to different institutional principles and exhibit different organizational and interorganizational structures that manifest those principles. The business organizations found in each of these economies are not corruptions of technically ideal organizational forms, but represent qualitatively distinct conceptualizations of what constitutes appropriate economic activity. Each economy rests on institutional principles that provide a coherent logic for competitive economic action. Socially constructed, accepted models of correct market behavior shape interfirm relations, prompting firms to behave with and against each other in characteristically homogeneous ways. To be "technically efficient," firms must consider and comply with the institutional setting in which they are embedded.

Each of the three market economies we examine has a distinct pattern of firm relations that express themselves as characteristic firm structures and interfirm networks. The networks are strikingly uniform or isomorphic within each economy, but different from each of the others—they express the organizing principles of that economy's environment. The institutional principles that shape organizational forms in these three countries do not hamper organizational efficiency, but rather provide a basis for market order and for competitive relations.

We organize our chapter in four sections. In the first section, we highlight the significance of institutionalization theory in accounting for patterns of intrasocietal isomorphism and intersocietal variation of large business groups in Japan, South Korea, and Taiwan, comparing it with other theories which would predict intrasocietal variation and with competing explanations of intersocietal differences. In the second section, we deal with data sources, methodology, and definitional problems. In the third section, we analyze the interfirm network structure of the major enterprise groups in each society, showing the distinctive organizational forms which obtain in each and proposing the "institutional principles" which provide the organizing logic for macro-organizational relations in each instance. Finally, we elaborate on the significance of the institutional approach for the study of organizational forms, by showing its relevance in the analysis of East Asian enterprise groups and by arguing in favor of a broader interpretation and application of the new institutionalism to encompass not only the study of predictably institutionalized organizational environments, but also, and more importantly, to include those organizational environments where the institutional aspects might appear to be secondary or altogether irrelevant. It is only by entering in the latter arena, we believe, that the new institutionalism can realize its full potential.

Isomorphism and Variation in Organizational Forms

Our thesis is but one of several that attempt to account for organizational form. For example, its classical formulation—the population ecology model of organizations—embraces Hawley's (1968) notion that "the diversity of organizational forms is isomorphic to the diversity of environments" (Hannan and Freeman 1977:939). Organizational variation is essential to this model, since such variation provides "the raw material from which selection is made" (Aldrich 1979:35). Summarizing the dominant views in the field, DiMaggio and Powell (1983:148) pointed out that "much of modern organizational theory posits a diverse and differentiated world of organizations and seeks to explain variation among organizations in structure and behavior." Arguments explaining organizational variation from a resource-dependence perspective have appealed to the growing interdependence which accompanies the "increased specialization and division of labor among organizational entities" (Pfeffer and Salancik 1978:43); population ecologists, instead, have emphasized the existence of "multiple, dynamic environments" which impose conflicting constraints on populations of organizations (Hannan and Freeman 1977:939). In both scenarios, one would expect the variation of organizational forms to be a dominant feature.

A transaction-cost perspective also predicts a diversity of organizational forms reflecting involvement in different industrial and nonindustrial sectors, varying accessibility to technologies, and differential access to financial resources and markets (Williamson 1981). The variation in market factors and technological factors should translate into a variation in organizational forms.

Despite the predictions of variation postulated by these theories, we have found that business groups in East Asian countries show a remarkable degree of intrasocietal isomorphism; more to the point, such isomorphism does not seem to hamper the organizations' economic fitness, but to enhance it. To be sure, population ecologists identified an isomorphic stage of competition in which "competitors become more similar as standard conditions of competition bring forth a uniform response" (Hannan and Freeman 1977:940); but this stage is followed, in the population ecology model, by the elimination of weaker competitors and their subsequent differentiation "either territorially or functionally." The isomorphism we identify in East Asian business groups, on the contrary, is far from episodic and shows remarkable continuity over time. The explanation for East Asian isomorphism cannot be found in competitive mechanisms alone (although they are a key source of isomorphic organizational behavior), but must be justified by the larger social and political contexts in each of the three countries.

The intersocietal variation of organizational forms is also amenable to alternative theoretical predictions and competing explanations. From an anthropological perspective which identifies broad cultural traits across East Asian societies (e.g., a common Confucian work ethic, obedience to authority, high rates of literacy, desire to achieve), one would predict the homogeneity of organizational forms across societies. But as we argued elsewhere when examining the anthropological arguments (Hamilton and Biggart 1988), cultural explanations at this broad level mislead us in focusing on "primordial constants that undergird everything." A similar prediction of homogeneity would obtain, for opposite reasons, if one postulated the automatic application of universal economic principles in the behavior of profit-seeking organizations. In this case, not the overwhelming emphasis on cultural factors but the upholding of a cross-cultural, undifferentiated economic ethic (which rests on the individuation of the *homo oeconomicus* as a universally applicable ideal type) would lead to prediction of nearly total homogeneity in organizational forms.

Both the cultural and the economic approach err in adopting a unidimensional view of the environment (either as a culture or as a market) to explain organizational forms which are subject to more articulated and detailed environmental factors. The new institutionalism is more sensitive to the details of environments because it escapes reductionism in either direction; it provides, one could say, a middle-range theory of organizational environments.

But even if the existence of identifiably different organizational forms in Japan, South Korea, and Taiwan is acknowledged, it would be far from obvious that such difference should be attributed to varying institutional characteristics across the three societies. Alternative theoretical explanations have focused on the different stage of development reached by each of the three economies (Cumings 1984), on the differing industrial structure in each country (Scitovsky 1985), and on the political and historical factors shaping organizational forms (Hamilton and Biggart 1988). These alternative explanations are not necessarily at odds with an institutional explanation of variation; on the contrary, the new institutionalism incorporates the roles of technological development, of the state, and of market factors in its study of organizational forms. Obviously, the level of economic development of Japan is far ahead of those of South Korea and Taiwan, but it is far from evident that either of the latter countries (especially Taiwan) will go on to develop organizational forms similar to Japan's. Moreover, the differential development argument would be less applicable in a comparison of South Korea and Taiwan; there, if anything, we identify not two different stages of development, but rather two different roads to development—two different, institutional notions of development.

The roles of the state and of historical, political events in each country are also paramount in explaining the development of different organizational forms. In our previous work (Hamilton and Biggart 1988) we amply illustrated such roles, but argued against a one-way causal flow from state action to organizational forms. Institutional arrangements influence political action as much as they are influenced by it; it would be misleading to see the state as an extra-societal entity which is unaffected by the social institutions of which it is a part. Therefore, rather than positing state action as the prime mover, we are inclined to see the state in each society as interacting (in different degrees and with different strategies) with the other organizational forms in that society.

As for the variation in the industrial composition of each country (where, for instance, South Korea concentrates on shipbuilding and steel whereas Taiwan specializes in metal products and textiles), it is clear that such variation would accompany a variation in organizational forms, but it is less evident, again, that the relation between the two should be one of cause and effect—or at least that the causal relation should be unidirectional. In fact we argue that an institutional environment which favors small-size, family-centered businesses as found in Taiwan, would also favor the concentration of production in light metal industries and textiles. The affinity between organizational forms and types of production is obvious, but the causal pattern influencing each is far from self-evident. It is here that a broadening of the institutionalization perspective to encompass both technical and sociocultural arguments, without presuming a priori causal directions, can show its full potential.

Methodology, Sources of Data, and Definitional Problems

In Japan, South Korea, and Taiwan there are numerous clusters of interlinked firms, or what we call enterprise groups. Enterprise groups are relatively stable and identifiable aggregates of firms which are related by way of shared ownership or management, mutual financial and market transactions, and other identifiable, patterned interdependencies. In each of the three countries, we have focused on the dominant enterprise groups in the private sector, since their existence, historical formation, and organizational patterns have been systematically documented. While firms in enterprise groups have stable relations over time, they might not have a legal status which externally sanctions such relations; however, the published literature available in each country on the exact configuration of these groups makes it possible to identify them fairly accurately. East Asian enterprise groups differ from the clusters of firms found in the United States, which are often short-term, episodic combinations of convenience (Pfeffer and

Salancik 1978). In each of the three East Asian societies a substantial journalistic and professional literature speculates about the shifting configurations of enterprise groups; in Japan, substantial scholarly literature has also focused on the exact configuration and implications of its domestic enterprise groups.

For each society we examined the complete set of organizational networks at the top of each economy, as they are identified in each setting, rather than a predetermined number of clusters (e.g., the top five). Instead of selecting equal numbers of enterprise groups across the border, we chose to analyze naturally occurring patterns within each economy. Our rationale is that the number of enterprise groups included in each society's set is itself a crucial variable in explaining the variation across societies; this approach helps provide institutional comparability.

For each cluster of enterprise groups within each society, we wanted to know what sorts of firms come to be identified with which groups and according to what criteria, what kinds of linkages exist among member firms, and how business-group firms differ from unaligned but similarly successful firms. In short, we wanted to know how the clusters were internally organized and how they related to the general economy. Our intent was to see if firms could be understood to align with each other in discernible patterns. To identify such patterns we resorted to measures of isomorphism, that is, measures of uniformity of group configurations.[1]

A Comparison of Enterprise Groups

While a firm-level analysis reveals distinctive organizational characteristics in each country (Fukuda 1983; Redding and Tam 1986), such an analysis is, by itself, insufficient. The wide availability of publications which identify groups of firms according to standardized patterns in each of the three countries is, in itself, an indication that group membership is a significant organizational phenomenon in East Asia. The aggregation of firm-level statistics according to indigenous enterprise groups dramatizes the organizational similarities within each country and the differences among them in a way that firm-level analysis cannot. The adoption of this unit of analysis led us to the identification of three distinct organizational sets. For Japan, we looked at the six major intermarket groups (*kigyo shudan*) and the ten largest independent industrial and financial groups (*keiretsu*); for South Korea we looked at the fifty largest enterprise groups, the so-called *chaebol;* for Taiwan, we examined the top ninety-six business groups, called *jituanqiye*.

As a preliminary identification of the significant variation across societies, selected general areas of difference among the business groups as a whole should be emphasized before we begin a detailed analysis of each organizational pattern. Table 15.1 provides a comparative statistical overview. First, the number and size of affiliated firms in each group differ markedly. Japan's busi-

Table 15.1   General Characteristics of Business Groups in Japan, South Korea, and Taiwan

	Japan 1982 (16 groups)	Korea 1983 (50 groups)	Taiwan 1983 (96 groups)
Total sales in lo-	217,033	54,663	633.7
cal currency	Billion ¥	Billion Won	Billion NT$
In billions US$	871.26	68.32	16.48
Total workers	2,841,000	795,000	330,000
Total firms	1,001	552	745
Firms per group	62.60	11.04	7.76
Workers per firm	2,838	1,440	444
Percentage of to-			
tal workforce	9.5	5.5	4.7

Sources: Dodwell 1984; *Hankook Ilbo* 1985; Zhonghua Zhenxinso 1985.

ness groups (the fewest in absolute terms) embrace the largest number of individual firms, with an average of over 112 firms for each of the six inter-market groups, and about 33 firms for each of the ten independent keiretsu. South Korea's chaebol, in contrast, include only an average of about 11 firms each. The largest (and often oldest) chaebol, however, include 20 or more firms on average, suggesting that the smaller, younger chaebol will perhaps grow with time. Taiwan's business groups are smaller still, typically having fewer than 8 affiliated firms each.

Second, the size of business-group firms also differs markedly from country to country. Firms in Japan's business groups are large, with an average of more than 2,800 workers. Korean chaebol firms are not as large, averaging less than 1,500 workers (although top chaebol firms can average up to 3,600 workers). Taiwan's groups, in contrast, comprise relatively small companies with only a few hundred workers.

Third, the economic impact of enterprise groups differs in each country, even accounting for the economies' relative size differences (Japan's GNP is 22 times greater and South Korea's is 1.3 times greater than Taiwan's GNP). Although our data set for Taiwan comprises more business groups than the other two countries combined, their collective economic importance is, by far, the smallest. The South Korean economy, only slightly larger than Taiwan's, is in contrast dominated by the chaebol. Japan's business groups are similarly important economic actors, representing an extraordinary US$871 billion in sales in 1982. Their relative contribution to GNP, however, is smaller than the Korean chaebol (Hahn, Kim, and Kim 1987:128).

JAPANESE ENTERPRISE GROUPS: A COMMUNITY OF FIRMS

Scholars agree that at the top of the Japanese economy there are a few well-defined clusters of firms (Futatsugi 1986; Kobayashi 1980; Okumura 1982,

1984, 1985; Sumiya 1986). These groups of firms are not conglomerates in the American sense of that term; they are social rather than legal entities (although there is joint stock ownership, as we describe below). Nonetheless, these clusters of firms take their social relationship seriously and are organized for the mutual benefit of all affiliated firms. Enterprise-group firms straightforwardly identify themselves as members of a community of corporations with a distinct identity; individual firms understand their relative ranking in the community and the economic role they are expected to play for the good of the whole group.

In recent years, analysts have identified two major types of enterprise groups in Japan—the intermarket groups and the independent groups (Dodwell 1984; Toyo Keizai Shimposha 1986a and 1986b). Each represents a distinct form of corporate community, although they share many features (see Orrù, Hamilton, and Suzuki 1989). Table 15.2 lists the six intermarket groups and the ten independent groups. While each has a distinctive "community character" which sets it apart from the other groups, all intermarket groups share at least four isomorphic features. First, all six groups are structured around a horizontally bound web of large firms, most of which occupy leading positions in different economic sectors. As table 15.3 shows, all intermarket groups contain a similar lineup of firms competing across sectors, but not within them. This is known as the one-set principle (Futatsugi 1986). In this way intermarket groups compete with each other for shares of the total economy. Accordingly, when new industrial areas appear, each intermarket group creates or attempts to include firms specializing in those areas. Second, all six groups have their own banking institutions, insurance companies, and trading firms that take care of the financial and market transaction needs of the group. Third, all the intermarket groups have a Presidents' Club: the president of each of the leading companies in the group belongs to a council which meets once a month to discuss the affairs of that group (Okumura 1985:15–16). Fourth, each Presidents' Club member firm maintains vertically aligned affiliate and subsidiary firms. These vertical alignments are conventionally called keiretsu. Affiliate and subsidiary firms, in

Table 15.2 Intermarket Groups
and Independent Groups in Japan

Intermarket Groups	Independent Groups
Mitsubishi	Tokai Bank
Mitsui	IBJ
Sumitomo	Nippon Steel
Fuyo	Hitachi
DKB	Nissan
Sanwa	Toyota
	Matsushita
	Toshiba-IHI
	Tokyu
	Seibu

Table 15.3   Presidents' Club Firms by Sector in Japan's Six Intermarket Groups, 1982

Sector	Mitsubishi	Mitsui	Sumitomo	Fuyo	DKB	Sanwa
Banking and insurance	****	****	****	****	*******	****
Trading and commerce	*	**	*	*	*****	****
Forestry and mining		*	**			
Construction	*	**	*	*	*	***
Food and beverages	*	*	*	***		**
Fibers and textiles	*	*		**	*	**
Pulp and paper	*	*		*	*	
Chemicals	*****	**	**	***	******	*******
Petroleum products	*			*	*	*
Rubber products					*	*
Glass and cement	**	*	**	*	*	*
Iron and steel	*	*	*	*	***	****
Nonferrous metals	**	*	****		***	*
Machinery—general	*		*	**	***	*
Electrical and electronics	*	*	*	***	*****	*****
Transportation machinery	**	**		*	***	***
Precision instruments	*			*	*	
Real estate	*	*	*	*		
Land transportation				**	*	**
Marine transportation	*	*		*	*	*
Warehousing	*	*	*		*	
Service industry					*	
Total number of firms	28	23	21	29	46	42

Source: Dodwell 1984: 53, 64–65, 74, 82, 91, 100.
Note: Each asterisk represents one firm.

addition, maintain numerous, differentially ranked long-term subcontract relationships with small- and middle-sized firms which are not counted as part of the intermarket keiretsu, but are nonetheless vital to the overall system of production (Okumura 1982, 1984; Ishida 1983; Shimokawa 1982, 1985). Subcontract relationships are ranked as primary, secondary, and tertiary, depending on the role they play in the production process. While they usually are not formal members of the keiretsu, subcontractors identify readily with the keiretsu community.

In contrast to the intermarket groups, independent groups represent a network of vertically integrated firms in one industrial sector. Independent groups tend to be structurally similar to the keiretsu within intermarket groups, each consisting of a very large, highly successful parent company and vertically aligned subordinate companies (Dodwell 1984). For example, Nissan Motor, the automotive giant and head of an important independent group, is often referred to as a keiretsu in its own right. It maintains long-term relations with parts subcontractors, many of which are located adjacent to or near Nissan plants, so that members of independent groups often form a geographic, as well as an economic and social, community.

Despite their label, the ten large independent groups are not, in fact, independent of each other or of the six intermarket groups. Independent groups maintain linkages to other enterprise groups through mutual shareholding by financial institutions. As we argue elsewhere (Orrù, Hamilton, and Suzuki 1989), these interlinkages closely resemble the sort of ties found among Presidents' Club firms within intermarket groups. Hence, the independent groups collectively form a super intermarket group, whose presidential club would include the leading firms of the independent groups and the leading financial institutions of the intermarket groups.

In summary, two important types of configurations occur within Japanese enterprise groups. The first configuration consists of stable horizontal linkages across noncompeting industrial sectors which result in a community of equals or near equals; in these horizontally aligned communities, no one firm dominates, but rather all firms exercise collective mutual control. The second configuration is a vertical alignment characterized by hierarchical relationships among firms, in terms of both production links and status positions.

The isomorphic qualities of these two types of configurations in intermarket groups can be evinced by comparing rates of intra- and intergroup stockholding for the six groups, and rates of stockholding for keiretsu (including both the very large keiretsu formed by the independent groups and the smaller ones formed around the Presidents' Club firms in intermarket groups). Table 15.4 shows the rates of intra- and intergroup stockholding for the intermarket groups. Here we can distinguish two patterns. First, all six intermarket groups have a similar substantial level of intragroup shareholding. For example, Mitsui group firms collectively own, on average, over 18 percent of all Mitsui firms' stock; likewise, members of the Sumitomo group own 28 percent of member companies' shares. Although individual firms typically only own between 2

Table 15.4 Percentage Crossholding of Stocks by Enterprise Groups, 1977

Owner	Owned						
	Mitsui	Mitsubishi	Sumitomo	Fuyo	DKB	Sanwa	Total
Mitsui	18.42	0.79	1.16	1.60	2.35	2.98	27.30
Mitsubishi	1.02	25.01	0.44	2.30	2.59	2.07	33.43
Sumitomo	1.06	0.17	28.24	1.24	0.98	1.03	32.72
Fuyo	0.96	1.02	1.00	16.59	2.92	8.36	30.85
DKB	1.47	1.96	0.68	2.27	13.73	10.21	30.32
Sanwa	0.72	0.63	1.06	1.39	2.10	17.35	23.25
Total	23.65	29.58	32.58	25.39	24.67	42.00	

Source: Okumura 1982:70.

Table 15.5   Selected Measures of Isomorphism for Japan's Intermarket Groups, 1982

Group	Relative Density: Top Five Firms	Relative Density: Council Firms	Internal Control: Council Firms
Sumitomo	.88 (1)	.128 (1)	72.5 (1)
Mitsubishi	.86 (2)	.063 (2)	64.6 (2)
Mitsui	.79 (3)	.050 (3)	53.1 (3)
Fuyo	.64 (4)	.022 (4)	42.1 (4)
Sanwa	.53 (5)	.010 (6)	39.0 (5)
DKB	.48 (6)	.020 (5)	38.2 (6)

Source: Dodwell 1984.
Note: Rank is given in parentheses.

percent and 7 percent of other member firms, the joint holdings of several members can be substantial, representing a controlling interest of 20–30 percent. In fact, as we show in table 15.5 above, 65 percent of the shares owned by the top ten shareholders of Mitsubishi firms belong to Mitsubishi firms. Second, firms in intermarket groups (especially financial firms) own small percentages of shares in other intermarket groups (between 1 percent and 2 percent on average). This pattern, like the first one, is remarkably stable across groups. Although there is some variation, the isomorphic pattern of mutual shareholding within and across enterprise groups is clear.

Table 15.5 gives additional evidence for a distinctive patterning of firm relations in Japan, providing measures of shareholding density for intermarket group members. A network with a value of 1.0 is one in which all members are individually connected to each other—in this case through ownership of shares. Column one shows the relative density of shareholding among the top five members of each intermarket group. The second column measures saturation for all other Presidents' Club firms within each group. The third column shows the percentage of member firms' shares in the top ten shareholders of each Presidents' Club firm in that group. This last figure measures the level of internal control of each intermarket group. In all instances, the three intermarket groups that date before World War II—Mitsubishi, Mitsui, and Sumitomo (still frequently referred to as *zaibatsu*)—show higher levels of internal cohesiveness. The postwar groups, instead, have relatively looser internal ties and more linkages outside the group, although the group density is still extraordinary when compared with U.S. firm clusters.

Not only do intermarket groups resemble each other in their level of intragroup and intergroup shareholdings; they are also isomorphic in the relative importance they attribute to the top shareholders in their group. Table 15.6 shows the top five firms in each intermarket group ranked according to the average shares they own in Presidents' Club firms and according to the number of Presidents' Club firms in which they own shares. For the former zaibatsu groups, Mitsui, Mitsubishi, and Sumitomo, the identity in rankings is startling. The top shareholder in all three groups is the mutual life insurance company of the group; in every instance, this company is privately owned (see Nishiyama 1984). The second shareholder is the city bank, and the third shareholder is the trust and banking firm. In the fourth and fifth spots are the marine and fire insurance and the trading companies of each group. The post–World War II groups (also called the bank groups) show a slightly different pattern, with the city banks as top shareholders, and the trust and banking and mutual life companies in either second or third ranking.

Tables 15.7 and 15.8 show vertical shareholding patterns within intermarket groups and within independent groups. In both instances, parent firms typically own 20–30 percent of stocks in their affiliate firms, but independent groups are characterized by a larger number of vertically aligned firms.

It is clear from these measures that Japan's large corporations, while legally independent of each other, are highly connected. Moreover, the nature of these connections is not idiosyncratic but forms distinctive patterns within each of two identifiable types of business groups. Our indicators of isomorphism are based on mutual shareholding, but other types of linkages exist that point to the same patterns (see Orrù, Suzuki and Hamilton 1989). For example, business-group firms have interlocking directorates, share logos and trademarks, exchange executives, participate in joint public relations activities, and in other ways act as a corporate community.

Having demonstrated the existence of isomorphic patterns in Japanese enterprise groups, we need to justify their occurrence. Japanese enterprise groups are clearly an economic success, and one might say that competitive isomorphism is the key to the striking homogeneity we have observed. We feel, however, that

Table 15.6   Top Five Stockholding Firms in Intermarket Groups, 1982

| | Former Zaibatzu Groups | | | | | | City Bank Groups | | | | | |
| | Mitsubishi | | Mitsui | | Sumitomo | | Fuyo | | DKB | | Sanwa | |
Rank	A	B	A	B	A	B	A	B	A	B	A	B
First	MLI	MLI	MLI	MLI	MLI	MLI	CTB	CTB	CTB	FKE	CTB	CTB
Second	CTB	CTB	CTB	CTB	CTB	CTB	T&B	MLI	MLI	CTB	MLI	MLI
Third	T&B	T&B	T&B	T&B	T&B	T&B	MLI	MFI	FKE	MLI	T&B	GTC
Fourth	MFI	MFI	MFI	MFI	GTC	GTC	MFI	T&B	FKC	FKC	HZC	HZC
Fifth	GTC	GTC	GTC	GTC	MFI	MFI	GTC	GTC	GTC	GTC	GTC	T&B

Source: Dodwell 1984.

Notes: A = rank according to average shares held in Presidents' Club firms; B = rank according to number of Presidents' Club firms in which shares are held; CTB = city bank; T&B = trust and banking; MLI = mutual life insurance company; MFI = marine and fire insurance company; GTC = general trading company; FKC = Furukawa Corporation; FKE = Furukawa Electric; and HZC = Hitachi Zosen Corporation.

Table 15.7 *Keiretsu* Isomorphism in Intermarket Groups, 1982

Mitsubishi Chem. Industries		Mitsui & Co. (Trading Company)		Sumitomo Metal Industries		Marubeni Corp. (Fuyo Group)		Fujitsu Ltd. (DKB Group)		Nisso Iwai Corp. (Sanwa Group)	
N. Kasei Ch.	37.4	N. Univac	34.2	Nippon Pipe	46.9	Marub Constr	34.1	Fanuc Ltd.	44.6	Kanoh Steel	33.4
Taiyo Sanso	36.3	F-One Ltd.	34.2	N. S. Steel	37.5	Toyo Sugar	33.7	Takeda Riken	21.5	Fuji Seito	43.9
N. Carbide	17.7	Showa Min.	16.7	Chuo Denki	30.1	Nankai Spinn	15.7	Fuji El-Chem	51.8	Goto Drop	23.2
Teikoku Kako	25.0	Chuo Build	20.5	Kanto Steel	33.6	Katakura Chi	34.0	Takamisawa	37.1	Nihon Mining	35.4
M. Plastics	51.0	N Feed Mfg.	12.1	Osaka Titan.	28.2	Japan Carlit	10.0	Towa Electr.	36.8	Japan Bridge	7.1
N. Synthetic	49.1	M. Sugar	26.6	S Lig Met In	28.9	Okamoto Rik.	7.1	Fuji Electr.	9.4		
Kodama Chem.	10.3	Taito Co.	26.1	Sumikura Ind	46.4	Amatei Inc.	32.7				
Nitto Kako	44.6	Mikuni CC	76.9	S Precision	50.1	Nippei Ind.	20.6				
Toyo Carbon	46.1	Hohnen Oil	9.3	Daikin Inds	16.9	Kaji Iron Wk	40.0				
		Daito Wool	9.5	S Spec Metal	52.1	Okano Valve	43.1				
		Takasaki P.	34.6								
		Honshu Chem	39.2								
		Kawakami Pt	6.0								
		Fuji Kisen	26.5								
		Utoku Expr	22.3								
		Tokai-Kanko	38.7								
		Asia Air s.	27.2								
Avg shares	35.3	Avg shares	27.1	Avg shares	37.1	Avg shares	27.1	Avg shares	33.5	Avg shares	28.6

Source: Dodwell 1984.

Table 15.8 *Keiretsu* Isomorphism
in Independent Groups, 1982

	Average Shares	No. of Firms
Financial groups		
Tokai Bank	6.46	22
IBJ	6.69	22
Industrial groups		
Nippon Steel	21.00	33
Hitachi	44.17	35
Nissan	34.48	30
Toyota	26.12	34
Matsushita	44.95	24
Toshiba-IHI	37.94	39
Tokyu	23.18	17
Seibu	34.80	14

Source: Dodwell 1984.

institutional factors are more relevant than competitive ones, although both are present. What is embodied in the isomorphism of Japanese enterprise groups is not simply organizational efficiency and effectiveness in the Western sense, but also a unique concern with group solidarity and cooperation. The economic philosophy of the groups is to merge the goals of profit maximization and risk sharing. In relations among equally ranked and unequally ranked firms, benevolence and good faith are not simply good economic policy; they are a duty (Dore 1983). Power is not perceived to be located in individual firms, but in the group as a whole. In the Japanese organizational environment, competition and cooperation do not pull in opposite directions, but are integrated in the structure of the enterprise groups. The crucial factor here is what DiMaggio and Powell (1983:150) call *coercive isomorphism*, as it pertains particularly to "the cultural expectations in the society within which organizations function."

The Japanese state had a distinctive role in clearing the way for the establishment of the large intermarket groups, once the Allied forces had disbanded the old, family-centered zaibatsu groups. But even the relation between the Japanese state and large enterprise groups is fashioned according to cultural expectations and mirrors the relation within enterprise groups; it is not a one-way domination of the groups by the state, but rather a collaborative partnership. It "reflects above all a recognized common interest between MITI [the Ministry of International Trade and Industry] and the leading firms in certain oligopolistic industries" (Caves and Uekusa 1976:54).

The theoretical importance of this convergence between technical and institutional environments, between the requirements of competition and of cooperation and conformity, is that it questions the Western assumption of an irreconcilable divergence between them. It is not despite their institutional iso-morphism that Japanese enterprise groups are economically fit, but because of the incorporation of institutional elements in their organizations that they are so successful.

SOUTH KOREAN BUSINESS GROUPS:
CORPORATE PATRIMONIALISM

On the surface, South Korean and Japanese business groups seem to show similar interfirm configurations, and in fact they are often compared favorably with each other (e.g., Lee 1986). A closer look, however, reveals substantial differences. South Korean enterprise groups are called *chaebol,* the Korean transliteration of the Japanese term *zaibatsu.* Like the prewar zaibatsu, most chaebol are usually owned and controlled by a single person or family and are organized through a central holding company. These similarities, however, are largely superficial. In fact, the chaebol have distinctive characteristics which set them apart from current intermarket groups in Japan.

First, the Japanese intermarket groups expanded through the pursuit of hori-zontal diversification as well as vertical integration; chaebol typically started their business in only a few related industrial sectors. As table 15.9 shows, chaebol firms are involved in a narrower range of industrial and commercial pursuits than the intermarket groups of Japan, and their resources are only un-evenly distributed across industrial sectors.

Chaebol resemble Japan's independent groups in their patterns of industrial-sector concentration, but also differ from them in important ways. For instance, chaebol do not rely on stable subcontracting relations with small firms, a dis-tinctive feature of Japanese keiretsu. Instead chaebol buy or start new firms to care for their own production needs, and to a large extent they rely on Japanese firms for the supply of production components. Consequently, the size of major member firms in the top chaebol is on average larger than those in Japanese intermarket groups. The tendency to internalize production within chaebol boundaries is particularly evident in the overall percentage contribution of the chaebol to the South Korean economy, a figure significantly higher than that of the Japanese business groups (Hahn, Kim, and Kim 1987).

The internalization of production sequences and of other transactions points to the major difference between Japanese and South Korean business groups: South Korean business groups, somewhat similar to U.S. corporations, repre-sent an integrated set of economic activities under a unified, centralized management structure. Japanese business groups, instead, represent genuine associations of firms, some more tightly bound to the group than others. Con-trol in Japanese business groups is, in principle, not centralized, but rather dispersed throughout the network of firms.

A number of indicators illustrate these differences. In Japan, interfirm rela-tionships are signified by a number of different horizontal and vertical

Table 15.9   Sector Distribution of Selected Firms in Top Six Korean *Chaebol*

Sector	Hyundai	Samsung	Lucky-GS	Sunkyung	Daewoo	Ssangyong
Banking and insurance	***	**	****		***	**
Trading and commerce	*	**	*	*	**	*
Forestry and mining			*			
Construction	**	***	*	*	*	*
Food and beverages		**				
Fibers and textiles	*	***		***	****	
Pulp and paper	*	***	*			*
Chemicals	*		*		**	
Petroleum products		*	*	*		****
Rubber products	*					
Glass and cement	**					*
Iron and steel	**					
Nonferrous metals	*					
Metal products	**				***	*
Machinery—general	*		***	*		*
Electrical and electronics		*****	*******	*	***	*
Transportation machinery	******	*		*	***	
Precision instruments		*	**		*	
Real estate	*	*		*	*	*
Land transportation				**		
Marine transportation	*					*
Warehousing				*		
Service industry			*			
Total number of firms	26	24	23	13	23	15

Source: *Hankook Ilbo* 1985; *Daily Economic News* 1986.
Note: Each asterisk represents one firm.

reciprocal ties. Joint stockholding is the most important of these and contributes to the fact that the Japanese stock markets are, by far, the largest and most important in all of Asia. In South Korea, instead, the stock market has, until recently, played a very minor role; it is small, and 70–80 percent of firms within chaebol groups are not listed (compared to only 10 percent of Japanese business-group firms). Unlisted firms are usually entirely owned by the individuals and families controlling the chaebol. The South Korean government has recently encouraged chaebol owners to put their firms on the stock market, thereby reducing the amount of debt financing that has gone into building South Korean capitalism. The emerging pattern, as joint stock firms are created, is not one of systematic reciprocal shareholding, as is the case in Japan, although it might come to resemble Japan's as more and more firms go public. For now, chaebol are listing only a few key firms (on average 20–25 percent of their firms), and then appear to be using the equity funds, as they had used the loans before, to create and buy out other firms. The stock market does not reinforce

Marco Orrù, Nicole Woolsey Biggart, and Gary G. Hamilton

community ownership, but rather hierarchical control by top corporations over smaller ones. The emphasis on control is reflected in the shareholding patterns of firms listed on the stock market. Major shareholders are (1) the chaebol leader (usually the founder or his son and his family); (2) the leading firm of the chaebol, typically the trading company or holding company; (3) one or more financial institutions in which the chaebol owns significant shares. The founders' control over the chaebol may be substantially greater than the figures in table 15.10 suggest, however, if the founders are significant partners in securities companies, many of which are privately owned.

Korean management structure reinforces the Korean isomorphic pattern of vertical domination. In Japanese keiretsu, the core firm is the major stockholder for affiliated and subsidiary firms; affiliated firms may in turn own some shares of the core firm and, more likely, of equally ranked affiliated and subsidiary firms. The core firm develops interlocking directorates with affiliated and subsidiary firms with much greater frequency than do Presidents' Club firms. In South Korea, however, the individual owner of the chaebol, a holding company, or a main firm usually owns most firms that are not joint stock firms, and owns or controls, through family and bank holdings, a very high percentage of all shares of those firms that are listed. In South Korea, there is little evidence of interlocking directorates among chaebol firms; instead, there is widespread use of family members as directors of key subordinate firms and use of professional managers for other firms. Significant interlocking directorates only obtain between the chaebol and the main, privately owned financial institutions with which the chaebol deal.

Chaebol do not own banks, but have minority shares in banks controlled by the government. This explains, in part, the reliance on vertical patterns of hierarchy in Korean chaebol and the reluctance to go public. The government, which historically supplied the chaebol with huge amounts of capital to stimulate their rapid growth, retains the right to appoint bank directors who are usually not chaebol executives. Japanese intermarket groups, in contrast, own their own banks. As table 15.11 shows, individual chaebol own, usually, between 5 percent and 15 percent of major banks' shares. The Korean government is the majority shareholder in most commercial banks, and the chaebol own substantial shares only in regional and local banks (see table 15.12). This pattern of bank ownership shows the strong influence of the Korean state on business concentration and on chaebol industrial policy and organizational structure. The centralized domination of the state over each chaebol is isomorphic with the centralized domination that obtains within each chaebol's organizational structure; in both instances, the pattern is one of a strong, vertical hierarchy of powers.

While we restricted our statistical analysis just to the top ten chaebol, we believe that similar patterns, except those related to size, continue through all chaebol. Size is an important factor, however, because the top five chaebol

Table 15.10   Stockholding Structure of Major Firms in Top Six *Chaebol*

Hyundai Corporation		*Hyundai Construction*	
Korea Securities	21.4	Chung Ju-Yung (founder)	54.6
Chung Ju-Yung (founder)	19.2	Hyundai Heavy Industries	7.9
Korea Inv. & Finance Co.	6.9	Hyundai Pipe Company	5.6
Hyundai Motor Services	3.4	Hyundai Wood Industries	5.6
Hyundai Cement	1.8	Hyundai Chung Jung-Gi	2.8
Gum Gang	0.6		
Samsung Corporation		*Samsung Electronics*	
Seoul Bank	15.2	Korea Securities	17.9
Lee Kun-Hee (son) & others	11.5	Seoul Bank	12.1
Shin Young Securities	8.1	Lee Kun-Hee (son)	9.9
Daewoo Securities	6.0	Daewoo Securities	6.6
Korea Fund	4.6	Dongbang Life Insurance	6.4
Lucky-Goldstar Corporation		*Goldstar Co.* (home appliances)	
Data not available		Seoul Bank	8.9
		Lucky Securities	8.0
		Kukje Gum Yung Gong Sha	7.6
		Lucky Ltd.	6.8
		Daewoo Securities	5.5
Sunkyong Ltd. (trading company)		*Yukong Ltd.* (petrol. products)	
Choi Jong-Hyun (chairman)	10.9	Sunkyong Ltd.	50.0
GongMoonWon KuanLi GongDan	3.9	Jae-Il Securities	6.1
HanRuk GoDeung KyoDeng KyoYuk	1.9	Hyundai Securities	4.0
		Daewoo Securities	3.6
		HanKuk SanUp Bank	3.5
Daewoo Corporation		*Daewoo Heavy Industries*	
Daewoo Jae Dan	19.2	Daewoo Corporation	17.4
Korea Investment and Finance	8.7	Daewoo Jae Dan	3.3
Daewoo Hak Won	3.3	Pung Guk Yung Yoo	2.8
Ssangyong Corporation		*Ssangyong Cement*	
Ssangyong Cement	29.0	Kim Suk-Won (founder)	17.9
Korea Securities	17.1	KumMin HakWon	3.2
Kim Suk-Won (founder)	9.2	SungYoo HakSul MunHwa	1.2
Seoul Bank	6.9		
Cho-Heung Bank	6.4		
Korea Invest. & Finance Co.	3.4		
Ssangyong Hau Un	0.4		

Source: *Daily Economic News* 1986.

alone account for 50 percent of the total manufacturing sales of the top fifty Korean chaebol combined.

If we discount the effects of size, the above analysis shows, for South Korean business groups, the predominance of one isomorphic network configuration: a centralized management and ownership structure controlled by a founding patriarch and his heirs. The uniformity is remarkable when one considers the rapid

Table 15.11   Percentage of *Chaebol* Stockholdings in Commercial Banks

Chaebol	Commercial Bank of Korea	Cho-Heung Bank	Korea First Bank	Bank of Seoul	Hanil Bank
Hyundai		2.4	10.3	12.0	11.7
Samsung	16.6	10.3	6.5		
Lucky-Goldstar		1.7	8.5		7.4
Daewoo			14.4		
Ssangyong		6.0			
Hankuk Hwayak					4.3
Han Jin					9.9
Daelim					12.4
Shin Dong Ha		4.8	6.0	9.9	
Dong Ah				10.0	
Tae Kwang Sun Up		11.4		4.6	
Hanil Hap Sung					
Dae Han				5.7	
Dongkuk				3.9	
Total shares	16.6	36.6	45.7	46.1	50.1

Source: *Hankook Ilbo* 1985.

change in the Korean economy in the past two decades. Horizontal linkages are few, but perhaps important, since they seem to be concentrated around regional and city banks. However, there seem to be no significant mutual webs among vertically integrated clusters of firms—a common practice of the Japanese business groups. Moreover, even within vertically integrated networks, there is little evidence of reciprocality (or "relational contracting," as Dore 1986 calls it) among hierarchically ranked firms—a characteristic of Japanese keiretsu.

Finally, the volatility of chaebol growth differs from Japanese business-group stability. Table 15.13 shows that in Japan the market share of major enterprise groups, while not fixed, is relatively stable (both in size and over time), and there seems little likelihood of great change in the near future.

In South Korea, however, the number of chaebol has grown rapidly as new economic sectors have opened. One of the most recent analyses of chaebol lists fifty such groups which include a total of 552 firms. Unlike the mature patterning that characterizes the Japanese case, the number of chaebol, their rank, and the number of firms in each chaebol change constantly. Table 15.14 shows that chaebol positions are subject to rapid changes not only in terms of relative ranking among the chaebol themselves, but also in absolute terms, in relation to other international industrial corporations. The difference in organizational structure between Japan and South Korea could be dismissed as simply showing the different stages of development reached by the two countries; we claim, however, that significant institutional factors account for the observed dif-

Table 15.12 Percentage of *Chaebol* Stockholdings in Regional Banks

Chaebol	Kangwon Bank	Daegu Bank	Kyungki Bank	Chung Buk Bank	Kwangju Bank	Gyeong Nam Bank	Bank of Pusan	Chung Chong Bank	Jeonbuk Bank
Hyundai	32.7								
Samsung		14.7							
Sun Kyung			11.0						
Daewoo				41.5					
Kukje					5.8	13.2	2.9		
Hankuk Hwa Yak								27.2	
Han Jin			23.0						
Hyo Sung						21.5			
Du San		11.8							
Lotte							31.0		
Kolon		7.7							
Kumho					24.4				
Shin Dong Ha			17.6						
Miwon									8.9
Dongkuk Jae Gang							17.4		
Sam Yung									23.5
Total shares	32.7	34.2	51.6	41.5	30.2	34.7	51.3	27.2	32.4

Source: Hankook Ilbo 1985.

Table 15.13 Assets of Intermarket Groups, 1955–1984
(Percentage of National Figures)

	1955	1965	1975	1984
Mitsui	6.1	5.0	2.9	2.4
Mitsubishi	5.0	7.2	3.4	2.6
Sumitomo	3.2	5.4	1.8	1.5
Fuyo	2.9	3.8	3.4	2.8
DKB	3.1	3.2	2.7	4.4
Sanwa	1.4	2.6	3.3	3.2

Sources: Caves and Uekusa 1976:64; *Toyo Keizai Shimposha* 1986a.

ferences. One factor, as we have observed, is the presence of a strong Korean state which is actively involved in the planning and enforcement of economic policies favoring industrial concentration and vertical lines of domination; this is the coercive isomorphism generated by the political influence of a strong state. A second factor has been the cultural impact, in South Korea, of American managerial practices brought through the institution of management programs in South Korean universities (Zo 1970). Third, and more broadly, we point to the persistence in South Korean society of what Norman Jacobs (1985) calls a "patrimonial social order." He explains: "The present situation is attributable to the desire of industrial decision-makers within and without the polity to use time-tested patrimonial techniques of controlling and prebendally exploiting an industrial economy" (1985:154). It is then far from self-evident that today's Japanese organizational forms are tomorrow's Korean ones; rather, we are inclined to think that the two are unlikely ever to resemble each other.

Table 15.14 Fortune International 500 Ranking of Top Korean *Chaebol*

Rank in 1976	Rank in 1980	Rank in 1984
209. Korea Oil	72. Hyundai	38. Samsung
278. Hyundai	101. Lucky	39. Hyundai
459. Ssangyong	125. Samsung	43. Lucky
	139. Korea Oil	48. Daewoo
	237. Hyosung	61. Sunkyong
	275. Ssangyong	139. Ssangyong
	297. Pohang Steel	185. Korea Explosives
	322. Sunkyong	209. Pohang Steel
	338. Kukje	216. Hyosung
	376. Korea Explosives	413. Doosan

Sources: *Fortune*, August 1976, August 1980, and August 1984 issues.

TAIWAN BUSINESS GROUPS:
FAMILIAL NETWORKS

A simple description of Taiwan's business groups (*jituanqiye* in Chinese) is enough to reveal sharp differences between the Taiwanese case and the other two. One of the most obvious differences is the size and importance of Taiwanese groups in that country's economy. Japanese and South Korean business groups are central features of their respective economies, and include, as member firms in some cluster, most leading industrial firms. In Taiwan, however, the business groups do not occupy nearly so central a position. Of the largest five hundred manufacturing firms in Taiwan, only about 40 percent belong to business groups; moreover, some of these firms are not leaders in their own sector of production. Instead, in Taiwan, many large enterprises remain single-unit operations and are not included within any business group at all. The lack of centrality is reflected in the total sales figure for the 743 firms which belong to the top 96 business groups, which only accounts for a modest percentage of Taiwan's GNP.

The differences in the size of business groups in Taiwan also testify to their lack of centrality. On average, Taiwanese groups have fewer and smaller member firms than do the business groups in Japan and Korea, and the total assets and sales figures of Taiwanese business groups are much lower than the figures for the other two countries.

The differences of size and centrality of the Taiwan business groups point to more fundamental organizational differences. First, Chinese business groups have none of the tightly coupled vertical ties (both in terms of production and ownership) that characterize, in different ways, Japanese keiretsu and Korean chaebol. Instead, although they have fewer firms per group and the firms themselves have a smaller percentage of total sales per industrial sector when compared to the other two cases, Taiwanese business groups typically diversify their holdings. As table 15.15 shows, Taiwanese business groups have, on average, 7.76 firms; those few firms are spread in an average of four different industrial sectors. Moreover, none of the ninety-six business groups are solely based on vertical linkages among member firms within the same business sector. Instead of being vertically integrated, tightly controlled sets of firms, Taiwanese business groups are agglomerations of different-size firms—mostly small—in different economic sectors.

Taiwanese groups have several isomorphic organizational features that set them off from South Korean and Japanese business groups. First, in contrast to Japan where 90 percent of business-group firms are publicly held, in Taiwan only 10 percent of all firms in the business groups are joint stock firms. Moreover, only 40 percent of the ninety-six business groups have one or more publicly listed firms. Instead, the prevailing ownership pattern is one of private family control. Taiwanese enterprise groups are owned either by a single family

Table 15.15   Summary Statistics of Taiwan's 96 Business Groups, 1983

Avg. no. core persons per business group	2.90
Avg. no. of firms per business group	7.76
Avg. positions in individual firms	7.18
Avg. no. of industrial sectors per group	4.00
Mean no. of workers per business group	3,456
Median no. of workers per group	1,396
Mean no. of workers per firm	459
Median no. of workers per firm	90
Avg. year of firm establishment	1971
Avg. sales per business group (million NT$)	633.68
Avg. sales per firm (million NT$)	103.20

Source: Zhonghua Zhengxinso 1985.

or by several individuals in limited partnership; in the Chinese context, partnerships amount to a form of family ownership (Wong 1985).

Second, firm financing in Taiwan differs from both Japan and South Korea. Japanese business groups rely heavily on equity markets and bank loans to raise funds, hence Japan's extraordinarily large financial markets. South Korean business groups instead rely heavily on debt financing, most of which is controlled by the state; South Korea is Asia's largest debtor nation. Taiwanese business groups, in contrast, rely largely on curb market financing. Financial institutions, including banks and cooperative credit associations, supply 31.2 percent of firm funds, usually in the form of short-term operating loans. The capital and money markets supply only 8.4 percent of funds. By far the largest source of money, more than 60 percent, comes from privately arranged loans from family and friends, as well as from retained earnings. The state-owned financial institutions invest very little in private enterprises; partly for this reason Taiwan has one of the largest foreign reserves of any country in the world.

Third, Taiwanese business-group firms are typically only loosely integrated. For example, according to our data there are only limited capital transfers (an average of 0.66 capital links per firm) and equally limited market transactions among firms in a group. Even more significant, the business groups lack a unified command or management structure. What occurs, instead, is that every firm duplicates a command structure (see table 15.16). The same set of people, usually the owners and their close relatives, holds multiple managerial, often identical positions in several firms within the group, and sometimes several positions within a single firm. Business groups are loosely coupled networks of firms owned by the same individual or related persons who join together in multiple enterprises. Although there are Taiwanese patriarchs, their control of enterprise groups is less certain, less centralized, and more circumscribed than is typical for heads of chaebol. South Korean chaebol owners, holding one position at the top, exercise their authority through all the firms in the group, all

Table 15.16   Management Isomorphism for Top Six Taiwanese *Jituanqiye*, 1983

Group	Firms	Core Persons	Relationship	Positions Held by Core Persons		
				Director	Manager	Stockholder
Formosa	18	2	two brothers	10	5	14
Linden	12	1	—	5	0	1
Tainan	33	11	two families	28	7	59
Yue Loong	10	1	—	7	2	4
Far Eastern	17	4	family and one friend	9	8	10
Shin Kong	21	5	one family	21	12	18

Source: Zhonghua Zhengxinso 1985.

the way down to the last employee in the smallest firm. The duplication of positions in Taiwanese business groups suggests the weakness or boundedness of authority structures in that economy and the necessity for maintaining face-to-face relations in order to sustain control.

Finally, like Japan, but unlike South Korea, Taiwanese business groups rely extensively on subcontracting relations with nongroup firms. Unlike Japan, however, subcontract relations are neither exclusive nor necessarily long lasting. Small firms typically supply goods or services for more than one firm. In fact, it is not unusual for several small- and middle-sized firms to create fairly short-lived production networks to provide components for assembly in a business-group company.

The unstructured character of Taiwanese business groups has several institutional sources (see Orrù 1991). First is the Chinese system of equal inheritance for all sons—a system which favors the fragmentation of family holdings from generation to generation (see Wong 1985). Second is the centrality of family relations in business activities, which allows new firms to be established over night, thanks to the pooling of financial and human resources of the extended family. The business groups in Taiwan are, after all, selected family firms which succeeded best in their economic activities. Third is the state policy of noninterference in the private sector. As Scitovsky describes it, "In Taiwan, today, government does not have the strong ascendancy it still has in Korea, and economic controls tend to be moderate" (1985:223). The Taiwanese policy is that market forces should be left to their own devices; competition is enhanced by the presence of large numbers of small firms, not by the presence of few, giant corporations. Accordingly, the Taiwanese state has reinforced the role of family-centered business groups by refusing to influence through direct intervention the growth of selected firms in selected industrial sectors.

The picture emerging on the Taiwanese case, then, is again one of isomorphic organizational structures which are surrounded, in the cultural and political arena, by institutionalized practices that reinforce organizational homogeneity. Most relevant to this pattern of organizational forms is that it well served Taiwan's role in the international market. Through their flexible organizational structures Taiwanese firms have been able to adjust readily to changing market demands in textiles, leather goods, electrical appliances, and small metal products. Again, meeting the demands of its institutional environment has favored, not hindered, Taiwan's organizational fitness in the technical environment.

Institutionalization and Isomorphism

Enterprise groups in Japan, South Korea, and Taiwan display distinctive organizational patterns of ownership, management, finance, and production. Measures of isomorphism confirm the uniformity of firm relations within each country and, equally, the differences among them. These distinctive characteristics are summarized in table 15.17. The economies of these nations are not reducible to the business groups we examined, of course, but these groups are significant economic actors in their respective economies and their isomorphism demands explanation.

Why are business groups so uniform within each market economy, yet so different in comparison with the others? Multiple answers are necessary for a full account, but they are not reducible to purely economic variables—the pressures of technical environments or patterns of competitive isomorphism. Business groups might be explained as competitive collusions—the opportunistic response to technical environmental pressures in northeast Asia. The organizational isomorphisms we identified, however, cannot simply be explained as the attempt to achieve market fitness. Business groups are too widespread and too isomorphic to be viewed as idiosyncratic responses to market factors. Moreover, multiple social institutions in each society support the

Table 15.17   Organizational Characteristics of Business Groups

	Japan	South Korea	Taiwan
Ownership patterns	Shareholding of group firms	State-financed family groups	Family ownership and partnership
Intragroup networks	Cross-shareholding mutual dominance	Strict hierarchical structure from top	Multiple positions of core personnel
Intergroup networks	Cross-shares, loans, and joint ventures	Coordination through banks and government	Cross-investment by individuals and firms
Subcontract relations	Structures or semiformal	Insignificant	Informal and highly flexible
Investment patterns	Vertical and horizontal integration	Vertical and horizontal integration	Vertical integration or diversification
Growth patterns	Bank-financed group activities	State-financed sector growth	Informal financing and reinvestment

formation of patterned firm relations, as we described, and do not press organizations toward the Western idea of autonomously competing firms. Technical requirements alone cannot explain East Asian isomorphism.

Following the arguments of institutional theorists, we claim that each society creates a context of fiscal, political, as well as social institutions that limit and direct the development of fit organizational forms. In all three economies we discussed, but especially in South Korea and Japan, the important role of the state in economic affairs leads us to believe that institutional and normative factors are particularly important to organizational viability in those nations. Asian firms, like all firms, operate in an institutional environment that presents a structure of constraints and possibilities, but, most importantly, of normative forms of economic action. Each of these economies, our data suggest, fashions itself after a distinctive institutional environment, generating a characteristic pattern of business relationships. These relationships are not simply ones of convenience or efficiency, but represent enactments of socially acceptable, institutionalized forms of economic behavior—they are the manifestations of a normative structure that underlies economic activity and provides market order. Clearly, the firms in these economies are capitalist and profit seeking, but they seek profit not abstractly, but with a knowledge of legitimate strategies for gaining market advantage. This they accomplish by merging together the technical and institutional requirements of their environments.

Different fundamental principles of control, which are not solely economic in character but rather are drawn from other institutional sources such as the state, the community, and the family, are at work in each society. These principles inform predictable social relations in multiple arenas, including the economic, and are supported in various ways by state agencies.

Japanese enterprise groups enact a communitarian ideal. Like residential, intellectual, and other forms of community, Japanese business groups maintain clearly defined status relations among firms, some of which are egalitarian and others hierarchical. While there are clearly more important and more influential firms within enterprise groups, the decision-making unit is the group, and command is exercised not by fiat but by consensus. Decisions are made considering what is best for the collectivity, not simply for individual firms, however powerful.

The South Korean chaebol are an expression of a patrimonial principle. The chaebol are, in a Weberian typology "patrimonial households"—organizations dominated by a patriarch and his children, but extending beyond them to include professional managers from outside the family. These industrial empires are the property of an authoritarian leader and his designees who manage not by consensus, but by centralized command supported by the state.

Taiwanese business groups enact yet another principle, that of the familial network. While they are based on family ties as in South Korea, the Taiwanese business groups do not express the will of a single patriarch but rather the interests of an extended family where division of financial holdings on the death of the patriarch is the rule (Cohen 1976). There is patriarchalism in Taiwan, to be sure, but it is more contested and less unified. Unlike Korean patriarchs who may direct their business empires even in the absence of a corporate position, Taiwanese business leaders assume multiple executive posts to reinforce their authority.

East Asian enterprise groups are both an expression and a product of these three organizing principles. None is a corruption of a mythical ideal of competitive market fitness; rather, each is an enactment of socially constructed technical and institutional requirements. While these three principles are subject to variation in each economy, exceptions are variations on a common theme. For example, the relatively nonpatriarchal character of the Daewoo chaebol is frequently noted because it breaks the expected and understood patriarchal pattern of chaebol organization (e.g., Hahn, Kim, and Kim 1987; Chang 1987).

The new institutionalism has been instrumental in calling attention to the cultural, political, and normative pressures present in the environment, and it has proven useful in the analysis of organizations which are particularly vulnerable to these pressures. Yet the new institutionalism seems to have shortchanged itself by claiming only partial relevance in the analysis of organizational environments. As we showed in this study, the new institutionalism is just as fruitful (if not more fruitful) in the analysis of organizational environments with a strong technical component. Institutional features need not be limited to explaining the achievement of legitimacy in organizations; institutional features can be shown to be just as crucial to achieving the technical and competitive fitness of organizations. We have demonstrated that this is indeed the case in East Asian enterprise groups.

If one assumes, in a Western vein, that firm individuation is the natural state of an orderly market, then the organizational principles we have described can only be understood as institutional obstacles to a successful and competitive economy. Indeed, the U.S. officials' breakup of the Japanese *zaibatsu* after World War II was an expression of this presumption. Today's success of East Asian economies, including Japan's adoption of the *kigyo shudan* arrangement, challenges this fundamental assumption of Western economic analyses. From a perspective which integrates institutional and technical requirements, we argue that the patterns of institutional isomorphism observed in Japan, Taiwan, and South Korea aim not only at achieving legitimacy, but also serve the function of market order by providing norms that channel economic activity. Indeed, breaches of institutional patterns of economic behavior would be disruptive in the respective economies in which they are found. Japanese firms that act without regard for the business group of which they are a part create chaos and impeded successful economic planning and investment strategy. Taiwanese executives who do not consider the interests of the lineage likewise disrupt an orderly market. East Asian economies have prospered not because they have unilaterally adapted to technical environmental requirements, but because they have successfully institutionalized the principles of market activity suited to their sociocultural environment and to their strategies of economic development.

Notes

1. Our sources of information differ for each society, but are roughly comparable. For Japan, we relied on annual reports of firms collected by private research institutes (Dodwell Marketing Consultants 1984; Toyo Keizai Shimposha 1986a and 1986b) and by the Japanese government (Kosei Torihiki Iinkai Jimukyoku 1983). Besides identifying firm membership in enterprise groups, these reports contain information on joint shareholding, bank loans, and interlocking directorates as well as the standard information on firm size, sales, and assets. For additional data sources as well as for their interpretation, we have drawn on the excellent discussions in Aoki 1984; Caves and Uekusa 1976; Futatsugi 1982, 1986; Hadley 1970; Kobayashi 1980; Nakatani 1982, 1984; Okumura 1982, 1984, 1985; Sumiya 1986; and Ueda 1983, 1986.

For South Korea, we relied on the statistics on enterprise groups collected by the *Hankook Ilbo* (Korean Daily News) and on those compiled in the 1986 *Korean Directory of Firms*. The first source contains the identification of firms in enterprise groups, statistics about each of the top fifty enterprise groups, and information about each individual firm. The second source lists owners, managers, and (when applicable) major shareholders and gives some information about product specialization as well as standard information on firm assets and liabilities. We supplemented these statistics with newspaper reports and journalistic accounts, and the few recent scholarly examinations (Lee 1986; Koo 1984; Hahn, Kim, and Kim 1987).

For Taiwan, we relied on the extensive survey done by the China Credit Information Service (Zhonghua Zhengxinso). Published on a yearly basis since 1971, this survey identifies firms within business groups and provides data on assets, liabilities, product specialization, management structure and key personnel in the business group, and a list of principal owners and managers in individual firms. These data are supplemented by journalistic, anecdotal accounts of specific enterprise groups and a few scholarly examinations on related topics (Gold 1986; Numazaki 1986). To add to our interpretation of the Taiwan material, we also drew upon Wong Siu-lun's (1985, 1988) and Redding and Tam's (1986) discussions of the similarly organized Chinese family-based enterprises in Hong Kong.

16 Institutional Change and Ecological Dynamics

JITENDRA V. SINGH,
DAVID J. TUCKER, AND
AGNES G. MEINHARD

During roughly the last decade, ecological and institutional theories of organization have generated considerable interest among students of organization. Organizational ecology has mainly been concerned with changes in populations of organizations over time (Aldrich 1979; Carroll 1984, 1987, 1988; Hannan and Freeman 1977, 1984, 1989; Singh, House, and Tucker 1986; Singh, Tucker, and House 1986; Singh and Lumsden 1990). For the most part, ecological studies have systematically examined founding and death rates of different organizational forms in various populations, although recently some work has also addressed endogenous change in individual organizations (Singh, Tucker, and Meinhard 1988) and proposed an expanded scope for organizational ecology which includes intraorganizational change (Burgelman and Singh 1988). Institutional theory, on the other hand, is mainly concerned with how the institutional environment, comprised of socially created beliefs and cognitions, widely held in society and reinforced by corporate actors, affects organizations. In an influential statement of these ideas, Meyer and Rowan (1977) argued that modern societies contain institutionalized rules in the form of rationalized myths, and these beliefs shape organizational forms. Thus, sociocultural pressures to conform to rationalized myths, rather than technical demands, affect organizations. This institutional isomorphism by which organizations assimilate institutional rules into their forms makes organizations in an organizational field more homogeneous over time (DiMaggio and Powell 1983). Through processes of institutionalization, the socially created beliefs and cognitions take on a taken-for-granted character and become the natural way to act (Zucker 1983).

In this chapter we explore the relationship between ecological and institutional approaches empirically by studying changes in a population of voluntary social service organizations over time. Although there has been some debate about whether institutional or technical and competitive forces better explain change in organizations (Astley and Van de Ven 1983; Scott 1987b: ch. 8), we premise our theoretical approach here firmly in the fundamental complementarity of the two approaches.

Related to the links between ecological and institutional theories of organization, two important questions can be raised. First, one may ask how changes in the institutional environment affect the ecological dynamics of population change. Second, one can also investigate the ecological processes that culminate in institutional change.[1] We concentrate here on the former question, treating institutional changes as exogenous and studying their impact on processes of population change. In general formulations of ecological theory, it is argued that population change can occur through processes of founding, death, and organizational change (Hannan and Freeman 1989: ch. 1; Singh, Tucker, and Meinhard 1988). Therefore, we study the impact of institutional changes on all three processes.

Some critics of the ecological approach (e.g., Perrow 1985a, 1986: ch. 6) have forcefully drawn attention to the lack of emphasis on power in this perspective. In a partial effort to redress this lack, we concentrate in particular on the role of the state in the institutional environment, especially through its various agencies and programs. In modern societies, the nation-state is a vital source of resources and coercive power (DiMaggio 1983; DiMaggio and Powell 1983) and often imposes uniform structures and procedures on organizations. Thus the state is an important source of isomorphism in organizational fields and in shaping the demography of organizational populations (Scott 1987: ch. 8). Therefore, this study also illustrates one way in which power considerations may fruitfully be incorporated into ecological approaches to organization.

Overview of Earlier Research

This chapter represents one more step in a series of studies examining change in a population of voluntary social service organizations (VSSOs) in the metropolitan Toronto, Canada, area during 1970–82. In earlier studies, we investigated the liability of newness—the higher propensity of young organizations to die—in this population (Tucker, Singh, and House 1984) and the processes underlying this propensity (Singh, Tucker, and House 1986). In a separate paper, we examined the impact of intraorganizational changes on mortality rates; the findings revealed that although core changes were disruptive to survival, peripheral changes were frequently adaptive, suggesting the complementarity of adaptation and selection ideas (Singh, House, and Tucker 1986). Another study addressed how changes in the institutional environment of VSSOs altered the ecological dynamics of founding and death patterns (Tucker et al. 1988) in the population. Tucker, Singh, and Meinhard (1990) extended the findings of this previous study by demonstrating that founding patterns of specialist and generalist VSSOs were differentially affected by institutional changes and ecological dynamics. The effects of ecological dynamics and institutional changes were much stronger for specialists than generalists, suggesting that founding patterns differ by organizational form. After controlling for environmental and life-cycle effects, Tucker, Singh, and Meinhard (1987) found that environmental and organizational conditions at founding systematically affected long-run organizational mortality. In another recent study, Singh, Tucker and Meinhard (1988), in a departure from most ecological studies of birth and death rates, examined competing theoretical models of rates of change in VSSOs and found that rates of change in some core organizational features decreased with age and rates of change in some peripheral organizational features increased with age. Based on these results, it was suggested that the scope of organizational ecology be expanded to encompass birth, death, and change rates in organizations (Burgelman and Singh 1988; Singh, Tucker, and Meinhard 1988). Here we summarize the results of several previous studies (Singh, Tucker, and House 1986; Tucker, Singh, and Meinhard 1990; Tucker et al. 1988) and also present new results on the effects of institutional changes on rates of change in organizational features.

THE NATURE OF VSSOs

We define voluntary social service organizations (VSSOs) as "organizations governed by a board of directors and that operate on a nonprofit basis and are concerned with changing, constraining and/or supporting human behavior" (Singh, Tucker, and House 1986:175). We regard the population of VSSOs studied here to be similar to other groups of human service organizations since they are quite diverse. Some are small and rely mostly on volunteer labor. Others are large, sophisticated organizations employing professional staff and using advanced computer technology. The services offered range from highly specialized legal, medical, and counseling services performed by professional staff to settlement and interpretation services provided by volunteers (Singh, Tucker, and House 1986:175).

Because VSSOs have somewhat indeterminate technologies (Tucker 1981:605; Singh, Tucker, and House 1986:174), they are limited in their ability to demonstrate their effectiveness in terms of conventional output, efficiency, or process criteria. Under these conditions, Daft (1983:107–8) argues that social criteria, like the satisfaction and approval of external constituencies, are more likely to be used to judge effectiveness. This suggests that VSSOs are specifically vulnerable to conditions and constraints that have their origins in the institutional environment, and that factors such as the acquisition of external institutional support significantly affect their survival chances (Singh, Tucker, and House 1986). Thus, VSSOs are higher on the institutional (Meyer and Rowan 1977; Meyer and Scott 1983a) than the technical dimension, which implies that this population is eminently suited to investigating the links between institutional and ecological theories.

CHANGE IN THE INSTITUTIONAL
ENVIRONMENT OF VSSOs

Based on the view that institutional environments can be conceptualized in terms of the decisions and activities of a few powerful institutional actors (Rowan 1982; Tolbert and Zucker 1983), we have argued elsewhere (Tucker et al. 1988) that the most significant actor in the institutional environment of VSSOs is the state and its respective agencies and programs. Because of its control over the authoritative allocation of values and resources in society, the state is considered by organization theorists (e.g., Aldrich 1979; Brown and Schneck 1979; Freeman 1979) to be the major factor accounting for patterns of population change. We contend that this is particularly true for the voluntary social services sector because historically it has had a close association with the state, frequently regarded as complementary to or, in some circumstances, an appendage of state-operated service systems (e.g., Webb and Webb 1912; Wilensky and Lebeaux 1958; Splane 1965; Kramer 1981).

In 1971, the Canadian federal government implemented a program called Opportunities for Youth (OFY), the most significant of a number of programs introduced by the government during the 1960s and early 1970s aimed at promoting increased citizen participation in solving social problems (Loney 1977). The relevance of OFY for our research is that its implementation elaborated an institutional rule that enhanced the legitimacy of dealing with social problems by creating new organizations. It also generated new resources supplied directly by the government. One implication is that the patterns of foundings and deaths of VSSOs may have been influenced by these changes in the institutional environment.

By 1970, the youth constituency had emerged as an important and visible object of political concern in Canada, due in part to demographic changes: young people had become a significantly larger proportion of the population (Committee on Youth 1971). Also among the young was an intense dissatisfaction with the status quo. This manifested itself in a variety of ways, including the organization of public-interest and advocacy groups, sit-ins and demonstrations, the articulation and pursuit of alternate life-styles, and the rejection of employment not seen as personally meaningful or socially relevant (Best 1974).

Concerned with growing signs of discontent among youth, the federal government appointed the Committee on Youth in 1968. Its draft report, presented to the government in 1970 (Best 1974:142), projected increasing rates of unemployment among youth and documented the alienation of youth from existing social institutions. In 1970–71, when unemployment among youth increased sharply, the federal government quickly instituted a program, first developed by the Company of Young Canadians in the mid-1960s, providing resources directly to local community groups to enable them to implement projects regarded as socially useful (Gwyn 1972). Specifically, the federal government supported demonstration projects that, while addressing various social problems and/or providing services to various community groups, were organized, implemented, and operated by the young themselves. These demonstration projects proved very successful, and the OFY program was subsequently launched with a budget of just over $14 million. Because of the popularity of OFY, the budget was increased by $10 million over the first summer. The following year in 1972, the national budget for the funding of youth-initiated projects was increased by 900 percent to $250 million and the "Great Ottawa Grant Boom" was under way (Gwyn 1972).

The rationale for the implementation of OFY constituting a major institutional change for the VSSO population is threefold. First, data on the initial funding sources of VSSOs show that of those organizations born in the OFY period, most did not receive funds from OFY at founding, or from other similar government programs. Further, a comparison of VSSOs founded in the OFY period with those founded later shows that a larger number of those founded in the non-OFY period received money in their first year of operation (28.5 percent as compared to 23.0 percent). A reasonable interpretation of these data is that the founding of VSSOs in the OFY period reflects the influence of symbolic considerations.

Second, the introduction of a new government funding program, like OFY, might normally be assumed to result in an expansion and diversification in the service delivery activities of existing organizations as opposed to the proliferation of new organizations. Since existing organizations are already in operation, their initial costs of organization have been met (Olsen 1965:47). Thus, compared to new organizations, existing organizations may be competitively advantaged in going after new funds. Two interrelated factors question the applicability of this argument to VSSOs. First, the voluntary sector is characterized by ease of entry. The material and human resources required to set up a VSSO are small. Most of the VSSOs in our population initially did not have a budget or paid staff, and the median board size was only six people. Also, the general characteristics of the voluntary sector—highly dispersed, not regarded as economically significant, and constrained by government legislation from engaging in self-interested political lobbying—are not the ones usually associated with high barriers to entry (Pfeffer and Salancik 1978; Aldrich 1979). Second, although OFY's selection criteria were not formalized, they did present the expectation that the work performed would be controlled by project participants themselves and be innovative in nature, that is, different from work done by existing organizations (Best 1974:144–60). This meant that for existing organizations to receive funds, they had at least to incur the cost of appearing to have changed, for example, by an adjustment in internal reporting relationships to accommodate a new, autonomous unit. Since there was an upper limit on the size of individual grants and no guarantee of future funding, this effectively lowered the value of the benefit to existing organizations while increasing the risks (Olsen 1965). Based on the above arguments, it seems reasonable to accept that OFY's endorsement of the legitimacy of local community groups engaging in independent organizational activity to achieve collective ends may have influenced the proliferation of VSSOs in metro Toronto.

Third, policy theorists argue that, in democratic societies, political decision making involves choices not only about the ends of policy but also about the means of ensuring compliance with political decisions (e.g., Lowi 1964, 1970, 1972; Salisbury and Heinz 1970; Sabatier 1975; Hayes 1981). This latter emphasis has focused attention on the content of policy, the different means used by government to ensure compliance with and/or social acceptance of its decisions. One legitimate means of coercion available to government is the use of symbolism (Edelman 1967; Lowi 1970). By the way a particular policy is presented and the meaning ascribed to it, government may consciously attempt to evoke and reinforce particular behaviors in policy constituents (also see Piven and Cloward 1977). Best (1974), in a study of the origin and nature of youth policy in Canada, addressed the question of the symbolic significance of OFY. He concluded that although OFY, by its nature and process, was a distributive policy (i.e., resources were distributed in a highly disaggregated form to individual projects), its impact at an aggregate level was intended to be mainly "constituent or symbolic" (Best 1974:160). While government was concerned about the value of projects supported by OFY in helping solve social problems, it was more concerned with the symbolic impact of OFY in convincing youth that the government was responding to their demands for meaningful participation and socially relevant work (Best 1974:162; see also Houston 1972, and Loney 1977). Thus the founding of VSSOs in the OFY period may reflect the influence of pressure on constituents to conform with government-initiated institutional rules that defined such behavior as socially legitimate.

While there was some initial resistance to and criticism of the federal government's administration of OFY by established voluntary organizations, and by other levels of government (Paris 1972; Best 1974; Loney 1977), conditions defining new organizational responses to social problems as legitimate persisted until 1975 (e.g., Wharf and Carter 1972; Social Planning Council of Metropolitan Toronto 1976). By the midseventies, however, some important changes were occurring. Concern with economic issues had replaced concern with social issues. Inflation in Canada was at record levels, and the view was emerging that if it was to be controlled, and economic recovery nurtured, governments were going to have to restrain and redirect their spending. The result was actions by the federal government, and by the Ontario provincial government, that undermined the support of local community groups in seeking organizational solutions to social problems.

Beginning in 1976, the federal government terminated OFY and replaced it with programs emphasizing the efficiency advantages of using established organizations, government agencies, and corporations as employment sites for youth and others (Economic Council of Canada 1976, 1977). The central thrusts of these programs were economic. They were designed to prepare persons for entry into the labor market and, coincidentally, support the productivity of the host organization (Economic Council of Canada 1977). From these developments, it was clear that the federal government had shifted its policy emphasis away from legitimating the founding and maintenance of nonprofit organizations, like VSSOs, that were controlled by project participants and mainly concerned with solving social problems.

Under the Canadian constitution, provincial governments are formally responsible for public policy dealing with social services and social welfare. In Ontario, the provincial government, in its 1975 budget (McKeough 1975), indicated that it would be moving to restrain growth in government expenditures. The following year a comprehensive expenditure restraint program was introduced (McKeough 1976). Social expenditures were singled out for restraint, resulting in most social services being limited to a 5.5 percent increase in funding for fiscal year 1976–77 (Puckett and Tucker 1976). Since the annual rate of inflation at the time was approximately 11 percent, this represented an actual reduction in levels of expenditure. In the same way that the introduction of OFY seemed to legitimate the founding of VSSOs, and provide opportunities and incentives favoring their creation, the introduction of the Ontario government's Restraint Program seemed to reduce legitimacy, limit opportunities, and be a disincentive to creating organizations.

Method

DATA COLLECTION

Sources of data used to identify and characterize the VSSO population and establish founding dates are mainly archival (Singh, Tucker, and House 1986; Singh, House, and Tucker 1986). They include (1) files, documents, and indexes maintained by the federal, provincial, and municipal levels of government; (2) files, lists, and documents made available by local planning, coordinating, and funding agencies (e.g., the United Way, the Community Information Centre); and (3) the annual reports of individual VSSOs.

The process of identifying the study population was an exhaustive one and was implemented in two phases, the first in 1981 and the second in 1983. Identical procedures were used in both phases. We began by compiling a comprehensive list of all the distinct voluntary associations and collectives that came into existence in metro Toronto in the period 1970–82. This list was compared to the *Provincial Index of Incorporated Non-share Organizations*, and all associations and collectives without incorporation numbers were eliminated, leaving a list of 681 organizations. Archival data were then reviewed to determine if each organization on the list was an independent operating unit and conformed to our definition of a VSSO. The number of organizations subsequently eliminated was 230, leaving a study population of 451.[2]

RESEARCH DESIGN

Given the nature of the questions raised in this chapter, our interest is in foundings, deaths, and organizational changes over time. Thus, it seemed unlikely that a cross-sectional design would be appropriate here. Cross-sectional designs implicitly assume that the process is in temporal equilibrium, that is, the phenomenon of interest is unchanging over time (Tuma and Hannan 1984). We used a longitudinal approach for the study of foundings, deaths, and changes. For the study of VSSO foundings, we used a time series design to analyze quarterly founding frequency data. For the study of deaths and changes, as in previous studies (Singh, Tucker, and House 1986; Singh, House, and Tucker 1986; Tucker et al. 1988), we used event history analysis to analyze the data (Tuma, Hannan, and Groeneveld 1979; Carroll and Delacroix 1982).

MEASUREMENT

Foundings

We define organizational founding as the date of formal incorporation of a VSSO. Our underlying premise is that incorporation is a clear signal from the founders of the VSSO of their intent to maintain the organization as an ongoing entity. The dependent variable in the analysis of foundings, the frequency of foundings, is the number of VSSOs founded every quarter from January 1970 to December 1982.

Deaths

We define a VSSO as dead when it ceases to exist as a legal entity. Thus, mergers count as organizational deaths. The frequency of deaths for this population is the quarterly number of deaths in the population during the period January 1970 to 1982.

Density

Density is the total number of VSSOs alive at any point in time in the population. It is useful to bear in mind the identity relationship:

$$\text{density}_t = \text{density}_{t-1} + (\text{foundings}_{t-1} - \text{deaths}_{t-1}).$$

Organizational Form

VSSOs differ from each other in terms of the number of domains in which they provide services. Some provide services in a single domain, while others operate in multiple domains. Approximately 48 percent of VSSOs offered services in a single domain (e.g., health, or leisure, or education), about 33 percent offered services in two domains, and the remaining 19 percent operated in three or more domains. For the purposes of these analyses, organizations that operated in a single domain were called specialists, and organizations that operated in three or more domains were called generalists. Thus, organizations that operated in two domains were omitted. This has two implications. One, dropping the intermediate group helps distinguish between the specialists and generalists more clearly. Two, the effects of the specialism and generalism dummy variables are relative to this intermediate group.

External Legitimacy

We use external legitimacy to mean an organization having its actions endorsed by powerful external collective actors (Stinchcombe 1968) and developing strong relationships with external constituencies. Legitimacy is a conferred status and, as such, is usually controlled by those outside the organization (Pfeffer and Salancik 1978). It results from a congruence between societal values and organizational actions (Dowling and Pfeffer 1975; Meyer and Rowan 1977).

We used three different indicators of legitimacy. A listing in the *Community Directory of Metropolitan Toronto,* an authoritative reference source on acceptable services in the metropolitan area which is frequently consulted by clients and referral services, was the first indicator. A dummy variable, which takes the value 1 when the organization is listed in the directory but is 0 otherwise, described this. The issuance of a charitable registration number by Revenue Canada was the second indicator of legitimacy. This registration number is only given out to bona fide charities after an intensive review. One important consequence of having a charitable registration number, in addition to having Revenue Canada's stamp of approval, is that all contributions to the VSSO become tax deductible. This increases the organization's access to resources. A dummy variable, receipt of charitable registration number, was created, similar to the one for community directory listing.

The third indicator of legitimacy was the size of an organization's board of directors at the time of founding. Earlier research has suggested that creating boards of directors is an important way in which organizations attempt to co-opt (Selznick 1949) important external constituencies. In addition to accessing more resources and developing interfirm commitments, firms use board of directors to establish legitimacy (Pfeffer and Salancik 1978:161) and gain the support of other institutional actors in the external environment.[3]

Institutional Changes

We defined institutional changes in terms of the occurrence of two historical events in the context of this population. As described above, the Opportunities for Youth period (OFY) lasted from 1971 to 1975, and the Provincial Restraint period (RES) lasted from 1976 to 1981. OFY and RES were treated as dummy variables coded 1 when present and 0 otherwise.

Death Rate

The death rate is described by the hazard rate, $h(t)$, which gives the instantaneous rate of death at each instant of a VSSO's life. The hazard rate is given by

$$h(t) = \lim_{\Delta t \to 0} \frac{\text{Pr[death } (t, \ t + \Delta t) \mid \text{alive until } t]}{\Delta t}.$$

Rates of Organizational Change

We gathered data on changes in name, sponsor, location, service area, goals, client groups, conditions-of-service provision, chief executive, and structure. The propensity of organizations to change was described by a stochastic function, the instantaneous transition rate, $r(t)$. Conceptually, this transition rate is similar to the instantaneous death rate, $h(t)$, the hazard of death described above, and used in earlier research (Carroll and Delacroix 1982; Freeman, Carroll, and Hannan 1983; Singh, Tucker, and House 1986), although substantive differences between death and change make for important peculiarities in estimating rates of change.[4] The instantaneous rate of change is given by

$$r(t) = \lim_{\Delta t \to 0} \frac{\text{Pr[change } (t, \ t + \Delta t)]}{\Delta t}.$$

Unlike the hazard of death, this rate is not conditional upon the event not having occurred until time t. Intuitively, higher rates of change imply shorter average waiting times between changes, and vice versa.

Name change referred to an actual change in the identifying title of the organization. Sponsor change referred to a change in the organization that supported, promoted, or otherwise actively sponsored the focal organization. Location change measured a change in the physical quarters of the organization. Service area change referred to a change in the domain in which an organization offered services, for example, legal, socio-rehabilitative, education, and so forth. Goal change measured whether the goals of the organization had changed, for example, advocacy, information and referral, raising and allocating funds, and so forth. Client group change referred to whether an organization had changed the body of clients to whom it was offering services, for example, families, elderly, children. Change in conditions of service measured whether there had been a change in the number of criteria or conditions to be satisfied by a client in order for services to be provided by the organization, for example, crime victim, physically handicapped, geographic location, economically disadvantaged. Chief executive change measured whether there had been a succession in the executive head of the organization. Finally, structural change referred to a change in the structure of the organization, either through the addition or deletion of subunits. All occurrences of these changes, and their timings, were noted. The change variables were coded 1 in the year the change occurred and 0 otherwise.

Institutional Effects on
Patterns of Founding

Ecological analyses of organizational foundings have examined founding patterns in relation to previous patterns of foundings and deaths (Delacroix and Carroll 1983) and density (Hannan and Freeman 1987). In a study of foundings of newspapers in Ireland and Argentina during 1800–1925, Delacroix and Carroll (1983) found curvilinear relationships between current foundings and prior foundings and prior deaths. The underlying argument was that, initially, organizational deaths create free-floating resources which can easily be reassembled into new organizations. But an increase in deaths signals a noxious environment to entrepreneurs, who stay away from creating organizations. In a similar fashion, organizational deaths initially signal a supportive environment and encourage new foundings. But as foundings increase, competition between the organizations increases, which depresses further foundings.

Hannan and Freeman (1987), in a study of foundings of labor unions in the United States during 1836–1975, argued that density is curvilinearly related with foundings of labor unions. Initially, increasing density enhances the legitimacy of the organizational form, thereby increasing foundings, but as density increases further, competitive pressures increase, which depresses foundings. Their findings supported these arguments.

Other studies have also focused on the impact of institutional environments on organizational foundings (Carroll and Huo 1986; Hannan 1986a). Carroll and Huo (1986), in a study of changes in the structure of a local newspaper industry in California over as 125-year period, found that institutional variables, especially political turmoil, affected foundings, but task environmental variables affected performance more. Hannan (1986a), in work related to Hannan and Freeman (1987), argued for the complementarity of ecological and institutional approaches to the study of foundings. While both studies emphasized the importance of examining the impact of institutional variables on organizational foundings, they did not address how institutional changes affect the ecological dynamics within the population. Here, summarizing earlier work (Tucker, Singh, and Meinhard 1990; Tucker et al. 1988), we report how ecological and institutional variables affect founding patterns of VSSOs and, in particular, how institutional changes affect the ecological dynamics in the population.

OVERALL FOUNDINGS OF VSSOs

Figure 16.1 presents the number of VSSOs founded per quarter during the period 1970–82. As may have been expected, given the findings of earlier research, the data showed cyclical founding patterns. But the overall trend was an increasing one, from 1970 to a high around 1975. Subsequently, except for a surge of foundings during 1981, the trend was a declining one.

We tested the empirical validity of the ecological and institutional arguments as explanations of the overall founding patterns of VSSOs by regressing the time series of quarterly foundings upon the independent variables. The first step in the data analysis was to use ordinary least squares (OLS) procedures. We estimated the coefficients using SHAZAM, an econometric package especially suited to time series analysis. All independent variables were lagged one time period, and the regression equations were of the form

$$B_t = \beta_1 + \beta_2 B_{t-1} + \beta_3 B^2_{t-1} + \beta_4 D_{t-1} + \beta_5 D^2_{t-1} + \beta_6 N_{t-1} + \beta_7 N^2_{t-1}$$
$$+ \beta_8 OFY_{t-1} + \beta_9 RES_{t-1} + U_t,$$

where B_t = number of VSSOs founded in period t;
      D_t = number of VSSO deaths in period t; and
      N_t = number of VSSOs alive in period t.

Frequently, with time series data, autocorrelation is a problem (Kennedy 1985). Therefore, we tested for the presence of first-order autocorrelation using the Durbin-Watson statistic. If the results showed significant first-order autocorrelation, we explicitly specified a first-order autoregressive error term and

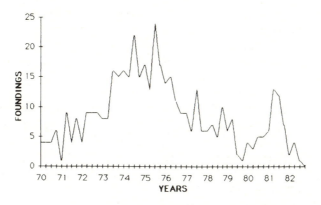

Fig. 16.1. Quarterly foundings of VSSOs, 1970–82.

used maximum likelihood methods to estimate both the autocorrelation parameter ρ and the regression coefficients β (Kennedy 1985:105). Thus,

$$U_t = \rho \, U_{t-1} + \epsilon_t,$$

where $|\rho| < 1$, *and* $E(\epsilon_t) = 0$;
$\qquad E(\epsilon_t \epsilon_s) = 0$, for $s = t$; and
$\qquad E(\epsilon_t \epsilon_s) = \sigma^2$, for $s \neq t$.

Unlike U_t, the autoregressive error term, the error term ϵ_t satisfies the usual OLS assumptions.

However, through exploratory data analysis, we found in some cases that the residuals from a first-order autocorrelation process were still autocorrelated. Since it is known that, with quarterly data, the error terms may be autocorrelated lagged four periods (Kennedy 1985:105; Wallis 1972), we evaluated higher-order autocorrelations as well. We chose the order of the autocorrelation process based on the significance of the autocorrelation coefficients, the explained variance, and the minimum sum of squared residuals, even though the results were not generally very different. Table 16.1 reports the estimates for both the OLS and GLS models.

Column 1 of table 16.1 reports the curvilinear effects of lagged foundings, deaths, density, and the lagged institutional changes on current foundings. The overall model was significant ($p < .01$) and explained 55.1 percent of the variance in current foundings. But there was significant autocorrelation, since the calculated Durbin-Watson statistic ($d = 2.504$) was lower than the upper bound of the appropriate criterion value at the 5 percent level of significance, a commonly accepted test for first-order autocorrelation (Johnston 1972: ch. 8). We next examined a generalized least squares (GLS) model with the same specification (column 2, table 16.1). A fourth-order autocorrelation process provided the best model, and the overall model was significant, explaining 71.2 percent of the variance in current foundings. Both lagged foundings and deaths had significant curvilinear affects on current foundings, although density did not. Lagged OFY, the favorable institutional change, significantly increased foundings, whereas lagged RES, the unfavorable institutional change, significantly decreased foundings, as was expected.

The next substantive question was how the institutional changes affected the ecological dynamics in this population. We were interested in determining whether OFY and RES simply raised or lowered the level of the ecological processes of imitation and competition, or if they changed the nature of the ecological processes. We introduced the OFY and RES dummy variables into both the slope and intercept terms of the previous model. However, due to multicollinearity problems, we were unable to estimate models with all the main effects and interaction terms together and were forced to run separate models for the affects of lagged OFY and lagged RES on the curvilinear dynamics of

Table 16.1 Least Squares Estimates: Ecological and Institutional Effects on Organizational Foundings

Independent Variables	Dependent Variable: Foundings				
	OLS	GLS	GLS	GLS	OLS
Constant	3.074 (3.603)	3.324* (1.980)	1.931** (1.337)	0.147 (1.277)	1.328 (2.508)
Foundings	0.571 (0.351)	1.141* (0.187)	−0.638 (0.425)	1.116** (0.307)	
Foundings²	−0.009 (0.015)	−0.019* (0.009)	0.005 (0.024)	−0.011 (0.013)	
Deaths	2.851* (1.182)	2.079** (0.488)	−0.029 (0.479)	0.401 (1.405)	
Deaths²	−0.340* (0.179)	−0.226** (0.072)	−0.004 (0.088)	−0.063 (0.434)	
Density	0.0005 (0.019)	−0.009 (0.010)			0.018 (0.014)
Density²	−0.000007 (0.00002)	0.000002 (0.00001)			−0.00001 (0.00002)
OFY	3.305* (1.686)	1.124* (0.604)	0.215 (4.285)		−164.59* (83.50)
RES	−2.970 (1.874)	−2.905** (0.789)		2.988 (11.243)	−592.3 (1649.7)
OFY × N					0.685* (0.368)
OFY × N²					−0.0007* (0.0004)
RES × N					2.087 (5.369)
RES × N²					−0.002 (0.004)
OFY × B			0.298 (0.852)		
OFY × B²			−0.032 (0.035)		
OFY × D			1.875 (2.847)		
OFY × D²			0.971 (1.285)		
RES × B				−0.473 (1.079)	
RES × B²				−0.051 (0.069)	
RES × D				−2.874 (4.537)	
RES × D²				0.254 (0.660)	
Adj R^2	0.551	0.712	0.694	0.590	0.578
F-ratio	8.653	16.808	13.580	9.011	9.74
p-level	<.01	<.01	<.01	<.01	<.01

Notes: Standard errors are in parentheses. GLS is at the fourth-order autocorrelation.
*$p < .05$.
**$p < .01$.

lagged foundings and deaths. But for the curvilinear effects of lagged density, we were able to model OFY and RES together. These results are reported in columns 3, 4, and 5 of table 16.1.

We first estimated the coefficients for the main effects of lagged foundings and lagged deaths, lagged OFY, and the interaction terms (column 3). Although a fourth-order autocorrelation process specification gave rise to a significant model overall (adjusted $R^2 = 0.694$), none of the coefficients were significant. This was unexpected and suggested the presence of multicollinearity, since it often gives rise to overall significant models with insignificant coefficients. Even though the presence of multicollinearity does not bias the regression estimates, their standard errors tend to be large, which understates the significance of the estimated coefficients (Johnston 1972; Kennedy 1985; Kmenta 1971). The next model, with the main effects of lagged foundings and deaths, lagged RES, and the interaction terms, with a fourth-order autocorrelation process (column 4), was again significant overall, although, with the exception of lagged foundings, none of the coefficients were significant.

We investigated the multicollinearity problem further by examining the correlation matrix for the independent variables. The correlations between foundings and foundings^2, and deaths and deaths^2 were both quite high (above .90), which was not surprising, because they are monotone functions of each other. The correlations of the interaction terms were also systematically very high (OFY $\times$ B and OFY $\times$ B^2, OFY $\times$ D and OFY $\times$ D^2, RES $\times$ B and RES $\times$ B^2, RES $\times$ D and RES $\times$ D^2). Thus it became clear that the multicollinearity problem was creating difficulties in the estimation of coefficients.[5]

In the final model, with the main effects of lagged density, lagged OFY and lagged RES, and the interaction terms (column 5), the results were somewhat different. An OLS model was adequate, since there was no significant autocorrelation problem. The overall model was significant (adjusted $R^2 = 0.578$), and lagged OFY and its interactions with the curvilinear effects of density were also significant. On the one hand, these results suggested that OFY had fundamentally altered the nature of the ecological dynamics of density dependence of foundings, because OFY significantly affected both the intercept and slope terms; on the other hand, we were troubled by the changed sign of the main effect of OFY and the magnitudes of the interaction terms.[6]

We examined the incremental contribution of the interaction terms by testing differences between the explained variances of nested regression models using an F-test (Kmenta 1971:371).[7] Thus we reestimated the model in column 3 of table 16.1 after deleting the interaction terms (OFY $\times$ B, OFY $\times$ B^2, OFY $\times$ D, OFY $\times$ D^2) and compared the two models. A statistical test showed that the interaction terms added significantly to the model ($F_{4,41} = 3.35$; $p < .05$). A similar test for the model in column 4 of table 16.1, however, showed that the interactions with RES (RES $\times$ B, RES $\times$ B^2, RES $\times$ D, RES $\times$ D^2) did not significantly add to the model ($F_{4,41} = 1.12$, n.s.). Finally, the incremental effect of the interaction terms for the model in column 5 of table 16.1 (OFY $\times$ N, OFY $\times N^2$, RES $\times N$, RES $\times N^2$) was also significant ($F_{4,42} = 6.75; p <$ .01).[8] This means that OFY significantly altered the nature of the founding and death dynamics, and OFY and RES significantly altered the nature of the density dynamics, even though we cannot comment on the specific signs of the coefficients for the interaction terms.

Overall, in spite of the complications arising due to problems of multicollinearity, the analysis of total foundings of VSSOs showed strong evidence of independent effects of institutional changes and ecological dynamics on VSSO foundings. A favorable institutional change, OFY, enhanced foundings, whereas an unfavorable institutional change, RES, depressed foundings. And prior foundings and deaths were curvilinearly related to current foundings. Despite multicollinearity problems, however, we were reliably able to conclude that the interactions between OFY and the founding and death dynamics, and between OFY and RES and the density dynamics were significant. Thus there is some evidence that, in addition to their independent effects, institutional changes significantly altered the pattern of the ecological dynamics of current foundings of VSSOs, even though we cannot obtain the precise coefficient estimates.

DIFFERENTIAL FOUNDING PATTERNS OF SPECIALIST AND GENERALIST VSSOs

Figure 16.2 shows the number of specialist and generalist VSSOs founded every quarter during the period 1970–82. In general terms, except for differences between the mean levels of foundings of specialists and generalists, with more specialists being founded in every period, the overall founding patterns of the two forms were roughly similar. The differences in mean levels of specialists and generalists founded per quarter were not surprising, since there were many more specialists than generalists in the population. An interesting aspect of the data was that specialist foundings peaked during 1975 and generalist foundings peaked during 1974, but both were near in time to the end of OFY in 1975. The other surge of foundings in 1981 coincided with the cessation of RES in 1981.

Our objective here was to elaborate our findings on overall founding patterns of VSSOs by examining whether the founding patterns of specialist and generalist VSSOs were different. Our theoretical expectation was that since specialists deal with narrower, less complex environments and, presumably, have simpler organization structures (Burns and Stalker 1961; Lawrence and Lorsch 1967), their creation should be more opportunistically motivated. Therefore, specialist foundings should be more responsive to the effects of institutional changes and ecological dynamics. Generalist organizations, on the other hand, are internally more complex than specialists, operate in wider environmental domains, and require more effort and talent to create. Therefore, the creation of generalists would not be as opportunistic, and their founding

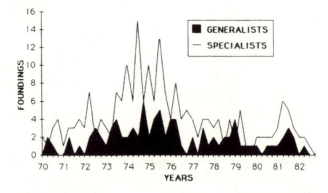

Fig. 16.2. Quarterly foundings of specialist and generalist VSSOs, 1970–82.

patterns would be less responsive to institutional changes and ecological dynamics.

As with the analysis of overall foundings of VSSOs, we used regression models for specialist and generalist foundings separately, and examined the independent effects of institutional changes and ecological dynamics, and the interactions between them. The OLS and GLS results, as appropriate, are presented in table 16.2.

The first model (column 1, table 16.2) reports the results for the curvilinear effects of lagged foundings, deaths, and density and lagged OFY and RES on current foundings of specialist organizations. A first-order autoregression model, in which the current error term is correlated with the error term from the previous period, was significant overall (adjusted $R^2 = 0.529$). Both lagged foundings and deaths had significant positive effects on current specialist foundings, and lagged OFY increased foundings, whereas lagged RES decreased foundings. These results were similar to the pattern for overall foundings, although lagged foundings and deaths did not have curvilinear effects here. But a similar analysis for foundings of generalist organizations (column 2, table 16.2) showed weaker and quite different results. Although a first-order autocorrelation process model was significant overall, the explained variance was much lower (adjusted $R^2 = 0.286$) and none of the coefficients were significant. In part, of course, the nonsignificance of the regression coefficients must be attributed to the multicollinearity between foundings, deaths, and density and their quadratic functions. Even so, because the same multicollinearity problems exist for the specialist data, these results show support for our expectation that specialist foundings would be affected more by institutional changes and ecological dynamics.

Next, we studied the interactions between the institutional changes and the ecological dynamics and their impacts on foundings of specialist and generalist VSSOs (columns 3–8, table 16.2). As in the analysis of overall foundings, we were forced by the collinearity among the variables to model the interactions in three separate sets—the interaction of OFY and RES with the curvilinear effects of lagged density (columns 3–4), the interaction of OFY with the curvilinear effects of lagged foundings and deaths (columns 5–6), and the interaction of RES with the curvilinear effects of lagged foundings and deaths.

The first model with the interaction effects (column 3, table 16.2) reports the results for the curvilinear effects of lagged density, and lagged OFY and RES and their interactions on current foundings of specialist VSSOs. A fourth-order autocorrelation model was significant overall (adjusted $R^2 = 0.585$), and there was a significant nonlinear interaction of lagged OFY with density. As in the case of overall foundings, however, the estimated coefficients were quite large, due to problems of being in a multicollinear environment. As stated earlier, these coefficients need to be interpreted quite cautiously, since their precise values can be misstated. But, as before, it is possible to use a more powerful test to see if all the interaction terms, taken together, add significantly to the model. We reestimated the model after deleting the interaction terms (OFY $\times N$, OFY $\times N^2$, RES $\times N$, RES $\times N^2$). The contribution of these interactions was significant ($F_{4,42} = 4.075; p < .01$). This meant that the occurrence of OFY and RES significantly altered the nature of the density dynamics for specialist foundings, even though we cannot reliably comment on the signs of the specific coefficients. But when we ran the same model for generalist foundings (column 4, table 16.2), the overall model was not significant, and the interaction terms did not add significantly to the model ($F_{4,42} = 1.72$, n.s.). Thus, OFY and RES did not significantly alter the nature of the density dynamics for generalist organizations.

The next four models (columns 5–8, table 16.2) report the results for the curvilinear effects of lagged foundings and deaths, the institutional changes, and their interactions for specialist and generalist foundings respectively. The pattern of results for these models was relatively consistent. With the exception of lagged foundings, none of the other variables were significant, even though all models were overall significant. We again tested whether the interaction effects added significantly to their respective models. The results were mixed, with the interaction effects being significant for one model of specialist foundings (column 5: $F_{4,41} = 2.617; p < .05$) and for one model of generalist foundings (column 8: $F_{4,41} = 3.27; p < .05$). These results did not unequivocally support our expectations.

But overall, the analysis of foundings of specialist and generalist VSSOs was supportive of our theoretical expectations that the founding patterns of specialists and generalists would be quite different. For specialist organizations, there was support for effects of both favorable and unfavorable institutional changes, and prior foundings and deaths, on current foundings. But one difference compared to overall founding patterns was that the effects of prior foundings and deaths were not curvilinear. Further, for specialist organizations,

Table 16.2 Parameter Estimates: Founding Patterns of Specialist and Generalist VSSOs

Independent Variables (t − 1)	Dependent Variables (t) Specialist and Generalist Foundings (qtrly)							
	Spec[a]	Gen[a]	Spec[b]	Gen[c]	Spec[a]	Gen[d]	Spec[a]	Gen[b]
Constant	-1.110 (2.092)	0.129 (1.201)	0.931 (1.778)	-0.374 (1.253)	0.732 (0.875)	0.531 (0.569)	0.423 (0.958)	-0.369 (0.418)
B	0.385** (0.188)	0.117 (0.113)			0.460* (0.252)	0.032 (0.162)	0.469* (0.218)	0.299** (0.100)
B^2	-0.004 (0.008)	-0.0007 (0.005)			-0.010 (0.015)	0.006 (0.009)	-0.005 (0.009)	-0.004 (0.004)
D	0.880* (0.503)	0.511 (0.344)			-0.218 (0.376)	0.272 (0.256)	1.364 (1.061)	-0.106 (0.443)
D^2	-0.102 (0.075)	-0.071 (0.052)			0.023 (0.066)	-0.044 (0.045)	-0.368 (0.315)	0.067 (0.135)
N	-0.0001 (0.011)	0.001 (0.006)	0.009 (0.009)	-0.006 (0.006)				
N^2	-0.000003 (0.00001)	-0.000002 (0.000007)	-0.000008 (0.00001)	-0.000005 (0.000008)				
OFY	1.197* (0.698)	0.543 (0.483)	-95.524** (35.954)	-41.448 (29.637)	-0.196 (2.461)	1.037 (1.598)		
RES	-1.290* (0.814)	-0.408 (0.554)	-429.97 (839.16)	-578.80 (585.24)			0.495 (6.884)	4.594 (3.609)
OFY × N			0.392** (0.159)	0.176 (0.131)				
OFY × N^2			-0.0004* (0.0002)	-0.0002 (0.0001)				
RES × N			1.482 (2.724)	1.876 (1.905)				

	(1)	(2)	(3)	(4)	(5)	(6)	(7)
RES × N²		-0.001 (0.002)	-0.002 (0.002)				
OFY × B				0.059 (0.494)	-0.039 (0.319)		
OFY × B²				-0.002 (0.021)	-0.005 (0.014)		
OFY × D				0.867 (1.757)	0.240 (1.213)		
OFY × D²				-0.395 (0.797)	0.267 (0.557)		
RES × B						-0.028 (0.567)	0.072 (0.334)
RES × B²						-0.001 (0.035)	-0.020 (0.021)
RES × D						-1.844 (3.099)	-1.705 (1.468)
RES × D²						0.427 (0.463)	0.123 (0.209)
Adj R^2	0.286	0.584	0.216	0.584	0.330	0.442	0.408
F-ratio	3.5	9.797	2.721	8.74	3.74	5.37	4.991
p-level	<.05	<.01	n.s.	<.01	<.05	<.01	<.01

Note: Standard errors are in parentheses.
a. First-order autocorrelation.
b. Fourth-order autocorrelation.
c. Ordinary least squares.
d. Second-order autocorrelation.
*p < .05.
**p < .01 (one-tail test).

despite problems of multicollinearity, we were able to conclude that the interaction between OFY and the curvilinear density dynamics was significant. Thus, there was some evidence that, in addition to the main effects of OFY and RES, OFY significantly altered the density dependence of current specialist foundings of VSSOs. On the other hand, with one exception, the results for foundings of generalist VSSOs were considerably weaker, and, for the most part, the coefficients were not significant. This generally supported our basic theoretical expectation that founding patterns of specialists and generalists would differ both for the institutional changes and the ecological dynamics.

Effects of Institutional Changes on Death Rates

Figure 16.3 shows the annual number of deaths in the VSSO population during the period 1970–82. The study population here was comprised of 389 organizations compared to the 451 studied for the analysis of founding patterns. This smaller population of 389 VSSOs was the number created during the period 1970–80. Death data for organizations founded during 1981–82 are currently unavailable. The death pattern showed that there were no organizational deaths in the first three years. After that, the number of deaths increased each year, reaching a high in 1977, and then declining steadily to 1980. The methodology used to analyze the death data is event history analysis (Tuma, Hannan, and Groeneveld 1979; Carroll and Delacroix 1982).

Similar to earlier studies of death rates in this population (Singh, Tucker, and House 1986; Singh, House, and Tucker 1986), we estimated parametric models of the death rate using Makeham-Gompertz models. After initially exploring period-dependent models of the death rates which were unsuccessful,[9] we chose a simple Gompertz model that was not period-dependent:

$$(1) \qquad\qquad h(t) = \exp{(\beta_0)} \exp{(\gamma_0)t}.$$

Time-varying covariates were entered into the β and γ vectors of the multiple spells models like equation (1). These were of the form

$$(2) \qquad\qquad h(t) = \exp\{\beta_0 + \Sigma_i \beta_i X_i(\tau)\} \exp{(\gamma_0)t},$$

and

$$(3) \qquad\qquad h(t) = \exp\beta_0 \exp\{\gamma_0 + \Sigma_i \gamma_i X_i(\tau)\}t,$$

where the X_i's are the time-varying ecological and institutional covariates. Table 16.3 presents the maximum likelihood estimates and standard errors for the parameters of the Gompertz models using RATE (Tuma 1980).

We first modeled the curvilinear effects of density on the instantaneous rate of death in order to investigate the validity of ecological arguments.[10] The results are shown in the first and second rows of table 16.2. When the effects of density

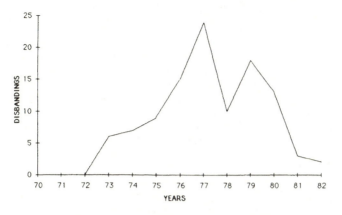

Fig. 16.3. Annual deaths of VSSOs, 1970–82.

were modeled in the β vector (row 1), the overall model was strongly significant compared to a constant-rate model, based on a chi-square likelihood ratio-test ($\chi^2_{3df} = 25.23; p = 1.32 \times 10^{-5}$). There was also a significant curvilinear effect of density. However, our findings contradicted findings in other populations (see, for example, Hannan and Freeman 1988), since death rates initially increased with density, but as density increased even further, they began to decline. This does not support arguments which suggest that for low levels of density, increases in density enhance the legitimacy of the organizational form, thereby decreasing the death rate. As density increases even further, however, the effects of competition take over and death rates increase. Further, in our population, density has a maximum impact on the death rate when it is approximately 524, which occurred during the year 1975–76.[11] Since density during the period of observation ranged between 359 and 668, the declining death rate at higher levels of density is within the observed range of density and occurred in this population during the study period. When these density effects were modeled in the γ vector, the results were more or less identical. The overall model was significant compared to a constant-rate model ($\chi^2_{3df} = 41.93; p = 4.15 \times 10^{-9}$), and density again had strong curvilinear effects.[12]

Next, we modeled the impact of the institutional changes on the death rates of VSSOs (rows 3 and 4 of table 16.2). When OFY and RES were modeled in the β term, the overall model was significant compared to a constant-rate model ($\chi^2_{3df} = 48.22; p = 1.92 \times 10^{-10}$). Both OFY and RES had significant effects on death rates. Whereas the positive effects of RES were as expected, the positive effect of OFY was surprising. Contrary to our expectations, OFY significantly increased death rates of VSSOs. The results were similar when OFY and RES were modeled in the γ vector, with both OFY and RES significantly increasing the death rate. As we have discussed elsewhere (Tucker, Singh, and Meinhard 1987), this result is consistent with the argument that favorable in-

Table 16.3 Maximum Likelihood Estimates: Ecological and Instituaional Effects on Death Rate (Multiple Spells Models)

Covariates in β or γ vector	β_0	γ_0	Density	Density^2	OFY	RES	χ^2	df	p-level
1. β	−29.12** (6.658)	0.159** (0.044)	0.099** (0.025)	−0.00009** (0.00002)			25.33	3	1.32×10^{-5}
2. γ	−3.977** (0.221)	−5.980** (2.024)	0.025** (0.007)	−0.00002** (0.000006)			41.93	3	4.15×10^{-9}
3. β	−6.139** (0.556)	0.182** (0.042)			2.447** (0.549)	2.387** (0.476)	48.22	3	1.92×10^{10}
4. γ	−3.871** (0.209)	−0.111* (0.068)			0.384** (0.100)	0.310** (0.065)	46.10	3	5.41×10^{10}
5. β	−16.95** (6.959)	0.215** (0.046)	0.049* (0.027)	−0.00005* (0.00003)	1.435* (0.785)	2.016** (0.505)	52.56	5	4.13×10^{10}
6. γ	−4.073** (0.027)	−1.483 (2.245)	0.009 (0.008)	−0.00001 (0.000007)	0.067 (0.170)	0.202** (0.071)	58.46	5	2.53×10^{11}

Note: Standard errors are in parentheses.

*$p < .05$.

**$p < .01$ (one-tail test).

stitutional environments may encourage the creation of organizations which would not normally be founded, and these may subsequently exhibit higher death rates.

We next modeled the impact of both the ecological and institutional variables together, in order to rule out problems of specification error. Row 5 of table 16.2 presents the results for all covariates modeled in the β vector. As before, the overall model was significant compared to a constant-rate model ($\chi^2_{5df} = 52.56; p = 4.13 \times 10^{-10}$), and all the variables continued to show the previous pattern of results. But when all the covariates were modeled in the γ vector (row 6 of table 16.2), with the exception of RES, the earlier results were eliminated, even though the overall model was highly significant. However, the overall pattern of results showed still some evidence that the ecological and institutional effects were present. Despite the unexpected effects of density and OFY, the evidence suggested that both ecological processes of competition and institutional changes significantly affected death rates.[13]

Overall, the analysis of death rates showed that both the ecological dynamics and institutional changes had significant independent effects on the death rate of VSSOs, although some of the effects ran counter to our intuitions. One interesting result was that favorable institutional changes enhanced death rates, suggesting that perhaps such organizations were subjected to weaker selection pressures at the time of founding and subsequently had higher death rates. However, because of estimation difficulties due to multicollinearity, we were unable conclusively to determine whether the institutional changes significantly altered the nature of the ecological dynamics, although some intermediate solutions presented evidence against the existence of these effects.

Organizational Legitimacy and Death Rates

In addition to the impact of institutional changes on death rates of VSSOs, another significant link between institutional and ecological theories of organization can be established by studying how institutional support affects selection pressures on organizations. A central feature of some institutional ideas is that structural isomorphism with rationalized myths in the institutional environment increases the legitimacy of the organization (Meyer and Rowan 1977; Meyer and Scott 1983b). This increased legitimacy provides greater access to resources and thereby enhances organizational survival. Despite the importance of this idea to the institutional approach, it has not, to the best of our knowledge, been the subject of much empirical investigation.

Interestingly, the same question is also of significant importance in the ecological approach. Empirical research has shown that one important way in which selection processes occur in organizations is that younger organizations have higher propensities to die. This liability of newness has been shown to exist in newspaper organizations (Carroll and Delacroix 1982), in labor unions and semiconductor firms (Freeman, Carroll, and Hannan 1983), in retail, wholesale, and manufacturing organizations (Carroll 1983), and in VSSOs (Tucker, Singh, and House 1984; Singh, Tucker, and House 1986). Hannan and Freeman (1984) have argued that, in addition to internal processes that increase reproducibility of structure as organizations age, external legitimation may also underlie the liability of newness. As organizations grow older, they are more likely to develop exchange relationships with other institutional actors, become embedded in the power hierarchy, and come to have their actions endorsed by powerful collective actors (Stinchcombe 1968).

In an earlier paper, we had investigated the importance of these processes in explaining the liability of newness in this population. We were interested in determining whether external legitimacy or internal coordination processes explained better the liability of newness. We report below some of the results for the impact of organizational legitimacy on organizational death rates, which showed that, for these organizations, the main reason young organizations had higher death rates was that they did not have external institutional support.

We investigated this question by introducing the indicators for external legitimacy into a Gompertz model of the death rate. As described earlier, we had three separate indicators of external legitimacy—community directory listing, charitable registration number, and board size. Since some VSSOs that lost their community directory listing or charitable registration during their lifetimes subsequently reacquired it, we treated both these indicators as time-varying variables. These dummy variables were 1 in the year the organization had the community directory listing or charitable registration number, and 0 otherwise. We were unable, however, to use board size as a time-varying covariate because the board-size data during the later years of a VSSO's life were not fully and reliably available. Therefore, we used board size at founding. The model was of the form

$$h(t) = \exp(\beta_0) \exp(\gamma_0 + \gamma_1 X_1(\tau) + \gamma_2 X_2(\tau) + \gamma_3 X_3)t,$$

where X_1 and X_2 are the time-varying variables for community directory listing and charitable registration number, and X_3 is the board size at founding. The overall model was significant compared to a constant-rate model ($X^2 4df = 28.22; p = .00001$), and the parameter estimates were as follows (standard errors in parentheses):

$$h(t) = \exp(-3.486^{***}) \exp .210^{***}$$
$$(.180) \qquad (.043)$$

$$- .108^{***} \text{ COMDIR } - .079^{***} \text{ CHAREG}$$
$$(.045) \qquad (.038)$$

$$- .012^{***} \text{ BOARD})t.$$
$$(.005) \qquad\qquad (** p < .05; *** p < .01)$$

These results show strong support for the view that acquiring legitimacy through support from the institutional environment significantly reduced the death rate. In order to rule out alternative explanations for these findings, we included dummy variables for organizational form at time of founding, specialist or generalist, time-varying dummy variables for the institutional changes, OFY and RES, and a time-varying variable for density as controls in the above model. The model was significant compared to a constant-rate model ($X^29df = 83.45; p = .00$), and the parameter estimates were as follows (standard errors in parentheses):

$$h(t) = \exp(-4.056^{***}) \exp(1.917^{***} - .115^{***} \text{ COMDIR}$$
$$(.228) \qquad (.559) \qquad (.048)$$

$$- .087^{**} \text{ CHAREG} - .010^{**} \text{ BOARD} - .026 \text{ SPEC}$$
$$(.040) \qquad\qquad (.005) \qquad\qquad (.043)$$

$$- .067 \text{ GEN} - .071 \text{ OFY} + .250^{***} \text{ RES}$$
$$(.063) \qquad (.179) \qquad (.068)$$

$$- .003^{***} \text{ DENS})t.$$
$$(.001) \qquad\qquad (^{**}p < .05; ^{***}p < .01)$$

Despite the inclusion of these control variables, the effects of the three indicators for legitimacy were unaltered. Our earlier inference that the acquisition of institutional support reduced death rates of VSSOs was still valid.

Institutional Effects on Rates of Change

We pointed out above that in general formulations of ecological theory, change in populations may occur through processes of founding, death, and organizational change (Hannan and Freeman 1989: ch. 1; Singh, Tucker, and Meinhard 1988). Having examined the impact of institutional changes on founding and death patterns, we turned our attention to rates of change in organizations. Our theoretical expectation of a relationship between rates of change in features of organizations and institutional changes was based on a dynamic formulation of institutional ideas. Since organizations attempt to align their structures with the institutional environment (Meyer and Rowan 1977), it seemed reasonable to us to expect that changes in the institutional environment would positively affect rates of change in organizations.

We also incorporated some realistic control variables into the parametric models of rates of change. In earlier studies, we had found that organizational form at founding, specialist or generalist, significantly influenced patterns of founding (Tucker, Singh, and Meinhard 1990) and had long-term impacts on death rates (Tucker, Singh, and Meinhard 1987). In another study we had also seen that board size of a VSSO significantly influenced death rates (Singh, Tucker, and House 1986). Finally, previous research has shown that density influences both founding (Hannan and Freeman 1987) and death rates (Hannan and Freeman 1988; Tucker, Singh, and Meinhard 1987) in organizational populations. Although the impact of these variables on rates of change has, to the best of our knowledge, not been explored in the literature, and our expectations were not clear, it seemed plausible that they would also affect change rates. The exception was board size, because of our expectation that a larger-sized board would bring multiple external influences to bear on the decisions within a VSSO, and this would presumably increase rates of change.

We used multiple spells models to estimate the impact of the institutional changes and control variables on rates of change, the length of each spell being determined by the timing of the successive changes, in order to account for the time-varying character of some of the variables. As we had mentioned earlier in the method section, we estimated rates of change in name, sponsor, location, service area, goals, client groups, conditions-of-service provision, chief executive, and structure. We used dummy variables for form at founding, specialist or generalist (the effects are relative to the excluded group of organizations that operated in two domains only), board size at founding, time-varying dummy variables for the institutional changes OFY and RES, and time-varying variables for density. Since we were not interested here in age dependence of rates of change, unlike another study (Singh, Tucker, and Meinhard 1988), we used models of the general form:

$$r(t) = \exp\{\alpha_0 + \Sigma_i \alpha_i X_i + \Sigma_j \alpha_j X_j(\tau)\},$$

where the X_i's are the exogenous variables at founding, and the X_j's are the time-varying exogenous variables. Table 16.4 presents the parameter estimates and standard errors for the various rates of change.

The results in table 16.4 show relatively strong patterns for the effects of the institutional changes on rates of change. The overall finding was that both OFY and RES significantly increased rates of change, although the results were more consistent for RES than for OFY. Although RES was significant for all nine rates of change, OFY was nonsignificant for service area, client groups, conditions of service, and structure. This suggests that rates of change in organizational features are affected by both favorable and unfavorable institutional changes, but these rates are affected for more organizational features in the case of unfavorable institutional change. Incidentally, these specific results bear out the assumption underlying much of organizational theory—that environmental turbulence and change have an impact on organizational propensities to change. To the best of our knowledge, this has not previously been demonstrated using dynamic methods. While not of central interest here, there was also some evidence that a larger-sized board at founding increased rates of change, and, with the exception of rate of goal change, density decreased rates of change.

Table 16.4 Maximum Likelihood Estimates: Makeham-Gompertz Models of Rates of Change with Control Variables (Multiple Spells Models)

Change type		Specialist	Generalist	Bd Size	OFY	RES	Density			
	α_0	α_1	α_2	α_3	α_4	α_5	α_6	χ^2	df	p-level
Name	2.062	−0.163	−0.194	0.106***	1.955**	2.610***	−0.013***	145.43	6	0.000
	(3.179)	(0.317)	(0.429)	(0.024)	(1.111)	(0.515)	(0.004)			
Sponsor	2.740	0.073	0.414	0.079***	1.816**	3.057***	−0.015***	125.17	6	0.000
	(3.018)	(0.358)	(0.450)	(0.033)	(1.089)	(0.575)	(0.005)			
Location	3.123***	−0.075	0.154	0.020**	0.617**	1.879***	−0.011***	346.93	6	0.000
	(0.941)	(0.140)	(0.159)	(0.012)	(0.345)	(0.188)	(0.001)			
Service area	1.949	0.189	−0.105	0.081**	0.250	2.059***	−0.013**	40.24	6	0.000
	(4.195)	(0.472)	(0.696)	(0.037)	(1.531)	(0.572)	(0.006)			
Goals	−13.84***	0.667***	1.090***	0.065***	5.420***	3.185***	0.011*	109.65	6	0.000
	(4.746)	(0.366)	(0.388)	(0.024)	(1.341)	(0.461)	(0.007)			
Client groups	8.034***	0.299	1.597	0.042	−15.05	1.815**	−0.025***	20.44	6	0.000
	(3.339)	(1.210)	(1.240)	(0.097)	(861.00)	(0.983)	(0.005)			
Conditions of service	4.912	0.045	0.098	0.082*	0.811	2.257***	−0.019***	45.56	6	0.000
	(3.643)	(0.625)	(0.872)	(0.059)	(1.362)	(0.848)	(0.006)			
Chief executive	1.955**	0.009	−0.008	0.003***	0.051*	1.588***	−0.001***	300.57	6	0.000
	(1.169)	(0.017)	(0.017)	(0.001)	(0.040)	(0.017)	(0.0002)			
Structure	3.158***	0.091	0.193	0.017*	0.420	1.033***	−0.009***	183.89	6	0.000
	(1.263)	(0.156)	(0.173)	(0.013)	(0.417)	(0.160)	(0.002)			

Note: Standard errors are in parentheses.

*$p < .10$.
**$p < .05$.
***$p < .01$.

Conclusion

In this chapter, we described how changes in the institutional environment of a VSSO population affected the ecological dynamics of founding, death, and change. The overall pattern of the results strongly supported our theoretical position that institutional change would have significant impacts on all three processes. First, the study of founding patterns of VSSOs showed that both prior foundings and deaths and institutional changes affect current foundings. And the institutional changes significantly altered the nature of the ecological dynamics, even though we were unable to obtain precise coefficient estimates due to problems of multicollinearity. Further, when we analyzed the founding patterns of specialist and generalist VSSOs separately, we found that, as expected, specialist founding patterns were influenced much more by institutional changes and ecological dynamics than generalist founding patterns. This is particularly interesting because it suggests the possibility that institutional changes may affect different organizational forms differentially, an idea worth pursuing further in future research.

Second, the study of death rates showed that both density and institutional changes significantly affected death rates of VSSOs. As expected, RES, the unfavorable institutional change, increased death rates, but OFY, the favorable institutional change, also increased death rates, which was surprising since it had increased foundings in the earlier analysis. As discussed in greater detail elsewhere (Tucker et al. 1988), the reason was that OFY increased foundings beyond the point where the competitive effects of density began to occur, increasing deaths in the population. This occurred during 1974–75, the last year of OFY. Ironically, OFY's success in creating new VSSOs increased deaths in the population. The implications of these findings for the study of population change are quite intriguing. It seems that, in general, the effects of institutional changes or processes of founding and death may not be symmetric. Thus, institutional changes that enhance foundings may not depress deaths, as one might expect. Rather, the relationship is more complex and depends upon whether increases in foundings make density exceed the threshold level beyond which competitive effects begin to occur and, therefore, death rates increase, instead of decreasing through enhanced legitimacy of the organizational form (Hannan 1986a). Furthermore, our study of death rates strongly supported the position that being externally legitimated and having the support of other institutional actors significantly lowered death rates of VSSOs.

Third, we also examined if institutional changes affected rates of change in organizational features. The evidence was again relatively clear that both institutional changes and density affected rates of change. However, there was stronger evidence for the effects of unfavorable institutional changes on rates of change than favorable institutional changes, and both increased rates of change. This was generally supportive of arguments which suggest that organizations attempt to alter their structure and features to reflect the changing institutional environment.

Overall, the results in this chapter demonstrate relatively clearly that both institutional and ecological effects led to changes in the VSSO population through their effects on founding, death, and change processes. And at least for the founding patterns, the institutional changes significantly altered the ecological dynamics in the population. The systematically supportive results appear to reinforce the veridicality of our underlying premise that ecological and institutional approaches are two quite complementary ways to study change in organizational populations.

Acknowledgments

The authors are indebted to Howard Aldrich, Paul DiMaggio, John Freeman, Hans Pennings, and V. Srinivasan for comments on and discussions of the ideas presented in this chapter and the statistical methods underlying the analyses.

Notes

1. This question has received some attention in the literature. We refer here to studies such as Warren, Rose, and Bergunder 1974—an analysis of community decision organizations in nine U.S. cities where, because of the emergence of density-based intraspecific competition, functionally similar human services organizations were found advocating for state-supported policies incorporating rules which effectively regulate the entry of new rivals for government funds into the human services sector. For analysis of similar behavior by economic organizations, see Stigler 1971 or Pfeffer 1974.

2. The number of organizations studied here, 451, differs from the 389 studied in earlier analyses of death rates (Singh, Tucker, and House 1986; Singh, House, and Tucker 1986). The 389 VSSOs studied in the analysis of differential death rates were the number created during the 1970–80 period. Updated death data were not available for VSSOs created during 1981 and 1982 when the earlier studies were done.

3. It may be argued that these three indicators of external legitimacy are also measures of human capital and preexisting networks. A listing in the *Community Directory* requires an awareness of the field and some minimum organizing ability, and acquiring a charitable registration number probably requires minimal human resources. Thus both may be measuring human capital at founding. And putting together a board of directors requires the ability to persuade people, which may indirectly measure preexisting networks. We think the argument is essentially correct but do not consider it problematic for two reasons. One, we are concerned primarily with whether organizations acquired institutional support, and less with what factors may have facilitated or hindered that process. Thus, as long as either human capital or preexisting networks enhance acquiring external institutional support, the measures continue to have integrity. Two, we view the indicators of external legitimacy as unobtrusive measures (Webb et al. 1966). Such

measures always contain noise, since they frequently carry information not related to the construct measured, but we assume, following proponents of such an approach, that the noise is low relative to the signal (Webb and Weick 1979:652).

4. Organizational death is an event unique in that the *same* organization cannot die more than once. But a structural change, say, can occur several times in the life of an organization. It is not meaningful to calculate the transition rate for only the first structural change, since we are interested in all such structural changes. What is needed is a transition rate that incorporates the information from all structural changes into one overall rate. This can be done by *not* specifying any origin state in the RATE program, but specifying structural change as the destination state. The program then estimates a composite transition rate for all transitions to this destination state, regardless of whether the origin state is "no structural change" or "structural change." This solution to the problem benefited from invaluable consultations with Terry Amburgey.

5. Discussions with Howard Aldrich were very helpful in identifying and dealing with this problem.

6. In subsequent explorations of the problem we concluded that there were multicollinearity problems here as well, since the interaction terms were again highly correlated with each other (r was about 0.99 for OFY $\times$ N with OFY $\times$ N^2, and RES $\times$ N with RES $\times$ N^2). In addition to inflating the standard errors and understating levels of significance, it is possible for multicollinearity to alter the coefficient estimates in sign and magnitude, even though the estimates are unbiased, that is, accurate in an expectational sense (Srinivasan, pers. com.). Unfortunately, there are relatively few satisfactory solutions to problems of multicollinearity. A common approach is to respecify the models by removing the offending terms (Kennedy 1985) and reestimating the coefficients. We thought it was inappropriate to do so in this study, since the theoretical ideas themselves specify curvilinear effects (Delacroix and Carroll 1983; Hannan and Freeman 1987). This, of course, also points to potential difficulties all studies in this genre probably face in the estimation of coefficients. Due to these problems of multicollinearity, the results of the model with interactions between institutional changes and ecological dynamics need to be interpreted cautiously. Since the inflated standard errors introduce a conservative bias in tests of significance, there may, in truth, be significant coefficients whose estimates appear to be insignificant. Further, in specific instances, the coefficient estimates may also be incorrect. Thus, we could not reliably conclude what were the signs of the interaction effects. However, it is still possible to test if the interaction terms add significantly to the model, using an F-test comparing nested regressions (Kmenta 1971:371); this is a useful test in a multicollinear environment (Srinivasan, pers. com.).

7. If there are two nested regression models, one with Q explanatory variables (including the constant term) and the other with K explanatory variables ($Q > K$), then

$$\frac{(R_Q^2 - R_K^2)\,(n - Q)}{(1 - R_Q^2)\,(Q - K)} \sim F_{Q-K,n-Q},$$

where n is the number of observations.

8. We also carried out a similar test using the more complete specification in column 2 of table 16.1. The incremental effect of the interaction terms was still significant, ruling out specification problems ($F_{4,38} = 6.653; p < .01$).

9. Unlike other studies (Carroll and Delacroix 1982; Freeman, Carroll, and Hannan 1983; Singh, Tucker, and House 1986), our primary emphasis here was on the effects of ecological dynamics and institutional changes on death rates, rather than the age dependence of death rates. Therefore, we thought it appropriate to use as a baseline model a two-time period model that best fitted the death rate data in this population (Singh, House, and Tucker 1986). This model was of the form

$$h(t) = \exp \{\beta_0 (p)\} \exp \{\gamma_0 (p)\} \, t,$$

where $p = 1,2$.

In order to estimate the effects of the institutional changes and ecological dynamics on the death rate, we entered the appropriate time-varying covariates into the above model. Further, since we used multiple spells models, with length of spells defined by the timing of the consecutive changes, it seemed equally meaningful to model the covariate in either the β or γ vectors, because, in such models, the substantive interpretations of the two vectors are not very different (Singh, House, and Tucker 1986). Unfortunately, all the models we estimated using the baseline model in the above equation ran into severe convergence problems and we were forced to change the baseline model in order to obtain results.

10. We modeled the effects of density in the current year rather than lagged density because we had only thirteen years of data. A one-year lag would have led to the loss of one year of data, which we considered excessive. Lagged foundings and deaths were not modeled for the same reason, nor were the lagged institutional variables.

11. Elementary differential calculus shows that this is the case, since, for a maxima, the first derivative of $h(t)$ with respect to density must be zero.

$$h(t) = \exp (\beta_0 + \beta_1 d + \beta_2 d^2) \exp (\gamma_0 t);$$

for a maxima,

$$\frac{\delta h}{\delta d} = 0 = (b_1 + 2b_2 d) \, h(t),$$

and, thus, $d^* = b_1 / 2b_2 = 524$.

12. A surprising finding is the positive and significant value of the γ_0 parameter, when the effects of density are modeled in the β term, since this does not support the well-accepted ideas of liability of newness. But when the density effects were modeled in the γ term, the γ_0 parameter was significant and negative, suggesting that the previous significant and positive value of γ_0 may be an artifact of the modeling. In any case, since the primary focus here was not on γ_0, we did not pursue this question any further.

13. We also asked, similar to the analysis of foundings, whether the institutional change influenced the nature of the ecological dynamics itself. We answered this question by introducing dummy variables for OFY and RES separately into the models in equations (2) and (3). Because more complex models did not converge, we had to introduce OFY and RES separately into both the constant terms and the coefficients of the density variables. None of these models converged, despite raising the number of iterations to 100. However, the intermediate solution for a model specifying the interaction of OFY with the curvilinear effects of density provided interpretable results. The overall

model fitted the data well ($\chi^2_{6df} = 33.79$; $p = 7.39 \times 10^{-6}$), although the fit was worse compared to the models without interaction effects in table 16.2. There was no significant interaction effect, although density still had a curvilinear relationship with death rate. It seems likely that the nonconvergence of the models is attributable to the multicollinearity between density and density^2 and their cross-product terms with OFY (OFY $\times$ N and OFY $\times$ N^2). Since the models with interaction terms did not converge, we cannot test whether the interaction terms added significantly to the model. However, the partial evidence available from the intermediate solution suggests that the institutional changes may not have affected the density dependence of death rate significantly. But, as we mentioned earlier, this result must be interpreted cautiously and is relatively tentative.

References

Abbott, Andrew. 1988. *The System of Professions: An Essay on the Division of Expert Labor*. Chicago: University of Chicago Press.

Abelson, Robert P. 1976. Script Processing in Attitude Formation and Decision Making. In *Cognition and Social Behavior*, ed. J. S. Carroll and J. W. Payne, 33–45. Hillsdale, N.J.: Erlbaum.

Abernathy, William. 1978. *The Productivity Dilemma*. Baltimore: Johns Hopkins University Press.

Abolafia, Mitchell. 1984. Structured Anarchy: Formal Organization in the Commodity Futures Market. In *The Social Dynamics of Financial Markets*, ed. Patricia Adler and Peter Adler, 129–50. Greenwich, Conn.: JAI Press.

Abrams, M. A. 1985. Art-as-Such: The Sociology of Modern Aesthetics. *Bulletin of the American Academy of Arts and Sciences* 38:8–33.

Adam, T. R. 1939. *The Museum and Popular Culture*. New York: American Association for Adult Education.

Aiken, Michael, and Jerald Hage. 1968. Organizational Interdependence and Intra-organizational Structure. *American Sociological Review* 33:912–30.

Akerlof, George. 1976. The Economics of Caste and of the Rat Race and Other Woeful Tales. *Quarterly Journal of Economics* 90:599–617.

Alchian, Armen, 1950. Uncertainty, Evolution, and Economic Theory. *Journal of Political Economy* 58:211–21.

Alchian, Armen A., and Harold Demsetz. 1972. Production, Information Cost, and Economic Organization. *American Economic Review* 62:777–95.

Aldrich, Howard E. 1972. An Organization-Environment Perspective on Cooperation and Conflict in the Manpower Training System. In *Conflict and Power in Complex Organizations*, ed. A. R. Negandhi, 11–37. Kent, Ohio: Center for Business and Economic Research.

———. 1978. Centralization versus Decentralization in the Design of Human Service Delivery Systems: A Response to Gouldner's Lament. In *The Management of Human Services*, ed. R. C. Sarri and Y. Hasenfeld, 51–79. New York: Columbia University Press.

———. 1979. *Organizations and Environments*. Englewood Cliffs, N.J.: Prentice-Hall.

Aldrich, Howard E., and Jeffrey Pfeffer. 1976. Environments of Organizations. *Annual Review of Sociology* 2:79–105.

Aldrich, Howard E., and Udo Staber. 1988. Organizing Business Interests: Patterns of Trade Association Foundings, Transformations and Death. In *Ecological Models of Organizations*, ed. Glenn R. Carroll, 111–26. Cambridge, Mass.: Ballinger.

Aldrich, Howard E., and David A. Whetten. 1981. Organization-sets, Action-sets, and

Networks: Making the Most of Simplicity. In *Handbook of Organization Design,* ed. P. C. Nystrom and W. H. Starbuck, 1:385–408. New York: Oxford University Press.

Alexander, C. N., Jr., L. G. Zucker, and C. Brody. 1970. Experimental Expectations and Autokinetic Experiences: Consistency Theories and Judgmental Convergence. *Sociometry* 33:108–22.

Alexander, Edward P. 1983. *Museum Masters: Their Museums and Their Influence.* Nashville: American Association for State and Local History.

Alexander, Jeffrey C. 1983. *The Modern Reconstruction of Classical Thought: Talcott Parsons.* Vol. 4 of *Theoretical Logic in Sociology.* Berkeley: University of California Press.

———. 1987. *Twenty Lectures: Sociological Theory since World War II.* New York: Columbia University Press.

Alexander, Jeffrey C., and W. Richard Scott. 1984. The Impact of Regulation on the Administrative Structure of Hospitals: Toward an Analytic Framework. *Hospital and Health Services Administration* 29:71–85.

Alexander, Victoria D. 1988. Aging as a Societal Sector: Causes and Consequences of the Structuration of the Aging Industry. Paper presented at the annual meetings of the Pacific Sociological Association, Las Vegas, April 5–8.

Alford, Robert R. 1975. *Health Care Politics: Ideological and Interest Group Barriers to Reform.* Chicago: University of Chicago Press.

Alford, Robert R., and Roger Friedland. 1985. *Powers of Theory: Capitalism, the State and Democracy.* Cambridge: Cambridge University Press.

Alinsky, Saul. 1969. *Rules for Radicals.* Chicago: University of Chicago Press.

Allison, Graham T. 1971. *Essence of Decision: Explaining the Cuban Missile Crisis.* Boston: Little, Brown.

Althusser, Louis. 1969. *For Marx.* London: Allan Lane.

Amburgey, Terry L., and Paul G. Lippert. 1989. Institutional Determinants of Strategy: The Legitimation and Diffusion of Management Buyouts. Manuscript. University of Wisconsin.

American Management Association. 1926. Marketing Policies and Sales Methods that Stabilize Business. Sales Executive Series No. 36. New York: American Management Association.

Anderson, Florence. 1941. *Memorandum on the Use of Art and Music Study Materials.* New York: Carnegie Corporation of New York.

Anderson, Perry. 1974. *Passages from Antiquity to Feudalism.* London: New Left Books.

Angell, Robert C. 1936. Discussion of the Ecological Aspect of Institutions. *American Sociological Review* 1:189–92.

Aoki, Masahiko. 1984. Aspects of the Japanese Firm. In *The Economic Analysis of the Japanese Firm,* ed. M. Aoki, 3–43. Amsterdam: Elsevier.

Aristotle. 1929. *Politics.* Trans. P. H. Wickstead and F. M. Cornford. London: W. Heinemann.

Arthur, W. Brian. 1987. Urban Systems and Historical Path-Dependence. In *Urban Systems and Infrastructure,* ed. R. Herman and J. Ausubel. Washington, D.C.: NAS/NAE.

———. 1988a. Competing Technologies: An Overview. In *Technical Change and Economic Theory,* ed. G. Dosi et al., 590–607. London: Pinter.

————. 1988b. Self-Reinforcing Mechanisms in Economics. In *The Economy as an Evolving Complex System*, ed. P. W. Anderson and K. J. Arrow, 9–32. Menlo Park, Calif.: Addison-Wesley.

————. 1989. Competing Technologies and Lock-in by Historical Events: The Dynamics of Allocation under Increasing Returns. *Economic Journal* 99(394):116–31.

————. 1990. Positive Feedbacks in the Economy. *Scientific American* 262(2):92–99.

Ashworth, William. 1975. *A Short History of the International Economy since 1850.* London: Longman.

Astley, W. Graham. 1985. The Two Ecologies: Population and Community Perspectives on Organizational Evolution. *Administrative Science Quarterly* 30:224–41.

Astley, W. Graham, and Andrew Van de Ven. 1983. Central Perspectives and Debates in Organization Theory. *Administrative Science Quarterly* 28:245–73.

Bach, Richard F. 1924. *The Place of the Arts in American Life.* Office Memorandum, ser. I, no. 9. Carnegie Corporation, New York.

Badie, Bertrand, and Pierre Birnbaum. 1983. *The Sociology of the State.* Chicago: University of Chicago Press.

Bailes, Kendall. 1978. *Technology and Society under Lenin and Stalin.* Princeton: Princeton University Press.

Baker, Frank, and Gregory O'Brien. 1971. Intersystems Relations and Coordination of Human Service Organizations. *American Journal of Public Health* 61:130–37.

Baker, Wayne. 1984. The Social Structure of a National Securities Market. *American Journal of Sociology* 89:775–811.

Bales, Robert F. 1953. The Equilibrium Problem in Small Groups. In *Working Papers in the Theory of Action*, ed. T. Parsons, R. F. Bales, and E. A. Shils, 111–50. Glencoe, Ill.: Free Press.

Ballarin, E. 1986. *Commercial Banks amid the Financial Revolution.* Cambridge, Mass.: Ballinger Press.

Bankston, Mary. 1982. Organizational Reporting in a School District: State and Federal Programs. Project Report No. 82-A10. Stanford, Calif.: Institute for Research on Educational Finance and Governance, Stanford University.

Barbagli, Mario. 1982. *Educating for Unemployment.* Trans. from the Italian by Robert H. Ross. New York: Columbia University Press.

Barbu, Zevedei. 1960. *Problems of Historical Psychology.* London: Routledge and Kegan Paul.

Bardach, Eugene. 1977. *The Implementation Game: What Happens after a Bill Becomes a Law.* Cambridge: MIT Press.

Barnard, Chester. 1938. *The Function of the Executive.* Cambridge: Harvard University Press.

Barnouw, Erik. 1966–70. *A History of Broadcasting in the United States.* 3 vols. New York: Oxford University Press.

Baron, James P., Frank Dobbin, and P. Devereaux Jennings. 1986. War and Peace: The Evolution of Modern Personnel Administration in U.S. Industry. *American Journal of Sociology* 92:250–83.

Barzelay, Michael, and Rogers Smith. 1987. The One Best System? A Political Analysis of Neoclassical Institutionalist Perspectives on the Modern Corporation. In *Corporations and Society,* ed. W. Samuels and A. S. Miller, 81–110. New York: Greenwood Press.

Becker, Gary. 1981. *A Treatise on the Family*. Cambridge: Harvard University Press.

Bell, Daniel. 1973. *The Coming of Post-Industrial Society*. New York: Basic Books.

———. 1976. *The Cultural Contradictions of Capitalism*. New York: Basic Books.

Bem, Daryl J. 1970. *Beliefs, Attitudes, and Human Affairs*. Belmont, Calif.: Brooks Cole.

Bendix, Reinhard. 1956. *Work and Authority in Industry*. Berkeley: University of California Press.

———. 1964. *Nation-Building and Citizenship*. New York: Wiley.

———. 1968. Bureaucracy. In *International Encyclopedia of the Social Sciences*, ed. David L. Sills, 206–19. New York: Macmillan.

Benson, J. Kenneth. 1975. The Interorganizational Network as a Political Economy. *Administrative Science Quarterly* 20:229–49.

———. 1981. Networks and Policy Sectors: A Framework for Policy Analysis. In *Interorganizational Coordination*, ed. D. L. Rogers and D. A. Whetten, 137–76. Ames: Iowa State University Press.

Berger, Joseph, B. P. Cohen, and Morris Zelditch. 1966. Status Characteristics and Expectation States. In *Sociological Theories in Progress*, ed. J. Berger et al., 29–46. Boston: Houghton Mifflin.

———. 1972. Status Characteristics and Social Interaction. *American Sociological Review* 37:241–44.

Berger, Peter L. 1968. *The Sacred Canopy: Elements of a Sociological Theory of Religion*. New York: Doubleday.

Berger, Peter L., Brigitte Berger, and Hansfried Kellner. 1973. *The Homeless Mind: Modernization and Consciousness*. New York: Random House.

Berger, Peter L., and Thomas Luckmann. 1967. *The Social Construction of Reality*. New York: Doubleday.

Berger, Suzanne D., ed. 1981. *Organizing Interests in Western Europe: Pluralism, Corporatism, and the Transformation of Politics*. Cambridge: Cambridge University Press.

Berk, Sarah Fenstermaker. 1985. *The Gender Factory*. New York: Plenum.

Berman, Paul, and Milbrey McLaughlin. 1975–78. *Federal Programs supporting Educational Change*. Vols. 1–8. Santa Monica, Calif.: Rand Corporation.

Berner, Roberta. 1983. Giving in Minnesota—1982: For Corporations, Foundations, Total Giving Tops 180 Million Dollars. *Giving Forum* 6(4):6.

Bernstein, Basil. 1971. *Class, Codes, and Control*. Vol. 1. Boston: Routledge and Kegan Paul.

Bertsch, Kenneth. 1982. *Corporate Philanthropy*. Washington, D.C.: Investor Responsibility Research Center, Inc.

Best, Robert S. 1974. Youth Policy. In *Issues in Canadian Public Policy*, ed. G. B. Doern and V. S. Wilson, 137–65. San Francisco: Macmillan.

Bierstedt, Robert. 1970. *The Social Order*. 3rd ed. New York: McGraw-Hill.

Bierstedt, Robert, E. J. Meehan, and P. A. Samuelson. 1964. *Modern Social Science*. New York: McGraw-Hill.

Bingham, Mary, comp. 1933. *Who's Who in the Membership of the American Association of Museums*. Washington, D.C.: American Association of Museums.

Blake, J., and K. Davis. 1964. Norms, Values and Sanctions. In *Handbook of Modern Sociology*, ed. R. E. L. Faris, 247–79. Chicago: Rand McNally.

Blau, Peter M. 1956. *Bureaucracy in Modern Society*. New York: Random House.

————. 1970. A Formal Theory of Differentiation in Organizations. *American Sociological Review* 35:201–18.

————. 1977. *Inequality and Heterogeneity*. New York: Free Press.

Blau, Peter M., and Richard A. Schoenherr. 1971. *The Structure of Organizations*. New York: Basic Books.

Blau, Peter M., and W. Richard Scott. 1962. *Formal Organizations*. San Francisco: Chandler.

Block, Fred. 1977. The Ruling Class Does Not Rule. *Socialist Revolution* 7:6–28.

Blum, Alan F., and Peter McHugh. 1971. The Social Ascription of Motives. *American Sociological Review* 36:98–109.

Boltanski, Luc. *The Making of a Class: Cadres in French Society*. Trans. Arthur Goldhammer. New York: Cambridge University Press.

Boomer, D. S. 1959. Subjective Certainty and Resistance to Change. *Journal of Abnormal and Social Psychology* 58:323–28.

Boorman, Scott A., and Paul R. Levitt. 1979. The Cascade Principle for General Disequilibrium Dynamics. Harvard-Yale Reprints in Mathematical Sociology, no. 15.

Borcherding, T. E., and R. T. Deacon. 1972. The Demand for the Services of Non-Federal Government. *American Economic Review* 62:891–901.

Bourdieu, Pierre. [1972] 1977. *Outline of a Theory of Practice*. Cambridge: Cambridge University Press.

————. 1981. Men and Machines. In *Advances in Social Theory and Methodology*, ed. K. Knorr-Cetina and A. Cicourel, 304–18. Boston: Routledge and Kegan Paul.

————. 1984. *Distinction: A Social Critique of the Judgement of Taste*. Trans. Richard Nice. Cambridge: Harvard University Press.

————. 1990. *The Logic of Practice*. Stanford: Stanford University Press.

Bourdieu, Pierre, and Luc Boltanski. 1975. Le titre et le poste: Rapports entre le système de reproduction. *Actes de la Recherche en Sciences Sociales* 2:95–107.

Bourdieu, Pierre, and Jean-Claude Passeron. 1977. *Reproduction in Education, Society, and Culture*. Trans. Richard Nice. Beverly Hills, Calif.: Sage.

Bourricaud, François. 1981. *The Sociology of Talcott Parsons*. Chicago: University of Chicago Press.

Bower, Gordon H., J. Black, and T. Turner. 1979. Scripts in Text Comprehension and Memory. *Cognitive Psychology* 11:177–220.

Bowles, Samuel, and Herbert Gintis. 1976. *Schooling in Capitalist America*. New York: Basic Books.

Braito, Rita, Steve Paulson, and Gerald Klonglon. 1972. Domain Consensus: A Key Variable in Interorganizational Analysis. In *Complex Organizations and Their Environments*, ed. M. B. Brinkerhoff and P. R. Kunz, 176–92. Dubuque, Iowa: Wm. C Brown.

Braudel, Fernand. 1982. *The Wheels of Commerce*. New York: Harper and Row.

Brint, Steven. 1984. "New Class" and Cumulative Trend Explanations of the Liberal Political Attitudes of Professionals. *American Journal of Sociology* 91:30–70.

Brint, Steven, and Jerome Karabel. 1989. *The Diverted Dream: Community Colleges and the Promise of Educational Opportunity in America, 1900–1985*. New York: Oxford University Press.

Brown, John L., and Rodney Schneck. 1979. A Structuralist Comparison between Canadian and American Industrial Organizations. *Administrative Science Quarterly* 24:24–47.

Brown, Lawrence D. 1983. *New Policies, New Politics: Government's Response to Government's Growth.* Washington, D.C.: Brookings Institute.

Brown, Richard H. 1978. Bureaucracy as Praxis: Toward a Phenomenology of Formal Organizations. *Administrative Science Quarterly* 23 (September):365–82.

Buckley, Walter. 1967. *Sociology and Modern Systems Theory.* Englewood Cliffs, N.J.: Prentice-Hall.

Bull, Hedley, and Alan Watson. 1984. *The Expansion of International Society.* Oxford: Oxford University Press.

Burawoy, Michael. 1983. Between the Labor Process and the State: The Changing Face of Factory Regimes under Advanced Capitalism. *American Sociological Review* 48:587–605.

Burgelman, Robert A., and Jitendra V. Singh. 1988. Strategy and Organization: An Evolutionary Approach. Wharton School, University of Pennsylvania. Manuscript.

Burns, Lawton R., and Douglas R. Wholey. 1990. The Diffusion of Matrix Management: Effects of Task Diversity and Interorganizational Networks. Manuscript. University of Arizona.

Burns, Tom, and Helen Flam. 1987. *The Shaping of Social Organization.* Newbury Park, Calif.: Sage.

Burns, Tom, and G. M. Stalker. 1961. *The Management of Innovation.* London: Tavistock.

Burt, Ronald S. 1983. *Corporate Profits and Cooptation.* New York: Academic Press.

Cahill, Holger. 1944. John Cotton Dana and the Newark Museum. Foreword to *The Newark Museum: A Museum in Action.* Newark, N.J.: Newark Museum.

Callahan, Raymond E. 1962. *Education and the Cult of Efficiency.* Chicago: University of Chicago Press.

Camic, Charles. 1986. The Matter of Habit. *American Journal of Sociology* 91(5):1039–87.

———. 1989. Structure after 50 Years: The Anatomy of a Charter. *American Journal of Sociology* 95(1):38–107.

Campbell, R. F., and T. L. Mazzoni, Jr. 1976. *State Policy Making for the Public Schools.* Berkeley, Calif.: McCutchan.

Cantor, Nancy, and Walter Mischel. 1977. Traits as Prototypes: Effects on Recognition Memory. *Journal of Personality and Social Psychology* 35:38–49.

Carlson, Richard O. 1962. *Executive Succession and Organizational Change.* Chicago: Midwest Administration Center, University of Chicago.

Carroll, Glenn. 1983. A Stochastic Model of Organizational Mortality: Review and Reanalysis. *Social Science Research* 12:303–29.

———. 1984. Organizational Ecology. *Annual Review of Sociology* 10:71–93.

———. 1987. *Publish and Perish: The Organizational Ecology of Newspaper Foundings.* Greenwich, Conn.: JAI Press.

———, ed. 1988. *Ecological Models of Organization.* Cambridge, Mass.: Ballinger.

Carroll, Glenn R., and Jacques Delacroix. 1982. Organizational Mortality in the Newspaper Industries of Argentina and Ireland: An Ecological Approach. *Administrative Science Quarterly* 27:169–98.

Carroll, Glenn R., J. Delacroix, and J. Goodstein. 1988. The Political Environment of

Organizations: An Ecological View. In *Research in Organizational Behavior*, vol. 10. Greenwich, Conn.: JAI Press.

Carroll, Glenn R., Jerry Goodstein, and Antal Gyenes. 1988. Organizations and the State: Effects of the Institutional Environment on Agricultural Cooperatives in Hungry. *Administrative Science Quarterly* 33(2):233–56.

Carroll, Glenn R., and Yang-chung Paul Huo. 1986. Organizational Task and Institutional Environments in Ecological Perspective: Findings from the Local Newspaper Industry. *American Journal of Sociology* 91:838–73.

Caves, Richard E., and Masu Uekusa. 1976. *Industrial Organization in Japan.* Washington, D.C.: Brookings Institute.

Chandler, Alfred D. 1961. *Strategy and Structure.* Cambridge: MIT Press.

———. 1977. *The Visible Hand: The Managerial Revolution in American Business.* Cambridge: Harvard University Press.

Chang, Chan-sup. 1987. Management of Chaebol: The Conglomerate in South Korea. In *Proceedings of the Pan-Pacific Conference IV*, 42–47. Taipei, Taiwan.

Child, John. 1972. Organization Structure, Environment and Performance: The Role of Strategic Choice. *Sociology* 6:1–22.

Child, John, and Alfred Kieser. 1981. Development of Organizations over Time. In *Handbook of Organizational Design*, ed. P. C. Nystrom and W. H. Starbuck, 28–64. New York: Oxford University Press.

Cicourel, Aaron. 1964. *Method and Measurement in Sociology.* New York: Free Press.

———. 1970. The Acquisition of Social Structure: Toward a Developmental Sociology of Language. In *Understanding Everyday Life*, ed. J. D. Douglas, 136–68. Chicago: Aldine.

———. 1974. *Cognitive Sociology.* New York: Free Press.

Ciniglio, Ada V. 1976. Pioneers in American Museums: Paul J. Sachs. *Museum News* 54:48–51, 68–71.

Clark, Burton R. 1956. *Adult Education in Transition.* Berkeley: University of California Press.

———. 1960a. The "Cooling-Out Function" in Higher Education. *American Journal of Sociology* 65:569–76.

———. 1960b. *The Open-Door Colleges: A Case Study.* New York: McGraw-Hill.

———. 1962. *Educating the Expert Society.* San Francisco: Chandler.

———. 1986. *The Higher Education System: Academic Organization in Cross-National Perspective.* Berkeley: University of California Press.

Coase, Ronald H. 1937. The Nature of the Firm. *Economica* 16:386–405.

———. 1960. The Problem of Social Cost. *Journal of Law and Economics* 3:1–44.

Cohen, Bernard P. 1980. *Developing Sociological Knowledge: Theory and Method.* Englewood Cliffs, N.J.: Prentice-Hall.

Cohen, Michael D., and James G. March. 1974. *Leadership and Ambiguity: The American College President.* New York: McGraw-Hill.

Cohen, Michael D., James G. March, and Johan P. Olsen. 1972. A Garbage Can Model of Organizational Choice. *Administrative Science Quarterly* 17:1–25.

Cohen, Myron L. 1976. *House United, House Divided: The Chinese Family in Taiwan.* New York: Columbia University Press.

Cole, Robert. 1985. The Macropolitics of Organizational Change: A Comparative Analysis of the Spread of Small-Group Activities. *Administrative Science Quarterly* 30:560–85.

Coleman, J. F., R. R. Blake, and J. S. Mouton. 1958. Task Difficulty and Conformity Pressures. *Journal of Abnormal and Social Psychology* 57:120–22.

Coleman, James S. 1964. *Introduction to Mathematical Sociology.* New York: Free Press.

———. 1974. *Power and the Structure of Society.* New York: Norton.

———. 1982. *The Asymmetric Society.* Syracuse, N.Y.: Syracuse University Press.

———. 1985. Micro Foundations and Macrosocial Theory. In *Approaches to Social Theory,* ed. S. Lindenberg et al., 345–63. New York: Russell Sage.

———. 1986. Social Theory, Social Research, and a Theory of Action. *American Journal of Sociology* 91:1309–35.

Coleman, James S., and Thomas Hoffer. 1987. *Public and Private High Schools: The Impact of Communities.* New York: Basic Books.

Coleman, Laurence Vail. 1932. Recent Progress and Condition of Museums. In U.S. Commissioner of Education, *Biennial Survey of Education in the United States, 1928–30.* Washington, D.C.: U.S. Government Printing Office.

———. 1939. *The Museum in America: A Critical Study.* Washington, D.C.: American Association of Museums.

Collins, N., and L. Preston. 1961. The Size Structure of the Largest Industrial Firms, 1900–1958. *American Economic Review* 51:986–1011.

Collins, Randall. 1975. *Conflict Sociology.* New York: Academic Press.

———. 1979. *The Credential Society.* New York: Academic Press.

———. 1981. On the Micro-Foundations of Macro-Sociology. *American Journal of Sociology* 86:984–1014.

———. 1986a. Is Sociology in the Doldrums? *American Journal of Sociology* 91:1336–55.

———. 1986b. The Weberian Revolution of the High Middle Ages. In *Weberian Sociology Theory,* 45–76. New York: Cambridge University Press.

———. 1988a. The Durkheimian Tradition in Conflict Sociology. In *Durkeimian Sociology: Cultural Studies,* ed. J. C. Alexander, 107–28. New York: Columbia University Press.

———. 1988b. The Micro Contribution to Macro Sociology. *Sociological Theory* 6:242–53.

Committee on Youth. 1971. *A Report to the Secretary of State: It's Your Turn.* Ottawa: Information Canada.

Cooke, Edmund. 1934. A Survey of the Educational Activities of Forty-seven Museums. *Museum News* 12:6.

Cooper, S. K., and D. R. Fraser. 1984. *Banking Deregulation and the New Competition in the Financial Services Industry.* Cambridge, Mass.: Ballinger Press.

Copeland, M. 1927. Marketing. In *Recent Economic Changes in the United States,* 321–424. New York: McGraw-Hill.

Cornwell, H. C. 1966. Personality Variables in Autokinetic Figure Writing. *Perceptual and Motor Skills* 22:731–35.

Coser, Lewis, Charles Kadushin, and Walter W. Powell. 1982. *Books: The Culture and Commerce of Publishing.* New York: Basic Books.

Covaleski, Mark A., and Mark W. Dirsmith. 1988. An Institutional Perspective on the

Rise, Social Transformation, and Fall of a University Budget Category. *Administrative Science Quarterly* 33(4):562–87.

Cross, K. Patricia. 1971. *Beyond the Open Door.* San Francisco: Jossey-Bass.

Cummings, Bruce. 1984. The Origins and Development of the Northeast Asian Political Economy: Industrial Sectors Product Cycles, and Political Consequences. *International Organization* 381:1–40.

Cyert, Richard M., and James G. March. 1963. *A Behavioral Theory of the Firm.* Englewood Cliffs, N.J.: Prentice-Hall.

Daft, Richard L. 1983. *Organization Theory and Design.* St. Paul, Minn.: West Publishing.

Dahrendorf, Ralf. 1964. *Class and Class Conflict in Industrial Society.* Stanford: Stanford University Press.

Daily Economic News. 1986. *Directory of Korean Firms for 1985.*

Dalton, Melville, 1959. *Men Who Manage.* New York: Wiley.

Dana, John Cotton. 1917. *The Gloom of the Museum.* Woodstock, Vt.: Elm Tree Press.

David, Paul. 1986. Understanding the Economics of QWERTY: The Necessity of History. In *Economic History and the Modern Historian,* ed. W. Parker, 30–49. London: Blackwell.

Davis, Keith. 1973. The Case for and against Business Assumption of Social Responsibilities. *Academy of Management Journal* 16:312–22.

Davis, Kingsley. 1949. *Human Society.* New York: Macmillan.

Davis, Stanley M., and Paul R. Lawrence. 1977. *Matrix.* Reading, Mass.: Addison-Wesley.

Deacon, R. T. 1978. A Demand Model for the Local Public Sector. *Review of Economics and Statistics* 50:184–92.

Deci, Edward L. 1971. Effects of Externally Mediated Rewards on Intrinsic Motivation. *Journal of Personality and Social Psychology* 18:105–15.

Delacroix, Jacques, and Glenn R. Carroll. 1983. Organizational Foundings: An Ecological Study of the Newspaper Industry of Argentina and Ireland. *Administrative Science Quarterly* 28:274–91.

Deleuze, Giles. 1988. *Foucault.* Minneapolis: University of Minnesota Press.

Derthick, Martha, 1972. *New Towns In-Town.* Washington, D.C.,: Urban Institute.

Dill, William R. 1958. Environment as an Influence on Managerial Autonomy. *Administrative Science Quarterly* 2:409–43.

DiMaggio, Paul J. 1977. Market Structures, the Creative Process, and Popular Culture. *Journal of Popular Culture* 11:436–52.

———. 1982a. Cultural Entrepreneurship in Nineteenth-Century Boston, Part I: The Creation of an Organizational Base for High Culture in America. *Media, Culture and Society* 4:33–50.

———. 1982b. Cultural Entrepreneurship in Nineteenth-Century Boston, Part II: The Classification and Framing of American Art. *Media, Culture and Society* 4:303–22.

———. 1983. State Expansion and Organizational Fields. In *Organizational Theory and Public Policy,* ed. R. H. Hall and R. E. Quinn, 147–61. Beverly Hills, Calif.: Sage.

———. 1986a. Structural Analysis of Organizational Fields: A Blockmodel Approach. In *Research in Organizational Behavior,* ed. Barry M. Staw and L. L. Cummings, 8:335–70. Greenwich, Conn.: JAI Press.

————. 1986b. Support for the Arts from Private Foundations. In *Nonprofit Enterprise in the Arts,* ed. Paul DiMaggio, 113–39. New York: Oxford University Press.

————. 1988a. Interest and Agency in Institutional Theory. In *Institutional Patterns and Organizations,* ed. L. G. Zucker, 3–22. Cambridge, Mass.: Ballinger.

————. 1988b. Progressivism in the Arts. *Society* 25:70–75.

DiMaggio, Paul J., and Walter W. Powell. 1983. The Iron Cage Revisited: Institutional Isomorphism and Collective Rationality in Organizational Fields. *American Sociological Review* 48:147–60.

————. 1984. Institutional Isomorphism and Structural Conformity. Paper presented at 1984 American Sociological Association Annual meetings, San Antonio, Tex.

Dobbin, Frank R. 1986. The Institutionalization of the State: Industrial Policy in Britain, France, and the United States. Ph.D. diss., Stanford University.

Dobbin, Frank R., Lauren Edelman, John W. Meyer, W. Richard Scott, and Ann Swidler. 1988. The Expansion of Due Process in Organizations. In *Institutional Patterns and Organizations,* ed. L. G. Zucker, 71–98. Cambridge, Mass.: Ballinger.

Dodwell Marketing Consultants, comp. 1984. *Industrial Groupings in Japan.* Rev. ed. Tokyo: Dodwell.

Domhoff, J. William. 1967. *Who Rules America?* Englewood Cliffs, N.J.: Prentice-Hall.

————. 1970. *The Higher Circles.* New York: Random House.

————. 1979. *The Powers That Be: Processes of Ruling Class Domination in America.* New York: Random House.

————. 1983. *Who Rules America Now?* Englewood Cliffs, N.J.: Prentice-Hall.

Donabedian, Avedis. 1966. Evaluating the Quality of Medical Care. *Milbank Memorial Fund Quarterly* 44(part 2):166–203.

Dore, Ronald P. 1976. *The Diploma Disease: Education, Qualifications and Development.* Berkeley: University of California Press.

————. 1983. Goodwill and the Spirit of Market Capitalism. *British Journal of Sociology* 34(4):459–82.

————. 1986. *Structural Adjustment in Japan, 1970–82.* Geneva: International Labour Office.

Dornbusch, Sanford, M., and W. Richard Scott. 1975. *Evaluation and the Exercise of Authority.* San Francisco: Jossey-Bass.

Douglas, Mary. 1986. *How Institutions Think.* Syracuse, N.Y.: Syracuse University Press.

Dowling, John, and Jeffrey Pfeffer. 1975. Organizational Legitimacy: Social Values and Organizational Behavior. *Pacific Sociological Review* 18:122–36.

Downs, Anthony. 1967. *Inside Bureaucracy.* Boston: Little, Brown.

Dumont, Louis. 1982. A Modified View of Our Origins: The Christian Beginnings of Modern Individualism. *Religion* 12:1–27.

Durkheim, Emile. [1901] 1950. *The Rules of Sociological Method.* Glencoe, Ill.: Free Press.

————. 1933. *The Division of Labor in Society.* New York: Macmillan.

Dye, Thomas R. 1981. *Understanding Public Policy.* 4th ed. Englewood Cliffs, N.J.: Prentice-Hall.

————. 1986. *Who's Running America? The Conservative Years.* 4th ed. Englewood Cliffs, N.J.: Prentice-Hall.

Dyson, Kenneth H. F. 1980. *The State Tradition in Western Europe*. Oxford: Oxford University Press.

Eccles, Robert G., and Harrison C. White. 1988. Price and Authority in Inter-Profit Center Transactions. *American Journal of Sociology* 94:517–52.

Economic Council of Canada. 1976. *People and Jobs: A Study of the Canadian Labour Market*. Ottawa: Information Canada.

————. 1977. *Into the 80s*. Ottawa: Information Canada.

Edelman, Lauren B. 1985. Organizational Governance and Due Process: The Expansion of Rights in the American Workplace. Ph.D. diss., Stanford University.

————. 1990. Legal Environments and Organizational Governance: The Expansion of Due Process in the American Workplace. *American Journal of Sociology* 95:1401–40.

Edelman, Murray. 1967. *The Symbolic Uses of Politics*. Urbana: University of Illinois Press.

Eis, C. 1978. *The 1919–1930 Merger Movement in American Industry*. New York: Arno Press.

Eisenstadt, Schmuel N. 1968. Social Institutions: The Concept. In *International Encyclopedia of the Social Sciences*, ed. D. L. Sills, 14:409–21. New York: Macmillan.

————. 1983. Transcendental Visions—Other Worldliness—And Its Transformations. *Religion* 13:1–17.

————. 1985. Civilizational Formations and Political Dynamics: The Stein Rokkan Lecture, 1985. *Scandinavian Political Studies* 8:231–51.

Elazar, Daniel J. 1972. *American Federalism: A View from the States*. 2d ed. New York: Harper and Row.

Elias, Norbert. 1978. *The Civilizing Process*. New York: Urizen Books.

Ellul, Jacques. 1964. *The Technological Society*. New York: Knopf.

Elster, Jon. 1982. Marxism, Functionalism, and Game Theory. *Theory and Society* 11:453–82.

————. 1985. *Making Sense of Marx*. Cambridge: Cambridge University Press.

————. 1986. Introduction. In *Rational Choice*, ed. John Elster, 1–33. New York: New York University Press.

Emery, Fred L., and Eric L. Trist. 1965. The Causal Texture of Organizational Environments. *Human Relations* 18:21–32.

Encarnation, Dennis J. 1983. Public Finance and Regulation of Non-Public Education: Retrospect and Prospect. In *Public Dollars for Private Schools*, ed. T. James and H. M. Levin, 175–95. Philadelphia: Temple University Press.

Estes, Carroll L. 1979. *The Aging Enterprise*. San Francisco: Jossey-Bass.

Evan, William M. 1966. The Organization Set: Toward a Theory of Interorganizational Relations. In *Approaches to Organizational Design*, ed. James D. Thompson, 173–88. Pittsburgh: University of Pittsburgh Press.

Everard, L. C., ed. 1932. *Handbook of American Museums*. Washington, D.C.: American Association of Museums.

Fararo, Thomas J., and John Skvoretz. 1986. Action and Institution, Network and Function: The Cybernetic Concept of Social Structure. *Sociological Forum* 1:219–50.

Farr, Robert M., and Serge Moscovici, eds. 1984. *Social Representations*. Cambridge: Cambridge University Press.

Farrow, B. J., J. F. Santos, J. R. Haines, and C. M. Solley. 1965. Influence of Repeated

Experience on the Latency and Extent of Autokinetic Movement. *Perceptual and Motor Skills* 20:1113–20.

Faucheux, Claude, Gilles Amado, and Andre Laurent. 1982. Organizational Development and Change. *Annual Review of Psychology* 33:343–70.

Federal Trade Commission. 1957. *Report on Industrial Concentration and Product Diversification in the 1000 Largest Manufacturing Companies.* Washington, D.C.: U.S. Government Printing Office.

Feinberg, Walter. 1980. *Revisionists Respond to Ravitch.* Washington, D. C.: National Academy of Education.

Fennell, Mary L. 1980. The Effects of Environmental Characteristics on the Structure of Hospital Clusters. *Administrative Science Quarterly* 25:484–510.

Field, Alexander J. 1979. On the Explanation of Rules Using Rational Choice Models. *Journal of Economic Issues* 13:49–72.

Firestone, William A. 1985. The Study of Loose Coupling: Problems, Progress, and Prospects. In *Research in Sociology of Education and Socialization,* ed. Ronald G. Corwin, 5:3–30. Greenwich, Conn.: JAI Press.

Fiske, Susan T. 1982. Schema-Triggered Affect: Applications to Social Perception. In *Affect and Cognition: The 17th Annual Carnegie Symposium on Cognition,* ed. M. S. Clarke and S. T. Fiske, 55–78. Hillsdale, N.J.: Erlbaum.

Fiske, Susan T., and Mark A. Pavelchak. 1986. Category-Based versus Piece-meal-Based Affective Responses: Developments in Schema-Triggered Affect. In *Handbook of Motivation and Cognition: Foundations of Social Behavior,* ed. R. M. Sorrentino and E. T. Higgins, 167–203. New York: Guilford.

Fitzpatrick, Sheila. 1979. *Education and Social Mobility in the Soviet Union, 1921–1934.* New York: Columbia University Press.

Flacks, Richard. 1988. *Making History vs. Making Life: Left and Mainstream in American Consciousness.* New York: Columbia University Press.

Fligstein, Neil. 1985. The Spread of the Multidivisional Form among Large Firms, 1919–1979. *American Sociological Review* 50:377–91.

———. 1987. The Intraorganizational Power Struggle: The Rise of Finance Presidents in Large Firms, 1919–79. *American Sociological Review* 52:44–58.

———. 1990a. Organizational, Economic, and Demographic Determinants of the Growth Patterns of Large Firms, 1919–79. In *Comparative Social Research,* ed. Craig Calhoun, 12:45–76. Greenwich, Conn.: JAI Press.

———. 1990b. *The Transformation of Corporate Control.* Cambridge: Harvard University Press.

Flora, Peter, and J. A. Heidenheimer. 1981. *The Development of Welfare States in Europe and America.* New Brunswick, N.J.: Transaction.

Foucault, Michel. 1978. *The History of Sexuality.* Vol. 1. New York: Vintage.

———. 1979. Governmentality. *Ideology and Consciousness* 6:5–21.

———. 1980. *Power/Knowledge.* Ed. Colin Gordon. New York: Pantheon.

———. 1983. The Subject and Power. In *Michel Foucault: Beyond Structuralism and Hermeneutics,* 2d ed., ed. H. Dreyfus and P. Rabinow, 208–23. Chicago: University of Chicago Press.

Fox, Daniel M. 1963. *Engines of Culture: Philanthropy and Art Museums.* Madison: Wisconsin State Historical Society.

Freedman, J. L., J. M. Carlsmith, and D. O. Sears. 1974. *Social Psychology*. 2d ed. Englewood Cliffs, N.J.: Prentice-Hall.

Freeman, John H. 1973. Environment, Technology and Administrative Intensity of Manufacturing Organizations. *American Sociological Review* 38:750–63.

———. 1979. Going to the Well: School District Administrative Intensity and Environmental Constraint. *Administrative Science Quarterly* 24:119–33.

———. 1982. Organizational Life Cycles and Natural Selection Processes. In *Research in Organizational Behavior,* ed. B. Staw and L. L. Cummings, 4:1–32. Greenwich, Conn.: JAI Press.

Freeman, John H., Glenn R. Carroll, and Michael T. Hannan. 1983. The Liability of Newness: Age Dependence in Organizational Death Rates. *American Sociological Review* 48:692–710.

Freeman, John H., and Michael T. Hannan. 1983. Niche Width and the Dynamics of Organizational Populations. *American Journal of Sociology* 88:1116–45.

Freidson, Eliot. 1986. *Professional Powers: A Study of the Institutionalization of Formal Knowledge*. Chicago: University of Chicago Press.

Friedland, Roger, and Richard D. Hecht. 1989. Rocks, Roads and Ramot Control: The Other War for Jerusalem. *Soundings* 72(2–3):227–73.

———. 1990. Jerusalem: Deconstructing the Politics of a Sacred City. Paper presented at the American Academy of Religion, New Orleans.

Friedland, Roger, and A. F. Robertson. 1990. Beyond the Marketplace. In *Beyond the Marketplace: Rethinking Economy and Society*. ed. Roger Friedland and A. F. Robertson, 2–52. New York: Aldine de Gruyter.

Friedman, Debra, and Michael Hechter. 1988. The Contribution of Rational Choice Theory to Macrosociological Research. Paper presented at the annual meetings of the American Sociological Association, Atlanta, Ga.

Friedman, Lawrence M. 1973. *A History of American Law*. New York: Simon and Schuster.

Fukuda, John K. 1983. Transfer of Management: Japanese Practices for the Orientals? *Management Decision* 21:17–26.

Futatsugi, Yusaku. 1982. *Nihon no kabushiki shoyu kozo* (The structure of shareholding in Japan). Tokyo: Dobunkan.

———. 1986. *Japanese Enterprise Groups*. Monograph No. 4. School of Business Administration, Kobe University.

Galaskiewicz, Joseph. 1984. Interorganizational Relations. *Annual Review of Sociology* 11:281–304.

———. 1985a. Professional Networks and the Institutionalization of a Single Mind Set. *American Sociological Review* 50:639–58.

———. 1985b. *Social Organization of an Urban Grants Economy: A Study of Business Philanthropy and Nonprofit Organizations*. Orlando, Fla.: Academic Press.

———. 1987. The Study of a Business Elite and Corporate Philanthropy in a U.S. Metropolitan Area. In *Research Methods for Elite Studies,* ed. G. Moyser and M. Wagstaffe, 147–65. London: Allen and Unwin.

Galaskiewicz, Joseph, and Ronald S. Burt. 1991. Interorganizational Contagion in Corporate Philanthropy. *Administrative Science Quarterly* 36(1):88–105.

Galaskiewicz, Joseph, and Stanley Wasserman. 1989. Mimetic and Normative Processes within an Interorganizational Field: An Empirical Test. *Administrative Science Quarterly* 34(3):454–79.

Galbraith, Jay. 1973. *Designing Complex Organizations*. Reading, Mass.: Addison-Wesley.

Gamson, William A. 1975. *The Strategy of Social Protest*. Homewood, Ill.: Dorsey Press.

Gans, Sheldon, and Gerald Horton. 1975. *Integration of Human Services: The State and Municipal Levels*. New York: Praeger.

Gardner, Elmer A., and James N. Snipe. 1970. Toward the Coordination and Integration of Personal Health Services. *American Journal of Public Health* 60:2068–78.

Garfinkel, Harold. 1967. *Studies in Ethnomethodology*. Englewood Cliffs, N.J.: Prentice-Hall.

GAUSS. 1985. Program and Documentation.

Geertz, Clifford. 1973. *The Interpretation of Cultures*. New York: Basic Books.

———. 1975. On the Nature of Anthropological Understanding. *American Scientist* 63:47–53.

———. 1983. *Local Knowledge*. New York: Basic Books.

Gerth, Hans, and C. Wright Mills. 1953. *Character and Social Structure*. New York: Harcourt Brace.

Giddens, Anthony. 1976. *The New Rules of the Sociological Method*. New York: Basic Books.

———. 1979. *Central Problems in Social Theory: Action, Structure, and Contradiction in Social Analysis*. Berkeley: University of California Press.

———. 1982. *Sociology*. New York: Harcourt Brace Jovanovich.

———. 1984. *The Constitution of Society*. Berkeley: University of California Press.

———. 1986. *The Nation-State and Violence*. Berkeley: University of California Press.

Gilman, Benjamin Ives. 1918. *Museum Ideals*. Cambridge: Harvard University Press for the Museum of Fine Arts.

Glasberg, Davita S., and Michael Schwartz. 1983. Ownership and Control of Corporations. *Annual Review of Sociology* 9:311–32.

Goffman, Erving. 1961. *Asylums: Essays on the Social Situation of Mental Patients and Other Inmates*. New York: Doubleday.

———. 1967. *Interaction Ritual*. Garden City, N.Y.: Anchor.

———. 1974. *Frame Analysis*. Cambridge: Harvard University Press.

Gold, Thomas B. 1986. *State and Society in the Taiwan Miracle*. New York: M. E. Sharpe.

Goldner, Fred, and Richard R. Ritti. 1967. Professionalism as Career Immobility. *American Journal of Sociology* 72:489–502.

Goode, George Brown. 1897. Memorial to George Brown Goode, Together with a Selection of His Papers on Museums and on the History of Science in America. In *Annual Report for 1897*. Smithsonian Institution, Washington, D.C.

Goodwin, Gregory. 1971. The Historical Development of the Community-Junior College Ideology. Ph.D. diss., Department of Education, University of Illinois.

Gort, M., 1961. *Diversification and Integration in American Industry*. Princeton: Princeton University Press.

Gouldner, Alvin W. 1954. *Patterns of Industrial Bureaucracy*. Glencoe, Ill.: Free Press.

———. 1962. Anti-Minotaur: The Myth of a Value-Free Sociology. *Social Problems* 9:199–213.

———. 1970. *The Coming Crisis of Western Sociology.* New York: Basic Books.

———. 1978. The New Class Project, I. *Theory and Society* 7:153–202.

———. 1979. *The Future of Intellectuals and the Rise of the New Class.* New York: Seabury.

Gramsci, Antonio. 1971. *Selections from the Prison Notebooks.* New York: International Publishers.

Grana, Cesar. 1963. *Fact and Symbol: Essays in the Sociology of Art and Literature.* New York: Oxford University Press.

Granovetter, Mark. 1973. The Strength of Weak Ties. *American Journal of Sociology* 78:1360–80.

———. 1978. Threshold Models of Collective Behavior. *American Journal of Sociology* 83:1420–43.

———. 1985. Economic Action and Social Structure: The Problem of Embeddedness. *American Journal of Sociology* 91:481–510.

Greenwood, Royston, and C. R. Hinings. 1988. Organizational Design Types, Tracks, and the Dynamics of Strategic Change. *Organization Studies* 9:293–316.

Gregory, R. L., and O. L. Zangweil. 1963. The Origin of the Autokinetic Effect. *Quarterly Journal of Experimental Psychology* 15:252–61.

Grodzins, Morton. 1961. Centralization and Decentralization in the Federal System. In *A Nation of States: Essays on the American Federal System,* ed. Robert A. Goldwin, 1–23. Chicago: Rand McNally.

———. 1966. *The American System.* Chicago: Rand McNally.

Grossman, Sanford J., and Oliver Hart. 1987. The Costs and Benefits of Ownership: A Theory of Vertical and Lateral Integration. *Journal of Political Economy* 94:691–719.

Gusfield, Joseph. 1955. Social Structure and Moral Reform: A Study of the Womens' Christian Temperance Union. *American Journal of Sociology* 61:221–32.

Gwyn, Sandra. 1972. The Great Ottawa Grant Boom (and How It Grew). *Saturday Night* 87(10):7–20.

Habermas, Jurgen. 1970. *Toward a Rational Society.* Boston: Beacon Press.

———. 1975. *Legitimation Crisis.* Boston: Beacon Press.

———. 1984. *The Theory of Communicative Action.* Boston: Beacon Press.

Hadley, Eleanor M. 1970. *Antitrust in Japan.* Princeton: Princeton University Press.

Hahn, Chan K., Yong H. Kim, and Jay S. Kim. 1987. An Analysis of Korean Chaebols: Formation and Growth Pattern. In *Proceedings of the Pan-Pacific Conference IV,* 128–33. Taipei, Taiwan.

Hall, John A. 1986. *Powers and Liberties: The Causes and Consequences of the Rise of the West.* New York: Penguin.

Hall, Peter. 1987. A Historical Overview of the Private Nonprofit Sector. In *The Nonprofit Sector: A Research Handbook,* ed. W. W. Powell, 3–26. New Haven: Yale University Press.

Hall, Richard. 1968. Professionalization and Bureaucratization. *American Sociological Review* 33:92–104.

Halperin, Mortin H. 1974. *Bureaucratic Politics and Foreign Policy.* Washington, D.C.: Brookings Institution.

Hamilton, Gary G., and Nicole Woolsey Biggart. 1988. Market, Culture, and Authority: A Comparative Analysis of Management and Organization in the Far East. *American Journal of Sociology* 94:S52–S94.

Hankook Ilbo. 1985. *Pal ship o nyndo hankook ui 50 dae jae bul* (The 50 top *chaebol* in Korea). Seoul, Korea.

Hannan, Michael T. 1986a. A Model of Competitive and Institutional Processes in Organizational Ecology. Technical Report No. 86-13. Department of Sociology, Cornell University.

———. 1986b. Uncertainty, Diversity, and Organizational Change. In *Behavioral and Social Sciences: Fifty Years of Discovery,* ed. N. Smelser and D. Gerstein, 73–94. Washington, D.C.: National Academy Press.

Hannan, Michael T., and John H. Freeman. 1977. The Population Ecology of Organizations. *American Journal of Sociology* 82:929–64.

———. 1981. Niche Width and the Dynamics of Organizational Populations. Technical Report No. 2. Institute for Mathematical Studies in the Social Sciences, Stanford University.

———. 1984. Structural Inertia and Organizational Change. *American Sociological Review* 49:149–64.

———. 1987. The Ecology of Organizational Founding: American Labor Unions, 1836–1985. *American Journal of Sociology* 92:910–43.

———. 1988. The Ecology of Organizational Mortality: American Labor Unions, 1836–1985. *American Journal of Sociology* 94:25–52.

———. 1989. *Organizational Ecology.* Cambridge: Harvard University Press.

Harris, Neil. 1962. The Gilded Age Revisited: Boston and the Museum Movement. *American Quarterly* 14:545–66.

Hastings, A., and C. R. Hinings. 1970. Role Relations and Value Adaptation: A Study of the Professional Accountant in Industry. *Sociology* 4:353–66.

Hatch, Elvin. 1989. Theories of Social Honor. *American Anthropologist* 91:341–53.

Hawley, Amos. 1968. Human Ecology. In *International Encyclopedia of the Social Sciences,* ed. David L. Sills, 328–37. New York: Macmillan.

Hawley, Ellis W. 1966. *The New Deal and the Problem of Monopoly: A Study in Economic Ambivalence.* Princeton: Princeton University Press.

Hay, Robert, and Ed Gray. 1974. Social Responsibilities of Business Managers. *Academy of Management Journal* 17:135–43.

Hayek, Friedrich August von. 1973. *Law, Legislation, and Liberty.* Vol. 1. London: Routledge and Kegan Paul.

Hayes, Michael T. 1981. *Lobbyists and Legislators: A Theory of Political Markets.* New Brunswick, N.J.: Rutgers University Press.

Hays, Samuel P. 1957. *The Response to Industrialism, 1985–1914.* Chicago: University of Chicago Press.

———. 1964. The Politics of Reform in Municipal Government in the Progressive Era. *Pacific Northwest Quarterly* 55:157–69.

———. 1972. The New Organizational Society. In *Building the Organizational Society,* ed. Jerry Israel, 1–9. New York: Free Press.

Hechter, Michael. 1975. *Internal Colonialism: The Celtic Fringe in British National Development, 1536–1966.* Berkeley: University of California Press.

————, ed. 1983. *The Micro Foundations of Macrosociology*. Philadelphia: Temple University Press.

Heintz, Kathleen. 1976. State Organizations for Human Services. *Evaluation* 3:106–10.

Heritage, John C. 1984. *Garfinkel and Ethnomethodology*. Cambridge, England: Polity Press.

————. 1987. Ethnomethodology. In *Social Theory Today*, ed. A. Giddens and J. Turner, 224–72. Stanford: Stanford University Press.

Hernes, Gudmund. 1976. Structural Change in Social Process. *American Journal of Sociology* 82:513–47.

Herriot, Robert E., and William A. Firestone. 1984. Two Images of Schools as Organizations: A Refinement and Elaboration. *Educational Administration Quarterly* 20:48–57.

Hicks, John. 1969. *A Theory of Economic History*. Oxford: Oxford University Press.

Hirsch, Paul M. 1972. Processing Fads and Fashions: An Organization-Set Analysis of Cultural Industry Systems. *American Journal of Sociology* 77:639–59.

————. 1975. Organizational Effectiveness and the Institutional Environment. *Administrative Science Quarterly* 20:327–44.

————. 1985. The Study of Industries. In *Research in the Sociology of Organizations*, ed. S. B. Bacharach and S. M. Mitchell, 4:271–309. Greenwich, Conn.: JAI Press.

————. 1986. From Ambushes to Golden Parachutes: Corporate Takeovers as an Instance of Cultural Framing and Institutional Integration. *American Journal of Sociology* 91:800–837.

Hirsch, Paul M., and Thomas Whisler. 1982. The View from the Boardroom. Paper presented at Academy of Management Meetings, New York, N.Y.

Hirschman, Albert O. 1972. *Exit, Voice, and Loyalty*. Cambridge: Harvard University Press.

————. 1986. The Concept of Interest: From Euphemis to Tautology. In *Rival Views of Market Society*, 35–55. New York: Viking.

Hiss, Priscilla, and Roberta Fansler. 1934. *Research in Fine Arts in the Colleges and Universities of the United States*. New York: Carnegie Corporation.

Hobbs, C. 1924. Why a Sales Training Makes a Good Manufacturer. *System*, August 1924, 147–49.

Hofstadter, Richard. 1955. *The Age of Reform*. New York: Knopf.

Hofstede, Geert. 1980. *Culture's Consequences: International Differences in Work-Related Values*. Beverly Hills, Calif.: Sage.

Hogan, Daniel J. 1985. *Class and Reform: School and Society in Chicago, 1880–1930*. Philadelphia: University of Pennsylvania Press.

Hollis, Martin. 1985. Of Masks and Men. In *The Category of the Person*, ed. Michael Carrithers et al., 217–33. New York: Cambridge University Press.

Holusha, John. 1987. Accounting in Factories Is Criticized as Outdated. *New York Times*, March 23.

Homans, George C. 1950. *The Human Group*. New York: Harcourt, Brace.

————. 1961. *Social Behavior: Its Elementary Forms*. New York: Harcourt Brace Jovanovich.

Hopwood, Anthony. 1983. On Trying to Study Accounting in the Contexts in Which It Operates. *Accounting, Organizations, and Society* 8:287–305.

Horwitz, Morton J. 1977. *The Transformation of American Law, 1780–1860.* Cambridge: Harvard University Press.

Houston, Lorne F. 1972. The Flowers of Power: A Critique of OFY and LIP Programmes. *Our Generation* 7:52–71.

Hughes, Everett C. 1936. The Ecological Aspect of Institutions. *American Sociological Review* 1:180–89.

———. 1937. Institutional Office and the Person. *American Journal of Sociology* 63:79–87.

Hunt, Lynn. 1984. *Politics, Culture, and Class in the French Revolution.* Berkeley: University of California Press.

Huntington, Samuel P. 1968. *Political Order in Changing Societies.* New Haven: Yale University Press.

Hurst, James Willard. 1982. *Law and Markets in United States History.* Madison: University of Wisconsin Press.

Inkeles, Alex, and David H. Smith. 1974. *Becoming Modern: Individual Change in Six Developing Countries.* Cambridge: Harvard University Press.

Ishida, Hideto. 1983. Anticompetitive Practices in the Distribution of Goods and Services in Japan: The Problem of Distribution *Keiretsu. Journal of Japanese Studies* 9:319–34.

Jacobs, David, M. Useem, and M. Zald. 1991. Firms, Industries, and Politics. In *Research in Political Sociology* 5:141–65. Greenwich, Conn.: JAI Press.

Jacobs, Norman. 1985. *The Korean Road to Modernization and Development.* Urbana: University of Illinois Press.

Jacobs, R. C., and D. T. Campbell. 1961. The Perpetuation of an Arbitrary Tradition through Successive Generations of a Laboratory Microculture. *Journal of Abnormal and Social Psychology* 62:649–58.

Jacoby, Sanford, 1985. *Employing Bureaucracy.* New York: Columbia University Press.

Janowitz, Morris. 1969. *Institution Building in Urban Education.* New York: Russell Sage Foundation.

———. 1978. *The Last Half Century: Societal Change and Politics in America.* Chicago: University of Chicago Press.

Johnston, John. 1972. *Econometric Methods.* 2d ed. New York: McGraw-Hill.

Jones, E. L. 1981. *The European Miracle.* New York: Cambridge University Press.

Jubin, Brenda. 1968. *Program in the Arts, 1911–1967.* New York: Carnegie Corporation.

Kalberg, Steven. 1980. Max Weber's Types of Rationality: Cornerstones for the Analysis of Rationalization Processes in History. *American Journal of Sociology* 85:1145–79.

Kamm, Henry. 1987. With Prague, Glasnost Comes in a Fainter Echo. *New York Times,* November 7, p. 4.

Kanter, Rosabeth Moss. 1972. *Commitment and Community.* Cambridge: Harvard University Press.

———. 1977. *Men and Women of the Corporation.* New York: Basic Books.

Karabel, Jerome. 1983. The Politics of Structural Change in American Higher Education: The Case of Open Admissions at the City University of New York. In *The Compleat University: Break from Tradition in Three Countries,* ed. H. Hermanns, U. Teichler, and H. Wasser, 21–58. Cambridge, Mass.: Schenkman Publishers.

———. 1984. Status Group Struggle, Organizational Interests, and the Limits of Institutional Autonomy: The Transformation of Harvard, Yale and Princeton, 1918–1940. *Theory and Society* 13:1–40.

Katz, Michael B. 1975. *Class, Bureaucracy, and Schools: The Illusion of Educational Change in America.* New York: Praeger.

Katz, Michael C., and Carl Shapiro. 1985. Network Externalities, Competition, and Compatibility. *American Economic Review* 75(3):424–40.

———. 1986. Technology Adoption in the Presence of Network Externalities. *Journal of Political Economy* 94(4):822–41.

Keim, Gerald D. 1978. Corporate Social Responsibility: An Assessment of the Enlightened Self-Interest Model. *Academy of Management Review* 3:32–39.

Kelley, Harold H. 1971. *Attribution in Social Interaction.* Morristown, N.J.: General Learning Press.

Kennedy, Peter. 1985. *A Guide to Econometrics.* 2d ed. Cambridge: MIT Press.

Keohane, Robert O. 1984. *After Hegemony.* Princeton: Princeton University Press.

———. 1988. International Institutions: Two Research Programs. *International Studies Quarterly* 32:379–96.

Keppel, Frederick P. 1926. *Education for Adults and Other Essays.* New York: Columbia University Press.

———. 1934. The Arts. In *Recent Social Trends in the United States,* ed. William F. Ogburn. New York: McGraw-Hill.

Keppel, Frederick P., and R. L. Duffus. 1933. *The Arts in American Life.* New York: McGraw-Hill.

Kestenbaum, Meyer, chair. 1955. *Final Report of the Commission on Intergovernmental Relations.* House Doc. 198, 84th Cong., 1st sess. Washington, D.C.: U.S. Government Printing Office.

Kiesler, Sara, and Lee Sproul. 1982. Managerial Responses to Changing Environments: Perspectives on Problem Sensing from Social Cognition. *Administrative Science Quarterly* 27(4):548–70.

Kimball, Fiske. 1929. Report of the Director of the Museum. In *Fifty-third Annual Report of the Pennsylvania Museum and School of Industrial Art.* Philadelphia.

———. 1933. Kimball Reviews Museum Study by Rea. *Museum News* 1:4–5.

Kimberly, John R. 1975. Environmental Constraints and Organizational Structure: A Comparative Analysis of Rehabilitation Organizations. *Administrative Science Quarterly* 20:1–9.

———. 1980. Initiation, Innovation and Institutionalization in the Creation Process. In *The Organizational Life Cycle,* ed. J. Kimberly Miles and B. Miles, 18–43. San Francisco: Jossey-Bass.

Kingdon, Frank. 1948. *John Cotton Dana: A Life.* Newark, N.J.: Public Library and Museum.

Kinzer, David M. 1977. *Health Controls out of Control: Warning to the Nation from Massachusetts.* Chicago: Teach'em.

Klahr, David, P. Langley, and R. Neches, eds. 1987. *Production System Models of Learning and Development.* Cambridge: MIT Press.

Kmenta, Jan. 1971. *Elements of Econometrics.* New York: Macmillan.

Knoke, David. 1981. Power Structures. In *Handbook of Political Behavior,* ed. Samuel L. Long, 3:275–332. New York: Plenum.

———. 1982. The Spread of Municipal Reform: Temporal, Spatial, and Social Dynamics. *American Journal of Sociology* 87:1314–39.

———. 1986. Associations and Interest Groups. *Annual Review of Sociology* 12:1–21.

Knoke, David, and Edward O. Laumann. 1982. The Social Organization of National Policy Domains. In *Social Structure and Network Analysis,* ed. P. Marsden and N. Lin. Beverly Hills, Calif.: Sage.

Kobayashi, Yoshihiro. 1980. Kigyo no gurupu no bunseki hoko: Kotorii jimukyoku *Kigyo shudan no jittai chosa ni tsuite o yonde* (A trend in the analysis of business groups: A comment on *About the research on the state of affairs in the business groups*). Tokyo: Bureau of Fair Trade Commission.

Kochan, Thomas, Harry Katz, and Robert McKersie. 1986. *The Transformation of American Industrial Relations.* New York: Basic Books.

Kohn, Melvin L. 1969. *Class and Conformity.* Homewood, Ill.: Dorsey.

Konrad, George, and Iven Szelenyi. 1979. *Intellectuals on the Road to Class Power.* New York: Harcourt Brace.

Koo, Hagen. 1984. The Political Economy of Income Distribution in South Korea: The Impact of the State's Industrialization Policies. *World Development* 12:1029–37.

Kosei Torihiki Iinkai Jimukyoku (Fair Trade Commission). 1983. *Kigyo shudan no jittai ni tsuite* (About the state of affairs in business groups). Tokyo: Bureau of Fair Trade Commission.

Kramer, Ralph M. 1981. *Voluntary Agencies in the Welfare State.* Berkeley: University of California Press.

Krasner, Stephen D., ed. 1983. *International Regimes.* Ithaca: Cornell University Press.

———. 1988. Sovereignty: An Institutional Perspective. *Comparative Political Studies* 21(1):66–94.

Kratochwil, Frederick, and J. G. Ruggie. 1986. International Organization: A State of the Art on the Art of the State. *International Organization* 40(4):753–76.

Kretch, D., and R. S. Crutchfield. 1962. *Individual in Society.* New York: McGraw-Hill.

Kulik, Carol. 1989. The Effects of Job Categorization on Judgments of the Motivating Potential of Jobs. *Administrative Science Quarterly* 34(1):68–90.

Kuran, Timur, 1988. The Tenacious Past: Theories of Personal and Collective Conservativism. *Journal of Economic Behavior and Organization* 10:143–71.

Lachmann, L. M. 1971. *The Legacy of Max Weber.* Berkeley, Calif.: Glendessary Press.

Lagemann, Ellen Condliffe. 1983. *Private Power for the Public Good: A History of the Carnegie Foundation for the Advancement of Teaching.* Middletown, Conn.: Wesleyan University Press.

Lammers, Cornelis J., and David J. Hickson. 1979. A Cross-national and Cross-institutional Typology of Organizations. In *Organizations Alike and Unlike,* ed. C. J. Lammers and D. J. Hickson, 420–34. London: Routledge and Kegan Paul.

Landau, Martin. 1969. Redundancy, Rationality, and the Problem of Duplications and Overlap. *Public Administration Review* 29:346–58.

Langlois, Richard, ed. 1986. *Economics as Process.* New York: Cambridge University Press.

Larson, Magali Sarfatti. 1977. *The Rise of Professionalism: A Sociological Analysis.* Berkeley: University of California Press.

Laumann, Edward O., Joseph Galaskiewicz, and Peter Marsden. 1978. Community Structure as Interorganizational Linkage. *Annual Review of Sociology* 4:455–84.

Laurent, André. 1983. The Cultural Diversity of Western Conceptions of Management. *International Studies of Management and Organization* 8:75–96.

Lawrence, Paul R., and Lorsch, Jay W. 1967. *Organization and Environment*. Boston: Harvard Business School Press.

Leblebici, Huseyin, and Gerald R. Salancik. 1982. Stability in Interorganizational Exchanges: Rulemaking Processes of the Chicago Board of Trade. *Administrative Science Quarterly* 27:227–42.

Lee, M. L. 1971. A Conspicuous Production Theory of Hospital Behavior. *Southern Economic Journal* 38:48–58.

Lee, Sang M. 1986. Management Style and Practice of Korean Chaebols. Decision Sciences Institute Meetings, Honolulu, Hawaii.

Lehman, Edward W. 1975. *Coordinating Health Services*. Beverly Hills, Calif.: Sage.

Lester, Robert S. 1940. The Corporation and Operating Agencies. In Frederick P. Keppel and and R. S. Lester, *Report of the President and of the Treasurer*, 37–49. New York: Carnegie Corporation.

Levine, Andrew, Elliot Sober, and Erik Olin Wright. 1987. Marxism and Methodological Individualism. *New Left Review* 162:67–84.

Lévi-Strauss, Claude. 1966. *The Savage Mind*. London: Weidenfeld and Nicholson.

Levitt, Barbara, and James G. March. 1988. Organizational Learning. *Annual Review of Sociology* 14:319–40.

Levy, R. I. 1973. *Tahitians: Mind and Experience in the Society Islands*. Chicago: University of Chicago Press.

Lindblom, Charles E. 1968. *The Policy-Making Process*. Englewood Cliffs, N.J.: Prentice-Hall.

———. 1977. *Politics and Markets*. New York: Basic Books.

Litwak, Eugene, and Lydia F. Hylton. 1962. Interorganizational Analysis: A Hypothesis on Coordinating Agencies. *Administrative Science Quarterly* 6:395–420.

Lombardi, John. 1978. The Resurgence of Occupational Education. Topical Paper No. 65. Los Angeles: ERIC Clearing House for Junior Colleges.

———. 1979. The Decline of Transfer Education. Topical Paper No. 70. Los Angeles: ERIC Clearing House for Junior Colleges.

Loney, Martin. 1977. The Political Economy of Citizen Participation. In *The Canadian State: Political Economy and Political Power*, ed. Leo Panitch, 346–72. Toronto: University of Toronto Press.

Lowi, Theodore J. 1964. American Business, Public Policy, Case Studies and Political Theory. *World Politics* 16:675–715.

———. 1969. *The End of Liberalism*. New York: Norton.

———. 1970. Decision Making vs. Policy Making: Toward an Antidote for Technocracy. *Public Administration Review* 30:298–310.

———. 1972. Four Systems of Policy, Politics and Choice. *Public Administration Review* 32:314–25.

Lukes, Steven. 1972. *Emile Durkheim, His Life and Work*. New York: Harper and Row.

———. 1974. *Power: A Radical View*. London: Macmillan.

Lynd, Robert, and Helen Lynd. 1929. *Middletown*. New York: Harcourt Brace and Jovanovich.

———. 1937. *Middletown in Transition*. New York: Harcourt Brace.

McCarthy, John, and Mayer Zald. 1977. Resource Mobilization and Social Movements: A Partial Theory. *American Journal of Sociology* 82:121–41.

McDonnell, Lorrain M., and Milbrey W. McLaughlin. 1982. *Education Policy and the Role of the States*. Santa Monica, Calif.: Rand.

McGuire, Joseph W. 1963. *Business and Society*. New York: McGraw-Hill.

MacIver, Robert M. 1931. *Society, Its Structure and Changes*. New York: Ray Long and Richard R. Smith.

McKelvey, William. 1982. *Organizational Systematics*. Berkeley: University of California Press.

McKeough, W. D. 1975. *Ontario Budget 1975*. Toronto: Ministry of Treasury, Economics and Intergovernmental Affairs.

———. 1976. *Ontario Budget 1976*. Toronto: Ministry of Treasury, Economics and Intergovernmental Affairs.

McNeil, William H. 1982. *The Pursuit of Power: Technology, Armed Force, and Society since A.D. 1000*. Chicago: University of Chicago Press.

Majone, Giandomenico. 1980. Professionalism and Non-Profit Organizations. Working Paper No. 24. New Haven: Yale Program on Non-Profit Organizations.

Mann, Michael. 1973. *Consciousness and Action in the Western Working Class*. London: Macmillan.

———. 1986. *The Sources of Social Power*. Vol. 1. New York: Cambridge University Press.

Marceau, Jane. 1989. *A Family Business? The Making of an International Business Elite*. New York: Cambridge University Press.

March, James C., and James G. March. 1977. Almost Random Careers: The Wisconsin School Superintendency, 1940–72. *Administrative Science Quarterly* 22:378–409.

March, James G. 1981. Decisions in Organizations and Theories of Choice. In *Perspectives on Organization Design and Behavior*, ed. A. H. Van de Van and W. F. Joyce, 205–44. New York: Wiley.

March, James G. and Michael Cohen. 1974. *Leadership and Ambiguity: The American College President*. New York: McGraw-Hill.

March, James G., and Johan P. Olsen. 1976. *Ambiguity and Choice in Organizations*. Bergen: Universitetsforlaget.

———. 1984. The New Institutionalism: Organizational Factors in Political Life. *American Political Science Review* 78:734–49.

March, James G., and Herbert A. Simon. 1958. *Organizations*. New York: Wiley.

March, James G., and Roger Weissinger-Baylon, eds. 1986. *Ambiguity and Command*. Cambridge, Mass.: Ballinger.

Marrett, Cora Bagley. 1980. Influences on the Rise of New Organizations: The Formation of Women's Medical Associations. *Administrative Science Quarterly* 25:189–99.

Marshall, J. E. 1966. Eye Movements and the Visual Autokinetic Phenomenon. *Perceptual and Motor Skills* 22:319–26.

Marshall, T. H. 1964. *Class, Citizenship, and Social Development*. New York: Doubleday.

Matthews, R. C. O. 1986. The Economics of Institutions and the Sources of Growth. *Economic Journal* 96:903–18.

Maurice, Marc, F. Sellier, and J. J. Silvestre. 1982. *Politique d'éducation et organization industrielle en France et en Allemagne*. Paris: Presses Universitaires de France.

Mauss, Marcel. 1985. A Category of the Human Mind: The Notion of Person; The Notion of Self. In *The Category of the Person*, ed. M. Carrithers et al., 1–25. New York: Cambridge University Press.

Mayhew, Bruce H. 1980. Structuralism versus Individualism. *Social Forces* 59:335–75, 627–48.

Mayhew, Leon. 1984. In Defense of Modernity: Talcott Parsons and the Utilitarian Tradition. *American Journal of Sociology* 89(6):1273–1305.

Mazur, P. 1928. Diversification in Industry. *Review of Reviews*, June, 631–34.

Mead, George Herbert. [1934] 1972. *Mind, Self, and Society*. Chicago: University of Chicago Press.

Meier, Norman Charles. 1926. *Aesthetic Judgment as a Measure of Art Talent*. Iowa City: University of Iowa.

Meiksins, Peter F. 1984. Scientific Management and Class Relations: A Dissenting View. *Theory and Society* 13:177–209.

Melton, Arthur. 1935. *Problems of Installation in Museums of Art*. Washington, D.C.: American Association of Museums.

Merkle, Judith. 1980. *Management and Ideology: The Legacy of the International Scientific Management Movement*. Berkeley: University of California Press.

Merton, Robert K. 1940. Bureaucratic Structure and Personality. *Social Forces* 18:560–68.

———. 1949. Patterns of Influence: A Study of Interpersonal Influence and of Communications Behavior in a Local Community. In *Communication Research, 1948–49*, ed. P. F. Lazarsfeld and F. Stanton, 16–22. New York: Harper.

Merton, Robert K., L. Brown, and L. S. Cottrell, Jr. 1959. *Sociology Today: Problems and Prospects*. New York: Basic Books.

Messinger, Sheldon. 1955. Organizational Transformation: A Case Study of a Declining Social Movement. *American Sociological Review* 20:3–10.

Meyer, John W. 1968. Collective Disturbances and Staff Organizations on Psychiatric Wards: A Formalization. *Sociometry* 31:180.

———. 1970. The Charter: Conditions of Diffuse Socialization in Schools. In *Social Processes and Social Structure*, ed. W. R. Scott, 564–78. New York: Holt, Rinehart, and Winston.

———. 1971. Institutionalization. Manuscript. Stanford University.

———. 1977. The Effects of Education as an Institution. *American Journal of Sociology* 83:53–77.

———. 1980. The World Polity and the Authority of the Nation State. In *Studies of the Modern World System*, ed. A. J. Bergesen. New York: Academic.

———. 1981. Remarks at ASA session: The Present Crisis and the Decline in World Hegemony. Toronto, Canada.

———. 1983a. Innovation and Knowledge Use in American Public Education. In *Organizational Environments*, ed. J. W. Meyer and W. R. Scott, 233–60. Beverly Hills, Calif.: Sage.

———. 1983b. Institutionalization and the Rationality of Formal Organizational Structure. In *Organizational Environments: Ritual and Rationality*, ed. J. W. Meyer and W. R. Scott, 261–82. Beverly Hills, Calif.: Sage.

———. 1986. Social Environments and Organizational Accounting. *Accounting, Organizations, and Society* 11:345–56.

———. 1987. The World Polity and the Authority of the Nation-State. In *Institutional Structure*, ed. George Thomas et al., 41–70. Newbury Park, Calif.: Sage.

———. 1988a. Conceptions of Christendom: Notes on the Distinctiveness of the West. In *Cross-National Research in Sociology*, ed. M. Kohn. Newbury Park, Calif.: Sage.

———. 1988b. Society without Culture: A Nineteenth-Century Legacy. In *Rethinking the Nineteenth Century: Contradictions and Movements*, ed. F. O. Ramirez, 193–202. Westport, Conn.: Greenwood Press.

Meyer, John W., John Boli, and George Thomas. 1987. Ontology and Rationalization in the Western Cultural Account. In *Institutional Structure*, ed. George Thomas et al., 12–37. Newbury Park, Calif.: Sage.

Meyer, John W., and Michael Hannan. 1979. *National Development and the World System*. Chicago: University of Chicago Press.

Meyer, John W., and Brian Rowan. 1977. Institutionalized Organizations: Formal Structure as Myth and Ceremony. *American Journal of Sociology* 83:340–63.

———. 1978. The Structure of Educational Organizations. In *Environments and Organizations*, ed. Marshall W. Meyer et al., 78–109. San Francisco: Jossey-Bass.

Meyer, John W., and W. Richard Scott. 1983a. Centralization and the Legitimacy Problems of Local Government. In *Organizational Environments: Ritual and Rationality*, ed. J. W. Meyer and W. R. Scott, 199–215. Beverly Hills, Calif.: Sage.

———, with the assistance of B. Rowan and T. Deal. 1983b. *Organizational Environments: Ritual and Rationality*. Beverly Hills, Calif.: Sage.

Meyer, John W., W. Richard Scott, Sally Cole, and Jo-Ann Intili. 1978. Instructional Dissensus and Institutional Consensus in Schools. In *Environments and Organizations*, ed. Marshall W. Meyer, 233–63. San Francisco: Jossey-Bass.

Meyer, John W., W. R. Scott, and T. E. Deal. 1981. Institutional and Technical Sources of Organizational Structure. In *Organization and the Human Services*, ed. H. D. Stein, 151–78. Philadelphia: Temple University Press.

Meyer, John W., W. Richard Scott, and David Strang. 1987. Centralization, Fragmentation, and School District Complexity. *Administrative Science Quarterly* 32:186–201.

Meyer, John W., W. Richard Scott, David Strang, and Andrew Creighton. 1988. Bureaucratization without Centralization: Changes in the Organizational System of American Public Education, 1940–1980. In *Institutional Patterns and Organizations,* ed. L. G. Zucker, 139–67. Cambridge, Mass.: Ballinger.

Meyer, John W., David Tyack, Joane Nagel, and Audri Gordon. 1979. Public Education as Nation-Building in America: Enrollments and Bureaucratization, 1870–1930. *American Journal of Sociology* 85:591–613.

Meyer, Marshall, and M. Craig Brown. 1977. The Process of Bureaucratization. *American Journal of Sociology* 83:364–85.

Meyer, Marshall, W. Stevenson, and S. Webster. 1985. *Limits to Bureaucratic Growth*. Berlin: Walter de Gruyter.

Meyer, Marshall, and Lynne G. Zucker. 1988. *Permanently Failing Organizations*. Huntington Park, Calif.: Sage.

Mezias, Stephen J. 1990. An Institutional Model of Organizational Practice: Financial Reporting at the Fortune 200. *Administrative Science Quarterly* 35(3):431–57.

Michels, Robert. [1915] 1962. *Political Parties*. Trans. from the German by Eden Paul and Cedar Paul. New York: Collier Press.

Milgram, Stanley. 1974. *Obedience to Authority: An Experimental View*. New York: Harper and Row.

Mills, C. Wright. 1940. Situated Actions and Vocabularies of Motive. *American Sociological Review* 5:904–13.

Milofsky, Carl. 1981. Structure and Process in Community Self-Help Organizations. Working Paper No. 17. New Haven: Yale Program on Non-Profit Organizations.

Miyazawa, Setsuo. 1986. Legal Departments of Japanese Corporations in the United States: A Study of Organizational Adaptation to Multiple Environments. *Kobe University Law Review* 20:99–162.

Moe, Terry. 1984. The New Economics of Organization. *American Journal of Political Science* 28(4):739–77.

———. 1987. Interests, Institutions, and Positive Theory: The Politics of the NLRB. In *Studies in American Political Development,* 2:236–99. New Haven: Yale University Press.

Molotch, Harvey L. 1976. The City as a Growth Machine: Toward a Political Economy of Place. *American Journal of Sociology* 82:309–32.

Molotch, Harvey L., and John R. Logan. 1987. *Urban Fortunes: The Political Economy of Place*. Berkeley: University of California Press.

Momigliano, Arnoldo. 1985. Marcel Mauss and the Quest for the Person in Greek Biography and Autobiography. In *The Category of the Person,* ed. M. Carrithers et al., 83–92. New York: Cambridge University Press.

Moody's Manuals of Industrials. 1920, 1930, 1940, 1950, 1950, 1970, 1980. New York: Moody's.

Moore, Wilbert E. 1979. *World Modernization*. New York: Elsevier.

Morris, Robert, and Ilana H. Lescohier. 1978. Service Integration: Real versus Illusory Solutions to Welfare Dilemmas. In *The Management of Human Services,* ed. R. C. Sarri and Y. Hasenfeld, 21–50. New York: Columbia University Press.

Morrissey, Joseph P., Richard H. Hall, and Michael L. Lindsey. 1982. *Interorganizational Relations: A Sourcebook of Measures for Mental Health Programs*. Washington, D.C.: National Institute of Mental Health.

Mott, Paul. 1970. The Role of the Absentee Owned Corporation in the Changing Community. In *The Structure of Community Power,* ed. M. Aiken and P. Mott, 170–80. New York: Random House.

Moynihan, Daniel P. 1969. *Maximum Feasible Misunderstanding*. New York: Free Press.

Mueller, W. 1979. The Celler-Kefauver Act: The First 27 Years. Washington, D. C.: U.S. Government Printing Office.

Münch, Richard. 1986. The American Creed in Sociological Theory: Exchange, Negotiated Order, Accommodated Individualism, and Contingency. *Sociological Theory* 4:41–60.

Murphy, Jerome T. 1981. The Paradox of State Government Reform. *Public Interest* 64:124–39.

Musto, David A. 1975. Whatever Happened to "Community Mental Health"? *Public Interest* 29:53–79.

Nadel, S. F. 1953. Social Control and Self-Regulation. *Social Forces* 31:265–73.

Nakatani, Iwao. 1982. Risuku shearingu kara mita nihon keizai: Kigyo shudan no keizai gorisei ni kansuru ichikosatsu (Japanese economy viewed from risk-sharing: A perspective on economic rationality in the business groups). *Osaka Daigaku Keizaigaku* 32:219–45.

———. 1984. The Economic Role of Financial Corporate Grouping. In *The Economic Analysis of the Japanese Firm,* ed. M. Aoki, 227–58. Amsterdam: Elsevier.

Nasaw, David. 1979. *Schooled to Order.* New York: Oxford University Press.

Nelson, Richard, and Sidney Winter. 1982. *An Evolutionary Theory of Economic Change.* Cambridge: Harvard University Press.

Neuhauser, Duncan. 1972. The Hospital as a Matrix Organization. *Hospital Administration* 17:8–25.

Neustadt, Richard, and Harvey Fineberg. 1978. *The Swine Flu Affair: Decision Making on a Slippery Disease.* Washington, D.C.: U.S. Government Printing Office.

Nishiyama, Tadonori. 1984. The Strucure of Managerial Control: Who Owns and Controls Japanese Business. In *The Anatomy of Japanese Business,* ed. Kazuo Sato and Yasuo Hoshino. Armonk, N.Y.: M. E. Sharpe.

Noll, Roger G. 1971. *Reforming Regulation.* Washington, D.C.: Brookings Institution.

North, Douglass C. 1981. *Structure and Change in Economic History.* New York: Norton.

———. 1983. A Theory of Institutional Change and the Economic History of the Western World. In *The Microfoundations of Macrosociology,* ed. M. Hechter, 190–215. Philadelphia: Temple University Press.

———. 1984. Government and the Cost of Exchange in History. *Journal of Economic History* 44:255–64.

———. 1986. The New Institutional Economics. *Journal of Institutional and Theoretical Economics* 142:230–37.

———. 1987. Institutions and Economic Growth: An Historical Introduction. Paper presented at Conference on Knowledge and Institutional Change, University of Minnesota.

———. 1990. *Institutions, Institutional Change and Economic Performance.* New York: Cambridge University Press.

North, Douglass, C., and Robert Thomas. 1973. *The Rise of the Western World: A New Economic History.* New York: Cambridge University Press.

Numazaki, Ichiro. 1986. Networks of Taiwanese Big Business. *Modern China* 12:487–534.

Nystrom, N. C., and William H. Starbuck. 1984. To Avoid Organizational Crisis, Unlearn. *Organizational Dynamics,* Spring, 53–65.

Offe, Claus. 1984. *Contradictions of the Welfare State.* Cambridge: MIT Press.

Office of Management and Budget. 1972. *Standard Industrial Classification Manual.* Washington, D.C.: U.S. Government Printing Office.

Okumura, Hiroshi. 1982. Interfirm Relations in an Enterprise Group: The Case of Mitsubishi. *Japanese Economic Studies* 10:53–82.

———. 1984. Enterprise Groups in Japan. *Shoken Keizai* 147:169–89.

———. 1985. *Shin nihon no rokudai kigyo shudan* (Japan's six major business groups). Rev. ed. Tokyo: Daiyamondo Sha.

Olson, Mancur. 1965. *The Logic of Collective Action*. Cambridge: Harvard University Press.

Orloff, Ann, and Theda Skocpol. 1984. Why Not Equal Protection? Explaining the Politics of Public Social Spending in Britain and the United States. *American Sociological Review* 49(6):726–50.

Orrù, Marco. 1991. The Institutional Logic of Small-Firm Economies in Italy and Taiwan. *Studies in Comparative International Development* 26(1):3–28.

Orrù, Marco, Gary G. Hamilton, and Mariko Suzuki. 1989. Patterns of Inter-Firm Control in Japanese Business. *Organizational Studies* 10:549–74.

Ostrom, Elinor, 1986. An Agenda for the Study of Institutions. *Public Choice* 48:3–25.

Ouchi, William G. 1980. Markets, Bureaucracies, and Clans. *Administrative Science Quarterly* 25:129–41.

———. 1984. *The M-Form Society*. Reading, Mass.: Addison-Wesley.

Ouchi, William, and Mary Ann Maguire. 1975. Organizational Control: Two Functions. *Administrative Science Quarterly* 20:559–69.

Paradis, Lenora Finn, and Scott Cummings. 1986. The Evolution of Hospice in America toward Organizational Homogeneity. *Journal of Health and Social Behavior* 27:370–86.

Paris, Edna. 1972. Are There Really Any Opportunities for Youth? *MacLean's*, 34.

Parsons, Talcott. 1937. *The Structure of Social Action*. New York: McGraw-Hill.

———. 1938. The Professions and the Social Structure. *Social Forces* 17:29–37.

———. 1940. The Motivation of Economic Activities. In *Essays in Sociological Theory Pure and Applied*. Glencoe, Ill.: Free Press.

———. 1945. The Present Position and Prospects of Systematic Theory in Sociology. In *Twentieth Century Sociology*, ed. G. Gurvitch and W. E. Moore. New York: Philosophical Library.

———. 1951. *The Social System*. Glencoe, Ill.: Free Press.

———. 1956. Suggestions for a Sociological Approach to the Theory of Organizations, Parts I and II. *Administrative Science Quarterly* 1:63–85, 225–39.

———. 1960. *Structure and Process in Modern Societies*. Glencoe, Ill.: Free Press.

———. 1971. *The System of Modern Societies*. Englewood Cliffs, N.J.: Prentice-Hall.

———. 1977. *The Evolution of Societies*. Englewood Cliffs, N.J.: Prentice-Hall.

———. 1982. *On Institutions and Social Evolution*. Ed. Leon H. Mayhew. Chicago: University of Chicago Press.

———. 1990. Prologomena to a Theory of Social Institutions. *American Sociological Review* 55(3):319–33.

Parsons, Talcott, and Robert F. Bales. 1960. *Family Socialization and Interaction Process*. Glencoe, Ill.: Free Press.

Parsons, Talcott, and Edward A. Shils, eds. 1951. *Towards a General Theory of Action*. Cambridge: Harvard University Press.

Perrow, Charles. 1963. Goals and Power Structures. In *The Hospital in Modern Society*, ed. Eliot Freidson, 112–46. New York: Free Press.

———. 1967. A Framework for the Comparative Analysis of Organizations. *American Sociological Review* 32:194–208.

————. 1970. *Organizational Analysis: A Sociological View.* Belmont, Calif.: Wadsworth.

————. 1974. Is Business Really Changing? *Organizational Dynamics*, Summer, 31–44.

————. 1976. Control in Organizations. Paper presented at American Sociological Association annual meetings, New York, N.Y.

————. 1977. The Bureaucratic Paradox: The Efficient Organization Centralizes in Order to Decentralize. *Organizational Dynamics* 5:2–14.

————. 1985a. Comments on Langton's Ecological Theory of Bureaucracy. *Administrative Science Quarterly* 30:278–83.

————. 1985b. Overboard with Myth and Symbols. *American Journal of Sociology* 91:151–55.

————. 1986. *Complex Organizations: A Critical Essay.* 3rd ed. New York: Random House.

Perrucci, Carolyn C., Robert Perrucci, Dana B. Targ, and Harry R. Targ. 1988. *Plant Closing: International Context and Social Costs.* New York: Aldine de Gruyter.

Perrucci, Robert, and Joel E. Gerstl. 1969. *Profession without Community: Engineers in American Society.* New York: Random House.

Peterson, Paul E. 1981. *City Limits.* Chicago: University of Chicago Press.

Pfeffer, Jeffrey. 1974. Administrative Regulation and Licensing: Social Problem or Solution? *Social Problems* 21:468–79.

————. 1981. *Power in Organizations.* Marshfield, Mass.: Pitman.

————. 1982. *Organizations and Organization Theory.* Marshfield, Mass.: Pitman Press.

Pfeffer, Jeffrey, and Gerald Salancik. 1978. *The External Control of Organizations: A Resource Dependence Perspective.* New York: Harper and Row.

Piore, Michael, and Charles Sable. 1984. *The Second Industrial Divide.* New York: Basic Books.

Piven, Frances Fox, and Richard A. Cloward. 1971. *Regulating the Poor: The Functions of Public Welfare.* New York: Pantheon.

————. 1977. *Poor People's Movements.* New York: Pantheon.

————. 1980. Social Policy and the Formation of Political Consciousness. In *Political Power and Social Theory*, ed. M. Zeitlin, 1:117–52. Greenwich, Conn.: JAI Press.

Posner, Richard A. 1981. *The Economics of Justice.* Cambridge: Harvard University Press.

Powell, Walter W. 1983. New Solutions to Perennial Problems of Bookselling: Whither the Local Bookstore? *Daedalus* 112(1):51–64.

————. 1985a. *Getting into Print: The Decision-Making Process in Scholarly Publishing.* Chicago: University of Chicago Press.

————. 1985b. The Institutionalization of Rational Organization: Review of *Organizational Environments. Contemporary Sociology* 14(5):564–66.

————. 1986. How the Past Informs the Present: The Uses and Liabilities of Organizational Memory. Paper presented at conference on Communication and Collective Memory, Annenberg School, University of Southern California.

————. 1988. Institutional Effects on Organizational Structure and Performance. In *Institutional Patterns and Organization*, ed. L. Zucker, 115–36. Cambridge, Mass.: Ballinger.

————. 1990. Neither Market nor Hierarchy: Network Forms of Organization. In *Research in Organizational Behavior,* ed. B. Staw and L. L. Cummings, 12:295–336. Greenwich, Conn.: JAI Press.

Powell, Walter W., and Rebecca Friedkin. 1986. Politics and Programs: Organizational Factors in Public Television Decision-Making. In *Nonprofit Enterprise in the Arts,* ed. P. J. DiMaggio, 245–69. New York: Oxford University Press.

Pressman, Jeffrey L., and Aaron Wildavsky. 1973. *Implementation.* Berkeley: University of California Press.

Przeworski, Adam. 1974. Contextual Models of Political Behavior. *Political Methodology* 1:27–61.

Przeworski, Adam, and John Sprague. 1971. Concepts in Search of Explicit Formulation. *Midwest Journal of Political Science* 15:183–218.

Przeworski, Adam, and Michael Wallerstein. 1986. Popular Sovereignty, State Autonomy, and Private Property. *Archives European Sociology* 27:215–59.

Puckett, Tom, and David J. Tucker. 1976. Hard Times for Ontario's Social Services. *Canadian Welfare* 52:8–11.

Pugh, D. S. 1976. The Aston Approach to the Study of Organizations. In *European Contributions to Organization Theory,* ed. G. Hofstede and M. S. Kassem. Assen, Netherlands: Van Gorcum.

Putnam, Robert D. 1976. *The Comparative Study of Political Elites.* Englewood Cliffs, N.J.: Prentice-Hall.

Putterman, Louis, ed. 1986. *The Economic Nature of the Firm.* New York: Cambridge University Press.

Radford, Neil A. 1984. *The Carnegie Corporation and the Development of American College Libraries, 1928–1941.* New York: American Library Association.

Ramsey, Grace Fisher. 1938. *Educational Work in Museums of the United States: Development, Methods and Trends.* New York: H. W. Wilson.

Ravitch, Diane. 1978. *The Revisionists Revised.* New York: Basic Books.

Rea, Paul Marshall. 1932. *The Museum and the Community: A Study of Social Laws and Consequences.* Lancaster, Pa.: Science Press.

Rechtschaffen, A., and O. Mednick. 1955. The Autokinetic Word Technique. *Journal of Abnormal and Social Psychology* 51:346–48.

Redding, Gordon, and Simon Tam. 1986. Networks and Molecular Organizations: An Exploratory View of Chinese Firms in Hong Kong. In *Proceedings of the Inaugural Meeting of the Southeast Asia Region Academy of International Business,* ed. K. C. Mun and T. S. Chan, 129–44. Chinese University of Hong Kong.

Reddy, William. 1987. *Money and Liberty in Modern Europe.* New York: Cambridge University Press.

Regier, Darrel A., Irving D. Goldberg, and Carl A. Taube. 1978. The De Facto U.S. Mental Health Services System: A Public Health Perspective. *Archives of General Psychiatry* 35:685–93.

Reid, William J. 1969. Inter-organizational Coordination in Social Welfare: A Theoretical Approach to Analysis and Intervention. In *Readings in Community Organization Practice,* ed. R. M. Kramer and H. Spect, 188–200. Englewood Cliffs, N.J.: Prentice-Hall.

Reynolds, Lloyd G., and Joseph Shister. 1949. *Job Horizons: A Study of Job Satisfaction and Labor Mobility.* New York: Harper.

Riesman, David. 1958. *Constraint and Variety in American Education*. Garden City, N.Y.: Anchor Books.

Riesman, David, and Ruell Denney. 1951. Football in America: Study in Culture Diffusion. *American Quarterly* 4:309–25.

Riker, William H. 1980. Implications from the Disequilibrium of Majority Rule for the Study of Institutions. *American Political Science Review* 74:432–446.

Ritti, R., R., and Fred H. Goldner. 1979. Professional Pluralism in an Industrial Organization. *Management Science* 16:233–46.

Roberts, George, and Mary Roberts. 1959. *Triumph on Fairmount: Fiske Kimball and the Philadelphia Museum of Art*. Philadelphia: J. B. Lippincott.

Robertson, A. F., Forthcoming. Reproduction and the Making of History: Time, the Family, and Modern Society. In Roger Friedland and Deirdre Boden, eds., *Nowhere: Time, Space and Modernity*.

Robinson, Edward S. 1928. *The Behavior of the Museum Visitor*. Washington, D. C.: American Association of Museums.

Rogers, David L., and David A. Whetten, eds. 1981. *Interorganizational Coordination*. Ames: Iowa State University Press.

Rogers, Everett M. 1962. *Diffusion of Innovations*. New York: Free Press.

Rokkan, Stein, with Agnus Campbell, Per Torsvik, and Henry Valen. 1970. *Citizens, Elections and Parties*. New York: McKay.

Rosaldo, Michelle Z. 1980. *Knowledge and Passion*. Cambridge: Cambridge University Press.

Rosch, Eleanor. 1978. Principle of Categorization. In *Cognition and Categorization*, ed. E. Rosch and B. B. Lloyd, 27–48. Hillsdale, N.J.: Erlbaum.

Rosch, Eleanor, Carolyn B. Mervis, Wayne D. Gray, David M. Johnson, and Penny Boyes-Braem. 1976. Basic Objects in Natural Categories. *Cognitive Psychology* 8:382–439.

Rose, Michael. 1985. Universalism, Culturalism, and the Aix Group: Promises and Problems of a Societal Approach to Economic Institutions. *European Sociological Review* 1:65–83.

Rosengren, William R., and Mark Lefton, eds. 1970. *Organizations and Clients*. Columbus, Ohio: Charles E. Merrill.

Rothman, David J. 1971. *The Discovery of the Asylum: The Social Order and Disorder in the New Republic*. Boston: Little, Brown.

Rothman, Mitchell. 1980. The Evolution of Forms of Legal Education. Manuscript. Department of Sociology, Yale University.

Rothschild-Whitt, Joyce. 1979. The Collectivist Organization: An Alternative to Rational Bureaucratic Models. *American Sociological Review* 44:509–27.

Rowan, Brian. 1981. The Effects of Institutionalized Rules on Administrators. In *Organizational Behavior in Schools and School Districts*, ed. S. B. Bacharach, 47–75. New York: Praeger.

———. 1982. Organizational Structure and the Institutional Environment: The Case of Public Schools. *Administrative Science Quarterly* 27:259–79.

Roy, William. 1986. Functional and Historical Logics: Explaining the Relationship between the Capitalist Class and the Rise of the Industrial Corporation. Manuscript.

Ruggie, John G., ed. 1983. *The Antinomies of Interdependence*. New York: Columbia University Press.

Rumelt, Richard. 1974. *Strategy, Structure, and Economic Performance*. Boston: Harvard Business School.

Sabatier, Paul. 1975. Social Movements and Regulatory Agencies: Toward a More Adequate—and Less Pessimistic—Theory of Clientele Capture. *Policy Sciences* 6:301–42.

Sahlins, Marshall. 1976. *Culture and Practical Reason*. Chicago: University of Chicago Press.

Salancik, Gerald R., and Jeffrey Pfeffer. 1974. The Bases and Use of Power in Organizational Decision Making. *Administrative Science Quarterly* 19:453–73.

Salisbury, Robert, and John Heinz. 1970. A Theory of Policy Analysis and Some Preliminary Applications. In *Policy Analysis in Political Science*, ed. I. Sharkansky, 39–60. Chicago: Markham.

Sartori, Giovanni. 1984. Guidelines for Concept Analysis. In *Social Science Concepts*, ed. G. Sartori, 15–85. Beverly Hills, Calif.: Sage.

Schank, Roger, and Robert Abelson. 1977. *Scripts, Plans, Goals and Understanding*. Hillsdale, N.J.: Erlbaum.

Schelling, Thomas. 1978. *Micromotives and Macrobehavior*. New York: Norton.

Schmidt, William E. 1987. For Displaced Farmers, More Than Sympathy. *New York Times*, December 8, p. 10.

Schmitter, Philippe C. 1974. Still the Century of Corporatism? In *The New Corporatism*, ed. F. B. Pike and T. Stritch, 85–131. Notre Dame: University of Notre Dame Press.

———. 1979. Modes of Interest Intermediation and Models of Societal Change in Western Europe. In *Trends toward Corporatist Intermediation*, ed. P. C. Schmitter and G. Lehmbruch, 63–95. Beverly Hills, Calif.: Sage.

Schneider, Mark A. 1987. Culture-as-Text in the Work of Clifford Geertz. *Theory and Society* 16:809–39.

Schotter, Andrew. 1981. *The Economic Theory of Social Institutions*. New York: Cambridge University Press.

Schulze, Robert. 1961. The Bifurcation of Power in a Satellite City. In *Community Political Systems*, ed. M. Janowitz, 19–80. New York: Free Press.

Schutz, Alfred. 1962. *Collected Papers I: The Problem of Social Reality*, ed. Maurice Natanson. The Hague: Martinus Nijhoff.

———. 1967. *The Phenomenology of the Social World*. Trans. G. Walsh and F. Lehnert. Evanston, Ill.: Northwestern University Press.

Scitovsky, Tibor. 1985. Economic Development in Taiwan and South Korea, 1965–81. *Food Research Institute Studies* 19(3):215–64.

Scott, Joan Wallace. 1984. Men and Women in the Parisian Garment Trades. In *The Power of the Past*, ed. P. Thane, G. Crossick, and R. Cloud, 67–93. Cambridge: Cambridge University Press.

Scott, Marvin B., and Stanford M. Lyman. 1968. Accounts. *American Sociological Review* 33:46–62.

Scott, W. Richard. 1975. Organizational Structure. *Annual Review of Sociology* 1:1–25.

———. 1977. Effectiveness of Organizational Effectiveness Studies. In *New Perspectives on Organizational Effectiveness*, ed. P. S. Goodman and J. M. Pennings, 63–95. San Francisco: Jossey-Bass.

————. 1981a. *Organizations: Rational, Natural, and Open Systems*. Englewood Cliffs, N.J.: Prentice Hall.

————. 1981b. Reform Movements and Organizations: The Case of Aging. In *Aging: Social Change*, ed. S. B. Kiesler et al., 331–45. New York: Academic Press.

————. 1982a. Health Care Organizations in the 1980s: The Convergence of Public and Professional Control Systems. In *Contemporary Health Services: Social Science Perspectives*, ed. A. W. Johnson et al., 177–95. Boston: Auburn House.

————. 1982b. Managing Professional Work: Three Models of Control for Health Organizations. *Health Services Research* 17:213–40.

————. 1983. The Organization of Environments: Network, Cultural, and Historical Elements. In *Organizational Environments*, ed. J. W. Meyer and W. R. Scott, 155–75. Beverly Hills, Calif.: Sage.

————. 1985. Conflicting Levels of Rationality: Regulators, Managers and Professionals in the Medical Care Sector. *Journal of Health Administration Education* 3, pt. 2:113–31.

————. 1986. Systems within Systems: The Mental Health Sector. In *The Organization of Mental Health Services: Societal and Community Systems*, ed. W. R. Scott and B. L. Black, 31–52. Beverly Hills, Calif.: Sage.

————. 1987a. The Adolescence of Institutional Theory. *Administrative Science Quarterly* 32:493–511.

————. 1987b. *Organizations: Rational, Natural and Open Systems*. 2d ed. Englewood Cliffs, N.J.: Prentice-Hall.

————. 1990. Symbols and Organizations: From Barnard to the Institutionalists. In *Organization Theory: From Chester Barnard to the Present and Beyond*, ed. O. E. Williams, 38–55. New York: Oxford University Press.

Scott, W. Richard, and Bruce L. Black, eds. 1986. *The Organization of Mental Health Services: Societal and Community Systems*. Beverly Hills, Calif.: Sage.

Scott, W. Richard, and John C. Lammers. 1985. Trends in Occupations and Organizations in the Medical Care and Mental Health Sectors. *Medical Care Review* 42:37–76.

Scott, W. Richard, and John W. Meyer. 1983. The Organization of Societal Sectors. In *Organizational Environments: Ritual and Rationality*, ed. J. W. Meyer and W. R. Scott, 129–53. Beverly Hills, Calif.: Sage.

————. 1988. Environmental Linkages and Organizational Complexity: Public and Private Schools. In *Comparing Public and Private Schools*, ed. H. M. Levin and T. James, 128–60. New York: Falmer Press.

Sedlak, Michael W. 1981. Youth Policy and Young Women, 1950–1972: The Impact of Private-Sector Programs for Pregnant and Wayward Girls on Public Policy. Paper presented at National Institute for Education Youth Policy Research Conference, Washington, D.C.

Selznick, Philip. 1949. *TVA and the Grass Roots*. Berkeley: University of California Press.

————. 1957. *Leadership in Administration*. Evanston, Ill.: Row, Peterson.

Sergiovanni, Thomas J., Martin Burlingame, Fred D. Coombs, and Paul Thurston. 1980. *Educational Governance and Administration*. Englewood Cliffs, N.J.: Prentice-Hall.

Sewell, William H., Jr. 1987. Theory of Action, Dialectic, and History. *American Journal of Sociology* 93(1):166–72.

Sharpe, L. J. 1973a. American Democracy Reconsidered: Part I. *British Journal of Political Science* 3:1–28.

———. 1973b. American Democracy Reconsidered: Part II. *British Journal of Political Science* 3:129–67.

Shaw, Clifford. 1940. The Chicago Area Project. In *Criminal Behavior*, ed. W. C. Reckless, 508–16. New York: McGraw-Hill.

Shefter, Martin, and Benjamin Ginsberg. 1985. Institutionalizing the Reagan Regime. Paper presented at the annual meeting of the American Political Science Association.

Shepsle, Kenneth A. 1986. Institutional Equilibrium and Equilibrium Institutions. In *Political Science: The Science of Politics*, ed. H. Weisburg, 51–82. New York: Agathon.

———. 1989. Studying Institutions: Some Lessons from the Rational Choice Approach. *Journal of Theoretical Politics* 1:131–47.

Shepsle, Kenneth A., and Barry Weingast. 1981. Structure-Induced Equilibria and Legislative Choice. *Public Choice* 37:503–19.

———. 1987. The Institutional Foundations of Committee Power. *American Political Science Review* 81:85–104.

Sherif, M. 1935. A Study of Some Social Factors in Perception. *Archives of Psychology* 187:45.

———. 1967. *Social Interaction: Process or Product*. Chicago: Aldine.

Sherman, Roger. 1974. *The Economics of Industry*. Boston: Little, Brown.

Shibutani, Tamotsu. 1986. *Social Processes*. Berkeley: University of California Press.

Shils, Edward. 1975. *Center and Periphery*. Chicago: University of Chicago Press.

Shimokawa, Koichi. 1982. Nihon ni okeru jidosha meka, buhin meka kankei to sono bungyo kozo no rekishiteki hatten to gendaiteki igi: Sono gijyutsu kakushin to seisan no junansei ni kanrenshite (The relationship between automobile manufacturers and parts producers, historical development and contemporary significance of such a division of labor: Issues of technological innovation and flexible production). *Keiei Shirin* 19:23–47.

———. 1985. Japan's Keiretsu System: The Case of the Automobile Industry. *Japanese Economic Studies* 12(4):3–31.

Shweder, Richard A., and Edmund J. Bourne. 1984. Does the Concept of the Person Vary Cross-Culturally? In *Culture Theory: Essays on Mind, Self, and Emotion*, ed. R. A. Shweder and R. A. Levine, 158–199. New York: Cambridge University Press.

Shweder, Richard, and Robert LeVine. 1984. *Culture Theory: Essays on Mind, Self, and Emotion*. Chicago: University of Chicago Press.

Siegfried, A. 1956. Stable Instability in France. *Foreign Affairs* 34:394–404.

Sills, David L. 1957. *The Volunteers: Means and Ends in a National Organization*. Glencoe, Ill.: Free Press.

Simon, Herbert A. 1945. *Administrative Behavior*. New York: Free Press.

———. 1962. The Architecture of Complexity. *Proceedings of the American Philosophical Society* 106:467–82.

Singh, Jitendra V., Robert J. House, and David J. Tucker. 1986. Organizational Change and Organizational Mortality. *Administrative Science Quarterly* 31:587–611.

Singh, Jitendra V., and Charles J. Lumsden. 1990. Theory and Research in Organizational Ecology. *Annual Review of Sociology* 16:161–95.

Singh, Jitendra V., David J. Tucker, and Robert J. House. 1986. Organizational Legitimacy and the Liability of Newness. *Administrative Science Quarterly* 31:171–93.

Singh, Jitendra V., David J. Tucker, and Agnes G. Meinhard. 1988. Are Voluntary Organizations Structurally Inert? Exploring an Assumption in Organizational Ecology. Paper presented at Academy of Management meetings, Anaheim, Calif.

Skocpol, Theda. 1979. *States and Social Revolution.* New York: Cambridge University Press.

———. 1985. Bringing the State Back In: Strategies of Analysis in Current Research. In *Bringing the State Back In,* ed. P. Evans et al., 3–43. New York: Cambridge University Press.

Skowronek, Stephen. 1981. *Building a New American State.* New York: Cambridge University Press.

Smelser, Neil. 1959. *Social Change in the Industrial Revolution.* Chicago: University of Chicago Press.

Smith, Lee. 1981. The Unsentimental Corporate Giver. *Fortune Magazine,* September 21, pp. 121ff.

Snell, Bruno. 1960. *The Discovery of the Mind.* New York: Harper and Row.

Social Planning Council of Metropolitan Toronto. 1976. *In Search of a Framework.* Toronto: Social Planning Council of Metropolitan Toronto.

Somers, Anne R. 1969. *Hospital Regulation: The Dilemma of Public Policy.* Princeton: Industrial Relations Section, Princeton University.

Spencer, Herbert. 1897. *Principles of Sociology.* New York: Appleton.

Splane, Richard. 1965. *Social Welfare in Ontario, 1791–1893.* Toronto: University of Toronto Press.

Sproull, Lee S. 1981. Response to Regulation: An Organizational Process Framework. *Administration and Society* 12:447–70.

Stackhouse, E. Ann. 1982. The Effects of State Centralization on Administrative and Macrotechnical Structure in Contemporary Secondary Schools. Project Report No. 82-A24. Stanford: Institute for Research on Educational Finance and Governance, Stanford University.

Starbuck, William H. 1976. Organizations and Their Environments. In *Handbook of Industrial and Organizational Psychology,* ed. Marvin D. Dunnette, 1069–1123. New York: Rand McNally.

Stark, David. 1980. Class Struggle and the Transformation of the Labor Process. *Theory and Society* 9:101–52.

———. 1986. Rethinking Internal Labor Markets: New Insights from a Comparative Perspective. *American Sociological Review* 51:492–504.

Starr, Paul. 1980. Medical Care and the Boundaries of Capitalist Organization. Manuscript. Program on Non-Profit Organizations, Yale University.

———. 1982. *The Social Transformation of American Medicine.* New York: Basic Books.

Staw, B. M. 1981. The Escalation of Commitment: A Review and Analysis. *Academy of Management* 6:577–87.

Staw, B. M., B. J. Calder, R. K. Hess, and L. E. Sandelands. 1980. Intrinsic Motivation and Norms about Payment. *Journal of Personality* 48:1–14.

Staw, B. M., and Ross, J. 1987. Behavior in Escalation Situations: Antecedents, Prototypes, and Solutions. In *Research in Organizational Behavior,* ed. B. M. Staw and L. L. Cummings, 9:39–78. Greenwich, Conn.: JAI Press.

Stein, Maurice. 1960. *The Eclipse of Community: An Interpretation of American Studies.* New York: Harper and Row.

Stenbeck, M. J. E. 1986. The Quality of Work Measurement. M. A. thesis, Department of Sociology, University of California, Santa Barbara.

Stepan, Alfred. 1978. *The State and Society: Peru in Comparative Perspective.* Princeton: Princeton University Press.

Stigler, George J. 1971. The Theory of Economic Regulation. *Bell Journal of Economics* 5:1–13.

Stinchcombe, Arthur L. 1965. Social Structure and Organizations. In *Handbook of Organizations,* ed. J. G. March, 142–93. Chicago: Rand McNally.

———. 1968. *Constructing Social Theories.* New York: Harcourt Brace.

———. 1973. Formal Organization. In *Sociology: An Introduction,* ed. Neil J. Smelser, 23–65. New York: Wiley.

———. 1986a. Milieu and Structure Updated. *Theory and Society* 15:901–13.

———. 1986b. Reason and Rationality. *Sociological Theory* 4:167–85.

Storer, N. W. 1973. *Focus on Society: An Introduction to Sociology.* Reading, Mass.: Addison-Wesley.

Streeck, Wolfgang, and Philippe C. Schmitter. 1985. Community, Market, State—and Associations?: The Prospective Contribution of Interest Governance to Social Order. In *Private Interest Government: Beyond Market and State,* 1–29. London: Sage Publications.

Suchman, Edward A. 1967. *Evaluative Research.* New York: Russell Sage Foundation.

Sudnow, David. 1964. Normal Crimes. *Social Problems* 12:255–75.

Sumiya, Toshio. 1986. *Gendai nihon shihon shugi no shihai kozo: Nihon kenzai to rokudai kigyo shudan* (The structure of domination in modern Japanese capitalism: Japanese economy and six major business groups). Tokyo: Shimpyoron.

Sumner, William G. 1906. *Folkways.* Boston: Ginn.

Sundquist, James L. 1969. *Making Federalism Work.* Washington, D.C.: Brookings Institution.

Sundstrom, William. 1988. Institutional Isomorphism: The Standardization of Rules and Contracts in Business Firms. Paper presented at Western Economic Association International Conference.

Suttles, Gerald D. 1984. The Cumulative Texture of Local Urban Culture. *American Journal of Sociology* 90:283–304.

Swanson, Guy. 1971. An Organizational Analysis of Collectivities. *American Sociological Review* 36:607–623.

———. 1986. Phobias and Related Symptoms: Some Social Sources. *Sociological Forum* 1:103–30.

Swidler, Ann. 1979. *Organization without Authority: Dilemmas of Social Control of Free Schools.* Cambridge: Harvard University Press.

———. 1986. Culture in Action: Symbols and Strategies. *American Sociological Review* 51:273–86.

Tamuz, Michal. 1982. Organizational Changes within the Mental Health Sector in California, 1940–1980. In *Institutional Sectors and Organizational Consequences:*

Schools and Other Public Organizations in a Federalist System, ed. J. W. Meyer and W. R. Scott. Final report to the National Institute of Education. Stanford: Institute for Research on Educational Finance and Governance, Stanford University.

Taub, Richard P. 1988. *Community Capitalism*. Boston: Harvard Business School Press.

Taylor, Shelley E., and Jennifer C. Crocker. 1980. Schematic Bases of Social Information Processing. In *The Ontario Symposium on Personality and Social Psychology*, ed. E. T. Higgins, P. Herman, and M. P. Zanna, 1:89–134. Hillsdale, N.J.: Erlbaum.

Terreberry, Shirley. 1968. The Evolution of Organizational Environments. *Administrative Science Quarterly* 12:590–613.

Thévenot, Laurent. 1984. Rules and Implements: Investment in Forms. *Social Science Information* 23:1–45.

Thomas, George M. 1989. *Revivalism and Cultural Change: Christianity, Nation Building, and the Market in the Nineteenth-Century United States*. Chicago: University of Chicago Press.

Thomas, George M., and John W. Meyer. 1984. The Expansion of the State. *Annual Review of Sociology* 10:461–82.

Thomas, George M., John Meyer, Francisco Ramirez, and John Boli. 1987. *Institutional Structure: Constituting State, Society and the Individual*. Newbury Park, Calif.: Sage.

Thompson, E. P. 1963. *The Making of the English Working Class*. New York: Random House.

Thompson, James D. 1967. *Organizations in Action*. New York: McGraw-Hill.

Tilly, Charles, ed. 1975. *The Formation of National States in Western Europe*. Princeton: Princeton University Press.

Tocqueville, Alexis de. [1856] 1955. *The Old Regime and the French Revolution*. Garden City, N.Y.: Doubleday.

Tolbert, Pamela S. 1985. Resource Dependence and Institutional Environments: Sources of Administrative Structure in Institutions of Higher Education. *Administrative Science Quarterly* 30:1–13.

———. 1988. Institutional Sources of Organizational Culture in Major Law Firms. In *Institutional Patterns and Organizations*, ed. L. G. Zucker, 101–13. Cambridge: Ballinger.

Tolbert, Pamela S., and Robert N. Stern. 1989. Organizations and Professions: Governance Structures in Large Law Firms. Manuscript. Cornell University.

Tolbert, Pamela S., and Lynne G. Zucker. 1983. Institutional Sources of Change in the Formal Structure of Organizations: The Diffusion of Civil Service Reform, 1880–1935. *Administrative Science Quarterly* 28:22–39.

Tomkins, Calvin. 1970. *Merchants and Masterpieces: The Story of the Metropolitan Museum of Art*. New York: Dutton.

Toyo Keizai Shimposha. 1986a. *Kigyo keiretsu soran* (Overview of firm alignments). Tokyo.

———. 1986b. *Nihon no kigyo gurupu*. (Business groups in Japan). Tokyo.

Troy, Kathryn. 1982. *The Corporate Contributions Function*. New York: The Conference Board.

Tucker, David J. 1981. Voluntary Auspices and the Behavior of Social Service Organizations. *Social Service Review* 55:603–27.

Tucker, David J., Jitendra V. Singh, and Robert J. House. 1984. The Liability of Newness in a Population of Voluntary Social Service Organizations. Paper presented at the 49th American Sociological Association Annual Meeting, San Antonio, Tex.

Tucker, David J., Jitendra V. Singh, and Agnes G. Meinhard. 1987. Founding Conditions, Environmental Change and Organizational Mortality. Manuscript. School of Social Work, McMaster University.

————. 1990. Organizational Form, Population Dynamics and Institutional Change: A Study of Birth Selection Processes. *Academy of Management Journal* 33:151–78.

Tucker, David, Jitendra Singh, Agnes Meinhard, and Robert House. 1988. Ecological and Institutional Sources of Change in Organizational Populations. In *Ecological Models of Organizations,* ed. G. R. Carroll, 127–51. Cambridge, Mass.: Ballinger.

Tuma, Nancy B. 1980. *Invoking Rate.* Menlo Park, Calif.: SRI International.

Tuma, Nancy B., and Andrew J. Grimes. 1981. A Comparison of Models of Role Orientations of Professionals in a Research-Oriented University. *Administrative Science Quarterly* 26:187–206.

Tuma, Nancy B., Michael T. Hannan, and Lyle P. Groeneveld. 1979. Dynamic Analysis of Event Histories. *American Journal of Sociology* 84:820–54.

Turk, Herman. 1977. *Organizations in Modern Life.* San Francisco: Jossey-Bass.

Tyack, David. 1974. *The One Best System: A History of American Urban Education.* Cambridge: Harvard University Press.

Tyack, David, and Elizabeth Hansot. 1982. *Managers of Virtue.* New York: Basic Books.

Udy, Stanley, H., Jr. 1970. *Work in Traditional and Modern Society.* Englewood Cliffs, N.J.: Prentice-Hall.

Ueda, Yoshiaki. 1983. Kigyo shudan ni okeru yakuin ken-nin no keiryo bunseki: Kigyokan kankei no sokutei (The mathematical analysis of interlocking directorates in enterprise groups: Measurement of interfirm relationships). *Shoken Keizai* 146: 25–48.

————. 1986. Intercorporate Networks in Japan: A Study of Interlocking Directorates in Modern Large Corporations. *Shoken Keizai* 157:236–54.

Useem, Michael. 1979. The Social Organization of the American Business Elite and Participation of Corporation Directors in the Governance of American Institutions. *American Sociological Review* 44:553–72.

————. 1987. Corporate Philanthropy. In *The Nonprofit Sector: A Research Handbook,* ed. W. W. Powell, 340–59. New Haven: Yale University Press.

Veblen, Thorstein. 1918. *The Higher Learning in America: A Memorandum on the Conduct of Universities by Business Men.* New York: B. W. Heubsch.

Walker, Jack. 1969. Diffusion of Innovations among the American States. *American Political Science Review* 63:880–99.

Wall, Wendy L. 1984. Companies Change the Ways They Make Charitable Donations. *Wall Street Journal,* June 21, pp. 1ff.

Wallerstein, Immanuel. 1974. *The Modern World System.* New York: Academic.

Wallich, H., and J. J. McGowan. 1970. Stockholder Interest and the Corporation's Role in Social Policy. In *A New Rationale for Corporate Social Policy,* 39–59. New York: Committee for Economic Development.

Wallis, K. 1972. Testing for Fourth Order Autocorrelation in Quarterly Regression Equations. *Econometrica* 40:617–36.

Warner, R. Stephen. 1978. Toward a Redefinition of Action Theory: Paying the Cognitive Element Its Due. *American Journal of Sociology* 83(6):1317–49.

Warner, W. Lloyd, and J. O. Low. 1947. *The Social System of the Modern Factory*. New Haven: Yale University Press.

Warren, Roland L. 1963. *The Community in America*. Chicago: Rand McNally.

———. 1967. The Interorganizational Field as a Focus for Investigation. *Administrative Science Quarterly* 12:396–419.

———. 1972. *The Community in America*. Rev. ed. Chicago: Rand McNally.

Warren, Roland L., Stephen Rose, and Ann Bergunder. 1974. *The Structure of Urban Reform*. Lexington, Mass.: D. C. Heath.

Weatherly, Richard A. 1979. *Reforming Special Education: Policy Implementation from State Level to Street Level*. Cambridge: MIT Press.

Webb, Eugene, D. T. Campbell, R. D. Schwartz, and L. Seechrest. 1966. *Unobtrusive Measures*. Chicago: Rand NcNally.

Webb, Eugene, and Karl E. Weick. 1979. Unobtrusive Measures in Organizational Theory: A Reminder. *Administrative Science Quarterly* 24:650–59.

Webb, Sidney, and Beatrice Webb. 1912. *The Prevention of Destitution*. London: Longmans, Green.

Weber, Max. [1919] 1946. Science as a Vocation. In *From Max Weber: Essays in Sociology*, ed. H. H. Gerth and C. W. Mills, 129–56. New York: Oxford University Press.

———. [1922] 1963. *The Sociology of Religion*. Boston: Beacon Press.

———. [1922] 1978. *Economy and Society*. Berkeley: University of California Press.

———. [1927] 1950. *General Economic History*. Glencoe, Ill.: Free Press.

———. 1947. *The Theory of Social and Economic Organization*. New York: Oxford University Press.

———. 1952. *The Protestant Ethic and the Spirit of Capitalism*. New York: Scribner.

Weick, Karl E. 1969. *The Social Psychology of Organizing*. Reading, Mass.: Addison-Wesley.

———. 1976. Educational Organizations as Loosely Coupled Systems. *Administrative Science Quarterly* 21:1–19.

Weick, Karl, and D. P. Gilfillan. 1971. Fate of Arbitrary Traditions in a Laboratory Microculture. *Journal of Personality and Social Psychology* 17:179–91.

Weingast, Barry, and William Marshall. 1988. The Industrial Organization of Congress; or, Why Legislatures, Like Firms, Are Not Organized as Markets. *Journal of Political Economy* 96:132–64.

Weinstein, James. 1968. *The Corporate Ideal in the Liberal State, 1900–1918*. Boston: Beacon Press.

Weiss, Janet. 1981. Substance versus Symbol in Administrative Reform: The Case of Human Service Coordination. *Policy Analysis* 7:21–46.

Welfling, Mary B. 1973. *Political Institutionalization: A Comparative Analysis of African Political Systems*. Beverly Hills, Calif.: Sage.

Westney, D. Eleanor. 1987. *Imitation and Innovation: The Transfer of Western Organizational Patterns to Meiji Japan*. Cambridge: Harvard University Press.

———. 1989. Institutionalization Theory and the Organizational Dilemma of Multinational Enterprise. Working paper. Sloan School of Management, MIT.

Wharf, Brian, and Novia Carter. 1972. *Planning for Social Services: Canadian Experiences.* Ottawa: Canadian Council on Social Development.

White, Harrison, C. 1981. Where Do Markets Come From? *American Journal of Sociology* 87:517–47.

White, Harrison C., Scott A. Boorman, and Ronald L. Breiger. 1976. Social Structure from Multiple Networks, I: Blockmodels of Roles and Positions. *American Journal of Sociology* 81:730–80.

White, Morton G. 1949. *Social Thought in America.* New York: McGraw-Hill.

Wiebe, Robert. 1967. *The Search for Order, 1877–1920.* New York: Hill and Wang.

Wiewel, Wim, and Albert Hunter. 1986. The Interorganizational Network as a Resource: A Comparative Case Study on Organizational Genesis. *Administrative Science Quarterly* 30:482–96.

Wildavsky, Aaron. 1964. *The Politics of the Budgetary Process.* Boston: Little, Brown.

———. 1979. *Speaking Truth to Power: The Art and Craft of Policy Analysis.* Boston: Little, Brown.

Wilensky, Harold L. 1964. The Professionalization of Everyone. *American Journal of Sociology* 70:137–58.

Wilensky, Harold L., and Charles Lebeaux. 1958. *Industrial Society and Social Welfare.* New York: Free Press.

Williamson, Oliver, E. 1975. *Markets and Hierarchies.* New York: Free Press.

———. 1979. Transaction-Cost Economics: The Governance of Contractual Relations. *Journal of Law and Economics* 22:233–61.

———. 1981. The Economics of Organization: The Transactions Cost Approach. *American Journal of Sociology* 87:548–77.

———. 1985. *The Economic Institutions of Capitalism.* New York: Free Press.

Wilson, James Q., ed. 1980. *The Politics of Regulation.* New York: Basic Books.

Winer, B. J. 1962. *Statistical Principles in Experimental Design.* New York: McGraw-Hill.

Winter, Sidney G. 1964. Economic "Natural Selection" and the Theory of the Firm. *Yale Economic Essays* 4:224–72.

———. 1975. Optimization and Evolution in the Theory of the Firm. In *Adaptive Economic Models,* ed. R. H. Day and T. Graves, 73–118. New York: Academic.

Wong, Siu-lun. 1985. The Chinese Family Firm: A Model. *British Journal of Sociology* 36:58–72.

———. Forthcoming. *Emigrant Entrepreneurs: Shanghai Industrialists in Hong Kong.* Hong Kong: Oxford University Press.

Woodward, C. Vann. 1957. *The Strange Career of Jim Crow.* New York: Oxford University Press.

Woodward, Joan. 1965. *Industrial Organization, Theory and Practice.* London: Oxford University Press.

Wright, Erik Olin. 1979. *Class Structure and Income Determination.* New York: Academic.

———. 1985. *Classes.* London: Verso.

Wrigley, Julia. 1982. *Class, Politics and Public Schools: Chicago, 1900–1950.* New Brunswick, N.J.: Rutgers University Press.

Wuthnow, Robert. 1980. The World-Economy and the Institutionalization of Science in

Seventeenth-Century Europe. In *Studies of the Modern World System,* ed. A. Bergesen, 25–56. New York: Academic.

———. 1987. *Meaning and Moral Order.* Berkeley: University of California Press.

Wuthnow, Robert, J. D. Hunter, A. Bergesen, and E. Kurzweil. 1984. *Cultural Analysis.* Boston: Routledge and Kegan Paul.

Wuthnow, Robert, and Marsha Witten. 1988. New Directions in the Study of Culture. *Annual Review of Sociology* 14:49–67.

Yang, Mayfair Mei-hui. 1989. The Gift Economy and State Power in China. *Comparative Studies in Society and History.* 31:25–54.

Young, Oran R. 1986. International Regimes: Toward a New Theory of Institutions. *World Politics* 39:104–22.

Youtz, Philip Newell. 1931. A Museum of the Twentieth Century. Paper presented at the May 21 meeting of the American Association of Museums, Pittsburgh, Pa. Manuscript in Philadelphia Museum of Art Archives, Record Group 6, PMA: 69th Street Branch—pamphlets, publications.

———. 1932. The Sixty-ninth Street Branch of the Pennsylvania Museum of Art. Paper presented at the May 13 meeting of the American Association of Museums, Boston, Mass. Carnegie Corporation Archives, filed under Pennsylvania Museum of Art.

Zald, Mayer N., and Patricia Denton. 1963. From Evangelism to General Service: The Transformation of the YMCA. *Administrative Science Quarterly* 8:214–34.

Zhonghua Zhengxinso, comp. 1985. *Taiwan diqu jituan qiye yanjiu* (Research on business groups in Taiwan). Taipei: China Credit Information Service.

Zimmerman, D. H., and M. Pollner. 1970. The Everyday World as a Phenomenon. In *Understanding Everyday Life,* ed. J. Douglas, 33–65. Chicago: Aldine.

Znaniecki, Florian. 1945. Social Organization and Institutions. In *Twentieth Century Sociology,* ed. G. Gurvitch and W. E. Moore, 172–217. New York: Philosophical Library.

Zo, Ki-zun. 1970. Development and Behavioral Patterns of Korean Entrepreneurs. *Korea Journal* 10:9–14.

Zolberg Vera L. 1974. The Art Institute of Chicago: The Sociology of a Cultural Institution. Ph.D. diss., Department of Sociology, University of Chicago.

———. 1986. Tensions of Mission in American Art Museums. In *Nonprofit Enterprise in the Arts: Studies in Mission and Constraint,* ed. P. J. DiMaggio, 184–98. New York: Oxford University Press.

Zucker, Lynne G. 1977. The Role of Institutionalization in Cultural Persistence. *American Sociological Review* 42:726–43.

———. 1983. Organizations as Institutions. In *Research in the Sociology of Organizations,* ed. S. B. Bacharach, 1–42. Greenwich, Conn.: JAI Press.

———. 1986. Production of Trust: Institutional Sources of Economic Structure, 1840–1920. In *Research in Organizational Behavior,* 8:53–111. Greenwich, Conn.: JAI Press.

———. 1987. Institutional Theories of Organizations. *Annual Review of Sociology* 13:443–64.

———, ed. 1988a. *Institutional Patterns and Organizations: Culture and Environment.* Cambridge, Mass.: Ballinger.

———. 1988b. Where Do Institutional Patterns Come From? Organizations as Actors in Social Systems. In *Institutional Patterns and Organizations,* ed. L. G. Zucker, 23–52. Cambridge, Mass.: Ballinger.

―――. 1989. Combining Institutional Theory and Population Ecology: No Legitimacy, No History. *American Sociological Review* 54(4):542–45.

Zwerling, L. Steven. 1976. *Second Best.* New York: McGraw-Hill.

Contributors

WALTER W. POWELL is professor of sociology at the University of Arizona and the current editor of *Contemporary Sociology*. He has taught previously at MIT, SUNY–Stony Brook, and Yale. He is coauthor of *Books: The Culture and Commerce of Publishing* (Chicago, 1985), editor of *The Nonprofit Sector: A Research Handbook* (Yale, 1987), and author of *Getting into Print: The Decision-Making Process in Scholarly Publishing* (Chicago, 1985). His research focuses on processes of change and persistence in organizational forms. He is currently studying business alliances in the biotechnology industry.

PAUL J. DIMAGGIO is professor of sociology at Princeton University. A former executive director of Yale's Program on Non-Profit Organizations, he is editor of *Nonprofit Enterprise in the Arts: Studies in Mission and Constraint* (Oxford, 1986) and *Structures of Capital: The Social Organization of Economic Life* (Cambridge, 1990; coedited with Sharon Zukin), and has written widely on organizational sociology and the sociology of culture.

ROBERT R. ALFORD is professor of sociology at the Graduate Center, City University of New York. He has taught previously at the University of California at Santa Cruz and the University of Wisconsin at Madison. He is author of *Powers of Theory* (Cambridge, 1985; coauthored with Roger Friedland), *Health Care Politics* (Chicago, 1975), *Bureaucracy and Participation* (Rand McNally, 1979), and *Party and Society* (Rand McNally, 1963), as well as numerous articles on urban politics, political participation, social policy, and social theory and methodology.

NICOLE WOOLSEY BIGGART is associate professor of management and sociology at the University of California, Davis. Her current interests include Asian business and the relationship of economic structure to social structure. She is author of *Charismatic Capitalism: Direct Selling Organizations in America* (Chicago, 1988) and coauthor with Gary Hamilton of *Governor Reagan, Governor Brown: A Sociology of Executive Power* (Columbia, 1984).

STEVEN BRINT is associate professor of sociology at Yale University. His current work focuses on national differences in the political outlooks of intellectuals and professional workers. He has also written on the professions and higher education in the United States. He is coauthor with Jerome Karabel of *The Diverted Dream: Community Colleges and the Promise of Educational Opportunity in America, 1900–1985* (Oxford, 1989) and author of *Retainers, Merchants and Priests: A Political Sociology of the Professional Middle Class in the United States* (California, 1991).

NEIL FLIGSTEIN, professor of sociology at the University of Arizona, has authored *The Transformation of Corporate Control* (Harvard, 1990). His chapter in this volume represents a part of that larger project. He is interested in the theoretical problems presented by the construction, maintenance, and transformation of organizational fields and the ways in which action in those fields is conceptualized. He is currently undertaking research to extend these ideas to the context of European corporations.

ROGER FRIEDLAND, professor of sociology at University of California, Santa Barbara, is working on the material and symbolic politics of time and space in the metropolitan area of Jerusalem (with Richard Hecht) and on the relationship between corporation, class, and space (with Donald Palmer). Friedland is coauthor (with Robert Alford) of *Powers of Theory* (Cambridge, 1985).

JOSEPH GALASKIEWICZ is professor of sociology and strategic management at the University of Minnesota. He is the author of *Exchange Networks and Community Politics* (Sage, 1979) and *Social Organization of an Urban Grants Economy: A Study of Business Philanthropoy and Nonprofit Organizations* (Academic, 1985). He and Wolfgang Bielefeld are currently working on a panel study of two hundred public charities in the Minneapolis–St. Paul area covering the years 1980, 1984, and 1988. They are especially interested in the strategic response of nonprofits to changes in their funding environments and the effects of these responses on organizational structure and process.

GARY G. HAMILTON is professor of sociology at the University of California, Davis. He has written widely on topics relating to the historical and comparative analysis of China. He has written, with Nicole Biggart, an organizational analysis of California state government, *Governor Reagan, Governor Brown: A Sociology of Executive Power* (Columbia, 1984). He, along with others at UC Davis, is working on a large research project on the institutional foundations of East Asian economies, in cooperation with research teams in Taiwan, Singapore, and Hong Kong. His chapter is a result of that research.

RONALD L. JEPPERSON is assistant professor of sociology at the University of Washington. At the time of writing, he was a Ph.D. candidate in sociology and political science at Yale University.

JEROME KARABEL is associate professor of sociology at the University of California, Berkeley, and a senior editor of *Theory and Society*. He is coauthor (with Steven Brint) of *The Diverted Dream: Community Colleges and the Promise of Educational Opportunity in America, 1900–1985* (Oxford, 1989) and has written widely on topics in the sociology of education, social stratification, and political sociology. His current research is about the politics of the intelligentsia under capitalism and socialism.

AGNES G. MEINHARD is assistant professor in the Faculty of Management at the University of Toronto. Her research interests include organizaitonal ecology, women in organizations, group processes, and intergroup relations. She received her Ph.D. in social psychology at the University of Tel Aviv.

JOHN W. MEYER is professor of sociology at Stanford University. He works in the areas of the sociology of education, comparative sociology, and formal organizations and is involved in cross-national research projects in each of these areas. He is coauthor of *National Development and the World System* (Chicago, 1979), *Environments and Organizations* (Jossey-Bass, 1978), *Organizational Environments* (Sage, 1983), and *Institutional Structure* (Sage, 1987).

MARCO ORRÙ is associate professor of sociology at the University of South Florida. He received his Ph.D. in 1984 from the University of California, Davis. His book, *Anomie,* was published by Allen and Unwin (1987), and his research has appeared in the *British Journal of Sociology, Archives européennes de sociologie, Journal of the History of Ideas,* and Japan's *Financial Economic Review.*

BRIAN ROWAN is associate professor of educational administration and teacher education at Michigan State University. His research interests currently focus on organizational analyses of schools and school districts, with particular attention to the consequences of school organization on student and teacher outcomes. His work on these issues has been published recently in the *American Educational Research Journal* and *Educational Researcher.*

W. RICHARD SCOTT is professor of sociology at Stanford University, with courtesy appointments in the Schools of Business, Education, and Medicine. He also serves as director of the Stanford Center for Organizations Research (SCOR) at Stanford University. Scott has specialized in the study of professional organizations, in particular, educational and medical organizations. His most recent books include *Organizational Environments: Ritual and Rationality* (Sage, 1983) with John W. Meyer; *Hospital Structure and Performance* (Johns Hopkins, 1987) with Ann Barry Flood; and *Organizations: Rational, Natural, and Open Systems* (Prentice-Hall, 1987, 2d ed.). Scott is recipient of the Distinguished Scholar Award for 1987 from the Organization and Management Theory Division of the Academy of Management and is current editor of the *Annual Review of Sociology.*

JITENDRA V. SINGH is Joseph Wharton Term Associate Professor of Management at the Wharton School, University of Pennsylvania. His current research interests involve modeling ecological processes in organizational popoulations and the link between ecological and institutional theories of organization. His articles have appeared in *Academy of Management Journal, Administrative Science Quarterly, American Sociological Review,* and the *Annual Review of Psychology.* He received his M.B.A. from the Indian Institute of Management, Ahmedabad, and his Ph.D. in organization theory and behavior from the Graduate School of Business, Stanford University.

DAVID J. TUCKER is professor at the School of Social Work, University of Michigan. His current research interests include the structural analysis of interorganizational service delivery systems, the ecology of human service organizations, and the critical analysis of selected public policy issues. He has published articles in various journals, including *Administrative Science Quarterly, Social Service Review, Administration in Social Work, Social Work Research and Abstracts, Canadian Social Work Review,* and *Canadian Public Policy. He recieved his Ph.D. in social work from the University of Toronto.*

LYNNE G. ZUCKER is professor of sociology and an affiliated faculty member with the School of Education and the Institute of Industrial Relations at UCLA. She is editor of and contributor to *Institutional Patterns and Organizations: Culture and Environment* (Ballinger, 1988). Together with Marshall Meyer she wrote *Permanently Failing Organizations* (Sage, 1989).

Index

Abbott, Andrew, 356
Abrams, M. A., 270
Accounting systems, 130–31, 177, 245
Acquisition process, 178
Action, theory of, 15–16, 202n.6
Adaptation theories, 358n.11
Africa, 230n.4
Aiken, Michael, 47
Akerlof, George, 4
Aldrich, Howard E., 66, 82n.6, 362
Alexander, Jeffrey, 36n.16, 37n.21
Alford, Robert R., 25, 28, 29–30, 122, 187
American Association of Adult Education, 279
American Association of Junior Colleges (AAJC), 339, 353
American Association of Museums (AAM), 274, 275, 276, 277, 279, 280, 284, 285
American Federation of Arts, 274, 275
American Library Association, 279
American Management Association, 319–20
Anthropology, 202n.6, 365
"Anticipatory subordination," 348
Antitrust suits, 321
Art museums, professionalization of, 267–89
Arthur, Brian, 193, 194, 203n.9
Assessment criteria, external, 51–52
Association, defined, 159n.1
Australia, 216
Austria, 217
Authority structures, 384–85
Authorization process, 175–76
Autokinetic phenomenon experiment, 88–101

Backman, Elaine, 135
Baker, Wayne, 185
Balinese cockfights, 247–48, 262n.18
Banks, 369, 378, 384
Bardach, Eugene, 115
Barnard, Chester, 36n.19
Barnouw, Erik, 64, 79
Belgium, 216
Beliefs, 180–81, 237, 390

Bell, Daniel, 25, 120–21
Bemis, Judson, 303
Benson, J. Kenneth, 120, 139
Berger, Brigitte, 165–66, 167–68
Berger, Peter L., 21, 151, 160n.8, 165–66, 167–68, 169, 179
Bergunder, Ann, 419n.1
Berk, Sarah Fenstermaker, 235
Best, Robert S., 395
Biggart, Nicole Woolsey, 32, 218, 231n.8, 312
Boli, John, 188–89
Boston Globe, 299
Boston Museum of Fine Arts, 269
Bounded rationality, 315
Bourdieu, Pierre, 25–26, 38nn. 27, 28
Bourne, Edmund J., 261n.7
Bourricaud, François, 35n.15
Braudel, Fernand, 183
Brint, Steven, 31, 287, 360n.22
Brown, Lawrence D., 116
Brown, Richard H., 170
Buckley, Walter, 160n.11
Bureaucracy, 63–64, 166, 167–68, 261n.12
Burma, 230n.4
Burns, Tom, 28
Burt, Ronald S., 171, 306
Business, structural power of, 347, 358n.10
Business domination model, 338, 340, 344
Business-state relations, 195–96

California, 339, 343, 353, 358n.7, 360n.18
Campbell, D. T., 89
Campbell, Doak, 339
Canada, 216; VSSOs, 126, 175–76, 390–419
Capitalism, 257–58, 259, 358n.10
Carnegie Corporation, 268, 269, 274–85
Carnegie Foundation's "State of Higher Education in California" (1932), 339
Carnegie school, 18, 19
Carroll, Glenn R., 66, 82n.6, 134, 188, 400
Cartels, 318

Categorical rules, 55–60
Catholic mass, 160n.10
Causal analysis, 295, 310
Celler-Kefauver Act, 321
"Center," 150, 161n.17
CEOs (chief executive officers), functional
    background of, 322–23, 324, 332–34
Chaebol (South Korean enterprise groups),
    367, 368, 376–82
Chandler, Alfred D., 356
Chicago Tribune, 299
China, 258–59
Christianity, 155, 210, 215, 230n.3, 240, 249,
    254, 261nn. 8, 9
Clark, Burton R., 358n.7, 360n.20
Class theory, 259
Cleveland Museum of Natural History, 280,
    285
Clique, 81n.1
Coercion, 67–69, 175, 375, 391
Cognition, 35n.10, 315–16, 335, 390
Cole, Robert, 198
Coleman, James S., 133, 297
Coleman, Laurence V., 277
Collective organization of the environment, 48
Collective rationality, 63–81
College Art Association, 274, 275
Collins, N., 336n.3
Collins, Randall, 20, 23–24, 37n.25, 70
Commodities markets, 184–85
Community colleges, vocationalization of, 31,
    287, 337–56
Community-corporate relations, 295–98
Community of firms (Japan), 368–76, 387
Community patterns, 111–13
Competition, 187, 202n.5, 364–65; and
    cooperation, 375; and efficiency, 32–33
Competitive isomorphism, 361, 362, 373–75
Compromise, 196
Conference Board, 299, 304
Conflict theory, 360n.21
Connectedness, 65, 81n.1
Constraints, 146, 197
Constructedness, 153–54, 156–57, 162n.28
Consumer-choice model, 337–38, 340, 344,
    357n.3
Contextuality, 149–50, 161n.12
Cooperation, 375
Corporate-community relations, 295–98
Corporate contributions professionals, 304–7,
    308, 310

Corporate grants economy, 299–300
Corporate patrimonialism, 376–82, 387
Corporate philanthropy, 287, 293–310
Corporatist polity, 121, 217, 222–23, 228
Coser, Lewis, 64
Council for Financial Aid to Education, 299
Cowles, John, Jr., 301
Cross, K. Patricia, 360n.17
Culture, 150–51, 165–67, 168–69;
    organizational, 155, 208; politics of, 253–
    56
Cultural analysis, 247–48
Cultural anthropology, 202n.6
Cultural controls, 180–81
Cultural persistence, 83–106
Cummings, Scott, 196
Curb market financing, 384
Czechoslovakia, 258

Daewoo, 388
Daft, Richard L., 392
Dahrendorf, Ralf, 148
Dana, John Cotton, 270, 279–82, 285
Data analysis, 324–26
David, Paul, 193
Davis, Jerry, 190
Dayton, Bruce, 303
Dayton, Kenneth, 301
Deal, T. E., 124, 184
Debt financing, 383–84
Decision making, 129–35
Decoupling structures and activities, 57–58
Deinstitutionalization, 105, 152
Delacroix, Jacques, 66, 82n.6, 188, 400
Deleuze, Giles, 253
Demographic changes, 354, 360n.17, 393
Dependency, 335
Depression, the, 320–21
Derthick, Martha, 130
Detroit Art Institute, 273
Development, differential, 365–66
Differentiation vs. isomorphism, 105
Diffusion processes, 268, 286–87, 335
DiMaggio, Paul J., 25, 29, 30, 31, 37n.23,
    64, 120, 171–75, 177, 184, 185–86, 190,
    191, 197, 244, 246, 247, 267, 306, 315,
    342–43, 362, 364, 375
Diversification, 171–72, 313–14, 325, 326–
    34, 335, 336n.6, 371, 376
Diverted Dream, The (Brint and Karabel),
    357n.1

Domhoff, J. William, 230n.5, 359n.14
Dornbusch, Sanford M., 176
Douglas, Mary, 24–25, 160n.9, 162n.22, 251–52, 262n.22
Downs, Anthony, 114
Dumont, Louis, 261n.9
Durkheim, Emile, 143, 158, 163n.32, 239, 247, 343–44

East Asia, 218–19, 361–89
Ecological processes, 188, 391. *See also* Population ecology
Economic sectors, resource-based/knowledge-based, 203n.9
Economy, 210–11
Economy effects, external, 193
Edelman, Lauren, 257
Educational programs, federal, 132, 176, 177
Eels, Walter Crosby, 339
Eighteenth Brumaire, The (Marx), 346
Eisenstadt, Schmuel N., 159n.2, 261n.8
Elites, 79, 237, 350–52, 353, 358n.8, 359n.14; philanthropic, 300–302, 307–9
Emery, Fred L., 47
Enlightened self-interest, 302–4, 309
Enterprise groups, 218–19, 366–68; in Japan, 368–76; in South Korea, 376–82; in Taiwan, 383–87
Entry barriers, 394
Environment, 48, 161n.14, 165–74, 179–80
Environmental adaptation theory, 348–49
Environmental Protection Agency (EPA), 136
Equity markets, 384
Ethnomethodology, 19–22, 85–88, 106n.1
Europe, 222, 230n.3, 246
Exogenous/endogenous variables, 162n.28, 225, 231n.9

Fararo, Thomas J., 156
Federal system, 114, 130, 132, 139, 176, 196, 200
Feminists, 256–57
Fennell, Mary L., 73
Financing, 384
Firestone, William A., 125
Flacks, Richard, 251
Flam, Helen, 28
Fligstein, Neil, 30, 31, 32, 178
Formal organizing, 150, 207–9, 213–14, 217–28
Formal structure, 42–53

Fortune, 298, 302, 336n.3
Foucault, Michel, 202n.6, 253, 254, 260, 262nn. 23, 24, 263n.28
France, 216, 223, 224, 227–28, 237, 250–51
Freedom, 146, 246
Freeman, John H., 65, 66, 126, 140, 187, 198, 358n.11, 400
Friedland, Roger, 25, 28, 29–30, 121, 187
Function of the Executive (Barnard), 36n.19
Functional organizational fields, 173
Funding, 130–31, 176–77, 393–94, 396

Galaskiewicz, Joseph, 30, 32, 65, 287, 298, 306
Garfinkel, Harold, 19–21, 37nn. 20, 21
Geertz, Clifford, 247–48
Generational uniformity, 87, 101–2; transmission experiment, 89–98
Germany, 217, 222, 228; Social Democratic party, 344
Giddens, Anthony, 22–23, 192, 262nn. 17, 20, 263n.30
Gilman, Benjamin Ives, 269, 270
Ginsberg, Benjamin, 162n.20
Goal displacement, 355, 360n.20
Goffman, Erving, 23, 150, 151
Goldner, Fred H., 67
Goode, George Brown, 233
Goodstein, Jerry, 134, 188
Gort, M., 332
Gouldner, Alvin W., 286, 360n.22
Gramsci, Antonio, 38n.29, 259
Granovetter, Mark, 252
Great Britain, 237
Greece, ancient, 238–39, 255
Greenwood, Royston, 29
Grodzins, Morton, 114, 139
Group interests, 344
Gusfield, Joseph, 358n.7
Gyenes, Antal, 134

Habermas, Jurgen, 259
Habitus, 25–26
Hage, Jerald, 47
Hall, Peter, 187
Hall, Richard H., 116–17
Hamilton, Gary G., 32, 218, 231n.8, 312
Hannan, Michael T., 65, 66, 126, 140, 187, 198, 358n.11, 400
Hansot, Elizabeth, 356, 359n.13
Harper, William Rainey, 338

Harvard Business Review, 299
Harvard University, 275, 276
Hawley, Amos, 47, 66, 364
Hawthorne, Bower, 301
Hechter, Michael, 255
Herriott, Robert E., 125
Higher Learning in America, The (Veblen), 358n.9
Hinings, C. R., 29
Hirsch, Paul M., 71, 120, 173
Hirschman, Albert O., 245, 261n.14, 296
Hoffer, Thomas, 133
Hofstede, Geert, 218
Hollis, Martin, 262n.25
Homeless Mind, The (Berger, Berger, and Kellner), 165–66
Homer, 239, 261n.3
Horizontal diversification, 371, 376
Horizontal/vertical patterns of relations, 112
Hospitals, 73, 175
House, Robert J., 126, 175–76
Households, 235
How Institutions Think (Douglas), 251
Human services systems, 115–17
Hungary, 258; agricultural cooperatives, 134
Hunt, Lynn, 250
Huntington, Samuel, 161n.20
Huo, Yang-chung Paul, 400

Ideologies, 262n.21
Imitation, unsuccessful, 199
Imprinting process, 178–79
India, 230n.4, 239, 261n.7
Individual roles, 188–90
Individualist imagery, 153, 154, 163n.29
Individuality, transformation of, 238–40
Inducement strategies, 176–77
Industry system, 120, 173
Inspection and evaluation, ceremonial, 59–60
Institution, 34n.3, 143, 145; and association distinguished, 159nn. 1, 2; and norm distinguished, 160n.6
Institution-building: corporate philanthropy, 293–310
Institutional analysis, 310
Institutional arguments and rational-choice arguments, 157
Institutional boundaries, 262n.20
Institutional change, 152–53, 254, 287; and ecological dynamics, 390–419; extrainstitutional sources of, 30–31; and institutional patterns, 197–200

Institutional commonalities and modern polity, 209–14
Institutional contradiction, 29–30, 241, 255, 256–59
Institutional definition (structuration), 65, 77, 171, 192, 267–68
Institutional development, 152
Institutional diffusion, 268, 286–87, 335
Institutional effects and institutionalism, 153–57
Institutional environments, 123, 184, 361–63; change in, 393–96, 415–16, 418; impact on organizations, 49–53; and organizational death rates, 410–15; and organizational foundings, 400–410; and organizational structures, 174–81; and population change, 391; and technical environments, 167–69
Institutional expectations, 188, 237
Institutional interests, 345–55
Institutional isomorphism, 186, 362, 376, 390; and collective rationality, 63–81; mechanisms of change, 67–74
Institutional origins and transformations, theory of, 345–55
Institutional patterns, 188; and institutional change, 197–200
Institutional reproduction, 189–94
Institutional sources of change in formal organizing, 225–28
Institutional structures and organizational activities, 54–60
Institutional terms, conceptualizations of, 149–50
Institutional theory, 153, 267, 390, 391; cultural persistence in, 84–89; microfoundations of, 19–22, 103–6; new directions in, 27–33
Institutional transformations, 246, 250–51; of individuality, 238–40
Institutionalism: and actors, 157–59; expanded, 186–89; and institutional effects, 153–57; and isomorphism, 386–89; restrictive, 183–86; and the theory of action, 15–19
Institutionalization, 145, 180, 390; and action contrasted, 148; binding power to a value, 161n.16; comparison of, 151, 161n.19; of corporate public service activity, 299–307; and cultural persistence, 87–88; degrees of, 104, 151–52; and diversification, 334; ethnomethodological approach to, 85–86; of formal organization, 213–14; forms of,

150–51; incomplete, 199; and legitimation, 149, 160n.11; of organizational forms, 267; versus resource dependence, 104; tensions within, 268; vulnerability to social intervention, 151–52; what it is not, 147–49

Institutionalized organizations, structural inconsistencies in, 55–56

Institutionalized rules, 42, 390

Institutions: how they operate, 146–47; and institutionalization, 144–50; logic of, 248–53; positive theory of, 5–6; as shapers of interest and politics, 28–30

Interdependencies, complex, 191–92

Interest structures, 214

Interfirm network structure, 363

Interinstitutional conflict, 29–30

Intermarket groups, Japanese (kigyo shudan), 367, 368–76

International Monetary Fund, 188

International regimes, 6–7

Interorganizational fields, 110, 173

Interorganizational network, 120

Intersocietal variation, 363, 365

Intrasocietal isomorphism, 363

Isomorphic change, predictors of, 74–77

Isomorphism, 47, 66, 81n.5, 171, 361, 391; versus differentiation, 105; and institutionalism, 386–89

Italy, 216, 358n.10

Jacobs, Norman, 382

Jacobs, R. C., 89

Janowitz, Morris, 294, 295

Japan, 218–19, 230n.4, 239, 262n.16, 363, 365–76, 386–88

Jepperson, Ronald L., 25, 28, 29, 30, 37n.23, 38n.28, 191

Jituanqiye (Taiwanese business groups), 367, 368, 383–86

Kadushin, Charles, 64

Kanter, Rosabeth Moss, 66, 72

Karabel, Jerome, 31, 287, 360n.21

Keim, Gerald D., 302

Keiretsu (Japanese independent industrial and financial groups), 367, 368–76

Kellner, Hansfried, 165–66, 167–68

Kent, Henry, 285

Keohane, Robert O., 7

Keppel, Frederick, 275, 276, 277, 279, 280, 281, 282–83, 285

Kigyo shudan (Japanese intermarket groups), 367, 368–76

Kimball, Fiske, 280, 281, 283, 284

Kimberly, John R., 179

Kinship networks, 383–86, 387–88

Knoke, David, 81n.3, 230n.5

Koch, David, 301

Komarek, Valtre, 258

Konrad, George, 360n.22

Koos, Leonard, 339

Kuran, Timur, 4

Labor, 257–58

Labor market, 341, 346–47, 352, 359n.15

Labor union foundings, 400

Lachmann, L. M., 160n.8

Landau, Martin, 139–40

Lange, Alexis P., 338

Larson, Magali Sarfatti, 70, 356

Latin America, 216, 224, 230n.4, 245

Laumann, Edward O., 65

Laurent, André, 218

Law firms, 105

Leadership efforts of local organizations, 48–49

Lee, M. L., 73

Legal environment, 67–68, 187–88

Legitimation, 169–70, 202n.5, 396, 398; and institutionalization, 149, 160n.11; and organizational death rates, 413–15

Levels of analysis, 153, 154, 240–42

Lévi-Strauss, Claude, 160n.9, 248, 253

Liberal/individualist polity, 216–17, 220–22, 227

Lindblom, Charles E., 347, 358n.9

Lindsey, Michael L., 116–17

Ling, Jim, 322

Lodge, George, 303

Logan, John R., 296

Logic of confidence and good faith, 58–59

Lombardi, John, 360n.17

Low, J. O., 295

Luckmann, Thomas, 21, 151, 160n.8, 165, 179

Lynd, Helen, 295

Lynd, Robert, 295

McClatchy, John H., 283, 284

McGowan, J. J., 30

McGuire, Joseph W., 302

MacIver, Robert M., 159n.1

Macroinstitutionalism, 103–4, 149, 154, 160n.13, 163n.29

Madness and Civilization (Foucault), 262n.23
Maintenance process, 87–88,98–99, 102
Managerial capacity, 353
Mann, Michael, 38n.29, 211
March, James C., 71
March, James G., 18–19, 35n.11, 71, 80, 179, 180
Market forces, 184–85, 234–35, 318, 341–42, 352, 363
Marsden, Peter, 65
Marshall, T. H., 152, 263n.27
Marxism, 38n.29, 78, 79, 163n.32, 202n.6, 213, 230n.5, 236, 247, 263n.27, 295, 346
Massachusetts, 355
Materialist-idealist dualism, 251
Mather, Frank Jewitt, 285
Matthews, R. C. O., 4
Mauss, Marcel, 238, 254, 261n.2
Mayhew, Leon, 35n.15
Means-end dualism, 251
Meinhard, Agnes G., 32, 391–92
Mental health clinics, 184
Mergers, 318, 320, 321–22
Messinger, Sheldon, 358n.7
Methodological structuralism, 163n.29
Metropolitan Museum of Art (New York), 273, 282, 285
Meyer, John W., 11–12, 21–22, 24, 25, 28, 30, 37n.23, 70, 75, 76, 79, 124, 125, 128, 134, 165–73, 176–77, 180, 184, 188–89, 190, 202n.2, 337, 342, 344, 362, 363, 390
Meyer, Marshall, 66
Michels, Robert, 344, 355
Microinstitutionalism, 16, 35n.12, 103–6, 154, 158, 163nn. 29, 32, 294–95
Minneapolis Chamber of Commerce: Business Action Resource Council, 305, 308; Two and Five Percent Clubs, 301, 307, 308
Minneapolis–St. Paul corporate philanthropy, 298–310
Minnesota Council on Foundations, 299, 305, 308
Minnesota Project on Corporate Responsibility (MPCR), 303–4, 307, 308–9
Minorities, 354, 360n.21
Mitsubishi, 372–73
Mitsui, 371, 372–73
Modeling, 70, 75
Modern polity and formal organizations, 204–30
Moe, Terry, 6

Molotch, Harvey L., 296
Morrissey, Joseph P., 116–17
"Multiplier" organizations, 198–99
Municipal civil service reform, 65–66, 81n.3, 175, 178, 243
Museum in America, The (Coleman), 277
Museum of Modern Art (New York), 279

Nation-states, 121–22, 150, 172, 176, 208–9, 391
National Education Association, 280
National Endowment for the Arts (NEA), 177
National Labor Relations Board, 6
National statist polity, 216, 223–24, 227–28
Natural selection, 78
Nelson, Richard, 4, 10, 34n.4, 78
Neoclassical economic theory, 233–34, 295
Neoinstitutionalism, micro-/macro-. *See* Macroinstitutionalism; Microinstitutionalism
Nepal, 230n.4
Networks, 156, 171, 252–53, 308, 310, 335, 367
"New class" theories, 360n.22
New institutional economics, 3–5, 163n.30
New institutional theory, gaps in, 343–45
New institutionalism, 143, 180, 242–47, 364; and community colleges, 342–45; and "old institutionalism," 11–15, 345, 356, 358n.8; points of divergence, 7–11; and sociological tradition, 11–27
New York Public Library, 283
New York Times, 299
Newspaper foundings, 400
Nissan Motor, 370–71
Nonmarket mechanisms, 357n.5
Nordic countries, 217
Normative pressures, 70–74, 75–76, 160n.6, 175, 344
North, Douglass C., 4–5, 211

Occupational diversity, 196–97
Offe, Claus, 259
Ogburn Commission, 272
"Old boy" network, 300–302, 307–9
"Old institutionalism" and new institutionalism, 11–15, 345, 356, 358n.8
Olsen, Johan P., 180
Open-Door Colleges, The (Clark), 360n.20
Open system theory, 127, 165, 170, 172, 179
Opportunity fields, 348–50

Order-affirming organizations, 342
Organization-environment models, 109–17
Organizational assets, 350
Organizational change, 65, 81n.2; and
    heterogeneity, 194–200; institutional effects
    on, 415–16, 418; rates of, 399–400
Organizational competition, 344, 354–55
Organizational cultures, 155, 208
Organizational density, 397
Organizational diversification, 64–74, 171–
    72, 311–35, 371, 376
Organizational ecology, 390
Organizational elites, 350–52, 353, 358n.8,
    359n.14
Organizational environments, 165–74, 361,
    364, 375
Organizational fields, 64–65, 120, 173, 174,
    391; and diversification, 313–14, 335;
    professionalization of, 267–89;
    recomposition of, 200, structuration of,
    267–68
Organizational forms, 287, 343, 363, 397–98.
    See also Organizational variation
Organizational foundings, 192, 397, 400–
    410, 418
Organizational heterogeneity and change,
    194–200
Organizational homogeneity, 243, 365, 385,
    390
Organizational interests, 355–56
Organizational isomorphism, 361, 385, 391
Organizational legitimacy, 169, 170, 396,
    398; and institutionalization, 149, 160n.11;
    and organizational death rates, 413–15
Organizational memory and learning
    processes, 192–93
Organizational mortality, 397, 399, 410–15,
    418
Organizational networks, 156, 171, 308, 310,
    367
Organizational rationalization, 207–8
Organizational relationships, stabilization of,
    52–53
"Organizational revolution," 211–12, 351,
    359n.13
Organizational stability, 314–15, 336n.7
Organizational strategies, 322–24, 334
Organizational structure, 175–81, 243; and
    diversification, 312–15; and myth and
    ceremony, 41–62
Organizational success and survival, 53

Organizational theory, 364; and organizational
    diversity, 64–74
Organizational variation, 217–25, 364–66
Organizations: and institutional environments,
    47; power-oriented, 235–38; types of, 54–
    55
Organization sets, 109, 173
Orloff, Ann, 237
Orrù, Marco, 32, 312

Paradis, Lenora Finn, 196
Parsons, Talcott, 15–18, 35nn. 13–15, 36nn.
    16–18, 47, 158, 160nn. 6, 9, 161n.15, 169,
    259, 263n.29
Path-dependent models, 191, 192, 193–94
Patrimonial principle, 376–82, 387
Peer pressures, 300–302, 307–9
Pennsylvania Museum of Art, 269, 273;
    Branch experiment, 279–82
Perrow, Charles, 38n.29, 79, 358n.7
Pfeffer, Jeffrey, 67–68, 74, 163n31, 169,
    359n15
Phenomenonological imagery, 153, 162nn.
    27, 28
Philanthropic elite, 300–302, 307–9
Pillsbury, John S., 303
Poland, 258
Policy choice vs. consumer choice, 357n.3
Political institutionalization, 161n.20
Political processes, 187–88
Political science institutionalism, 5–7
Politics of culture, 253–56
Politics of institutional contradiction, 256–59
Population change, 391
Population ecology, 32, 109–10, 173, 235,
    361, 364
Positive theory of institutions, 5–6
Powell, Walter W., 25, 29, 30, 32, 37n.23,
    64, 120, 127–28, 139, 171, 172, 173, 175,
    184, 185–86, 190, 197, 267, 306, 312,
    342–43, 362, 364, 375
Power, 191, 246, 254, 255, 262n.24, 391
Power and the Structure of Society (Coleman),
    297
Power centers, 346–48
Power structures, 214, 230n.5, 346–48
Powers of Theory (Alford and Friedland), 241,
    261n.10
Practical action, theory of, 22–27
Pressman, Jeffrey L., 115
Preston, L., 336n.3

Price setting, 318–19
Princeton University, 276
"Private interest government," 133
Process controls, 136
Product-dominant/product-related/product-
  unrelated diversification patterns, 325, 326–
  34, 336n.6
Production, types of, and organizational
  forms, 366
Professional diversity, 196–97
Professionalization, 70–72, 77, 130, 172,
  356, 360n.22; of art museums, 267–89; of
  corporate philanthropy, 304–7, 308, 310
Profit maximization, 375
Programmatic decision, 176–77
Protestant Ethic and the Spirit of Capitalism
  (Weber), 63
Przeworski, Adam, 230n.5
Public-choice theory, 233, 252, 260
Public opinion, 237
Public policy, 113–15, 120
Publishers, 127–28
Putterman, Louis, 34n.4

Ramirez, Francisco, 160n.10
Rational-choice theory, 157, 232–33, 251,
  255
Rational myths, 47–49, 166–67, 390
Rationality, 315; collective, 63–81; individual
  instrumental, 232–35; institutionalizing,
  304–7
Rationalization, organizational/social, 207–8
Rationalized society, 207
Rea, Paul Marshall, 280–81, 282, 284, 285
Reagan era, 162n.20, 200
Realist imagery, 153, 162n.26
Recombination, 199
Reductionism, 365; historical limits of, 238–
  40
Regimes, and international relations, 6–7, 150
Reinstitutionalization, 152
Relational frameworks, 171
Relational networks, elaboration of, 48
Resistance to change, 88, 102–3; experiment,
  99–101
Resource dependency, 76, 104, 195, 235, 353,
  359n.15, 361, 364, 391
Rewards, 145, 160n.6
Richards, Charles R., 279
Riesman, David, 348

Risk, 246, 375
Ritti, R. R., 67
Ritual, 250
Rockefeller philanthropies, 274, 279
Role theory, 255
Roman Empire, 230n.2, 261n.2
Rose, Stephen, 419n.1
Rothman, Mitchell, 64
Rowan, Brian, 21–22, 30, 75, 125, 128, 131,
  165, 166, 169, 180, 190, 337, 390
Roy, William, 187
Rumelt, Richard, 324, 336n.5

Sachs, Paul J., 275, 276, 279, 285
Salancik, Gerald, 67–68, 74, 359n.15
Sales and marketing strategy, 320–21
Sanctions, 37n.23, 102, 145, 160n.6
Sappho, 261n.4
Schacht, Henry, 303
Schelling, Thomas, 65
Schmitter, Philippe C., 121–22, 133
Schneider, Mark A., 363n.18
School policy, 125, 127, 128–29, 133–35,
  180–81
Schotter, Andrew, 162n.21
Scitovsky, Tibor, 385
Scott, Joan Wallace, 257
Scott, W. Richard, 12, 25, 28, 29, 30, 32,
  37n.23, 124, 128, 134, 159n.2, 167, 168,
  170, 171–72, 173, 176–77, 184, 190, 197,
  202n.2, 362, 363
Sectors: controls, 135–37; decision making,
  129–35; levels, 126–29; organization, 122–
  37
Selection pressures, 66, 81n.4
Selznick, Philip, 12, 16, 34n.9, 35n.13, 65,
  124, 180, 344, 355, 358nn. 7, 8
Sergiovanni, Thomas J., 132
Shareholding, mutual, 371–73, 377, 378
Shefter, Martin, 162n.20
Shepsle, Kenneth A., 5, 10
Sherif, M., 88–89
Shin, Don, 38n.29
Shweder, Richard A., 261n.7
Simon, Herbert A., 18–19, 35n.11, 80
Singh, Jitendra V., 32, 126, 175–76, 391–92
Skocpol, Theda, 236, 237, 238, 260n.1
Skowronek, Stephen, 222
Skvortez, John, 156
Smelser, Neil, 257

Social Construction of Reality (Berger and Luckmann), 21
Social controls, 150, 297, 307–10
Social networks, 252–53
Social orders or patterns, 145, 294, 295, 310; reproduction of, 148
Social psychology, 156
Social Security Administration (SSA), 133
Social structure, 153–54, 156–57
Social theory, 78–80, 247
Socialization, 203n.10
Societal sectors, 108–40, 173
Society-centered theory, 232–35
Sociology, 143; of institutional forms/institutional change, 343–45
South Korea, 219, 363, 365–68, 376–82, 386, 387, 388
Specialist/generalist organizations, 398, 418; differential founding patterns, 405–10
Spencer, Edson, 303
Sri Lanka, 358n.10
Stackhouse, E. Ann, 134
Standard Industrial Classification (SIC), 118, 119
Starr, Paul, 64, 346, 356
State, the, 347–48; intervention of, 195–96; and organizational diversification, 314, 321, 336n.1; role of, 187–88, 366, 375, 378, 380–82, 385, 391, 393
State-centered theory, 235–38
Statist polity, 216, 223–24, 227–28
Status deprivation/competition/conflict, 351, 353–54, 360n.19
Staw, B. M., 37n.22
Stenbeck, M. J. E., 261n.11
Step or stage models, 295
Stepan, Alfred, 216
Stinchcombe, Arthur L., 160nn.7, 9, 161n.16, 178, 191, 200, 344
Stock markets, 377–78
Strang, David, 134, 177
Strategic variation in response to institutional environments, 105
Streeck, Wolfgang, 121–22, 133
Structural controls, 136
Structural elements, introduction of, 171–72
Structural equivalence, 65, 81n.1
Structural isomorphism, 171
Structural power of business, 347, 358n.10
Structuralist imagery, 153, 154

Structuration, 65, 77, 171, 192, 267–68
Subcontracting relations, 370, 385
Sudnow, David, 358n.7
Sumitomo, 371, 372–73
Summer, James A., 304
Sundquist, James L., 116, 137–38
Sundstrom, William, 203n.8
Swidler, Ann, 28, 169
Switzerland, 217
Symbolism, 250, 394, 395
Szelenyi, Iven, 360n.22

Taiwan, 219, 363, 365–68, 386–88
Taken-for-grantedness, 147, 152, 165, 179, 191, 390
Tamuz, Michal, 135
Task-performance, 342
Technical environments, 122–26, 167–69, 184, 361, 362–63
Television stations, 127–28, 139
Tennessee Valley Authority, 12, 344
Theory of action, 15–19
Thévenot, Laurent, 38n.28
Thomas, George, 188–89, 344
Thompson, E. P., 255
Thompson, James D., 47, 74, 125, 191
Thompson, Wayne, 301
Time, 299
Tocqueville, Alexis de, 145, 220
Tolbert, Pamela S., 65, 105, 178, 184, 243
Total institutions/institutionalization, 151
Townsend movement, 358n.7
Training markets, 346–47
Transaction-cost perspective, 364
Tribal systems, 160n.9
Trist, Eric L., 47
Troy, Kathryn, 304–5
Tucker, David J., 32, 126, 175–76, 391–92
TVA and the Grass Roots (Selznick), 34n.9, 35n.13, 358n.7
Tyack, David, 64, 351, 356, 359n.13

Udy, Stanley H., Jr., 47
United Kingdom, 216
United States: art museums, 272; Congress, 5–6; freedom in, 246; liberal/individualist polity, 220, 227; welfare state, 237
USSR, 230n.4
Utilitarian individual, 232–35
Utilitarian theory, 17, 35n.15

Utility formation theory, 233–35
Utility maximization, 245

Variation, sources of, 195–97
Veblen, Thorstein, 358n.9
Vertical integration, 318, 370, 376
Vertical/lateral differentiation, 219
Voluntary social service organizations
  (VSSOs), 126, 175–76, 390–419

Wall Street Journal, 298, 299, 302
Wallerstein, Michael, 230n.5
Wallich, H., 302
Warner, R. Stephen, 36n.17
Warner, W. Lloyd, 295
Warren, Roland L., 111–13, 419n.1
Weber, Max, 42, 43, 63, 67, 78, 247, 344,
  355
Weick, Karl E., 37n.22, 163
Weinstein, James, 79
Welfare state, 237
Welfing, Mary B., 161n.20
Westney, D. Eleanor, 29
Whisler, Thomas, 71
Wildavsky, Aaron, 115, 120–21, 122
Williamson, Oliver E., 4, 74, 163n.30, 178

Winter, Sidney, 4, 10, 78
Wissler, Clark, 279, 280, 282
Women and Foundations/Corporate
  Philanthropy, 305–6, 308
Women's Christian Temperance Union,
  358n.7
Work, decision to, 234
Workers and capitalists, 257–58
Workplace reform, 198
World Health Organization, 188
World system and formal organizing, 208–9
World War I, 357n.2, 360n.18
Wuthnow, Robert, 210
Wyman, Thomas, 303

Yale University, 276, 280
Yang, Mayfair Mei-hui, 258, 263n.28
YMCA, 358n.7
Young, Oran R., 8, 34n.5
Youtz, Philip, 283–84, 285

Zaibatsu groups, 372–73, 375
Znaniecki, Florian, 159n.2
Zucker, Lynne G., 12, 25, 29, 37n.23, 65,
  160n.5, 166, 178, 184, 190, 243, 342

52299199R00291

Made in the USA
Lexington, KY
23 May 2016